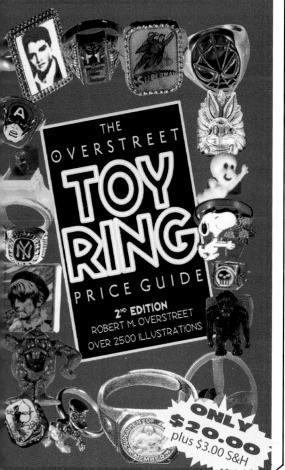

Ted Hake, in 1967, founded Hake's Americana & Collectibles, the first auction house to specialize in 20th century American popular culture. His early initiatives in hundreds of collecting areas contributed significantly to establishing collectibles as a major pastime for millions of Americans. Over the years, Hake has shared his expertise by writing fifteen reference/price guides covering such subjects as television collectibles, presidential campaigns, advertising, comic characters, and cowboy characters. These books are recognized by collectors and dealers as informative, useful, and accurate. Hake produces his books, sales lists, and auction catalogues from his hometown of York, Pennsylvania.

OTHER BOOKS BY TED HAKE:

THE BUTTON BOOK
(out of print)

BUTTONS IN SETS
with Marshall N. Levin

COLLECTIBLE PIN-BACK BUTTONS 1896-1986: AN ILLUSTRATED PRICE GUIDE
with Russ King

THE ENCYCLOPEDIA OF POLITICAL BUTTONS 1896-1972;
POLITICAL BUTTONS BOOK II 1920-1976;
POLITICAL BUTTONS BOOK III 1789-1916

THE ENCYCLOPEDIA OF POLITICAL BUTTONS:
1991 REVISED PRICES FOR BOOKS I, II AND III

HAKE'S GUIDE TO ADVERTISING COLLECTIBLES
100 Years of Advertising from 100 Famous Companies

HAKE'S GUIDE TO COMIC CHARACTER COLLECTIBLES
An Illustrated Price Guide to 100 Years of Comic Strip Characters

HAKE'S GUIDE TO COWBOY CHARACTER COLLECTIBLES
An Illustrated Price Guide Covering 50 Years of Movie & TV Cowboy Heroes

HAKE'S GUIDE TO PRESIDENTIAL CAMPAIGN COLLECTIBLES
An Illustrated Price Guide to Artifacts from 1789-1988

HAKE'S GUIDE TO TV COLLECTIBLES: AN ILLUSTRATED PRICE GUIDE

NON-PAPER SPORTS COLLECTIBLES: AN ILLUSTRATED PRICE GUIDE
with Roger Steckler

SIXGUN HEROES: A PRICE GUIDE TO MOVIE COWBOY COLLECTIBLES
with Robert Cauler

A TREASURY OF ADVERTISING COLLECTIBLES
(out of print)

For ordering information write the author at P.O. Box 1444-PG York, PA 17405

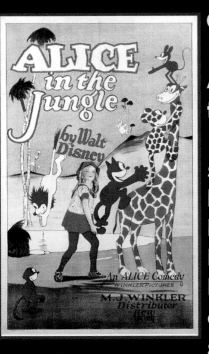

Overstreet Presents:

Hake's Price Guide to
Character
Toy
Premiums

Including Comic, Cereal, TV, Movies, Radio & Related Store Bought Items

HAKE'S PRICE GUIDE TO CHARACTER TOY PREMIUMS
(1st Edition) is an original publication by Gemstone Publishing, Inc.

Distributed to the book trade by
Collector Books
P.O. Box 3009
5801 Kentucky Dam Road
Paducah, KY 42001
PH: (502) 898-6211

Single editions of this book are available directly from the publisher. To order, send $24.95 plus $4.00 shipping & handling to the following address:

Gemstone Publishing, Inc.,
1966 Greenspring Drive
Timonium, MD 21093
Attn: Hake Guide

or call (410) 560-5806

(Bulk purchases may qualify for special quantity discounts. Please inquire.)

Cover design by Jeff Dillon

Printed in the United States Of America.

First Printing: October 1996

10 9 8 7 6 5 4 3 2 1

Many people contributed to making this book possible. My appreciation goes to Marshall Levin who researched and wrote the majority of the histories that precede each subject entry. George Hagenauer contributed the informative biographical section on premium designers Fred Voges and Wally Weist. Gordon Gold provided fascinating information on the premium industry in which he and his father, Sam Gold, were major forces for many decades. Harry Matetsky's interview offers an informative perspective on the collecting mentality. For their support and many contributions, special thanks are due my wife Jonell, my son Ted and my staff at Hake's Americana & Collectibles: Vonnie Burkins, Joan Carbaugh, Russ King, Charlie Roberts, Jeff Robison, Deak Stagemyer and Alex Winter.

Special acknowledgment is extended to Steve Geppi, President and Chief Executive Officer, Gemstone Publishing, Inc. for making this book possible. My thanks also go to John K. Snyder, President, Diamond International Galleries, who convinced me to undertake this project and served as a consultant on evaluations. John also contributed an article on the historical development of premiums and generously made available hundreds of rare items from his collection. Bob Overstreet kindly allowed the use of values determined by himself and his advisors, including this author, for premium rings and premium comic books. My gratitude to Bob and his staff at Gemstone Publishing Inc. for the many hours needed to turn a voluminous manuscript and thousands of photographs into a finished book. The contributions of Carol Overstreet, Tony Overstreet, Arnold T. Blumberg, Cathy Disbrow, John Frizzera, Jr. and Mike Renegar are gratefully acknowledged.

The advertisers in the first edition of this guide are due a special thank you for their support.

The final acknowledgment and my gratitude goes to the many collectors who contributed information and photographs useful in this project. Some contributions were made recently, others were made years ago in fanzines, articles or books--all generously shared their knowledge to make our understanding of this fascinating hobby more complete.

Gary Alexander
Andy Anderson
Dave Anderson
Bob Barrett
Robert Bruce
Scott Bruce
Bill Campbell
Bob Cauler
Ken Chapman
Mike Cherry
Tom Claggett
Jerry Cook
Dan Coviello
Joe Cywinski
Jimmy Dempsey
Jerry Doxey
Mark Drennen
Tony Evangelista
Joe Fair
John Fawcett
Lee Felbinger
Keif Fromm
Danny Fuchs
Tony Goodstone
Rick Gronquist
Robert Hall
Phil Hecht
Joe Hehn
Bob Hencey
John Hintz
Bob Hritz
Steve Ison
Harvey Kamins
Fred L. King
Walter Koenig
Ray La Briola
Bob Lesser
Richard Leibner
Don Lineberger
Larry Lowery
Hy Mandelowitz
Don Maris
Harry Matetsky
Jack Melcher
Richard Merkin
Peter Merolo
Rex Miller
Pat Morgan
DeWayne Nall
M. G. 'Bud' Norris
Richard Olson
Don Phelps
Ralph Plumb
Ed Pragler
Harry Rinker
Scott Rona
Bruce Rosen
Frank Salacuse
Joe Sarno
Jay Scarfone
Gene Seger
Joel Siegel
Jim Silva
Joel Smilgis
William Stillman
Ernest Trova
Tom Tumbusch
Howard C. Weinberger
Mike West
Evelyn Wilson
Larry Zdeb

My world first intersected with the premium concept in 1948, at the age of five. Roy Rogers, aided by Quaker Oats, sent me a postcard featuring a color picture of himself and Trigger. The card thanked me for my contest entry, "being given careful consideration by our judges." Alas, I was not among the 22,501 eventual winners, but I still have and treasure that postcard.

Although a prolific comic book reader, and with more than my share of hours as a 1950s kid spent in front of the radio and television, the rest of my youth was influenced little by premiums. Roy and Quaker Oats did come through once more in 1950 with the Roy Rogers Deputy Star badge. Quaker, Cheerios and Wheaties pocket size premium comic books joined my Dell Comics collection; and somehow, at thirteen, I acquired the Rin-Tin-Tin rifle pen. Most importantly for my future, during this time I became fascinated by the past. My mother's antiques and the local auctions we attended, my father's revelation when I was eight that people collected coins and so could I, and innumerable family visits to museums were all unsuspected precursors to the founding of Hake's Americana & Collectibles.

In 1960, my interest in coin collecting ended when I discovered presidential campaign buttons. As small as coins, but ever more so graphic and colorful, these artifacts of history captured my collecting energies. By 1965, to help with graduate school expenses, I issued my first sales lists devoted to presidential campaign collectibles. Along the way, I also discovered "non-political" buttons, many with even more graphic appeal than the political issues. Although there was practically no collector interest in non-political buttons, I began including them in my sales catalogues.

My awakening to the world of premiums came in 1967. The sales lists evolved into the nation's first mail and telephone bid auctions focusing on 20th century collectibles. Campaign items had a small but serious base of collectors, while the non-political buttons and related small collectibles often went unsold and seldom drew bids exceeding five dollars.

To my astonishment, a brass badge inscribed "Buck Rogers Solar Scouts" received a bid of twenty dollars from Ernest Trova of St. Louis, who I later discovered was a world famous artist and sculptor. Mr. Trova's interest initiated my quest for more premiums and more collectors.

As the first wave of interest in popular culture collectibles developed around 1967, premiums joined campaign items, advertising, sports, Disneyana, comic characters and movie cowboy heroes in Hake's Americana & Collectibles growing list of specialties.

This book has been in the making ever since. The project almost happened in 1976. I made plans to author a price guide based on premiums appearing in my auction catalogues augmented by examples from several advanced collectors. However, my auction catalogue schedule and two books documenting 8,000 presidential campaign collectibles put the idea on a slow track. The idea de-railed with the 1977 publication of Tom Tumbusch's **Illustrated Radio Premium Catalog and Price Guide**. Twenty-nine years is a long wait, but **Hake's Price Guide to Character Toy Premiums** is now a reality. Over the years, thousands of premiums have been documented in Hake's auction catalogues and many collectors contributed to the body of premium knowledge. Time has given us the needed perspective to assess what premiums were issued and their rarity, desirability and value.

The past several years have seen remarkable changes in the marketplace, particularly for the rarest, most desirable premiums in the top condition grade of near mint. Long-time collectors may find some values shockingly high, but these prices reflect actual transactions in the marketplace and the maturation of the hobby. Whatever your collecting interests may be, I hope this book will contribute to your enjoyment of this field of collecting.

Ted Hake
August, 1996

USING THIS
GUIDE

This guide is composed of 302 categories from the collecting areas related to advertising characters, cereal companies, comic books, comic strip and cartoon characters, movies, music, pulps, radio and television. The categories are arranged in alphabetical order by name of the character, company, person, product, program or publication. The most basic name form is used. This applies to character names, in particular, because a given character often appears in several mediums, frequently with a variety of titles.

Each category is introduced by a brief history of the subject. Within each category, each item is illustrated and given a brief descriptive title. Quotation marks in the title denote words actually appearing on the item. Where possible, the exact name assigned by the sponsor to the item is used in the descriptive title, although these are not indicated by quotation marks unless the words actually appear on the item.

All items in a category are arranged in chronological order, with minor exceptions due to photo layout restrictions. The item's title is followed by an exact year of issue, an approximate year of issue, an exact decade of issue or an approximate decade of issue. Accordingly, within each category, items with the earliest specific year of the earliest decade come first. These are followed by items approximated to the earliest specific year. Following all items with an exact or approximate specific year come those items dated exactly or approximately to the earliest decade. The sequence begins anew with items dated to the earliest specific year of the next decade.

The 302 catagories in this book are arranged in alphabetical order by name of character, company, person, product, program, or publication.

Date information is followed by the name of the sponsor or issuer, if known, for the majority of the premiums. However, this information is not listed for certain categories where it would merely be redundant. For example, Cracker Jack items are all issued by Cracker Jack and Ovaltine issued all Captain Midnight premiums between 1941-1989, with a few exceptions which are specified. In categories where sponsors are not noted, refer to the historical information introducing that category. Some categories include items that were store-bought or vending machine issues. Some items saw use both as store items and premiums. Where known, this type of information is included in the description.

Following the date or sponsor information, any descriptive text necessary to explain the item is included. The description ends with three values for the item in Good, Fine and Near Mint condition. It is most important to read the section defining these condition terms to properly understand and use the values specified for each item.

TYPES OF ITEMS CATALOGUED

For this guide book, "Comic" and "Premiums" are broadly defined.

"Comic" includes not only characters from newspapers, comic books, animated cartoons but also a gamut of entertainment-related personalities--created or actual—ranging from animated Speedy Alka-Seltzer to live-action Zorro.

"Premiums" includes items by sponsors given away directly—as package insert or loosely—plus items requested and obtained by mail, sometimes requiring small payment and/or purchase proof of the sponsor's product. True premiums were rarely available as an outright store purchase and store bought items are considered "Non-Premiums."

Non-Premiums are largely excluded from this book unless closely associated to premium interest by the collecting fraternity. Examples of allied non-premiums in this reference include Syroco (composition wood) figures, other three-dimensional figures capturing the spirit of the particular character, plus related store displays such as signs or standees. Also included as non-premiums are instances typified by movie serial posters, originally intended for movie theater use only, not as a sale item in any way.

Premiums and related items in this book are confined to those of U.S. origin, other than foreign items issued under authorized U.S. copyright. Prominent examples are the popular 1930s bisque character figures made in Germany or Japan.

This book's listing is comprehensive but not all-inclusive. Omitted items should not be assumed to be either common and inexpensive or rare and costly.

DATING

Premiums of each category are listed chronologically. The majority of premiums are specifically dated by (a) copyright year on the item, (b) dated source such as a premium catalogue, newspaper or comic book ad, or similar period source. General references of films or broadcast dates were also consulted. In a few instances, an item's patent date (not the copyright date) is used to document its age, when the patent date only is indicated.

Premiums offered in overlapping years, for more than one year, or re-issued in later years are dated to the earliest year the item was available. Conversely, a few premiums are known to have a copyright year earlier than the actual issue of the item. In these limited examples, the exact or approximate issue date is indicated rather than the copyright year.

If an exact year could not be determined, the item is dated to an approximate year or the known exact decade. When an exact year or decade specification is open to question, the date is denoted by the abbreviation c. for circa to indicate an approximation of issue date.

Using these criteria, the sequence of items within each category is: earliest specific year of the earliest decade followed by earliest approximate year of the earliest decade. After all items with an exact or approximate year are listed, the remaining items dated exactly or approximately to the earliest decade are listed. The sequence begins anew with items dated to the earliest specific year of the next decade.

ABBREVIATIONS, DEFINITIONS, SIZES

Most frequent abbreviations, with definitions:

Three abbreviations are used very frequently for recurring descriptive purposes:

c. = circa. An approximate date.

If an item cannot be dated exactly, an approximate year or exact known decade is shown. When the exact year or decade is open to question, the date is abbreviated c. for circa to indicate an approximation of the issue date.

cello. = celluloid. Usually referring to a pinback button or other small collectible having a protective covering of this substance. The term and abbreviation are also used for convenience to indicate similar latter day substances, such as acetate or thin plastic, which gradually replaced the use of flammable celluloid coverings after World War II.

litho. = lithographed process. Usually referring to a pinback button or other small collectible with the design printed directly on metal, usually tin, rather than "cello" version wherein the design is printed on paper with a celluloid protective covering.

Additional abbreviations:

ABC = American Broadcasting Companies, Inc.
BLB = Big Little Book series by Whitman Publishing Co.
BTLB = Better Little Book series by Whitman Publishing Co.
CBS = Columbia Broadcasting System, Inc.
KFS = King Features Syndicate
K.K.Publications = Kay Kamen Publications
MGM = Metro-Goldwyn-Mayer Studios, Inc.
NBC = National Broadcasting Co.
NPP = National Periodical Publications, Inc.
RCA = Radio Corporation of America
WDE = Walt Disney Enterprises
WDP = Walt Disney Productions

The highest grade evaluated for each item in the book is Near Mint, i.e. nearly perfect, like-new condition with only the slightest detectable wear on close inspection

Sizes

For the majority of items, sizes are not specified with these exceptions. Sizes are specified for pinback buttons measuring two inches in diameter or larger. Sizes are also specified for display signs, maps, posters, standees, items produced in more than one size, and items where size was deemed an important distinguishing factor.

Condition Definitions

Physical condition and appearance of a premium are primary factors in determining its value, along with rarity, demand and packaging (see next two sections). Condition judgments are certain to have some subjective nuances between individuals. Still, general criteria exist in the collecting community.

Only a small fraction of items, unless recently produced or stored away at time of issue, can properly be termed mint, i.e. in original new condition with absolutely no flaws. Items evaluated in this guide will very seldom be encountered in mint condition. Therefore, the highest grade evaluated for each item is Near Mint, i.e. nearly perfect like new condition with only the slightest detectable wear on close inspection. Additional values are provided for each item in the grades of Fine and Good.

Condition concerns vary according to an item's basic material, and the items in this guide fall into four basic categories. Accurately determining an item's condition is the crucial step in arriving at a price equitable to both the seller and buyer. Because of the wide value gap, particularly for rarer items, between Near Mint condition and the lower grades, it's essential for the proper use of this book to understand and apply the following condition definitions, in the complete absence of wishful thinking.

Paper and Cardboard

Near Mint: Fresh, bright, original crisply-inked appearance with only the slightest perceptible evidence of wear, soil, fade or creases. The item should lay flat, corners must be close to perfectly square and any staples must be rust free.

Fine: An above average example with attractive appearance but moderately noticeable aging or wear including: small creases and a few small edge tears; lightly worn corners; minimal browning, yellowing, dust or soiling; light staple rust but no stain on surrounding areas, no more than a few tiny paper flakes missing, small tears repaired on blank reverse side are generally acceptable if the front image is not badly affected.

Good: A complete item with no more than a few small pieces missing. Although showing obvious aging, accumulated flaws such as: creases, tears, dust and other soiling, repairs, insect damage, mildew, and brittleness must not combine to render the item unsound and too unattractive for display.

Metal (primarily club badges and rings)

Near Mint: Item retains 90% or more of its original bright finish metallic luster as well as any accent coloring on the lettering or design. Badges must have the original pin intact and rings must have near perfect circular bands. Any small areas missing original luster must be free of rust, corrosion, dark tarnish or any other defect that stands out enough to render the naked eye appearance of the piece less than almost perfect.

Fine: An above average item with moderate wear to original luster but should retain at least 50%. There may be small, isolated areas with pinpoint corrosion spotting, tarnish or similar evidences of aging. Badges must have the original pin, although perhaps slightly bent, and rings must have bands with no worse than minor bends. Although general wear does show, the item retains an overall attractive appearance with noticeable luster.

Good: An average well-used or aged item missing nearly all luster and color accents. Badges may have a replaced pin and ring bands may be distorted or obviously reshaped. There may be moderate, not totally defacing, evidence of bends, dents, scratches, corrosion, etc. Aside from a replaced pin, completeness is still essential.

• Condition can vary
• according to an
• item's basic materi-
• al. Items in this
• guide fall into four
• basic catagories.

Celluloid or Lithographed Tin Pinback Buttons

Near Mint: Both celluloid and lithographed tin pinbacks retain the original, bright appearance without visual defect. For celluloid, this means the total absence of stain (known as foxing to button collectors). There can be no apparent surface scratches when the button is viewed directly; although when viewed at an angle in reflected light, there may be a few very shallow and small hairline marks on the celluloid surface. The celluloid covering must be totally intact with no splits, even on the reverse where the button paper and celluloid covering are folded under the collet. Lithographed tin buttons may have no more than two or three missing pinpoint-size dots of color and no visible scratches. Even in Near Mint condition, a button image noticeably off-center, as made, reduces desirability and therefore value to some price below Near Mint depending on the severity of the off-centering.

Fine: Both styles of buttons may have a few apparent scattered small scratches. Some minor flattening or a tiny dent noticeable to the touch, but not visually, is also acceptable. Celluloids may have a very minimal amount of age spotting or moisture stain, largely confined to the rim area, not distracting from the graphics and not dark in color. There may be a small celluloid split on the reverse by the collet, but the celluloid covering must still lay flat enough not to cause a noticeable bump on the side edge. Lithographed tin buttons may have only the slightest traces of paint roughness, or actual rust, visible on the front.

A variation of the celluloid pinback is the celluloid covered pocket mirror which holds a glass mirror on the reverse rather than a fastener pin. Condition definitions for pocket mirrors match those for celluloid buttons except a fine condition item may have a clouded or smoked mirror and some streaks on the silvering. A cracked mirror typically reduces desireability to the level of Good condition.

Good: Celluloid pinbacks may have moderately dark spotting or moisture stain not exceeding 25% of the surface area. There could be some slight evidence of color fade, a small nick on the front celluloid, or a small celluloid split by the reverse collet causing a small edge bump. Dark extensive stain, deep or numerous scratches and extensive crazing of the celluloid covering each render the button to a condition status of less than good and essentially unsalable. Lithographed tin buttons must retain strong color and be at least 75% free of noticeable surface wear or they too fall into the likely unsalable range.

Other materials: Ceramic, Glass, Wood, Fabric, Composition, Rubber, Plastic, Vinyl, Etc.

Toy premium collectibles in this guide are typically composed of paper and cardboard; metal; celluloid or lithographed tin buttons; or other materials.

Near Mint: Regardless of the substance, the item retains its fresh, original appearance and condition without defect. Only the slightest traces of visually non-distracting wear are acceptable.

Fine: Each material has its inherent weakness in withstanding age, typical use or actual abuse.

Ceramic, porcelain, china, bisque and other similar clay-based objects are susceptible to edge chips. These are acceptable if minimal. Glazed items very typically develop hairline crazing not considered a flaw unless hairlines have also darkened.

Glass is fragile and obviously susceptible to missing chips, flakes or hairline fractures but acceptable in modest quantity.

Wood items, as well as the faithful likeness composition wood, generally withstand aging and use well. Small stress fractures or a few small missing flakes are acceptable if the overall integrity of the item is not affected.

Fabric easily suffers from weave splits or snags plus stain spots are frequently indelible. Weaving breaks are generally acceptable in limited numbers but fabric holes are not. Stains may not exceed a small area and only a blush of color change.

Composition items, typically dolls or figurines, tend to acquire hairline cracks of the thin surface coating. This is commonly expected and normally acceptable to the point of obvious severity. Color loss should not exceed 20% and not involve critical facial details.

Rubber items, either of solid or hollow variety, tend to lose original pliability and evolve into a rigid hardness that frequently results in a warped or deformed appearance. Some degree of original flexibility is preferred or, at least, minimal distortion.

Plastic and vinyl items have a tendency to split at areas of high stress or frequent use. This is frequently expected and excused by collectors up to the point of distracting from overall appearance or function.

Good: Items of any material are expected to be complete and/or functional. Obvious wear is noticeable, but the item retains its structural soundness. Wear or damage must not exceed the lower limits of being reasonably attractive for display purposes.

Rarity and demand determine value

A premium's value rests largely on its degree of rarity plus collector demand. Rarity is a constant--either few examples of a given object were produced originally or few are known to remain.

Demand, however, is influenced by a number of variables. An item must have popular appeal, otherwise rarity is not a salient consideration. Appeal is typically based on the subject matter of the item or the type of item. Superman appeals to more collectors than Rocky Jones, Space Ranger and more collectors specialize in rings than pedometers.

Following popular appeal, with rarity being equal, the condition of an item is the primary factor in determining value. Whatever the rarity factor may be, only a very small percentage of known specimens of any item will still exist in high grade condition. The desire to own items in close-to-new condition is a commonly-shared trait among collectors. The resulting competition accounts for the wide gap in value between an example in fine condition and one in near mint condition. The rarer the item, the greater this value differential is likely to be. Collectors willing to forego top condition examples and the inherent competition-driven high prices may add much purchasing power to available funds if lesser grade examples are acceptable.

Among the remaining factors that create value are cross-over interest, emotional factors and geographic variation.

Cross-over interest occurs when a premium has the same appeal but for a different reason to various collectors. A Lone Ranger Frontier Town cereal box may appeal to a cereal box collector, a generalist premium collector, a Lone Ranger collector and a collector specializing in cut-out toys. Cross-over interest frequently increases demand and therefore prices for those kinds of items.

Emotional factors include the determination to acquire a premium once owned and lost, the desire to finally own an item never acquired during childhood or the desire to "complete" a particular collection. For others, collecting premiums may spring from aesthetic considerations or perceived investment potential. Emotions play the role of a wild card in the factors establishing value.

Geographical factors also play some role in fixing values. Radio premiums of the 1930s were likely offered and distributed in larger numbers in the most populous areas, frequently in the Eastern United States. Even today, premiums may be offered on a regional or local basis generating a sense of scarcity and increased value among those outside the distribution area. Ultimately, geographic differences diminish as old and new premiums are distributed among collectors by sales and auction catalogues, publications with buy and sell advertising, and collectibles shows attended by collectors and dealers from all points.

> *Emotional factors, such as the desire to acquire a premium once owned and lost, are the 'wild-card' in establishing value.*

Valuations in this book

Values in this guide are based on the author's 29 years experience in auctioning premiums. Also considered were results of other auctions, sales lists, show prices, known transactions between individuals and advice from collectors with various specialties. The values listed are for retail sales, not prices paid by dealers (see Selling Your Items).

The Near Mint, Fine and Good condition grades used in this book cover the vast majority of premiums. The value for an item can be determined only in conjunction with the standards for each grade outlined in the section on Condition Definitions.

For items falling between the three grades, i.e. Very Fine or Very Good, an approximate value is the mid-point value between the two grades closest to the condition of the item under consideration.

Truly mint items, like new and with absolutely no wear or defect, could command a price 10% or even greater than the Near Mint listed value. Conversely, an item with severe damage or missing parts may lose 50% or more of the Good listed value.

The final consideration in establishing valuations is packaging. Most collectors highly value items complete with original packaging, box or carton, when applicable.

Earlier premiums of the 1930s to mid-1950s--before the collectibles era we know now--were generally saved by the recipient without regard to packaging or other contents. This is particularly true of mail order premiums. Mailing boxes and envelopes from this era were seldom graphic but frequently held instruction sheets, other paper inserts such as a premium catalogue, or an order form for re-ordering another of the premium at hand. A "complete" premium package—assuming acceptable condition—can command up to 25% more value than the actual premium item alone. Many of the most desirable instruction sheets, or similar papers, are included and priced in this guide. Many items are also assigned a separate value for an example boxed and complete with papers, all in Near Mint condition.

Needless to say, premiums of the mid-50s and after are also enhanced approximately 25% in value if all original packaging is present.

The range of items covered by this guide is vast and assigned values are as low as a few dollars to as high as many thousands. Within this collecting universe are subjects and areas of specialization to match any collecting budget.

Truly mint items, like new and with absolutely no wear or defect, could command a price 10% or more greater than the Near Mint listed value

Restored items

Original premiums damaged and restored are marketable, particularly scarcer examples, due to continuing demand as available examples leave the marketplace and enter private collections.

Restoration takes many forms depending on the material substance of the premium. Examples range from simply cleaning an item to completely refinishing one. In between, typical restorations include book rebinding, refilling minor chips or flakes, color or scratch retouching, replacement of missing part(s).

Responsible dealers and collectors volunteer full disclosure on restorations at the time offered for sale. Even an expertly restored item will seldom exceed the value of another example in unrestored fine condition.

Proper restoration is a delicate process often overlooked by the well-meaning but inexperienced restorer. Countless items drop dramatically in value by a devout scrubbing that removes not only soiling but character as well. Paint restorations may be neatly done but in a color hue so unfaithful to the original that distracting appearance results. Repairs using improper tapes or glues usually turn brown, radically diminishing the appearance and value of the "restored" premium.

Wisdom will leave repairs and restorations to proven professionals unless an individual is confident of his or her restoration skills and willing to accept the marketplace judgment of these skills.

Reproductions and Fantasies

Every hobby with valuable items attracts thieves who operate by deception. Premiums and popular culture collectibles in general are not exempt from this immoral practice. A collector may avoid being deceived by acquiring some basic knowledge about the chosen specialty, by exercising reasoned judgment when faced with an apparent bargain and by patronizing dealers who unconditionally guarantee their merchandise as authentic.

Deceptive items usually take the form of reproductions and fantasies. The fantasy item is an object, never licensed by the copyright owner, that did not even exist during the time period that produced original and authorized collectibles. Fantasy collectibles are produced after the fact, typically when a person, character, movie, etc. is the subject of collector interest. The people making fantasy items intend them to appeal to, or intentionally defraud, collectors unaware of the item's unauthorized status and relative newness. Frequently such items bear illegitimate copyright notices and spurious dates. The best defenses are familiarity with authentic items issued in a particular category or a guarantee from a reputable dealer.

Reproductions, undated and unmarked as such, will undoubtedly be encountered by active collectors. Unlike a fantasy item, the reproduction has its original, authentic counterpart. In some circumstances, a questionable item may be compared directly to a known original to determine any difference. Producing reproductions doesn't require ethics, but it does require some care and skill to produce a copy with most, if not all, the distinguishing features of the original. Careful observation of originals, some appreciation of the materials and manufacturing techniques in use when the original was produced and a healthy degree of skepticism are potent weapons against reproductions. Copied items very seldom match all the characteristics of the original. If any doubts surface, postpone the purchase and get a second opinion, or at least obtain a written receipt with the seller's money-back guarantee of authenticity.

Here are a few basic warnings and tips to keep in mind regarding reproductions:

Tin Signs--many authentic signs have been reproduced and many fantasy signs created. The reproductions are frequently executed in a size different than the originals. Buyers need personal expertise or the guarantee of a reputable dealer knowledgeable in this area.

Framed Items--covering an item with glass, or even shrink wrap, may hide a multitude of problems. A generous layer of grime or highly reflective glare may obscure the image enough to hide what proves to be a photocopy, color laser copy or printed reproduction.

- *A 'fantasy item' is an object, never licensed by the copyright owner, that didn't even exist during the period in which original and authorized collectibles were produced. A 'reproduction' is, basically, a copy of an original.*

A collector may avoid being deceived by acquiring some basic knowledge about the chosen specialty, by exercising reasoned judgment, and by patronizing dealers who unconditionally gurantee authentic merchandise.

Printed Items--small single sheet paper items and cards are easy to reproduce. Color laser copies are particularly deceptive, but detectable on close inspection. Sometimes this technology is put to use to reproduce wrist or pocket watch dials as well as other deceptions. Both color and black/white reproductions of paper items sometimes reproduce small tears, creases or other flaws on the paper of the original item being copied. These defects may show on the copy while the paper used to produce the copy is actually not torn, not creased or otherwise flawed.

Pinback Buttons--very few buttons were made in both celluloid and lithographed tin varieties. However, a small number of lithographed tin buttons have been reproduced as celluloids. Nearly all buttons described in this guide as lithographed tin (litho.) should be regarded with much suspicion if encountered as a celluloid version. Most button reproductions are celluloid copies made by photographing celluloid originals. This sometimes results in a slightly blurred appearance, sometimes the dot screen fills in on the reproduction and sometimes the covering of plastic is noticeably different than the celluloid of the 1950s and earlier. A shiny metal back doesn't prove much. The metal used now may quickly oxidize while the metal used in the 1960s and earlier may retain its shine.

Metal Badges--these are more costly to copy than paper items or buttons but a limited number have been subject to reproduction. These are typically very exact copies of the front image. However, most originals had a soldered bar pin on the reverse. Most reproductions feature a small oval metal plate with two small raised areas used to anchor the bottom bar of the pin.

Reproductions and fantasies are an annoying aspect of nearly all hobbies, but not cause for despair. In the normal course of enjoying and learning about a particular specialization, the ability to discern the small number of deceptive items is acquired almost automatically. Just proceed with a bit of caution at the outset and rely on fellow collector for advice concerning reputable dealers.

The first premium?--truly a trivia question without answer. The word in the context of this guide means something offered free or at a reduced price as an inducement to buy. The concept of a premium is ancient and certainly dates to the days of barter when some clever trader offered an extra "free" item to clinch a deal.

For much of history and in America's earliest years, premiums were not needed. Merchants offered only very basic necessities that could not be home-grown or home-made. The premium came to America with the industrial revolution when towns formed, work became more specialized and competition arose among merchants offering virtually the same products at the same prices. The premium became the means to gain an edge over the competition.

Paper was somewhat a luxury commodity in the infancy of America. Paper production—still from rag content rather than wood pulp— became less scarce in the early 1800s, common by the 1850s, abundant following the Civil War. The use of illustrated advertisements increased after the War although still by primitive printing or engraving processes enabling only black on white reproduction.

The effectiveness of supplemental color also was limited only to printers with proper lithographing equipment and skilled craftsmen. Mass-produced color was still distant as was the ability to color-print in large sizes. These factors contributed to the immense popularity of give-away advertising trade cards of the 1870s-1890s, the first mass-produced premiums. Card inserts in product packaging began in the late years of the century.

The development of celluloid for commercial use in the mid-1890s opened the way for an entirely new, cost effective, and well-received way of advertising, particularly suited for premiums.

Paper and celluloid, along with brass for metal items, became the mainstays of comic premiums until World War II. However, celluloid buttons lost ground in the 1930s Depression era to the even less expensive lithographed tin button.

Certainly the most notable early combination of comic character and premiums rests on the scrawny shoulders of a homely and bald street waif attired only in a nightshirt, The Yellow Kid. He appeared on buttons, gum cards and postcards by various sponsors in ubiquitous fashion. The Yellow Kid was followed closely by another popular comic character—also created by R.F. Outcault—namely Buster Brown and his faithful sidekick dog Tige. Buster was traditionally associated with the shoe line bearing his name, although lending his endorsement popularity to tonics and several other products.

In 1904, the Brown Shoe Company issued what is considered the first comic book premium--**Brown's Blue Ribbon Book of Jokes and Jingles**. This first of four 5"x7" books featuring Outcault art, issued in a Jokes and Jingles series between 1904 and 1910, was printed in two versions. The earliest version includes Pore Li'l Mose with Buster Brown and other characters while the second version replaces Mose with the Yellow Kid.

Kellogg's, another prolific premium sponsor, issued their apparent first premium in 1909. The 3-1/2"x4-3/4" two-fold booklet carries a 1907 patent date and a 1909 W.K. Kellogg copyright date. The color booklet features three interior pages picturing costumed animals in

DEVELOPMENT OF
PREMIUM
USE

"...the most notable early combination of comic character and premiums rests on the scrawny shoulders of a homely and bald street waif attired only in a nightshirt, The Yellow Kid."

various activities. Two additional pages, with similar pictures printed on each side, are each cut horizontally into five strips allowing the use to create numerous pictorial variations of the animals by alternating the strips depicting heads, mid-sections and legs. Kellogg must have been very satisfied with this premium as the company soon produced a new edition in a 6"x8" size and offered the booklet well into the 1930s.

The early characters from comic strip land were followed by live entertainment stars: silent movie serial buttons emerged c. 1916; the first radio premiums directed to adult listeners began in the early 1920s and the early 1930s began the Golden Age of radio and related premiums dominated by Little Orphan Annie (Ovaltine) and Tom Mix (Ralston). Premiums had become a widespread marketing tool by both radio and print mediums aimed at youngsters, who in turn, beseeched parents to buy the sponsoring product.

World War II curtailed the quantity and quality of premiums although not eliminating them. Following the war, a new mass entertainment medium—television—quickly grew from infancy to a giant, overpowering radio and newspapers.

1948 marks the first use of a television premium associated with a character destined to become a popular culture icon. Howdy Doody began his television career in 1947. Shortly into the presidential election year of 1948, the show's producers decided to conduct their own Howdy Doody for President campaign. On March 23rd, Buffalo Bob Smith offered his audience an "I'm For Howdy Doody" 1-1/4" celluloid pinback button (picturing Howdy as he first appeared, not as we know him today). Only five stations carried the show at the time and the offer was announced only seven times. An astonishing 60,000 request poured into the NBC mail room. The power of TV advertising aimed at the juvenile market was proven and Colgate, Continental Baking, Ovaltine and Mars candy quickly signed as long-term Howdy Doody sponsors.

On March 23, 1948 Buffalo Bob Smith offered his audience an "I'm For Howdy Doody" (for president.) 1-1/4" celluloid pinback button An astonishing 60,000 requests poured into the NBC mail room.

The premium tradition continued briefly in the early TV years—principally Howdy Doody, Cisco Kid, Hopalong Cassidy and Roy Rogers—but by the mid-1950s, the mail premium heyday dissipated due to media costs (limiting advertisers from sponsoring entire programs) coupled with escalated premium manufacturing costs.

Premiums for youngsters continue, of course, from the mid-1950s to the present, although almost universally made of plastic or paper. More elaborate premiums for adults include radios, watches and figural objects.

Throughout the years, cereals have been the most prominent and faithful sponsor of youth premiums, followed by a host of other food products. Since the 1960s, fast food franchises have joined the ranks. From the thousands of premium creations over the last century, the ring is the most popular with collectors today. The 1990s saw the revival of rings used as premiums and several firms currently issue limited edition rings as collectibles.

Over the decades, premiums have changed their forms but lost none of their appeal. They certainly still exist in profusion and will continue to do so as long as sponsors seek to find that certain incentive to gain an edge on the competition.

History of Premium Collecting

Premiums of all types have been consciously preserved in collections, or at least saved due to benign neglect by original owners and their descendants since the 1870s. At various times, these objects were appreciated for their beauty, novelty or association with a favorite character. Adults and children accumulated premiums as they were encountered on a daily basis. There existed virtually no marketplace wherein collectors bought, sold and traded premiums.

The marketplace for premiums first began in the mid-1960s with the advent of nostalgia memorabilia collecting. Why this occurred at this time is open to interpretation and speculation. Disposable income is certainly one of the factors. Rational people don't buy Radio Orphan Annie decoder badges unless the bills are paid. The age range of these new collectors is another key factor.

The mid to late 1960s was a prosperous time for many Americans. The vanguard of collectors motivated by nostalgia was largely between the ages of 30 and 45. These people had many of life's crucial decisions--marriage, family, home buying, behind them. They were in control of their lives with established jobs and professions. Disposable income was available. They also had memories: memories of childhood, memories of the time they were not in control, memories of hard times and sacrifice.

Being 30 to 45 years old, this group spent part or all of their childhood under the cloud of the Depression and World War II. One might well assume these stressful years be best forgotten, and millions tried. However, for the new collectors still in touch with their childhoods, these very years became the focus of their collecting interests.

Many of today's most established collectible hobbies trace their roots to nostalgia memorabilia collecting begun in the mid-1960s.

The passions of these people while approximately ten to twelve years old in the 1930s and 1940s form the original foundation for collecting premiums, Disneyana, comic books, comic strip characters, science fiction, cowboys, space and superheroes, movie posters, sport and non-sport cards, many toy categories and more.

Although the objects collected in the mid-1960s, and now, have no inherent value, the memories associated with them are invaluable. Most frequently, the collector of 1930s-1940s items was attempting to acquire a beloved item once owned and lost or an item much desired in childhood but never acquired. The motivations remain much the same for later generations.

Ted Hake's specialty was sales lists of presidential campaign items in the mid-1960s when nostalgia memorabilia collecting first developed. In 1967, Hake's Americana & Collectibles began, with an auction format, adding premiums and similar non-political items to the catalogue. Hake's became the first collectibles business in the United States specializing in the sale of 20th century popular culture collectibles through a mail and telephone bid auction.

About the same time, comic book conventions were established--small and isolated by current standards. For roughly six years, the premium marketplace was limited to Hake's, the occasional comic book convention, pot-luck at local antiques shops or shows, and classifieds in the few national hobby-oriented publications such as **The Antique Trader** and **Collectors News**.

> *Most frequently, the collector of 1930s-1940s items was attempting to acquire a beloved item once owned and lost or an item much desired in childhood but never acquired.*

The first convention devoted to premiums was organized by Jimmy Dempsey and held in Evansville, Indiana July, 1984. To the joy of some and sorrow of others, this proved to be the exact weekend selected by General Mills in Minneapolis to auction off their premium archive as a benefit for the city's Como Zoo.

The first attempt to bring premium collectors together was Jack Melcher's **Radio Premium Collectors Newsletter**, published in January, 1973 and continued approximately two years. Additional efforts in the 1970s included: Tom Claggett's **The Premium Exchange**, 1976; Hy Mandelowitz's **The Premium Guide**, 1977; Ted Hake's **Collectibles Monthly**, 1977; Joe Sarno's **Space Academy Newsletter**, 1978.

The biggest event of the 1970s was the publication of the first radio premium price guide by Tom Tumbusch in 1977 titled **Illustrated Radio Premium Catalog and Price Guide**. This book, and later editions, gave collectors and dealers an organized survey of available radio premiums and brought many new collectors into the hobby.

Another 1970s event was the 1974 discovery of old stocks from the Brownie Manufacturing Company and the Robbins Company. The Brownie find involved c. 1950 plastic premiums while the Robbins find consisted of c. 1936-1941 metal premiums, a few dies and a small number of unique prototype premiums. While both finds were reputedly "large," from that time until now there has been no perceptible impact on prices. Whatever was found seemed to be immediately absorbed by collectors of that era and further dissipated in the ensuing years. The minor exception is an abundant supply of the 1950 Straight Arrow cave ring missing the photo inserts.

The premium hobby continued to grow in the 1980s. Joel Smilgis began publishing **Box Top Bonanza** in 1983 and continued until 1991. The first convention devoted to premiums was organized by Jimmy Dempsey and held in Evansville, Indiana July, 1984. To the joy of some and sorrow of others, this proved to be the exact weekend selected by General Mills in Minneapolis to auction off their premium archive as a benefit for the city's Como Zoo. The decade was capped by the 1987 inaugural of a regularly scheduled specialty show for premium collectors. Organized by Don Maris and now known as the Dallas Big D Show, this event occurs each July and November.

1990 brought a new specialty publication. Scott Bruce's **Flake The Breakfast Nostalgia Magazine** was devoted to cereal box collecting and related premiums. (Bruce ceased publication in 1996 in favor of a web site devoted to cereal-related collecting.) In 1992, Hake's Americana & Collectibles auctioned Jimmy Dempsey's premium ring collection and received then-record prices. In 1993, the Supermen of America contest prize ring in near mint condition established a record of $125,000 as the most expensive comic premium sold to date. These events heralded the 1994 publication of the **Overstreet Premium Ring Price Guide** which joined the **Overstreet Comic Book Price Guide** as the accepted references for these collecting fields. The second edition of Overstreet's Ring Guide was published in 1996.

Most significantly, the 1990s saw increasing recognition of the rarity of many premiums, particularly in high grade condition. This is especially true regarding the historical importance of premiums associated with certain comic book titles. This book recognizes the price increases of the 1990s and the growing appeal of premiums to collectors across the fields of radio, television, comic books, pulps, cereal boxes, movies, music and advertising.

Building a Collection

Any dedicated collector will attest to the joys and satisfaction of being one. Even the most experienced were newcomers at the outset and most will admit to mistakes and judgment errors along the way. Most are still driven by the exciting possibility of a "new find" regardless of the years and depth of their collection.

Beginning collectors often explore various fields of interest, casually or intensely, before generally settling into a specific choice of collectible within financial means. This guide book will hopefully demonstrate to beginning premium collectors the wide range of specialization options to fit any budget.

Needless to say, unseasoned collectors can benefit by purchasing from dealers who guarantee their collectibles as authentic and have a clear return policy in the event of an error in representation.

The first step in collection building is to acquire the appropriate reference books. References show at least a segment of the universe of collectibles in a given area and often provide the author's opinion regarding value.

Armed with some basic knowledge, the next step is to see, handle and price the collectibles of interest. Typically, this occurs at a local flea market or perhaps a more specialized collectibles show. This participation in the marketplace, whether as a buyer or merely as an observer, brings the new collector in contact with the collecting fraternity. Meeting collectors and dealers with a shared interest, learning about collector clubs and discovering any relevant specialized publications will provide the information necessary to focus collecting interests. This focus must be acquired to minimize the number of errors that occur in every learning process.

When collection building begins in earnest there are many sources. Locally, successful finds can occur at estate auctions, garage sales, flea markets, general line antiques shops and collectibles co-operative stores. An advertisement in the local newspaper could yield a bonanza--or nothing.

Regional sources likely include larger flea markets and general line antiques shows. Hopefully, for a greater concentration of interesting items, there may be some shows of a specialized nature such as paper Americana, sport and non-sport cards, comic books, toys and advertising memorabilia.

National sources for premium collectibles include many magazines and newspaper format publications that carry display and classified advertising. There are also mail and telephone bid auctions such as we offer at Hake's Americana & Collectibles, specialists in comic artifacts and premiums such as Diamond International Galleries, and any of the dealers advertising in this book.

Beginning collectors often explore various fields of interest, casually or intensely, before generally settling into a specific choice of collectible within financial means.

Selling a Collection

The collectibles marketplace necessarily relies on sellers as well as buyers. The prices in this book are retail values. Dealers will pay a percentage of these prices based on their own business practices, operational costs and assessment of value.

Sellers with a collection, as opposed to a few random items, must decide whether to wholesale to a dealer in a single transaction or whether to invest the time, energy and financial costs inherent in retailing the collection piece by piece to collectors. Each approach has advantages and disadvantages. Prospective sellers can well use the resources described in the section Building A Collection for the opposite purpose of selling a collection.

If selling to a dealer, the sale price will likely be maximized by selling all the items--the good with the bad--all at once, all for one price. The dealer's offer, or reaction to a price asked by the seller, will be based on quantity, quality, condition and the dealer's instincts as to how easily and quickly the items may be marketed to his clientele.

An in-person transaction is ideal--it becomes the dealer's responsibility to evaluate exactly what he is buying. Conversely, a transaction by mail will require the seller to list, photograph, photocopy and/or video tape the items as well as to evaluate and make representations regarding condition. The dealer cannot react to a price or make an offer without this essential information. A tentative price agreement still leaves the seller the chore of packing and shipping. The dealer will want to see what he is buying before accepting the transaction as complete and making payment.

Should a seller aspire to full retail prices, the role of "dealer" is assumed by necessity. The choices become in-person sales or mail order sales.

A seller may elect to become a vendor at local, regional or national shows. Assuming the size of the collection warrants this option, the seller must balance hopes of obtaining retail prices against the costs of personal time, transportation expense, booth rental fee, lodging and food; all the while assuming adequate show publicity or tradition and acceptable weather, when a factor, for crowd turn-out. In addition are sales tax and income tax reporting requirements.

If a seller chooses the mail order option, travel and booth expenses trade place with advertising costs. Personal time costs likely increase and certainly extend into weeks and months as the process unfolds: advertising copy preparation with descriptions and perhaps photos, mail and telephone orders with attendant correspondence, packing, shipping and fielding complaints from some percentage of customers dissatisfied with a purchase. Taxes remain a constant.

Whether selling in-person or via mail, don't count on a sell-out. The highest quality items and obviously under-priced items will sell quickly.

The novice seller, aiming for retail prices, faces a final hurdle. Whether selling in-person or via mail, don't count on a sell-out. The highest quality items and obviously under-priced items will sell quickly. The seller will soon be left with an inventory, probably the bulk of the collection, comprised of average, damaged and low grade items. To move this material will require repeated show participation or advertising. Offering a dealer what remains of the "collection" at this point will probably be met with a polite "I'll pass" response.

In summation, selling an intact collection to a dealer offers immediate cash in a single payment and elimination of time and expenses required for retailing. A higher profit could be realized by retailing to collectors, if the time and expenses required are accurately calculated with regard to the collection's realistic retail value.

TRACING THE HISTORY OF
COLLECTIBLE PREMIUMS

by John K. Snyder, Jr.

The 1945 Superman radio show featured one of the most sought-after premiums, the Pep beanie, with the comic & military buttons.

Today's comic collectible market can be divided into three separate classifications: books, art, and toys. Toys can be split into two categories: store bought or premiums.

Store bought toys are manufactured for mass market outlets, with large production runs. Most of the time premium toys, on the other hand, are not produced until all the orders have been received by the sponsoring company. As a result, they are produced on a fraction of the scale of store bought toys.

The majority of articles dealing with premium toys begin with the familiar tag line, "And now, a word from our sponsor." This article is no exception!

During the heyday of radio and early television shows, this phrase would thrill kids across America. What new and exciting ring, badge, or toy would they soon have the chance to own?

A ring from the Supermen of America club? A Dick Tracy Paper Machine Gun? Perhaps a patch from the Captain Marvel Club? Maybe a Mysto-Matic Decoder from Radio Orphan Annie's Secret Society?

No matter what the prize, children would collect and mail in stamps, box tops, proofs-of-purchase, and small change. Then there was the anticipation, waiting for the mailman to drop off that special box, wrapped in brown paper and containing the latest treasure.

Today, these cherished giveaways and premiums have become highly collectible and entire magazines and trade shows are dedicated to the pursuit of these trinkets.

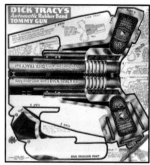

One of the rarest Dick Tracy premiums is the DT Tommy gun.

The history of these collectibles and the characters which inspired them are closely related with the history of America. As each new generation faced the trials and tribulations of a changing world, comic characters entertained, informed, and most importantly, reflected the social trends and situations of America.

Classic example of the use of a fairy tale to promote the sale of shoes.

The "Yellow" Age of Comics

The fact that American and comic character history share so much common ground can be attributed to several factors. A chief influence was the Civil War, which, at its close, left a large majority of Americans angry, hurt, bitter, and polarized by the conflict.

These resentments began to lessen as America changed from a rural to an urban society due to the Industrial Revolution. Various premiums created during this time reflected the denizens of fairy tales which in some instances took the form of insects, animals, and reptiles to promote products.

Early examples of animals, insects, and amphibians used to promote sewing products.

One of the first major groups of comic characters were The Brownies, created by Palmer Cox. These whimsical creatures endorsed an amazing amount of products, including cough drops, food, stoves and the World's Fair in both 1892 and 1893.

As the cities began to grow and change, newspapers—which until then contained few advertisements and barely any graphics—

An early postcard from 1883 Quaker Oats. Cereal companies would play a major role later on in promoting comic characters.

sprang to the forefront of urban culture. William Randolph Hearst was one of the first entrepreneurs to enter the publishing fray on a large scale. As he bought newspaper companies in major cities, Americans on both coasts began to look to their newspapers for information _and_ entertainment.

Responding to this new audience in 1895 was the talented artist Richard Outcault and his Yellow Kid, who was one of the first comic characters geared specifically towards adults.

Brownies were used to promote Luden's cough drops and the Worlds Fair in 1892.

This strangely rendered orphan—who initially found success in New York—was the first solo character to appear in newspapers, and also provided a test case for the use of color in a newspaper.

Outcault's creation—which marked its 100th birthday in 1995—sparked a variety of mimics, none of which were able to find the same success as the orphan in the yellow nightshirt.

The appearance of Palmer Cox's Brownie box and illustration book _Queer People_ (over right) gave the impression a change was in the wind in the late 1800s.

However, Outcault himself did create another extremely popular comics character.

The Yellow Kid gave rise to Buster Brown, which Outcault promoted at the World's Fair in 1904. Having learned a lesson in the need to have copyrights from the Yellow Kid, Outcault, who completely owned the character, offered his newest sensation to companies; one of them, the Brown Shoe Company, bought the rights to use Buster as a mascot to promote their line of shoes.

The licensing of Buster Brown marked one of the first times

New York based Yellow Kid promotes clothing in early 1900s in Missouri.

that a comic character was licensed out on a national level, and the impact was enormous. By the end of 1905, Brown Shoe Company was the number one shoe company in America.

Both characters inspired long lists of "licensed" merchandise, from posters and comic books advertising Buster Brown shoes to metal cigarette stands and pin backs bearing the Yellow Kid's visage.

As America began to prosper economically and technologically, people found there was more time for entertainment,

1910 Yellow Kid ad die.

1945 Buster Brown Comics #1.

Buster Brown
Mirror

Buster Brown promo postcard.

Brotherhood of Bulls
(MILWAUKEE CHAPTER)

Barney Google's Brotherhood of
Bulls member card.

and comic strips began to gain popularity and so did the production of premiums. The basic cartoon now centered around the man of the house being in trouble, the wife settling things—sometimes with a rolling pin—and the children being boisterous, but lovable.

This depiction of the family, especially of the father, was a far cry from the way society was structured during the Victorian era. Examples of this type of comic strip genre included **Gasoline Alley, Barney Google, The Gumps, Polly and Her Pals, Bringing Up Father, The Captain and The Kids**, and **Happy Hooligan**—all of which helped Americans look at themselves differently and realize that their lives and problems were similar. Many newspaper companies organized clubs around these popular comic strips and gave away related premiums in well-prepared and organized contests featured in the newspapers.

Statues of the Captain & his
kids, Hans & Fritz.

On the Air

Comic characters, already popular from their exposure in newspapers, made the next logical leap in the evolution of entertainment, thanks to Marconi's wireless radio. Broadcasters were quick to recognize the popularity of these characters, and soon the airwaves were flooded with tales of adventure, mystery, and comedy.

In 1927 Charles "Lucky" Lindbergh astounded the world and inspired a generation of young boys when he flew non-stop from New York to Paris in the first trans-Atlantic crossing. Almost overnight, clubs promoting aviation sprang up around the country. Examples include Sky Climbers, Sky Riders, Junior Birdmen of America, Flying Aces Club, Sky Blazers, and Jimmie Allen. Club members sent away for patches, pins, badges, and manuals—all reflecting the aviation craze. Many of the aviation premiums offered from 1928-40 are very scarce.

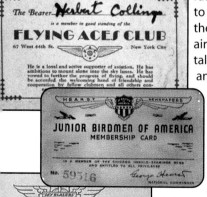

One of the many club cards given to members following Charles Lindbergh's flight across the Atlantic.

Two different newspaper giveaways and sheet music featuring Foxy Grandpa.

Perhaps the most famous character to gallop through the imagination of America was the Lone Ranger, who first aired in 1933 on WXYZ in Detroit. Proceeds from sponsorships enabled the Mutual Radio Network, which carried the Lone Ranger, to create a country-wide network of radio stations.

Radio and comic strips were becoming increasingly popular, offering Americans the chance to escape increasingly dark times. Another famous comics-based radio personality, Little Orphan Annie, was introduced when Americans were feeling the effects of the Great Depression.

1930s Sky Rider's Club pocket knife.

This was also the era when Mickey Mouse became very popular as he traveled to far away places, discovering treasure and adventure. (Escapism in its purest form). While Mickey's adventures in movie theater cartoons at the movies were popular, his daily exploits in newspapers across the country were what solidified his continuing popularity. Many premiums were offered in theaters and newspapers promoting the Mickey Mouse Clubs across the United States.

Kix Cereal contest poster for The Lone Ranger.

Before superheroes like Superman and Captain Marvel, children in the 1930s had been transported to distant galaxies by space operas such as Buck Rogers, who appeared in comic books, newspapers, and radio programs. His followers were dubbed Solar

Left: 1935 gold plated Buck Rogers badge. Right: 1928 Chicago Tribune giveaway.

1950s General Mills premium shirt, mask, and cardboard shield for the Lone Ranger.

1939 Mickey comic giveaway.

Cocomalt Buck Rogers Adventure Book 1933.

Scarce oil cloth doll from the 1930s.

Scouts and sent away for all types of collectibles produced by several different companies including Kellogg's, Cocomalt, and Cream of Wheat.

One of the most well-known crime fighters of that day, the sinister Shadow began his famous fight against evil-doers in 1930. The adventures of Lamont Cranston would inspire various premiums—many of which are now considered rare and important—available through radio giveaways and, later, **The Shadow** magazine.

Besides the far reaches of space, children of all ages were transported to the steamy reaches of the Dark

Above: The Shadow glow-in-the-dark badge is one of the most sought-after pinbacks.

Left: The Shadow was unmasked in this giveaway from Street & Smith in 1933.

Continent in 1932, by Edgar Rice Burrough's creation: Tarzan, Lord of the Apes. The jungle hero endorsed a variety of products, the majority of which were related to food.

In October of 1933, a new action hero debuted on newsstands across America. His name was The Spider and he waged a relentless war against the overlords of crime in the pages of **The Spider—Master of Men**. Dressed in a black hat and a cape, this crime fighter sported a ring that bore the image of a crimson spider.

Clubs were the trend of the day and creators of the Spider wasted little time forming "The Spider League for Crime Prevention." Members were called Spiders—and were enlisted to help America's G-men ferret out criminals and alert authorities—and a column called "The Web" was featured in each issue of the magazine.

Spiders could order a Spider ring just like the one The Spider wore when he left his mark on the jaw of a despicable gangster. The cost of the ring was 25¢. Today, with less than 20 of these original rings documented, a high grade ring can bring up to $10,000.

In April of 1934 a new kind of hero followed the Spider to instill patriotism in an America that was reeling from the Great Depression. His name was Jimmy Christopher, a special agent with the United States Secret

Tarzan of the Jungle buttons and free masks poster.

The rare Spider pencil with the spider emblem carved into the eraser.

The Spider ring.

Service. Christopher's code number was Operator 5 and his mission was to discover subversive elements bent on the ultimate destruction of the United States. His secret symbol was a skull with a number five centered in its forehead, signifying membership in an elite covert strike force.

Operator-5 Pulp premium ring.

Operator 5 Magazine was an instant hit and a club for kids called "The Secret Sentinels of America" was formed, which gave members the chance to purchase the famous ring with the Operator 5 secret symbol on it for 25¢, in currency or stamps. Today this premium ring (in high grade condition) sells for over $20,000, and there are only six documented owners of the originals.

As Franklin Delano Roosevelt's social programs began to turn the tide, and as Americans slowly recovered from the Depression, Little Orphan Annie's popularity began to decline. However, the imminent war in Europe and fear of conflict were used to attempt to breathe new life into the character.

The Orphan Annie Secret Guard ring ad.

Annie donned an iron helmet, and the Radio Orphan Annie Junior Commandos of the Secret Guard were created. However, they never became popular and the radio show was quickly canceled. Consequently, the Secret Guard premiums and materials offered by Quaker Oats' Rice Sparkies Cereal are incredibly rare—and extremely collectible because of the show's cancellation.

Rare 1940 Superman Member ring. 1600 of these were offered as a prize in the first Superman contest in late 1939.

After the Depression, the specter of war on the horizon brought along a classic American invention in 1938: the superhero, the first of whom is still fighting evil and injustice today.

It's easy to imagine Joe Shuster and Jerry Siegel sitting in their drawing room, passing ideas back and forth for a new character. Gradually, they probably mixed the science-fiction heroes—such as John Carter of Mars and Flash Gordon—with pulp fiction characters. The result is Superman, The Man of Steel, who has thrilled millions of readers for more than 50 years.

It could be said that Superman saved the comic character and gave birth to the expansion of the comic book industry. His popularity brought superheroes to the forefront of entertainment, and signaled a major shift from science fiction, crime, and adventure.

Besides comics, Superman found fame on the airwaves. By 1940, he was on radios nationwide, complemented by a variety of premiums from a host of cereal companies, which gave away badges, rings, and buttons.

1950s Superman Tim premium.

1946 Superman calendar.

1950 Superman standee promo for the movie serial.

First ad promoting the Captain Marvel club October 1941, from Whiz Comics #23.

1942 Club letter

In the early 1940s, there was another superhero even more popular than Superman for a short time during the war years. Captain Marvel, who first appeared in **Whiz Comics**, became a fan favorite via comics and the movies. The Captain Marvel Club produced a wide range of give-aways, which included buttons, cards, ties, and other products.

During the war years, children sought to escape the stress of the world-wide conflict through the exploits of comic characters. One such group created in 1942 to fill this demand was The Junior Justice Society of America—first appearing in **All Star Comics**—which united a variety of heroes into one crime-fighting group.

Another hero that gained in popularity during the war years was Captain Midnight, who soared across the airwaves until the early 1950s, thrilling children with his constant battles against the forces of evil. Kids who flew with Captain Midnight collected numerous premiums, including everything from badges to buttons to rings and decoders.

Ad in All Star #10 for Wonder Woman button offer featured in 1942.

1941 U.S. Jones Cadets Club kit

Superman's influence was such that, by the time World War II was over, more than 400 separate costumed heroes had been introduced to the American public. Most of them were shown battling the world's leading enemy, the notorious Axis Powers. The rarest of all superhero premiums kits was the U.S. Jones Cadets kit that was offered as a premium in several Fox titles.

Television, Rock and Roll, and the Fantastic Four

As American soldiers returned from overseas, and American women grudgingly (if temporarily) gave up their place in the work force, love filled the air. With the return of the fighting men, the United States experienced its first baby boom, which dovetailed quite nicely with the invention and marketing of television.

1954 Howdy Doody merchandise catalog.

Comic-inspired characters were at the forefront of this enter-tainment medium. All of the puppet shows—including **Howdy Doody, Kukla, Fran and Ollie**, and **Foodini and Pinhead**—were basically comic characters, and many west-ern and comic radio stars crossed over to the small screen.

However, Howdy Doody proved to be the king of the puppets, and his overwhelming popularity brought mil-lions of kids in front of the television set, where they were instructed to send away for a wide selection of premiums.

This period in American history also saw the popularity of cowboys hit a new high. With the Axis defeated, the world had become a safer place, but Americans had retained an interest in romance, violence, and adventure. The cowboy movies, television shows, and comics were safe outlets for these impulses.

Already firmly entrenched in American popular culture was the famous cowboy, Tom Mix. The most popular, and highest paid, movie star of the 1920s, this gunslinger experienced the same success in radio and would continue his reign well into the 1950s after his death in 1940. His popularity is mirrored in an astounding number of collectibles and Ralston premiums.

Above top: Howdy Doody 1955 merchandise manual.
Across far right: Many consider the Howdy Doody periscope as the rarest of the giveaways associated with his popular television show.

Another important cowboy was Hopalong Cassidy, who inspired hundreds of collectible premiums. He was fol-lowed by legends Gene Autry and Roy Rogers, who in turn helped pave the way for a horde of Western characters over the next decade.

As America grew older, the next wave of entertainment crashed down on the younger generation: rock and roll, in all of its sneer-ing, leering, rebellious glory. Kids who had grown up with comics were now entranced by the likes of Elvis Presley, Jerry Lee Lewis, Buddy Holly, and Little Richard.

Ralston offerings for Tom Mix.

Pillsbury Farina ad offers a gun for the boys & a doll for the girls.

Gene Autry Honor Medal.

Roy Rogers newspaper promo.

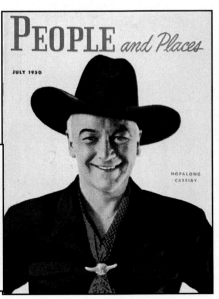

Car promo from 1950, features the television sen-sation, Hopalong Cassidy.

However, by the beginning of 1960, Presley was in the Army, Holly had died in a plane crash, Little Richard gave up his piano for a Bible and became a preacher, and Lewis had been scandalized by his marriage to his 13-year-old cousin. The initial tremors from rock and roll had subsided, but comics experienced a fresh, new approach to the young reader's sense of emotion, thanks largely to the creators at Marvel Comics.

The creation of the Fantastic Four and Spider-Man brought a human element to superhuman characters. For example, in an early issue of **The Fantastic Four**, the Thing returns after a hard day. Feeling alone and depressed, his eyes light up when he spots a present with a big ribbon waiting for him. Opening the box, he's punched by a spring-loaded boxing glove with a note which reads, "From the Yancy Street Gang." The reader both laughs and feels sorry for the Thing, looking forward to buying the next issue to follow his exploits.

Spider-Man was another good example of the new brand of hero. He had money problems which forced him to get a part-time job, didn't get along with his peers, was shy with girls, and there was illness in his family. These were problems experienced by teenagers, and they identified and imagined themselves as the wall-crawling human, Peter Parker.

An example of jewelry items offered to promote teen idols and singers by Dick Clark.

In order to capitalize on the popularity of its characters and expand its base of readers, Marvel Comics invented the Merry Marvel Marching Society. This club operated on the same basic tenants as the clubs formed for popular radio and television characters.

WELCOME TO THE ANCIENT AND HONORABLE ORDER OF

The Merry Marvel Marching Society

be it known

The Merry Marvel Marching Society

MAKE MINE MARVEL

The Bullpen G

The 1967 Marvel kit was a great hit with kids.

SCREAM ALONG WITH

MARVEL

WHO *SAYS* THIS ISN'T THE MARVEL AGE OF RIOTOUS RECORDINGS?

As clubs began to once again grow in popularity, fast food chains like McDonald's, Bob's Big Boy, and Burger King formed clubs geared towards children, with special premiums and giveaways—all with strong ties to each business's food

be it known

The Merry Marvel Marching Society

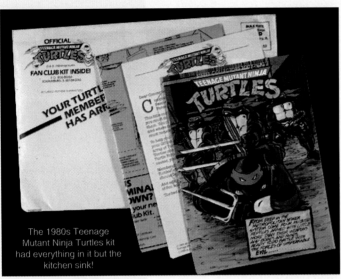

The 1980s Teenage Mutant Ninja Turtles kit had everything in it but the kitchen sink!

product. Later incarnations of these clubs were formed around The Teenage Mutant Ninja Turtles and the popular **Goosebumps** collection of stories.

Even today, premiums and giveaways remain popular. It can be said that the appeal of these inexpensive toys and gadgets have never lost their luster.

A Living Piece of History

Clearly, comic characters have reflected American history since their inception, and so have the wonderful items which were produced to advertise them. Original paintings, statues, toys, premiums, and other items have become popular with collectors of all ages and backgrounds.

Museums and educational centers are beginning to recognize the historical importance of these collectibles and the demand for information on the subject is constantly growing.

Radio premiums and collectibles have become extremely popular among all types of collectors. It's not hard to understand why grown men and women are so dedicated to this hobby. Youth is a time of few responsibilities and, as one progresses into adulthood, there's a yearning for the carefree past. Collectors rediscover these memories by immersing themselves in this pastime.

There's also a special bond felt by collectors. As

Model of the International Museum of Cartoon Art located in Florida.

children, future collectors were interested in comics and related areas that some of society didn't understand or care about. This sentiment developed into a good-natured "Us versus Them" mentality in adulthood which has forged strong friendships and mutual support among collectors of these artifacts.

There's also an overall feeling of excitement involved with collectibles. No two collections are exactly alike, and one of the true joys of this hobby is that there is no "right way" to collect. Each collection reflects the owner's personality.

Another aspect of the collectible market is the shared sense of history. The current comic book industry has achieved new heights, thanks to the framework built by the founding fathers of comics and premiums. Creators like Hal Foster, Floyd Gottfredson, Alex Raymond, Winsor McCay, Jimmy Swinnerton, Cliff Sterrett, and the team of Siegel and Shuster were keystone in the creation and development of the comic character. In the area of premiums many important people like Sam and Gordon Gold, Orin Armstrong, Fred Voges, and Wally Weist are just a few who helped design and promote the wonderful world of premiums.

As in comics' and radio's earliest days, people still want the world to be like it was in the comics, radio shows, and on television, where readers and listeners could always feel a spirit of humor and happiness and where, of course, the good guys always won. ■

Rare lead proofs of Tom Mix and Jack Armstrong badges.

Below: Jack Armstrong, All-American Boy ring.

Our Gang premium photo ad for Blatz's gum offered in the 1930s.
It doesn't get any better than this!

THE PREMIUM HISTORY OF SAM & GORDON GOLD

GOOD AS GOLD

Since the 1920s, premiums have had a long and colorful history. From the PEP cereal pins to the Cracker Jack toys, these "sales incentives" have touched all of our lives at some point. That's what makes this collectible field so special. Almost everyone can remember eating the whole box of cereal to reach that valuable "prize" and convincing a loved one that just one more box would save our lives. It's no small surprise that these companies sold millions of dollars worth of product. But who was responsible for this premium craze and its after-effects? That pioneer was Sam Gold.

Sam Gold was born in 1900. In 1920, at the age of 20, Sam Gold went to work for Whitman Publishing Company, one of the largest publishers in the country, where he created and developed children's books. By 1922, Sam had moved to Chicago and started his own company, known as American Advertising & Research Corporation, which produced children's books, premiums, direct mail and displays. Sam believed that the "world's greatest super-salesman" was a child, able to sell to mom and dad when no one else could. This concept was the principle that Sam used as the foundation of his business. He would go to large national food companies (mostly cereal companies), stating that the child could help them sell their product. Sam said, "You've tried radio, you've tried newspaper and you've tried displays in the store, now let's try another way of selling your product." His idea was simple, use the child as the salesman. He compared this sales tech-

Sam Gold, considered to be the father of children's premiums in the United States. Gold was called the "Premium King" by large national advertisers and ad agencies and named the top idea man in the premium industry by *Life Magazine* (April 19, 1949).

nique to going to a house, trying the front door and the side door and not getting in. What he wanted to do was use children as a back door entrance into that house. This was a revolutionary idea at the time because, in those days, children weren't listened to by the family as they are today. Many customers felt a child wouldn't be able to influence an adult to buy a product, but Sam was convinced that if you "sell" the child, you can get the child to help "sell" the parents. To implement this idea, Sam created a total marketing plan that included point of purchase displays, posters, direct mail and radio scripts aimed at selling these products to kids.

In 1934, American Advertising & Research Corporation, located in Chicago, had a ten man art department who worked on premiums for kids and related displays. Sam Gold was the owner and Art Director. As Art Director, he would divide assignments, giving one artist the layout, another artist the inking on the layout, another the color in the ink drawing and so on. Sam would personally be in the art department each day directing and working with the artists. Sam also had a full-time copywriter by the name of Hugh Stevenson, his background included working for the General Mills ad agency in Minneapolis. With these core people, the development of these premiums was really a team effort, involving many people. But it was the Art Director and the Creator who had the responsibility of creating the original idea and deciding which idea or premium to develop and how to produce it.

Gordon Gold, considered "a premium legend in his own time," has created and produced over 3,000 children's premiums. Mr. Gold's customers sound like a list of who's who, General Foods, Best Foods, Borden, Nabisco, Cracker Jack, General Mills, Pillsbury, Quaker Oats, Kellogg's cereal, Campbell's Soup, Johnson & Johnson, Vicks, Beech-Nut Foods, Kool-Aid, just to name a few. Gordon Gold was licensed to use some of the most famous names in the world, namely Rin-Tin-Tin, Walt Disney characters, Range Rider, King Comics characters, Flintstones, Jackson 5, Quaker Oats characters, General Mills characters, and others.

During this time, there were very few people in the development of children's premiums. The industry consisted mostly of toy companies, who went into a specific premium promotion, or of individuals that came up with one big idea in their lifetime. Many times these individuals would sell the premium from a hand-made model, but when actually mass produced, the premium wouldn't work like the original dummy model. Therefore, the actual production of a premium was a difficult job. It had to be planned and coordinated so the production premium worked when all the parts were finally manufactured, including rubber bands, balloons, etc. If everything didn't fit together and the premium wouldn't assemble correctly and it wasn't delivered in time, it was a really big problem. If companies took an order from a cereal company for $25,000 to $100,000, which in those days was big money, and then if they couldn't produce it, they would be sued. Many times, when food companies originally issued a purchase order, they made the manufacturer personally responsible. If the manufacturer didn't have a big company, the food companies held the manu-

Display room of Gordon Gold's Florida office in 1969.

Gordon Gold's main Florida offices in 1969.

facturer personally responsible for all their losses including radio time, newspaper coverage, and loss of production. Even the premium buyers for the food companies could get fired if the premiums were late. Because of Sam and Gordon Gold's dedication and ingenuity, however, neither Sam Gold or his son Gordon Gold were ever sued by a customer, and they always came through on delivery.

In 1934 Sam Gold created and produced the **Mickey Mouse Waddle Book** for Blue Ribbon books. Sam arranged the licensing of Mickey Mouse with the Disney studio and also signed Disney to do the artwork on this book. He also later arranged the license for **The Wizard of Oz Waddle Book**. Sam's creation and development of the **Mickey Mouse Waddle Book** let him work with Disney's top marketing man, Kay Kamen, who became one of his dearest friends. Unfortunately this friendship came to a tragic end. When Kay Kamen was in Europe, he had planned a lunch date with Sam when he got back. Before they could meet, Sam received a call from Kay's secretary saying that the plane had crashed and that Kay was killed flying back to the USA on the same plane with Marcel Cerdan (a world famous fighter).

It was also in 1934 that Sam created and produced a pop-up book containing comic characters for, once again, Blue Ribbon books. He handled the creation and marketing and negotiated the licensing with the comic characters. He arranged the licensing and comic character's artwork with his friend Al Leowenthal, head of the Famous Artists Syndicate, and his friend John Dille on the **Buck Rogers** pop-up book. **Tarzan, Orphan Annie, Mother Goose** and **Little Red Riding Hood** titles were also produced. Sam did the marketing plan for the salesmen on how to sell these books in different circulars and advertisements, and he even designed and produced the display counter stand. Sam specialized in the complete marketing package for

everything that he did because he wanted to be sure the item was successful.

On an interesting note, during this time Sam also started collecting antique toys. He had people looking for these toys in both the USA and Europe, and at the time of his death in 1965, he had one of the largest and finest antique toy collections in the country. Mrs. Sam Gold and Gordon Gold, his son, both felt that this collection should be given to a museum so that kids and adults could see the toy collection that took Sam Gold 40 years to collect and be thrilled by the creativity and the ability of the old time toy makers. Both the Strong Museum in Rochester and the Museum of the City of New York wanted this collection for permanent exhibit. In 1975 Gordon Gold presented this toy collection, called the Gold Toy Collection, to the Museum of the City of New York. The museum had a huge cocktail party for the occasion and invited 3,000 of their museum members for the opening day. After this official opening, over 500,000 paid to see this exhibit. The museum still has the collection, and, with a total of 2,500 items, it is one of the finest antique toy collections in the country.

In 1942 Gordon Gold started working for his father on Sundays helping with the filing of dummies, samples and so forth. Born in 1926, Gordon, with premium creation in his blood, would eventually learn the market while Sam was very busy selling premiums to General Foods, Kellogg's, Quaker Oats and others. By 1943 Sam Gold was known as the "Premium King" in the advertising field to customers and ad agencies in the United States. In 1944 Sam Gold set up a new company with Einson-

1950 Western Badges banner produced by Gordon Gold's Premium Specialties Company.

1937 Pillsbury's Farina 3 Stooges promo.

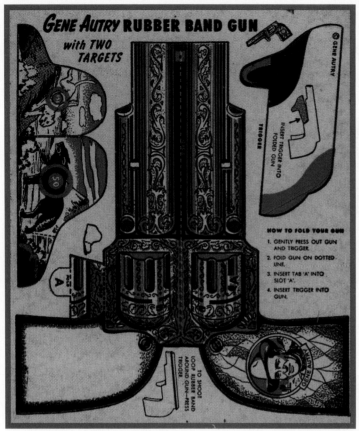

GENE AUTRY RUBBER BAND GUN with TWO TARGETS

HOW TO FOLD YOUR GUN
1. GENTLY PRESS OUT GUN AND TRIGGER.
2. FOLD GUN ON DOTTED LINE.
3. INSERT TAB 'A' INTO SLOT 'A'.
4. INSERT TRIGGER INTO GUN.

1950 Gene Autry Rubber Band Gun sold by Gordon Gold's Premium Specialty Co. Licensed by Gordon by Fortune Merchandising.

Below: **General Mills, Lucky Leprechaun Kite.** An actual miniature kite that would fly like a big one, but could be packaged in the advertiser's cereal box. Produced by Gold Premium International in 1971.

Freeman, who was considered the top display company. They manufactured paper displays, cardboard displays and were also known as a very fine printer. They had a huge 14 building plant in Fairlawn, New Jersey. The new company was named the Gold-Einson Freeman Company, with Sam owning two-thirds and Einson owning the rest. Since Sam was the top premium man in the United States and Einson the top printer, this was a marriage made in heaven. And because Einson had a large sales force and Sam was the only salesman in his company, they really needed each other at that time.

Sam then renovated an old four-story brownstone in Chicago and made it his headquarters. He had his ten man art department, sales production staff, and accounting department all in this building. Of this group, Sam was really the only salesman. It was during this time that Sam decided to move into other fields besides the cereal premium business. Sam thought that since the child was the world's greatest salesman, mom and dad could be sold into buying other products besides cereal. The child would beg, plead, and cry to get the parent to do what he wanted, namely come into the show room to see the product in order to get the premium. This led Sam to develop the Traffic Builder Program.

When the adult brought the child to the showroom, the dealer would give the child a terrific premium. Sam went to General Electric, one of the biggest companies in America, to explain how the child was the world's great salesman and how a company could put that child to work for them selling their product. Of course General Electric believed that idea was ridiculous. How could a child sell a refrigerator or a television set? Though still disbelieving, they gave Sam a chance to prove himself. Sam's Traffic Builder Promotion would be put into action.

If the adult would bring their child into a General Electric store to view the new line of General Electric refrigerators, GE would give the child a General Electric Circus—a full color, cardboard and die-cut playset. This gave salesmen a chance to show off their newest refrigerators. This promotion was so successful that Sam also sold the idea to General Motors and many other large companies. Because the traffic builder concept worked so well, he went from a company that sold mostly to cereal companies, to selling hard products for some of the largest companies in America. He created the General Electric Western Rodeo, General Electric Circus, the Admiral TV Walt Disney Peter Pan Theater and many others. This concept changed the entire premium business. Companies would pay anywhere from 33 to 50 cents each for a traffic building premium and would buy 500,000 to a million on the first order!

In 1945, the War was over and Gordon Gold returned from the service and joined Gold-Einson Freeman Company as a salesman selling premiums and displays. The next year Sam created the idea of full-color comic character pinback buttons. Working with the Tribune Comic Syndicate, he then sold this button idea to the Kellogg's cereal company. The original orders were for 100 million buttons. The Kellogg's PEP set of 86 buttons are still considered to be one of the most successful premiums ever produced.

Sam believed very much in comic characters and he promoted them when other companies thought that comic characters were not that important. Though this was before comics had taken off, Sam already realized the link between these characters and the kids.

Around 1947, Gordon Gold, after creating and selling the Baby Snooks premium for Tums, resigned from Gold-Einson Freeman and started his own company called Premium Specialties. There he made up a line of children's stock premiums that any company could use. When Sam Gold did a job, companies had to buy in very large quantities. If you didn't need a lot, he couldn't work with you. Gordon's approach with the line of stock items was to sell them to the advertising specialty jobbers throughout the country. Companies could buy 10,000, 20,000, or 25,000 and imprint their name on the premium. Gordon would sell to the smaller or medium-sized companies while his father would handle the larger companies. Gordon's company also produced character premiums such as a Gene Autry button, the Gene Autry rubber band gun and Hopalong Cassidy badges.

Above: **Howard Johnson's Menu and Construction Model.** A complete children's menu out of cardboard with the added plus of providing a die cut facsimile of the famous restaurant landmark. Produced in 1966 for Gold Premium of New York.
Left: **Nabisco Foods Walt Disney Productions Love Bug and Launcher from 1966.** An example from the foreign licensee in Canada, used to help sell a cereal product. One car and launcher was packed inside the cereal.
Below: **H.P. Hood & Sons Funny Face Mask.** A colorful and inexpensive paper giveaway designed to promote and stimulate the sale of clients' novelty ice cream bars.

In 1948 Sam Gold started licensing companies in other countries to sell premiums on a 50/50 partnership basis. He had licensing deals in England, Italy, France, Germany, South America, Holland, and Mexico, in which Sam would send these associates premium items. They would then approach the counterparts of cereal companies, General Electric and other companies to see if the overseas branch would use the same item that had been so successful in the United States. The orders weren't as large as in the United States, but it was a successful international business. Because of his success in premiums, *Life* magazine (April 19, 1949) had a write-up on the cereal premium phenomenon and called Sam Gold the top idea man of the premium business. It was also during this time

that Sam came up with the Post Cereals comic character tin rings. Sam enjoyed cheap cigars. He would often take the band that goes around cigars and put it on his finger. These cigar bands were very colorful. One day Sam looked down and decided that this concept would make a great kid's ring premium. He talked with Post and the rest was history. Sam once admitted that his success and his ideas were due to that fact that he was "mentally a kid."

This attitude led to Sam Gold selling the Cracker Jack company premiums in 1950. Later in 1954, Sam Gold and Einson-Freeman broke up their joint company, Gold-Einson Freeman, and Sam Gold moved into the Gordon Gold Premium Specialty Company offices in Chicago. Gordon had an office building in Chicago on Illinois St. at this time and had begun to create plastic premiums. Because most other companies were still doing paper and cardboard, Sam was truly seeing the future of premiums by being open to a transition into plastics.

Together, Sam and Gordon wanted to do some of their own manufacturing as well as start a big push in plastic premiums. Even though their experience and background was in paper and cardboard premiums, Sam and Gordon both agreed that the kids wanted more toys made of plastic than paper and cardboard.

Now, in 1956, Gordon Gold's company, Premium Specialties, merged with Sam Gold Associates (created after Sam left the Gold-Einson Freeman company). Gordon became Vice President and moved to New York City to open up the New York office. Gordon Gold's plan was to set up separate offices in Chicago and New York to give the customers faster service in creating and selling ideas. The food companies wanted ideas and dummies fast, and they wouldn't wait. This also offered Gordon and Sam an opportunity to get into manufacturing certain key parts to the premium that would allow them better control of production and final product quality. At this point they were working with many different types of material, and because of this, there was no way to manufacture the entire premium. For example, they had balsa gliders one week, the next week metal buttons, then rubber bands. If they became locked into one type of manufacturing, they would be stuck. Their flexibility in manufacturing was one of the many things that made their company successful.

In 1957 Gordon Gold sold his first order to Nabisco cereal, a large (6,000,000) order of the Rin-Tin-Tin telegraph key premiums. Gordon had just received the Rin-Tin-Tin license from Ed Justin of Screen Gems in New York. Gordon and Sam began making

Sam Gold created and produced a Buck Roger's Space Ranger Kit premium offered and pictured on this display. Sam was licensed by John Dille, owner of Buck Rogers. This was a Traffic Builder premium.

Nabisco's premiums and soon became Nabisco's largest supplier of premiums. At this time, they also created the Best Foods Easter Kit. Gordon then set up Shields Plastic, in 1957, in Chicago. This company only did the packaging of the premiums because all of the premiums had to be put in a paper or cellophane bag ready for insertion in cereal boxes. They also set up a large plastic die-cutting and packaging plant at 40 West 20th Street in New York City and specialized in vacuum forming. One of the first to do vacuum forming in the display and premium business, examples of their early product include the Nabisco Rin-Tin-Tin totem poles and insignia patches. From 100 to 300 people were employed in the plant depending on the time of the year.

Later that year, they started a New York corporation called Gold Premium of New York and Gold Manufacturing Corp. Gordon became President of both companies while Sam Gold acted Vice President. Sam did not like running the day to day business, he liked selling and creating new ideas. Gordon Gold felt the same way, but he was also stuck with the business end, although his love was creating and selling to customers.

Above: **Quaker Oats Company Cap'n Crunch Wiggle Figures.** A series of plastic figures, each complete with a spring produced in 1969 by Gold Premium International. Figures were adapted from their established characters and designed to nod and shake with the slightest movement.
Left: **Best Foods Bosco Bear Rocket Chute.** An unusual toy produced by Gold Premium of New York that helped sell this chocolate mix. The toy was prominently displayed and attached on the outside of the product jar.
Below: **General Foods Archie's Car.** This toy car package insert is a copy of the one driven by the famous comic character. As an added feature, the figures and garage were included for the child to cut and fold out of the cereal box. Produced by Gold Premium International in 1969.

As a result, the New York office rented two large floors at 40 West 20th Street and set up a plant specializing in premiums, displays and toys. Now it was a two-fold business plant. The plan was that Sam Gold would design, sell and manufacture in Chicago and surrounding areas with customers such as General Foods, Kellogg's, and Quaker while New York would do the same thing—create, sell and manufacture to customers in New York and its surrounding areas. New York, however, would manufacture and package in its own plant.

It was in 1957 that Gordon Gold created and developed a product called Sculpture Contact, a vac-u-form. It was a three dimensional wall covering that could be put on a surface to make a beautiful brick or fieldstone, etc. wall. It was plastic and it was around a half inch deep. This was produced in the New York plant (which was helpful during the slower premium times). With premiums, the Golds were sometimes flooded with orders while at other times it was slow. To keep their people busy, as they didn't want to let anybody go, they developed a wall product which ended up doing ten million dollars a year in retail sales (Sculpture Contact).

"I loved the child appeal premium business. What other business would enable an adult to play with children's premiums (toys) for his entire career."
-Gordon Gold

In 1962 things started getting very slow in the premium business. To be more effective, Gordon asked Sam to move to New York where the larger market was at the time. Unfortunately, in 1963, Gordon's apartment in New York burned down. So, taking his wife and three children, he decided to move to Miami Beach, Florida. Sam and Gordon liquidated their companies and each started a new company. Sam's company was Gold Premium of Illinois and Gordon's company was the Gordon Premium Corporation. They split their customers, with Gordon taking Nabisco, General Mills, and Best Foods and Sam taking General Foods.

Late in 1965, Sam Gold died at the age of 64 in Chicago, during a premium presentation to the Cracker Jack Company. He always told Gordon that he wanted to die with his "boots on." At the time of his death, he'd already established 15 factories in Hong Kong making premiums for Cracker Jack. After Sam died, Gordon purchased the company from Sam's wife, Gordon's mother, who wanted no role in the premium business. He later merged Sam's company with his own at the end of 1965. At this time, Gordon Gold's company was the largest premium company in the United States, and was shipping nine to twelve million premiums a week to Cracker Jack alone. Gordon's excitement about premiums and the perceptions of others can be best described in a story that Gordon was fond of telling, "In 1967 I sold Post Cereal a jet action balloon boat for use in their Alpha Bits cereal. I brought the production plastic shots for approval to Post Cereal at White Plains, NY. I met with Tom Irwin the Product Manager and Stu Melville the Purchasing Manager; we took these plastic boats and balloons into the bathroom at Post's main building and preceded to blow up the balloon and try them out in the wash bowl filled with water. A group of men came in the room and used the facility and looked at us like we were nuts. When the men left the bathroom they looked at each other and shook their heads, they thought that we were playing with toys in the Post's Cereal Co. bathroom."

Gordon would continue to run the business successfully until 1974, when he decided to liquidate his assets and move to North Carolina to retire. His retirement would not last long. Still attached to the premium business, Gordon would come out of retirement in 1976, 1980 and 1981 to sell huge premium promotions to Post Cereal and Burger King (Burger King called him "the legendary Gordon Gold").

Because of his success in the children's premium business, Gordon Gold's premium empire was displayed at Duke University in 1989. Creating the display to honor his father, Gordon would put together an exhibit of premiums that three generations could see and enjoy.

Sam and Gordon Gold have left their mark on the hearts of children and adults everywhere, creating memorable premiums for over 60 years. They successfully changed the face of promotions and showed companies better ways to promote their product. Always on the cutting edge, Sam and Gordon Gold welcomed new technology but still retained the quality that built their reputation. Sam and Gordon Gold and the premiums they created have taken their place in history, making the Golds the "Kings of Premiums." ■

PAPER WIZARDS
FRED VOGES AND WALLY WEIST
THE ART OF PAPER PREMIUMS
by George Hagenauer

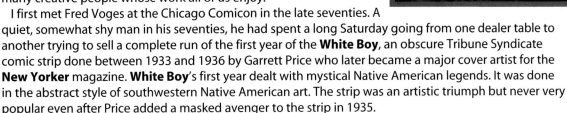

In Japan, origami and kirigami, the arts of folding and cutting paper have long been recognized as forms of serious artistic expression. In America, on the other hand, creative uses for folding and cutting paper have usually been viewed as disposable art - pieces to be created today and tossed into the garbage tomorrow. In America, the art of paper folding and cutting has been limited to the ghettos of paper dolls, punch out books and paper premiums. Today many of these objects, especially the ones with cartoon characters, are collector's items.

However, the creative talent behind these ingenious and beautiful premiums is largely unknown and lost to history. While the objects are valued, the creators are largely ignored. There is more published about the least important artist in the 1940s sweatshops that produced the earliest comic books than there is of the major premium creators and designers. Fortunately, several years ago, I had the opportunity to meet Fred Voges, one of the masters of this field. He got me interested in paper premiums and in the search to uncover the many creative people whose work all of us enjoy.

I first met Fred Voges at the Chicago Comicon in the late seventies. A quiet, somewhat shy man in his seventies, he had spent a long Saturday going from one dealer table to another trying to sell a complete run of the first year of the **White Boy**, an obscure Tribune Syndicate comic strip done between 1933 and 1936 by Garrett Price who later became a major cover artist for the **New Yorker** magazine. **White Boy**'s first year dealt with mystical Native American legends. It was done in the abstract style of southwestern Native American art. The strip was an artistic triumph but never very popular even after Price added a masked avenger to the strip in 1935.

Fred hadn't run into any dealer at the Con who had even heard of **White Boy** until he stopped at my table. I said that if the price was right that I would take the run. We then talked a bit about Price's work after which I asked him "what else do you have?" "Oh, **Prince Valiant, Flash Gordon, Superman, Captain Easy**..." said Fred. I was at Fred's house within a few days.

At that time, I didn't own a car or have a driver's license. As such, I was limited to buying two shopping bags of Sunday pages on each visit. Since I didn't have a lot of money, two shopping bags were about what I could afford. As a result, it took me almost a year to clean out Fred's comic strips and the few comic books that he still owned. (In the 1950s he either tossed out or gave away as Halloween treats near complete runs of most major Golden Age titles!) Selling the material was painful for Fred so each purchase took a couple of hours since we'd sit and sort strips, talking the whole time about the characters and the styles of the artists.

Usually about an hour into every visit, Fred would amble off into a closet and bring out a paper toy. One time, it was a perfectly spherical paper globe that was assembled as a punch out toy. Another time it was a huge Man from Mars mask or a paper Davy Crockett hat. He'd start talking about how he created and designed each piece. After a few visits, I was hooked on the paper wizardry of Fred Voges. When I ran out of comic strips to buy, I began buying premiums. And that's how I got to know this remarkable man and his work – as well as being introduced to the many creative staff members who worked on the paper punch outs that I and many others enjoyed as a child.

Fred Voges was born just after the turn of the century in the Chicago community of Ravenswood. He grew up less than a mile from where I lived when I met him. At the time, Ravenswood was a German neighborhood. It was home to independent craftsmen, small businessmen and a number of creative people including writer, Carl Sandburg.

Fred went to Trumbull Elementary School, a "modern" school built around the turn of the century. Architecturally, Trumbull resembles closely Joliet State Prison or the old Chicago Bridewell Jail. Trumbull's thick fortress like walls and barred windows made for less than an ideal educational atmosphere. Fred talked little of his early years in school. He did remember a lot about what he learned in the school yard and on the street. He had an incredible memory for the games and homemade toys the children created. He also had a fascination for things mechanical and spent hours studying horse drawn steam fire engines and other machines in the neighborhood.

Fred did well enough to enter Lane Technical Institute, a local public high school which only accepted students with above average skills. Fred had an incredible curiosity about everything which was fueled by the range of science and technical courses offered at Lane. In drafting class, he became close friends with Herb Block who later went on to be a Pulitzer Prize winning editorial cartoonist. Fred's creative talents began to emerge at this time. He wrote and acted in plays through the school Drama Club.

High school, however, was as far as Fred went in school. Fred's father needed help with the family business – a small die-cutting business on Chicago's north side.

His father specialized in producing die-cut items out of cardboard or light chip board. When Fred began working for him, his father was mainly producing punchboards. Punchboards were multiple sheets of cardboard with the top sheet perforated in a hundred or more tiny circles. Each circle was sold as a separate chance. When you paid you had the chance to punch out one of the circles and see what, if anything, you had won. While some of these boards made their way to church or charity bazaars, most of them were used in speakeasys, bars and small casinos during prohibition. People would play them for money or free drinks.

The Depression (abetted by Eliot Ness' raids on speakeasys) slowed down the punchboard business. The business found a new market when it was visited by Sam Gold. Sam Gold had worked for Whitman Publishing Company, one of the earliest publishers of comic related reprint books and other children's books. By this time he had formed his own company, American Advertising and Research Corporation. In addition to creating advertising premiums, Sam's company also produced a wide range of different paper toys for various businesses.

Sam had come up with an idea for a new type of pop-up book which he had sold to Blue Ribbon Books. Most pop-up books are quite simple. They often consist of one sheet of thin cardboard. Two pages are printed on the sheets and it is creased and folded. The top half is die-cut and creased so that the figure or foreground comes away ("pops up") from the background. While Sam was going to use these types of pop-ups in the Blue Ribbon books, the center of his proposal were many far more complex pop-ups: an

Fred Voges on the left and Wally Weist on the right strut their stuff.

incredible 3-D monster leaping up at Buck Rogers; Sandy jumping through a hoop held by Little Orphan Annie; the Tournament of Death rising from the center of the Flash Gordon book; and Popeye in a rowboat exploding from the center of another book; and many more. These were to be very complex pop-ups requiring not only difficult die-cuts but precise pasting of the pop-ups to the book.

Sam was trying to find a company to do the complicated die-cutting at a reasonable cost. This was in the early part of the Depression and money was very tight. Blue Ribbon wanted to sell these books, most featuring licensed comic characters, with three elaborate pop-ups in each book along with a full story and many black and white illustrations for only 20 cents each.

Fred Voges, daughter Lynn, and wife Elizabeth in the 1940s.

To get the job, Fred's father had to come up with a way to do the job cheaply. Fred was fascinated by the early pop-up books he read as a child. Fred still owned several books from his childhood – one was a beautiful punch out book based on John Tenniel's illustrations for **Alice In Wonderland**; the other was an early pop-up book by the 19th century German artist Lothar Meggendorfer. Meggendorfer spent his life creating elaborate pop-up and action books. His work was extremely well known in the German community in Chicago where even in the 1980s German reprints of the books still were sold.

Fred's father took the prototypes from Gold, younger Fred worked to figure out how they could be produced cheaply. This involved making some changes in the basic design and suggesting some improvements to Gold that reduced some of the assembly costs. Gold was pleased with the suggestions and gave them the job of die-cutting the pop-ups.

The pop-up books were a great success. Blue Ribbon asked Gold for some similar books. He came up with the idea of the Waddle Books, quite elaborate story books that had punch out figures and a runway. When assembled, the figures would walk down the runway. The first Waddle Book was to feature Mickey Mouse. Fred's father again got a die-cutting job for this and the **Wizard of Oz Waddle Book**. Because the Waddle Books required punching out the figures, complete and intact Waddle Books are among the scarcest of all Disney and Oz items.

The early 1930s saw an increased demand for premiums of all types. Part of this was due to the rise of radio as a major entertainment medium. By the early 1930s, there were several major national networks offering a full range of programs for the whole family. The advertisers, especially on the children programs, found premium offers increased sales. The program producers also found that including premiums in children's shows helped to maintain their audience; especially when the premium, like the decoders, actually played a continuing role in the stories. Advertising for everyday products actually increases during times of economic decline as companies compete in a limited consumer market. During the Depression, paper premiums were a very cheap way of giving consumers something extra with their purchase. Some of the paper premiums cost less than a tenth of a cent each to produce! That tenth of a cent bought a lot of product recognition since children often played with the premiums for months after they arrived.

Another factor in the growth of premiums was the more aggressive licensing of cartoon characters. Licensing comic characters to other media is as old as the comic strip. **The Yellow Kid** was not only the first comic strip, but it was one of the most licensed characters in comic history. Literally hundreds of items were licensed during the Kid's relatively short reign after his creation by R.F. Outcault. With the exception of Outcault's equally successful run of Buster Brown material, no other early strips were extensively licensed. That's not to say there weren't Little Buddy Tucker, Mutt & Jeff, Nemo and other toys, buttons etc. Peripheral material was produced from any number of strips. For the most part, none of it appeared in any great quantity.

The dearth of early licensing was partly due to the fact that licensing was usually done by the artist as opposed to the syndicate. Most artists did not have the time or the inclination to expend a lot of time on developing other outlets for their characters. By the 1920s there was also no incentive as most artists no longer owned the characters they created and the syndicate did not aggressively license their characters. Things changed in the late '20s when the Disney company went into licensing with a vengeance with Mickey Mouse. Licensing became the job of departments of companies as opposed to individual artists. Disney's licensing strategy resulted in a deluge of Mickey Mouse material. Other syndicates and even individual agents saw high profits in licensing. The end result was that the comic character market was beginning to boom about the time radio and the new sound "talkie" movies entered the scene.

As a result, Sam Gold's business greatly increased and Fred's father's business increased with Gold's success. At this point, there were two facets to the paper toy market. The first was the traditional outlet of punch out books, die-cut games and other paper items which were sold in dime stores. The second was the premium market where the toys were just given away as prizes or sales incentives. Sam Gold sold both to the toy and premium market. Part of Gold's business was a partnership company with Einson-Freeman. Gold owned two-thirds of the company called Gold-Einson Freeman and this company was the giant in the premium business.

Fred Voges files contained dozens of Sam Gold premiums from this period. From this period there are also indications that Fred may have worked for other premium producers as well since there are prototypes and multiple samples of premiums like the Ralston Tom Mix Indian Villages that were not released by Gold.

It's known when Fred's father died in the late 1930s, Gold hired Voges as a full-time staff member. While Fred was brilliant in his ability to solve technical problems and to create wonderful ideas, he was not very good at managing a small factory. Without his father's business skills, the factory closed and Fred began working directly for Gold who by then was known nationally as the "Premium King."

Since Fred was not an artist, his job duties involved mainly writing copy (instruction and other text) for premiums and doing mechanical design work similar to what he had done at his father's factory. Fred went to work at $25 a week – a nice salary for a time when a six bedroom apartment in a good Chicago neighborhood cost $29 a month. As part of the deal, Fred signed a work for hire clause which meant that anything he created during his 40 hour work week became the property of Gold's company.

Fred shared an office with an artist, Wally Weist. Wally was pushing fifty – considerably older than Fred. Weist was an incredible commercial artist, fast, creative and versatile. He was able to draw almost anything with minimal reference. His excellence gave him the ability to copy a wide range of different artists' styles. This was of great use on the comic related premiums where Weist had to mimic Chester Gould, Milt Caniff, Harold Gray and others. There were even times when he needed to do several comic characters by different artists in one promotion!

Most of the examples I have show that Fred and Wally would work on a premium together. Gold's company was a continuous flurry of activity as Gold produced thousands of different premiums over the years. The process of selling premiums to clients usually involved several different drafts of a premium. Initially Gold would write a proposal to the client, usually an advertising agency, or directly to a store or company. If the written proposal was accepted, a tight rough was made of the premium as it would look unpunched as well as a prototype that was fully assembled. After approval, the final script and art was completed and sent for final review.

In some cases the process was relatively simple. Premiums needed to be produced cheaply as they were either given away for free or for a box top and a dime. The simplest jobs were already produced premiums where all that had to be done was changing the name of the store or sponsor. In those cases, a sample of the finished premium already done for another client in another market could be sent to a potential client with total final production involving just the addition of a logo or trademark. Next simplest were premiums where the art only needed to be changed. Sam Gold had a standard design for a rubber band gun. Fred had copies of this gun used as a generic policeman's pistol, for the **Howie Wing** radio show, for the Dick Tracy hat promotion and several other campaigns. In these situations, an artist like Weist would just

1950s - Fred Voges (left) with Elizabeth and Pulitzer Prize winning cartoonist Herb Block.

Fred Voges outside Chicago's
Science and Industry Museum.

draw Dick Tracy and paste his head on the original policeman gun's grip. For Howie Wing, Dick Tracy would come off and Howie the aviator would go on (and the gangster targets would become airplanes). The same dies (and in some cases the same negatives) could be re-used for project after project.

More elaborate and expensive premiums involved a lot more work even if based on past ideas. For instance, Gold used the idea of a punch out training cockpit several times during the war. The first trainer was the Jack Armstrong Flight Trainer, a simple cardboard box with a stick that you moved to steer the paper airplane inside the box. The next piece was the Captain Sparks training cockpit done for the **Little Orphan Annie show**. This was a complete punch out replica of an airplane cockpit. The final incarnation was a full size table top cockpit made out of very thick cardboard and sold through Einson-Freeman in a box for $2.

In each of these flight cockpits, not only did the premium need to be designed mechanically so that it would work properly but entire handbooks and instructions needed to be developed that were accurate. Also, Sam Gold usually did not just design premiums but entire campaigns. In addition to the cockpit, store posters would be made, ad slicks developed for magazines, and instructions devised for sales people pitching it to stores as promotion. Dozens of pages of instructions and many pieces of art could be created for one premium.

Fortunately, Fred and Wally worked extremely well together. They soon became close friends. Some of the major campaigns they worked on for Gold included: a series of 15 promotional posters for Sealtest each month featuring a different **Chicago Tribune** comic character; the Pep paper airplane promotion; several Dick Tracy detective kits; at least one Captain Midnight manual; the Terry and the Pirates periscope, airspotter and Genghis Khan book; the Sears Christmas comic books and numerous punch out planes. Weist's graphics for many of these are incredible.

At the end of the war, Fred and Wally decided to team up with a friend H.O. Hipwell as business manager and President to form their own small firm, Advertising Ingenuities. Fred now had a family and wanted to earn more money and own any patents that he created. They initially pitched ideas to many of the same clients that had purchased premiums from Sam Gold. Their work level remained just as intense. In 1948 they created over 24 different games and cut-out toys a month as cereal box backs for Kellogg's! While that sounds like a lot of work, it is only one of several projects they were doing on a monthly basis.

Once the business was established, Fred decided to finally move his family into a house in a nice suburban neighborhood. This was to prove a challenge since they had only a few thousand dollars in savings. Fred purchased a lot in Park Ridge, a reasonably exclusive suburb, and proceeded to build the house himself! This caused quite a stir in the community since it was the first (and last!) owner built home since Park Ridge ceased being a farm community.

As could be expected, it was not your ordinary house. First of all, Fred wanted a maintenance free building. Learning that the Tucker Torpedo car factory had gone bankrupt, Fred scavenged their remaining windshields. These he used as windows after inventing both special curved frames for them and a ventilation system which enabled air to circulate without opening the windows. Fred was very proud of these windows and always kept a hammer on hand to show that they were unbreakable! Other innovations included hidden paneled closets (twelve in the master bedroom alone!), window valances created from scraps of 19th century carved furniture and a living room parquet floor made from several 50 cent barrels of maple end scraps.

Shortly after he built his house, Advertising Ingenuities almost went out of business. They were producing a set of three action books for Simple Simon bread. These books were the size of Golden books except that every other page was die-cut to do some form of action. Simple Simon was going to sell them at cost as a promotion. They accepted one book and two others were at the printers (including **Action Stories of the Bible**!) when Simple Simon went bankrupt. Fred and Wally faced the problem of having to pay for tens of thousands of expensive books! Hipwell saved the day by having the covers changed, deleting Simple Simon's name, and wholesaling the books through Dyco Books as publishers.

The 1950s saw many changes in the premium business. Radio serial programs were on the decline, killed by the advent of television. As a result, several Advertising Ingenuity projects began as radio promotions for Tom Mix (the Tom Mix Circus) or the Lone Ranger (Magic Indian Totem Pole) but saw print years later as generic cowboy cereal box backs. They did a host of bread label campaigns. The bread labels were designed to be collected like bubble gum cards or mounted on display boards. They did a series of different Disney labels including a set that were pasted on punch out puppet heads, a group that formed a Panorama of Peter Pan's Island with all of the characters standing on it; labels that were mounted to form a set of 3-D Snow White pictures; and a weird set where Jiminy Cricket taught safety on flip cards.

Fred ran into censorship problems on two occasions in the 1950s. He had created a Howdy Doody haunted house promotion for Mars candy. This was a spooky house (with a beautiful punch out haunted forest background) which had a rubber band noisemaker to make it bounce and shriek. Unfortunately, the promotion was being produced when Frederic Wertham had just started a new publicity campaign about the evils of horror and ghost comics. Mars decided they did not want to release the premium. Since Mars was under contract with Advertising Ingenuities for the job, Wally redrew the house as the Super Circus Snickers Shack. This was a house with a happy face and Mary Hartline in the window. For some reason never explained, the happy house bounced up and down. This was probably one of the most demented premiums of all time. Movable paper puppets and magic kits were other standard premiums produced by the firm.

Super Circus was involved in another headache for the firm. Mars had decided to issue a pair of moving puppets of **Super Circus's** two main characters, Mary Hartline and Cliffy the Clown. Mary was every pre-pubescent boy's dream girl, a beautiful voluptuous blonde in a short majorette outfit. Wally did an excellent portrait of her for the puppet, the dies had been cut and the first proofs run off the press. Fred shipped copies to the **Super Circus** show and Mars candy. That afternoon he received an irate call from an executive of the show who also happened to be Mary Hartline's boy friend. Mary's breasts were too large on the puppet! Fred stopped the job until Wally redrew Mary's breasts. This was Advertising Ingenuities last job for **Super Circus**!

By the mid-1950s, the firm was facing increased competition from cheap plastic premiums. Most of the airplanes, trucks, boats, etc. that appeared in paper during the 1940s were now produced in plastic. Kids liked the plastic premiums because they were similar to the more elaborate plastic toys in the dime stores. In 1957, Wally suddenly took ill. All his life, he had been a heavy smoker. His lungs finally had worn out. Wally retired to spend the last ten years of his life resting and gardening at a house he bought in rural Indiana. Fred did the art on their final premium, a display for a Chicago beer company. He then decided to close the company. Fred had the perfect working relationship for seventeen years with Wally. He decided that he didn't want to break in a new partner during a bad time for the business.

Fred freelanced for a short while and invented the only patent that he ever owned, a punch out globe. This he sold to the Beckley Cardy school supply company. He received royalties from the globes for several years. He then took a job at a cardboard plant where he designed displays and packages. When it closed in the 1970s, Fred found himself out of work. Few places were using paper displays, and no one wanted to hire a quiet old man in his seventies even if he was a genius.

Though Fred continued to look for work, he essentially retired and lived on social security. He worked at home on various projects for his own enjoyment. Money was tight but he and his wife, Elizabeth, happily survived. Suddenly members of Elizabeth's family began mysteriously dying. They had retired to a senior citizen community at the urging of Elizabeth's nephew-in-law, Frank Albanese. Elizabeth became suspicious as Albanese slowly gained control of her mother's business, a small trophy factory. Elizabeth had the bodies exhumed and autopsies performed. All of her relatives had died of arsenic poisoning! Albanese was investigated and arrested. Death threats were made against Elizabeth and Fred. For a while, they lived under police protection. The stress of this and the long trial caused Fred to have a stroke. The mind that could solve almost any problem was condemned to live out his years in a nursing home where he died in 1986. Albanese was later convicted, and after many appeals was executed in late 1995. ■

(George Hagenauer relaxes from his day job advocating for children by reading comics and collecting comic art. He is the author of the **Collecting Original Comic Art Handbook** *which will be published in 1997 by Kitchen Sink Press. He is continuing to research the life and work of Fred Voges and Wally Weist for a possible book. If you have information related to them, their associates (especially Sam Gold, Einson-Freeman and other premiums companies) and their work, you can contact Hagenauer at Box 930093, Verona WI 53593.)*

As a hobby, comic collecting is easy. There are plenty of places to buy new and old comics, price guides are reliable and accurate, and even the comics themselves are easy to track, thanks to issue numbers and a host of fan-oriented magazines and publications.

But what about other collectible items like toys and premiums? True, there are several price guides dedicated to these collectible items, but the history of these collectibles is not as clearly defined as comic books. There were a large number of premiums and related toys produced by a wide variety of companies, from Post Cereal to Ovaltine, but unfortunately, the toys and collectibles were produced in low numbers, and for every new collectible "discovered," there are a great many that still remain lost. The history of these treasures is constantly growing and becoming richer as collectors begin to discover new collectibles and pay closer attention to marketing campaigns and business practices forty years ago.

Take, for example, Roy Rogers, one of the greatest movie-star cowboys ever to ride across the silver screen. His likeness appeared on hundreds of documented collectibles as companies paid to use his face on products including bread, milk, beverages and cereal. Taking a close look at the marketing plan behind Roy Rogers, it's easy to see that every possible media outlet was included, along with detailed plans to use Rogers' likeness on a multitude of products and collectibles. While many of these collectibles have been listed in price guides, there remains a great deal of Roy Rogers memorabilia that has yet to be found.

The future of collectibles is sure to change in the next several years. Toys and figurines have already begun to gain wide popularity with collectors, as have rings, movie posters, buttons, and other comic-related products. As these new areas of collecting gain popularity, it's important to note that collectors themselves will be helping to write history with each new discovery.

It's also interesting to note that many of the comic characters we have come to know and love began their lives as advertising icons. It was only after achieving fame from the popularity of their primary media that they were then spun off into

KNOWLEDGE IS
POWER
by John G. Frizzera, Jr.

Premiums were produced to sell a wide variety of products, the most common of which were bread, cereal, milk, and beverages. Several examples are illustrated on the following pages, from Lone Ranger selling Schmidt's Blue Ribbon Bread to the Kool-Aid Junior Aviation Corps.

Below left: Terry and the Pirates Canada Dry ad.
Below right: The Adventures of Big Boy #1.

LOOK WHAT'S BEHIND EVERY ROY ROGERS PROMOTION IN YOUR STORE

THE ROY ROGERS ORGANIZATION

ROY ROGERS "King of the Cowboys"
DALE EVANS "Queen of the West"

SPONSORS POST CEREAL DIVISION GENERAL FOODS CORP.		MOTION PICTURES NO. 1 WESTERN BOX OFFICE STAR 10TH CONSECUTIVE YEAR
BENTON & BOWLES, Inc. ADVERTISING AGENCY	ART RUSH Incorporated W. Arthur Rush, Pres. • Larry Kent, Vice-Pres. EXECUTIVE MANAGEMENT	"SON OF PALEFACE" A PARAMOUNT PICTURE
NBC Exclusively		NEWSPAPER COMICS DAILY AND SUNDAY
TELEVISION	ROY ROGERS PRODUCTIONS TELEVISION FILMS	RCA VICTOR RECORDS
RADIO	OSBORNE & WARD FINANCIAL MANAGEMENT	RODEOS & Pers. Appearances
National Advertising		COMIC BOOKS

ROY ROGERS Enterprises   DALE EVANS Enterprises

EXECUTIVE MANAGEMENT
W. ARTHUR RUSH
LARRY KENT

AL RACKIN ADVERTISING PUBLICITY DIRECTOR	DON GARDNER MERCHANDISE MANAGER	CONRAD KREBS SALES PROMOTION MANAGER

THE BOGERTS Inc.
MERCHANDISING & ADVERTISING AGENCY

66 LICENSEES

Newspapers	Magazines	Safety Awards	Fan Mail	Trade Papers	Disc Jockeys

THE POWER TO PROMOTE FOR PROFIT

This organization chart of the Roy Rogers empire was published in the 1953 merchandising catalog shown above. It's interesting to see the extensive media coverage given Roy & Dale.

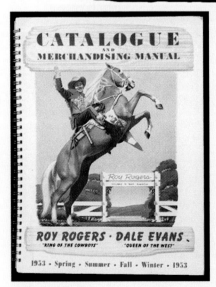

The 1953 Roy Rogers merchandising catalog.

comic books and related products. Once these characters became popular, however, smaller companies couldn't afford the cost of having them on their products. In response to this, new characters were constantly being created to hawk everything from shoe polish to cigarettes. These creations only added to the constantly growing pantheon of comic-related characters which give us such a rich and varied history today.

As an example, consider the modern-day icon of the Energizer Bunny. Over time, as he's made his way through commercials, people have begun to associate more with the mechanical rabbit than with the battery. Who knows? In fifty years, an Energizer Bunny giveaway could be one very sought-after collectible.

The Energizer Bunny is, of course, only one example of a modern-day character with possible long-term potential. Another aspect of collecting today to consider is that, recently, people have started to collect objects which they can display in their homes, three-dimensional objects which can be admired by everyone. As these different products become popular, demand increases, and the market becomes volatile, with prices rising almost overnight.

As the popularity of comic-related premiums and toys grows, collectors are constantly asking, " Where does this piece fit into he history of the character? Were more of these produced by ifferent companies? What was the thinking and marketing hich went into the creation of these intriguing collectibles?"

The purpose of **Hake's Price Guide to Character Toy remiums** is both to chronicle the many toys and premiums hat were produced and to educate collectors about these prod- cts, specifically how they were produced and how they npacted society at that time. With the kind of knowlege about oys and premiums found in books like the **Hake Guide**, there is reduction in wildly high prices being asked for commonly vailable items. By expanding the knowledge base about this cet of collecting, a common reference point is provided for oth collectors and dealers in regards to price, condition, and uthenticity.

With more collectors entering the hobby and new discoveries eing made every day, the importance of publications like the ake Guide can not be overestimated. It's important to note, owever, as more questions are answered and history is rewrit- n, even more questions will continue to arise.

Until then, make sure you hold onto that Energizer Bunny veaway... ■

Above: This Lone Ranger wrapper promotes Schmidt's Blue Ribbon Bread.
Left: The Kool-Aid Junior Aviation Corps Cap.
Below left: Elsie the Cow for Borden's Cheese.
Below right: Kellogg's 'Pop' Cloth Cut-Out Doll.

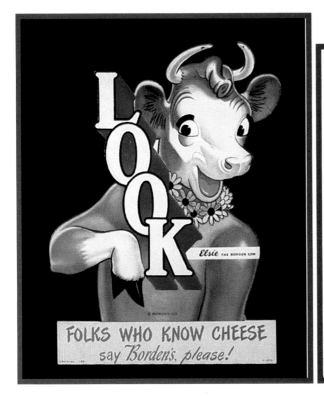

A CONVERSATION WITH PREMIUM COLLECTOR

HARRY MATETSKY

Former magazine and book publisher, Harry Matetsky is a collector and recognized expert in the premium, art and comic fields.

"...even though we're doing the same thing, there is an enormous amount of competition; everybody's out to get the best deal and the best piece."

How did you get started collecting premiums?

As soon as I came out of the womb [laughter]. As a kid, I was a closet collector who didn't know any other collecters, and who'd go to the newsstand, buy comic books, save them, and trade a little here and there. As the old story goes, after I had amassed a couple hundred comics, my Mom got rid of most of them.

As a teenager, I wanted to be a cartoonist. After writing to all the newspaper syndicates and having my letters forwarded to the various cartoonists, they sent me daily strips of their cartoons that had been appearing in the newspapers.

After graduating without the talent to be a cartoonist, I ended up starting at the bottom of various comic companies. While working for Fawcett Publications in 1954, right before they folded up the comic line as a result of the DC lawsuit, I met a bunch of guys who worked on the comics. This resulted in me becoming involved with the editorial end of the magazine business and starting out as an art assistant before working myself up to art director. From there, I ultimately started to publish my own stuff in the magazine business, a lot of teen magazines and one-shots like **Michael Jackson**, **Elvis**, **The Rolling Stones**. These experiences helped me develop an awareness of premiums on a collectible level. Phil Seuling [creator of the comic book direct market] had just started his conventions. The first one, with all the comic books and dealers, was like heaven to me. And that got me started again. During this time, I met a lot of people who are still friends and associates, people like Ted Hake, Steve Geppi, Bob Overstreet, and John Snyder.

So, after starting back with Golden Age comics and building up a very big collection, I started to expand my original art collection while continuing to collect comics. At that period of time, guys like Russ Cochran [publisher of EC Comics] and Bruce Hamilton [publisher of Gladstone] were selling original art work at conventions. My collecting came to include more types of collectibles. During the early seventies, around '72-'73, a guy named Robert Lesser published a book on collecting comic memorabilia, which was called **A Celebration of Comic Art and Memorabilia**. That book displayed a lot of peripheral stuff, toys, watches, games, figurines, advertising pieces, books, so on and so forth. This helped to broaden my collecting. If there was a comic character on it, I was interested. So my collecting expanded to comic character toys, advertising pieces, and comic character gum cards (my collection of these is extensive), and the thing got crazier and crazier. The collection just kept growing and growing, and it's still growing [laughter].

Was there something that really motivated you to move into the premiums?

As a kid,during the 40s, I sent away for a Shadow ring, which became one of my first re-acquisition premiums. It's still one of my favorite premiums. Broadening my collecting helped me realize that there was a whole other world out there besides comics and original art.

Do you still collect comics?
Oh, yes. My collection is pretty decent, and it spans many different collectible fields.

Why do you think there aren't a lot of comic collectors in the premium hobby?
They're not really familiar with what's out there and what's been a crossover between say, a **Phantom** premium and a **Phantom** comic book, or a **Flash Gordon** premium and a **Flash Gordon** comic book, or a **Superman** premium and a **Superman** comic book. They're integrated and one supports the other. The premium situation is really going to explode once the **Hake Guide** comes out, it will open up a lot of people's eyes. Also, in many cases, the stuff is so rare that most people are not even aware that the premiums exist. There hasn't been enough exposure throughout the years on premiums like there has been with comic books, especially since **Overstreet** started the comic book price guide. The **Hake Guide** will do for premiums what the **Overstreet Guide** did for comic books.

Why do you think there's this jealousy between collectors from one hobby to the other?
There's competition in everything, whether it's in business or collecting. With some of the collectibles, you're dealing with competitive people who want the best examples of things, and in some cases only very few examples exist. As far as competition, or one person saying one thing about another part of the hobby, one reason that happens so much is due to an unfamiliarity with the subject. In many cases, it's almost a defensive reaction more than anything else. I know people that collect comic books as much as they collect original art and I know other collectors who do it all, and even though they're doing the same thing, there's an enormous amount of competition; everybody's out to get the best deal and the best piece. In some cases, you're fighting for one or two of a kind.

Who would you say were the major players in the beginning of the premium hobby?
A lot of credit goes to guys like Robert Lesser, Charles Crane and Mel Birnkrant, who were collecting in the '60s and going out and buying this stuff before it was popular to do so.

They were the ones who really stimulated other people into collecting premiums. When people visited them, they became motivated. It motivated me.

Even though I had comic books and original art, I was totally unaware that there were so many people out there that had already begun to collect premiums ten years earlier than me. When I got to know these people and to see some of the stuff they had, I wanted my own and started collecting. I puchased a lot of pieces at shows and conventions and through the mail via networks of other collectors and dealers. I bought all related magazines to find out what was going on. One thing led to another and I became friends with some big time collectors like Charlie Crane (who has an enormous and varied collection) Don Phelps and Russ Cochran. It was a great ride, and it still is.

What do you think some of the turning points were in premium collecting?
When items that people never knew existed were discovered and shared with other collectors, that generated a lot of interest. Ted Hake and John Snyder, of course, were instrumental in that. They motivated a lot of people into collecting. My turning point was when I walked into collector Bob Lesser's apartment back in the early '70s and saw what he had, I was so envious at that point. I hoped that one day I would be able to have a really extensive collection, and now, twenty years later, I do.

Why collect toy premiums?
The best reason is that people collect things from their generation. Guys who are collecting stuff from the '60s and '70s are in their forties, so they go back to their youth and collect the toys and things they had that they want back. By the time they're grown and they have their own money, most of the stuff they played with when they were kids is broken or thrown away. So it's really revisiting your past to a large extent, and if you've got a collector mentality, which many of us have, it becomes a drive, it becomes insatiable. If you're prone to wanting more, once the bug bites you it never ends.

What is the difference between mail premiums and store bought premiums?

The only difference is that premiums you sent away for by listening to **Superman** on the radio, or the **Lone Ranger** or any of the other shows that always had offers, and store-bought is that you would walk into a store and buy a box of cereal or a toy. Cereal and food promotions are really where it all began, where the first promotions were done. Premiums began around the turn of the century. You'd walk into a grocery store and buy a box of Corn Flakes or a box of Kellogg's Pep, and on the front it would be a picture of a Superman button and a caption saying "Buy this cereal, the button's in the box." You'd not only go home with the cereal, my mother bought it for me [laughter], you couldn't wait to eat that Pep because you wanted her to buy another box so you could complete that set! And so that would be a store-bought item. You walk into a toy store and you see a toy that you want and your parents buy it for you, that's store bought as well, just as the name implies. All this stuff is integrated in one way. Whether you go into a store and get instant gratification by purchasing something or you send away ten cents and a box top and wait six weeks and look into your mail box everyday and hope it was going to appear one day, it's the same thing.

So your pleasure could come about in a lot of different ways, whether it be through the mail, by passing the window of a toy store and seeing something you need and going in and buying it, or by reading books on the subject that would inform you about something you didn't know existed. Just when you think you've seen it all, along comes a few other things you haven't seen.

What are a few of your favorite characters or areas of collecting?

I have an extensive collection of Captain Marvel and Fawcett premiums. Probably the most complete collection, that I'm aware of, in existence. I was always a big fan of the Big Cheese (Captain Marvel). Actually, Steve Geppi played a large part in why I got a lot of those collectibles. He purchased the Fawcett warehouse, and in there was a lot of the Fawcett premiums and information on the licensing and distribution of these premiums that I still have in my records and files to this day. So I was always very fond of Fawcett premiums and Captain Marvel. Superman premiums, of course. Superman was

licensed pretty much from when he first appeared in the comic books, it wasn't until a year later that the first store-bought Superman doll was manufactured, unlike Batman. They never really did anything with him until 1966. You can count on one hand the Batman premiums that exist from the '40s as opposed to the thousands that exist in the Superman license, so there's a number of Superman buttons and Superman rings that exist. However, that's not the case with Batman, so when you do find something Batman from the '40s, it's far and few between.

Do you think the general prices of a lot of premiums are realistic in today's market?

No one really understands the value, and the **Hake Guide** will probably shed a good bit of light on the rarity of these collectibles. The book will also show when an item is really sharp and in mint condition, and there are only two or three examples of it known, how rare it really is. This rarity will definitely be reflected in the price, because it's that way in the market today. The prices are realistic and should, in some way, be explained as to why they are where they are. It's really not that hard to figure out: if you have a multitude of the same thing, the price is going to be lower; if there are very few pieces of that particular item, that becomes a super-rare thing, and the price will go up.

How should pricing be done on the rare pieces?

First, you have to take into consideration how many examples of that rare piece exist. Second, condition of course, plays into it. And third, what did it sell for before and how much are you being offered for it now. All of those conditions really determine the value.

Do you have an idea where the market is going in the premium hobby?

The market is very strong in every area of the high end. In other words, the stuff that there are multiples of, those prices won't rise unless they are in very high grade, that's just simple supply and demand. Once this book comes out, the prices in 1996 are going to be very low in comparison to the prices four years from now, when this book generates attention.

As in any hobby, when item values begin to rise "knock-offs" are almost always sure to follow.

Should the people who produce premium knock-offs be prosecuted?

If it's a copyrighted item, and it's a blatant rip-off, that's wrong. The people who own the copyright should be made aware of that, and they should try to stop it. Somebody trying to pass off something that's not real is definitely not good, I'm opposed to that. If it's something that's licensed, that stuff will be licensed forever. There's new stuff being bought by kids today. There'll be a lot more Phantom stuff coming out with the new movie, and it's all legitimate stuff. I just don't like seeing repros and knock-offs that are being done purely to rip people off. And a lot of people are unscrupulous, just like in everything else, once the money starts getting up there, a lot of fakes turn up. You have to know what you're doing, and if you don't, talk to someone who knows what's going on.

You mentioned the Phantom and the new stuff. Are there bargains in the new premium market from places like McDonalds, Burger King and 7-11?

Yes, you just have to be selective. If you go into McDonalds buy a Happy Meal and take home a premium, you can't go wrong as long as you bought it because you like it. I believe in buying from your heart, stuff that turns you on, stuff that you love. Every time I've done that, I've always done very well. If you try to play this market just for monetary reasons, you'll make more mistakes than you will have successes. You really have to know what you're doing. It's a learning experience, and you can't teach somebody overnight. This book will help a lot of people get into it and understand what's happening.

We often hear that you shouldn't collect character premiums because when people look back years from now, they're not going to remember them. Is there any truth to that statement?

The younger collector today, a collector in his thirties collecting stuff from the '70s because that's when he was a kid, is going to start buying stuff from the '60s. Before you know it, the more knowledgeable he becomes, he'll be going back all the way because it just becomes more and more addictive. So age plays into collecting by periods of time, but at the same time, if you really want to get into serious collecting, you can't collect Superman from the '80s or the '70s and not look at Superman from the '40s. So if you're talking about popularity in characters, a lot has to do with your own personal tastes and how far you want to go into the area you're in. A lot of that comes from doing it for a time. You get into it more and more. The stuff that's 50 and 60 years old, a young guy is going to be less motivated to be involved in that because he's not familiar with it, but as he continues to collect, he's going to become more aware of these things, and once he becomes aware of them, he's going to familiarize himself with them and want them.

If you had to start over today, what advice would you give to beginning collectors?

Don't sell [laughter]. Seriously, I would say to the beginning collector, "Buy from your heart. You're going to make mistakes, I still make them, but the trick is to make as few as you can. If you buy enough and you're diverse in your purchasing, you'll have much more pleasure. But you have to educate yourself about the hobby." Again, I keep referring to the book that's coming out because it's really going to wake up a lot of people and motivate them in this area which has not been exposed as much as other areas of collecting. ■

*Note: I asked Harry what his favorite premiums were. He told me that he would get back with me and later faxed me the following list:

Fleischer cartoon Superman standee, 1941; Buck Rogers Solar Scouts patch; Superman Prize ring; Captain Marvel Syroco, both varieties, Captain Marvel Jr. and Mary Marvel Syrocos; Shadow Blue Coal ring and instructions in mailer; **Buck Rogers Cut-Out Adventure Book**; Superman **Action Comics** patch, large patch; U.S. Jones button, membership card in mailer; Captain Battle button, membership card, letter in mailer; Captain America badge, membership card, in mailer; Golden Age Flash button; Golden Age Wonder Woman button; Doc Savage medal of honor; The Shadow glow-in-the-dark button on card; Junior Justice Society membership kit; Great Comics Victory Club button and membership card, in mailer; Superman World's Fair 1940 die-cut pin; American Eagle button and membership card, in mailer; Green Lama membership kit; Buck Rogers metal dog tag; Little Orphan Annie Altascope ring; Captain Marvel boxed set of four statuettes, and sign.

POP CULTURE

A NEVER ENDING STORY

by Michael Renegar

When people think of premiums, the first thing that comes to mind is older cereal toys from their childhood. Images of whistle rings and plastic toys remind us of a simpler time of adventure and surprise. So what ever happened to those premiums and why aren't those great toys available today? Well, hold on to your Atom Bomb rings, because they are.

Every year companies look for new and exciting ways to promote their products. What would surprise consumers is that most of these ideas have been done before in some form or fashion. Sure they may look different, but ultimately, they're the same. So what was the motivation behind the creation of these products and what were the "idea men" thinking in the early stages of the premium boom? To discover the answer to our questions, let's flashback 45 years and take a look at this article from the Aug. 1951 issue of **Sponsor** magazine.

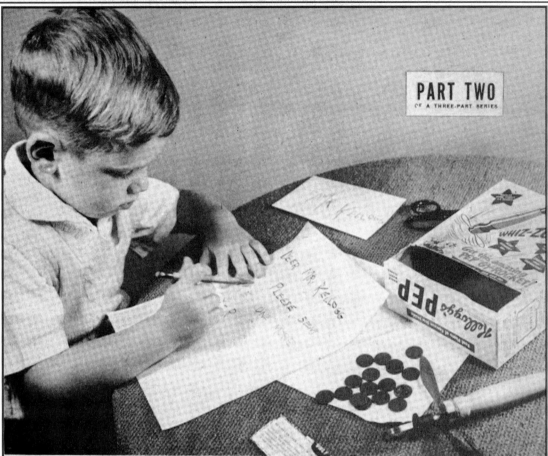

PREMIUMS ARE BIG FACTOR IN MAKING YOUNGSTERS BRAND CONSCIOUS. KIDS SWAY 90% OF PACKAGE CEREAL PURCHASES

PART TWO
OF A THREE-PART SERIES

Sponsors cash in on kid premiums

Never underestimate the power of a child in influencing sales.

Here's how premiums promoted via air get junior on your side

over-all "I swiped this from Harry S. Truman!"

The President has that engraved on fountain pens he presents as gifts. Any premium advertiser can tell you why. The inscription's "excitement value" exerts a strong appeal. Consequently, those pens are desired and prized beyond any relationship to their monetary worth.

Project this psychological strategy to air-advertised premiums for chil-

dren and you get the same result—only more so. Their reaction to excitement value is the dominant factor in the success of premium deals directed at them. It has even impelled them to respond to comic-book offers on such CBS adult shows as *Lowell Thomas, Big Sister, Ma Perkins,* and *Beulah.*

How important are these promotions?

A survey conducted by the Daniel

Starch Organization for Fawcett Comics Groups provides statistical proof that Junior is, among other things, the autocrat of the breakfast table. *He dictates the choice of 64% of the packaged cereals consumed in this country.* The report, based on over 2,000 personal interviews, "asked the mothers if they ever bought certain products because their children asked them to." They found that "children do ask for specific brands" and that

SPONSOR

"their mothers almost always buy them." Over 35,000,000 young Americans between the ages of six and 19 years spend billions of dollars and influence the spending of many more billions. That stacks up as a potential box-top bonanza.

Premiums for juveniles are most important—if you want their business.

"How do you go about finding a suitable item for a self-liquidating offer?" Sidney B. Silleck, Jr., Kenyon and Eckhardt promotion manager on the Kellogg account, poses the question—and the keynote of the answer. "The first and most important thing is to have a plan."

You'll do well to base your plan on these five fundamentals. Choose:

1. The most effective psychological factor in selling premiums to children.

2. The most effective advertising media in selling premiums to children.

3. The most effective operational precautions in selling premiums to children.

4. The most effective techniques in selling premiums to children.

5. The most effective kinds of premiums in selling products to children.

"I give that I may get" is the philosophy of box-top merchandising. You give something extra; you get extra sales in return. That gives the advertiser a justifiable reason for making an offer. But it doesn't necessarily give the kids a justifiable reason to go for it.

What does?

For practical purposes, excitement value is the only thing that induces

Rings are big hit with kids

Product: Quaker Oats
Description: Roy Rogers branding iron ring
Price: $.25 and 1 boxtop
Program: "Roy Rogers show," MBS-radio

Product: Cheerios
Description: Movie Film ring
Price: $.25 and 1 boxtop
Program: "Lone Ranger," ABC-radio

Product: Peter Pan peanut butter
Description: Ball point pen and magnifying glass ring
Price: $.25 and 1 label
Program: "Sky King," MBS-radio

Product: Cheerios
Description: Lone Ranger flashlight ring
Price: $.25 and 1 boxtop
Program: "Lone Ranger," ABC-radio

Product: Kellogg Pep
Description: Donald Duck ring
Price: $.25 and 1 boxtop
Program: "Singing Lady," ABC-TV and radio spots

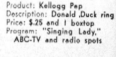

Product: Shredded Ralston
Description: Magic-light tiger-eye ring (in combo with miniature TV set)
Price: $.20 and 1 boxtop
Program: "Tom Mix," MBS-radio

Product : Kellogg Pep
Description: Rocket ring
Price: Free package insert
Program: "Space Cadet," ABC-TV and spot radio

Product: Kix
Description: Atomic bomb ring
Price: $.15 and 1 boxtop
Program: "Lone Ranger," ABC-radio

Product: Kellogg Corn Flakes
Description: Baseball ring
Price: $.25 and 1 boxtop
Program: Spot radio

Product: Kellogg Pep
Description: Plastic ring
Price: Free package insert
Program: "Mark Trail," ABC-radio, "Space Cadet," ABC-TV and spot radio

Product: Peter Pan peanut butter
Description: Television ring
Price: $.25 and wrapper
Program: "Sky King," MBS-radio

Product: Post Grape-Nuts Flakes
Description: Hopalong Cassidy Concho
Price: $.15 and 1 boxtop
Program: "Hopalong Cassidy," CBS-radio

Impact of kid premiums is pointed up by figures below which show how often mothers cater to children's wishes

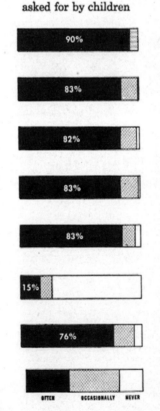

Percent of children who ask for specific brands

	YES
Cereals	71%
Desserts (Packaged)	44%
Milk Fortifiers	35%
Tooth Paste	32%
Hair Tonic	17%
Automobiles	17%
Tooth Powder	9%

Mother said she bought brands asked for by children

	OFTEN
Cereals	90%
Desserts (Packaged)	83%
Milk Fortifiers	82%
Tooth Paste	83%
Hair Tonic	83%
Automobiles	15%
Tooth Powder	76%

From the A B C's of Comics Magazines—Fawcett Comics Group, 1947

Young America to respond to premium promotions. The pulling power of an offer is in direct relation to this factor. It plays the star role. The other four fundamentals are the supporting cast. Consequently, a deal is a dead duck if it doesn't engender excitement. As one youngster put it, "It don't mean a thing if it ain't got that ping."

You don't have to be the seventh son of a seventh son to understand "that ping." In principle, children follow the identical pattern of susceptibility to excitement value as adults. The difference is only in the details.

We don't have to leave the family circle to find examples of the similarity between adults and children's desires. Let's assume the child sends for (1) a *Roy Rogers Western* branding-iron ring and (2) *The Lone Ranger* Western saddle ring. The items correspond pretty much to those his mother sent for a short time ago. They were (1) *My True Story* double horseshoe brooch and (2) *The Second Mrs. Burton* black rose pin.

★ ★ ★ ★ ★ ★ ★ ★
"Color television will be more revolutionary in its effect upon the people of America than was the transfer of silent motion pictures to sound."
JOHN W. HANES,
President,
Ecusta Paper Company
★ ★ ★ ★ ★ ★ ★ ★

While he's on the subject of premium rings, the child may talk about some which have "a secret compartment," "a magic signalling mirror," "a scientific reflector," "a plastic dome" and other fabulous-sounding devices. Actually, they involve varying combinations of magnifying lens, mirror, sun dial, magnet, compass, and whistle. But the descriptive terms aren't irresponsible hokum. They're related to those his father uses when he speaks of, say, "free wheeling" or "fluid drive." It's astute advertising lingo designed to appeal to the imagination. And isn't imagination the springboard of excitement?

Detailed methods of making a premium exciting will be discussed in another part of this article.

Right now let's face this: if you select the right item but the wrong advertising media you start with two strikes against you. It's an irrefutable fact that potential customers won't send coins and proofs of purchase if they don't know about the offer. In formulating the blueprint of your operation, bear in mind that (a) the youngest small fry don't know how to read; (b) the next segment hasn't gotten beyond one-syllable words; (c) their immediate seniors consider the comic section the only part of a newspaper worth scanning; (d) the next group looks at the headlines—then the girls skim through the Hollywood gossip columns, and the boys glance at the sports section; (e) the upper bracket is too busy with schoolwork, dates, and other activities to have time for more than sporadic newspaper reading. From an objective viewpoint, the odds are against printed ads.

The very opposite applies to air exploitation. Youngsters are avid radio and/or TV fans. Listening to broadcasts is an integral part of their daily lives. The first two groups of the preceding paragraphs don't have any difficulty understanding the spoken word. The older segments have developed an amazing versatility which enables them to listen and do their homework simultaneously. In all age categories, broadcast commercials register on childrens' trigger-quick minds, particularly if they involve special offers.

Mind you, broadcast publicity of a premium deal is not an automatic guarantee of success. As with all advertising and selling operations, there aren't any formulas that can't fail. But by exercising these four precautions you can conduct a reasonably safe campaign:

1. Don't expect astronomical returns on each offer. No one hits the jackpot every time. There's no need of purchasing a huge quantity of the premium to be presented. K & E's Sidney Silleck's common-sense advice is "Buy as few as you have to in order to get the rock-bottom price; and then reorder as often as necessary." In that way, you aren't hurt if the deal doesn't set the world afire. On the other hand, if it does click you can capitalize on it as long as the returns roll in.

2. Don't abuse the patience of your customers. Compton Advertising's premium specialist John W. Cantwell has two rules for this phase of the box-top business. They are: "Have the premium available before advertising it." and "Have facilities to mail it promptly." Children become disgruntled if the item doesn't reach them in two to three weeks. If the waiting period drags on, their enthusiasm wanes—

for both premium and product. The operation of delivery schedules can be summed up in four words: the quicker the better.

3. Don't misrepresent a premium. Youngsters generate terrific enthusiasm over an article that fits their specifications. They generate a corresponding degree of disapproval if it doesn't measure up to their standards of quality. In either case, the memory may remain with them for years. As expressed by John M. Davidson, premium manager of Colgate-Palmolive-Peet Company and former president of the Premium Advertising Association of America, "Good will is a volatile and fickle thing—hard to gain but easy to lose. And lose it we will if we do not guard against inferior quality, false claims, inflated values and other obvious evils."

4. Don't feature things that are available in stores. Inasmuch as the actual selling depends on the excitement factor rather than the article itself, a retail display of the item deflates it to the status of the ordinary. That can put the Indian sign on a promotion in jig time. It isn't difficult to guard against that contingency. You can get exclusive rights to an article for a long-enough period to protect your deal.

That brings us back to excitement value. The creation and development of this all-important element is achieved in the process of presenting the offer. There are about as many techniques of accomplishing this as there are approaches to writing commercial copy.

One of the most popular is to build up the item for weeks as an integral part of a dramatic program. It is invariably the hero's indispensable prop. He'd be lost without it. It helps him wade through tribulations to triumphs. Each broadcast enhances its desirability. To the kids it becomes a symbol of adventure, action, victory for our side—and an ideal instrument for having fun. Then with a figurative—and sometimes literal—fanfare of trumpets and roll of drums the momentous news is announced: the thing is available to the listeners.

Here are a couple of quick illustrations of this technique in action. Both were offers made by General Mills and required 25¢ plus the usual proof of purchase. Some years ago an offer of pedometers was featured on *Jack Armstrong* (ABC). During the build-up and the campaign the all-American boy and his pals were involved in suspense-laden episodes where the distance between various places was of crucial importance. They measured almost every step of the miles they hiked. The theme of their dialogue was: How far had they walked. How much farther did they have to go? Would they arrive in time? The kids ate it up. Result: the deal went over big.

Last year a flashlight pistol was presented on *The Lone Ranger* (ABC). It was publicized as a model of the masked rider's own six-gun. During the promotion, the storyline used every device of speech and sound to highlight the hero's blazing revolver. The effect brought a flood of requests for the premium.

Bristol-Myers Company stimulated Ipana toothpaste sales with a deal on *Lucky Pup* (CBS-TV). A ring, featuring a character from the program, was offered on 12 stations for 10¢ and the usual tear from the product package. The puppets did the selling on the commercials. It pulled 40,000 returns. What's more, a survey showed that only 22% of the respondents had used Ipana before the promotion.

The technique works equally well with premiums unrelated to any character of the show. Bob Emery, "Big Brother" of the *Small Fry Club* (Du-Mont) created sales-inducing excitement with his demonstrations of an Indian mask. Whitehall Pharmacal Company offered the "Injun hats" for 25¢ and a Kolynos toothpaste carton. Alice O'Hare, Emery's secretary, reported that "within a week more had been sold than anticipated for the whole campaign." The total response, resulting from 14 demonstrations in six weeks, was 25,000. That didn't hurt anyone—other than Kolynos' competitors.

Another way to make a premium exciting is by giving it pseudo-scientific glamor. Children are fascinated by imaginative jargon. They don't know what "space symbols" are, but they go for them. That and the appeal of hero worship are combined in Kellogg Company's recent offer on *Tom Corbett, Space Cadet* (ABC-TV). For 25¢ and a Pep or Corn Flakes box top they receive a Space Cadet Club membership card with movable space symbols. They also get a picture of the cast, a copy of *Space Cadet News*, and a membership button, certificate, and armband. The deal is drawing excellent returns.

Last summer Quaker Oats Company featured a "natural" in behalf of Quaker and Mother's Oats. It represented a smooth blend of three exciting elements: law and order, Western glamor, a Western personality. The first two were really one—for the item was a "Sheriff Badge." The third was the radio program used to push the offer —*Roy Rogers* (MBS). The badge, plated with 14-karat gold, had "a secret compartment, built-in mirror and hidden signal whistle." The combination induced moppets to mail quarters and trademarks.

Advertising copy based on what makes kids tick makes premiums click. A 25¢ disguise kit—plastic nose, stick-on goatee, false ears, etc.—was demonstrated on Kellogg's *Space Cadet* last February. Emphasis on impressing others, on being the life of the party, roused enthusiastic response. The deal helped move a lot of Pep and Corn Flakes.

Broadcast ballyhoo heightens the excitement inherent in comic books. Procter and Gamble used that to advantage last summer by offering six books for 15¢ and two trademarks on *Lowell Thomas, Big Sister, Ma Perkins,* and *Beulah.* Although two of the products involved don't ordinarily interest youngsters, the deal impelled them to influence their mothers to buy Dreft and Oxydol. That shows what effective selling of a premium can do.

Mind you, it has to be the right kind of premium. Air exploitation can't be expected to generate excitement if the item doesn't have any exciting qualities. Another factor to be considered is the age of the children for whom it is intended.

There are two distinctly separate divisions of offers for minors. An article that fascinates a seven-year-old doesn't have the same effect on an adolescent 17 years of age. For the most part, the cleavage in interests begins when the individual becomes a teenager. We'll deal with the teenage contingent later.

In the six to 12 group there isn't any notable differentiation between premiums for boys and for girls. Junior and little sister send for the same things. This doesn't imply that everything which appeals to one automatically appeals to the other. It simply means there is a wide variety of articles suitable for both. Without getting involved in Kinsey connotations, some of the differences between their interests may have commercial possibilities. So advertisers may be shortchanging themselves by treating the small fry as a sexless entity.

The selection of a suitable item doesn't have to be a hit-or-miss gamble. All other factors being equal, some *types* of things have strong pulling power; some do not. For that reason, there is a growing tendency among premium specialists to study the record of the type represented by the article under consideration. It can help answer such vital questions as: (a) Does it fit the requirements of your sales problem? (b) Does it have excitement value? (c) Does it have immediate appeal or will it need a lengthy build-up? (d) Is the price right for your purpose? The experience of others can serve as guideposts —but there aren't any infallible formulas in this field.

With that in mind, here are some items which have figured in successful self-liquidating promotions.

Comic books have been perennial favorites. One General Mills' offer, handled by Dancer Fitzgerald-Sample, involved a set of four pocket-size Disney books for 10¢ and a Kix, Cheerios, or Wheaties box top. There were four different sets from which to choose. Many youngsters ordered all 16 books.

Magic tricks have clicked for years. A recent deal on *Howdy Doody* featured a magic kit for 15¢ and a wrapper from Mars Candy Company's Snickers or Three Musketeers. The consistent use of magic tricks by Gold Medal Candy Corporation on *The Magic Clown* (NBC-TV) has played a big role in upping the volume of Bonomo's Turkish Taffy. According to sales-promotion manager Tico Bonomo, "Sales figures seem to go along with the response figures."

A very recent Kellogg promotion that drew excellent returns was a miniature plastic aircraft carrier for 25¢. It catapulted a plane, fired a rocket, and helped sell Corn Flakes and Pep. The selling vehicles were *Mark Train* (MBS) and *Space Cadet.*

A parade of puppets has done well for their sponsors, especially on *Howdy Doody.* Prices have ranged from 10 to 50¢. The half-dollar puppet is the current Colgate-Palmolive-Peet offer in behalf of Palmolive soap.

A long list of rings has helped up sales of a long list of products. And their postwar price trend reflects the upswing in the amount of money required for all items featured in box-top merchandising. This is the story: 1947, Atomic Bomb Ring—15¢; 1948, Jet Plane Ring—20¢; 1949, Flying Saucer Ring—20¢; 1950, Movie Film Ring—20¢; 1951, Flasher Ring, 25¢.

The significant thing is that returns have increased much more than prices. In the period from 1947 through 1950 the box-top industry's income rose from $450,000,000 to $1,500,000,000. It's the fastest-growing branch of advertising.

The preceding sentence does not apply to premiums for teenagers. There is an almost-total absence of offers suited to their interests. Deals are either for small fry or housewives. Costume jewelry is about the only thing

★ ★ ★ ★ ★ ★ ★
"Washington, D. C., no longer sees the adman as a stand-in for Mephistopheles —on the contrary, he is often embarrassed at being mistaken for the Angel Gabriel and being asked to accomplish miracles with advertising that a host of angels would find mighty tough to put over."

ALLAN M. WILSON
*Vice president,
Advertising Council,
Atlanta Advertising Club*

★ ★ ★ ★ ★ ★ ★

to which teenage girls respond. The boys have been limited to football and baseball books. They are the step-children of premium operations.

A survey conducted by the Gilbert Youth Research Organization (New York) for NBC uncovered some high-

ly interesting facts. In brief, the findings showed that teenagers are enthusiastic radio listeners. Approximately 64% of them have AM sets of their own. Their total buying power is about $10,000,000,000.

Why do premium advertisers overlook them? Isn't their money any good? Obviously, here is a field which is ripe for aggressive promotion.

Whether dealing with children or adults, premium merchandising is a sound and logical system of stimulating sales. This year marks the centennial anniversary of this form of "aggressive selling by good will methods." From all indications in the days ahead the use of premiums will be a steadily expanding factor in inducing consumer demand for sponsored products.

★ ★ ★

nice example of a movie tie-in with a milk promotion. This poster was given away at the movie premier of *The Phantom*.

Now that we've seen some of the promotions that companies have done in the past, let's take a look at what companies are doing in the present.

Movie companies have always been big on promotion. It seems Hollywood is always coming up with bigger and better ways to push its product. This has led to many unique and collectible items being offered to the public. For instance, movie-goers were given western badges for the movies **Bad Girls** and **Tombstone**, sew-on military-style patches for the blockbuster movie **Independence Day**, and a collectible watch for the video release of the movie **Waterworld**. Promotions like these are designed to help the release of the movie at the theater and sometimes on video cassette. Buttons for movies like **The Shadow, The Crow** and **Jurassic Park** have all increased awareness for the movies while at the same time becoming collectible items. Almost every movie released today has some sort of premium promotion involved. The surprising thing to most new collectors is the fact that most of these advance premiums were not original in origin, but variations of promotions used as early as the 1950s.

Using the past as a guide, many promoters have updated the style of premiums so that they relate and attract consumers today. Countless premiums, offered in the cereal market years ago, have begun to find homes in the new market. Collectible premium buttons, pogs, posters and even the cereal boxes themselves are being offered to consumers today, with more scheduled for the future. Just walk down the cereal aisle at your local food store. Every month new and exciting premiums are being offered to kids and adults in countless food products. Comic book heroes, long used in the '40s and '50s, have started to appear on canned goods and other food products offering everything from premium comic books to trading cards. Even for the release of the **Batman** movie, a special cereal was made and a Batman bank was shrink wrapped to the box.

The fast food chains are even getting into the swing of things. What was once a toy just for kids has now become a collectible for thousands of adults everywhere. High quality products like the Burger King **Pocahontas** glasses, the Burger King **Hunchback of Notre Dame** figurines, the McDonald's Happy Meal Disney toys, McDonald's Happy Meal Marvel Super Heroes, Hardee's X-Men figure sets and the Pizza Hut X-Men videos have all been produced with the collector in mind. Even though this practice has been in effect for the last several years, it is only now that the quality and collectibility have begun to play an important role in these premiums.

When you registered at a Holiday Inn during the summer of 1996, you received a free Izzy figure.

Patches are highly collected and this one is sure to be winner. Used to promote the blockbuster hit movie *Independence Day*.

With so many collectors looking for new premiums, will the market ever run dry? Not likely. Each year, thousands of different types of premiums are being offered with no end in sight. And for all the premiums we know about, there are hundreds that are unknown. That's one of the things that makes collecting premiums so exciting, you never know what you're going to find around the corner. What also surprises most collectors is the fact that premiums are all around us, we just aren't always aware of them. Sure we see some of the obvious ones in things like cereal, but what about mail-in offers? Things like the exclusive Batman action figure you received for buying the animated movie collection or the Star Trek figure you received for buying the video game

A fine example of using a cereal box to relive baseball's past. Note hat offer on side of box.

Glasses have been given away regularly since the 1930s. Now they come in a nice colorful box. Note Colors of the Wind Collection

sometimes pass us by. Collectors need to learn to really look at this new premium market and the many wonderful pieces it offers. With so many premiums being produced today, collectors, while exploring the past, can look forward to a bright and exciting future of premiums. Make no mistake about it, Pop Culture is definitely here to stay. ∎

Cowboy movies made a strong comeback in the 90s. Note premium badges for *Tombstone* and *Bad Girls*. The *Shadow* movie pinback and 1st Disney convention badge pictured as well.

When you ordered a quantity of *Waterworld* video tapes, you could also receive this beautiful limited edition watch.

MARKET REPORT

by Bob Overstreet

The market for toy premiums and related store bought items has come of age and there's been a dramatic increase in the number of collectors of all types of comic character memorabilia in the 1990s. Fueled by the large number of promotions in the entertainment industry, it seems everyone is collecting premiums, old and new.

Every week various fast food chains are giving away new items to collect with the purchase of their products. Taco Bell had a promotion for the comic character the Tick, McDonald's has offered a variety of Disney toys, the Seven-Eleven chain offered free Phantom rings and Burger King couldn't keep the **Toy Story** figurines in stock. The movie industry is cranking out all kinds of buttons, badges and posters to coincide with the release of new movies. Cereal companies are now producing limited edition boxes and using the opportunity to offer unique premiums including rings, decoders, pins and figures. Hotels and motels are also getting into the act with Howard Johnson's staging a big Marvel Comics campaign which is giving away cool memorabilia from the Fantastic Four and the X-Men. The Holiday Inn chains are passing out different free figurines of Izzy, the 1996 mascot for the summer Olympics. In other words, more premiums are being produced than ever before.

What all this means is that kids are continuing to follow in the footsteps of the adults accumulating toys as artifacts. These campaigns and giveaways help maintain the interest in collecting popular culture artifacts and strengthens the overall hobby.

Adding to the interest in older toy premiums has been the dispersal of several important collections in the last few years which has sparked higher prices and more participation of auction bidders than ever before.

Availability of scarcer items has always been important in maintaining and increasing demand in the market. The investors that move and shake the comic book market have expanded their buying habits and are purchasing posters, premiums, advertising and promotional comic book giveaways. The prices listed in this guide for items that are scarce and rare are believed accurate, although perhaps conservative for select items where there has been a lack of known sales transactions. In those instances, it is possible seldom-offered premiums may realize a higher price than guide value.

Despite higher prices, the demand for older toy premiums and advertising items has continued to increase. Another reason for the increased demand is the constant addition of new players that are interested in the past and want to buy back their childhood memories with the purchase of these items. The number of auctions that sell comic character toy premiums and other related store bought items continues to grow and has risen 300% over the last five years. Hake's Americana has been joined by auction hous-

It seems everyone is collecting premiums, old and new.

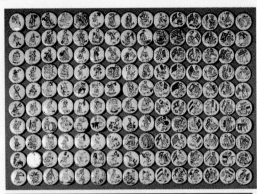

Near complete Yellow Kid button set, late 1890s.
Sells at auction for $3,737!

es such as Sotheby's and Christie's who now sell premiums in their comic-related auctions. Dozens of magazines and tabloids publish articles and price information on premiums every month. Another spectacular development is the increased buying by international collectors from Japan, Canada and Europe who are purchasing premiums, art, and books at a record pace.

In 1995 our industry celebrated the 100th anniversary of the first comic character introduced in the newspapers, The Yellow Kid. This activity brought renewed interest in toy premiums related to the Kid and other characters from the early Platinum Age of comic

Demand for older toy premiums and advertising items has continued to increase!

Group of Yellow Kid periodicals, late 1890s.
Sells at auction for $1,995!

Superman "Leader" Patch
Sells for $15,000!

characters. In July, 1996 Sotheby's auctioned off 31 lots of Yellow Kid artifacts. The prices realized were extremely strong and the following list represents what was paid for some of the Yellow Kid material. H.A. Thomas & Wylie Yellow Kid lithograph poster for the **New York Journal's** colored comic supplement, late 1890s $5,750; McLoughlin Bros. Yellow Kid puzzle the McFadden's Row of Flats, copyright 1896 $1,380; Pulver one cent chewing gum machine with the Yellow Kid figure $747; near complete Yellow Kid pin collection (150), late 1890s $3,73; seven Yellow Kid composition head and cloth dolls, late 1890s $4,025; group of Yellow Kid periodicals (7) late 1890s $1,995; group of Yellow Kid smoking related premiums (13), late 1890's $2,185; Yellow Kid high chair, late 1890s $690.

Costume superhero toys and paper items continued their advance in various sales and auctions with Superman leading the way and forcing record prices for these scarce premiums. 1940s Superman savings bond war poster $14,950; Superman 1950s "television" poster $10,000; 1941 Superman horizontal Fleisher Studio poster $15,000; 1940 Superman large wooden socks box $3,600; 1940 Superman lollypops box $6,000; 1940 Superman Kellogg's Pep poster $20,000; 1950s Superman doll box $2,800; 1940 Superman "Leader" patch $15,000; 1940 Superman letter that came with **Action Comics** patch $5,000; 1945 Superman Pep brochure $3,500; 1945 Superman candy wrapper (1940) $500; 1950s Superman-Tim celluloid die-cut pin $2,000; 1950s Superman-Tim bracelet $1,000; 1950s Superman Christmas cards $500; 1950s Superman window card $3,000; 1940s Superman World's Fair certificate $800; **Superman's Christmas Adventure** 1940 Comic $2,000 in Fine; 1940 Superman newspaper window card $3,000; Superman McDowells promotional button $3,000; "Superman of America"

1940 Superman Christmas Comic sells for $2,000 in Fine!

Superman Tim Bracelet brings $1,000!

/8" size 1940s club button $764; "Supermen of America" 1 1/4" black and white club button $2,300, "Supermen of America" 2 X 2 1/2" premium patch $5,000 in Very Fine (VF); Superman painted version syroco-style figure $5,000; Superman secret initialing with paper image 15,000 in Very Good (VG); Superman muscle building pinback $500; Supermen of America prize ring $22,500 in Good; Superman Fleischer Studio cartoon poster $12,500; Superman 1941 membership kit $150;

Supermen of America prize ring $100,000 in Very Fine (VF). Club kits which included pins, decoders, letters and membership

Red Ryder Victory Patrol in VF fetches $6,000!

cards that were offered in Golden and Silver Age comic books are very hot and in high demand. Premium comic books sold across the board at shows and from dealer's lists at over **Overstreet Guide** prices. Here are a few examples: **Bob's Big Boy** #1 $450 in VF; **Red Ryder Victory Patrol** $6,000 in VF; **Funnies on Parade** $5,000 in FN; **Famous Funnies Carnival of Comics** $7,500 in NM; **Century of Comics** $8,500 in VG Plus; **Skippy's Own Book of Comics** $3,000 in FN; **Tarzan** #988 1933 in VF $1,000; **Roy Rogers Riders Club** 1952 $150 in FN; **Donald Ducks Surprise Party** $1,000 in FN; **Lone Ranger Comics** (Ice Cream) 1939 $4,000 in VF; and **March of Comics** #4 $7,500. Premium rings continue their advance at various auctions across the country. Here are some examples of important sales of rings sold in a major auction: Radio Orphan Annie Altascope FN $12,650; Captain Marvel Compass FN $3,163; Shadow Carey Salt VF $1,555; Green Hornet Secret Compartment VF $3,450; Frank Buck World's Fair FN $6,000.

For years, a small group of collectors have enjoyed seeking out and putting together collections of a very rare collectible that has touched all of us–the cereal box. Only a small number of mint finds of flats have surfaced over the past 10 years. When they did, anxious collectors bought up the entire supply. With the recent publication of **Cerealizing America** by Scott Bruce and Bill Crawford which focuses on the development of the cereal empire, interest in this new collectible should explode. Recently, an auction was held offering a large selection of cereal boxes from 1958 to the 1970s period. These boxes were mostly mint in flats. Bidding was hot with many boxes setting record prices! A few sales are: Tarzan

Quick Draw McGraw cereal box flat from 1961 sells for $1,043!

1946 Pep calendar/blotter sells for $1,200!

1933 **Mickey Mouse milk magazine** brings $600!

1930s cereal box $1,000; Kellogg's Sugar Smacks (Quick Draw McGraw cover/USS Nautilus Submarine) 9oz. flat 2/23/61 $1,043; Kellogg's Puffa Puffa Rice (Banana Splits pin-up posters/Banana Splits record offer) 8oz. flat 3/11/69 $691; Kellogg's Sugar Frosted Flakes (Tony rescue copter/Batman periscope on side panel) 15oz. flat $572; Kellogg's Apple Jacks (Free inside "Crater Creatures" from Outer Space) 7oz. flat 3/25/69 $585; Kellogg's Froot Loops (Free inside "Funny Fringes") 7oz. flat 10/3/72 $403.

Hake's Guide lists over three hundred programs and characters and over a hundred different categories of collectibles. The following is a list of some recent important sales compiled from various auction houses and major dealers; many of these prices are reflected in the values in this book. DC Comics ten-pocket comic book rack 1941 $10,000; original art for Dick Tracy song sheet $2,500; Don Winslow Fleer bubble-gum advertising poster $1,500; Shmoo flicker picture in frame $800; 1946 Pep calendar/blotter $1,200 in VF; 1933 Mickey Mouse Milk Comic Book #1 $600 in FN; 1925 Orphan Annie song sheet $200; Dick Tracy and Smilin' Jack penny candy boxes $600; **All the Funny Folks** book with dust jacket $1,000; Big Thrill gum advertising poster $2,000; Flash Gordon bubble gum die-cut cardboard gun $500; Fearless Fosdick Wildroot Cream Oil advertising standee $900 in VF; Buck Rogers Post Toasties advertising poster $2,000; Shadow secret message advertising card $1,800; **Red Ryder** original Sunday page $2,500; Metro Comics pop-up comic character advertising die-cut standee $1,000.

Frank Frazetta original watercolor art for greeting cards: Little Abner & Daisy Mae $5,000, Shmoo $5,000, Moonbeam McSwine $5,000, Mammy & Pappy $5,000. Other examples of sales include a Batman mask (newspaper premium) $2,000; **Evening Ledger Comics** Mickey Mouse 1 1/4" pin-back $826; Shield G-Men Club 1-3/4" pin-back $1,052; sign for Fawcett statues $4,000; Orphan Annie "Cunningham's Ice Cream..." pinback $596; Captain Midnight Mystic Sun God ring $1,800; Pinocchio Weatherbird Shoes Tell The Truth ring $596; Don Winslow Squadron of Peace ring (Fine) $1,035; Jerry

Buster Brown Blue Ribbon Shoes 1912 boxed pocketwatch sells for $1,569!

Kellogg's Pep set of 86 comic character pinbacks sells for $1,295!

Sign for Fawcett statues brings $4,000!

Captain Battle Boys' Brigade button sells for $1,600!

Lewis/Dean Martin double face puppet $402; Pez figural boy/girl tin clicker (U.S. Zone Germany) $506; Orphan Annie Secret Guard nurse outfit $567; Hopalong Cassidy boxed film w/viewer $575; Prince Valiant syroco figure $500; Lost In Space Switch N Go set $2,222; James Bond attache case (complete) $625; Orphan Annie Magnifying ring $2,381; The Mighty Hercules Magic ring $310; Buster Brown Blue Ribbon Shoes 1912 boxed pocketwatch $1,569; Mickey Mouse Movie Stars gum wrapper $849; Howdy Doody ceramic bust bank $587; the Shadow radio program advertising sign $1,200; Mr. Peanut painted metal figural paperweight $622; "Chief" Mickey Mouse early 1930s movie club officer's button $2,434; Shadow Glow-in Dark Blue Coal ring $580; The Yellow Kid tin litho sand pail $1,800; Kellogg's Pep set of 86 comic characters $1,295; Woodstock Music Festival poster $847; Reddy Kilowatt and cloud vinyl bank $918; Wizard of Oz "Hecht Month" department store button $914; Donald Duck Jackets button $700; **Freaks** MGM movie button $838; Tracy/Annie "Genung's" department store button $1,357; Buck Rogers movie serial button $1,397;

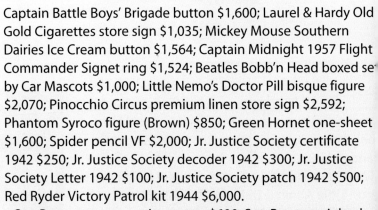

Don Winslow Golden Torpedo decoder brings $2,100!

Captain Battle Boys' Brigade button $1,600; Laurel & Hardy Old Gold Cigarettes store sign $1,035; Mickey Mouse Southern Dairies Ice Cream button $1,564; Captain Midnight 1957 Flight Commander Signet ring $1,524; Beatles Bobb'n Head boxed set by Car Mascots $1,000; Little Nemo's Doctor Pill bisque figure $2,070; Pinocchio Circus premium linen store sign $2,592; Phantom Syroco figure (Brown) $850; Green Hornet one-sheet $1,600; Spider pencil VF $2,000; Jr. Justice Society certificate 1942 $250; Jr. Justice Society decoder 1942 $300; Jr. Justice Society Letter 1942 $100; Jr. Justice Society patch 1942 $500; Red Ryder Victory Patrol kit 1944 $6,000.

Sgt. Preston contest prize poster $600; Sgt. Preston pinback 1950 (Yellow) $5,000; Sgt. Preston pinback (White) $2,800 in VF Don Winslow "Squadron of Peace" Lt. Cmdr. Pin $1,500; **Drums of Fu Manchu** (One-Sheet) $850; Red Ryder Playmate gloves trading cards $75; Lone Ranger Safety Club secret code card $75; Space Patrol cards (16) $300; **McFadden's Flats** Book (Yellow Kid 1897) $7,500; Captain Midnight "SQ" Secret Squadron patch $55; Tarzan 3-D card set $83; Straight Arrow neckerchief $50; Don Winslow Golden Torpedo decoder $2,100 Operator 5 ring $20,000; Tarzan 1930s cereal box $1,000;

Captain Marvel plastic figure sells for $5,000!

Orphan Annie Secret Guard Initial ring $5,000; Quake World ring $1,500; 1946 Captain Marvel plastic figure $5,000; Capt. Marvel 5" figure $8,000; Li'l Abner & Daisy Mae candy machine $650; 1933 **Big Little Paint Book** $1,000; 1935 **Dick Tracy Paint Book** $750; 1936 **Flash Gordon Paint Book** $750; Wonder Woman pinback $3,000; 1941 Captain America badge $935; circular Pep cereal sign promoting comic pinbacks $5,500 in Fine; Shadow game $700; Dick Tracy Inspector General badge $850 in VF; 1941 Shadow ring paper with mailer $941; Lone Ranger Town Cheerios box complete $500; Sunset Carson pennant $150; Annie Oakley hat $100; Shadow glow in dark pinback $1,200; Ranger Joe bowl $50; Roy Rogers Grape-Nuts cereal box $500; Batman Christmas card $750; Batman ice cream poster $500; Batman cola bottle $500; 1950 DC wooden comics rack $5,000; Captain Midnight 1957 decoder $450; Captain Midnight wings $700, Melvin Purvis Scarab ring $1,500 in VF; Radio Orphan Annie Triple Mystery ring $1,300; Shadow Carey Salt ring

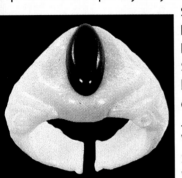

$1,300; Hopalong Cassidy clock $800; Hopalong Cassidy radio $850; Hopalong Cassidy chalk statue $1,100; Hopalong Cassidy blue bust bank $325; Hopalong Cassidy pudding package $200; Howdy Doody Jack-in-the-Box ring $4,200 in Fine/VF; Valric of the Vikings ring $5,000 in VF; Sylvania Lightbulb ring $2,500 in VF; Whistle Bomb ring $2,500 in VF; 1941 Captain America membership card $900 in FN; 1960s Batman print set, mint in box $175; 1950s Tom Corbett card button & decoder $375; Captain Midnight 1949 decoder w/key $225 in VF; Capt. Marvel power sirens (full store card) $5,500; Capt. Marvel wartime comic mailer $800; Hopalong Cassidy hat $1,200; **Superman vs. Atom Man** movie serial promo booklet $800; Phantom serial ring $3,000; Pep beanie in mailer $225; Don Winslow member kit, mint in mailer $500; Capt. Marvel code wheel $700; Doc Savage lapel stud $350; **King of the Royal Mounted** poster $250; Jack Armstrong Talisman game $250; Hopalong Cassidy Troopers Club member kit $225; Capt. Midnight 1949 decoder with key $230; Capt. Video Mysto Decoder $465; Capt. Marvel secret code/magic membership card $185; **Skippy Mystic Code Book** $125; Space Patrol baking soda gun $255; Lord's Gang Buster badge $150 FN; Tarzan 1932 writing pad notebook $125; Captain Marvel patch, shield type $125; **Captain Marvel Coloring Book** $175; Captain Gallant membership kit in mailer $300. Tom Mix belt with box $250; Mandrake The Magician club kit $450; Lone Ranger Black-Out kit $400; Space Patrol rocket with film in box $500; Space Patrol walkie-talkie in box $375; Space Patrol pistol in

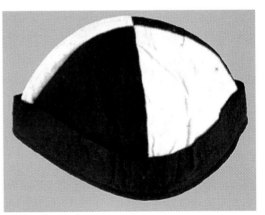

box $500; Tom Mix blow gun complete $450; Tom Mix Gold Straight Shooters badge $135; Tom Mix Signal Arrowhead box only with papers $185.

In summary, the toy premium market is very strong with record sales occurring every month. The field continues to grow with more collectors entering every day! With **Hake's Price Guide to Character Toy Premiums** available for the first time, collectors now have accurate information readily available. The alphabetical listings are easy to use with thousands of collectibles now identifiable with descriptions and prices. ∎

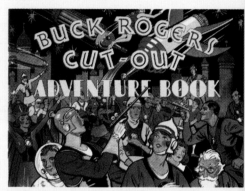

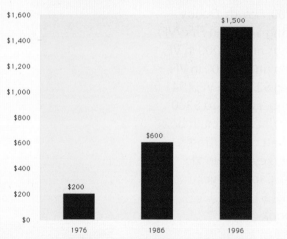

20 year growth of the 1943 Batman mask.

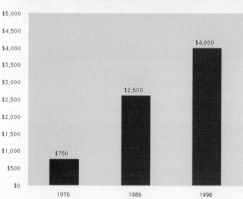

20 year growth of the 1933 **Buck Rogers Cut-Out Book**.

Top Ten Most Desirable Paper Items

1.	Superman Fleischer Cartoon Standee	1941	$25,000
2.	Buck Rogers Cut-Out Book	1933	$4,000
3.	Mickey Mouse Cereal Box	1934	$2,500
4.	Space Patrol Hanging Mobile	1953	$1,200
5.	Cisco Kid War Game	1950s	$800
6.	Terry & the Pirates Terryscope	1941	$600
7.	U. S. Jones Decoder	1941	$500
8.	Howdy Doody Periscope	1950	$375
9.	Sherlock Holmes Map	1930s	$320
10.	Silver Streak Photo	1941	$300

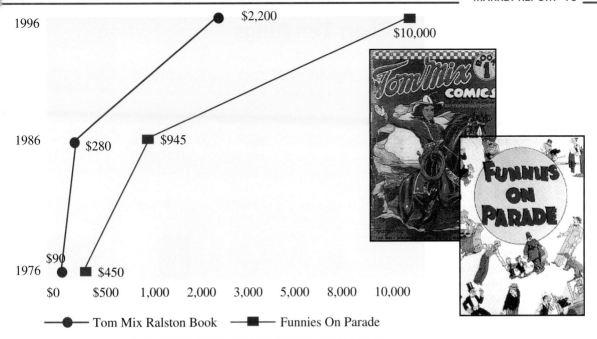

20 year growth comparison of the 1933 **Funnies On Parade** and the 1940 **Tom Mix Ralston Book** #1.

Top Ten Most Desirable Premium Comics

1. **Century of Comics** (100 pages)	1933	$16,000
2. **Motion Picture Funnies Weekly**	1939	$14,000
3. **Funnies on Parade**	1933	$10,000
4. **March of Comics #4**		
(Donald Duck by Barks)	1946	$6,800
5. **Lone Ranger Ice Cream**	1939	$3,500
6. **Superman's Christmas Adventure**	1940	$3,400
7. **Buster Brown Blue Ribbon Book of Jokes**	1904	$3,200
8. **Donald Duck Icy-Frost Giveaway**	1948	$2,000
9. **Terry & the Pirates** (Libby's)	1941	$1,600
10. **Merry Christmas for Mickey Mouse**	1939	$1,400

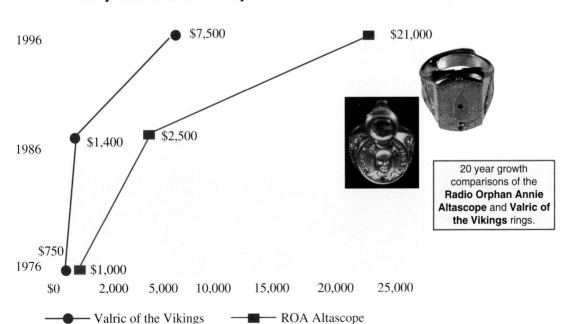

20 year growth comparisons of the **Radio Orphan Annie Altascope** and **Valric of the Vikings** rings.

Top Ten Rings

1.	**Superman Prize**	1940	$100,000
2.	**Superman Secret Compartment** (Gum)	1940	$50,000
3.	**Superman Secret Compartment** (Candy)	1940	$40,000
4.	**Operator 5**	1934	$22,000
5.	**Little Orphan Annie Altascope**	1942	$21,000
6.	**Superman/Tim**	1949	$14,000
7.	**Sky King Kaleidoscope**	1940s	$9,500
8.	**Spider**	1930s	$9,000
9.	**Cisco Kid Secret Compartment**	1950s	$8,500
10.	**Valric of the Vikings Magnifying**	1940s	$7,500

Superman Circular Patch ■ Superman Rectangular Patch

20 year growth comparison between the 1940 Superman rectangular patch and the Superman large **Action Comics** patch for getting 3 members to sign up for **Superman** comic subscriptions.

Top Twenty Most Desirable Character Items

1.	Superman Leader Patch	1940	$15,000
2.	Captain Marvel Syroco Statuette	1945	$8,100
3.	Marvel Bunny Statuette	1946	$6,500
4.	Buck Rogers Solar Scouts Sweater Patch	1936	$5,000
5.	Superman Rectangular Patch	1940	$5,000
6.	Jack Armstrong Crocodile Whistle	1942	$4,000
7.	Captain America Club Kit (4 pieces)	1941	$3,150
8.	Lone Ranger Town	1948	$3,075
9.	Doc Savage Award Bronze Medallion	1930s	$3,000
10.	Don Winslow Golden Torpedo Decoder	1942	$3,000
11.	Space Patrol Lunar Fleet Base	1952	$2,500
12.	Junior Justice League Solid Brass Badge	1942	$2,000
13.	Roy Rogers Prize Poster	1949	$1,700
14.	Jack Armstrong "Captain" Brass Badge	1940	$1,200
15.	Lone Ranger Ice Cream Bracelet	1938	$1,200
16.	Sgt. Preston Camp Stove and Tent	1952	$1,000
17.	Captain Midnight Airline Map	1940	$600
18.	Green Lama Kit	1945	$500
19.	Junior Justice League Certificate	1945	$500
20.	Little Orphan Annie "Safety Guard" Glow-in-the-Dark Plastic Badge	1941	$350

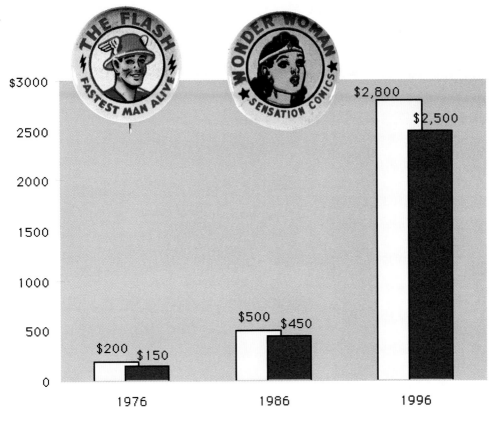

Flash Pinback ■ Wonder Woman Pinback

20 year growth comparisons of the 1942 Flash pinback and the 1942 Wonder Woman pinback from **Sensation Comics**.

Top 10 Celluloid
or Litho Pin-Back Buttons

1. "Sergeant Preston Of The Yukon" red/black on yellow	$5,000
2. "U.S. Jones Cadets" comic book club	$4,500
3. "The Flash" **Flash Comics** (1000 produced)	$2,800
4. "The Scarecrow Of Oz" for Baum book	$2,500
5. "Wonder Woman" **Sensation Comics**	$2,500
6. "Sergeant Preston Of The Yukon" full color	$2,000
7. "Sincerely Yours, Mickey Mouse" 3-1/2" for store employees	$2,000
8. "Buck Rogers 25th Century Acousticon" Dictagraph Products Co.	$1,800
9. "Captain Battle Boys' Brigade" **Silver Streak Comics**	$1,500
10. Dick Tracy/Little Orphan Annie "Genung's" department store	$1,500

HARRY MATETSKY CONGRATULATES GEMSTONE FOR PUBLISHING THE STUFF THAT DREAMS ARE MADE OF!

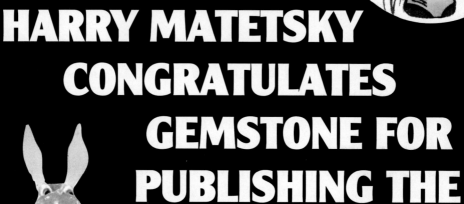

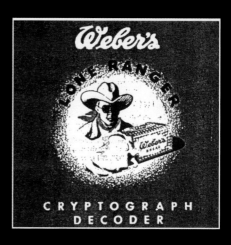

PACIFIC COMIC EXCHANGE, INC.

World Wide Web page at *http://www.pcei.com/*

WANTED!

SELLERS: The following comics and others are wanted by collectors trading on the Pacific Comic Exchange. Please contact The Exchange if you would like to *consign* these or other books at full market value. All books should be graded according to CGSA standards.

CGSA	M	NM/M	NM	VFN/NM	VFN	FN/VFN	FN	VG/FN	VG	G/VG	G	Fr	Pr
	100-91	90	88,85,80,75	70	65,60,55	50	45,40,35	30	25,20	15	10	6	3
PgQ	0 1 2	2.5	3	3.3	4	5	6	6.5	7	7.5	8	8.5	9 9.5 10

Wanted immediately in all grades

Action Comics 1 © DC

Detective Comics 27 © DC

Marvel Comics 1 © MEG

	G 10	VG 20	FN 40	VFN 60	NM 80	NM/M 90
Action Comics 1	$25,000	$50,000	$80,000	$130,000	$260,000	$450,000
Detective Comics 27	$22,000	$45,000	$75,000	$115,000	$225,000	$375,000
Marvel Comics 1	$15,000	$25,000	$45,000	$65,000	$130,000	$260,000

Wanted Immediately in VFN 60 - NM/M 90

	VFN 60	NM 80	NM/M 90		VFN 60	NM 80	NM/M 90
Action Comics 1	$130,000	$260,000	$450,000	Green Lantern 1 (SA)	$1,800	$4,000	$7,500
Adventure Comics 40	$30,000	$60,000	$100,000	Green Lantern 1 (GA)	$15,000	$30,000	$60,000
Adventure Comics 210	$2,000	$5,000	$7,500	Incredible Hulk 1	$5,000	$12,000	$25,000
Adventure Comics 247	$2,500	$6,000	$10,000	Jimmy Olsen 1	$3,500	$10,000	$15,000
All Star Comics 3	$30,000	$60,000	$120,000	Journey Into Mystery 83	$2,500	$6,000	$12,000
All Star Comics 8	$25,000	$50,000	$75,000	Justice League 1	$2,000	$5,500	$10,000
All-American Comics 16	$50,000	$100,000	$175,000	Lois Lane 1	$2,000	$4,500	$8,500
Amazing Fantasy 15	---------	$25,000	$50,000	Marvel Comics 1	$65,000	$130,000	$260,000
Amazing Spider-Man 1	---------	$20,000	$35,000	More Fun Comics 52	$50,000	$100,000	$150,000
Batman 1	$40,000	$80,000	$130,000	More Fun Comics 55	$10,000	$20,000	$40,000
Batman 100	$1,200	$3,000	$6,000	Sensation Comics 1	$13,000	$25,000	$50,000
Captain America 1	$35,000	$70,000	$110,000	Showcase 4	$18,000	$35,000	$70,000
Detective Comics 1	$75,000	$150,000	$225,000	Showcase 22	$3,000	$8,000	$12,000
Detective Comics 27	$115,000	$225,000	$375,000	Sub-Mariner Comics 1	$12,000	$25,000	$50,000
Detective Comics 33	$25,000	$50,000	$100,000	Superman 1	$75,000	$125,000	$250,000
Detective Comics 38	$25,000	$50,000	$100,000	Superman 100	$1,500	$3,500	$6,000
Fantastic Four 1	---------	$20,000	$40,000	Suspense Comics 3	$7,000	$14,000	$21,000
Flash Comics 1	$40,000	$80,000	$140,000	Wonder Woman 1	$12,000	$30,000	$60,000
Flash Comics 104	$5,000	$10,000	$20,000	X-Men 1	---------	$6,000	$12,000

Pacific Comic Exchange, Inc.
E-Mail: sales@pcei.com

Corporate Office:
337 S. Robertson Blvd. Suite 203, Beverly Hills, CA 90211
Tel: (310) 836-7234 (PCEI)

Shipping Address:
P.O. Box 34849 Los Angeles, CA 90034
Fax: (310) 836-7127

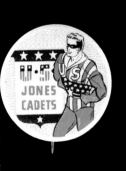

BILL 'N ANNE CAMPBELL

1221 Littlebrook Lane

Birmingham, AL 35235

BUYING – SELLING – TRADING

Radio and Box Top Premiums (Rings, Badges, Decoders, Manuals)

Character Watches, Boxes, Inserts, Bands, Parts, Hands, Dials

Western Hero Items including Cap Guns and Holsters

Comics, Big Little Books, Pop-Ups

Capt. Marvel, Capt. Midnight, Capt. Video, Buck Rogers, Tom Corbett Space Cadet, Doc Savage, Shadow, Tom Mix, Lone Ranger, Superman, Batman, Little Orphan Annie, Mickey Mouse, Donald Duck, Popeye, Howdy Doody, Hopalong Cassidy, Roy Rogers, G-Man, Gene Autry, Jack Armstrong, Davy Crockett, Paladin, Rin Tin Tin, Sgt. Preston, Zorro, Green Hornet, Sky King, Straight Arrow, Buster Brown, Flash Gordon

For personal collection: Capt. Marvel items wanted. Also especially need Whistle Bomb Ring, Big Bad Wolf and Donald Duck 1934 Wrist Watches with leather bands.

BIG-D COLLECTIBLE SHOW
❖ ❖ ❖ Dallas, Texas ❖ ❖ ❖

Flying rodents, political pundits, fat cats and more than a few super heroes...

(just another day at the International Museum of Cartoon Art.)

• • • • • • • • • • • • • • • • • • •

The only museum of its kind anywhere in the world featuring
masterpieces of animation, editorial cartoons, comic strips,
comic books, sports cartoons and more
displayed in permanent and changing exhibition galleries.
Visit the theater and Create-a-Toon Center.

• • • • • • • • • • • • • • • • • • •

**Drop by and visit the International Museum of Cartoon Art.
We're in Mizner Park- 201 Plaza Real, Boca Raton, Florida
or call 561-391-2200 for more information.**

Wallace-Homestead presents a trio of value and identification guides authored by Ted Hake—respected authority on Americana and 20th-century collectibles.

Descriptions, photos, and values for more than 1,500 items. Ted covers 65 of your favorite cowboy heroes of the movies and TV over a 50-year span—Roy Rogers, Hopalong Cassidy, Gene Autry, the Lone Ranger, Tom Mix, Annie Oakley, Paladin, and many more!

Hake's Guide to Cowboy Character Collectibles
192 pages, plus 8 pages in color
ISBN: 0-87069-647-5
$17.95, plus $2.50 shipping and handling

Your familiar friends from the Sunday funnies and comics get star treatment from Ted in this cavalcade of toys, dolls, figurals, and paper collectibles. Over 1,500 items from 75 strips and comics covering a hundred-year span are presented with vivid descriptions and values.

Hake's Guide to Comic Character Collectibles
192 pages, plus 8 pages in color
ISBN: 0-87069-646-7
$17.95, plus $2.50 shipping and handling

Tons of figurals, dolls, cars 'n' trucks, die-cuts, and more— 1,500 items in all—to delight the advertising collector. One hundred famous American brand names are represented —from Alka-Seltzer to Wrigley's gum. All items are pictured, described, and priced.

Hake's Guide to Advertising Collectibles
192 pages, plus 8 pages in color
ISBN: 0-87069-645-9
$17.95, plus $2.50 shipping and handling

Wallace-Homestead Book Company One Chilton Way Radnor, PA 19087-0230

WALLACE-HOMESTEAD

Check with your dealer or local bookstore first, or order direct with your Mastercard or VISA by calling 1-800-695-1214, 9:00 AM - 4:30 PM ET, Mon.-Fri. Dealer inquiries welcomed.

DIRECTORY OF SHOPS
(PAID ADVERTISING – STORE LISTING)

You can have your store listed here for very reasonable rates. Send for details and deadline for the next Guide. The following list of stores have paid to be included in this list. We cannot assume any responsibility in your dealings with these shops. This list is provided for your information only. When planning your trip, it would be advisable to make appointments in advance.

CALIFORNIA
Happy Trails
1606 Haight St.
San Francisco, CA 94117
PH: (415) 431-7232

Brian Rachfal
1177 Branham Ln., Ste. 359
San Jose, CA 95118
PH: (408) 629-3980

FLORIDA
Whiz Bang! Collectibles
948 E. Semoran Blvd.
Casselberry, FL 32707
PH: (407) 260-8869

Tropic Comics East Inc.
5439 N. Federal Hwy.
Ft. Lauderdale, FL 33308
PH: (954) 351-0001

Tropic Comics South Inc.
742 N. E. 167th. St.
N. Miami Beach, FL 33162
PH: (305) 940-8700

Tropic Comics Inc.
313 S. State RD 7
Plantation, FL 33317
PH: (954) 587-8878

ILLINOIS
Jack Melcher, Buy Where The Dealers Buy
P. O. Box 14
Waukegan, IL 60079-0014
PH: (847) 249-5626

June Moon Collectibles
245 N. Northwest Hwy.
Park Ridge, IL 60068
PH: (847) 825-1411

MASSACHUSETTS
Robert DeCenzo
P. O. Box 2266
Framingham, MA 01703
PH: (508) 879-8541

MISSOURI
Decades Of Toys
3315 Woodson
Breckenridge Hills, MO 63114-4718
PH: (314) 427-8693

OHIO
Toys Toys Toys
110 Main St.
Bellville, OH 44813
PH: (419) 886-4782

TEXAS
Bedrock City Comic Co.
6521 Westheimer
Houston, TX 77057
PH: (713) 780-0675

VIRGINIA
Richmond Book Shop
808 W. Broad Street
Richmond, VA 23220
PH: (804) 644-9970

CLASSIFIED ADVERTISING

$*$*SUPERMAN COLLECTIBLES WANTED!*$*$
BUYING ALL SUPERMAN ITEMS FROM 1938-1966:
TOYS, GAMES, FIGURES, BUTTONS, RINGS, PREMIUMS, ADV.
MATERIALS,... ANYTHING!!!!
DANNY FUCHS, 209-80 18TH AVE., BAYSIDE, NY 11360.
718-225-9030 FAX: 718-225-3688.
"AMERICA'S FOREMOST SUPERMAN COLLECTOR"

Forget Antique stores! Visit my American Junk Shop! Fun & Affordable! Call Gretchen at Happy Trails SF, CA.
415-431-7232

Premium Display Case: Display, Organize, and Protect up to 35 collectibles per case! $10.00 ea. plus S & H, 4 or more ONLY $7.95 plus S & H Visa/MC Accepted. Shelf or wall mount, lock together when stacked. L. S. A. S. E. Dept. PH Collectors Display Case Co., RT2 Box 73, Fremont NE 68025-9635 (402-721-4765)

AUTOMOBILE/TRUCK/MOTORCYCLE Literature
Wanted: 1900-1975. I buy sales brochures, manuals, toys, racing memorabilia, etc. Walter Miller, 6710 Brooklawn, Syracuse, NY 13211 (315) 432-8282. FAX (315) 432-8256.

Arne Johnsen • Crestwood Village I
151-D Azalia Drive • Whiting, NJ 08759 • (908) 849-0555
Premium Collector of Capt. Marvel, The Lone Ranger,
Tom Mix and Capt. Midnight.

COMIC BOOKS FOR SALE
One of the world's largest catalogues selling Golden Age, DC, Marvel, Dell, Classic Illustrated, plus BLB's, Sunday pages, original art. We supply Canadians with all types of plastic bags, acid free boxes and boards, etc. Send $2.00 for catalogue.

COMIC BOOKS WANTED
Highest prices paid for comic books, BLB's, newspaper comics before 1959. 40 years as a collector and dealer. Contact us before selling.
INTERNATIONAL COMIC BOOK COMPANY
CALVIN AND ELEANOR SLOBODIAN
74 WATERLOO CRES., BRANDON, MANITOBA
CANADA R7B3W7 PHONE 204-728-4337

MAD and Alfred E. Neuman collectible items wanted: jewelry (lapel pin, tie pin, cuff links, key chain, charm bracelet) Halloween costumes, hardback and paperback books, A. E. N. for President campaign kits, more recent pinback buttons, Hallmark greeting cards, FLIP skateboards, plus other MAD-related items and anything with A. E. N. face or likeness. Also need a variety of old annuals (Worst from MAD, More Trash from MAD, MAD Follies, MAD Special) with bonuses intact, as well as magazines (#24-300), including Humbug and Panic comics and magazines, in NM or better condition. Bennett Barsk, 13-A Sunset Drive, Alexandria, V. 22301 (703) 299-8749.

LARGE SELECTION OF RINGS, CEREAL PREMIUMS & CHARACTER TOYS. BUY & SELL. DON WILSON
(612) 789-5498.

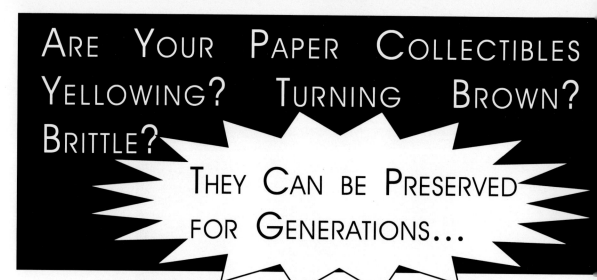
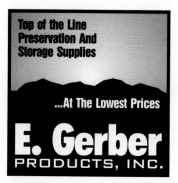

(Prices listed represent **GOOD**, **FINE**, and **NEAR MINT** conditions.)

ACE DRUMMOND

World War I air ace Eddie Rickenbacker created the story line for this aviation strip, with illustrations by Clayton Knight, for King Features in 1934. The strip was not a major success and was dropped in the late 1930s. A 13-episode adventure serial based on the strip was produced by Universal Pictures in 1936, with John King as Drummond and Noah Beery, Jr., as Jerry, his mechanic. The serial was released to TV in 1949.

ACE-1

ACE-1. "Ace Drummond" Cello. Button, 1936. Universal Pictures. For 13-chapter movie serial "Ace Drummond" with added inscription "Capt. Eddie Rickenbacker's Junior Pilot's Club". - **$60 $150 $300**

ADMIRAL BYRD

Richard E. Byrd (1888-1957), American aviator and preeminent polar explorer, flew to the North Pole and back in 1926, made a spectacular transatlantic flight in 1927, and starting in 1928, led several important expeditions to Antarctica. The second such expedition featured weekly on-site short wave broadcasts - *The Adventures of Admiral Byrd* - over the CBS network from November 1933 to January 1935. The program was sponsored by Grape-Nuts Flakes.

ADM-1   ADM-2

ADM-1. Commander Byrd Cello. Button, 1928. Identified "Commander Richard E. Byrd". - **$10 $20 $30**

ADM-2. Admiral Byrd Cello. Button, 1930. Profile picture inscribed "Rear Admiral Richard Evelyn Byrd, U.S.N." - **$8 $15 $25**

ADM-3

ADM-3. "Authorized Map Of The Second Byrd Antarctic Expedition", c. 1933. General Foods. 18x24" opened. - **$15 $25 $60**

(front)   ADM-4   (back)

ADM-4. Byrd Map Hard Cardboard Version, c. 1933. Thick cardboard back with two hangers. - **$30 $60 $120**

ADM-6

ADM-5

ADM-5. "South Pole Radio News" Photo Newspaper, c. 1933. Grape-Nuts, "The Cereal Byrd Took To Little America". Issue #3 shown. At least three issues known. Each - **$8 $24 $40**

ADM-6. "To The South Pole With Byrd" Booklet, 1933. Ralston Purina Co. - **$10 $15 $20**

ADM-7

ADM-7. Admiral Byrd Grape Nuts Booklet, 1930s. - **$10 $20 $40**

ADVENTURE COMICS

Major Malcolm Wheeler-Nicholson got into the comic book publishing business in early 1935 with *New Fun*. Although sales weren't very good, he decided to try a second title. *New Comics* #1 appeared in late 1935 with paper covers and 80 pages of color and black and white stories and art. Siegel and Shuster did Federal Men and Sheldon Mayer and Walt Kelly also contributed. Starting with issue #12, the title became *New Adventure* and finally *Adventure Comics* with issue #32. Like *New Fun*, *Adventure Comics* was part of the foundation of DC Comics. DC cancelled the title in 1983.

ADC-2

ADC-1   ADC-3

ADC-1. "Special Operator" Cello. Button,
c. 1937. New Adventure Comics magazine. -
$35 $100 $200

ADC-2. Club Member Cello. Button,
c. 1937. Inscribed "Special Operator/Junior Federal Men
Club/New Adventure Comics Magazine." - **$35 $100 $200**

ADC-3. "Special Operator" Cello. Button,
c. 1939. Adventure Comics magazine. - **$40 $120 $240**

ADC-4

ADC-4. "Junior Federal Men Club" Member Card,
c. 1939. Adventure Comics magazine. Ink stamped Chief
Operator's name "Steve Carson". - **$40 $80 $150**

ADVERTISING MISCELLANEOUS

Literally thousands of product makers in the past century
have offered premiums in token or sporadic fashion. An
absolute listing of all known advertising premiums would
necessitate a massive set of volumes in book form while still
leaving gaps of information lost in time. This section offers
an overview of advertising premiums and similar items of
established appeal to collectors. Represented are some of
the most famous trademark characters of our popular culture.
A more comprehensive listing is contained in *Hake's Guide
To Advertising Collectibles/100 Years of Advertising From
100 Famous Companies* published in 1992.

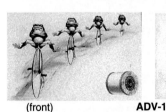 

(front)   ADV-1   (back)

ADV-1. Frogs Thread J & P Coats Trade Card,
1890s. - **$20 $40 $80**

(closed)   ADV-2   (open)

**ADV-2. Mother Goose Series - Mother in Shoes
Trade Card,**
1890s. Nestle's Chocolate. - **$30 $60 $90**

(front)   ADV-3   (back)

ADV-3. Spider's Spool Cotton Trade Card,
1890s. - **$20 $40 $80**

ADV-4

**ADV-4. Mother Goose Series - Mother in Shoes
Trade Card,**
1900s. Nestle's Food. - **$10 $20 $40**

ADV-5

ADV-5. Red Goose Alarm Clock,
1920s. - **$150 $300 $600**

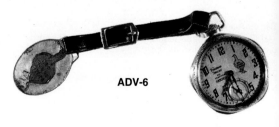

ADV-6

ADV-6. Red Goose Pocket Watch & Fob,
1927. Watch - **$200 $400 $600**
Fob - **$50 $100 $150**

ADV-7

ADV-8

ADV-15   ADV-16

ADV-17

ADV-7. H. C. B. (Hot Cereal Breakfast) Club Grand Award Certificate,
1935. Cream-of-Wheat premium. - **$20 $40 $60**

ADV-8. H. C. B. (Hot Cereal Breakfast) Club Letter/Poster-on-Back,
1935. Cream-of-Wheat premium. - **$20 $40 $60**

ADV-15. Kool-Aid 10x12" Sign,
1930s. Has attached membership certificate for Junior Aviation Corps. - **$50 $100 $200**

ADV-16. T.W.A. Kool-Aid Club Instruction Form,
1930s. - **$20 $40 $60**

ADV-17. Kool-Aid Aviation Club Cap,
1930s. - **$30 $60 $90**

ADV-10   ADV-11

ADV-9

ADV-18

ADV-19

ADV-9. Rippled Wheat - Jack Dempsey 6" Standee,
1930s. - **$50 $125 $250**

ADV-10. "Light Up A Kool" Willie Penguin Iron Cigarette Lighter,
1930s. - **$75 $150 $275**

ADV-11. "RCA" Cardboard Fan,
1930s. Radio Corp. of America. - **$35 $60 $100**

ADV-18. "Campbell's Kid Club" Cello. Button,
c. 1930s. 1-1/2" "Official Badge". - **$35 $65 $125**

ADV-19. ESKO-GRAM Sign,
1930s. With promo list that promotes premiums. - **$30 $60 $120**

ADV-12   ADV-13   ADV-14

ADV-20

ADV-20. Chiquita Banana Fabric Doll Pattern With Envelope,
c. 1944. Kellogg's Corn Flakes. First version offered.
Near Mint Packaged - **$100**
Loose Uncut - **$20 $40 $60**

ADV-12. "Michelin" Plastic Ashtray,
1930s. - **$35 $70 $100**

ADV-13. Nipper Papier Mache Store Display,
1930s. Victor Talking Machine Co. - **$150 $225 $350**

ADV-14. Aristocrat Tomato Composition Figure,
1930s. White base or black base. - **$125 $250 $400**

ADV-21

ADV-22

ADV-21. "RCA Victor Little Nipper" Cello. Button,
c. 1948. "Club Member" designation for children's records series. - **$15 $25 $50**

ADV-22. Fearless Fosdick Matches,
1949. - **$20 $40 $80**

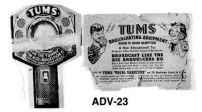

ADV-23   ADV-24

ADV-23. Tums Broadcasting Equipment,
1940s. Radio premium with mailer. - **$25 $50 $75**

ADV-24. Macy's Red Star Club Badge,
1940s. Scarce. - **$20 $40 $60**

ADV-25   ADV-26

ADV-27

ADV-25. Red Goose Tin Whistle,
1940s. Shoe premium. - **$10 $20 $40**

ADV-26. War Bond Matchbook Promo,
1940s. Striking surface on Hitler's rear end. - **$30 $60 $90**

ADV-27. Rocket Gyro X-3 with Mailer,
1940s. Sponsor Hometown Grocers. - **$20 $40 $60**

ADV-28   ADV-29   ADV-30

ADV-28. Campbell Kid Plaster Wall Plaque With Thermometer,
c. 1940s. - **$60 $100 $150**

ADV-29. "Dr. Kool" Plaster Figure Paperweight,
1940s. - **$75 $150 $225**

ADV-30. Kool Plastic Salt & Pepper Set,
1951. Boxed - **$20 $50 $80**
Loose - **$10 $18 $30**

ADV-31   ADV-32   ADV-33

ADV-31. 7up "Fresh Up Freddie" Litho. Button,
c. 1959. - **$10 $20 $30**

ADV-32. 7up "Fresh-Up Freddie" Soft Rubber Doll,
c. 1959. - **$50 $125 $250**

ADV-33 Campbell Kids Silver Plate Spoons,
1950s. Each - **$5 $8 $10**

ADV-34   ADV-35

ADV-34. "Oscar Mayer" Plastic Weinermobile,
1950s. "Little Oscar" figure rises and lowers. - **$75 $140 $250**

ADV-35. Missile Game Set,
1950s. Consists of map, punch-outs, manual, instructions, game board, and mailer. Hi-C Minute Maid premium. - **$20 $40 $80**

ADV-36   ADV-37

ADV-36. Red Goose Shoe,
1950s. St. Louis Zoo punch-outs. - **$30 $60 $90**

ADV-37. Flap Happy Bird with Mailer,
1950s. Post Toasties premium. - **$20 $40 $60**

ADV-38

ADV-38. Esso Space Captain Sign (Silver Wings),
1950s. Canada. - **$20 $40 $80**

ADV-40

ADV-46 ADV-47 ADV-48

ADV-46. Fearless Fosdick 15x36" Standee,
1950s. Scarce. Wildroot Hair Tonic. Five pieces attached to box. - **$300 $600 $1200**

ADV-47. Mr. Clean Vinyl Doll,
c. 1961. Procter & Gamble. - **$25 $40 $65**

ADV-48. Robin Hood Decoder and Mailer,
1963. ARO Milk premium. - **$30 $60 $120**

ADV-39

DV-39. Fireball Twigg Midget Kite Kit with Mailer,
950s. 6 Kites. - **$15 $30 $60**

DV-40. Grape Nuts Flakes Fireball Twigg Kite Premium ign,
950s. - **$20 $40 $80**

ADV-41 ADV-42

DV-41. "RCA" Victor Plastic Salt & Pepper Set,
950s. RCA Victor Corp. - **$20 $35 $50**

DV-42. Bardahl Detective Club 10x15" Sign,
950s. Rare. Shows all the villains. - **$100 $200 $400**

ADV-50 ADV-51

ADV-49

ADV-49. "Bud Man" Ceramic Stein,
c. 1969. Re-issued in 1990s. Original marked under base. Ceramarte made in Brazil. - **$150 $225 $350**

ADV-50. Marky Maypo Vinyl Figure,
1960s. Maypo Cereal. - **$25 $50 $75**

ADV-51. Campbell Kid Plastic Salt & Pepper Set,
1960s. - **$15 $25 $45**

ADV-43

ADV-45 ADV-44

DV-43. Bardahl Club Shield Litho. Tab,
50s. - **$5 $10 $20**

DV-44. Red Goose Display Goose,
50s. Scarce. Goose lays plastic golden eggs. - **00 $600 $900**

DV-45. Red Goose Gold Plastic Egg-Bank,
50s. Bank contained prize, listed as previous item. - **0 $20 $30**

ADV-53 ADV-54 ADV-55

ADV-52

ADV-52. SpaghettiOs Spoon Premium,
1960s. - **$20 $30 $40**

ADV-53 Colonel Sanders Composition Bobbing Head,
1960s. - **$75 $130 $200**

ADV-54. Bud Man Foam Rubber Doll,
c. 1970. - **$100 $140 $175**

ADV-55. "Chicken Hungry" Flexible Plastic Ring,
1972. Red Barn System. - **$10 $20 $35**

ADV-56   ADV-57

ADV-56. Indian Sticker Badges,
1972. Ovaltine premium. 6 different. Each - **$2 $4 $10**

ADV-57. "Bazooka Joe" Cloth Doll,
c. 1973. Bazooka Gum. 19" tall. - **$8 $15 $25**

ADV-59

ADV-58

ADV-58. "Heinz" Talking Plastic Alarm Clock,
1980s. Battery operated. - **$50 $100 $150**

ADV-59. Raid Bug Plastic Wind-Up,
1980s. - **$35 $75 $125**

ADV-60   ADV-61

ADV-60. Raid Battery Operated Plastic Robot With Remote Control,
1980s. - **$125 $250 $300**

ADV-61. Hershey "Messy Marvin Magic Decoder",
1980s. Hershey's Chocolate Syrup. Mechanical cardboard with two diecut letter openings. - **$5 $12 $20**

ADV-63

ADV-62

ADV-62. Twinkie the Kid 4' Anniversary Standee,
1990. - **$30 $60 $120**

ADV-63. "Oscar Mayer" Weinermobile,
c. 1991. Re-issue without Little Oscar figure. - **$10 $15 $2●**

AIR JUNIORS

One of the earliest radio clubs designed to encourage happ●
boys and girls to learn about flying airplanes and aspire to
become pilots when they grew up, the *Air Juniors* club was
formed in 1929. It was sponsored by the Common Wealth
Edison Electric Shops. The project was promoted on the
WENR Radio station broadcasting out of Chicago. The ide●
for the club piggy-backed on the popularity of Charles
Lindbergh's flight from New York to Paris in May of 1927.

AIR-1

AIR-1. Member's Card,
1929. - **$20 $40 $80**

AIR-2

AIR-3

AIR-2. Club Letter,
1929. - **$10 $15 $30**

AIR-3. Club Member Pin,
1929. Scarce. - **$75 $100 $200**

ALPHONSE AND GASTON

"You first, my dear Gaston!" "After you, my dear Alphons●
Frederick Opper's pair of acutely polite Frenchmen and th●
friend Leon first appeared in the Hearst Syndicate Sund●
pages in 1902. The strip was a hit with readers, but a●
1904 the characters appeared only occasionally in Opp●
other strips, particulary *Happy Hooligan* and *And Her Na●
Was Maud.* An early collection of color reprints was p●
lished by the *N.Y. American & Journal.*

ALP-1

ALP-2

ALP-1. "Alfonse & Gaston" Cut-Out Supplement,
1902. New York American & Journal newspaper.
Uncut - **$25 $50 $75**

ALP-2. Cello. Button,
1903. Advertises South Dakota State Fair. - **$8 $15 $30**

ALP-3

ALP-3. Handkerchief,
1903. Probable store item. - **$10 $20 $35**

ALP-4

ALP-5

ALP-6

ALP-4. Cello. Button,
1903. Advertises Omaha Grocers and Butchers picnic. -
$10 $20 $35

ALP-5. Alfonse Tinted White Metal Charm,
1904. There is a matching Gaston. Each - **$5 $12 $20**

ALP-6. Aluminum Cartoon Card,
1904. Store item set of 10 aluminum cards, only one featuring Alphonse & Gaston. Card pictures lady waiting at her and as they deliberate who should go first. - **$15 $25 $40**

ALP-7

ALP-7. Postcard,
1906. American Journal Newspapers. - **$5 $10 $15**

AMERICAN BANDSTAND

started in 1952 on WFIL, a Philadelphia ABC affiliate, and went on to become one of television's longest-running and most successful shows. Dick Clark brought *American Bandstand* to prime-time ABC in 1957, where it ran for 13 weeks from October through December. Since then, under

various names and in different formats and time slots, Clark's program has showcased thousands of contemporary bands, singers and dancers. Promotional items associated with the show typically carry an American Broadcasting Co. copyright.

AME-1

AME-2

AME-1. "Dick Clark Yearbook",
1957. - **$10 $18 $30**

AME-2. "This Week Magazine" Cover Article,
November 16, 1958. Sunday supplement magazine of various newspapers. - **$5 $8 $12**

AME-3

AME-4

AME-3. "Dick Clark Yearbook",
c. 1959. - **$10 $20 $30**

AME-4. Store Display With Jewelry,
1950s. Scarce. Displays 17 pieces including necklace, cuff links and tie clasps. Complete - **$150 $300 $600**

AME-5

AME-6

AME-7

AME-5. Dick Clark Doll,
1950s. Store item by Juro. - **$150 $300 $400**

AME-6. "Platterpuss" Cat Cloth Doll With Tag,
1950s. Store item. 14" tall with tag inscription "Official Autograph Mascot/Dick Clark American Bandstand". -
$40 $75 $125

AME-7. "Secret Diary",
1950s. Store item. - **$20 $35 $50**

AME-8

AME-9

AME-10

AME-8. Cello. Button,
1950s. WFIL-TV (Philadelphia). - **$10 $20 $35**

AME-9. Cardboard Record Case,
1950s. Store item. - **$25 $60 $90**

AME-10. "Caravan Of Stars" Program,
c. 1964. - **$15 $20 $30**

AME-11

AME-12

AME-11. "Where The Action Is" TV Show Program,
c. 1966. - **$12 $20 $30**

AME-12. "Caravan Of Stars" Concert Program,
1967. - **$15 $25 $35**

AME-13

AME-13. "20 Years Of Rock And Roll Yearbook",
1973. - **$8 $12 $18**

AMOS 'N' ANDY

Amos Jones and Andrew H. Brown, rustic blacks striving to succeed in the big city, were born in the imaginations of Freeman Gosden and Charles Correll, two white show business producers. Amos and Andy ran the Fresh Air Taxicab Co. and - together with George Stevens, the Kingfish of the Mystic Knights of the Sea Lodge - enchanted and entranced a huge radio audience in the 1930s. The program, probably the most successful radio series ever, was aired locally in Chicago beginning in March 1928 and went to the NBC network in August 1929. Sponsors included Pepsodent toothpaste until 1937, Campbell's soup until 1943, and Rinso soap, Rexall drugs and Chrysler automobiles. *The Amos and Andy Music Hall* ran on CBS radio from 1954 to 1960,

and a prime-time television series with a black cast appeared on CBS from 1951 to 1953.

AMO-1

AMO-2

AMO-3

AMO-1. Cast Photo & Mailer,
1929. Pepsodent Co. Photo Only - **$5 $15 $30**
With Mailer And Letter - **$30 $50 $100**

AMO-2. Gosden & Correll Biography Folder,
1930. Accompanied Pepsodent cardboard standup figure set of two. - **$5 $15 $25**

AMO-3. Pepsodent Cardboard Standup Figure Set,
1930. Each - **$20 $35 $50**

AMO-4

AMO-4. Cardboard Candy Box,
1930. Williamson Candy Co. - **$50 $100 $200**

AMO-5

AMO-5. Cardboard Standup Figures With Letters And Envelope,
1931. Set of six figures with two letters promoting Pepsodent toothpaste and urging dental visit.
Near Mint In Envelope - **$250**
Each Standup - **$10 $20 $30**

AMO-6

AMO-7

MO-6. Puzzle,
932. Pepsodent Co. - **$25 $40 $85**

MO-7. Radio Episode Script,
ecember 25, 1935. Pepsodent. For episode "Amos'
/edding". - **$10 $20 $30**

AMO-8

MO-8. "Eagle's-Eye View Of Weber City (Inc.)" Map,
)35. Pepsodent Co. Prize to each entrant of "Why I Like
epsodent Toothpaste" contest.
ear Mint In Envelope - **$100**
ap Only - **$20 $40 $75**

AMO-9

AMO-10

IO-9. Pepsodent Contest Winner Check,
36. Rare. - **$400 $600 $900**

IO-10. "Campbell's Soup" 13x20" Paper Poster,
1938. - **$40 $75 $125**

AMO-11

AMO-12

AMO-13

IO-11. "Amos" Wood Jointed Doll,
30s. Store item. - **$75 $125 $200**

IO-12. "Andy" Wood Jointed Doll,
30s. Store item. - **$75 $125 $200**

AMO-13. Bisque Figurines,
1930s. Store item. Pair - **$100 $225 $350**

AMO-14

AMO-15

AMO-14. Detroit Sunday Times Supplement Photo,
1930s. - **$15 $25 $40**

AMO-15. "Fresh Air Taxicab Company" Stock Certificate,
1930s. - **$75 $140 $200**

AMO-17

AMO-16

AMO-18

AMO-16. Lead Ashtray,
1930s. Store item. - **$100 $225 $400**

AMO-17. "Free Ride In Fresh Air Taxi" Litho. Button,
1930s. Amos 'N Andy Fresh Air Candy. From known series
of 19 with different slogan on each including one example
picturing the taxi. Each - **$10 $20 $40**

AMO-18. Amos and Andy Broadcast Sign,
1940s. - **$50 $100 $200**

AMO-19

AMO-19. Amos and Andy Plenamins Promo Band,
1940s. - **$20 $40 $60**

THE ARCHIES

Archie Andrews, typical American teen, first appeared in
December 1941 in *Pep Comics* and in more than 50 years
has not yet aged a day. Artist Bob Montana created Archie,
his girlfriends Betty and Veronica, his pal Jughead, his rival
Reggie, and dozens of other students at Riverdale High.
They have appeared in comic books, a syndicated newspaper strip, paperback books, 15-and 30-minute radio shows
(from 1943 to 1953 on the Mutual and NBC networks), and,
starting in 1968, a continuing succession of TV cartoons on
CBS or NBC. Archie became a merchandising success as
well as a cartoon phenomenon: his bubblegum rock band
even produced three hit songs.

ARC-1

ARC-2

ARC-1. Magazines,
1948. Archie Comics Publications Inc. Each - **$15 $25 $40**

ARC-2. Club Member Cello. Button,
1950s. Version without accent border. - **$5 $10 $15**

ARC-3

ARC-3. Archie Spring-Loaded Plastic Head,
1969. Post Cereals. - **$5 $10 $20**

ARC-4

ARC-4. "Post Super Sugar Crisp" Box With "The Archies Record",
1969. Example from set of four boxes. Each - **$15 $35 $70**

ARC-5

ARC-5. Comic Book Club Kit,
1960s. Includes envelope, letter, card, cello. button.
Set - **$20 $40 $60**

ARC-6

ARC-7

ARC-8

ARC-6. "Official Member Archie Club" Cello. Button,
c. 1960s. For comic book club. - **$3 $8 $12**

ARC-7. Club Member Cello. Button,
c. 1960s. One of at least two versions accented by rim color.
$5 $10 $15

ARC-8. Archie Club Felt Beanie,
1960s. - **$25 $60 $100**

ARC-10

ARC-9

ARC-9. Picture Or Slogan Litho. Buttons,
1970. Store item vending machine set of sixteen.
Each Picture - **$2 $4 $8**
Each Slogan - **$1 $3 $5**

ARC-10. Welch's Jelly Glasses,
1971. Set of eight. Each - **$3 $5 $10**

AUNT JEMIMA

Aunt Jemima Pancake Flour was formulated in 1889 in St Joseph Missouri, but it was the 1892 Columbian Exposition Chicago that made Jemima a national figure. The R.T. Davis Mill & Manufacturing Co. hired Nancy Green, a black cook from Kentucky to stand outside its exposition booth and cook pancakes - more than a million, it is claimed - during the course of the fair. Ms. Green traveled the country making personal appearances as Aunt Jemima for the next 30 years until her death in 1923. Quaker Oats bought the product and name in 1924, and today there are over three dozen Aunt Jemima breakfast products. Various Aunt Jemima varied programs ran on CBS between 1929 and 1953 in either minute or 15-minute versions. The trademark face has been re-drawn a number of times, most recently in 1989.

AUN-1

AUN-1. Cello. Button,
c. 1896. First issue is not inscribed "Pancake Flour."
Without Inscription - **$35 $65 $125**
With Inscription - **$25 $40 $75**

AUN-2

AUN-2. Aunt Jemima, Uncle Mose Doll Fabrics With Envelope,
1915. Scarce. Aunt Jemima Mills Co.
Near Mint Uncut In Mailer - **$800**
Each Cut Or Assembled - **$100 $175 $250**

AUN-3   **AUN-4**

AUN-5

AUN-3. Cloth Doll,
1929. Scarce. Near Mint Uncut - **$500**
Assembled - **$75 $150 $300**

AUN-4. Hard Plastic Salt & Pepper Set,
1949. - **$15 $25 $40**

AUN-5. Premium Doll (unstuffed) and Instructions,
1948. - **$30 $60 $125**

AUN-6

AUN-7

AUN-6. Plastic Syrup Pitcher With Box,
1949. Boxed - **$30 $50 $75**
Loose - **$15 $35 $60**

AUN-7. Plastic Cookie Jar,
1950s. - **$100 $250 $350**

AUN-8

AUN-8. Vinyl Stuffed Doll Set,
1950s. Set of four - **$75 $150 $250**

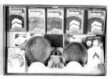

AUN-9

AUN-9. "Pastry Mix Set",
1950s. Store item by Junior Chef. Complete - **$35 $60 $125**

AUN-10   **AUN-11**

AUN-12

AUN-10. Chrome Metal Cigarette Lighter,
1960s. - **$25 $50 $75**

AUN-11. "Breakfast Club" 4" Litho Button,
1960s. - **$10 $20 $30**

AUN-12. Litho. Tab With Color Portrait,
1960s. - **$5 $8 $12**

AUNT JENNY'S REAL LIFE STORIES

Known under a number of names - *Aunt Jenny, Aunt Jenny's Real Life Stories, Aunt Jenny's Thrilling Real Life Stories, Aunt Jenny's True-Life Stories*, and in Canada as *Aunt Lucy* - this 15-minute serial drama ran five times a week on CBS radio for almost 20 years, from 1937 to 1956. Jenny, played by Edith Spencer and Agnes Young, was assisted by her announcer Danny, played by Dan Seymour, in relating the troubles of her friends and neighbors, providing a golden thought of the day, and offering cooking tips, invariably involving Spry, her longtime sponsor.

AJR-1   **AJR-2**

AJR-1. Cast Member Photo With Mailer Envelope,
c. 1937. Lever Brothers. Facsimile signature "Best Wishes/Dan Seymour-Sincerely Jennifer F. Wheeler (Aunt Jenny)". Mailer - **$3 $5 $10**
Photo - **$8 $12 $20**

AJR-2. "Complete Birthday Kit" With Mailer Box,
1940s. Spry Cooking Oil. Contents include small candles, candle holders, cake frosting tints, cake recipe leaflet, birthday scroll piece for cake. - **$8 $12 $20**

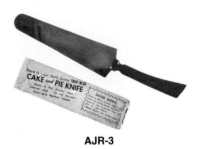

AJR-3

AJR-3. Cake Knife With Advertising On Cardboard Cover,
c. 1940s. Scarce. - **$30 $60 $100**

AJR-4

AJR-4. "Aunt Jenny's Recipe Book-12 Pies Husbands Like Best",
1952. Lever Brothers. - **$5 $12 $25**

BABE RUTH

George Herman "Babe" Ruth (1895-1948), baseball legend and American national hero, began playing professionally in 1914 for the old Baltimore Orioles before being purchased by the Boston Red Sox. He was a formidable pitcher, but it was his bat that propelled him to greatness. He led the major leagues in home runs in 10 of the 12 years between 1919 and 1930, and in 1927 he hit a record 60. He played in the outfield for the New York Yankees from 1920 to 1935 and Yankee Stadium became known as "The House That Ruth Built." The Babe appeared on several network radio shows: *Play Ball* and *The Adventures of Babe Ruth* sponsored by Quaker cereals in 1934, the *Sinclair Babe Ruth Program* in 1937, *Here's Babe Ruth* in 1943 and *Baseball Quiz* in 1943 and 1944. Eleven issues of *Babe Ruth Sports Comics* were published by Harvey Publications from 1949 to 1951.

BAB-1   **BAB-2**

BAB-1. "Babe Ruth Song" Litho. Button,
1928. Promotes sheet music for song following his 1927 record-breaking year of 60 home runs in season. -
$15 $30 $60

BAB-2. "Babe's Musical Bat",
c. 1930. German made store item. 4" long wood replica bat with insert harmonica reeds. - **$50 $85 $150**

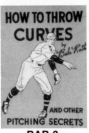  

BAB-3   **BAB-4**   **BAB-5**

BAB-3. Quaker Cereal "How To Throw Curves" Booklet,
1934. - **$15 $30 $75**

BAB-4. Quaker Cereal "How To Knock Home Runs" Booklet,
1934. Two additional "How To" booklets (not shown) are "Play The Infield" and "Play The Outfield". Each -
$15 $30 $75

BAB-5. Quaker Oats "Babe Ruth Hitting A Homer" Flip Booklet,
1934. Pages flip for batting sequence. - **$30 $65 $125**

BAB-6   **BAB-7**   **BAB-8**

BAB-6. Cello. Baseball Scorer Fob,
1934. Quaker Cereals. Pictures him in Boston cap, back has scoring wheel. - **$50 $100 $300**

BAB-7. Quaker Cello. Club Button,
1934. - **$25 $50 $85**

BAB-8. Quaker Cereal Patch,
1934. - **$20 $40 $75**

BAB-9   **BAB-10**   **BAB-11**

BAB-9. "Babe Ruth Club" Litho. Button,
c. 1934. - **$40 $75 $125**

BAB-10. Cello. Baseball Scorer Fob,
1934. Quaker Cereals. Pictures him in New York cap, back has scorer wheel. - **$50 $100 $250**

BAB-11. "Ask Me" 3" Cello. Button,
c. 1934. Store employee button promoting Quaker premium card game "Ask Me-The Game Of Baseball Facts". -
$100 $200 $300

BAB-12

AB-12. Ask Me Game,
. 1934. Scarce. Quaker Cereals. Includes mailer, cards and
nstructions. Complete - **$75 $150 $300**

BAB-13   BAB-14   BAB-15

AB-13. Babe Ruth Brass Ring,
935. Quaker Cereals. No inscriptions but Babe Ruth Club
remium picturing baseball symbols. - **$75 $135 $200**

**AB-14. Quaker "Babe Ruth Champions" Brass Club
adge,**
935. - **$25 $50 $85**

**AB-15. Quaker "Babe Ruth Champions" Cello. Club
utton,**
935. Pictures him in Boston cap. - **$25 $50 $85**

BAB-16   BAB-17   BAB-18

AB-16. "Babe Ruth" Brass Belt Buckle,
930s. Store item by "Harris Belts" marked on reverse. -
0 **$75 $150**

AB-17. "Esso Boys Club" Silvered Metal Badge,
930s. Figural baseball accented in red/blue with inscription
harter Member". - **$25 $50 $85**

AB-18. "Play Ball With Babe Ruth" Cello. Button,
930s. Universal Pictures. Promotion for "Christy Walsh All
merica Sports Reels" movie feature. - **$50 $85 $175**

BAB-19

**AB-19. "Babe Ruth" Cello./Steel Bat Replica
ocketknife,**
930s. Name inscribed on one side plus tiny baseball depic-
n. - **$40 $75 $125**

BAB-20

BAB-21

**BAB-20. Esso Gasoline "Babe Ruth Boys Club" Contest
Coupon,**
1930s. Offers premium for acquiring new members. -
$15 $25 $40

BAB-21. Club 3" Fabric Patch,
1930s. Possibly Quaker Cereals. - **$15 $30 $50**

BAB-22

**BAB-22. "Official Babe Ruth Wrist Watch" With Display
Case,**
1949. Store item by Exacta Time. Plastic display case is
replica baseball.
Near Mint In Case With Coupons And Box - **$1500**
Watch Only - **$100 $200 $600**

BAB-23

BAB-23. "Babe Ruth" Plastic Ring,
c. 1949. Inset picture of him swinging bat. From Kellogg's set
of sixteen picturing sports and movie stars, airplanes and
19th century western personalities. - **$25 $42 $60**

BABY SNOOKS

Baby Snooks was a 7-year-old brat and America's radio listeners loved her. Born in the imagination of Ziegfeld Follies
star Fanny Brice, the irrepressible imp was introduced to the
world on February 29, 1936, in *The Ziegfeld Follies of the Air,*
a lavish 60-minute extravaganza on CBS. The program had
a brief life, but Baby Snooks was to appear continuously on
one network program or another for the next 15 years until
Fanny Brice's death in 1951. Sponsors included Maxwell
House coffee, Post Toasties cereal, Sanka, Jell-O and Turns.

BSN-1.   BSN-2.

BSN-3.

BSN-1. "Radio Guide" Magazine With Fannie Brice Cover,
1938.- **$5 $10 $20**

BSN-2. Composition/Wood/Wire "Flexy" Doll With Outfit And Tag,
1939. Store item by Ideal Toy & Novelty Co. -
$100 $200 $300

BSN-3. Whitman Cut-Out Doll Book,
1940. Store item. Designs by Queen Holden. -
$100 $200 $300

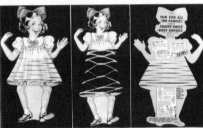

BSN-4.   BSN-5.

BSN-4. Plastic Figure On Metal Bar Pin,
c. 1940s. Figure finished in gold color. - **$10 $20 $35**

BSN-5. Cardboard Dancing Puppet,
1950. Tums. Flexible diecut paper mid-section. -
$30 $75 $150

BACHELOR'S CHILDREN

Radio's beloved serial, *Bachelor's Children* tells the story of Dr. Bob Graham and the twin teenage girls he promised to raise. In true soap opera form, he eventually marries one of them. The popular series, which won awards for "realism," aired on CBS from 1936 to 1946, sponsored by Old Dutch cleanser, Wonder bread, and Colgate.

BCH-1.

BCH-1. Wonder Bread Fan Newsletter,
c. 1945. - **$10 $20 $35**

BAMBI

One of Disney's most endearing creatures, *Bambi* debuted as a Technicolor feature cartoon at New York City's Radio City Music Hall on August 21, 1942. Since then, Bambi the deer, Thumper the rabbit, Flower the skunk and the Wise Old Owl have continued to enchant young and old audiences alike. Based on the Felix Salten story, Disney's Bambi was also published as a Better Little Book in 1942 and in comic book form several times in the early 1940s and as recently as 1984.

BAM-1.

BAM-2.

BAM-3.

BAM-1. "Prevent Forest Fires" 14x20" Poster,
1943. U.S. Forest Service. - **$100 $225 $400**

BAM-2. Paper Bookmark,
c. 1943. U.S. Department of Agriculture-Forest Service.-
$8 $15 $25

BAM-3. Wristwatch,
1949. Store item by US Time. - **$50 $125 $200**

BAM-4.

BAM-4. Signed Studio Fan Card,
1940s. Signed by Disney staff artist. - **$50 $75 $125**

THE BANANA SPLITS

This imaginative live-action show consisted of four people wardrobed in outfits of Fleegle the dog, Bingo the gorilla, Drooper the lion and Snorky the baby elephant. The group was musically inclined in addition to adventuresome and appeared in 60-minute shows produced by Hanna-Barbera on NBC, sponsored by Kellogg's, from 1968 to 1970. The show's official title was a lengthy *Kellogg's of Battle Creek Presents The Banana Splits Adventure Hour.* Characters were voiced by Paul Winchell (Fleegle), Daws Butler (Bingo), Allan Melvin (Drooper) and Don Messick (Snorky).

BSP-1

BSP-1. Club Kit,
1968. Mailing envelope plus pennant, membership book, code machine, certificate, group portrait, membership card, sticker. Complete - **$100 $250 $400**

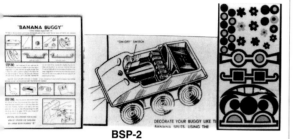

BSP-2

BSP-2. "Banana Buggy" Model Kit,
1968. Kellogg's. Yellow vinyl with motor and sticker sheet.
Mint Boxed - **$750**
Assembled - **$100 $200 $400**

BSP-3

BSP-3. Record In Sleeve,
1969. Kellogg's. Includes song "Doin' The Banana Split" and three others. With Mailer - **$25 $50 $75**
No Mailer - **$15 $40 $65**

BSP-4   BSP-5

BSP-4. Fleer Gum "Tattoo" Vending Machine Card,
1969.- **$5 $10 $15**

BSP-5. Record With Sleeve,
1969. Kellogg's. Song "Tra-La-La Song" and three others.
With Mailer - **$25 $50 $75**
No Mailer - **$15 $40 $65**

BSP-6   BSP-7

BSP-6. Fleegle Vinyl Figure,
1971. Store item by Sutton. Bagged - **$25 $50 $85**
Loose - **$15 $35 $70**

BSP-7. Drooper Vinyl Figure,
1971. Store item by Sutton. Bagged - **$25 $50 $85**
Loose - **$15 $35 $70**

BSP-8

BSP-8. 7-Eleven Plastic Cups,
1976. Each - **$15 $25 $35**

BARBIE

Until 1959, when Barbie first appeared, dolls were pretty much the same for hundreds of years. They were baby dolls to be mothered and nurtured by their youthful owners who would probably be mothers with their own real babies someday. Dolls came on the market with eyes that opened, movable arms and legs and finally dolls that wet and needed to be fed and changed. Not too exciting. Barbie started a revolutionary trend. Not a baby doll, but a young lady out in the world with fashionable clothes, cars, boyfriends and apparently some cash to throw around. And she had a bosom! The doll world was getting exciting. Ruth Handler, Barbie's creator, has been quoted as saying "Barbie was originally created to project every little girl's dream of the future." Barbie's boyfriend Ken came along in 1961, her best friend Midge arrived in 1963. Little sister Skipper was introduced in 1964 as were her male friend Ricky and girlfriend Skooter. The Barbie product line by Mattel continues to rank among the most successful offerings of the toy industry.

BAR-1

BAR-1. "Mattel Dolls For Fall '64" Retailer's Catalogue,
1964. - **$40 $75 $125**

BAR-2.

BAR-3. **BAR-4.**

BAR-2. Fan Club Membership Card,
1964.- **$10 $20 $35**

BAR-3. Wristwatch,
1964. Store item. - **$35 $65 $100**

BAR-4. "Barbie" Magazine,
March-April, 1965. One of a series by Mattel.
Each - **$5 $10 $20**

BAR-5

BAR-7

BAR-6

**BAR-5. Barbie & Friends 6x10x30" Glass And Metal
Mattel Electrical Display Sign,**
1960s. Florescent lighted. - **$100 $200 $300**

BAR-6. Silvered Metal Adjustable Ring,
1960s. Rhinestones around Barbie's profile in brass.
$35 $60 $100

BAR-7. Necklace With Metal Pendant,
1974. - **$10 $20 $35**

BARNEY GOOGLE

"Barney Google, with his Goo-Goo-Googly Eyes," the 1923
hit song by Billy Rose and Con Conrad, was about a feisty little sport in a top hat, the cartoon creation of Billy De Beck
that has been called one of the 10 greatest American comic
strips of all time. The daily Barney strip first appeared in
1919 on the sports page of the Chicago Herald-Examiner,
where he was soon joined by his pitiful racehorse Spark
Plug. Readers loved them. Snuffy Smith, a Kentucky hillbilly, was introduced to the strip in 1934; his name was added
to the title a few years later and by the mid-1940s he had
taken full title. Fred Lasswell continued the strip after De
Beck's death in 1942. A series of movie shorts was produced in the 1920s and a few animated TV cartoons were
produced in the 1960s.

BNG-1

BNG-2

BNG-1. Fabric Doll,
1922. Store item. - **$50 $75 $150**

BNG-2. "Spark Plug" Glass Candy Container,
1923. Store item. Saddle blanket area originally had orange
paint. - **$75 $150 $300**

BNG-4

BNG-3

BNG-5

**BNG-3. "Official Song Of The Secret And Mysterious
Order Of Billygoats" Sheet Music,**
1928. - **$20 $40 $60**

BNG-4. Brotherhood Of Bulls Membership Card,
1920s. Scarce. Chicago Herald and Examiner. -
$30 $60 $120

BNG-5. Brotherhood Of Billy Goats Membership Card,
1920s. Scarce. Chicago Herald and Examiner. -
$15 $30 $90

BNG-6   **BNG-7**

BNG-8

**BNG-6. "The Atlanta Georgian's Silver Anniversary"
Litho. Button,**
1937. Named newspaper. From set of various characters. -
$20 $50 $75

BNG-7. "Sunday Herald And Examiner" Litho. Button,
1930s. Chicago newspaper. From "30 Comics" set of vario
characters. - **$15 $25 $40**

BNG-8. Enamel On Silvered Brass Pin,
c. 1930s.- **$ 50 $75 $150**

BNG-9

BNG-10

NG-9. Boston Sunday Advertiser 11x17" Cardboard
Display Sign,
930s. - **$75 $150 $250**

NG-10. "Buy War Stamps" 14x18" Poster,
1944. U.S. Government. - **$40 $75 $125**

BATMAN

he legendary Batman - and the huge Bat-industry he was to
pawn - was introduced in *Detective Comics* #27 of May
939. Since then, the Caped Crusader and his sidekick,
obin the Boy Wonder, have battled crime and the forces of
il in comic strips, in live-action and animated cartoon TV
eries, on the radio, on prime-time network television, in
mic books, movie serials, feature films and in the hearts of
illions of fans, young and old. Artist Bob Kane and writer
l Finger also produced an array of notable knaves, among
em the Riddler, Penguin, the Joker and Catwoman.
atman's two greatest successes were the 1966-1967 ABC
levision series with Adam West and Burt Ward as the
ynamic Duo and a string of famous actors as the various
llains; and the 1989 blockbuster film starring Michael
eaton, Kim Basinger and Jack Nicholson. Both productions
enerated hundreds of toys, premiums, posters, games,
odels, dolls, etc., etc. Extensive licensing and premiums
so accompanied the 1995 Warner Bros. film *Batman*
orever, starring Val Kilmer and Jim Carrey. Holy
erchandise, Batman!

BAT-1

AT-1. Paper Mask,
1943. Scarce. Philadelphia Record newspaper, probably
ners. Back announces new daily and Sunday comic
ips. - **$200 $800 $1600**

BAT-2

AT-2. "Full Color Transfers",
44. Rare. Not a premium but earliest known merchandise
) cents) item for Batman. Back of sheet has ad for
tective Comics. - **$300 $600 $1200**

BAT-3

BAT-4

BAT-3. "Batman's Last Chance" One-Sheet,
1949. Columbia Pictures serial. - **$700 $1400 $2800**

BAT-4. "New Adventures of Batman & Robin Three-
Sheet,
1949. Columbia Pictures serial. - **$1500 $5000 $8000**

(1943 front)

(1947 front)

(back)

BAT-5

BAT-5. Batman Infantile Paralysis Card,
1940s. Scarce. March of Dimes premium. Small version
offered in 1943, large version in 1947.
1943 version - **$100 $200 $500**
1947 version - **$30 $90 $180**

BAT-6

BAT-7

BAT-6. Batman/Superman X-Mas Card,
1940s. Rare. - **$500 $1000 $1500**

BAT-7. DC Comics Fan Card,
1960. - **$30 $50 $90**

BAT-8

BAT-9

BAT-8. Batman Beanie,
1966. - **$10 $20 $30**

BAT-9. Batman Periscope,
1966. Kellogg's OKs cereal premium. - **$30 $60 $90**

| (front) | BAT-10 | (back) |

BAT-10. Batman Kellogg's Frosted Flakes Box (Flat),
1966. promotes Batman printing set premium. -
$300 $600 $1000

| (front) | BAT-11 | (back) |

BAT-11. Batman Kellogg's OKs Cereal Box (Flat),
1966. features Yogi Bear on front, Batman on back.
Promotes Batman periscope premium. - **$400 $800 $1600**

BAT-12   **BAT-13**

BAT-14

BAT-12. "Crimefighter" 1-3/8" Litho. Button,
1966.- **$5 $10 $15**

BAT-13. "Batman And Robin Deputy Crimefighter,
1966. Cello. button 3-1/2", store item. - **$8 $15 $25**

BAT-14. "Batman Golden Records" Boxed Set,
1966. N.P.P. Inc. Includes comic book, LP record, Batman
Crimefighters litho. button, flicker ring and club membership
card with secret code. Complete - **$20 $40 $75**

BAT-15

**BAT-15. "My Batman Collection" Metal Coin Set With
Plastic Holders,**
1966. Set of 20 coins.
Set In Holders - **$100 $200 $325**
Each Coin - **$3 $7 $12**

BAT-16

BAT-17

BAT-16. "Batman" Litho. Button,
1966. From red, white and blue set of 14 in 7/8" size, also
issued in similar set colored red, green, yellow, black.
Each - **$3 $8 $12**

BAT-17. GE Mask,
1966. One mask on front, other on reverse. - **$5 $10 $15**

BAT-18

BAT-19

**BAT-18. "Batman And Robin Buttons" Vending Machine
Display Paper,**
1966. - **$5 $8 $15**

BAT-19. Batman 1" Size Litho. Button Set,
1966. Vending machines but scarcer than 7/8" size. 14 different. Red/White/Blue Style Each - **$12 $20 $45**
Red/Green/Yellow Style Each - **$12 $25 $50**

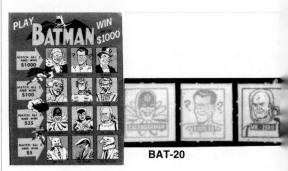

BAT-20

BAT-20. Contest Card With Three Picture Playing Piece
1966. Safeway Or Merit Gasoline. Shows both TV and com
book characters. - **$60 $125 $250**

BAT-22

BAT-21

AT-21. "Batman Coins" On Card,
)66. Store item by Transogram.
omplete On Card - **$20 $40 $75**
)ose Coin - **$1 $2 $3**

AT-22. Fan Photo,
)66. Adam West and Burt Ward with facsimile signatures. -
!5 **$40 $65**

BAT-23

AT-23. All Star Dairies 24x44" Cardboard Sign,
)66.- **$100 $200 $300**

BAT-24

BAT-25

AT-24. Metal License Plate,
66. Store item by Groff Signs. - **$10 $20 $35**

AT-25. Metal License Plate,
66. Store item by Groff Signs. - **$10 $20 $35**

BAT-26

AT-26. "Batman Ring Club" 4x5" Flicker Display Card,
'66. Showing both images. - **$15 $35 $60**

BAT-27

BAT-28

BAT-27. Metal License Plate,
1966. Store item. - **$10 $20 $35**

BAT-28. "Flicker Pictures" Vending Machine Display Paper,
1966. - **$10 $20 $35**

BAT-29

BAT-29. Flicker Miniature Pictures,
1966. Vending machine set of six. Each- **$5 $12 $18**

BAT-30

BAT-30. Plastic Flicker Rings,
1966. Set of 12 in either silver or blue base.
Silver Base Each - **$8 $15 $25**
Blue Base Each - **$8 $12 $15**

BAT-31

BAT-31. "Batman Candy & Toy" Boxes,
1966. Store item by Phoenix Candy Co. Set of eight with front and back numbered pictures (1-16).
Each Box - **$10 $20 $30**

BAT-33

BAT-32

BAT-32. Holloway Candies 17x22" Cardboard Store Sign,
1966. Milk Duds, Black Cow, Slo-Poke candies. Offered
three different coloring books with six-pack candy purchase.-
$60 $100 $150

BAT-33. "Batman" English Cello. Button,
1966. A&BC Chewing Gum Ltd. - **$10 $20 $35**

BAT-34

BAT-34. Pop Tarts Comic Booklet,
1966. "The Mad Hatter's Hat Crimes" from set of four. -
$5 $10 $18

BAT-35

BAT-35. Pop Tarts Comic Booklet,
1966. "The Penguin's Fowl Play" from set of four. -
$5 $10 $18

BAT-36

BAT-36. Pop Tarts Comic Booklet,
1966. "The Catwoman's Catnapping Caper" from set of four.-
$5 $10 $18

BAT-37

BAT-37. Pop Tarts Comic Booklet,
1966. "The Man In The Iron Mask" from set of four. -
$5 $10 $18

BAT-39

BAT-38

BAT-40

BAT-38. Composition Bobbing Head Figure,
c. 1966. Store item. - **$100 $350 $600**

BAT-39. "Robin" English Cello. Button,
1966. A&BC Chewing Gum Ltd. - **$10 $20 $35**

BAT-40. Batman Glass Tumbler,
1966. - **$5 $10 $15**

BAT-42

BAT-41

BAT-41. Robin Glass Tumbler,
1966. - **$8 $12 $20**

BAT-42. "Curly Wurly/Blam" Litho. Button,
c. 1966. English product. - **$8 $12 $20**

(sticker, card, button shown)
BAT-43

BAT-44

BAT-43. "Batman Club" Items,
c. 1966. Ron Riley's Batman Club of WLS/WBKB-TV, Chicago. Includes 2" litho. button, 3-1/2" sticker plus card.
Button - **$3 $6 $10**
Sticker - **$5 $10 $15**
Card - **$8 $12 $20**

BAT-44. Batman 6' Standee,
1966.- **$125 $250 $350**

BAT-45

BAT-45. High Relief Plastic 33x48" Store Display Sign,
1969. Issued to promote Aurora Batmobile kit offered as premium by Burry's cookies. - **$250 $600 $900**

BAT-46

BAT-46. Photo And Record,
1960s. DC Comics. Photo reads "To All My Batman Fans-Bats' Wishes Bob Kane." Record co-written by Kane titled "Have Faith In Me". Pair - **$50 $85 $150**

BAT-48

BAT-47

BAT-47. "Batman And, Of Course, Robin" Movie Serial Re-Release 27x41 " Poster,
1960s. Columbia Pictures. For reissue of original 1943 serial. **$50 $125 $250**

BAT-48. "Super Heroes Magnetic Dart Game",
1977. Cheerios. - **$10 $25 $50**

BAT-49

BAT-49. "The Dark Knight" Plastic Display Sign With Press Release,
1986. Press release on mini-series by Frank Miller.
Display - **$20 $35 $60**
Press Release - **$3 $5 $10**

BAT-50   BAT-51

BAT-50. McDonald's Happy Meals 14x14" Plastic Translight Panel,
1992. Depicts eight figures and vehicles. - **$25 $60 $100**

BAT-51. McDonald's Happy Meals 14x14" Plastic Translight Panel,
1992. Depicts six cups. - **$10 $20 $30**

BAT-52

BAT-53

BAT-52. McDonald's Happy Meals 14x14" Plastic Translight Panel,
1992. Depicts four vehicles. - **$10 $20 $30**

BAT-53. Batman Standee With Cups,
1990s. - **$100 $200 $300**

THE BEATLES

The Beatles, four gifted schoolboys from Liverpool, England, were the dominant musical force of the turbulent 1960s and have remained cultural icons to this day. The Fab Four burst on the American scene in an explosive live appearance on the Ed Sullivan Show on CBS-TV in February 1964, and though their last public concert was less than three years later, Beatles records and tapes still sell in the millions. Their movies - *A Hard Day's Night* (1964), *Help!* (1965) and the psychedelic animated feature *Yellow Submarine* (1968) - an animated Saturday morning series produced by King Features (1965-1969) and sponsored primarily by the A. C. Gilbert toy company, and comic books all added to the luster; but it was the brilliance and charm of the music that revolutionized rock and roll. Beatles memorabilia of all sorts, both original issues and later reproductions, are usually copyrighted NEMS Enterprises or SELTAEB.

BEA-1

BEA-1. "The Cavern" Ashtray,
c. 1963. Souvenir item. From Liverpool club where Beatles made January 1961 debut. - **$50 $100 $150**

BEA-2

BEA-2. Vinyl Doll Set,
1964. Store item by Remco Plastics. Each has life-like hair.
Each - **$30 $60 $90**

BEA-3

BEA-3. "Beatle Dolls" 7x18" Paper Store Poster,
1964. Remco Industries. - **$100 $200 $300**

BEA-4

BEA-4. "The Bobb'n Head Beatles" Boxed Set,
1964. Store item. Composition figures by Car Mascots Inc.
Boxed Set - **$200 $400 $600**
Each Loose - **$60 $90 $125**

BEA-5

BEA-5. Cincinnati Concert Program,
1964. - **$15 $30 $60**

BEA-6

BEA-6. Calendar Cards,
1964. Various advertisers.
Each - **$8 $12 $20**

BEA-7

BEA-7. "Color Oil Portraits" Set Of 4,
1964. Store item. Cut-out "Buddies Club" card on header.
Packaged With Uncut Card - **$50 $75 $100**

BEA-8

BEA-9

BEA-8. Vending Machine Litho. Button,
1964. Set of nine (four pictures/five slogans) either in
black/white/red, blue/orange, red/white/blue, or
black/white/blue. Pictures - **$3 $8 $15**
Slogans- **$3 $6 $10**

BEA-9. "Life Member" Fan Club Patch,
. 1964. - **$15 $30 $60**

BEA-10

BEA-10. "I Love" 3-1/2" Cello. Buttons,
. 1964. Each - **$8 $15 $25**

BEA-11

BEA-11. "Official Fan Club News Bulletin",
. 1964. Includes six stapled photo pages. - **$25 $40 $75**

BEA-12   BEA-13   BEA-14

BEA-12. Flicker Ring Set,
1964. Set of four.
Silver Base Each - **$8 $12 $15**
Blue Base Each - **$5 $7 $10**

BEA-13. "Ringo Starr" Soaky Bottle,
1965. Colgate-Palmolive. Only Ringo and Paul were produced. - **$40 $75 $100**

BEA-14. "Paul McCartney" Soaky,
1965. Colgate-Palmolive. Only Paul and Ringo were produced. - **$30 $60 $100**

BEA-15

BEA-16

BEA-15. "Help" Packaged Bandage,
c. 1965. Movie promotion on Curad bandage. - **$10 $20 $35**

BEA-16. Nestle's Quik Container,
1966. Has offer for inflatable doll set. - **$150 $300 $600**

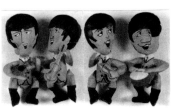

BEA-17

BEA-18

BEA-17. Beatles Inflatable Vinyl Dolls Set,
1966. Store item, also Nestle's Quik and Lux Soap.
Each - **$15 $25 $45**

BEA-18. "Yellow Submarine Magazine",
1968. Store item published jointly by Pyramid Publications
and King Features. - **$20 $40 $75**

BEA-19

BEA-19. Corgi "Yellow Submarine" Replica,
1968.
Near Mint Boxed - **$600**
Loose - **$150 $300 $450**

BEA-20

BEA-20. Yellow Submarine Rub-Ons,
1969. Nabisco Wheat (Or Rice) Honeys. Set of eight.
Each - **$15 $25 $40**

BETTY BOOP

Max Fleischer created the Boop-Oop-a-Doop girl as an animated cartoon in 1931. The sexy little flirt, modeled on singer Helen Kane and actress Mae West, was an immediate success and became Paramount's leading cartoon feature. Along with her dog Bimbo and her pal Koko the clown, Betty vamped and sang her way through comedies and adventures throughout the 1930s. Several actresses provided Betty's voice but Mae Questel is most closely identified with the character. A Sunday comic strip was distributed by King Features (1935-1938) and published as an Avon paperback in 1975. A children's show, *Betty Boop Fables*, had a brief run on NBC radio in 1932-1933, and the cartoons were packaged for TV in 1956 and re-released in color in 1971. Many merchandised items appeared in the 1930s at the height of Betty's popularity. Her continuing appeal produced an even wider range of licensed items in the 1980s-1990s.

BTY-1   BTY-2

BTY-1. Betty Boop/Gus Gorilla Fan Card,
1933. Fleischer Studios. Text refers to Paramount Pictures and NBC. - **$35 $75 $150**

BTY-2. Fleischer Studios Fan Card,
c. 1933. Personalized by first name of recipient. Text refers to Paramount, not NBC. - **$35 $60 $100**

BTY-3

BTY-3. Mask,
1930s. "Bob-O-Link Shoes" ad on reverse.
$30 $60 $125

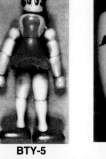

BTY-4   BTY-5   BTY-6

BTY-4. Composition/Wood Jointed Doll,
1930s. Scarce in high grade. Store item by Cameo Products. 12-1/2" tall. - **$250 $600 $1200**

BTY-5. Wood Jointed Doll,
1930s. Store item, 4-1/2" tall.- **$5 $10 $175**

BTY-6. China Wall Sconce,
1930s. Store item. - **$75 $150 $200**

BTY-7   BTY-8

BTY-7. Bisque Figure,
1930s. Store item. 3" size. - **$50 $100 $150**

BTY-8. China Ashtray,
1930s. Store item. - **$50 $75 $150**

BTY-9   BTY-10   BTY-11

BTY-9. Spanish Envelope,
1930s. Held transfer.
Envelope Only - **$10 $20 $35**
Complete - **$15 $30 $60**

BTY-10. "Bimbo" Cello. Button,
1930s. Inscribed "A Paramount Star Created By Fleischer Studios". - **$15 $25 $60**

BTY-11. Cello. Button,
1930s. Rim inscription "A Paramount Star Created By Fleischer Studios".- **$35 $75 $150**

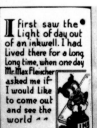

BTY-12

BTY-12. "Socks Appeal By Bimbo" Booklet,
1930s. Given with pair of Bimbo socks. - **$50 $90 $135**

BTY-13   BTY-14   BTY-15

BTY-13. "Saturday Chicago American" Litho. Button,
1930s. From set of 10 various characters. - $20 $45 $75

BTY-14. "Ko-Ko/Max Fleischer's Talkatoons" Litho.
Button #25,
1930s. Western Theater Premium Co. From numbered set of
50 either black, white, red or with additional yellow accent. -
$10 $20 $35

BTY-15. Betty Boop Postcard with Mickey Rooney,
1930s. - $30 $60 $120

BIG BOY

In 1936 Bob Wian, running a little diner called Bob's Pantry in
Glendale, California, added a double-decker cheeseburger to
his menu. A few weeks later, according to legend, a chubby
little boy wearing oversize pants and suspenders walked in.
Wian was enchanted, dubbed him Big Boy, changed the
name of the diner and began using an image of the boy as
his advertising logo. Wian sold his first franchise to the Elias
Brothers in Michigan in 1952, and other franchises quickly
followed. The Marriott Corp. bought the business in 1967,
and there are now more than 300 Big Boy restaurants in
North America and Japan. A giveaway comic book was
started in 1956 and continues to this day.

BIG-1   BIG-2

BIG-1. Big Boy Die-Cut Promo,
1949. - $20 $40 $80

BIG-2. Big Boy Ad Card,
1956. For Free comic. - $10 $20 $40

BIG-3   BIG-4   BIG-5

BIG-3. "Adventures Of The Big Boy" Comic Book #1,
1956. Art by Bill Everett. - $60 $180 $480

BIG-4. Early Litho. Button,
1950s. Light green rim. - $15 $35 $60

BIG-5. "Nat'l Big Boy Club" Litho. Member Button,
c. 1960. - $10 $20 $35

BIG-6

BIG-6. Ceramic Salt & Pepper Set,
1960s. - $60 $150 $250

BIG-7   BIG-8   BIG-9

BIG-7. Club Member Litho. Button,
c. 1960s. - $5 $10 $20

BIG-8. Silvered Metal Tie Bar,
c. 1960s. "Big Boy" name on miniature figure. - $10 $20 $35

BIG-9. Vinyl Figure By Dakin,
1970. - $50 $80 $130

BIG-10   BIG-11

BIG-10. Cloth Dolls,
c. 1978. Dolls are Big Boy, Dolly and Nugget.
Each - $5 $10 $15

BIG-11. "Adventures Of The Big Boy" Comic Book,
1978. Over 400 issues. See The Overstreet Comic Book
Price Guide for values of Issue 2 and above.

BIG-12   BIG-13   BIG-14

BIG-12. Watch,
c. 1970s. - **$25 $50 $75**

BIG-13. Vinyl Figure Night Light,
1970s. Electrical. - **$25 $50 $100**

BIG-14. Limited Edition 5" Metal Figure,
1980s. - **$20 $40 $80**

BILL BARNES

Street and Smith began publication of its pulp *Bill Barnes Air Trails* in the early 1930s and shortened the name of the magazine to *Air Trails* around 1937. Issues contained Bill Barnes air adventure stories, aviation news and features, and information on model planes. Barnes made his comic book debut in issue #1 of *Shadow Comics* in 1940 and had his own book from 1940 to 1943 under various titles: *Bill Barnes Comics, America's Air Ace Comics* and *Air Ace.*

BBR-1   BBR-2

BBR-1. "Bill Barnes Air Adventurer" Pulp Magazine,
September 1935. Published by Street & Smith. -
$15 $25 $50

BBR-2. "Bill Barnes/Air Adventurer" Gummed Paper Envelope Sticker,
1930s. Street & Smith Co., publisher of Bill Barnes pulp magazine. - **$20 $40 $65**

BBR-3

BBR-3. "Air Warden Cadets" Club Kit,
c. 1943. Cello. Button - **$15 $30 $50**
Airplane Spotting Booklet - **$8 $15 $30**
Group Of Six Related Sheets - **$15 $20 $30**

BILLY AND RUTH

Billed as America's Famous Toy Children, Billy and Ruth and their dog Terry were the fictional stars of annual pre-Christmas toy catalogues published for the toy industry as early as 1936. Created by Philadelphia-based L.A. Hoeflich, the catalogues promoted the toys of different participating manufacturers. Retailers who subscribed to the service printed their own store information on the front cover and thus had a ready-made catalogue for their customers. In the late 1950s, as independent toy retailers went out of business, Billy and Ruth became casualties of the new marketplace.

BLR-1

BLR-1. "In Toy World With Billy And Ruth" Catalogue,
1936. 32 pages of illustrated and priced period toys. -
$50 $100 $150

BLR-2   BLR-3

BLR-2. Promotional Cello. Button,
c. 1936. - **$15 $30 $60**

BLR-3. Club Member Button,
1940s. - **$12 $20 $35**

BLR-4

BLR-4. Christmas Toy Catalogue,
1951. - **$20 $35 $60**

BLR-5

BLR-5. Christmas Toy Catalogue,
1952. - **$20 $35 $60**

BLR-6   BLR-7

BLR-6. Christmas Toy Catalogue,
1954. - **$15 $25 $50**

BLR-7. Christmas Toy Catalogue,
1955. - **$12 $25 $50**

BILLY BOUNCE

Little is known of this comic strip rotund youngster other than he briefly had his own strip in 1905 based on various youthful charaters created by C. W. Kahles. Apparently Billy Bounce earned some syndication beyond home base of the *New York World*, as known premiums are mostly a few newspaper advertising pin-back buttons. A *Billy Bounce* hardcover book exists crediting W.W. Denslow, noted for his *Wizard of Oz* Illustrations, as both author and illustrator.

BYB-1   BYB-2

BYB-3

BYB-1. "Philadelphia Press" Cello. Button,
c. 1905. - **$35 $75 $150**

BYB-2. "Billy Bounce In The Sunday Sentinel" Cello. Button,
c. 1905. Also comes with "Washington Times" imprint. - **$75 $150 $250**

BYB-3. "Billy Bounce" Hardcover Book,
1906. Store item published by Donohue Co. Story by Denslow & Bragdon with pictures by Denslow (noted "Oz" artist). - **$60 $125 $200**

BLACK FLAME OF THE AMAZON

This radio adventure series was produced in California but apparently found air time only in the Midwest on the Mutual network. The syndicated program dramatized the adventures of explorer Harold Noice in the jungles of South America. Accompanied by his young friends Jim and Jean Brady, his aid Pedro, and the native guide Keyto, Noice did battle with lawless types and dealt with wild animals and strange savage customs. Sponsors included Mayrose processed meats and Hi-Speed Gasoline. In Detroit the series aired on station WXYZ from February to May 1938, sponsored by Hi-Speed.

BLF-1

BLF-2

BLF-1. Paper Mask,
1930s. Hi-Speed Gasoline. - **$20 $40 $80**

BLF-2. Cardboard Ruler,
1930s. Rare. Mayrose Meats. - **$40 $80 $120**

BLF-3   BLF-4   BLF-5

BLF-3. "Hi-Speed Explorer" Litho. Button,
1930s. Hi-Speed gasoline. - **$10 $15 $25**

BLF-4. "Hi-Speed Explorer" Brass Compass Ring,
1930s. - **$125 $235 $350**

BLF-5. "Paco Explorer" Litho. Club Button,
1930s. - **$12 $25 $40**

BLONDIE

One of the world's most popular comic strips, Blondie was created by Chic Young for King Features in 1930. This family comedy centers on the hectic misadventures of the Bumsteads - Blondie and Dagwood, their children Cookie and Alexander (originally Baby Dumpling), their dog Daisy and her pups, the neighbors Herb and Tootsie Woodley, Dagwood's boss Mr. Dithers and his wife Cora and the indestructible mailman Mr. Beasley. Hollywood turned out more than two dozen Blondie films with Penny Singleton and Arthur Lake in the lead roles and a half-hour radio program ran from 1939 to 1950, sponsored by Camel cigarettes, Super Suds and Colgate. Two TV series, in 1957 and again in 1968, failed to match the success of the strip or the movies.

BLD-1

BLD-1. "Sunday Examiner" Newspaper Contest Litho. Button,
1930s. Part of a set. - **$10 $20 $30**

BLD-2

BLD-2. Esso Ad Folder,
1940. - **$15 $30 $50**

BLD-4

BLD-3

BLD-3. "Blondie Goes To Leisureland" Paper Game,
1940. Westinghouse Co. - **$15 $25 $35**

BLD-4. "Comic Togs" Litho. Button,
1947. From clothing maker series of various characters. -
$25 $40 $75

BLD-5

BLD-5. "Penny Singleton" Photo,
1940s. Radio and films Blondie portrayer. - **$5 $10 $15**

BOB HOPE

From a small-time vaudeville comic, Bob Hope went on to become one of the world's most beloved performers. His *Pepsodent Show*, which premiered on NBC in 1938, was one of radio's biggest hits for a dozen years. He made a series of successful "Road" movies with Bing Crosby and Dorothy Lamour from 1940 to 1962 and has made countless TV appearances since 1950. He has also devoted much time and energy entertaining American troops all over the world. Thanks for the memories, Bob.

BOB-1

BOB-2

BOB-1. "They Got Me Covered" Book,
1941. Pepsodent toothpaste. - **$5 $15 $30**

BOB-2. Hair Pin Card,
1940s. Store item. - **$8 $12 $18**

BOB-3

BOB-3. Hope-Lamour Birthday Card,
1940s. Store item. - **$8 $15 $30**

BOB-4

BOB-4. Biography Booklet,
c. 1960. NBC/Chrysler Corp. For Chrysler Theater series on NBC-TV. - **$8 $15 $25**

BOB-5

BOB-5. "Popsicle" 8x20" Contest Poster,
1961. Joe Lowe Corp. Pictures water recreation prizes including grand prize of a swimming pool. - **$25 $40 $70**

BOBBY BENSON

...obby was the 12-year-old owner of a ranch in south Texas. ...ith his cowgirl pal Polly and a cast of regulars, *Bobby ...enson's Adventures* started riding the airwaves on CBS in ...932. As long as the show was sponsored by H-O (Hecker's ...ats) cereal, the ranch was called the H-Bar-O. When H-O ...ropped out as sponsor in 1936, the ranch became the B-...ar-B and the show continued briefly. It was revived as ...obby Benson and the B-Bar-B Riders* on the Mutual net-...ork from 1949 to 1955. Among the early cast members ...ere Dead-End Kid Billy Halop as Bobby and Tex Ritter, Don ...notts and Al Hodge. A series of comic books was pub-...shed by Magazine Enterprises from 1950 to 1953.

BNS-5

BNS-6

BNS-5. Certificate,
1934. Hecker H-O Cereal. - **$12 $20 $35**

BNS-6. H-Bar-O Newspaper Vol. 1 #3,
1934. Hecker Oats cereal. - **$10 $20 $35**

BNS-2

BNS-1

BNS-7

BNS-7. Code Rule,
1935. - **$20 $35 $60**

|NS-1. Fan Club Photo,
. 1932. - **$10 $20 $35**

|NS-2. "H-Bar-O Transfer Book",
...933. Paper cover holding strip of 12 sheets of transfer pic-...res to be cut apart and applied by water. - **$15 $60 $100**

BNS-8

BNS-3

BNS-8. Code Book,
1935. - **$15 $30 $50**

|NS-3. "H-Bar-O Herald" Vol. 1 #1 Newspaper,
...eptember 1933. Contents mention Benson radio broadcasts ...o begin September 18. - **$15 $30 $50**

BNS-11

BNS-9

BNS-10

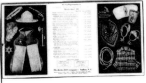

BNS-4

BNS-9. "Bobby Benson In The Tunnel Of Gold" Booklet,
1936. Hecker Cereals. - **$5 $20 $40**

BNS-10. "Bobby Benson And The Lost Herd" Book,
1936. Hecker Cereals. - **$5 $20 $40**

|NS-4. "H-Bar-O Rangers/Bobby Benson" Premium
)ffer Folder,
...934. - **$25 $50 $75**

BNS-11. Glass Bowl,
1930s. Comes in green, yellow or red. Each - **$8 $15 $30**

BNS-12

BNS-12. Photos With Envelope,
1930s. Envelope Or Each Photo - **$5 $8 $12**

BNS-14

BNS-13

BNS-13. "Bobby Benson And The H-O Rangers In Africa" 19x25" Map,
1930s. Map - **$75 $150 $300**
Envelope - **$30 $60 $120**

BNS-14. "Bobby Benson Ranger/H-Bar-O" Foil On Metal Badge,
1930s. - **$15 $25 $60**

BNS-15

BNS-15. Store Display Box With Glass Tumblers,
1930s. Tumblers were obtained with two boxes of Force Toasted Wheat Flakes, six different characters.
Boxed Display - **$100 $150 $300**
Each - **$5 $8 $12**

BNS-16   BNS-17   BNS-18

BNS-16. "H-Bar-O Rangers Club" Cello. Button,
1930s. - **$10 $15 $20**

BNS-17. "H-Bar-O Ranger" Enameled Brass Star Badge,
1930s. Scarce. - **$100 $200 $400**

BNS-18. "Special Captain" Cello. Club Rank Button,
1930s. - **$20 $40 $60**

BNS-19

BNS-19. "H-Bar-O" Card Game,
1930s. Deck of 32 playing cards and instruction leaflet for 18 games.- **$10 $20 $35**

BNS-20

BNS-21

BNS-20. "H-Bar-O Ranger" Enameled Brass Bracelet,
1930s. - **$50 $100 $200**

BNS-21. "H-Bar-O Ranger/808" 2" Long Enamel Brass Tie Clip,
1930s. Near Mint On Card With Mailer - **$300**
Tie Clip Only - **$50 $100 $200**

BNS-22

BNS-22. B-Bar-B Riders Club Kit With Mailer Envelope,
c. 1948. Contents of Bobby Benson humming lariat, photo, membership certificate. Each Item - **$15 $30 $65**

BONANZA

The story of the Cartwright family, set on their Ponderosa Ranch in Nevada in the 1860s, premiered on NBC in September 1959 and aired weekly until 1973 - the second longest Western series on television. One of the nation's most popular shows during most of the 1960s, it was also the first Western to be televised in color. The Ponderosa was a man's world, with Lorne Greene as the widowed father Ben and Pernell Roberts, Dan Blocker and Michael Landon as his sons Adam, Hoss and Little Joe. The program often focused on the relationships between the characters rather than on typical Western violence. It can still be seen in re-runs.

BON-1

BON-2

BON-3

BON-1. "Bonanza Booster" 2-1/4" Cello. Button,
c. 1960. - **$60 $125 $200**

BON-2. Fort Madison Iowa 2-1/4" Rodeo Button,
1964. From series of event buttons beginning in 1957. -
$40 $75 $125

BON-3. "Bonanza Days" 3" Cello. Button,
1964. For celebration in site city of series, picturing all four
original cast members. - **$20 $40 $65**

BON-4

BON-5

BON-4. 33 RPM Record,
1964. Chevrolet. - **$5 $10 $20**

BON-5. "Bonanza" Enamel Diecut Brass Stickpin,
c. 1965. European made, depicts Ben Cartwright on horseback. - **$25 $50 $75**

BON-6

BON-6. "Ponderosa Ranch" Tin Cup,
c. 1965. Store item. Pictures all four original stars. -
$12 $20 $40

BON-7

**BON-7. "Adam" And "Joe" European Litho. 2-1/2"
Stickpin Buttons,**
c. 1965. Each - **$15 $25 $50**

BON-8

BON-8. "The Ponderosa Ranch Story" Booklet,
1969. Ranch souvenir. - **$15 $25 $40**

BON-9

BON-10

BON-9. "Michael Landon/Little Joe" Fan Photo,
1960s. - **$15 $25 $40**

BON-10. "I Met Hoss Cartwright" Litho. Tin Tab,
c. 1970s. Nickey Chevrolet, as spelled. - **$8 $15 $30**

BOZO THE CLOWN

Bozo, a children's popular favorite since 1950 through Dell
comic books and endorsement of Capitol Records for youngsters, added television prominence by the syndicated series
developed and marketed beginning in 1959 by Larry
Harmon. The TV series combined an extensive library of
cartoon films and/or a live segment, also franchised by
Harmon, featuring a local host portraying the likeable circus
clown.

BOZ-1

BOZ-2

BOZ-1. Glass With Lid,
1965. Held peanut butter. Set of five.
Each - **$5 $10 $15**
Lid - **$2 $5 $10**

BOZ-2. "I Am A Bozo Pal" Cello. Button,
1960s. WDSM-TV (Superior, Wisconsin). Contest button,
match number to win prize.- **$5 $10 $15**

BOZ-4

BOZ-5

BOZ-3

BOZ-3. Plastic Push Puppet,
c. 1960s. Store item by Kohner. - **$10 $15 $30**

BOZ-4. Plastic Portrait Ring,
1960s. - **$20 $50 $80**

BOZ-5. "I Visited Bozo's Circus" Litho. Button,
c. 1970s. WGN-TV (Chicago). - **$3 $6 $10**

BOZ-6

BOZ-7

BOZ-6. Illuminated Plastic Snow Dome,
c. 1970s. Store item, battery operated. - **$40 $75 $150**

BOZ-7. "Bozo Is Love" 3" Cello. Button,
c. 1970s. Various TV stations. Pictured example from Grand Rapids, Michigan station. - **$3 $8 $12**

THE BREAKFAST CLUB

Don McNeill's *Breakfast Club*, a happy blend of Midwestern corn and audience participation, ruled morning radio for most of its 24 years on the air (1933 to 1968) - one of the longest-running network radio shows ever. The program, broadcast from Chicago, was essentially spontaneous and unrehearsed, combining contributions sent in by listeners, songs, prayers, marches around the breakfast table, poetry, anecdotes and occasional interviews with guest stars. There were many sponsors over the years. McNeill's familiar closing line - "Be good to yourself" - typified the warmth and charm of this popular and successful program. A TV simulcast in 1954 did not catch on.

BRK-1

BRK-1. Club Member Folder Kit,
c. 1944. Folder has contest and new member forms, comes with "Victory Garden" card.
Folder - **$8 $12 $20**
Card - **$3 $6 $10**

BRK-2

BRK-3

BRK-4

BRK-2. "Don McNeill For President" Litho. Button,
c. 1948. ABC Breakfast Clubs. - **$3 $5 $10**

BRK-3. Club Charter Member Card,
1940s.- **$5 $10 $15**

BRK-4. "Don McNeill Sent Me" Litho. Button,
c. 1950. Apparently to be worn to grocery or other retail store. - **$3 $6 $10**

BRK-5

BRK-6

BRK-5. Fan Club Folder,
1940s. - **$5 $10 $15**

BRK-6. "20 Years Of Corn" Booklet,
c. 1953. - **$10 $20 $35**

BRK-7

BRK-7. "Kiddie Party Ideas" Booklet,
c. 1950s. Fritos. - **$20 $40 $60**

BRK-8

BRK-8. Various Yearbooks,
1940s-1950s. Issued annually.
1942 - **$10 $20 $40**
1947 - **$8 $15 $30**
1948 - **$8 $15 $30**
1950 - **$7 $15 $30**

THE BROWNIES

Palmer Cox (1840-1924) tried cartooning in San Francisco in the 1860s and early 1870s then set up a studio in 1875 in New York City. He had some success being published in early *Life* humor magazines but his main claim to fame grew out of cartoons of Brownieland beginning in the *St. Nicholas* monthly children's magazine. Cox had been inspired by Scottish immigrant folk tales he heard as a boy in Granby, Canada. The frontispiece in the first book *The Brownies: Their Book* from 1887 reads: "Brownies, like fairies and goblins, are imaginary little sprites who are supposed to delight in harmless pranks and helpful deeds. They work and sport while weary households sleep and never allow themselves to be seen by mortal eyes." The Brownies world was a microcosm of society at its best and worst, all portrayed most skillfully through the mind and pen of Palmer Cox and his intricate work throughout the Victorian era and into the early 20th century. Brownieland complemented the times and most probably influenced the creation of *Little Nemo, Kewpies, Teenie-Weenies, Bucky Bug, Raggedy Ann* and other characters set in the world of fantasy.

BRW-1

BRW-1. Estey Organs and Pianos Trade Card, 1890. - **$15 $30 $60**

BRW-2

BRW-2. "Palmer Cox's Brownie Paper Dolls", 1892. Brownies Chocolate Cream Drops. Each - **$10 $25 $40**

BRW-3

BRW-3. World's Fair Trade Card - Chairs, 1892. - **$20 $40 $80**

BRW-4

BRW-4. World's Fair Pin, Needle & Thread Booklet, 1892. - **$20 $40 $80**

BRW-5

BRW-5. World's Fair Trade Card - Stoves/Furnaces, 1893. Scarce. - **$30 $60 $120**

BRW-6

BRW-6. "Palmer Cox Primers" Booklets, 1897. Jersey Coffee and others. Set of 12. Each - **$8 $15 $25**

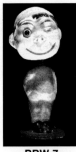

BRW-7

BRW-8

BRW-7. Brownie Type Bobbing Head with Glass Eye,
1890s. Made in Germany. - **$75 $200 $600**

BRW-8. Candy Fig Box,
1890s. - **$40 $80 $160**

BRW-9

BRW-9. Luden's Cough Drop Sign 6x9",
1890s. Rare. - **$250 $500 $1000**

BRW-10

BRW-11

BRW-10. Brownies Song Book,
1890s. - **$25 $60 $100**

BRW-11. Lion's Coffee Cut-Outs,
1890s. Each - **$10 $20 $40**

BRW-12

BRW-12. Advertising Cards,
1890s. Buttermilk Toilet Soap. Each - **$10 $20 $40**

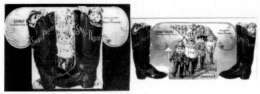

BRW-13

BRW-13. Advertising Trade Card,
1890s. Snag-Proof Boots. Card opens to Brownies as sportsmen using boots. - **$15 $30 $60**

BRW-14

BRW-15

BRW-16

BRW-14. "Merry Christmas From The Brownies" Cardboard Box,
1890s. Probably held candy or dates. - **$40 $75 $150**

BRW-15. Metal Figure Stickpin,
1890s. Tinted luster. - **$10 $15 $25**

BRW-16. "Libretto Of Palmer Cox's Brownies" Booklet,
c. 1904. 16-page song folio from stage production. - **$20 $40 $60**

BUCK JONES

Movie serials, known then as chapter plays, blossomed i the 1930s, drawing countless thousands of youngsters local movie palaces every Saturday to find out how their he would save himself from the perilous predicament at the en of the previous episode. Buck Jones was king of th Western serials. Charles Gebhart (1889-1942) was a cov puncher, a mechanic, a soldier and a trick rider. Aroun 1917 he found work as a Hollywood stuntman. Three year later, as Buck Jones, he had his first starring role. In a Buck Jones was to make more than 125 movies, but it wa as the hero of six chapter plays released between 1933 an 1941 that he was to find his greatest success. Kids ever where waited breathlessly for the next Buck Jones serial. radio series, *Hoofbeats*, sponsored by Grape-Nuts Flake ran for 39 episodes in 1937-1938. In the early 1940s Buc Jones starred with Tim McCoy and Raymond Hatton Monogram Pictures' *Rough Riders* movies.

BKJ-1

BKJ-2

BKJ-1. Rangers' Club Newsletter,
c. 1931. Columbia Pictures. - **$25 $60 $100**

BKJ-2. "Rangers' Club Of America" Cello. Button,
c. 1931. - **$20 $40 $80**

BKJ-3   BKJ-4

BKJ-3. Ranger's Club Member Application Card,
c. 1931. - **$10 $15 $30**

BKJ-4. "Buck Jones Rangers' Club Of America" Cello. Button,
c. 1931. Version of blue photo with red rim. - **$15 $25 $50**

BKJ-5

BKJ-5. Ranger Club Card With Fabric Patch,
c. 1931. Card - **$10 $25 $40**
Patch - **$20 $40 $80**

BKJ-6

BKJ-6. "Rangers Club Of America" Cowboy Outfit,
c. 1931. Hat - **$20 $35 $60**
Bandanna. - **$25 $40 $75**
Chaps, Includes Metal Buttons And Club Logo -
$75 $150 $300

BKJ-7   BKJ-8

BKJ-7. "Buck Jones Ranger" Enameled Brass Badge,
1931. Scarce. - **$50 $85 $175**

BKJ-8. "Buck Jones Rangers Club Of America" Leather Holster With Belt,
1931. Photo pictures embossed club symbol on holster over panel. - **$75 $125 $200**

BKJ-9

BKJ-9. Song Folio/Club Manual,
1932. Published by Bibo-Lang. Copyright "Book No. 1" with club ranks, pledge, etc. - **$20 $60 $120**

BKJ-10   BKJ-11

BKJ-10. "The Red Rider" Cello. Button,
1934. Universal Pictures. For 15-chapter movie serial "The Red Rider". - **$75 $150 $300**

BKJ-11. "The Phantom Rider Club" Cello. Button,
1936. Scarce. Universal Pictures. For 15-chapter movie serial "The Phantom Rider". - **$100 $225 $400**

BKJ-12

BKJ-12. "No. 107 Daisy Buck Jones Special" Air Rifle,
c. 1936. Store item by Daisy Mfg. Co., also used as premium. Compass and sundial on stock, sundial pointer often missing. - **$75 $150 $250**

BKJ-13

BKJ-15

BKJ-14

BKJ-13. Horseshoe Brass Badge,
1937. Grape-Nuts Flakes. - **$15 $25 $40**

BKJ-14. Grape-Nuts Flakes Premium Catalogue Folder Sheet,
1937. Offers about 40 premiums with expiration date December 31. - **$15 $35 $60**

BKJ-15. "Buck Jones Club" Brass Ring,
1937. Grape-Nuts Flakes. - **$75 $120 $160**

BKJ-16

BKJ-16. Cello. Over Brass 3-1/4" Bullet Holder For Pencil,
c. 1937. Grape-Nuts Flakes. Inscription "From Buck Jones To His Pal" followed by personalized name designated by orderer. - **$60 $120 $175**

BKJ-17

BKJ-17. "Buck Jones In The Cowboy Masquerade" Booklet,
1938. Ice cream cone premium, Buddy Book #8. - **$10 $20 $35**

BKJ-18

BKJ-18. "Buck Jones Movie Book",
1938. Daisy Mfg. Co. - **$20 $30 $60**

BKJ-19

BKJ-19. "UCA Salve" Premium Catalogue Folder Sheet,
c. 1938. Has endorsement of Buck Jones and opens to 9x20" with air rifle only related premium to him. - **$20 $50 $75**

BKJ-20

BKJ-21

BKJ-22

BKJ-20. Fan Photo,
1930s. - **$8 $15 $25**

BKJ-21. Portrait Photo,
1930s. Probably a premium photo. - **$10 $25 $35**

BKJ-22. "Chicago Stadium Rodeo" Cello. Button,
1930s. Single event issue. - **$20 $50 $75**

BKJ-23   BKJ-24   BKJ-25

BKJ-23. "For U.S. Marshal/Buck Jones" Cello. Button,
1930s. - **$40 $80 $150**

BKJ-24. "Buck Jones Club" Cello. Button,
1930s. Probably movie serial club. - **$40 $75 $125**

BKJ-25. "Riders Of Death Valley Club" Cello. Button,
1941. Universal Pictures. For 15-chapter movie serial "Riders Of Death Valley". - **$50 $80 $150**

BUCK ROGERS IN THE 25TH CENTURY

Buck Rogers was the first American comic strip to plunge into science fiction and it enjoyed great success after it was introduced in January 1929. The story was adapted by Ph. Nowlan from his futuristic novel, illustrated by Dick Calkins and syndicated by the John F. Dille Co. Buck wakes after 500 years of suspended animation and, along with young Wilma Deering and the scientist Dr. Huer, battles to save America and the earth from various enemies, in particular Killer Kane and Ardala Valmar, who want to conquer the world. The strip ran until 1967 (a companion Sunday strip appeared from 1930 to 1965) and both were revived in 1979 to 1983. A successful radio adaptation was broadcast from 1932 to 1947, sponsored first by Kellogg, then Cocomalt Cream of Wheat, Popsicle and General Foods. A TV version had a brief run in 1950-1951 and a revised series lasted from 1979 to 1983. Movie adaptations appeared in 1939 with Buster Crabbe and 1979, and there have been a variety of Big Little Books and comic books over the years.

BRG-1

BRG-1. "Amazing Stories" Pulp Magazine With First Buck Rogers Story ,
1928. Vol. 3 #5, August issue with story "Armeggedon-2419 A.D." (Sequel "Airlords of Han" appeared here May, 1929.) - **$150 $250 $500**

BRG-3

BRG-2

RG-2. "With My Very Best Regards" Fan Picture,
1929. Newspaper premium, black on green paper 6x9".
arge 11-1/2x17-1/2" black on orange paper version
peared 1931. Each - **$150 $250 $400**

RG-3. Newspaper Comic Strip Portraits Premiums,
32. Black and white, each about 8x10-1/2". Each -
5 **$150 $300**

BRG-4

RG-4. "Pep" Leaflet With Radio Show Ad,
32. Kellogg's. - **$20 $40 $60**

BRG-5

G-5. Radio Broadcast Publicity Leaflet,
1932. Kellogg's Corn Flakes. Sponsorship indicated for
ck Rogers and Singing Lady programs. - **$12 $25 $40**

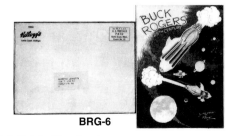

BRG-6

RG-6. Origin Storybook,
33. Kellogg's. Near Mint With Envelope - **$375**
ose - **$46 $140 $325**
ite Paper Letter (2 Versions) Each - **$40 $80 $125**

BRG-7

BRG-7. "Buck Rogers 25th Century A.D." BLB,
1933. Softcover with Cocomalt ad on back cover. -
$20 $60 $150

BRG-8

BRG-9

BRG-8. Mailer And Letter For Cocomalt BLB,
1933. Mailer - **$20 $50 $75**
Yellow Paper Letter - **$40 $80 $125**

BRG-9. "Solar System Map" Letter,
1933. Cocomalt. Orange paper. - **$35 $75 $125**

BRG-10

BRG-10. Solar System Map 18x25",
1933. Cocomalt. - **$250 $500 $800**

BRG-11

BRG-12

BRG-11. Buck And Wilma Cocomalt Picture,
1933. - **$50 $100 $150**
Blue Paper Letter **$35 $75 $125**

BRG-12. "Wilma" Paper Mask,
1933. Cocomalt. Curly hair version. Also issued for Buck
Rogers. Each - **$75 $150 $250**

BRG-13

BRG-13. "Buck Rogers" Cardboard Helmet,
1933. Cocomalt. Helmet - **$75 $125 $200**
Mailer - **$25 $50 $100**
Blue Paper Letter **$35 $75 $125**

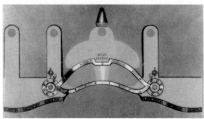

BRG-14

BRG-14. "Wilma Deering" Cardboard Helmet,
1933. Cocomalt. Helmet - **$75 $125 $200**
Mailer - **$25 $50 $100**
Blue Paper Letter **$35 $75 $125**

BRG-15

BRG-15. Cardboard Pop Gun,
1933. Cocomalt. Came with Buck or Wilma paper helmet.
Gun - **$75 $125 $200**
Mailer (Two styles) - **$25 $50 $100**

BRG-16

BRG-16. Painted Lead Figure,
1933. Cocomalt. Wilma and Killer Kane also issued. Came in
cellophane bag. With Leaflet - **$25 $50 $100**
Each Figure Only - **$15 $25 $40**

BRG-17

**BRG-17. Cocomalt "Buck Rogers Cut-Out Adventure
Book" Order Folder,**
1933. Full color 9x13" - **$75 $150 $300**

BRG-18

**BRG-18. Cocomalt "Buck Rogers Cut-Out Adventure
Book",**
1933. Rare. Came with cover letter and separate cardboard
sheet for theater stage.
Complete Uncut - **$1000 $2500 $4000**
Complete, Figures Cut - **$300 $600 $1200**

BRG-19

(patch on vest
enlarged above)

BRG-20

BRG-19. "Buck Rogers On The Air" Radio Station Listing Sheet,
c. 1933. Cocomalt. Three versions or more on blue or white paper, sizes vary. Each - **$25 $60 $100**

BRG-20. Child's Playsuit,
1934. Scarce. Store item and Cream of Wheat. Came with helmet.
Uniform, Complete Except Helmet - **$250 $600 $1200**
Vest Only With Patch - **$100 $200 $300**

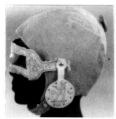
BRG-21

BRG-21. "Buck Rogers 25th Century" Space Helmet,
1934. Store item (brown suede cloth version) and Cream of Wheat (leather version). - **$150 $300 $750**

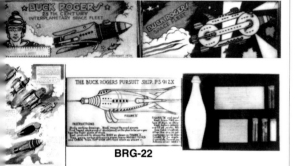
BRG-22

BRG-22. Rocketship Balsa Wood Model,
1934. Six in set (#6 shown), each boxed ready-made or unfinished with color/bw instruction sheet. Sold in stores (Sears offered #1,3,and 4) or as newspaper premium. Only #4 "Super Dreadnought" was available (unfinished) as Cream of Wheat premium.
Each Boxed - **$200 $350 $600**
Instruction Sheet - **$50 $80 $150**

BRG-23   BRG-24

BRG-23. "Buck Rogers Thwarting Ancient Demons" Booklet,
1934. Big Thrill Chewing Gum. Booklet #1 of six Buck Rogers titles in set of 24. 2-3/8x3" with eight pages. Each - **$25 $50 $75**

BRG-24. "Ardala" Metal Alloy Figure By Britains,
1934. Cream of Wheat. Each with moveable arm. Set (with name under base) of Buck, Wilma, Killer Kane, Ardala, Dr. Huer, Robot. Robot - **$250 $500 $750**
Others, Each - **$150 $300 $450**

BRG-25   (handle enlarged)

BRG-25. Rocket Pistol XZ-31 By Daisy,
1934. Store item. 9-1/2" long with black finish and cocking handle. - **$60 $150 $300**

BRG-26

BRG-26. Scientific Laboratory,
1934. Store item by Porter Chemical Co. Pictured are envelope that holds instruction manuals (three) and envelope for slide covers. Many other items came in boxed set. No complete sets known. Items Shown - **$100 $200 $300**

(enlarged view of label above)
BRG-27

BRG-27. "Buck Rogers Telescope",
1934. Store item, part of Scientific Laboratory set. - **$100 $250 $400**

BRG-28

BRG-29

BRG-30

BRG-28. "A Century Of Progress" Chicago World's Fair Litho. Button,
1934. - **$75 $150 $350**

BRG-29. Birthstone Initial Ring,
1934. Cocomalt. Unmarked brass Buck Rogers issue and other non-Buck offers, top has personalized single initial designated by orderer. Also offered by Popsicle, 1939. - **$200 $325 $450**

BRG-30. Saturday Chicago American Litho. Button,
c. 1934. - **$40 $75 $150**

BRG-31

BRG-31. "Caster" Booklet,
c. 1935. Boxed Caster sets were store item by Rapaport Brothers. Three booklet versions. Booklet includes cartoon story and photos of caster and mold sets.
Each - **$75 $150 $250**

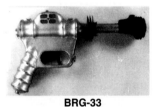

BRG-32   BRG-33

BRG-32. Rocket Pistol XZ-35 By Daisy,
1935. Store item. 7-1/2" long with black finish and cocking handle. - **$75 $175 $350**

BRG-33. Disintegrator Pistol XZ-38 By Daisy,
1935. Store item and Cream of Wheat. Used in 1939 as Popsicle premium. Copper finish. Flint produces spark. - **$125 $250 $500**

BRG-34

BRG-35

BRG-34. Dixie Ice Cream Lid,
1935. Browntone photo. Inscribed for Cream of Wheat radio series. - **$25 $40 $60**

BRG-35. Dixie Ice Cream Picture,
1935. Photo of Matthew Crowley, radio portrayer. Full color, obtained by redeeming lids. - **$40 $75 $150**

BRG-36

BRG-36. "Rocket Ship Knife" Box,
1935. Cream of Wheat and store item.
Box Only - **$150 $250 $400**

BRG-37

BRG-37. "Buck Rogers" Steel/Cello. Pocketknife,
1935. Scarce. Store item by Camillus Cutlery Co. and premium from Cream of Wheat. Two blades. Same image on both sides in red, green or blue styles. Color easily worn off. - **$300 $750 $1500**

BRG-38

BRG-38. "Irwin Projector" With Comic Character Films,
1935. Unmarked but offered as premium with six films (from group of 13 titles) in Cream of Wheat Buck Rogers Solar Scouts Club Manual. Boxed Projector - **$50 $80 $150**
Each Boxed Film - **$5 $10 $15**

BRG-39

BRG-39. Set of Three Board Games,
1935. Store item and Cream of Wheat premium. Came with 40 cards and 12 miniature bowling pin-shaped wood markers. Complete Boxed Set - **$250 $450 $700**
Each Board - **$50 $100 $150**

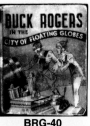

BRG-40   BRG-41

BRG-40. "Buck Rogers In The City Of Floating Globes" BLB,
1935. Cocomalt. Issued only as softcover. - **$75 $200 $400**

BRG-41. "Tarzan Cups" Premium Booklet Featuring Buck Rogers,
1935. Tarzan Ice Cream Cups. From Whitman set of six different characters, each obtained for 12 cup lids. -
$75 $150 $300

BRG-42   BRG-43

BRG-42. "Punch-O-Bag",
1935. Morton's Salt premium by Lou Fox, Chicago. Various colors each showing a different character. Balloon typically missing or disintegrated. - **$20 $30 $50**

BRG-43. "Buck Rogers 25th Century Adventures" Printing Set,
1935. Store item and Cream of Wheat. Set No. 4080 by StamperKraft Co. Includes 14 character stamps. -
$150 $400 $750

BRG-44

BRG-44. "Cosmic Conquests" Boxed Printing Set,
1935. Store item by StamperKraft Co. Set #4090-S with 22 character stamps. Boxed - **$150 $300 $500**

BRG-45

BRG-45. Pocketwatch,
1935. Store item by Ingraham Co. Lightning bolt hands and case back pictures Comet Man. Boxed With Gold Cardboard Insert - **$500 $1500 $2500**
Watch Only - **$300 $700 $1300**

BRG-46

BRG-47

BRG-46. "Buck Rogers In The 25th Century" Cello. Button,
1935. Cream of Wheat. - **$30 $60 $100**

BRG-47. "Buck Rogers On The Air For Cream Of Wheat" Gummed Back Paper Sticker,
c. 1935. Dark blue and yellow. - **$50 $100 $150**

BRG-48

BRG-48. Liquid Helium Water Pistol XZ-44 By Daisy,
1936. Store item. Used in 1939 as Popsicle premium. Nonfunctional due to aging of bladder.
Red and Yellow Version - **$200 $400 $800**
Copper Colored Version - **$250 $500 $1000**

BRG-49

BRG-49. Boxed Card Game,
1936. Store item by All-Fair. Box comes in two sizes, larger one shown. 35 cards and instructions. - **$150 $300 $500**

BRG-50

BRG-50. "Solar Scouts" Radio Club Manual,
1936. Cream Of Wheat. Offers 18 premiums. -
$75 $150 $300

BRG-51

BRG-52

BRG-53

BRG-51. Repeller Ray Brass Ring With Green Stone,
1936. Cream Of Wheat and newspaper premium offer. -
$500 $1750 $3000

BRG-52. "Solar Scouts" Sweater Patch,
1936. Rare. Less than 10 known. Cream of Wheat. -
$1500 $3500 $5000

BRG-53. Solar Scouts Member Brass Badge,
1936. Cream of Wheat and newspaper premium offer.
Facsimile Buck Rogers signature on reverse.. -
$25 $60 $100

BRG-56

BRG-54

BRG-55

BRG-54. "Spaceship Commander/Buck Rogers Solar Scouts" Silvered Brass Badge,
1936. Cream of Wheat and newspaper premium offer.
Metallic blue accent paint, holed at bottom to serve as whistle. - $85 $175 $300

BRG-55. "Spaceship Commander" Leaflet,
1936. Cream of Wheat. Offers badge, banner, magnetic
compass, stationery, Wilma handkerchief. - $75 $150 $250

BRG-56. "Chief Explorer/Buck Rogers Solar Scouts" Badge,
1936. Cream of Wheat and newspaper premium offer. Red
enamel paint background. Badge inscribed on back
"Awarded For Distinguished Achievement" with facsimile
Buck Rogers signature. - $100 $200 $350

BRG-57

BRG-58

BRG-57. "Chief Explorer" Brass Badge,
1936. Scarce. Cream of Wheat and newspaper premium
offer. Variety with gold luster and no red enamel paint. -
$150 $300 $500

BRG-58. Wilma Deering Brass Pendant With Chain,
1936. Rare. Cream of Wheat and newspaper premium offer.
Back inscription "To My Pal In The Solar Scouts". -
$300 $1000 $1500

BRG-59

BRG-59. "Buck Rogers Rocketship" Balsa Flying Toy With Mailer Envelope,
1936. Mrs. Karl's Bread by Spotswood Specialty Co., also
Cream of Wheat premium. Envelope is plain, comes with
wood stick and rubber band launcher. - $100 $250 $500

BRG-61

BRG-60

BRG-60. "Daisy Comics",
1936. Daisy Mfg. Co. Contents include Buck Rogers comic
story and shows guns for him plus features on cowboys Buck
Jones and Tim McCoy. - $30 $90 $210

BRG-61. "25th Century Acousticon Jr." 2-1/4" Cello. Button,
1936. Rare. Hearing aid device by Dictagraph Products
Co. - $300 $1000 $1800

BRG-62

BRG-62. Chemical Laboratory Boxed Set,
1937. Store item in two sizes by Gropper Toy Co.
Small Set - $350 $750 $1250
Large Set - $500 $1000 $1500

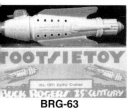

BRG-63

BRG-64

RG-63. Tootsietoy #1031 "Battle Cruiser",
937. Metal "Buck Rogers Battle Cruiser TSDDM3030."
sed as Popsicle premium in 1939.
ear Mint Boxed - **$350**
oose - **$75 $150 $225**

RG-64. Tootsietoy #1032 "Destroyer" With Box,
937. Metal "Buck Rogers Venus Duo-Destroyer MK 24 L".
sed as Popsicle premium in 1939.
ear Mint Boxed - **$350**
oose - **$75 $150 $225**

BRG-65

BRG-66

RG-65. Tootsietoy #1033 "Attack Ship",
37. Metal "Buck Rogers Flash Blast Attack Ship TS 310 Z".
sed as Popsicle premium in 1939.
ear Mint Boxed - **$350**
oose - **$75 $150 $225**

RG-66. Metal Figure 1-3/4" Tall,
37. Packaged with Tootsietoy rocketships. Buck (Silver
olor) Or Wilma (Gold Color) Each - **$60 $125 $175**

BRG-67

RG-67. Vicks Comic Book,
1938. Vicks Chemical Co. with local store imprint. Reprint
ries from earlier Famous Funnies comic books. -
5 **$200 $525**

BRG-68

BRG-69

BRG-68. "Rocket Rangers" Club Member Card,
c. 1939. Pictures "Inter-Planetary Battle Cruiser" on yellow
card. Five later versions were on blue or white cards, the last
issued in 1980. First Version - **$75 $150 $275**
Later Versions - **$20 $50 $100.**

**BRG-69. "Strange World Adventures Club" Serial Club
Button,**
1939. Scarce. Universal. One of the rarest and most desirable movie serial club buttons. - **$300 $750 $1500**

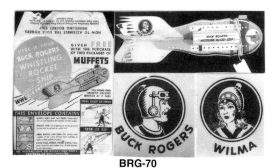

BRG-70

**BRG-70. "Whistling Rocketship" Cardboard Punch-Out
Assembly Kit With Envelope,**
1939. Scarce. Muffets cereal. Example photo shows portrait
details from tail fins.
Unused With Envelope - **$250 $500 $750**
Assembled - **$200 $400 $600**

BRG-71

BRG-72

BRG-71. Wilma Unlicensed Mask,
1930s. Store item, marked "Made In Japan". Unlike Cocomalt
premium, hair is not curly. - **$40 $80 $150**

BRG-72. School Map,
1930s. Probable Dixon Pencil Co. Paper sheet came folded
with Buck Rogers art in red bordering map of North America.-
$200 $400 $600

BRG-73

BRG-74

BRG-75

BRG-73. "Buffalo Evening News" Cello. Button,
1930s. From series of newspaper contest buttons, match number to win prize.- **$50 $100 $150**

BRG-74. "Buck Rogers Gang" Club Member Cello. Button,
1930s. Issuer unknown. - **$200 $400 $600**

BRG-75. Canadian Club Member Cello. Button,
1930s. Issuer unknown but 1" in blue/white/orange. Curl reads "Shaw Mfg. Toronto." - **$250 $600 $1200**

BRG-76   BRG-77

BRG-76. Matchbook,
1940. Popsicle/Creamsicle. May 4th version for new radio sponsorship. Also issued with April 6 date in either 1939 or 1940. - **$10 $20 $40**

BRG-77. Matchbook,
1940. Popsicle. May 4th version for new radio sponsorship. Also issued with April 6 date in either 1939 or 1940. - **$10 $20 $40**

BRG-78

BRG-78. "Onward School Supplies" 18x24" Paper Hanger Sign,
1940. Printed both sides. - **$150 $250 $400**

BRG-79

BRG-79. School Supplies 11x16" Paper Store Poster,
1940. Onward School Supplies. Announces rubber band gun free with school supply purchase. - **$150 $350 $750**

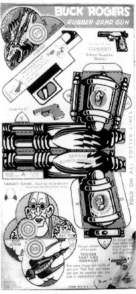

BRG-80

BRG-80. Cardboard Punch-Out Rubber Band Gun,
1940. Onward School Supplies. Punch-out sheet includes standup targets of Sea Monster, Wing Bat Wu, Spaceship. Unpunched - **$35 $60 $100**

BRG-81

BRG-81. "School Sale" Newspaper Circular,
1940. Photo examples are page details. - **$35 $60 $100**

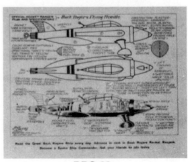

BRG-82

BRG-82. "Flying Needle" Airship Diagram Sheet,
c. 1941. Probable various newspapers. For "Buck Rogers Rocket Rangers" club of aspiring "Spaceship Commander" readers. - **$100 $200 $350**

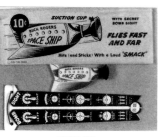

BRG-83

BRG-84

BRG-83. Cardboard Spaceship With Envelope,
1942. Morton's Salt. Includes cardboard "Secret Bomb Sight". - **$50 $100 $250**

BRG-84. "Buck Rogers Ranger" Aluminum Dog Tag With Chain,
c. 1942. Rare. Item has 1935 copyright but probably issued a few years later. - **$250 $600 $1000**

BRG-85

BRG-85. Atomic Pistol U-235 By Daisy,
1945. Store item. Silver color finish. Gun - **$75 $200 $350**
Box - **$75 $200 $350**
2-Page Story Folder - **$40 $75 $150**

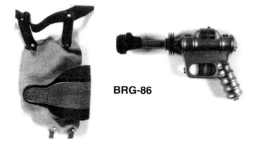

BRG-86

BRG-86. Atomic Pistol U-238 By Daisy,
1946. Store item. Gold color finish. Gun - **$100 $250 $400**
Holster - **$100 $250 $400**
Box - **$75 $200 $350**
2-Page Story Folder $40 $75 $150**

BRG-87

BRG-88

BRG-87. Glow-In-Dark Ring Of Saturn,
1946. Post's Corn Toasties radio premium. White plastic topped by red plastic stone. - **$325 $580 $850**

BRG-88. "Ring Of Saturn" Instruction Folder,
1946. Post's Corn Toasties radio premium. - **$50 $80 $150**

BRG-89

BRG-90

BRG-89. Cardboard "Flying Saucer",
c. 1940s. Store item by unknown maker. Has metal rim. - **$35 $75 $150**

BRG-90. Space Ranger Kit,
1952. Sylvania Electric Products Inc. Six full color punch-out sheets, each 10-1/2x14-1/2". Unpunched In Envelope - **$50 $100 $150**

BRG-91

BRG-92

BRG-91. "Buck Rogers/Satellite Pioneers" Litho. Tin 2" Tab,
c. 1957. - **$20 $40 $65**

BRG-92. "Satellite Pioneers" Cadet Bulletin Folder,
c. 1957. Various newspapers. - **$15 $35 $60**

BRG-93

BRG-94

BRG-93. Satellite Pioneers Club Bulletin,
c. 1957. Various newspapers. Cover portrait faces right. Includes "Map of the Solar System." - **$20 $30 $50**

BRG-94. "Satellite Pioneers" Picture Card,
c. 1960. Various newspapers. - **$15 $25 $40**

BUGS BUNNY

Probably the world's best-known rabbit, Bugs Bunny evolved into the brash character we know in the late 1930s in the Leon Schlesinger cartoon studios. He first uttered his memorable "Eh...What's up, doc?" to Elmer Fudd in *The Wild Hare* of 1940, and the mischievous wabbit has been asking it ever since in the voice made famous by Mel Blanc. Until 1969 the cartoons were released or produced by Warner Brothers. Bugs' first comic book appearance was in 1941 in the first issue of *Looney Tunes and Merrie Melodies* and a Sunday newspaper strip started in 1943. Many cartoons, comic books and animated TV specials in the years since have been accompanied by a seemingly endless parade of merchandise, usually copyrighted by Warner Brothers.

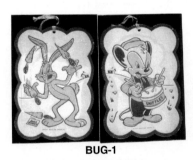

BUG-1

BUG-2

BUG-1. Bugs, Sniffles Cardboard Plaques,
1940s. Store items. Glows in the dark. Each - **$15 $25 $40**

BUG-2. Rubber Squeaker Figure,
1940s. Store item by Oak Rubber Co. - **$25 $50 $90**

BUG-3

BUG-3. Dell Comics Picture,
1940s. - **$15 $30 $50**

BUG-4

BUG-4. Dell Comics Christmas Card,
1940s. - **$20 $50 $70**

BUG-5

BUG-6

BUG-7

BUG-5. "What's Up Doc?" Litho. Button,
1959. Came on doll. - **$25 $50 $80**

BUG-6. "Help Crippled Children" Litho. Tin Tab,
c. 1950s. - **$3 $8 $12**

BUG-7. Bugs Bunny Beanie,
1950s. - **$30 $60 $120**

BUG-8

BUG-9

BUG-8. "Magic Paint Book",
1961. Kool-Aid. Includes offer for "Smiling Pitcher".-
$8 $15 $35

BUG-9. "March Of Comics" #273,
1965. Various sponsers. - $3 $8 $15

BULLWINKLE AND ROCKY

Rocky the flying squirrel and his pal Bullwinkle the moose were created by Jay Ward in one of television's successful early animated cartoons. From 1959 to 1963 they battled the evil little Mr. Big and his cohorts Boris and Natasha in *Rocky and His Friends* on ABC, in *The Bullwinkle Show* from 1961 to 1964 on NBC and then back to ABC until 1973. Other regulars included Mr. Peabody the beagle, his human friend Sherman, the inept Mountie Dudley Do-Right and his criminal foe Snidely Whiplash. Comic books started appearing in the early 1960s. Toys, games and other merchandise usually carry the copyright of P.A.T.-Ward Productions.

BUL-2

BUL-1

BUL-1. "P-F Flyers" Bullwinkle & Rocky 12x21"
Cardboard Store Sign,
1959. B. F. Goodrich Co. Also promotes Rin-Tin-Tin, The Lone Ranger, Captain Gallant. - $50 $100 $150

BUL-2. "Sewing Cards" Kit With Envelope,
1961. Set of six cards for yarn threading.
Near Mint In Mailer - $150
Each Card- $5 $10 $15

BUL-3

BUL-3. Bullwinkle's Safety Coloring Book,
1963. General Mills. - $10 $25 $50

BUL-4

BUL-4. "Electric Quiz Fun Game",
1963. General Mills. Battery operated. - $25 $40 $75

BUL-5 (close-up)

BUL-5. Cheerios 21x28" Double-Sided Paper Sign,
c. 1963. - $40 $75 $125

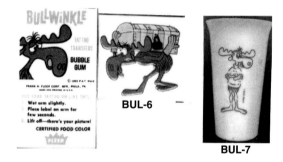

BUL-6

BUL-7

BUL-6. "Tattoo" Fleer Gum Wrapper,
1965. Example from set with different tattoo images. -
$8 $15 $25

BUL-7. Plastic Tumbler,
1960s. Issuer unknown. - $15 $25 $40

BUL-8

BUL-9

BUL-10

BUL-8. Bullwinkle Trading Coin,
1960s. Old London Dipsy Doodles and Corn Doodles. Numbered set of 60 plastic coins with paper inserts picturing Bullwinkle characters. Each - $5 $10 $15

BUL-9. Pepsi Collector Series Glasses,
1970s. Each - $8 $12 $18

BUL-10. Bullwinkle Pez Dispenser,
1970s. Issue with yellow or brown antlers. - **$40 $125 $175**

BURNS AND ALLEN

Longtime vaudeville stars, George Burns and Gracie Allen made a successful transition to radio in 1932 and broadcast continuously on CBS or NBC until Gracie decided to retire in 1958. George was the straight man, Gracie the scatterbrain and the show ranged from standup gags to situation comedy. The program also introduced Mel Blanc's Happy Postman character. Sponsors over the years included Robert Burns and White Owl cigars, Campbell's soup, Grape-Nuts Flakes, Chesterfield cigarettes, Hinds lotion, Hormel Packing Co., Swan soap, Maxwell House coffee and Block Drugs. A popular half-hour TV show aired from 1950 to 1958 on CBS. "Say goodnight, Gracie."

BUR-1

BUR-2

BUR-3

BUR-1. "Gracie Allen's Anniversary Gift To Guy Lombardo" Booklet,
1933. General Cigar Co., maker of Robert Burns cigars. Humor dialogue between Gracie and George Burns on what to buy orchestra leader Lombardo for his fourth anniversary of radio broadcasts.- **$10 $18 $25**

BUR-2. Grape-Nuts 12x18" Sign,
1930s. Scarce. Printed on both sides and with hanging cord. - **$300 $600 $1200**

BUR-3. Fan Photo,
1930s. Campbell's Soups. - **$15 $25 $40**

BUR-4

BUR-5

BUR-4. Fan Photo,
1930s. Columbia Broadcasting System. - **$10 $20 $30**

BUR-5. Radio Broadcast Listing Folder,
1930s. Grape-Nuts. - **$10 $20 $30**

BUR-6

BUR-6. "Gracie Allen's Missing Brother" Boxed Jigsaw Puzzle,
1930s. Store item by Commanday-Roth Co. Comes with leaflet describing the search for him in pictured crowd scene.
Boxed - **$15 $25 $40**
Loose - **$8 $15 $25**

BUR-7

BUR-7. "Motorola TV Coffee Servers" Boxed Set,
1950s. Motorola, maker of TV sets. Offered at 99 cents per set, glass items by Pyrex. Boxed - **$15 $25 $40**

BUSTER BROWN

Buster Brown was the creation of R. F. Outcault. The colo strip first appeared in the Sunday New York Herald of May 1902, a half-dozen years after Outcault's first great strip, Tf Yellow Kid. Buster was a pint-size prankster, constant bedeviling those around him, then apologizing. His ever-pre sent companion was Tige, a Boston terrier with an evil tootl grin. The strip was a huge success and ran until 1920. number of newspaper strip reprint books and advertisir booklets featuring cartoon panels appeared in the early pa of the century. Outcault sold merchandising rights to tf Buster Brown character to more than 50 manufacturers everything from bread to soap to harmonicas; today we c still buy Buster Brown shoes and children's clothes. A wee ly drama based on the strip ran on CBS in 1929 and w revived as *Smilin' Ed McConnell's Buster Brown Gang* NBC. It aired from 1943 to 1953, when it transferred to te vision, retaining Buster Brown Shoes as sponsor. C McConnell's death in 1954, Andy Devine took his place a the show was re-named *Andy's Gang*. The star of the shc was Froggy the Gremlin. Buster Brown has been a ri source of toys, comic books and premiums for 90 yea "Plunk your magic twanger, Froggy!"

BWN-1

BWN-2

BWN-1. "New York Herald/Young Folks" Cello. Button,
1902. Early newspaper issue. - **$75 $150 $275**

BWN-2. "Buster Brown And His Bubble" Postcard,
1903. From numbered set of 10, each including The Yellow
Kid. Each - **$25 $50 $75**

BWN-3

BWN-3. "Brown's Blue Ribbon Book Of Jokes And
Jingles",
1904. Scarce. Brown Shoe Co. Considered the first comic
book premium. First of four in 5x7" format. Two versions of
book #1: Early version includes Pore Li'l Mose, second version replaces Mose with the Yellow Kid. -
$450 $1370 $3200

BWN-4   BWN-5   BWN-6

BWN-4. "Buster Brown's Experiences With Pond's
Extract" Booklet,
1904. - **$75 $125 $200**

BWN-5. "Buster Brown Bread" Cello. Button,
1905. Issued in both yellow and gray rim variations. -
$10 $20 $35

BWN-6. "Buster Brown Shoes" Cello. Pocket Mirror,
1905. - **$75 $175 $300**

BWN-7   BWN-8

BWN-7. Enamel And Brass Stickpin,
1905. Initials on bottom edge stand for 'Buster Brown Blue
Ribbon Shoes'. - **$60 $150 $225**

BWN-8. "Quick Meal Steel Ranges" Booklet,
1905. - **$20 $40 $65**

BWN-9

BWN-9. "Buster Brown's Blue Ribbon Book Of Jokes &
Jingles No. 2",
1905. One of earliest premium comic books. -
$200 $600 $1400

BWN-10

BWN-10. Paper Mask,
c. 1905. - **$40 $75 $125**

BWN-11   BWN-12

BWN-11. "Buster Brown Stocking Magazine",
1906. - **$25 $50 $85**

BWN-12. Buster Brown Mirror,
1900s. Shoe Premium. - **$40 $80 $160**

BWN-13

BWN-13. Assortment of Postcards from several series,
1900s. Buster Brown and his Bubble series - **$25 $50 $75**
Others - **$10 $20 $30**

BWN-14

BWN-14. "Buster's Book Of Jokes And Jingles No. 3",
1900s. Third of four in series. - **$200 $600 $1400**

BWN-15   BWN-16

BWN-15. "Buster Brown Shoes" Cello. Button,
c. 1910. Red background. - **$60 $125 $200**

BWN-16. Black Background Version Cello. Button,
c. 1910. - **$60 $125 $200**

BWN-17   BWN-19

BWN-18

BWN-17. Cigar Tin,
c. 1910 Store item. Price includes lid. - **$400 $1000 $1600**

BWN-18. Entry Card For Pocketwatch Premium,
c. 1912. - **$20 $40 $80**

BWN-19. Buster And Tige Pocketwatch,
c. 1912. - **$100 $300 $600**

BWN-20

BWN-20. "Buster Brown's Book Of Travels",
1912. Brown Shoe Co. 12 pages 3-1/2x5". - **$80 $250 $575**

BWN-21

BWN-22

BWN-21. "Buster Brown Walking Club" Oval Cello. Button,
c. 1920s. Includes "Tread Straight" trademark arrow symbol. - **$20 $40 $65**

BWN-22. Magic Kit,
1934. Includes "Magic Ball, My Magic Ink, My Secret Ink, Trick Hospital Bandage". In Mailer - **$15 $25 $50**

BWN-23   BWN-24

BWN-23. Cello. Fob,
1930s. - **$25 $60 $125**

BWN-24. Litho. Tin Clicker,
1930s. - **$10 $20 $35**

BWN-25   BWN-26

BWN-25. Felt Patch,
1930s. - **$10 $20 $35**

BWN-26. Buster Brown Blotter,
1930s. - **$20 $40 $60**

BWN-27   BWN-28

BWN-27. Tin Whistle,
1930s. - **$20 $40 $60**

BWN-28. Buster Brown Comics #1,
1945. Scarce. Brown Shoe Co. No number and no date, covers refer to various shoe stores. - **$60 $200 $500**

BWN-30

BWN-29

BWN-29. Toy Currency,
1940s. Various denominations collected for prizes.
Each - **$2 $4 $6**

BWN-30. Buster Brown Knife,
1940s. Shoe premium, rare. - **$30 $60 $120**

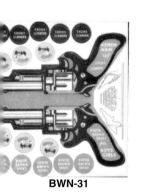

BWN-31

BWN-32

BWN-31. Punch-Out Gun Sheet,
1940s. Unpunched - **$15 $25 $40**

BWN-32. "Captain Kangaroo's Grandfather Clock" Punch-Out Sheet,
1956. Buster Brown Shoes, copyright Keeshan-Miller Enterprises. Unpunched - **$10 $20 $30**

BWN-33

BWN-33. Buster Brown Beanie,
1950s. - **$10 $20 $30**

BWN-34

BWN-34. Buster Brown Secret Agent Periscope,
1950s. - **$20 $40 $60**

BWN-35

BWN-35. Buster Brown/Capt. Kangaroo Hat Punch-out,
1960s. - **$20 $30 $40**

BWN-36 **BWN-37**

BWN-38

BWN-36. Palm Puzzle,
1960s. - **$5 $12 $20**

BWN-37. Plastic Flicker Ring,
1960s. Image changes from Buster and Tige to "Stop" and "Go" signs. - **$30 $45 $60**

BWN-38. "Buster Brown Big Foot" Plastic Whistle Ring,
c. 1960s. Blowing into big toe creates whistling sound. -
$10 $15 $20

CALIFORNIA RAISINS

In the mid-1980s much of America was captivated by a bunch of cool raisins with an irresistable beat—the California Raisins had arrived. Created in clay by Will Vinton for the California Raisin Advisory Board (CALRAB) and animated for musical television commercials by the Claymation process, these diminutive sports were anything but dry. The commercials began in 1986, featuring the raisins' signature song *I Heard It Through The Grapevine*. Small vinyl figures of the raisins were widely promoted as premiums or giveaways by CALRAB.

CAL-1

CAL-1. Store Display,
1988. Hardee's Food Systems. Came with six vinyl figures.
Complete - **$40 $75 $125**

CAL-2

CAL-3

CAL-2. Vinyl Bank,
1987. - **$5 $12 $25**

CAL-3. Vinyl Tote Bag,
1988. - **$5 $10 $15**

CAL-4

CAL-4. Plastic Radio,
1988. Flexible rubber arms and legs, microphone in hand. -
$15 $25 $35

CAP'N CRUNCH

Cap'n Crunch, a sweetened breakfast cereal that is supposed to stay crunchy down to the bottom of the bowl, was introduced in 1963 by Quaker Oats. In an unusual twist, the name of the cereal was also the name of the cartoon character created to promote it. The Cap'n was created in-house by Quaker and the TV ad campaign was designed by Jay Ward Productions, best known for Bullwinkle and Rocky animated cartoons. Other characters include Seadog, Jean LaFoote, Wilma the White Whale, Harry S. Hippo and Soggie. There have been many premium offers and giveaways. A Saturday morning animated cartoon was still running well into the 1990s.

CRN-1

CRN-1. "I'm Dreaming Of A Wide Isthmus" Comic Booklet,
1963. From set of three. Each - **$5 $10 $15**

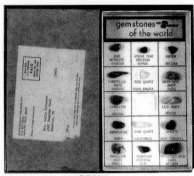

CRN-2

CRN-2. "Treasure Kit",
c. 1965. Contains 14 "Gemstones Of The World." -
$5 $15 $35

CRN-4

CRN-3

CRN-3. "Cap'n Crunch Coloring Book",
1968. - **$8 $15 $25**

CRN-4. "Sticky Wicket" Target Game,
1970. - **$10 $20 $35**

CRN-5

CRN-6

CRN-5. "Jean LaFoote" Vinyl Bank,
1972. - **$30 $50 $100**

CRN-6. Vinyl Bank,
1972. - **$25 $50 $75**

CRN-7

CRN-8

CRN-7. Seadog Spy Kit,
1974. Kit - **$10** **$20** **$35**
Instructions - **$5** **$10** **$15**

CRN-8. Fabric Doll,
1976. - **$10** **$20** **$30**

CRN-11

CRN-10

CRN-9

CRN-9. Figural Plastic Ring,
1970s. - **$150** **$240** **$325**

CRN-10. Cannon Plastic Ring,
1970s. - **$30** **$45** **$60**

CRN-11. Whistle Plastic Ring,
1970s - **$30** **$45** **$60**

CRN-12

CRN-13

CRN-12. Ship In Bottle Plastic Ring,
1970s. - **$30** **$45** **$60**

CRN-13. Plastic Treasure Chest Bank,
1970s. - **$10** **$20** **$35**

CRN-14

CRN-14. Plastic Sea Cycle Model,
1970s. Near Mint Boxed - **$35**
Assembled - **$10** **$20** **$30**

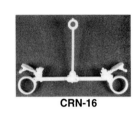

CRN-16

CRN-15

CRN-15. "Detective Crunch Squad" Paper Wallet,
1970s. - **$8** **$12** **$25**

CRN-16. Finger Tennis Game,
1970s. Plastic agility toy for two players. - **$5** **$10** **$15**

CRN-18

CRN-17

CRN-17. "La Foote" Miniature Plastic Vehicles,
1970s. Balloon operated for movement. Each - **$5** **$10** **$15**

CRN-18. Story Scope With Disks,
1970s. At least three disks cut from box backs. Scope Unit -
$8 **$15** **$30**
Each Disk - **$2** **$5** **$10**

CRN-19

**CRN-19. "Cap'n Crunch" 15x17x21" Treasure Chest
Toy Box,**
1987. Believed to be contest prize. - **$25** **$50** **$75**

CRN-20   CRN-21

CRN-20. Frame Tray Puzzle,
1987. - **$3 $5 $8**

CRN-21. Crunch The Soggie Target Game,
1987. Came with three balls covered with velcro strips. -
$5 $8 $12

CRN-22

CRN-22. Flicker Button 2-1/4",
1980s. - **$8 $12 $18**

CAPTAIN AMERICA

Captain America, World War II superhero and defender of democracy, was the creation of the legendary comic book team of Jack Kirby and Joe Simon. He made his bow in *Captain America Comics* #1 of March 1941 and spent the war years defeating the Axis foes. The book ceased publication in 1949 and was revived briefly in 1954 and again, more successfully, in 1964. Stan Lee is credited with writing some of the strip's best material. A 15-episode serial was produced by Republic Pictures in 1944, an animated cartoon series aired in 1966 and a TV movie for CBS ran in 1979, with the nature of the character altered to suit the times and the medium.

CAP-1

CAP-1. Membership Card,
1941. Scarce. - **$200 $600 $800**

CAP-2   CAP-3

CAP-2. Mailer Envelope,
1941. Rare. Held membership card and/or badge. -
$100 $300 $500

CAP-3. "Captain America/Sentinels Of Liberty" Enameled Brass Badge,
1941. Also issued in copper luster. Brass Finish -
$200 $400 $800
Copper Finish - **$200 $450 $850**

CAP-4   CAP-5

CAP-4. Three-Sheet,
1944. Scarce. Republic Pictures serial. 41" by 81". -
$2000 $4000 $6000

CAP-5. "Return Of Captain America" 27x41" Movie Poster,
1953. Republic Pictures. Example is 1953 re-issue of 1944 serial. - **$150 $300 $500**

CAP-6

CAP-7

CAP-6. "Captain America" 3-1/2" Cello. Button,
1966. Store item. #3 from numbered series. Near Mint Bagged - **$35**
Loose - **$10 $15 $25**

CAP-7. Litho. Metal Bicycle Attachment Plate,
1967. Store item by Marx Toys. - **$12 $25 $50**

CAP-8

CAP-9

CAP-8. Limited Edition Of Badge In Holder,
1990. Marked repro on back. Mint - **$35**

CAP-9. 50th Anniversary Pin Set,
1990. 1500 produced. Three in a holder. Mint - **$80**

CAPTAIN BATTLE

Captain Battle had a brief run as a superpatriot comic book hero in the early 1940s. He made his first appearance in *Silver Streak Comics* #10 in May 1941, then in Captain Battle Comics from 1941 to 1943. Readers who promised to uphold the principles of Americanism and the Constitution could join the Captain Battle Boys' Brigade. Two issues of *Captain Battle Jr.* were published in 1943-1944.

CBT-1

CBT-1. "Captain Battle Boys' Brigade" Cello. Button, 1941. Scarce. Silver Streak Comics. - **$300 $750 $1500**

CAPTAIN 11

Following the success of Captain Video and Space Patrol, the Rocket Ranger Club was formed in 1955. This club was designed to encourage children to watch Channel 11, a Midwestern station. Premiums issued for the club were only produced and distributed on a regional basis and are quite rare. The creed of the club focused on telling children to obey the laws and their parents at all times. The kit included a variety of decoders and planet credits, which enabled the young listeners to receive special messages and follow the exploits of the Rocket Ranger.

CVN-1

CVN-2

CVN-1. Membership Card, 1955. - **$15 $30 $50**

CVN-2. Mailer, 1955. - **$10 $20 $30**

CVN-3

CVN-3. Membership Certificate And Creed, 1955. - **$20 $40 $60**

CVN-4

CVN-5

CVN-4. Super Zoom Decoder, 1955. Rare. - **$60 $120 $240**

CVN-5. Zoom Code Card, 1955. - **$40 $80 $120**

CVN-6

CVN-6. Venus Credits Play Money, 1955. Six different. Each - **$3 $5 $10**

CVN-7

CVN-7. Martian Credits Play Money, 1955. Seven different. Each - **$3 $5 $10**

CAPTAIN EZRA DIAMOND

Captain Diamond's Adventures aired on the NBC Blue radio network from 1932 to 1937, offering weekly tales of sea adventures as related by Captain Diamond in his lighthouse. Al Swenson played the Captain, and his young visitor each week was Tiny Ruffner. Diamond Salt was the sponsor.

CEZ-1   CEZ-2

**CEZ-1. "Adventure Map Of Captain Ezra Diamond"
17x22",**
1932. - **$15 $25 $50**

**CEZ-2. "Adventure Map Of Captain Ezra Diamond"
16x22",**
1933. - **$15 $25 $50**

CEZ-3

CEZ-4

CEZ-3. Fan Photo Of Cast,
c. 1933. - **$5 $10 $15**

CEZ-4. Weather Forecast Card,
c. 1933. Lighthouse window area holds litmus paper. -
$20 $40 $60

CAPTAIN FRANK HAWKS

Frank Hawks (1897-1938) was a skilled pilot and an air
instructor for the army during World War I. He set a number
of speed records, including two in nonstop flights from Los
Angeles to New York in 1929 and 1933. As a spokesman for
Post cereals in the 1930s he made guest appearances on
the radio and was always available to speak to the press.
Boys and girls were urged to join Capt. Hawks' Sky Patrol to
win free prizes. Ironically, Hawks was killed in an airplane
crash.

CFH-1

CFH-2

CFH-1. Photo With Achievement Inscription,
c. 1935. Facsimile signature includes "Snapped Over The
Andes At 19,000 Feet Altitude On May 4 1935". -
$10 $25 $40

CFH-2. Club Manual,
1935. Post's 40% Bran Flakes. - **$15 $30 $60**

CFH-3

CFH-4

CFH-3. Sky Patrol Propeller Badge,
1935. Three ranks. Member - **$10 $15 $30**
Flight Lieutenant - **$15 $25 $60**
Flight Captain - **$20 $35 $80**

CFH-4. "Capt. Hawks Sky Patrol" Brass Ring,
1936. Depicts portrait, cloud and propeller design. -
$75 $190 $300

CFH-5

CFH-7

CFH-6

CFH-5. "Capt. Frank's Air Hawks" Brass Ring,
1936. - **$50 $100 $150**

CFH-6. Fan Photo,
c. 1936. - **$10 $20 $30**

CFH-7. Air Hawks Wings Badge,
1936. Three ranks. Silver - "Member" - **$10 $15 $30**
Brass - "Squadron Leader" - **$15 $25 $60**
Bronze - "Flight Commander" - **$20 $35 $80**

CFH-8

CFH-9

CFH-8. Sacred Scarab Ring,
1937. Post's Bran Flakes. Scarab in green. Also issued for
Melvin Purvis. - **$250 $500 $1200**

CFH-9. Sky Patrol Premium Booklet,
1937. Post's 40% Bran Flakes. Offers eight premiums including club badge, manual, ring, ID bracelet.- **$15 $25 $50**

CFH-10

CFH-10. "Sacred Scarab Ring" Newspaper Ad,
1937. Post's Bran Flakes. Ring offer expiration date December 31. Scarab in green, also issued for Melvin Purvis. Newspaper Ad - **$8 $12 $20**

CFH-11

CFH-11. Bracelet With Photo Picture,
1930s. Rare. Assumed to be related to Capt. Hawks cereal campaign. - **$100 $200 $400**

CAPTAIN GALLANT

Two-fisted Captain Gallant, played by Olympic gold medalist and seasoned actor Buster Crabbe, premiered in a black-and-white series on NBC-TV in February 1955. Filmed originally in Morocco and later in Libya and Italy, the show was essentially a Western in Arab garb, with the Captain chasing camel thieves rather than cattle rustlers. Crabbe's son Cullen was featured as Cuffy Sanders, his ward. The show was sponsored by Heinz Foods until 1957, then by General Mills in repeats from 1960 to 1963. The following year it was syndicated to local stations as *Foreign Legionnaire*. Items are usually copyrighted by Frantel Inc.

CGL-1

CGL-1. Comic Book,
1955. Heinz Foods. Membership certificate on back cover. - **$2 $5 $9**

CGL-2

CGL-3

CGL-2. "Tim Magazine For Boys" Cover Article,
June 1957. - **$15 $25 $40**

CGL-3. Captain Gallant And Cuffy Photos,
1950s. Each - **$10 $15 $25**

CGL-4

CGL-4. "Junior Legionnaires" Club Card,
1950s. - **$15 $30 $50**

CGL-5

CGL-6

CGL-7

CGL-5. "Junior Legionnaire" Litho. Tab,
1950s. - **$12 $25 $50**

CGL-6. TV Sponsor Paper Store Pennant,
1950s. P.F. footwear of B.F. Goodrich. - **$20 $40 $60**

CGL-7. "Captain Gallant" Cuffy Cello. Button,
1950s. Holsum Bread. - **$20 $50 $75**

CGL-8

CGL-9

CGL-10

CGL-8. "Captain Gallant Junior Legionnaire" Silvered Metal Badge,
1950s. Cardboard insert photo. Probably came with store bought gun set. - **$30 $60 $100**

CGL-9. Heinz Diecut Embossed Metal Member Badge,
1950s. "57" numeral under flame image. For mounting on Heinz premium Legionnaire's hat. Scarce. - **$50 $100 $250**

CGL-10. "The Italy Star" Metal And Fabric Award Medal,
1950s. Back has Captain Gallant logo and name. - **$10 $20 $50**

CGL-11   CGL-12

CGL-11. Foreign Legion Replica Award Medal,
1950s. Fabric ribbon holding gold luster metal pendant with military motifs and "GRI" inscription. - **$15 $25 $50**

CGL-12. Foreign Legion Replica Award Medal,
1950s. Fabric ribbon suspending silver luster metal pendant depicting cat-like animal killing dragon-like creature with commemorative date 1939-1945. - **$15 $25 $75**

CAPTAIN MARVEL

Young Billy Batson, a homeless orphan, only had to utter the name of the wizard Shazam to be transformed into Captain Marvel, the World's Mightiest Mortal. Created by artist C. C. Beck and writer Bill Parker, Captain Marvel was introduced in *Whiz Comics* #2 in February 1940. It was a huge success, outselling all its competition and generating a Mary Marvel, Captain Marvel Jr., Uncle Marvel, several Lt. Marvels and Hoppy the Marvel Bunny. The Captain subdued criminals and mad scientists for 13 years until a costly lawsuit for copyright infringement of the Superman character ended his run in 1954, but not before dozens of toys, novelties and premiums had been issued. Several comic book revivals and spinoffs have been published over the years. *The Adventures of Captain Marvel*, a 12-episode chapter play starring Tom Tyler as the Captain and Frank Coghlan Jr. as Billy was released by Republic Pictures in 1941. In 1974 a television series with Michael Gray as Billy was produced by Filmation Studios. SHAZAM - Solomon, Hercules, Atlas, Zeus, Achilles, Mercury.

CMR-1

CMR-1. Captain Marvel Title Card (Chapter 1 of 12),
1941. Rare. Less than 10 known. 1st title card is all color. - **$600 $900 $1500**
Chapters 2-12, two-color title cards - **$150 $250 $400**

CMR-2   CMR-3   CMR-4

CMR-2. "Captain Marvel Club/Shazam" Club Litho. Button,
1941. - **$20 $35 $50**

CMR-3. Yellow Rectangular Patch,
c. 1941. Rare. Fawcett premium. - **$50 $100 $250**

CMR-4. Blue Rectangular Patch,
c. 1941. Fawcett premium. - **$25 $50 $100**

CMR-5

CMR-5. "Captain Marvel Comic Hero Punch-Outs Book"
1942. Store item by Samuel Lowe Co. - **$50 $125 $200**

CMR-6

CMR-6. Captain Marvel Jr. #1 Promotional Kit,
1942. Rare. 6 pieces. - **$100 $250 $500**

CMR-7

CMR-8

CMR-7. "Secret Message Postcard",
1943. Scarce. - **$50 $100 $200**

CMR-8. "E.-Z. Code Finder",
c. 1943. Scarce. - **$100 $300 $600**

CMR-9

CMR-10

CMR-9. "Captain Marvel Club/Shazam" Cello. Club Button,
1943. - **$20 $40 $65**

CMR-10. "Captain Marvel Comic Story Paint Book",
c. 1943. Store item by Samuel Lowe Co. - **$50 $125 $200**

CMR-11

CMR-12

CMR-11. "Captain Marvel's Fun Book",
1944. Store item. - **$35 $100 $225**

CMR-12. "Captain Marvel Well Known Comics" Booklet,
1944. Bestmaid give-away published by Samuel Lowe Co. -
$15 $40 $80

CMR-13

CMR-14

CMR-15

CMR-13. "Captain Marvel Club/Shazam" Litho. Button,
1944. - **$20 $50 $85**

CMR-14. "Captain Marvel Painting Book",
c. 1944. Store item by L. Miller & Sons, London, England. -
$50 $75 $125

CMR-15. "Captain Marvel Club/Shazam" Cello. Button,
1944.- **$15 $30 $50**

CMR-16

CMR-17

CMR-16. "Captain Marvel" Canadian Comics Offer Folder,
c. 1944. Lightning bolt glows in dark. - **$25 $60 $100**

CMR-17. "Captain Marvel's Rocket Raider" Paper Toy Kit,
c. 1944. Store item and club premium.
Unused - **$10 $15 $20**

CMR-18

CMR-19

CMR-18. "Flying Captain Marvel" Punch-Out With Envelope,
c. 1944. Store item and club premium.
Unused - **$10 $15 $20**

CMR-19. "Fawcett's Comic Stars",
c. 1944. Store item with three metal stars depicting Captain
Marvel, Hoppy The Marvel Bunny, Sherlock Monk. -
$25 $60 $100

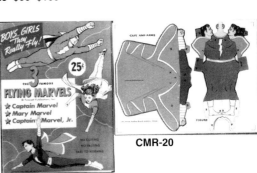

CMR-20

CMR-20. "The Three Famous Flying Marvels" Punch-Outs,
c. 1944. Store item and club premium. Unused - **$8 $12 $20**

CMR-21

CMR-21. "One Against Many" Picture Puzzle,
c. 1944. Store item and club premium. - **$10 $25 $40**

CMR-23

CMR-22

CMR-22. Punch-Out "Magic Eyes" Picture With Envelope,
c. 1944. Store item and club premium.
Unused - **$10 $15 $20**

CMR-23. "Buzz Bomb" Punch-Out Toy,
c. 1944. Store item and club premium.
Unused - **$10 $20 $35**

CMR-24

CMR-24. "Hoppy And Millie In Musical Evening" Cardboard Toy,
c. 1944. Store item and club premium. Unused - **$8 $12 $20**

CMR-25

CMR-25. "Shazam" Punch-Out Game With Envelope,
c. 1944. Store item and club premium.
Unused - **$10 $20 $30**

CMR-26

CMR-26. "Magic Picture" Cardboard Toy,
c. 1944. Store item and club premium. Scarcer than others in series. Unused - **$25 $40 $100**

CMR-27

CMR-28

CMR-27. "Captain Marvel, Jr. Ski Jump" Paper Assembly Toy In Envelope,
c. 1944. Store item and club premium. - **$10 $15 $20**

CMR-28. "Magic Lightning Box" Punch-Out Paper Toy In Envelope,
c. 1944. Store item and club premium. Captain Marvel figure moves up and down inside box, scarcest item in punch-out series. - **$40 $75 $125**

CMR-29

CMR-30

CMR-31

CMR-29. Skull Cap,
1945. Scarce. Fawcett Premium. No brim. - **$75 $150 $300**

CMR-30. Girl's Pink Felt Beanie,
1945. Rare. Marked Capt. Marvel with figure on front and back. Fawcett premium. - **$150 $300 $600**

CMR-31. Boy's Blue Felt Beanie,
1945. Fawcett premium. - **$75 $150 $300**

CMR-32

CMR-33

CMR-34

CMR-35

CMR-32. Captain Marvel Syroco-Style 5" Figure,
1945. Rare. Fawcett premium by Multi Products, Chicago. "Captain" spelled out on base. No box produced. Less than 10 known. - **$2700 $5400 $8100**

CMR-33. Captain Marvel 5" Figure,
1946. Rare. Fawcett premium by Kerr Co. of unknown substance. "Capt." on base. No box produced. Less than 10 known. - **$2700 $5400 $8100**

CMR-34. Captain Marvel Jr. 5" Figure,
1946. Fawcett premium by Kerr Co. of unknown substance. No box produced. - **$850 $1700 $2550**

CMR-35. Mary Marvel 5" Figure,
1946. Fawcett premium by Kerr Co. of unknown substance. Light color hair. No box produced. - **$775 $1550 $2350**

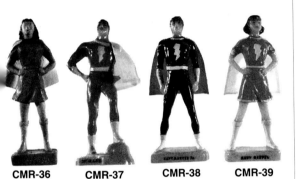

CMR-36   CMR-37   CMR-38   CMR-39

CMR-36. Mary Marvel 5" Figure,
1946. Rare. Similar to previous item. Hair may be light or dark. Wearing red dress with red belt and red lightning bolt. - **$1200 $2400 $3550**

CMR-37. Captain Marvel 6-1/2" Figure,
1946. Scarce. Fawcett premium by Kerr Co. of plastic. For C.C. Beck designed box in Near Mint add $750. - **$1700 $3400 $5100**

CMR-38. Captain Marvel Jr. 6-1/2" Figure,
1946. Scarce. Fawcett premium by Kerr Co. of plastic. For C.C. Beck designed box in Near Mint add $750. - **$1100 $2200 $3250**

CMR-39. Mary Marvel 6-1/2" Figure,
1946. Scarce. Fawcett premium by Kerr Co. of plastic. For C.C. Beck designed box in Near Mint add $750. - **$1000 $2000 $3100**

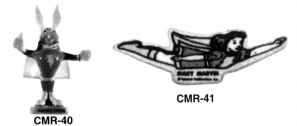

CMR-40

CMR-41

CMR-40. Marvel Bunny 6" Figure,
1946. Rare. Fawcett premium by Kerr Co. of plastic. Most examples have damaged or repaired ears. For C.C. Beck designed box in Near Mint add $750. - **$2200 $4500 $6500**

CMR-41. "Mary Marvel" Diecut Fiberboard Figure Badge,
1946. Full color litho. paper front. - **$100 $200 $350**

CMR-42

CMR-43

CMR-42. Mary Marvel Promo Card,
1946. Rare. - **$30 $60 $90**

CMR-43. Tie-Clip,
1946. On Card - **$25 $50 $75**
Clip Only - **$15 $25 $40**

CMR-44

CMR-44. "Captain Marvel Adventures" Vol. 10 #55,
1946. Scarce. Atlas Theater, Detroit. Theater replaced original cover of issue #55 with their own cover picturing generic heroes. - **$50 $150 $300**

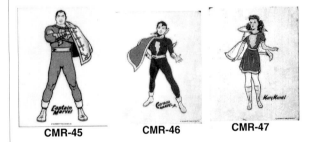

CMR-45   CMR-46   CMR-47

CMR-45. Captain Marvel Glow-In-The-Dark Picture,
1946. - **$75 $150 $300**

CMR-46. Captain Marvel Jr. Glow-In-The-Dark Picture,
1946. - **$75 $150 $250**

CMR-47. Mary Marvel Glow-In-The-Dark Picture,
1946.- **$75 $150 $250**

CMR-48

CMR-49

CMR-48. Hoppy Glow-In-The-Dark Picture,
1946. Came unframed. - **$50 $75 $150**

CMR-49. Statuettes Store Sign,
1946. Rare. R. W. Kerr Co. Art by C. C. Beck. 6 known. -
$1000 $2500 $4000

CMR-50   CMR-51

**CMR-50. "Captain Marvel Adventures" Wheaties Comic
Book,**
1946. Copies were taped to box. Good - **$50**
About Fine - **$150**

CMR-51. "Note Paper" Boxed Set,
1946. Held 18 sheets and envelopes.
Near Mint Boxed - **$300**
Each Sheet - **$5 $10 $15**

CMR-52   CMR-53
                          CMR-54

CMR-52. "Captain Marvel" Litho. Button,
1946. From set of 10 picturing Fawcett characters. -
$40 $75 $125

CMR-53. "Mary Marvel" Litho. Button,
1946. From set of 10 picturing Fawcett characters. -
$40 $75 $125

CMR-54. "Captain Marvel Jr." Litho. Button,
1946. From set of 10 picturing Fawcett characters. -
$20 $50 $75

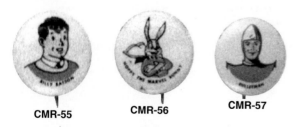

CMR-55   CMR-56
                          CMR-57

CMR-55. "Billy Batson" Litho. Button,
1946. From set of 10 picturing Fawcett characters. -
$20 $50 $90

CMR-56. "Hoppy The Marvel Bunny" Litho. Button,
1946. From set of 10 picturing Fawcett characters. -
$20 $35 $60

CMR-57. "Bulletman" Litho. Button,
1946. From set of 10 picturing Fawcett characters. -
$20 $35 $60

CMR-58   CMR-59   CMR-60

CMR-58. "Golden Arrow" Litho. Button,
1946. From set of 10 picturing Fawcett characters. -
$15 $30 $60

CMR-59. "Ibis" Litho. Button,
1946. From set of 10 picturing Fawcett characters. -
$15 $30 $60

CMR-60. "Nyoka" Litho. Button,
1946. From set of 10 picturing Fawcett characters. -
$15 $30 $60

CMR-61
                  CMR-62   CMR-63

CMR-61. "Radar" Litho. Button,
1946. From set of 10 picturing Fawcett characters. -
$15 $30 $50

CMR-62. Captain Marvel Felt Club Patch,
1946. - **$30 $60 $100**

CMR-63. Captain Marvel Jr. Felt Patch,
1946. Blue - **$25 $50 $100**
Dark Green (Scarce) - **$50 $75 $150**

CMR-64   CMR-65

CMR-64. "Mary Marvel" Felt Patch,
1946. Scarce. Fawcett Publications. - **$75 $125 $250**

CMR-65. Felt Pennant,
1946. Blue - **$40 $80 $150**
Yellow - **$50 $100 $200**

CMR-67

CMR-66

CMR-68

CMR-66. Plastic Keychain Fob,
1946. Back inscription "This Certifies That The Holder Of This Key Ring Is A Bonafied Member Of The Captain Marvel Club". - **$30 $75 $150**

CMR-67. Rocket Raider Compass Ring,
c. 1946. Red and black enamel paint on brass, unmarked but attributed to Captain Marvel. - **$625 $1250 $2500**

CMR-68. Sweater,
1947. Store item by Somerset Knitting Mills, Philadelphia. - **$100 $200 $300**

CMR-69

CMR-70

CMR-69. Tin Wind-Up Race Car #2,
1947. Store item by Automatic Toy Co. Numbered set of four.
Boxed With Keys - **$250 $600 $1200**
Each Car Loose, No Keys - **$60 $125 $225**

CMR-70. Capt. Marvel Jr. Die Cast Figure,
1947. Unauthorized 3-1/8" tall white metal figure by H & B Toys of New Jersey. Known as "Robe Boy" and only two examples known. A matching Captain Marvel is unknown. - **$1500 $2500 $5000**

CMR-71

CMR-72

CMR-73

CMR-71. "Captain Marvel" Watch,
1948. Store item and probable premium. Made in two sizes.
Boxed - **$200 $500 $750**
Watch Only - **$100 $200 $400**

CMR-72. "Capt. Marvel Jr." Wristwatch,
1948. Scarce. Offered by the Fawcett Club and not known with a box. Luminous hands and blue plastic strap. - **$300 $600 $1250**

CMR-73. "Mary Marvel" Wristwatch,
1948. Fawcett Publications copyright.
Boxed - **$150 $300 $600**
Watch Only - **$75 $150 $250**

CMR-74

CMR-75

CMR-74. "Captain Marvel's Secret Message" Paper Code Slip,
c. 1948. Master Comics. Code message deciphers into ad text for Captain Marvel Jr. appearance. - **$20 $40 $60**

CMR-75. Toss Bag,
1940s. Five varieties: Captain Marvel or Mary Marvel either flying or standing plus Hoppy. Each - **$15 $35 $75**

CMR-76

CMR-77

CMR-76. Portrait Picture,
1940s. Comes with blank bottom margin or with "Capt. Marvel Appears Monthly In Whiz Comics."
Blank - **$40 $75 $125**
Text - **$50 $100 $150**

CMR-77. Merchandise Sheet,
1940s. Regularly issued by Captain Marvel Club. - **$10 $20 $30**

CMR-78   **CMR-79**

CMR-78. Club Letter,
1940s. Example of many sent to club members. -
$15 $30 $60

CMR-79. "Shazam" Paper Pop-Up String Toy,
1940s. Fawcett Publications. - **$40 $75 $125**

CMR-81

CMR-80

CMR-80. Club Letter With Envelope,
1940s. Text for Jack Armstrong contest by Wheaties offering
actual Piper Cub airplane as grand prize.
Envelope - **$10 $30 $50**
Letter- **$20 $40 $75**

CMR-81. Pencil,
1940s. Scarce. - **$35 $100 $200**

CMR-82

CMR-82. "Magic Membership Card",
1940s. - **$40 $80 $125**

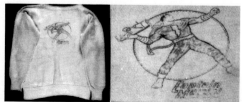

CMR-83

CMR-83. Child's Sweatshirt,
1940s. Scarce. - **$50 $100 $200**

CMR-84

CMR-84. "Jig-Saw" Puzzle #1,
1940s. Store item by L. Miller & Son Ltd., England. Boxed -
$35 $75 $150

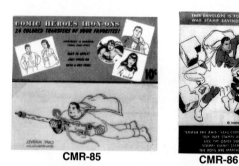

CMR-85   **CMR-86**

CMR-85. "Comic Heroes Iron-Ons" Packet,
1940s. Envelope held 24 transfers. Complete In Envelope -
$100 $150 $200

CMR-86. "War Stamps Savings Book" Envelope,
1940s. Held World War II savings stamp booklet. -
$40 $100 $200

CMR-88

CMR-87

**CMR-87. "Mechanix Illustrated" Magazine Subscription
Handbill,**
1940s. Captain Marvel pictorial endorsement for magazine
subscription. - **$20 $40 $75**

CMR-88. "Magic Whistle" Diecut Cardboard,
1940s. American Seed Co., Lancaster, Pennsylvania.
Working whistle that opens to show premiums earned by
selling seed products. - **$25 $60 $100**

CMR-89

CMR-89. Club Christmas Kit In Mailer Envelope,
1940s. Came with cover letter and sheet of 20 Fawcett character gummed stamps.
Near Mint In Mailer - **$150**
Letter - **15 $35 $60**
Stamp Sheet - **$15 $35 $60**

CMR-91

CMR-90

CMR-92

CMR-90. "Captain Marvel/Shazam" Cello. On Silvered Brass Pencil Clip ,
1940s.- **$30 $50 $75**

CMR-91. Captain Marvel "Power Siren",
1940s. Store item. Red plastic siren whistle with metal loop ring. - **$85 $175 $350**

CMR-92. "Captain Marvel And The Good Humor Man" Movie Comic,
1950. Jack Carson on cover. - **$40 $120 $275**

CMR-93

CMR-94

CMR-95

CMR-93. "Captain Marvel And The Lieutenants Of Safety" Comic Book #1 ,
1950. Rare. Fawcett Publications/Ebasco Services. - **$100 $300 $750**

CMR-94. "Captain Marvel And The Lieutenants Of Safety" Comic Book #2 ,
1950. Rare. Fawcett Publications/Ebasco Services. - **$100 $300 $750**

CMR-95. "Captain Marvel And The Lieutenants Of Safety" Comic Book #3 ,
1951. Rare. Fawcett Publications/Ebasco Services. - **$100 $300 $750**

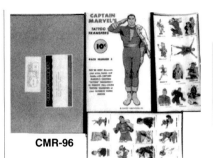

CMR-96

CMR-97

CMR-96. Coco-Wheats "Tattoo Transfers" Kit With Mailer Envelope,
1956. Mailer - **$10 $15 $25**
Illustrated Inner Envelope With Two Sheets - **$25 $50 $75**

CMR-97. "Shazam Is Coming" 4" Cello. Button,
1972. N.P.P. Inc. - **$10 $25 $50**

CAPTAIN MIDNIGHT

A shadowy plane and a mysterious pilot...diving furiously from the night sky...Captain Midnight and his Secret Squadron battled the sinister forces of evil on radio during most of the 1940s. The program originated in 1939 over WGN in Chicago, sponsored by the Skelly Oil Co. and broadcast in the Midwest. The following year it went national on the Mutual network sponsored by Ovaltine, which had just dropped Little Orphan Annie. Captain Midnight's Secret Squadron was one of radio's major producers of premiums. For an Ovaltine seal and a dime kids became Secret Squadron members. Decoder badges, pins, patches, mugs, maps, booklets, wings and rings followed in great profusion until the show closed in 1949.

The Captain made his first comic book appearance in *The Funnies* #57 in July 1941, moved to *Popular Comics* a year later and had his own book from September 1942 to September 1948. A 15-episode chapter play was released by Columbia Pictures in 1942. The *Captain Midnight* TV series premiered in 1953, starring Richard Webb as the American superhero and aired for four years on ABC and CBS, still sponsored by Ovaltine, still offering Secret Squadron mugs and decoder badges. The Secret Squadron logo, SS, was changed to SQ.

In the late 1950s, after Ovaltine declined to give up the copyrighted Captain Midnight name, the show was syndicated in reruns as *Jet Jackson, Flying Commando*. In 1988 Ovaltine offered a Captain Midnight SQ Secret Squadron watch in exchange for a proof-of-purchase seal.

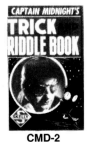

CMD-1

CMD-2

CMD-3

CMD-1. Skelly Large 36x84" Cardboard Display Sign,
1939. Rare. Has three brass grommet holes to aid in displaying. - **$800 $1500 $3000**

CMD-2. "Trick And Riddle Book",
1939. Skelly Oil Co. - **$10 $40 $60**

CMD-3. Skelly Oil "Flight Patrol Reporter" Vol. 1 #1 Newspaper,
Spring 1939. Six issues between Spring 1939 and March 1940. First Issue - **$40 $100 $175**
Other 5 Issues - **$25 $75 $125**

CMD-4

CMD-4. Skelly Oil "Flight Patrol Reporter" Vol. 1 #2 Newspaper,
June 15, 1939.- **$25 $75 $125**

CMD-5

CMD-5. Membership Card,
1939. Skelly Oil Co. - **$15 $30 $75**

CMD-6

CMD-6. "Air Heroes" Stamp Album,
1939. Skelly Oil. Holds 16 stamps. Empty - **$10 $20 $35**
Complete - **$25 $50 $75**

CMD-7

CMD-8

CMD-9

CMD-7. Portrait Photo,
1939. Skelly Oil Co. - **$25 $50 $85**

CMD-8. "Happy Landings" Photo,
1939. Skelly Oil Co. Captain Midnight with Patsy and Chuck. - **$20 $40 $75**

CMD-9. "Chuck Ramsey" Portrait Photo,
1939. Skelly Oil Co. - **$20 $40 $65**

CMD-10

CMD-11

CMD-10. Portrait Photo With Treasure Hunt Back,
1939. Skelly Oil Co. - **$60 $110 $160**

CMD-11. Unmarked Known As 'Chuck's Treasure Map' 9x11".
1939. Skelly Oil Co. - **$50 $125 $200**

CMD-12

CMD-13

CMD-12. Mysto-Magic Weather Forecasting Flight Wings Badge,
1939. Skelly Oil Co. With litmus paper - **$15 $30 $50**
Without litmus paper - **$10 $20 $30**

CMD-13. "Flight Patrol Commander" Brass Badge,
1939. Rare. Skelly Oil Co. One of the rarest Captain Midnight badges. - **$300 $900 $1500**

CMD-15

CMD-14

CMD-14. Skelly Oil "Fly With Captain Midnight" Radio Sponsorship Announcement Brochure,
1940. Pictures Captain Midnight, Chuck, Patsy, Steve, Ivan Shark. Skelly president announces show with list of midwest stations. - **$100 $250 $400**

CMD-15. Skelly Flight Patrol Member Card,
1940. - **$25 $50 $100**

CMD-16

CMD-17

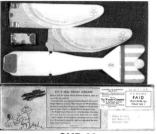

CMD-22

CMD-16. Membership Card,
1940. Skelly Oil Co. - **$15 $30 $75**

CMD-17. Skelly Flight Patrol Brass Spinner Medal,
1940. Spinner disk pictures Captain Midnight, Patsy Donovan, Chuck Ramsey, propeller design. - **$10 $15 $30**

CMD-22. "Wright Airplane" Balsa/Paper Assembly Kit With Box ,
1940. Scarce. Wings inscribed "Captain Midnight SS-1" and "Wright Aerial Torpedo". Near Mint Boxed - **$300**
Assembled - **$50 $125 $200**

CMD-19

CMD-18

CMD-23

CMD-18. "Mexican Jumping Beans" Paper Bag,
1940. Skelly Oil Co. For premium game utilizing jumping beans. - **$75 $125 $200**

CMD-19. "Mexican Ringo-Jumpo" Game Sheet,
1940. Skelly Oil Co. For jumping bean game. -
$100 $150 $250

CMD-23. Club Manual With Member Papers,
1941. With card and parents letter.
Complete Near Mint - **$225**
Manual Only - **$60 $110 $160**

CMD-20

CMD-25

CMD-24

CMD-20. "Captain Midnight's Flight Patrol Reporter" Vol.
#6 Newspaper,
1940. Skelly Oil Co. Last issue. - **$25 $75 $125**

CMD-24. Mystery Dial Code-O-Graph Brass Decoder,
1941. First Captain Midnight decoder. - **$25 $50 $80**

CMD-25. "Detect-O-Scope",
1941. Cardboard tube holds metal piece to judge altitudes. Also see item CMD-27. - **$35 $75 $125**

CMD-21

CMD-26

CMD-21. Skelly Oil "Flight Patrol" Airline Map,
1940. Scarce. 11x17" opened. - **$150 $300 $600**

CMD-26. American Flag Loyalty Pin With Paper,
1941. Patriotic text paper held in tube on pin reverse.
Badge - **$40 $100 $150**
Paper - **25 $50 $75**

CMD-27 **CMD-28**

CMD-34 **CMD-35** **CMD-36**

CMD-27. "Detect-O-Scope" Instruction Leaflet,
1941. - **$35** **$75** **$125**

CMD-28. Whirlwind Whistling Brass Ring,
1941. No Captain Midnight markings. - **$150** **$340** **$525**

CMD-34. Photomatic Decoder Brass Badge,
1942. Original glossy black and white photo usually missing or replaced as club manual instructed owner to insert a photo of themselves. With Original Photo - **$75** **$150** **$250**
Without Original Photo - **$35** **$65** **$100**

CMD-35. Flight Commander Flying Cross Brass Badge,
1942. - **$50** **$100** **$200**

CMD-36. Mystic Eye Detector Look-In Brass Ring,
1942. Brass eagle cover over viewer mirror, issued by Captain Midnight, Radio Orphan Annie, The Lone Ranger. - **$75** **$115** **$150**

CMD-29

CMD-29. "Whirlwind Whistling Ring" Instruction Sheet,
1941. - **$80** **$90** **$100**

CMD-37 **CMD-38**

CMD-37. Sliding Secret Compartment Brass Ring,
1942. - **$75** **$115** **$175**

CMD-38. Marine Corps Insignia Brass Ring,
1942. - **$150** **$310** **$475**

CMD-30 **CMD-31** **CMD-32**

CMD-30. Flight Commander Brass Decoder Ring,
1941. Inner side has "Captain Midnight Super Code 3". - **$200** **$350** **$500**

CMD-31. "Super Book Of Comics" Comic Book #3,
1941. Various sponsors. - **$15** **$50** **$110**

CMD-32. Club Manual,
1942. - **$60** **$125** **$200**

CMD-39

CMD-39. "Magic Blackout Lite-Ups" Kit With Envelope,
1942. Near Mint In Mailer - **$500**
Illustrated Folder Only - **$75** **$150** **$250**

CMD-33

CMD-33. "Flight Commander" Handbook,
1942. - **$75** **$150** **$250**

CMD-40

CMD-40. MJC-10 Plane-Detector Set,
1942. Rare. Tube with seven disk inserts and 12 airplane silhouettes. Complete - **$175** **$400** **$750**
Tube Only - **$50** **$100** **$200**

CMD-42

CMD-41

CMD-47

CMD-48

CMD-41. Newspaper Comic Strip Introduction Page,
1942. Full page ad from Chicago Sun edition of Sunday,
July 5. - **$25 $60 $100**

CMD-42. Shoulder Insignia 3-1/2" Wide Fabric Patch,
1943. - **$50 $100 $160**

CMD-47. "Invention Patent" Acknowledgement Postcard,
1944. Fawcett comic book premium. Assigns registration
number for unknown invention by youthful fan. -
$40 $85 $140

CMD-48. Club Manual,
1945. - **$40 $100 $175**

CMD-43

CMD-44

CMD-49

CMD-50

CMD-51

CMD-49. Magni-Matic Decoder Metal Badge,
1945. - **$40 $75 $200**

CMD-50. Mirro-Flash Code-O-Graph Brass Decoder,
1946. - **$35 $60 $125**

CMD-51. Mystic Sun God Ring,
1946. - **$400 $1000 $1600**

CMD-43. Army "Sleeve Insignia" Folder With Envelope,
1943. Came with Captain Midnight insignia.
Folder - **$50 $100 $150**
Envelope - **$10 $20 $30**

CMD-44. "Pilot's Badge" With Order Sheet,
1943. Brass wings badge. Badge - **$50 $125 $200**
Coupon - **$25 $50 $75**

CMD-45

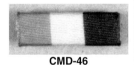

CMD-46

CMD-52

CMD-53

CMD-45. Pilot's Badge "Award Of Merit" Certificate,
1943. - **$75 $150 $200**

CMD-46. Distinguished Service Ribbon,
1944. - **$75 $125 $200**

CMD-52. Mystic Sun-God Ring Leaflet,
1946. - **$75 $90 $100**

CMD-53. Club Manual,
1946. - **$50 $90 $160**

CMD-55

CMD-54

CMD-54. Shake-Up Mug,
1947. Portrait on orange plastic with blue lid. -
$40 $85 $175

CMD-55. Whistling Code-O-Graph Plastic Decoder,
1947. Whistle with movable code wheel. - **$40 $75 $125**

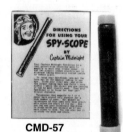

CMD-56

CMD-57

CMD-56. Manual,
1947. First of smaller format. - **$25 $50 $75**

CMD-57. "Spy-Scope" With Instructions,
1947. Plastic small telescope in two varieties of plastic rims.
Rare Blue Rims - **$40 $75 $150**
Orange Rims - **$30 $60 $110**
Instructions - **$15 $25 $40**

CMD-58

CMD-59

CMD-58. Manual,
1948 - **$25 $50 $100**

CMD-59. Mirro-Magic Brass/Plastic Decoder,
1948. Red plastic reverse usually warped and often
missing. - **$75 $135 $225**

CMD-60

CMD-61

CMD-60. Initial Printing Ring,
1948. Brass ring with personalized single initial designated
by orderer. - **$150 $325 $500**

CMD-61. Iron-On Transfer With Mailer Envelope,
1948. Scarce. Cellophane transfer on tissue sheet with
reverse lettering for application to fabric.
Envelope - **$15 $25 $40**
Transfer - **$35 $75 $125**

CMD-62

CMD-62. "Tattoo Transfers" Kit,
c. 1948. "Pack No. 8" with both Fawcett and Wander Co.
(Ovaltine) copyright. Two sheets with 22 transfers. -
$20 $50 $100

CMD-63

CMD-63. Club Manual,
1949. - **$50 $100 $200**

CMD-65

CMD-66

CMD-64

CMD-64. Key-O-Matic Code-O-Graph Brass Decoder,
1949. Without key. - **$35 $70 $125**

CMD-65. Key-O-Matic Code-O-Graph Brass Key,
1949. Used with decoder to set letter and number combina
tions. - **$50 $75 $125**

CMD-66. "Captain Midnight" Litho. Button,
1940s. Scarce. Issuer unknown. Pictures him at radio micro
phone, no identification other than his name. -
$150 $350 $600

CMD-67

CMD-68

CMD-67. Plaster Figure,
1940s. Store item from series of characters (76 known). Issued between 1941-1947 in white plaster to be painted. Captain Midnight - **$50 $100 $150**
Most Others- **$5 $10 $15**

CMD-68. Three-Sheet,
1940s. Scarce. Columbia Pictures serial. 41" by 81". - **$2000 $4000 $6000**

CMD-69

CMD-70

CMD-69. Plastic Mug With Decal,
1953. - **$15 $25 $50**

CMD-70. Manual,
1955-56. Scarce. - **$60 $200 $350**

CMD-71

CMD-74

CMD-72

CMD-73

CMD-71. Membership Card,
1955-56. - **$30 $60 $100**

CMD-72. "SQ" Plane Puzzle Decoder Plastic Badge,
1955-56. Near Mint Decoder With Mailer And Cardboard Holder- **$600**
Decoder Only - **$75 $200 $400**

CMD-73. "SQ" Cloth Peel-Off Patch,
1955-56. Unused - **$10 $30 $60**

CMD-74. Flight Commander Handbook,
1955-56. - **$80 $225 $450**

CMD-75

CMD-75. "Secret Squadron" Membership Kit,
1957. Complete With Envelope - **$175 $475 $800**
Club Manual - **$60 $200 $325**
Member Card - **$30 $60 $100**
Silver Dart Decoder - **$50 $175 $350**

CMD-76   CMD-77   CMD-78

CMD-76. Silver Dart "SQ" Jet Plane Decoder Plastic Badge,
1957. - **$50 $175 $350**

CMD-77. Peel-Off Cloth Patch,
1957. Unused - **$10 $20 $40**

CMD-78. Flight Commander Signet Ring,
1957. Silvered plastic depicting jet plane inscribed "SQFC". - **$400 $800 $1200**

CMD-79

CMD-80

CMD-79. Plastic Shake-Up Mug,
1957. - **$25 $45 $75**

CMD-80. "Flight Commander's Handbook",
1957. - **$50 $125 $225**

CMD-81.

CMD-82.

CMD-86

CMD-86. Cover Letter And Patch,
1989. Ovaltine offer from preceding 30th anniversary year of
1988. Letter - **$3 $5 $8**
Patch - **$5 $10 $15**

CMD-81. Flexible Record With Sleeve,
c. 1970. Longines Symphonette Society. Set of eight.
Each - **$3 $5 $8**

CMD-82. Flight Commander Commission Certificate,
c. 1970. Longines Symphonette Society. Accompanied vinyl
records re-issue of radio programs. - **$10 $18 $30**

CAPTAIN TIM HEALY

Kids interested in collecting postage stamps in the 1930s and
1940s could tune in their radios to the Tim Healy programs.
From 1934 to 1945 under a variety of names - *Stamp Club,
Ivory Stamp Club, Captain Tim's Adventures, Calling All
Stamp Collectors* and *Captain Tim Healy's Adventure Stories*
- and sponsored by Ivory soap or Kellogg's Pep cereal, Tim
Healy described the romance of stamps and encouraged
kids to become collectors. The few premiums offered were,
naturally, stamp-related.

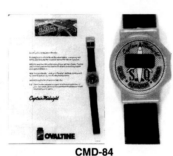

CMD-84

CMD-83

CTH-1

CTH-2

CMD-83. Punch-Out Decoder,
c. 1970. Longines Symphonette Society.
Unpunched - **$8 $12 $20**

CMD-84. Cover Letter And Watch,
1987. Offered for Ovaltine 30th anniversary year of 1988.
Letter - **$10 $12 $25**
Watch- **$20 $50 $125**

**CTH-1. Ivory Soap Stamp Club Album With Letter And
Envelope,**
1934. Cover Letter - **$3 $5 $10**
Album - **$5 $10 $15**

CTH-2. Member's Stamp-Shaped Brass Pin,
1934. Ivory Soap. Red Background - **$5 $15 $30**
Black Background - **$10 $20 $40**

CMD-85

CTH-3

CTH-4

CMD-85. Cover Letter And T-Shirt,
1988. Ovaltine 30th Anniversary Premium.
Letter - **$3 $6 $12**
T-Shirt- **$5 $15 $25**

'H-3. Ivory Stamp Club Album With Envelope,
1935. Ivory Soap. - **$5 $10 $15**

'H-4. "Spies I Have Known" Booklet,
36. Ivory Soap. Photo-illustrated stories about famous ies known by Captain Tim Healy. - **$10 $20 $35**

CTH-5   CTH-6

'H-5. Autographed Captain Tim Healy Photo,
1938. Ivory Soap. - **$10 $20 $35**

'H-6. Dixie Ice Cream Picture,
1940. - **$8 $15 $25**

CAPTAIN VIDEO

ptain Video was television's first venture into the solar sys-
n, beating Buck Rogers by a year. The show premiered
the Dumont network in June 1949 with Richard Coogan
the super cop, a role taken over in 1951 by Al Hodge.
e series, one of the most popular children's shows of its
ne, was notoriously low-budget, with props made of card-
ard or household items, but it featured such futuristic
vices as an Opticon Scillometer, a Radio Scillograph, an
omic Rifle, a Discatron and a Cosmic Ray Vibrator.
onsors such as Post cereals and Power House candy bars
ered many premiums—rings, a plastic ray gun, a Captain
Jeo helmet, a Rite-O-Lite flashlight and Luma-Glo card for
iting secret messages. The series ended its network run in
55, went local in New York City in 1956 and finally dis-
lved in 1957. The Captain appeared in comic books in
49-1951 and a 15-episode chapter play with Judd Holdren
the title role was released by Columbia Pictures in 1951.

CVD-1

CVD-2

'D-1. Picture Ring,
1950. Power House candy bars. Brass holding plastic
me over black/white photo of Richard Coogan holding ray
n. - **$100 $225 $350**

'D-2. "Picture Ring" Instruction Leaflet,
1950. Power House candy bars. - **$25 $50 $75**

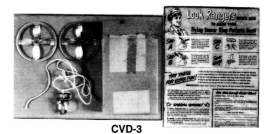

CVD-3

CVD-3. Post Toasties "Flying Saucer Ring" Set,
1951. Saucers of metal or plastic, non-glow or glow-in-dark.
Near Mint Boxed - **$1500**
Ring And Two Saucers - **$775 $1040 $1300**

CVD-5

CVD-4

CVD-6

CVD-4. "Flying Saucer Ring" Instruction Sheet,
1951. Post Toasties. Includes order coupon for additional
rings with expiration date March 31, 1952.- **$120 $135 $150**

CVD-5. "CV" Secret Seal Brass Ring,
1951. Top is designed to emboss in paper "CV" initials, also
pictures tiny rocketship and three stars. - **$150 $335 $525**

CVD-6. "Secret Seal Ring" Leaflet And Card,
1951. Power House candy bar. Instructions plus identification
card. - **$300 $450 $600**

 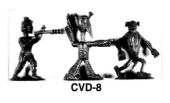

CVD-8

CVD-7

CVD-7. Cast Photo,
c. 1951. Facsimile signatures of Al Hodge and Don
Hastings. - **$15 $25 $60**

CVD-8. Captain Video Space Man,
1953. Post's Raisin Bran. Hard plastic set of 12.
Each - **$5 $12 $20**

CVD-9

CVD-9. "Secret Ray Gun",
1950s. Power House candy bars. Includes instruction sheet and "Luma-Glo" card. Complete - **$40 $75 $120**
Gun Only - **$15 $25 $40**

CVD-10

CVD-10. "Electronic Video Goggles" With Envelope,
1950s. Power House candy bars.
In Envelope - **$100 $150 $300**
Loose - **$75 $150 $250**

CVD-11

CVD-12

CVD-11. "Video Ranger" Club Member Card,
1950s. Scarce. Probable Post's Cereals. - **$25 $50 $75**

CVD-12. Purity Bread Litho. Tin Tab,
1950s. - **$15 $35 $65**

CVD-14

CVD-13

CVD-13. Mysto-Coder Brass Decoder With Clip Fastener,
1950s. Front has red plastic removable dome over Captain Video photo, back has two plastic code wheels. -
$75 $175 $300

CVD-14. Plastic Rocket Ring/Pendant With Keychain,
1950s. Rocketship includes glow portrait of Captain Video, magnifying glass and whistle. - **$500 $800 $1000**

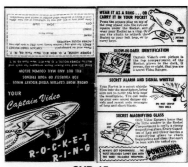

CVD-15

CVD-15. "Rocket Ring" Instruction Sheet,
1950s. Scarce. Power House candy bars. - **$150 $175 $2(**

CASEY, CRIME PHOTOGRAPHER

Flashgun Casey, Press Photographer, Crime Photographe under whatever name, "the ace cameraman who covers th crime news of a great city" for the Morning Express was fir broadcast on CBS in 1943. With Staats Cotsworth as th crusading crime fighter, the program ran until 1950, then w revived from 1953 to 1955. Sponsors included the Anch Hocking Glass Co., Toni Home Permanents and Philip Mor cigarettes. A television adaptation for CBS (1951-1952) fe tured Richard Carlyle, then Darren McGavin, in the title ro A brief run of comic books appeared in 1949-1950.

CCP-1

CCP-1. Photo Of Cast,
1940s. - **$25 $50 $75**

CEREAL BOXES

See entries by name of company, program and character.

CHANDU, THE MAGICIAN

Chandu was actually Frank Chandler, an American sec agent who used ancient occult powers he learned from Hindu yogi to combat evil. The 15-minute program originat on Los Angeles radio station KHJ in 1932 and ran on Mutu until 1936, sponsored in the west by White King soap and the east by Beech-Nut products. The series was revived 1948, based on the original scripts, with White King again sponsor. It had a final run as a half-hour weekly show on t ABC network in 1949-1950.

CHA-1

CHA-1. "The Return Of Chandu" Movie Serial Pressbook,
1934. Principal Distributing Corp. - **$100 $200 $350**

CHA-3 CHA-4

CHA-2

CHA-2. "The Return Of Chandu" 27x41" Movie Serial
Poster,
1934. Principal Distributing Corp. - **$150 $300 $600**

CHA-3. Fan Photo,
1930s. Pictures four unidentified cast members. -
$50 $125 $200

CHA-4. Radio Listing Folder,
1930s. White King Soap. Contents include listing of stations
in Central and Western United States carrying Chandu
broadcasts. - **$75 $140 $200**

CHA-6 CHA-7

CHA-5

CHA-5. Paper Mask,
1930s. Possible Beech-Nut Gum. Probable give-away. -
$25 $60 $125

CHA-6. Chandu Club Cello Button,
1930s. - **$75 $150 $300**

CHA-7. "Chandu Magicians Club" Cello. Member Button,
1930s. - **$75 $150 $250**

CHA-8

CHA-9

CHA-8. "Beech-Nut's King Of Magic" Leaflet,
1930s. Contents include radio cast photo, magic trick offer. -
$20 $40 $60

CHA-9. Magic Slate,
1930s. Ernst Kerr Co., Detroit department store radio sponsor on WJR. Comes with wood stylus marker. -
$50 $125 $200

CHA-10 CHA-11

CHA-10. "Beech-Nut Holiday Trick" Greeting Postcard,
1930s. Back lists radio cast members with holiday
message. - **$25 $50 $75**

CHA-11. Beech-Nut Galloping Coin Trick,
1930s. Boxed Set - **$25 $50 $90**

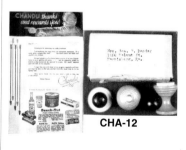

CHA-12

CHA-13

CHA-12. "Chandu Ball And Base" Boxed Trick,
1930s. Beech-Nut Gum. With letter and instruction leaflet. -
$25 $50 $75

CHA-13. "Chinese Coin On String" Trick With Mailer
Envelope,
1930s. Beech-Nut Gum. - **$25 $50 $75**

CHA-14

CHA-14. "Svengali Mind Reading Trick",
1930s. Beech-Nut Gum. Boxed - **$25 $50 $100**

CHA-15

CHA-16

CHA-15. "The Great Beech-Nut Buddha Money Mystery" Packet,
1930s. Magic trick based on Chandu radio series. -
$20 $40 $60

CHA-16. "Hypnotized Silver Sphere" Trick With Box And Order Sheet,
1930s. Beech-Nut Gum. - **$25 $50 $75**

CHA-17

CHA-17. "Chandu White King Of Magic" Boxed Trick Set,
1930s. White King Soap. Complete - **$100 $150 $250**

CHA-18

CHA-18. "Card Miracles" Boxed Set,
1930s. White King Soap. - **$25 $50 $75**

CHA-19

CHA-20

CHA-19. "Assyrian Money Changer" Trick With Mailer Envelope,
1930s. White King Soap. With instruction card, wooden block, two metal bands for holding penny. - **$25 $50 $75**

CHA-20. "Brazilian Beads" Trick With Mailer Envelope,
1930s. White King Soap. Comes with instructions, glass vial containing beads and cork. - **$25 $50 $75**

CHARLIE McCARTHY

Edgar Bergen and Charlie McCarthy accomplished th
seemingly impossible—a successful ventriloquist act o
radio. After years of knocking around vaudeville, Bergen an
Charlie broke into radio with a guest appearance on Rud
Vallee's show in 1936. They were an instant hit and fiv
months later they were stars on the Chase & Sanborn Hou
Week after week Charlie feuded with W. C. Fields and flirte
with Dorothy Lamour and America loved him. Anothe
dummy, Mortimer Snerd, was added in 1939 and Effi
Klinker joined the crew in 1944 but Charlie ruled suprem
Chase & Sanborn's sponsorship ended in 1948 and othe
sponsors (Coca-Cola, Hudnut, Kraft cheese) carried th
show until it ended in 1956. Charlie made an early T
appearance on the *Hour Glass* variety show in 1946 an
along with Bergen, hosted *Do You Trust Your Wife?* in 195
1957 and *Who Do You Trust?* on daytime TV from 195
1963. A comic strip had a brief run in the late 1930s an
comic books were published in the late 1940s and ear
1950s.

CHE-1

CHE-1. "Chase & Sanborn Radio News" Newsletter,
c. 1937. - **$25 $50 $75**

CHE-2

CHE-2. "Adventure Pops" Cardboard Folder,
1938. Held six lollipops by E. Rosen Co. From a set of five.
Each - **$25 $60 $100**

CHE-3

CHE-3. "Radio Party" Game,
1938. Chase & Sanborn Coffee. Includes spinner and 21
figures. Complete - **$20 $40 $65**

CHE-4   CHE-5   CHE-6

CHE-4. Animated Alarm Clock,
1938. Store item by Gilbert. - **$300 $600 $1200**

CHE-5. Cardboard Figure,
1938. Chase & Sanborn Coffee. - **$25 $50 $125**

CHE-6. Mortimer Snerd Cardboard Figure,
1938. Chase & Sanborn Coffee. - **$40 $100 $200**

CHE-7

CHE-8

**CHE-7. Effanbee Doll "Edgar Bergen's Charlie McCarthy"
Cello. Button,**
1938. For "An Effanbee Play-Product". - **$30 $60 $100**

CHE-8. Ventriloquist Doll Detective Outfit,
1938. Store item believed to be Effanbee. -
$200 $400 $700

CHE-9   CHE-10

CHE-9. Ventriloquist Doll In Tuxedo,
c. 1938. Store item believed to be Effanbee. -
$200 $400 $700

CHE-10. "Speaking For Myself On Life And Love" Book,
1939. Chase & Sanborn Coffee. - **$10 $20 $35**

CHE-11

CHE-12

CHE-11. Silver Plate Spoon With Mailer,
c. 1939. Mailer Only - **$10 $15 $25**
Standard Tuxedo Design Spoon - **$5 $10 $15**

CHE-12. Detective Outfit Design Spoon,
c. 1939. - **$20 $40 $75**

CHE-13   CHE-14   CHE-15

CHE-13. Painted Plastic Portrait Pin,
c. 1939. - **$15 $30 $60**

CHE-14. "Goldwyn Follies Club" Cello. Button,
1930s. Metro-Goldwyn-Mayer. - **$15 $30 $50**

CHE-15. Bust Portrait Brass Ring,
1940. Chase and Sanborn coffee. - **$150 $240 $325**

CHE-16   CHE-17   CHE-18

CHE-16. "Gold-Plated Ring" Coupon Sheet,
1940. Scarce. Clipping from can wrapper of Chase &
Sanborn Coffee offering ring for 10 cents plus the clipping. -
$10 $20 $30

CHE-17. Composition Bank,
c. 1940. Store item. - **$40 $75 $150**

CHE-18. Bergan/McCarthy Glass,
c. 1940. - **$15 $30 $50**

CHE-19

CHE-19. Contest Card,
1944. - **$12 $25 $50**

CHARLIE THE TUNA

Charlie is the out-of-luck character created for Star-Kist Foods in the 1960s. Charlie's ambition was to impress Star-Kist (and viewers) with his demonstrations of esthetic "good taste," inevitably rejected by "Sorry, Charlie. Star-Kist doesn't want tuna with good taste. Star-Kist wants tuna that tastes good." Despite - or because of - his loser image, Charlie became a winner in premium popularity.

CTU-1   **CTU-2**

CTU-3

CTU-1. Talking Cloth Doll,
1969. - **$35 $60 $100**

CTU-2. Metal Alarm Clock,
1969. - **$20 $50 $100**

CTU-3. "Charlie For President" Litho. Button,
1960s. - **$8 $15 $25**

CTU-6

CTU-4   **CTU-5**

CTU-4. Plastic Radio,
1970. Battery operated, base often missing.
Complete - **$40 $60 $90**
No Base - **$15 $25 $40**

CTU-5. Plastic Figural Camera,
1971. - **$20 $20 $75**

CTU-6. Oval Bathroom Scale,
1972. - **$20 $40 $75**

CTU-8

CTU-7   **CTU-9**   **CTU-10**

CTU-7. Metal Wristwatch,
1973. - **$25 $40 $65**

CTU-8. Mug,
1977. - **$5 $15 $25**

CTU-9. Plastic Telephone,
1987. - **$10 $20 $35**

CTU-10. Ceramic Bank,
1988. - **$25 $50 $75**

CHEERIOS MISCELLANEOUS

Cheerios ready-to-eat oat cereal was introduced by General Mills as Cheerioats in 1941 and has remained a perennial favorite with kids and adults ever since. Over the years the Cheerios box has carried cutout toys and promotions for a wide variety of merchandisers, notably the Lone Ranger, Wyatt Earp, Superman, the Muppets, Bugs Bunny, Snoopy and Peanuts, Star Trek, Star Wars and Mickey Mouse. Disney comic books and 3-D glasses were featured giveaways in the 1940s and 1950s. The items in this secion are primarily a selection of Cheerios non-character premiums.

CEE-1   **CEE-2**

CEE-1. "Hall Of Fun/Groucho Marx" 3-D Picture,
c. 1942. Assembled from box back. Set of eight.
Box Panel Or Assembled - **$25 $40 $60**

CEE-2. "Hall Of Fun/Joe E. Brown" 3-D Picture,
c. 1942. Assembled from box back. Set of eight.
Box Panel Or Assembled - **$10 $15 $25**

CEE-3

CEE-3. "Confederate Currency" Album With Envelope, 1954. Reproductions of Confederate money. - $40 $80 $150

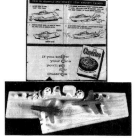

CEE-4

CEE-5

CEE-4 Cheerios Kid Statue, 1950s. Scarce. - $40 $80 $160

CEE-5. Aircraft Carrier And Planes Plastic Toy With Instructions And Box, 1960s. Planes are launched by rubber band. Near Mint In Mailer - $75

CEE-6

CEE-6. "Cape Cheerios Rocket Base" Box Panel Set, 1960s. Completed by parts from five box backs. Uncut Backs Each - $15 $30 $50

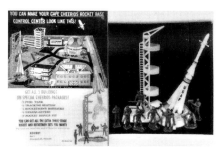

CEE-7

CEE-7. "Cape Cheerios Rocket Base", 1960s. Premium by Marx. Complete Boxed - $30 $50 $75

CHICK CARTER

Like father, like son, for detective work done. Nick Carter, a youth of considerable prominence to readers of pulp magazines and hardbound novels of the 1930s, fathered a son in his image—at least for purposes of radio and movie serial producers. The elder Carter, by name, was avoided for reasons unknown in broadcast and screen versions. *Chick Carter, Boy Detective* began as a radio drama on the Mutual network July 5, 1943 and ran until July 6, 1945. *Chick Carter, Detective*, a 1946 Columbia Pictures 15-episode serial, dropped all pretense that Chick was a youngster. Chick was an instant adult, portrayed by Lyle Talbot, a veteran actor of gangster and crime movie roles.

CCK-1

CCK-1. Chick Carter Club Card, 1944. - $15 $30 $60

CCK-2

CCK-2. Radio Club Promo Booklet, 1945. - $20 $40 $80

CCK-3

CCK-3. Club Kit Folder, 1945. - $30 $60 $120

CCK-4

CCK-4. Club Kit Card, 1945. Rare. - $15 $30 $60

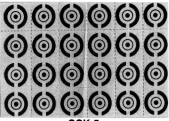

CCK-5

CCK-5. Set of 24 Inner Circle Logo Stickers,
1945. - **$10 $20 $48**
Each - **$2**

CHINA CLIPPER

In spite of the early 1930s Depression years, air travel demand continued almost unabated. The enterprising Pan American Airways offered a challenge based on need: a transport aircraft capable of 2,500 mile non-stop flight to span the Pacific. Aircraft makers responded quickly. On November 22, 1935 the first of the romantically-named "China Clipper" flights began to the Orient. The selected aircraft, one by Martin and one by Boeing, were masterpieces of huge payload capacity, incredible size and magnificent interior elegance for crew and passengers. So remarkable was this advance in aviation technology, a 1936 movie starring Pat O'Brien detailed the account of the initial flight that compared in public stature to Lindbergh's earlier solo flight of the Atlantic. The "China Clipper" mystique and adulation resulted in several tribute premiums issued by Quaker Oats.

CLP-1

CLP-2

CLP-1. China Clipper Brass Ring,
1935. Quaker Puffed Wheat and Rice. - **$40 $80 $120**

CLP-2. China Clipper 2" Brass Bar Badge,
1935. Quaker Puffed Wheat and Rice. - **$20 $40 $75**

CLP-3

CLP-4

CLP-3. Quaker "China Clipper" Balsa Model,
1935. Quaker Puffed Wheat and Rice. 12" wing span. Assembled - **$25 $50 $80**

CLP-4. "Giant Model Of The Famous China Clipper" Cardboard Punch-Out Folder,
1939. Pan-American Airways. Folder opens to 11x30". - **$40 $75 $150**

THE CINNAMON BEAR

First aired in 1937, *The Cinnamon Bear* was a syndicated children's Christmas tale broadcast five times a week between Thanksgiving and Christmas. In 26 chapters it followed the adventures of Judy and Jimmy Barton and Paddy O'Cinnamon as they travel through Maybe Land in search of their stolen Silver Star - across the Root Beer Ocean, face-

to-face with the Wintergreen Witch and Captain Taffy the Pirate. The show was sponsored by department stores, principally Wieboldt's of Chicago, and ran annually for many years.

CIN-1

CIN-2

CIN-3

CIN-1. Wieboldt's Litho. Tin Tab,
1940s. Rare. - **$75 $200 $400**

CIN-2. Foil Silver Star Picturing Paddy,
c. 1940s. - **$50 $75 $150**

CIN-3. "TV Club" Litho. Button With Cardboard Bear Attachment,
1950s. Wieboldt's department store. - **$40 $75 $125**

THE CISCO KID

The beloved bandito and his sidekick Pancho were create by O. Henry in a short story, *The Caballero's Way*, in th early 1900s and have lived a long entertainment life. The appeared in several silent movies and in 23 sound feature between 1929 and 1950, starring either Warner Baxter (wh won an Oscar for *In Old Arizona* in 1929), Cesar Romer Duncan Renaldo or Gilbert Roland. A radio series aired o Mutual from 1942 to 1956 and a popular television versio with Renaldo and Leo Carrillo was syndicated between 195 and 1956. Over 150 half-hour episodes were filmed by Z Television - in color, though at the time TV could broadca only in black and white. Comic books appeared in the 194 and 1950s and a daily comic strip ran from 1951 to 196 Most premiums date from the successful broadcast period the 1950s. "Oh Pancho! Ooooh Ceesco!"

CIS-1

CIS-2

CIS-1. "Safety Club Member" Cello. Button,
c. 1948. - **$25 $50 $75**

CIS-2. Cisco Kid Paper Mask,
1949. Various sponsors. Pictured example for Cisco Kid cookies, Cisco Kid sweet buns by Schofer's Bakery. - **$10 $20 $35**

CIS-3

CIS-3. Pancho Paper Mask,
1949. Various bakeries. - **$10 $20 $35**

CIS-4

CIS-4. Merchandising Portfolio,
1949. ZIV Co. Radio Productions . Contains over 25 promo-
onal items such as bw photos, sample ads, source list for
premiums. Complete - **$100 $300 $500**

CIS-5

CIS-5. Range War Game With Punch-Outs,
1949. Rare. - **$200 $400 $800**

CIS-6   CIS-7   CIS-8

CIS-6. "Wrigley's Cisco Kid Signal Arrowhead",
c. 1949. - **$125 $250 $400**

CIS-7. "Cisco Kid" Ring,
c. 1940s. Name appears on each side. - **$100 $210 $325**

CIS-8. "Cisco Kid" Aluminum Saddle Ring,
1950. Name in raised letters on saddle seat. -
$200 $425 $650

CIS-9   CIS-10

CIS-9. Cisco Kid Humming Lariat,
1950. Eddy's Bread. Cardboard rectangle with string and
streamer roll of crepe paper to "Execute The Thrilling Rope
Tricks Done By The Famous Cisco Kid". - **$20 $40 $80**

CIS-10. Secret Compartment Photo Ring,
c. 1950. Rare. Brass bands holding plastic compartment with
brass lid over bw picture. - **$1500 $4500 $8500**

CIS-12
CIS-11

CIS-11. "Cisco Kid Ranchers Club" Kit,
c. 1950. Dan-Dee Pretzel And Potato Chip Co.
Certificate - **$15 $40 $75**
Card - **$10 $20 $30**
Button - **$10 $25 $50**
Letter - **$15 $40 $75**

CIS-12. Freihofer's Bread Labels,
c. 1950. From a set. Each - **$10 $15 $20**

CIS-13

CIS-13. Mylar Reflective Mask With Envelope,
c. 1950. Scarce. Dolly Madison Ice Cream.
In Envelope - **$50 $150 $200**
Loose - **$25 $60 $100**

CIS-14

CIS-15

CIS-16

CIS-14. Glass,
c. 1950. Probably held diary product. Seen in lime green/black or yellow/brown. Each - **$25 $50 $75**

CIS-15. Cello. Button,
c. 1950. Possibly for rodeo appearance. - **$20 $40 $75**

CIS-16. "Cisco Kid On TV-Radio" Litho. Tin Tab,
c. 1950. Various sponsors. Various hat colors. - **$10 $20 $30**

CIS-17

CIS-18

CIS-19

CIS-17. TV-Radio Pancho Litho. Tab,
c. 1950. Various sponsors. Various hat colors. - **$10 $20 $30**

CIS-18. Kern's Bread Postcard,
1951. - **$12 $20 $35**

CIS-19. Triple "S" Club Litho. Button,
c. 1951. - **$15 $25 $50**

CIS-20

CIS-21

CIS-20. Kern's Bread "Triple S Club" Clothing Transfer,
c. 1951. Tissue paper with reverse image to be applied by warm iron on fabric. - **$10 $15 $30**

CIS-21. Portrait Photo,
1952. Butter-Nut Bread. - **$10 $20 $30**

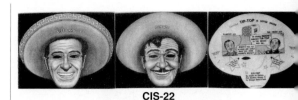

CIS-22

CIS-22. Paper Masks Set,
1953. Tip-Top Bread. Each - **$10 $20 $30**

CIS-23

CIS-23. Tip-Top Bread Puzzle,
1953. With Envelope - **$20 $40 $60**
Puzzle Only - **$8 $15 $25**

CIS-24

CIS-25

CIS-26

CIS-24. Photo,
1950s. Farm Crest Bakery. - **$15 $30 $75**

CIS-25. Plastic Tumbler,
1950s. Leatherwood Dairy. - **$15 $30 $75**

CIS-26. Glass Bowl,
1950s. Dairy product container. - **$10 $15 $25**

CIS-27

CIS-27. Tip-Top Bread Labels,
1950s. At least 28 in set. Each - **$5 $8 $12**

CIS-28 | CIS-29

CIS-28. Photo Cards,
1950s. Tip-Top Bread but various sponsors. Each -
$5 $10 $15

CIS-29. Cardboard Clicker Gun,
1950s. Dr. Swetts beverages but various sponsors. -
$20 $35 $60

CIS-30

Thruway Plaza

CIS-31

CIS-30. Cardboard Clicker Gun,
1950s. Tip-Top Bread. - $15 $25 $40

CIS-31. Shopping Mall Photo,
1950s. Printed for "Thruway Plaza," likely various mall sponsors. - $12 $20 $35

CIS-32

CIS-32. "Cisco Kid Ranchers Club" Member Kit,
1950s. Probable various breads. Includes two certificates,
manual, application, "Cattle Brand" card.
Complete - $75 $125 $250

CIS-33 | CIS-34

CIS-33. TV "Sponsor's Name" 10x18" Cardboard Sample Store Sign,
1950s. - $40 $75 $125

CIS-34. "Cisco Kid" Silvered Brass Hat Ring,
1950s. Name on brim. - $200 $425 $650

CIS-35 | CIS-36

CIS-35. "TV Channel 10" Member Cello. Button,
1950s. Dolly Madison and Aristocrat. Comes with beige or
green background. Green - $25 $50 $75
Beige - $40 $90 $140

CIS-36. "Cisco Kid" Silvered Brass Keychain Fob,
1950s. Store item stamped "Japan". - $15 $25 $40

CLARA, LU 'N' EM

This low-key comedy about three gossipy housewives was
created by three Northwestern University coeds to amuse
their sorority sisters. After graduation they took it to Chicago
radio station WGN, which ran it locally in 1930-1931 and then
as an evening program on NBC until 1932 when it became
the nation's first daytime soap opera. The sponsor was
Colgate. The program ran until 1936 and was revived for a
short run on CBS in 1942 for Pillsbury flour.

CLN-1

CLN-1. "Clara, Lu' n' Em" Puzzle,
c. 1933. Colgate. Envelope - $5 $10 $25
Puzzle - $10 $20 $40

CLYDE BEATTY

Clyde Beatty (1903-1965), world-famous wild animal trapper
and trainer, played himself in two chapter plays: *The Lost
Jungle* for Mascot in 1934 and *Darkest Africa* for Republic in
1936. In both he defeats hostile forces, human and animal,
and wins the girl. His *Clyde Beatty Show* on radio, on the
other hand, was said to dramatize actual incidents from his
life in the wild and at his circus. The program was syndicated in the late 1940s and ran on the Mutual network from
1950 to 1952, sponsored by Kellogg's cereal. Scattered
comic book appearances included a 1937 giveaway by
Malto-Meal and a 1956 giveaway by Richfield Oil.

CLY-1 | CLY-2

CLY-1. Lion Head Brass Ring,
1935. Quaker Wheat Crackels. Unmarked Clyde Beatty premium. - **$200 $350 $500**

CLY-2. Jungle Animal Brass Link Charm Bracelet,
1935. Scarce. Quaker Wheat Crackels. Unmarked Clyde Beatty premium. - **$50 $150 $300**

CLY-3

CLY-3. "Clyde Beatty & His Wild Animal Act" Punch-Out Album,
1935. Scarce. Quaker Wheat Crackels. Made by Fold-A-Way Toys. Unpunched - **$50 $150 $300**

CLY-4

CLY-5

CLY-4. Quaker Oats Circus Book,
1935. Inside front offers punch-out animal act, lion head ring, jungle bracelet, bullwhip.
$20 $50 $75

CLY-5. "Cole Bros. Circus" Cello. Button,
1930s. - **$8 $12 $25**

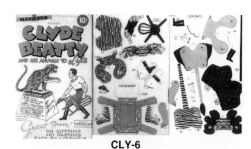
CLY-6

CLY-6. "Hingees" Punch-Out Kit In Envelope,
1945. Store item. Unused - **$25 $40 $75**

COCA-COLA

Since the mid-1890s, Coca-Cola has distributed premiums in staggering numbers and almost every conceivable material and variety. What started as a patent medicine tonic soon evolved into a soda fountain or bottled drink sold in more than 160 countries globally. Coca-Cola premiums never lack for distinct self-advertising but over the years have frequently been related to war, entertainment and comic characters, sports, toy trucks, educational materials and much more. Hundreds of items intended originally as only convenience items to stores and customers now swell the ranks of advertising collectibles. The quantity of Coca-Cola premiums issued in the past century have resulted in several reference books devoted solely to this output.

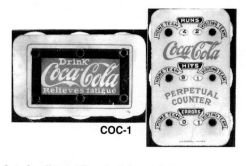
COC-1

COC-1. Cardboard Baseball Score Counter,
c. 1907. - **$20 $40 $60**

COC-2

COC-3

COC-2. Cello. Pocket Mirror,
1909. Illustration by Hamilton King. - **$150 $250 $500**

COC-3. Cello. Pocket Mirror,
1917. Pictures World War I era girl. - **$150 $250 $500**

COC-4

COC-5

COC-4. "Toonerville Refreshment Palace" Leaflet,
1931. From a series for distribution by salesman. -
$15 $30 $45

COC-5. Cleveland Press "Big Wheels Club" Cello. Button,
1930s. - **$15 $25 $40**

COC-6

COC-7

COC-6. "Bottlers Club" Cello. Button,
1930s. - **$40 $85 $150**

COC-7. Warplane 13x15" Cardboard Sign,
1943. From series bordered in white and gold.
Each - **$20 $40 $60**

COC-8

COC-8. "Know Your War Planes" Booklet,
c. 1943. Coca-Cola. - **$20 $35 $60**

COC-9

COC-9. Warplane Cards,
1943. Set of 20. Set - **$40 $60 $100**

COC-10   COC-11

COC-10. Warplane 13x15" Cardboard Sign,
1943. From series bordered in simulated wood.
Each - **$20 $40 $60**

COC-11. Felt Fabric Beanie,
1940s. - **$20 $50 $75**

COC-12   COC-13

COC-12. "Kit Carson Kerchief" 16x24" Cardboard Store Poster,
1953. Coca-Cola. - **$25 $75 $150**

COC-13. "Kit Carson" Fabric Kerchief,
1953. Picturing Bill Williams, TV series star. - **$15 $25 $50**

COC-14   COC-15

COC-14. "hi fi Club" Member Litho. Button,
c. 1959. - **$12 $18 $30**

COC-15. Celluloid 9" Wall Sign,
1950s. - **$40 $65 $125**

COC-16   COC-17

COC-16. Plastic Cooler Replica,
c. 1950s. 4x4x5" wide. - **$35 $75 $110**

COC-17. Diecut 5' Standee,
1960s. - **$75 $200 $400**

COC-18   COC-19

COC-18. Christmas Elf Cloth Doll,
1980s. - **$15 $25 $35**

COC-19. Canadian 3" Cello. Endorsement Button,
1980s. By Coca-Cola Ltd. of Canada picturing Bill Cosby. - **$5 $10 $15**

COMIC CHARACTER MISCELLANEOUS

Comic strip characters, particularly prior to World War II and the following early years of television, could almost be considered "family" to readers. No surprise, then, that advertisers sensed that premiums based on such familiar and well-loved characters would boost sales. Historically, the Yellow Kid and Buster Brown led the way. These and 73 others of intense popularity are listed in *Hake's Guide To Comic Character Collectibles* published in 1993, as well as other pages of this book. This section is devoted to comic characters that may have a large number of associated collectibles but relatively few offered as actual premiums.

COM-1

COM-1. "Little Sammy Sneeze" Book,
1905. Rare. By Winsor McCay. Rarely found better than very good. - **$400 $1000 $1800**

COM-2

COM-3

COM-2. Little Nemo Postcard,
1900s. From a series. Scarce. - **$30 $60 $120**

COM-3. "Krazy Kat" Stuffed Doll,
c. 1915. Store item by Averill Co. - **$300 $600 $1000**

COM-4

COM-5

COM-4. "Don't Be A Krazy Kat" Cello. Button,
c. 1915. Cigarette purchase give-away. Art by character creator George Herriman. - **$15 $25 $40**

COM-5. "Krazy Kat Kiddies Klub" Member Card,
c. 1920s. Art is unsigned, issuer is unknown. - **$100 $250 $350**

COM-6

COM-7

COM-6. Little Jimmy Writing Tablet,
1920s. Scarce. - **$20 $40 $80**

COM-7. Sunday Comic Section 7x11" Cardboard Sign With Jiggs,
c. 1920s. Boston Sunday Advertiser. - **$35 $65 $100**

COM-8

COM-9

COM-10

COM-8. "Ignatz" Flexible Figure,
c. 1930. Store item. Composition/wood/wire by Cameo Doll Co. - **$150 $250 $400**

COM-9. "Reg'lar Fellers" BLB,
1933. - **$10 $25 $50**

COM-10. "Tillie The Toiler" Jigsaw Puzzle,
1933. Various newspapers supplement. - **$8 $12 $20**

COM-11

COM-12

COM-11. "Funnies on Parade" #1,
1933. Scarce. Probably the 1st regular format comic book. Proctor & Gamble giveaway. - **$1100 $3300 $10000**

COM-12. "Century of Comics" #1,
1933. Scarce. 100 pages. Probably the third comic book. Wheatena/Malt-O-Milk giveaway. - **$3200 $9600 $16000**

COM-13

COM-14

COM-13. "Smitty Golden Gloves Tournament" BLB,
1934. Cocomalt. - **$10 $25 $50**

COM-14. Sears, Roebuck "Funny Paper Puppets" Punch Out Sheet,
1935. Unpunched - **$60 $100 $175**

COM-15

COM-16

COM-17

COM-15. "Tailspin Tommy In The Great Air Mystery/A Universal Picture " Cello. Button,
1935. For movie serial picturing cast members Clark Williams, Noah Beery, Jr., Jean Rogers. - **$30 $60 $100**

COM-16. "Tailspin Tommy Club" Cello. Button,
. 1935. Evening Sun newspaper. - **$20 $40 $75**

COM-17. "Tailspin Tommy" Cello. Button,
. 1935. Newark Star-Eagle. From series of newspaper contest buttons, match number to win prize. - **$5 $10 $15**

COM-18

M-18. "Scrappy's Animated Puppet Theater" Punch-ut Kit,
936. Pillsbury's Farina cereal. Unpunched - **$30 $75 $125**

COM-19

OM-19. Red Falcon Adventures,
937. Rare. 8 page comic premium, Seal Right Ice Cream.
sue #1 - **$100 $200 $300**
sues #2-#5 - **$60 $120 $200**
sues #6-#10 - **$50 $100 $150**
sues #11-#50 - **$30 $60 $100**

COM-20

OM-20. Federal Agent Fingerprint Outfit,
938. Gold Medal toy. - **$30 $60 $120**

COM-21	COM-22	COM-23

COM-21. Harold Teen Bat-O-Ball,
1938. Morton Salt premium. - **$20 $40 $80**

COM-22. Lillums Bat-O-Ball,
1938. Morton Salt premium. - **$20 $40 $80**

COM-23. Shadow Bat-O-Ball,
1938. Morton Salt premium. - **$20 $40 $80**

COM-24

COM-24. "Sears Toyland" Christmas Comic Book,
1939. Scarce. Features Chicago Tribune Syndicate characters. - **$75 $225 $700**

COM-26	COM-27

COM-25

COM-25. "Joe Palooka" Wood Jointed Doll,
1930s. Store item. - **$40 $60 $125**

COM-26. "Krazy Kat/New York Evening Journal" Cello. Button,
1930s. From series of newspaper contest buttons, match number to win prize. - **$25 $50 $75**

COM-27. "Krazy Kat/New York Evening Journal" Cello. Button,
1930s. From series of newspaper contest buttons, match number to win prize. - **$10 $25 $50**

COM-28	COM-29	COM-30

COM-28. "Ignatz Mouse/New York Evening Journal" Cello. Button,
1930s. From series of newspaper contest buttons, match number to win prize. - **$10 $25 $50**

COM-29. "Sky Roads" Cello. Button,
1930s. Buffalo Evening News. From series of newspaper contest buttons, match number to win prize. - **$10 $15 $30**

COM-30. "Ella Cinders Spinner",
1930s. United Features Syndicate. Cello. over metal disk that has underside center bump for spinning. - **$50 $100 $150**

COM-31

COM-32

COM-31. "Sky Roads Flying Club" Silvered Brass Wings Badge,
1930s. - **$20 $30 $50**

COM-32. Sky Pilot Pin Brass Wings,
1930s. - **$15 $30 $45**

COM-33   COM-34   COM-35

COM-33. Aviation Department Boy Flight Commander Brass Badge,
1930s. - **$10 $30 $60**

COM-34. Boy Chief of Police Brass Badge,
1930s. - **$10 $30 $60**

COM-35. Fire Department Boy Chief Brass Badge,
1930s. - **$10 $30 $60**

COM-36

COM-37

COM-36. Junior Sheriff Brass Badge,
1930s. - **$10 $20 $40**

COM-37. Herby Cloth Doll,
1930s. Back view showing artist's facsimile signature on leg area. - **$30 $60 $90**

COM-38

COM-38. "Smilin' Jack's Victory Bombers" Assembly/Play Game,
c. 1943. Store item by Plane Facts, Inc. - **$75 $150 $300**

COM-39

COM-39. "Santa's Christmas Comic Variety Show" Book
1943. Sears, Roebuck & Co. Features Dick Tracy, Orphan Annie, Terry and the Pirates, many others. - **$30 $90 $200**

COM-40   COM-41

COM-40. Kings Features Stationary Sheet,
1944. - **$10 $20 $40**

COM-41. Alley Oop (Test) Product Statuette,
1945. Rare. - **$500 $1200 $2500**

COM-42   COM-43

COM-42. Joe Palooka Matchbook,
1948. - $10 $20 $40

COM-43. "Black Cat" Comic Book Ad Matchbook,
1940s. Harvey Comics. - $10 $20 $40

COM-44

COM-45

COM-46

COM-44. Royal Northwest Mounted Police Brass Badge,
1940s. Scarce. - $30 $60 $120

COM-45. Moon Mullins Cloth Doll,
1940s. - $30 $60 $90

COM-46. Smitty Cloth Doll,
1940s. - $30 $60 $90

COM-47

COM-48

COM-49

COM-47. "Joe Palooka Championship Belt" Metal
Buckle,
1940s. Store item by Ham Fisher Belt Rite Leather Goods.
Buckle - $25 $50 $75
With Belt - $40 $75 $125

COM-48. Joe Palooka "Tangle Comics" Cello. Button,
1940s. Philadelphia Sunday Bulletin. - $10 $20 $35

COM-49. "New Funnies/Andy Panda" Cello. Button,
c. 1940s. New Funnies Comics. - $25 $60 $100

COM-50

COM-50. Metro Sunday Promo,
1951. Rare. Features 29 comic characters from Metro
Sunday newspapers. - $200 $400 $800

COM-51

COM-52

COM-51. Billy West Promo Card,
1950. Scarce. - $20 $40 $60

COM-52. Sparky's Fire Dept. Inspector Silvered Brass
Badge,
1950s. - $20 $40 $60

COM-53

COM-53. Kool-Pops "Captain Action" Card Game With
Mailer Box,
1967. - $35 $75 $125

COM-54

COM-54. Vending Machine Display Paper,
1960s. Depicts Casper and shows three monsters appearing
on flicker rings. - $30 $35 $40

COUNTERSPY

Washington calling David Harding, Counterspy! In 1942,
with the nation at war, the call was answered. One of radio's
long-running adventure series, *Counterspy* aired on ABC,
NBC or Mutual from 1942 to 1957. With Don MacLaughlin
as the ace agent, Counterspy fought Axis enemies during the
war and other security threats once the war was won.
Sponsors over the years included Mail Pouch chewing tobacco, Schutter Candies, Pepsi-Cola and Gulf Oil.

COU-1

COU-1. Pepsi-Cola 8x19" Paper Store Sign,
1949. - **$50 $100 $200**

COU-3

COU-2

COU-2. Club Member Certificate,
1949. Scarce. Pepsi-Cola. For "Counter-Spy Junior Agents Club". - **$15 $30 $50**

COU-3. Junior Agent Glow-In-Dark Brass Badge,
1949. Pepsi-Cola. Centered by plastic lens over bw glow portrait. - **$25 $45 $75**

COU-4

COU-4. Matchbook,
1940s. Old Nick candy bars. - **$10 $30 $60**

COU-5

COU-5. "Junior Counterspy" Activity Booklet,
1951. Gulf Oil. Story pages feature David Harding, Counterspy. - **$10 $25 $40**

CRACKER JACK

This blend of popcorn, peanuts and molasses candy has been a best-selling snack food for about 100 years. F. W. Rueckheim, a German immigrant, had opened a small popcorn stand in Chicago in 1872. He sold the first version of his candy combination at the 1893 Columbian Exposition; the product proved to be popular, but the kernels stuck together. By 1896 the company had found not only a process to keep the kernels separate, but also a name - cracker jack was a new slang term for excellent or superior, and F. W. promptly trademarked it for his sweet.

By 1899 Cracker Jack was being packaged in a waxed sealed box to keep it fresh, by 1902 it was listed in the Sears catalogue and in 1908 it became part of sports Americana in the song *Take Me Out to the Ball Game*. A happy customer is said to have contributed the company slogan, The More You Eat, The More You Want. In 1910 the company started inserting coupons in the packages to be traded in for prizes and two years later the coupons were replaced by the prizes themselves.

Since 1912 every package has contained a toy surprise inside. Sailor Jack, modeled after F. W.'s grandson, appeared in advertisements in 1916 with his dog Bingo and made it onto the box in 1919. The company was sold to Borden in 1972 and today Cracker Jack, still with a toy in every box, is marketed worldwide.

CRJ-2

CRJ-1

CRJ-1. "The Cracker Jack Bears" Postcard,
1907. Example from set of 16. - **$12 $20 $30**

CRJ-2. Portrait Cello. Button,
c. 1908. With "Cracker Jack" back paper. One of a series also issued by tobacco companies. - **$10 $20 $35**

CRJ-3

CRJ-3. "Cracker Jack" Wagon In White Metal,
c. 1910. Scarce. Metal has gold luster and wagon interior has cardboard insert floor. Horse's legs are usually broken. - **$75 $150 $250**

CRJ-4

CRJ-4. "Cracker Jack Riddles" Booklet,
c. 1920s. - **$10 $20 $30**

CRJ-5

CRJ-5. "Cracker Jack Drawing Book",
c. 1920s. - **$20 $30 $60**

CRJ-6

CRJ-6. Miniature Litho. Tin Wagon,
c. 1920s. - **$15 $30 $70**

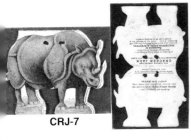 

CRJ-7   CRJ-8

CRJ-7. Rhinoceros Paper Prize,
c. 1920s. From set of 16 "Jumping Animals" to fold.
Each - **$35 $75 $125**

CRJ-8. "Cracker Jack/The Famous Confection" Top,
c. 1920s. Silver finish with incised lettering and slightly thicker metal than later versions. - **$40 $75 $125**

CRJ-9

CRJ-9. Cardboard String Toy,
c. 1920s. - **$25 $60 $90**

CRJ-10

CRJ-10. Chicago World's Fair Miniature Booklet,
1933. Ten pictures. - **$40 $80 $175**

CRJ-11   CRJ-12

CRJ-11. "Magnetic Fortune Teller" With Envelope,
c. 1930s. Gold printing on thin cellophane of various solid colors. - **$15 $25 $50**

CRJ-12. Litho. Tin Spinner Top,
c. 1930s. - **$15 $25 $40**

CRJ-13   CRJ-14

CRJ-13. Litho. Tin Top,
c. 1930s. - **$10 $20 $35**

CRJ-14. Toy Cart,
c. 1930s. Litho. tin with wood shaft. - **$10 $20 $30**

CRJ-15   CRJ-16   CRJ-17

CRJ-15. Tin Litho. Pocketwatch Replica,
c. 1930s. - **$20 $40 $75**

CRJ-16. Aluminum Snapper,
1930s. - **$10 $25 $35**

CRJ-17. Tin Litho. Standup,
1930s. From a set of 10: Chester, Harold Teen, Herby, Kayo, Moon Mullins, Orphan Annie, Perry, Skeezix, Smitty, Uncle Walt. Each - **$25 $50 $75**

CRJ-18

CRJ-18. "The Cracker Jack Line" Litho. Tin Train Engine,
1930s. - **$40 $75 $125**

CRJ-19 CRJ-20

CRJ-19. Litho. Tin Delivery Truck,
1930s. - **$40 $75 $125**

CRJ-20. "Tune In With Cracker Jack" Litho. Tin Miniature Desk Radio Replica,
1930s. Scarce. - **$65 $140 $200**

CRJ-21

CRJ-22

CRJ-21. "Cracker Jack Shows" Tin Circus Wagon,
c. 1930s. Depicts caged lion on each side. - **$30 $60 $100**

CRJ-22. Diecut Paper Frog,
1930s. - **$20 $40 $75**

CRJ-24

CRJ-23

CRJ-23. Tin Miniature Book Bank,
1930s. - **$50 $80 $150**

CRJ-24. Tin Bank,
c. 1930s. Brass luster. - **$25 $50 $75**

CRJ-25

CRJ-26 CRJ-27

CRJ-25. Litho. Tin Diecut Bookmark,
1930s. One of scarcer in series. - **$15 $30 $60**

CRJ-26. Litho. Tin Fortune Wheel,
1930s. Reveals fortune words by revolving upper disk to spell name of fortune-seeker. - **$15 $25 $40**

CRJ-27. Paper Fortune Wheel,
c. 1930s. Similar design and function to litho. tin version. - **$10 $20 $35**

CRJ-28

CRJ-29

CRJ-28. "Cracker Jack Air Corps" Dark Metal Wings,
1930s. Lapel stud reverse. - **$ 15 $30 $50**

CRJ-29. "Midget Auto Race" Paper Prize,
1940s. - **$15 $25 $40**

CRJ-30

CRJ-30. "Cracker Jack" Transfer Sheet Set,
1940s. 25 in set. - **$50 $125 $200**

CRJ-31

CRJ-31. Baseball Card Sheet 8x11".
1991. Uncut 36 card sheet with miniature replicas of Topps Gum "40 Years Of Baseball" cards. Uncut - **$25 $50 $75**

DAIRY QUEEN

Sales of soft ice cream dispensed from a spigot blossomed in the 1950s, not only from ice cream trucks but also from drive-in retail outlets. Thousands of these outlets were opened on the nation's highways by such retail chains as Dairy Queen, Tastee Freeze, and Carvel. By the end of the decade hard ice cream was making a comeback, but the soft ice cream chains had established themselves as a continuing roadside fixture. Dairy Queen promotions featured an anthropomorphic Mister Softee figure. "Did you DQ today?"

DAI-1   DAI-3

DAI-2

DAI-1. "Mister Softee Safety Club" Litho. Button,
c. 1950s. Softee Ice Cream. - $5 $8 $15

DAI-2. "Mister Softee" Enameled Brass Keychain Tag,
c. 1960s. - $10 $25 $40

DAI-3. "Mister Softee" Plastic Ring,
c. 1960s. - $10 $15 $20

DAI-4. "Adventures Of Captain Chapel" Space Cards,
1960s. Mister Softee. Cards 1-10 are numbered, following cards are unnumbered from unknown set total. - $1 $2 $3

DANIEL BOONE

Dan'l Boone (1734-1820), legendary Kentucky frontiersman, hunter, farmer and wilderness scout, was brought to life by 20th Century-Fox in a successful adventure series on CBS-TV from 1964 to 1970. The show starred Fess Parker, who a decade earlier had found fame playing Davy Crockett on the *Disneyland* series. The stories were centered on Boone's Kentucky settlement days, his expeditions and his struggles with the Indians. Other featured actors included Patricia Blair, Ed Ames, Albert Salmi and Roosevelt Grier. Merchandised items are usually copyrighted by 20th Century-Fox TV. An hour-long animated TV special sponsored by Kenner toys premiered on CBS in 1981 with Richard Crenna as the voice of Boone.

DNL-2

DNL-1

DNL-1. Fess Parker As Daniel Boone 5" Hard Plastic Doll,
1964. American Tradition Co. Store item. Accessories of fur hat, plastic rifle and strap with bag and powder horn. - $35 $60 $125

DNL-2. Trail Blazers Game,
1964. N.B.C. tie-in with Milton Bradley. Includes Trail Blazers Club application. - $20 $40 $75

DNL-3

DNL-3. Vinyl Zippered Pencil Case,
1964. Fess Parker/Daniel Boone Trail Blazers Club. Includes NBC premium leaflet offering wallet, ring binder, kaboodle kit, etc. - $10 $20 $35

DNL-4   DNL-5

DNL-4. "Fess Parker As Daniel Boone" Vinyl Wallet,
1964. N.B.C. Holds miniature magic slate and four photos from TV series. - $15 $30 $50

DNL-5. "Official Daniel Boone Fess Parker Woodland Whistle",
c. 1964. Autolite. - $20 $40 $60

DAVEY ADAMS, SON OF THE SEA

Details on this pre-World War II radio drama starring Franklin Adams are scarce but the program offered listeners membership in the DASC, the Davey Adams Shipmates Club, along with such premiums as a siren ring, a secret compartment members badge and a manual showing sailor knots and marine codes. Lava soap was the sponsor of this short-lived 1939 series.

DVM-1

DVM-2

DVM-1. Club Charter Member Certificate,
1939. Scarce. Lava soap. - **$25 $50 $75**

DVM-2. Club Letter,
1939. Lava soap. Offers Secret Compartment Shipmate's Badge. - **$5 $12 $20**

DVM-3

DVM-4

DVM-3. "D.A.S.C." Siren Ring,
1939. Scarce. Initials for "Davey Adams Shipmates Club." - **$175 $340 $500**

DVM-4. Shipmates Club Brass Decoder Badge,
1939. Lava Soap. Decoder wheel front, back has secret compartment. - **$40 $100 $200**

DAVY CROCKETT

Frontier scout, Indian fighter, bear killer, congressman, statesman, martyred at the Alamo, Davy Crockett (1786-1836) was a natural for television. Five fictionalized episodes from his life were broadcast on the *Disneyland* series on ABC in 1954 and 1955, starring Fess Parker in a coonskin cap and carrying his trusty rifle Old Betsy. Parker became an instant star, Crockett became an idol to an estimated 40 million viewers, *The Ballad Of Davy Crockett* landed on the *Hit Parade* and a merchandising mania swept the country. Some 500 products were licensed by Disney—toys, games, rifles, books, lunch boxes, costumes, coonskin caps—and unlicensed merchandise capitalizing on the craze followed in great profusion. Disney re-edited the films and released them to theaters as *Davy Crockett, King of the Wild Frontier* in 1955 and *Davy Crockett and the River Pirates* in 1956 and the original episodes were rebroadcast a half-dozen times over the next 20 years. An animated TV special sponsored by Kenner toys aired on CBS in 1976.

DVY-1

DVY-1. Gimbel's Club Kit In Mailer Envelope,
1955. Gimbel's department store. Disney authorized contents include photo and member card.
Near Mint In Mailer - **$90**
Photo - **$15 $25 $40**
Card - **$8 $15 $25**

DVY-2

DVY-2. "Davy Crockett In The Raid At Piney Creek" Comic,
1955. American Motors give-away. - **$10 $20 $40**

DVY-3

(enlarged view)

DVY-3. "Frontier Action Ring" On Card,
1955. Karo Syrup. Plastic ring holds flicker portrait.
On Card - **$160 $300 $450**
Loose - **$150 $275 $400**

DVY-4

DVY-5

DVY-4. Plastic Bank,
c. 1955. Various local sponsors. - **$10 $20 $35**

DVY-5. Ceramic Cookie Jar,
c. 1955. Store item. - **$150 $300 $500**

DVY-6

DVY-6. Frosted Glass,
c. 1955. Farmers Dairy Milk Ice Cream. - **$8 $15 $25**

DVY-7

DVY-8

DVY-14   DVY-15   DVY-16

DVY-7. "Candies And Toy" Box,
c. 1955. Super Novelty Candy Co. with Disney copyright. Cut-out cards on box back. Uncut Box - **$10 $40 $80**

DVY-8. "Davy Crockett Cookies" Box,
1950s. Federal Sweets & Biscuit Co. - **$25 $60 $125**

DVY-14. "Davy Crockett Frontier Club" Cello. Button,
1950s. - **$20 $35 $ 60**

DVY-15. "Big Yank Frontiersman" Litho. Button,
1950s. Clothing company. - **$10 $20 $30**

DVY-16. "Pfeifers Davy Crockett Fan Club" Litho. Button,
1950s. - **$20 $40 $80**

DVY-9   DVY-10

DVY-17   DVY-18   DVY-19

DVY-9. "Frontier Bread" Waxed Paper Bread Wrapper,
1950s. - **$15 $30 $50**

DVY-10. Coonskin Cap Punch-Out Sheet,
1950s. Nabisco. With simulated fur design. Unused With Tail - **$15 $30 $60**

DVY-17. "King Of The Wild Frontier" Cello. Button,
1950s. Disney authorized. - **$10 $20 $40**

DVY-18. "Frontiersman" Litho. Button,
1950s. Disney authorized. - **$15 $30 $50**

DVY-19. "Walt Disney's Davy Crockett" Metal Compass Ring,
1950s. Peter Pan Peanut Butter. - **$150 $260 $375**

DVY-11

DVY-11. Cardboard Money Saver,
1950s. Various sponsors. - **$12 $20 $35**

DVY-12   DVY-13

DVY-20

DVY-21

DVY-12. Deed of Land,
1950s. Scarce. - **$30 $60 $90**

DVY-13. "Jackson Daily News Fan Club" 2-1/4" Cello. Button,
1950s. - **$35 $75 $125**

DVY-20. Fess Parker/Crockett English Metal Badge,
1950s. Store item by "DCMT Ltd." of England. Silver finish, red lettering, black/white insert photo. - **$20 $50 $80**

DVY-21. Composition Bobbing Head,
1950s. Store item. - **$75 $125 $200**

DC COMICS

Former pulp magazine writer and army cavalry officer Major Malcolm Wheeler Nicholson published the first issue of *New Fun* (subsequent issues became *More Fun*) in 1935. Tabloid size with a full color cover and 32 black and white pages, it was the first comic book with original material in a Sunday comic page format. Although he wasn't making any money, the Major added *New Comics* (later to become *Adventure Comics* late in 1935). Most notable is that these two titles featured art by Walt Kelly as well as stories by Jerry Siegel and Joe Shuster in their pre-Superman days.

Next came *Detective Comics* in early 1937. The Major was so broke by now he was forced to take a partner, his printer. The new company was called Detective Comics, Inc. or DC Comics. Nicholson left soon afterwards. The new owners decided to add another title, *Action Comics*. Editor Vincent Sullivan was looking for new material when he saw samples of Superman by co-workers Siegel and Shuster. He decided to use the character. *Action #1* debuted in June 1938 and the comic book world was changed forever.

Sullivan also edited *Detective Comics* and after he suggested artist Bob Kane come up with something, Batman came out in issue #27 in 1939. Within one year editor Vincent Sullivan oversaw the beginnings of the two greatest comic book characters to ever see print. These characters are covered in their own sections while this section touches on additional DC characters.

DCM-1   DCM-2   DCM-3

DCM-1. "Green Lantern" 3-1/2" Cello. Button,
1966. #13 from series. Near Mint Bagged - **$35**
Loose - **$10 $15 $25**

DCM-2. "Aquaman" 3-1/2" Cello. Button,
1966. #15 from series. Near Mint Bagged - **$35**
Loose - **$10 $15 $25**

DCM-3. "Hawkman" 3-1/2" Cello. Button,
1966. #16 from series. Near Mint Bagged - **$35**
Loose - **$10 $15 $25**

DCM-4

DCM-5

DCM-4. "DC/Keebler President's Drug Awareness Campaign" Kit,
1983. Various paper items including those with facsimile endorsement signature of Nancy Reagan.
Complete - **$5 $10 $15**

DCM-5. Green Lantern Glow-In-Dark Plastic Ring,
1992. DC Comics re-introduction of the character. -
$1 $2 $4

DEATH VALLEY DAYS

One of the earliest radio dramas, *Death Valley Days* premiered on NBC in 1930. The stories of miners and homesteaders in the California desert, told by a character called the Old Ranger, were based on actual happenings and the show earned a reputation for historical accuracy. The program moved to CBS in 1941 and evolved into *Death Valley Sheriff* and then *The Sheriff* in 1945 when it aired on ABC. It ended its long radio life in 1951, sponsored from the beginning by 20 Mule Team Borax and Boraxo soap products. A syndicated television adaptation ran for 558 episodes, from 1952 to 1975, with Ronald Reagan, Robert Taylor, Dale Robertson or Merle Haggard playing the Old Ranger. The series has been rerun under a variety of titles.

DTH-1   DTH-2

DTH-1. "Radio Stars" Leaflet,
1930. Pictures John White, Old Ranger, Virginia Gardiner. -
$8 $15 $25

DTH-2. "Death Valley Days" Storybook,
1931. - **$5 $8 $12**

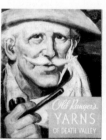 

DTH-3   DTH-4

DTH-3. "Old Ranger's Yarns Of Death Valley" Magazine,
1933. - **$5 $8 $12**

DTH-4. "Hauling 20 Mule Team Borax Out Of Death Valley" Puzzle,
1933. - **$15 $30 $60**

DTH-5

DTH-6

DTH-5. "Picture Sheet" Newspaper Style Folder Promoting Radio Show,
1933. - **$8 $12 $15**

DTH-6. "Death Valley Days" Charles Marshall Song Book,
1934. - **$5 $8 $12**

DTH-7   DTH-8

DTH-7. "Cowboy Songs As Sung By John White...",
1934. - **$5 $8 $12**

DTH-8. "Death Valley Tales" Storybook,
1934. - **$5 $8 $15**

DTH-9

DTH-10

DTH-9. "The World's Biggest Job" Radio Broadcast Script With Cover Folder And Envelope,
1935. For April 11 episode about construction of Boulder Dam. - **$8 $15 $25**

DTH-10. "High Spots Of Death Valley Days" Vol. 1 #1 Booklet With Envelope,
1939. Includes six previous broadcast stories plus radio script for May 19, 1939 episode.
Booklet - **$10 $20 $35**
Envelope - **$3 $5 $10**

DTH-11

DTH-11. "20 Mule Team" Model Kit,
1950s. Borax. Issued for many years from the 1950s through 1970s. Packaged in one or two boxes.
Near Mint In Box - **$35**

DELL COMICS

Dell Publishing Company founder George Delacorte started in the comic book business in 1929 with *The Funnies*, a 24-page weekly tabloid with eight pages in color, all original features and a ten cent price. 36 issues appeared, then Delacorte tried a few black and white titles in the early 1930s. Late in 1935 he introduced *Popular Comics*, the first Sunday comic page reprint title to compete with *Famous Funnies*. This proved successful enough for Delacorte to begin *The Funnies*, using the title a second time, the summer of 1936. Both titles used original material in conjunction with reprints. Next came *The Comics* in March 1937. The Four Color series began in 1939. Delacorte really began rolling in 1940 as Dell published *Walt Disney's Comics and Stories,* followed by *Looney Tunes and Merrie Melodies* in 1941 and original stories featuring Captain Midnight and Andy Panda in *The Funnies* of 1942. Four Color #9 (the first Donald Duck comic with original story and art) appeared in 1942. Carl Barks, Walt Kelly, *Marge's Little Lulu, The Lone Ranger, Roy Rogers, Gene Autry, Tarzan* and a host of others appeared in comics with the Dell logo. Many paper premiums to promote comic book subscriptions are listed in this book under sections for specific characters.

DEL-1

DEL-2

DEL-1. Dell Characters 8x10" Color Print,
1950. - **$50 $125 $225**

DEL-2. "KE" Plastic Puzzle Game,
1952. Played by pegs with "Secret Formula" instruction sheet. Complete Puzzle Only - **$10 $40 $60**

DEL-3

DEL-3. Club Membership Card,
1952. - **$8 $15 $30**

DEL-4

DEL-4. Dell Comic Club Promo & Club Card,
1953. Scarce. Barks cover. Folder - **$25 $60 $100**
Card - **$10 $20 $35**

DEL-5   DEL-6

DEL-5. "Walt Disney Comics And Stories" Christmas Gift Subscription Certificate,
c. 1950s. - **$20 $60 $100**

DEL-6. "Official Dell Comics Club/Member" Aluminum Cased Lincoln Penny,
1950s. Pictured example has 1953 penny, rim inscription "Keep Me And You Will Have Good Luck". - **$8 $12 $20**

DENNIS THE MENACE

Mischief-maker supreme, Dennis the Menace made his first appearance as a daily cartoon panel in 1951 and as a Sunday page the following year. Based on cartoonist Hank Ketcham's own son, Dennis, trailed by his dog Ruff, has been harassing his suburban neighborhood ever since. Frequent victims include his parents, Henry and Alice Mitchell and their neighbor, cantankerous George Wilson. The strip has been a consistent winner, so much so that the title itself has entered the language. Many paperback and hardcover reprints have been published and the first of many Dennis comic books appeared in 1953. A prime-time television series starring Jay North as Dennis ran on CBS from 1959 to 1963 and was rerun on NBC from 1963 to 1965. Most merchandised items are related to the comic strip; those based on the TV series are usually copyrighted by Screen Gems Inc.

DNS-1

DNS-2

DNS-1. "Dennis The Menace On Safety" Booklet,
1956. National Safety Council. - **$5 $10 $25**

DNS-2. Spoon Offer Kellogg's Sugar Pops Cereal Box,
1961. - **$40 $80 $160**

DNS-3

DNS-4

DNS-3. Spoon Ad Paper With Silver Plate Spoon,
1961. Kellogg's Rice Krispies. Ad - **$3 $5 $8**
Spoon - **$5 $10 $20**

DNS-4. "Dennis The Menace Takes A Poke At Poison",
1961. Food and Drug Administration.
Original 1961 Edition - **$1 $3 $6**
Later Reprints - **$1 $2 $4**

DNS-5

DNS-6

DNS-5. "Cast Your Ballot" Litho. Button,
1968. Sears. - **$8 $12 $20**

DNS-6. Fan Photo,
1960s. - **$5 $10 $15**

DNS-7

DNS-7. "..And Away We Go!" Comic Book,
1970. Caladryl medication. - $1 $3 $6

DETECTIVES BLACK AND BLUE

Adventures of Detectives Black and Blue, an early syndicated comedy crime show from Los Angeles radio station KHJ, aired from 1932 to 1934. The series followed the adventures of a pair of shipping clerks/amateur sleuths in their bumbling attempts at criminology. "Detec-a-tives Black and Blue, good men tried and true."

DTC-1   DTC-2   DTC-3

DTC-1. Fabric Double-Billed Detective Cap,
1932. Iodent toothpaste. Front bill names radio show and sponsor. - $20 $40 $65

DTC-2. "Detectives Black & Blue/Iodent Toothpaste" Brass Badge,
1932. - $20 $50 $85

DTC-3. "Detectives Black & Blue/Folger's Coffee" Brass Badge,
c. 1932. - $20 $50 $85

DEVIL DOGS OF THE AIR

The combination early in 1935 of a Warner Brothers real life U.S. Marine Flying Corps action adventure movie *Devil Dogs of the Air* and James Cagney in the starring role was quickly seized by Quaker Oats as a likely basis for premiums. A March 3, 1935 Sunday newspaper ad by Quaker offered Devil Dog ring, emblem badge and model airplane kit premiums based specifically on the movie plus closely related premiums of aviator goggles and leatherette flying helmet. Quaker Oats was thoroughly identified as Cagney's favorite cereal and the premium offer expiration date was May 15, 1935.

DVL-1   DVL-2

DVL-1. Quaker Oats Cardboard Sign,
1935. Rare. Displays the premiums and pictures James Cagney. - $1000 $1800 $2400

DVL-2. Ad Sign for Premiums,
1935. Scarce. Regular paper, color. - $50 $100 $200

DVL-3   DVL-4

DVL-3. Quaker Cereals "Man's Wings/How To Fly" Booklet,
1935. Scarce. Includes photo strip with James Cagney plus flight instruction pages. - $30 $60 $120

DVL-4. Quaker Oats Premium Order Blank,
1935. - $10 $18 $30

DVL-5   DVL-6   DVL-7

DVL-5. "Devil Dogs" Brass Badge,
1935. Quaker Cereals. - $20 $40 $75

DVL-6. "Military Order Of Devil Dogs" Brass Identification Tag,
c. 1935. Probably Quaker Cereals. - $30 $50 $85

DVL-7. Brass Ring,
1935. Quaker Cereals. - $50 $125 $200

DICK DARING'S ADVENTURES

Merrill Fugit played Dick Daring and Donald Briggs was Coach Greatguy in this 15-minute afternoon adventure series that had a brief run in 1933 on the NBC Blue network. Quaker Oats sponsored the show and offered merchandised and generic premiums in exchange for boxtops.

DDA-2

DDA-1

DDA-1. "Bag Of Tricks" Book,
1933. Quaker Oats. - **$5 $20 $50**

DDA-2. Quaker Underground Cavern Headquarters Map, Matching Puzzle,
c. 1933. Paper map and cardboard puzzle with identical design. Each - **$20 $50 $100**

DDA-3

DDA-4

DDA-3. Quaker Jigsaw Puzzle,
c. 1933. Puzzle scene of headquarters beneath city. - **$20 $50 $100**

DDA-4. "New Bag Of Tricks" Book,
1934. Quaker Oats. - **$8 $15 $40**

DICK STEEL, BOY REPORTER

Fresh from his role as Dick Daring, Merrill Fugit moved on to portray boy reporter Dick Steel in another 15-minute adventure series aired on NBC in 1934. The Educator Biscuit company was the sponsor and premiums included membership badges, booklets revealing secrets of police reporting and how to start a newspaper and such detective paraphernalia as a false mustache, invisible ink and handcuffs.

DST-1

DST-2

DST-1. "Secrets Of Police Reporting" Manual,
1934. Scarce. Educator Hammered Wheat Thinsies. - **$30 $100 $200**

DST-2. "Neighborhood News" Vol. 1 #1 Newspaper,
February 15, 1934. Envelope Mailer - **$5 $10 $15** Newspaper - **$50 $100 $150**

DST-3

DST-4

DST-3. Radio Cast Photo,
c. 1934. Shown entering United Airlines airplane. - **$20 $40 $75**

DST-4. Premium Order Sheet,
c. 1934. Hammered Wheat Thinsies and Toasted Cheese Thins. Ten premiums offered. - **$10 $20 $30**

DST-5

DST-6

DST-5. "Chief Editor" Silvered Metal Badge,
c. 1934. Rare. Awarded to "Reporter" advancing in rank. - **$50 $100 $250**

DST-6. "Reporter" Badge only,
c. 1934. - **$10 $20 $40**

DST-7

DST-8

DST-7. Dick Steel Whistle,
1934. Scarce. - **$20 $40 $60**

DST-8. "Dick Steel News Service/Special Police Reporter" Brass Badge,
c. 1934. Design includes radio front, lightning bolts, portrait, eagle. - **$25 $50 $80**

DICK TRACY

October 4, 1931 saw the birth of *Dick Tracy* in the Sunday Chicago Tribune. Eight days later the first daily strip appeared. So began Chester Gould's continuing saga of crime and violence that has produced a collection of appropriately named rogues and villains from Boris Arson to the Brow, Pruneface to Littleface, Flattop to the Mole, Gravel Gertie and B.O. Plenty and many others. Teamed with Tracy were his sidekicks Pat Patton and Sam Catchem and his enduring fiancee Tess Trueheart.

Despite the fanciful characters, the strip has been recognized for its realism and attention to details of police procedure and crime prevention. Tracy's popularity spread out into other media as well. Radio series ran on the CBS, Mutual and NBC networks from 1935 to 1939 sponsored by Sterling Products and Quaker cereals. The majority of early premiums came from Quaker in 1938-39. The show was revived on ABC from 1943 to 1948 sponsored by Tootsie Rolls candy.

Four 15-episode chapter plays with Ralph Byrd as Tracy were released between 1937 and 1941, followed by four full-length films between 1945 and 1947 and ultimately the 1990 Disney blockbuster with Warren Beatty, Madonna as Breathless Mahoney and Al Pacino as Big Boy Caprice. A live-action television series with Ralph Byrd again in the title role ran for a season (1950-1951) on ABC and was syndicated throughout the 1950s and 130 five-minute animated comic cartoons were released in the 1960s. Tracy cartoons were also reprised as segments of *Archie's TV Funnies* (1971-1973) on CBS.

The fearless crimefighter's first comic book appearance of many was in 1936 in *Popular Comics #1*. *The Celebrated Cases of Dick Tracy*, a hardbound anthology, was published in 1970. There have been countless Dick Tracy premiums over the years.

DCY-1

DCY-2

DCY-1. Paper Mask,
1933. Text on back tab reads "Free with one package of Handi-Tape." Published by Einson-Freeman Co. - $75 $150 $300

DCY-2. "Dick Tracy And Dick Tracy, Jr." Book,
1933. Perkins Products Co. - $15 $30 $60

DCY-3

DCY-4

DCY-3. "Dick Tracy/Junior" Cello. Button,
c. 1933. Unknown sponsor but made by Parisian Novelty Co. - $100 $200 $350

DCY-4. Belt Attachment With Link Chain And Loop,
1934. Scarce. Dated and inscribed "Dick Tracy Detective Agency." - $75 $150 $300

DCY-5

DCY-6

DCY-7

DCY-5. "Big Thrill" Chewing Gum Booklets,
1934. Goudey Gum Co. Set Of Six, Each - $10 $20 $40

DCY-6. "Dick Tracy Detective Club" Brass Shield Badge,
c. 1937. Reverse has leather cover slotted to wear on belt. - $40 $75 $150

DCY-7. "Dick Tracy Detective Club" Brass Shield Badge,
c. 1937. Reverse has leather coin pouch with snap shut flap.- $30 $65 $125

DCY-8

DCY-9

DCY-8. "Diamond Theatre Dick Tracy Club" Cello. Badge,
c. 1937. - $50 $80 $150

DCY-9. Club Manual,
1938. - $60 $100 $150

DCY-10

DCY-11

DCY-10. Quaker Two-Sided Sign,
1938. Rare. Shows the 1938 premiums. - $200 $400 $600

DCY-11. Quaker Silvered Brass Initial Ring,
1938. No Tracy inscriptions, personalized initials as designated by orderer. - $300 $600 $1200

DCY-12

(enlarged view)

DCY-12. Newspaper Premium Ad,
1938. Quaker Cereals. - **$5 $10 $20**

DCY-13

DCY-14

DCY-13. "Secret Service Patrol" Litho. Club Button,
1938. Quaker Cereals. - **$15 $30 $50**

DCY-14. "Secret Service Patrol" Cello. Button,
1938. Rare celluloid version, probably for Canadian membership. - **$75 $150 $300**

DCY-15

DCY-16

DCY-15. "Secret Service Patrol Promotion Certificate",
1938. Quaker Cereals. Add $20 for each applied promotion foil sticker. Without Stickers - **$15 $30 $50**

DCY-16. Sergeant 2-3/4" Tall Brass Badge,
1938. - **$40 $75 $150**

DCY-17

DCY-18

DCY-19

DCY-17. Sergeant Promotion Letter,
1938. Congratulatory letter also listing qualification for next rank of Lieutenant. - **$15 $35 $75**

DCY-18. Lieutenant Silvered Brass Badge,
1938. - **$40 $100 $200**

DCY-19. "Captain" 2-1/2" Brass Rank Badge,
1938. - **$75 $150 $300**

DCY-20

DCY-21

DCY-20. "Inspector General" 2-1/2" Brass Badge,
1938. Scarce. - **$200 $400 $800**

DCY-21. Secret Service Secret Compartment Brass Ring
1938. -**$150 $300 $450**

DCY-22

DCY-23

DCY-22. Patrol Leader Brass Bar,
1938. Rare. Awarded after "Inspector General" rank. -
$200 $400 $600

DCY-23. Lucky Bangle Brass Bracelet,
1938. Scarce. Charms of Tracy, Junior and four-leaf clover.
$60 $125 $200

DCY-24

DCY-25

DCY-24. "Dick Tracy Air Detective" Brass Wings Badge
1938. - **$25 $50 $85**

DCY-25. "Dick Tracy Air Detective" Brass Wing Bracele
1938. Scarce. Top of bracelet opens to place on wrist. -
$100 $300 $600

DCY-26

DCY-26. Rocket Gyro X-3 with Mailer,
1938. Rare. - **$100 $200 $400**

DCY-27

DCY-27. Official Detecto Kit,
1938. Scarce. Quaker Cereals. Includes mailer, bottle of "Q-11 Secret Formula", four negative-like black photos and instructions. Complete - **$100 $200 $400**

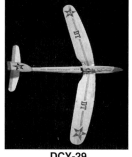

DCY-28   DCY-29

DCY-28. Secret Service Cardboard And Metal Phones,
1938. Scarce. Quaker Cereals. Pair - **$75 $150 $300**

DCY-29. Dick Tracy Flagship Balsa Wood Plane,
1938. Scarce. - **$100 $200 $400**

DCY-30   DCY-31   DCY-32

DCY-30. "Dick Tracy Returns" Movie Serial Handbill,
1938. Republic Pictures. - **$20 $45 $75**

DCY-31. "Secret Code Book Revised Edition",
1939. Quaker Puffed Wheat & Puffed Rice. - **$30 $60 $100**

DCY-32. Quaker Radio Play Script,
1939. "Dick Tracy And The Invisible Man" first of two books. - **$20 $50 $100**

DCY-33   DCY-34

DCY-33. Quaker "Dick Tracy's Ghost Ship" Booklet,
1939. By Whitman with actual radio broadcast script. - **$30 $75 $125**

DCY-34. Quaker Fold-Out Premium Sheet,
1939. Pictures 11 premiums including Tracy Flag Ship Rocket Plane, Pocket Flashlight, Radio Adventures Booklet, Siren Code Pencil. - **$30 $60 $100**

DCY-35   DCY-36

DCY-35. Quaker "Secret Detective Methods And Magic Tricks" Booklet,
1939. Picture example shows both covers. - **$30 $60 $100**

DCY-36. "Dick Tracy Secret Service" 3" Pen Light,
1939. Metal tube and plastic end cap. Seen with green or red tube - **$25 $60 $100**

DCY-37   DCY-38   DCY-39

DCY-37. "Dick Tracy Junior Secret Service" Brass Attachment,
1939. Originally attached by cord to Dick Tracy pen light. - **$15 $30 $65**

DCY-38. "Member" Brass Badge,
1939. - **$15 $30 $60**

DCY-39. "Second Year Member" Brass Badge,
1939. - **$20 $40 $75**

DCY-40   **DCY-41**

DCY-40. "Dick Tracy Secret Service Patrol/Girls Division" Brass Badge,
1939. - **$25 $60 $100**

DCY-41. Signal Code Siren Cap Pencil With Envelope,
1939. Near Mint In Mailer - **$175**
Pencil Only - **$50 $100 $150**

DCY-42   **DCY-43**

DCY-42. "Girls Dick Tracy Club" Silvered Brass Chain Link Bracelet,
c. 1939. Shield charm has red enamel accents (shown without chain). - **$40 $75 $150**

DCY-43. Wood Pencil And Wood Pen,
c. 1939. Each - **$20 $40 $75**

DCY-44

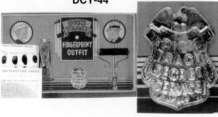

DCY-44. Detective Set,
1930s. Store item. Includes tin badge. - **$50 $80 $125**

DCY-45   **DCY-46**   **DCY-47**

DCY-45. "Detective" Cello. Button Facing Left, No Gun,
1930s. Back paper advertises comic strip in "The Chicago Tribune" or sometimes with name of New York City newspaper. - **$20 $35 $75**

DCY-46. "Detective" Cello. Button Facing Left With Gun,
1930s. Promoted newspaper comic strip with various newspapers indicated on back paper. - **$15 $30 $60**

DCY-47. "Detective" Cello. Button Facing Forward,
1930s. Chicago Tribune back paper. Promotes comic strip appearing in that newspaper. - **$20 $35 $60**

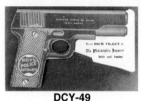

DCY-48   **DCY-49**

DCY-48. Foil Paper Shield Card,
1930s. Depicts badge inscribed "Dick Tracy Badge" and "Junior Detective First Grade". - **$40 $90 $150**

DCY-49. "Boy's Police Automatic" Cardboard Noisemaker Gun,
1930s. Philadelphia Inquirer. - **$20 $40 $60**

DCY-51

DCY-52

DCY-50

DCY-50. Pocketknife,
1930s. Celluloid grips on steel made by Imperial Co. - **$50 $75 $150**

DCY-51. Genung's Store Advertising Cello. Button With Dick Tracy/Little Orphan Annie,
Early 1930s. Rare. Considered one of the rarest and most desirable comic character buttons. - **$400 $900 $1500**

DCY-52. "Dick Tracy/A Republic Picture" Enameled Brass Shield Badge,
1930s. - **$25 $60 $90**

DCY-53   **DCY-54**

DCY-53. "Detective/Dick Tracy Club/Sun Papers" Silvered Embossed Tin Badge,
1930s. Probably Baltimore newspaper. - **$25 $60 $100**

DCY-54. "Cleveland News Dick Tracy Club" Brass Badge,
1930s. - **$25 $50 $80**

DCY-55

DCY-56

DCY-57

DCY-55. "Dick Tracy" Enameled Brass Hat Ring,
1930s. - **$100 $200 $300**

DCY-56. "Family Fun Book",
1940. Tip-Top Bread. - **$20 $50 $90**

DCY-57. "Dick Tracy Detective Club" Enameled Brass Diecut Tab,
1942. - **$25 $60 $100**

DCY-58

DCY-58. "Junior Dick Tracy Crime Detection Folio",
1942. Includes detective's notebook, jigsaw puzzle, card-board code finder, etc. Near Mint Set - **$250**

DCY-59

DCY-59. Junior Detective Kit Newspaper Advertisement,
1944. Tootsie V-M Chocolate Drink Mix. - **$8 $12 $20**

DCY-60

DCY-60. Junior Detective Kit,
1944. Tootsie V-M Chocolate Drink Mix. Includes manual, decoder, membership card, suspect sheets, ruler, line-up chart, badge. Two manual varieties: Type 1 includes anti-Japanese propaganda, Type 2 eliminates this and has differ-ent mailer. See color section for other differences.
Type 1 Near Mint Complete - **$500**
Type 2 Near Mint Complete - **$400**

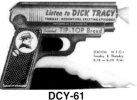

DCY-62

DCY-61

DCY-61. Tip-Top Bread Cardboard Noisemaker Gun,
1944. Urges radio broadcast listenership. - **$20 $45 $85**

DCY-62. "Dick Tracy's G Men" Cardboard Blotter/Ruler Card,
1945. Local theaters for 15-week movie serial. - **$35 $75 $125**

DCY-63

DCY-64

DCY-63. Cardboard Rubber Band Pistol,
1949. Dick Tracy Hat premium. Unpunched - **$20 $40 $80**

DCY-64. Cardboard Tommy Gun,
1949. Rare. Dick Tracy Hat premium. Unpunched - **$200 $400 $800**

DCY-65

DCY-65. "Straight From The Shoulder" Anti-Crime Booklet,
c. 1949. Crime Prevention Council of Illinois. Chester Gould art, printed in Illinois Penitentiary. - **$25 $50 $75**

DCY-66

DCY-67

DCY-66. "Hatfull Of Fun!" Game Book,
1940s. Miller Brothers Hats. - **$13 $41 $95**

DCY-67. "Dick Tracy Jr./Detective Agency" Silvered Brass Tie Clip,
1940s. Store item. - **$30 $50 $75**

DCY-68

DCY-68. Sparkle Plenty Plaster Bank,
1940s. Store item by Jayess Co. - **$150 $300 $600**

DCY-69

DCY-70

DCY-69. "Sunday Post-Gazette" 3" Cello. Button,
c. 1950. - **$50 $100 $150**

DCY-70. Dick Tracy And B.O. Plenty Knife,
c. 1950. Store item includes whistle, magnifier and grips that glow in the dark. Grips usually cracked by rivet. - **$20 $40 $75**

DCY-71

DCY-72

DCY-71. "Dick Tracy Crimestopper" Tin Shield Badge,
c. 1950. Lettering in black and red. - **$35 $70 $125**

DCY-72. "Dick Tracy TV Detective Club" Member Certificate,
1952. Copyright Chicago Tribune. - **$20 $30 $40**

DCY-73

DCY-73. Cardboard Flip Badge,
1952. Ward's Tip-Top Bread. - **$20 $40 $90**

DCY-74

DCY-74. Coco-Wheats Iron-On Transfers Set With Mailer Envelope,
1956. Inner envelope holding two transfer sheets picturing Tracy friends and villains. Mailer - **$10 $15 $25**
Illustrated Envelope With Two Sheets - **$25 $50 $75**

DCY-75

DCY-76

DCY-75. Post's Cereals "Red" Decoder Card,
1957. To decode answers to red "Crimestopper" messages on cereal box. - **$15 $25 $40**

DCY-76. Post's Cereals "Green" Decoder Card,
1957. To decode answers to green "Crimstopper" messages on cereal box. - **$15 $25 $40**

DCY-77   DCY-78   DCY-79

CY-77. Detective Club 2-1/4" Tall Fabric Sticker Patch,
1950s. - **$40 $85 $150**

CY-78. Enameled Brass Suspender Gripper,
1950s. From set of elastic fabric suspenders, store item. -
0 $20 $35

**CY-79. "Dick Tracy/Crimestopper" Silvered Metal
adge,**
961. Came with next item. - **$5 $12 $20**

DCY-80

Y-80. Crimestopper Club Kit,
61. Sponsor unknown. Many contents including badge
ee previous item). Fairly common due to warehouse find.
ar Mint Boxed - **$50**

DCY-81

Y-81. Sweepstakes Contest Packet,
62. Procter & Gamble. Includes leaflet, instruction sheet,
re purchase coupons. - **$30 $60 $90**

DCY-83

DCY-82

DCY-82. Soaky Bottle,
1965. Colgate-Palmolive. - **$5 $10 $25**

DCY-83. "WGN-TV" Crimestopper Litho. Tin Tab,
1960s. Chicago TV station. - **$10 $25 $50**

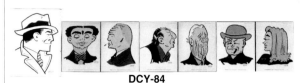

DCY-84

DCY-84. Tracy Villains Stationery Sample Kit,
c. 1971. Boise Cascade Paper Group. Six 11x14" posters,
stationery sheets and envelope. - **$20 $35 $50**

DCY-85

DCY-86

DCY-85. Dick Tracy/Detective Badge On Card,
1990. Store item. Carded - **$10**
Loose - **$1 $2 $4**

DCY-86. "Dick Tracy Party Rings" On Card,
1990. Total of eight. Store Item.
Carded Set - **$10**
Each Ring - **$1**

DIONNE QUINTUPLETS

Their names were Annette, Cecile, Emilie, Marie and Yvonne
and their combined weight at birth was less than 10 pounds.
They were born on May 28, 1934, in Callander, Ontario.
They were the Dionne quintuplets and they created an international sensation. Tourists and entrepreneurs flocked to
see them, they were made wards of the government to protect them from exploitation, it was said, and a promotional
and merchandising bonanza was born. The Quints appeared
in three films between 1936 and 1938 with Jean Hersholt as
Dr. Allan Roy Dafoe, the country doctor who delivered and
cared for them and they earned fees in exchange for lending
their names and images to promote a wide range of products, from soup to margarine to Karo syrup. Marketers took
full advantage of the age of these charming little girls.
Palmolive beauty soap, for example, offered adult pur-
chasers a Dionne quintuplets cutout book - especially for the
children.

DIO-1

DIO-1. Quaker 15x32" Paper Store Poster,
1935. Offered photo portrait set. - **$40 $75 $125**

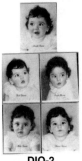

DIO-3

DIO-2

DIO-2. Quaker Cereals Color Photo Portrait Set,
1935. - **$15 $30 $60**

DIO-3. Chrome Finish Metal Cereal Bowl,
1935. Quaker Oats. - **$10 $20 $30**

DIO-4

DIO-5

DIO-4. Ink Blotter,
1935. Various sponsors. - **$3 $8 $12**

DIO-5. Cardboard Fan,
1935. Various advertisers. - **$8 $12 $20**

DIO-6

DIO-6. "Quintland",
c. 1935. Canadian published visit souvenir in mailer cover. -
$10 $20 $30

DIO-7

DIO-8

DIO-7. Silver Plate Spoons,
c. 1935. Probably Quaker Cereals. Set of five.
Each - **$5 $10 $15**

DIO-8. "Dionne Pops" Display Box,
1936. Vitamin Candy Co. - **$40 $100 $200**

DIO-9

DIO-10

DIO-9. Portrait Fan,
1936. Various advertisers. - **$10 $15 $30**

DIO-10. Cardboard Fan,
1936. Various advertisers. - **$8 $12 $20**

DIO-11

DIO-12

DIO-11. Ink Blotter Pad,
c. 1936. Various advertisers. Clear plastic cover. -
$12 $20 $35

DIO-12. Dionne Quintuplet Bread 3-1/2" Cello. Button,
c. 1936. - **$15 $35 $60**

DIO-13

DIO-14

DIO-13. "Quintuplet Bread" Paper Hanger,
c. 1936. Schulz Baking Co. Went on door knob. -
$10 $20 $35

DIO-14. Shirley Temple/Dionnes 9x12" Store Card,
1937. Modern Screen magazine. - **$50 $125 $225**

DIO-15

DIO-15. "Dionne Quin Cutout Book",
937. Palmolive Soap. With Mailer - **$25 $50 $100**
No Mailer - **$20 $40 $75**

DIO-16   DIO-17

DIO-16. Cardboard Wall Calendar,
938. Published by Brown & Bigelow with local imprints. -
5 **$12 $20**

DIO-17. "Souvenir Of Callander" China Tray,
1938. Birthplace souvenir. - **$25 $50 $75**

DIO-18

DIO-18. "Lysol Vs. Germs" Booklet,
938. Lehn & Fink Products. - **$8 $12 $20**

DIO-19

O-19. Dionne Quintuplets Wood Pin,
1938. Birthplace souvenir. - **$25 $50 $90**

DISNEY CHARACTERS MISCELLANEOUS

alter Elias Disney (1901-1966) and his talented skills domi-
ted the animation field throughout his working career and
tablished the monumental success of the current Disney
ernational empire. Entering animation shortly after World
ar I, Disney and his associates created dozens of house-
ld name animated characters headed, of course, by
ckey Mouse, but including Oswald The Rabbit, Donald
ck, Goofy, Pluto, Snow White and The Seven Dwarfs,
mbo, Bambi, Cinderella, Alice In Wonderland, Peter Pan
d Sleeping Beauty to name only the most obvious. Disney
s the leader in creating full-length animated films—Snow
hite (1937), Pinocchio and Fantasia (1940)—and joined
ese successes with live-action films starting in the late
40s including classics Treasure Island, 20,000 Leagues
der The Sea, Davy Crockett and Mary Poppins.

Children's TV entertainment during the 1950s-1960s was
dominated by Disney's Mickey Mouse Club and Zorro in
addition to the popular family series beginning under the
Disneyland title. Over the years, the quantity and beloved
quality of Disney characters have prompted more premiums
than any other single source.

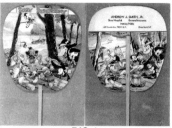

DIS-1

DIS-2

DIS-1. "Silly Symphony" Cardboard Fan,
c. 1935. Various sponsors. - **$75 $150 $300**

DIS-2. Department Store 18x25" Christmas Hanger Sign,
c. 1935. Various stores for toy departments. Paper printed
identically both sides. - **$150 $400 $750**

DIS-3

DIS-3. Goofy Ink Blotter,
1939. Sunoco. Igloo and polar bear. - **$15 $35 $60**

DIS-4

DIS-4. Morrell Hams "Walt Disney Calendar",
1942. 12 Disney character scenes. - **$100 $250 $400**

DIS-5

DIS-5. War Bond Certificate,
1944. United States Treasury Finance Committee. Also see Donald Duck items DNL-17 & 18. - **$40 $75 $150**

DIS-6

DIS-6. "Winter Draws On" Safety Booklet,
c. 1944. Safety Education Division Flight Control Command. - **$25 $50 $80**

DIS-7

DIS-8

DIS-7. "Cinderella" Movie Promotion 6" Cello. Button,
1950. RKO movie theaters. - **$25 $50 $75**

DIS-8. "Wheaties" Box With "Walt Disney Comic Books" Ad,
1950. 32 comics offered 1950-1951.
Complete Box - **$20 $50 $100**

DIS-9

DIS-10

DIS-9. Wheaties Comic Set A,
1950. Set of eight. #8 not shown. Each - **$4 $12 $25**

DIS-10. Wheaties Comic Set B,
1950. Set of eight. Each - **$5 $10 $15**

DIS-11

DIS-11. Wheaties Comic Set C,
1951. Set of eight. Each - **$5 $12 $25**
(Set D, Not Shown, Same Values)

DIS-12

DIS-13

DIS-12. "Walt Disney's Comics And Stories" Gift Subscription Christmas Card,
c. 1951. Dell Publishing Co. - **$35 $60 $100**

DIS-13. Cheerios 3-D Comics,
1954. 24 in set. Each - **$8 $25 $50**

DIS-14

DIS-15

DIS-14. Brer Rabbit "Ice Cream For The Party As Told B Uncle Remus" Comic Booklet,
1955. American Dairy Association. - **$40 $115 $265**

DIS-15. Lady And The Tramp "Butter Late Than Never" Comic Booklet,
1955. American Dairy Association. - **$10 $30 $75**

DIS-16

DIS-16. Plastic Dogs Newspaper Advertisement,
1955. Scotch Tape. Set of seven. Each - **$3 $5 $10**

DIS-17

DIS-18

IS-17. "Walt Disney's Magazine" Vol. 4 #1,
1958. Example issue. Published 6/57 - 10/59. Continuation of Walt Disney's Mickey Mouse Club Magazine.
Each - **$5 $14 $28**

IS-18. Sleeping Beauty Prince Philip Ring,
1959. Plastic topped by sword on shield inscribed "Truth/Virtue". - **$25 $50 $75**

DIS-20   DIS-21

DIS-19

IS-19. Disneykins Boxed Set,
1961. RCA Victor. - **$35 $60 $100**

IS-20. Sword In The Stone Character Plastic Ring,
1963. Depicts Sir Ector. Eight in set. Each - **$10 $15 $20**

IS-21. Sword In The Stone Character Plastic Ring,
1963. Depicts Wart as "Fish". Eight in set.
Each - **$10 $15 $20**

DIS-22

DIS-23

DIS-24

S-22. Sword In The Stone Character Plastic Ring,
1963. Depicts Wart as "Squirrel". Eight in set.
Each - **$10 $15 $20**

S-23. Sword In The Stone Mechanical Plastic Ring,
1963. Miniature sword withdraws from holder. -
$0 $30 $75

S-24. Jungle Book Swingers Plastic Figures,
1966. Nabisco Wheat and Rice Honeys. Set of six: Mowgli, Baloo, King Louie, Buzzy, Bagheera, Kaa. Each - **$3 $8 $12**

DIS-25

S-25. "Jungle Book Swap Cards",
1967. Nabisco. Australian numbered set of 24.
Set - **$15 $30 $50**

DIS-26

DIS-26. "The Love Bug Coloring Book",
1969. Hunt's Ketchup. - **$5 $8 $15**

DIS-27

DIS-27. "Crazy College Pennant Collector's" 17x22"
Poster With Pennants,
1975. Wonder Bread. Poster Only - **$5 $8 $15**
Complete - **$20 $40 $60**

DIS-28

DIS-28. "Crazy License Plates Collectors'" 22x26" Poster
With Stickers,
c. 1975. Wonder Bread. Poster Only - **$5 $8 $15**
Complete - **$20 $40 $60**

DIS-30

DIS-29

DIS-29. "NSDA Convention/Anaheim, California" Glass
Soda Bottle,
1977. National Soft Drink Association. - **$8 $15 $35**

DIS-30. "The Jungle Book Fun Book",
1978. Baskin-Robbins Ice Cream. - **$5 $8 $12**

DISNEYLAND

Sunday, July 17, 1955 began a new concept in Disney entertainment. The day officially opened Disneyland, a 230-acre complex in Anaheim, California on ground that was flat orange groves only a year before. The park's major components - Main Street U.S.A., Fantasyland, Frontierland, Adventureland, Tomorrowland - have been continuously refined and expanded annually to assure fresh entertainment year by year. Disneyland shops, of course, retail a virtually endless array of souvenir items with ceramics and jewelry quite popular. Giveaway premiums of paper items, buttons and the like, are quite frequent.

DIY-1.   DIY-2.   DIY-3.

DIY-1. "The Story Of Disneyland" Guide Book,
1955. The first guide book. - **$50 $80 $150**

DIY-2. "The Disneyland News" Vol. 1 #1,
1955. - **$50 $100 $175**

DIY-3. "Fly TWA To Disneyland" Schedule Book,
1955. Effective July 1 for July 17 opening day. -
$35 $75 $150

DIY-4.

DIY-4. Disney Studio Christmas Card,
1955. Features illustrated aerial view of Disneyland with 1956 calendar. - **$75 $125 $250**

DIY-5.

DIY-5. Guide Book,
1956. Second annual issue. - **$40 $75 $125**

DIY-6.   DIY-7.

DIY-6. "Sleeping Beauty Castle" Souvenir Book,
1957. Sold at Disneyland. - **$15 $30 $60**

DIY-7. Flicker Picture Card,
c. 1958. 2x2-1/2" "Souvenir From The Art Corner At Disneyland" picturing Tinkerbell at castle. - **$15 $25 $40**

DIY-8.   DIY-9.

DIY-8. "Disneyland And Santa Fe" Brochure,
1950s. Park brochure with Santa Fe advertising. -
$10 $20 $40

DIY-9. "Chesterfriend Chocolate Cigarettes" Plastic Pack,
1950s. Disneyland Candy Palace. Park souvenir. -
$15 $30 $50

DIY-10.   DIY-11.

DIY-10. "Butter Mints" Tin Container,
1950s. Disneyland Candy Palace. Park souvenir. -
$20 $40 $60

DIY-11. "Walt Disney's Guide To Disneyland" Book,
1960. Sold at Disneyland. - **$15 $35 $75**

DIY-12

DIY-13

DIY-12. "Win A Trip To Disneyland" Donald Duck Contest Form,
1960. - **$5 $10 $18**

DIY-13. Souvenir Guide,
1968. Park souvenir. - **$10 $25 $40**

DIY-14

DIY-14. "Pirate Party Kit",
1960s. Chicken of the Sea. Based on Pirate Ship Restaurant at Disneyland. Many pieces including eight place mats, paper game, hats, eye patches, etc.
Complete In Envelope - **$25 $50 $75**

DIY-15

DIY-16

DIY-15. Pepsi "I've Been To The Golden Horseshoe" 2" Litho. Button,
1960s. - **$15 $25 $50**

DIY-16. "Disneyland 25th Birthday Party" 2-1/4" Cello. Button,
1980. - **$5 $12 $20**

DIXIE ICE CREAM

The disposable paper drinking cup, called the Health Cup, had been around for 15 years when the Individual Drinking Cup Company changed its name to the Dixie Cup and began offering ice cream franchises in Cleveland in 1923. Dixie Cup has since become part of the language. Lithographed photographs printed on the underside of the cup lids helped sell the five-cent ice cream. The first were a set of 24 animals featured on the Dixie Circus radio program (Blue network, 1929-1930, and CBS, 1930-1931 and 1934). In the early 1930s a set of 24 MGM movie stars followed, with an offer of enlarged photographs in exchange for a number of

lids. A "Defend America" lid series in the early 1940s featured pictures of tanks and battleships, also available as enlarged full color pictures in exchange for lids. The company continued offering lids and picture sets into the early 1950s.

DIX-1

DIX-1. Early Waxed Cardboard Lid,
c. 1920. Scarce. Patent date of 1918. Lid reads "This Lunch Box Dixie Made By The Individual Drinking Cup Co., Inc." - **$10 $25 $50**

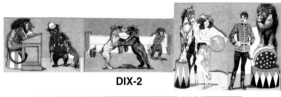

DIX-2

DIX-2. Circus Punch-Out Set,
1929. Stage and cut-outs in Series A-F and possibly more.
Stage - **$25 $60 $100**
Each Cut-Out - **$3 $5 $10**

DIX-3

DIX-4

DIX-3. "Portraits" 12x17" Cardboard Store Sign,
c. 1935. Easel sign picturing example of Barbara Stanwyck from "Annie Oakley" 1935 movie. - **$75 $175 $300**

DIX-4. "Movie Stars Ice Cream Dixie Lids" 6x18" Paper Sign,
c. 1930s. - **$50 $100 $150**

DIX-5

DIX-5. "America's Fighting Forces" Dixie Pictures,
c. 1942. Four examples from set. Each - **$3 $6 $12**

DIX-6

DIX-6. "United Nations At War" Dixie Pictures,
c. 1944. Four examples from set. Each - **$5 $10 $18**

DIX-7

DIX-8

DIX-7. "United Nations At War" Lid Set,
c. 1944. Set of 24. Each - **$3 $5 $10**

DIX-8. Al "Lash" LaRue Dixie Picture,
1947. - **$8 $12 $20**

DIZZY DEAN

Baseball's Jerome Herman Dean or Jay Hanna Dean (1911-1974), known to all as "Dizzy," was an outstanding pitcher for the St. Louis Cardinals from 1932 to 1938 and then for the Chicago Cubs (1938-1940). He was named the National League's Most Valuable Player in 1934, when his win-loss record of 30-7 helped carry the Cardinals to the World Championship. In 1952 his life story was the basis of the movie *Pride of St. Louis* and he was elected to the Baseball Hall of Fame in 1953. Dean did the radio broadcasts of St. Louis games from 1941 to 1949, where his grammar proved to be as challenging as his pitching - "he slud into third!" In 1948 Dean did a dozen weekly shows on NBC radio for Johnson Wax. His *Dizzy Dean Winners*, sponsored by Post cereals in the 1930s and promoted in Sunday comic sections, offered pins, rings and other premiums to young fans.

DZY-1

DZY-2

DZY-1. Sepiatone Facsimile Autographed Portrait,
1935. - **$10 $20 $35**

DZY-2. Grape-Nuts Booklet,
1935. - **$15 $25 $50**

DZY-3

DZY-4

DZY-3. "Dizzy Dean Winners" Club Brass Badge And Certificate,
1935. Post Cereals. Example picture shows badge on certifi cate. Badge - **$15 $40 $75**
Certificate - **$15 $25 $40**

DZY-4. Post's "Dizzy Dean Winners" Brass Club Badge,
1935. Figural baseball with profile portrait. - **$15 $40 $75**

DZY-5

DZY-6

DZY-5. Post's "Dizzy Dean Winners" Brass Bat Figural Pin,
1935. - **$15 $40 $75**

DZY-6. "Win With Dizzy Dean" Brass Ring,
1935. Raised portrait and other baseball symbols. -
$75 $160 $250

DZY-9

DZY-7

DZY-8

DZY-7. "Dizzy Dean Winners" Brass Baseball Charm,
1935. - **$10 $15 $25**

DZY-8. "Dizzy Dean-Good Luck" Brass Token,
1935. Portrait in horseshoe, back has short inspirational sports text. - **$20 $40 $60**

DZY-9. Post's "Dizzy Dean Winners" Brass Ring,
1936. - **$75 $160 $250**

DZY-10

DZY-10. "Dizzy Dean Winners" Premium Leaflet,
1936. Grape-Nuts. Pictures "49 nifty free prizes." -
$20 $45 $75

DOC SAVAGE

oc Savage was the superhero of popular pulp magazine tories by Lester Dent and others, published by Street & mith starting in March 1933. He made his first comic ppearance in *Shadow Comics* #1 of March 1940. Two months later he had his own comic book, which lasted only ntil October 1943, but he continued to show up occasionally *Shadow Comics* until 1949. There were brief excursions nto radio in 1934-1935 and 1942-1943, Warner Brothers made a film - *Doc Savage, Man of Bronze* - starring Ron Ely 1975 and there have been comic book revivals into the 990s, but nothing equaled the success of the original pulps. ans who joined the Doc Savage Club and followed the membership code could obtain badges and other premiums.

DOC-1   DOC-2   DOC-3

OC-1. "Doc Savage Magazine" 11x14" Cardboard
Window Poster,
930s. Scarce. Promotes "Doc Savage Radio Program ponsored By Cystex". - **$125 $250 $500**

OC-2. Pulp Magazine Ad Sticker,
930s. Example shown has trimmed margins. -
0 **$75 $150**

OC-3. Pulp Subscriber Portrait,
930s. Doc Savage Magazine. Color print of painting by alter M. Baumhofer especially for magazine. -
25 **$150 $350**

DOC-4   DOC-5

OC-4. Pulp Subscriber Portrait,
30s. Scarce. Doc Savage Magazine. Print of painting lieved by Walter M. Baumhofer especially for magazine. -
5 **$140 $200**

OC-5. "The Code Of Doc Savage" Wallet Card,
30s. Street & Smith Publishing Co. - **$40 $85 $135**

DOC-6   DOC-7   DOC-8

DOC-6. "Doc Savage Club" Member's Bronze Lapel Stud,
1930s. - **$75 $150 $300**

DOC-7. "Doc Savage Club/Member" Rubber On Wood Stamp Block,
1930s. Photo example includes image of ink stamped picture. - **$85 $175 $275**

DOC-8. "Doc Savage Award" Bronze Medallion,
1930s. Rare. Less than 10 known. Doc Savage pulp magazine. Inscribed "Service-Loyalty-Integrity" below portrait. -
$500 $1500 $3000

DOC-9   DOC-10

DOC-9. Lapel Stud Card With Envelope,
1930s. Pair - **$75 $150 $250**

DOC-10. Application For Doc Savage Award,
1930s. Scarce. - **$50 $100 $200**

DOC-11   DOC-12

DOC-11. Movie Card,
1975. Warner Bros. - **$5 $10 $20**

DOC-12. Commemorative Certificate,
1975. Warner Bros. From "The Man Of Bronze" film kit. -
$10 $25 $40

DONALD DUCK

Donald Duck was born in 1934 as a minor character in *The Wise Little Hen*, a Disney animated short and comic strip. By his second cartoon appearance he was a star. Clarence Nash, a milk salesman, was the voice of Donald and Dick Lundy did the animation. The irascible duck's first solo performance in the comics was in a Sunday feature in August 1936, drawn by Al Taliaferro and written by Bob Karp and a daily strip started in 1938. Nephews Huey, Louie and Dewey were introduced in 1937. Comic books, reprints of the strip, 64-page comic magazines as well as three decades of animated films and cartoons in theaters and on television have kept Donald a major Disney star. *Donald Duck's 50th Birthday*, a 60-minute spectacular on CBS-TV in 1984, reviewed his illustrious career.

DNL-1

DNL-2

DNL-1. "Donald Duck Jackets" Cello. Button,
c. 1935. Scarce. Norwich Knitting Co. - **$200 $400 $750**

DNL-2. Butter Creams 11x14" Cardboard Advertising Sign,
1937. - **$100 $200 $350**

DNL-3

DNL-4

DNL-3. "Walt Disney's 1939 All Star Parade" Announcement Folder,
1939. Sheffield Cottage Cheese. Pictures 10 glass tumblers distributed over 10 weeks picturing total of 45 Disney characters. - **$40 $75 $125**

DNL-4. Pint Milk Bottle,
c. 1939. Various milk companies. - **$75 $150 $250**

DNL-6

DNL-5

DNL-7

DNL-5. Long-Billed Donald Bisque Toothbrush Holder,
1930s. Store item. - **$80 $250 $500**

DNL-6. Long-Billed Double Figure Toothbrush Holder,
1930s. Store item. - **$125 $400 $600**

DNL-7. Mickey And Minnie With Donald Toothbrush Holder,
1930s. Store item. - **$100 $250 $400**

DNL-8

DNL-9

DNL-8. "Wanna Fight" Cello. Button,
1930s. Scarce. Image of irate long-billed Donald. - **$200 $500 $1000**

DNL-9. Dell Comic Book Promo,
1940. - **$30 $60 $90**

DNL-10

DNL-11

DNL-10. Sunoco Ink Blotter,
1942. Donald with adding machine. - **$15 $25 $60**

DNL-11. Sunoco Ink Blotter,
1942. Donald driving from garage. - **$15 $25 $60**

DNL-12

DNL-13

DNL-14

DNL-12. "The Spirit Of '43" 27x41" Government Movie Poster,
1943. Donald war-time patriotic cartoon used as added attraction to featured films. - **$200 $500 $750**

DNL-13. "USCG Patrol" Booklet,
1943. U.S. Coast Guard. - **$25 $50 $75**

DNL-14. Goodyear "Donald Duck Says:" Booklet,
c. 1943. Donald demonstrates how to make synthetic rubber. - **$25 $40 $75**

DNL-15

DNL-16

DNL-15. "Saludos" Studio Fan Card,
c. 1943. - **$30 $50 $70**

DNL-16. War Bond Poster,
1944. Scarce. - **$100 $200 $400**

DNL-18
(front)

DNL-17

DNL-18
(back)

DNL-17. War Bond Certificate with Paper Frame,
1944. United States Treasury War Bond Committee. Also
see Disney Miscellaneous item DIS-5. - **$60 $100 $200**
Certificate Only - **$40 $75 $150**

DNL-18. War Bond with Cardboard Stand-Up Frame,
1944. Scarce. - **$40 $80 $160**

DNL-19

DNL-19. Three Caballeros Studio Fan Card,
. 1945. - **$15 $35 $75**

DNL-20

**DNL-20. "Walt Disney's Comics And Stories" Comic
Book Gift Subscription Postcard,**
1946. - **$20 $50 $75**

DNL-21

DNL-22

DNL-21. Dell Comics Christmas Mailer,
1947. Inner panels picture comic book cover faced by subscription offer. - **$25 $50 $100**

DNL-22. "Donald Duck In Bringing Up The Boys" Book,
1948. Store item and K.K. Publications premium.
With Mailer - **$25 $50 $90**
Book Only - **$10 $20 $35**

DNL-23   DNL-24

DNL-23. Kellogg's Pep Plastic Magnetized Ring,
1949. Donald's head and miniature cereal box both have
magnets for moving his head, also known as "Living Toy
Ring". Complete - **$250 $325 $400**
Ring Only - **$150 $200 $250**

DNL-24. "Living Toy Ring" Newspaper Advertisement,
1949. Kellogg's Pep. - **$10 $20 $35**

DNL-25   DNL-26

DNL-25. "Living Toy Ring" Instruction Sheet,
1949. Kellogg's Pep. - **$125 $150 $175**

DNL-26. Mustard Product Glass Jar/Bank,
1940s. Nash Mustard. With Label And Lid - **$50 $100 $150**
\With Lid, No Label - **$20 $35 $60**

DNL-27

DNL-28

DNL-27. "Nu-Blue Sunoco" Cardboard Blotter,
1940s. Donald with smiling gasoline pump. - **$15 $25 $60**

DNL-28. Sylvania Radio Bulbs 18x28" Sign,
1940s. Rare. This Version - **$400 $800 $1600**
Smaller Version (scarce) - **$100 $200 $400**

DNL-29   DNL-30

DNL-29. Sunoco Ink Blotter,
1940s. Donald being hit by punching bag. - **$15 $25 $50**

**DNL-30. "Walt Disney's Comics And Stories" Gift
Subscription Card,**
1940s. - **$40 $80 $125**

DNL-31

DNL-31. Sunoco "How's Your I.Q." Booklet,
1940s. Automotive quiz. - **$30 $60 $100**

DNL-32

**DNL-32. Dell Comics/K.K. Publications Pictures With
Envelope,**
1940s. Set of 10. Near Mint In Mailer - **$600**
Each - **$15 $30 $50**

DNL-33   DNL-34   DNL-35

DNL-33. "Donald Duck Peanut Butter" Litho. Button,
1940s. Sponsor inscription on reverse, probable set of eight
also including Mickey Mouse, Minnie Mouse, Joe Carioca,
Pinocchio, Snow White, Bambi, Dumbo.
Each - **$10 $20 $40**

**DNL-34. "Ducky Dubble Club Of America/Member" Cello
Button,**
1950. Scarce. Depicts Donald eating Twin popsicle. -
$100 $175 $300

DNL-35. Decal Window Sign,
1950. Ice Cream Novelties, Inc. - **$20 $50 $75**

DNL-36

DNL-36. Premium Catalogue,
1950. Ice Cream Novelties, Inc. - **$10 $20 $35**

DNL-37

DNL-38

DNL-43

DNL-44

DNL-37. Icy-Frost Beanie,
1950. Rare. - **$100 $200 $400**

DNL-38. Icy-Frost Twins Cardboard Sign,
1950. - **$50 $100 $200**

DNL-43. Donald Duck Beverages Cola Glass,
1950s. - **$10 $20 $50**

DNL-44. "Donald Duck Cola" Cardboard 9x10-1/2" Store Counter Sign,
1950s. Printed in Canada. This Example - **$30 $50 $100**
Larger Version - **$50 $100 $175**

DNL-39

DNL-40

DNL-45

DNL-46

DNL-39. "Walt Disney's Comics And Stories" Comic Book Subscription Folder,
1953. - **$25 $60 $100**

DNL-40. "Donald Duck Bread" 30x38" Cardboard Standee Sign,
1950s. - **$125 $200 $350**

DNL-45. Beverages Trade Show 2-1/2" Cello. Button,
1950s. Canadian issue. Matte finish with center strip blank to write name. - **$200 $400 $600**

DNL-46. Orange Juice 6x13" Cardboard Display Sign,
1950s. - **$40 $90 $175**

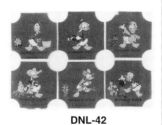

DNL-42

DNL-41

DNL-47

DNL-41. Donald Duck Bread Cardboard Bank,
1950s. - **$25 $50 $75**

DNL-42. Bread Labels,
1950s. Examples shown from state and country sets.
Each - **$3 $5 $10**

DNL-47. Donald & Ludwig Ceramic Mug Set,
1961. RCA Victor. Each - **$10 $20 $30**

DNL-48

DNL-49

DNL-48. Place Mats & Offer,
1964. RCA. Set - **$20 $40 $60**

DNL-49. Donald Duck Puppets Wheat Puffs Cereal Container/Bank,
1966. Vinyl with metal lid by Nabisco. - **$8 $15 $30**

 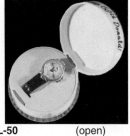

(closed)   DNL-50   (open)

DNL-50. 60th Anniversary Watch,
1994. Boxed - **$30 $60 $90**

DNL-51

DNL-51. Donald Duck with Gong,
1995. Disneyana convention premium. - **$100 $200 $300**

DON WINSLOW OF THE NAVY

Don Winslow was conceived by Lt. Commander Frank V. Martinek in the early 1930s as the hero of a series of novels written to promote navy recruiting. A Bell Syndicate comic strip, also originally written by Martinek and drawn by Leon Beroth and Carl Hammond, premiered in March 1934 and ran until July 1955. Winslow made his comic book debut in *Popular Comics* #1 of February 1936 and appeared in various Dell and Fawcett comics, among others, into the 1950s. Don Terry starred in two chapter plays, *Don Winslow of the Navy* in 1942 and *Don Winslow of the Coast Guard* in 1943, both of which were released to television in 1949. Winslow, along with his pal Lt. Red Pennington and his girlfriend Mercedes Colby, also fought the forces of evil on the radio from 1937 to 1943. His Squadron of Peace first did battle with the international Scorpia spy network, then turned its attention to the Axis menace of World War II. The series originated on WMAQ in Chicago and was aired on the NBC Blue network from 1937 to 1939 sponsored by Kellogg's cereals and Ipana toothpaste and on ABC in 1942-1943 sponsored by Post cereals and Red Goose shoes.

DON-1   DON-2

DON-1. Club Manual And Creed,
1939. Kellogg's. Near Mint In Mailer - **$150**
Manual - **$25 $50 $75**
Creed - **$10 $20 $35**

DON-2. "Squadron Of Peace" Member Card,
1939. Kellogg's Wheat Krispies. - **$15 $25 $50**

DON-3   DON-4   DON-5

DON-3. "Ensign/Squadron Of Peace" Silvered Brass Badge,
1939. Kellogg's. - **$10 $20 $35**

DON-4. "Lt. Commander/Squadron Of Peace" Silvered Brass Badge,
1939. Kellogg's. Scarce. Highest rank of series. -
$300 $900 $1200

DON-5. Honor Coin,
c. 1939. Kellogg's. Center has spinner disk, back inscription is "Take Me For Luck". - **$50 $100 $150**

DON-6

DON-6. Kellogg's Cardboard Periscope,
1939. Scarce. Slanted mirrors in each end. - **$50 $150 $30**

DON-7   DON-8

DON-7. "Guardians Of Peace" Cereal Box Backs,
c. 1939. Kellogg's Wheat Krispies.
Each Back - **$8 $12 $20**

DON-8. Winslow & Red Pennington Photo,
c. 1939. Scarce. - **$30 $75 $100**

DON-9   DON-10

DON-9. "Don Winslow's Secret And Private Code" Paper Sheet,
c. 1939. Includes Creed and decipher instructions. -
$20 $40 $60

DON-10. Identification Stamp Miniature Kit,
c. 1940. 1" tin container holding ink pad and rubber stamp personalized by initials designated by orderer with anchor design. - **$30 $60 $120**

DON-11   DON-12

DON-11. "League For Defense" Kit,
1940. Fleer's Dubble Bubble Gum. Includes pencil autograph of "Don And Red" on card with Navy text plus member card. Each - **$20 $40 $60**

DON-12. "Group Leader" Cello. Button,
1940. Scarce. Fleer's Dubble Bubble Gum. Radio club premium for League For Defense. - **$125 $200 $350**

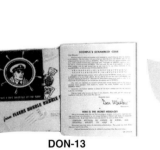

DON-13   DON-14   DON-15

DON-13. "Scorpio's Scrambled Code" Cardboard Sheet With Mailer Envelope,
1940. Scarce. Fleer's Dubble Bubble Gum. Explains code system with secret message to be deciphered.
Mailer - **$15 $25 $40**
Code Sheet - **$20 $40 $60**

DON-14. Catapult Bomber,
1942. Scarce. Post Toasties. - **$100 $200 $400**

DON-15. Golden Torpedo Decoder,
1942. Rare. Post Toasties. - **$500 $1500 $3000**

(front)

DON-16   (back)

DON-16. Undercover Deputy Certificate With Instructions,
1942. Scarce. Post Toasties. Goes with Golden Torpedo Decoder. - **$100 $150 $300**

DON-17   DON-18

DON-17. Don Winslow & Red Pennington Plaster Salt & Pepper Set,
1940s. Store item. From series of character sets. -
$25 $50 $90

DON-18. Coco-Wheats "Tattoo Transfers" With Mailer Envelope,
1956. Transfer sheets picture 22 characters.
Mailer - **$10 $15 $25**
Illustrated Inner Envelope With Two Sheets - **$25 $50 $75**

DON-19

DON-19. Secret Code Booklet with Shirt/Box,
1950s. Set - **$30 $60 $120**

DOROTHY HART, SUNBRITE JR. NURSE CORPS

Junior Nurse Corps was broadcast on CBS radio in 1936-1937 and on the Blue network in 1937-1938. The series, sponsored by Sunbrite cleanser and Quick Arrow soap flakes, both products of Swift and Company, centered on the activities of teen nursing student Dorothy Hart and her Aunt Jane. The program was aimed at an audience of teenage girls, focusing on the nurse's life and the importance of knowing first aid, as well as on historical events. There were many premiums offered in exchange for Sunbrite and Quick Arrow labels; most of the premiums were nursing-oriented.

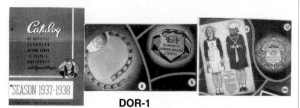

DOR-1

DOR-1. Club Premium Catalogue Fold-Out Sheet,
1937. For 1937-1938 season. - **$35 $60 $100**

DOR-2

DOR-3

DOR-2. Club Newspaper,
September 1937. - **$10 $20 $30**

DOR-3. Indian Princess Sa-ca-ja-wea Photo,
1937. Radio cast member. - **$8 $15 $25**

DOR-4

DOR-5

DOR-4. Cast Member Photo,
1937. - **$8 $15 $25**

DOR-5. Cello. Club Button,
1937. - **$5 $12 $20**

DOR-6

DOR-7

DOR-8

DOR-6. "Sunbrite Junior Nurse Corps" Brass Ring,
1937. - **$30 $60 $125**

DOR-7. "Sunbrite Junior Nurse Corps" Brass Badge,
1937. - **$15 $25 $40**

DOR-8. "Graduate" Highest Rank Brass Badge,
1937. - **$25 $40 $75**

DOR-9

DOR-10

DOR-9. "Sunbrite Junior Nurse Corps" Silvered Brass Bracelet,
1937. - **$20 $60 $100**

DOR-10. Cardboard Ink Blotter,
1937. - **$5 $10 $15**

DUFFY'S TAVERN

"Where the elite meet to eat," *Duffy's Tavern* was the radio creation of actor/director Ed Gardner in 1940. Gardner played Archie, the manager and with Abe Burrows did most of the writing. Shirley Booth originated the role of Miss Duffy, daughter of the never-present proprietor. The program was a 30-minute comedy variety with show-business guests dropping by each week for banter with Archie. It premiered on CBS in March 1941, went to the Blue network in 1942, to NBC in 1944 and was last heard in 1951. Sponsors included Schick, Sanka, Ipana toothpaste and Blatz beer. A 1945 Paramount film was essentially a reprise of the radio show.

DUF-1

DUF-1. "Duffy's First Reader By Archie" Booklet,
1943. Bristol-Myers Co. - **$15 $25 $40**

DUF-2

DUF-2. "Ed (Archie) Gardner" Record Album,
1947. Monitor, an appliance maker. Set of four 78 rpm records of actual broadcasts. - **$10 $25 $50**

DUF-3

DUF-4

DUF-3. Ed Gardner As Archie Fan Photo,
1940s. - **$5 $10 $20**

DUF-4. "Meet 'Archie' Thursday Night" Cello. Button,
1940s. Promotion for Archie's Tavern radio show. -
$10 $20 $35

DUMBO

The enchanting cartoon feature film of a baby circus elephant
with big ears, Walt Disney's Dumbo was released in 1941 to
great popular acclaim. Critics praised it and the public
flocked to see the delightful tale of a flying elephant and his
pal Timothy the Mouse. The musical score won Oscars for
Frank Churchill and Oliver Wallace - most notable were the
Pink Elephants on Parade dream sequence, the crows' song,
and *When I See An Elephant Fly*. There have been a number of Dumbo comic-book presentations, including early giveaways by Weatherbird shoes (1941) and multiple issues of
the *Dumbo Weekly* by Diamond D-X gas stations (1942).
Other premiums and merchandised items followed.

DMB-1

DMB-2

DMB-1. Song Book,
1941. Various sponsors. - **$10 $25 $40**

DMB-2. "The Gossipy Elephants" Glass Tumbler,
1941. Probably held dairy product. Set of six.
Each - **$35 $65 $100**

DMB-3

DMB-4

DMB-3. Dumbo Cloth Beanie,
1941. Probable premium. - **$100 $200 $300**

DMB-4. "Dumbo Song Book" 2-1/4" Litho. Button,
1941. Various sponsors. - **$40 $80 $125**

DMB-5

DMB-6

**DMB-5. "The Adventures Of Walt Disney's Dumbo"
Binder Folder With Issues,**
1942. Diamond D-X Gasoline. Folder for 16 "Dumbo Weekly"
four-page color comics. Folder - **$35 $100 $240**
First Issue - **$40 $120 $280**
Other Issues - **$15 $40 $90**

DMB-6. D-X Gasoline Mask,
1942. Rare. - **$30 $60 $120**

DMB-7

DMB-8

DMB-7. "D-X" Gasoline Station Cello. Button,
1942. - **$20 $30 $60**

DMB-8. "D-X Dumbo Club" Member Card,
1942. Diamond D-X Gasoline. Card includes chart to mark
off first 16 copies of "Dumbo Weekly" obtained plus signature
line for adult sponsor pledging a trial purchase of D-X products. - **$15 $40 $75**

DMB-9

DMB-9. Cardboard Bookmark,
1940s. Heath Publishing Co. - **$20 $40 $60**

THE EAGLE

The first appearance of this patriotic hero was in issue #1 of *Science Comics* in February 1940. He then showed up in issue #8 of *Weird Comics*; in four issues of his own book, *The Eagle*, in 1941-1942; and in a second *Eagle* series of two issues in early 1945. The 1941-1942 membership club for fans was known as American Eagle Defenders.

EAG-1

EAG-1. Member's Cello. Button,
1942. Scarce. - **$100 $375 $1000**

EDDIE CANTOR

Over a span of more than 50 years in show business, Eddie Cantor (1892-1964) went from singing waiter to radio super-star. Cantor juggled, sang, played in blackface in vaudeville and on the stage, made movies, hosted television series and toured Europe, but it was on the radio in the 1930s that the banjo-eyed comic achieved his greatest success. He pre-miered on the comedy-variety *Chase & Sanborn Hour* on NBC in September 1931 and during the next 20 years in vari-ous shows, mainly on NBC, he had a succession of major sponsors: Pebeco toothpaste (1935-1936), Texaco gasoline (1936-1938), Camel cigarettes (1938-1939), Sal Hepatica laxative (1940-1946), Pabst beer (1946-1949) and Philip Morris cigarettes (1951-1952). The manic comic often joked about his wife, Ida, and their five daughters, introduced many young performers and featured such accented characters as the Mad Russian and Parkyakarkas. On television he hosted *The Colgate Comedy Hour* (NBC, 1950-1954) and the *Eddie Cantor Comedy Theatre* (syndicated, 1954-1955).

EDD-1

EDD-1. "Eddie Cantor's Picture Book",
1933. Chase & Sanborn Coffee. - **$3 $8 $15**

EDD-2

EDD-3

EDD-2. Ink Blotter,
1934. Various advertisers. - **$5 $8 $12**

EDD-3. Calendar Postcard,
1934. Various advertisers. - **$5 $10 $15**

EDD-4

EDD-5

EDD-4. Magic Club Book And Trick,
1935. Pebeco Milk of Magnesia. Trick includes 12 cards and two instruction sheets. Book - **$10 $20 $35**
Trick Packet - **$5 $10 $20**

EDD-5. "Eddie Cantor Magic Club" Enameled Brass Club Badge,
1935. Pebeco toothpaste. - **$15 $40 $65**

EDD-6

EDD-7

EDD-8

EDD-6. Jokes Booklet,
1936. Pebeco Toothpaste. - **$10 $20 $35**

EDD-7. Pebeco Toothpaste 12x19" Paper Store Sign,
c. 1936. - **$40 $65 $110**

EDD-8. "Eddie Cantor For President" Litho. Button,
1948. - **$8 $12 $25**

ED WYNN

Ed Wynn (1886-1966) came to radio after a long career as a headliner in vaudeville and on Broadway. He was reluctant to try radio but he successfully made the transition from the visual comedy of his stage character, *The Perfect Fool*, to his radio persona, *The Fire Chief*, sponsored by Texaco "Fire Chief" gasoline, on NBC from 1932 to 1935. Wynn had several other radio shows in the 1930s and a brief run on *Happy Island* in 1944-1945 for Borden's milk, did comedy variety shows on television in 1949-1950 and 1958-1959 and appeared in a number of dramatic roles on television in the 1950s and 1960s.

EDW-1   EDW-2

EDW-1. Texaco Fire Chief Cardboard Mask,
c. 1933. - **$20 $60 $120**

EDW-2. Wood Jointed Figure,
c. 1935. Store item. - **$40 $75 $125**

 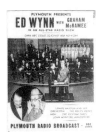

EDW-3   EDW-4

EDW-3. "The Grab Bag" Movie Promotion,
1930s. Cloth bag holding 10 paper figures based on movie "The Perfect Fool". - **$40 $75 $125**

EDW-4. "All Star Radio Show-Plymouth Radio Broadcast" Folder,
1930s. Plymouth Motors. - **$12 $20 $30**

ELLERY QUEEN

Sophisticated detective and mystery writer Ellery Queen was the hero of a number of popular novels written by Frederic Dannay and Manfred Lee. He had several incarnations on radio, beginning with Hugh Marlowe in *The Adventures of Ellery Queen* on CBS in 1939 and ending on ABC in 1948. Sponsors included Gulf Oil, Bromo-Seltzer and Anacin. Live-action TV series appeared on DuMont and ABC from 1950 to 1952 and on NBC 1958-1959 and 1975-1976. Queen's first comic book appearance was in *Crackajack Funnies* #23 in May 1940 and he had his own book in the late 1940s and early 1950s. A number of second-feature Ellery Queen films were released between 1935 and 1952, most starring Ralph Bellamy or William Gargan as the gentleman detective.

ELL-1

ELL-2

ELL-1. "Ellery Queen Club Member" Cello. Button,
c. 1939. - **$50 $120 $200**

ELL-2. "The Adventure Of The Last Man Club" BTLB,
1940. Store item. Whitman #1406. - **$15 $30 $50**

ELSIE THE COW

In the late 1930s the Borden Company ran a series of advertisements for its milk featuring a herd of cartoon cows. One - dubbed Elsie - became a star at the 1939 New York World's Fair when visitors to the Borden exhibit insisted on knowing which of the cows there was Elsie. Borden put Elsie to work during World War II touring the country to sell war bonds and promote its milk. Contests to name Elsie's calf in 1947 and twins in 1957 brought overwhelming public responses. Elsie is still appearing in Borden advertising and in bovine appearances around the country. Merchandising has included giveaway comic books, fun activity books and a wide variety of glass and ceramic items related to food and drink such as bowls, glasses and mugs.

ELS-1

ELS-2

ELS-1. Brass 2-1/4" Badge,
c. 1939. Likely issued during 1939 New York World's Fair. - **$15 $30 $65**

ELS-2. Wood Pull Toy,
1944. Store item by Wood Commodities Corp.
Boxed - **$100 $200 $350**
Loose - **$50 $100 $200**

ELS-3

ELS-4

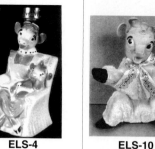

ELS-10

ELS-11

ELS-12

ELS-3. Store Display Poster,
1945. 30x45". - **$20 $40 $75**

ELS-4. Elsie And Baby China Lamp,
c. 1947. Store item. - **$75 $150 $250**

ELS-10. Plush Doll With Rubber Head,
1950s. 15" tall. - **$25 $50 $100**

ELS-11. "Elsie's Fun Book",
1950s. - **$12 $35 $85**

ELS-12. Plastic Ring,
1950s. - **$15 $20 $30**

ELS-5

ELS-6

ELS-7

ELS-5. "Elsie" Ceramic Mug,
1940s. - **$15 $30 $50**

ELS-6. "Beulah" Ceramic Mug,
1940s. - **$10 $20 $30**

ELS-7. "Borden's" Glass Tumbler,
1940s. - **$15 $25 $40**

ELS-13

ELS-14

ELS-13. "A Trip Through Space" Booklet,
1950s. - **$10 $30 $60**

ELS-14. Ceramic Cookie Jar,
c. 1950s. - **$100 $150 $200**

ELS-8

ELS-9

ELS-8. Elsie Ceramic Mug,
1950s. - **$10 $20 $35**

ELS-9. Elsie Diecut Sign,
1950s. - **$50 $100 $200**

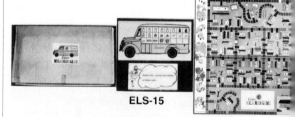

ELS-15

ELS-15. "Elsie's Milkman Game",
1963. - **$25 $40 $70**

ELS-16

ELS-16. "Elsie The Borden Cow" Litho. Button,
1960s. - **$5 $10 $18**

ELVIS PRESLEY

Elvis Presley was born in a two-room house in Tupelo, Mississippi, in 1935. He died in his Memphis, Tennessee, mansion in 1977 with an estate valued at more than $30 million. In his lifetime - and since his death - the rock 'n' roll legend spawned a merchandising cornucopia that has yet to subside. The national mania exploded in 1956 when Presley appeared on *The Ed Sullivan Show* and items from that period generate great collector interest. But the King lives on: in addition to frequent Elvis sightings at shopping malls and county fairs, Elvis Presley Enterprises continues to license countless memorial and commemorative items...still takin' care of business.

ELV-1   **ELV-2**   **ELV-3**

ELV-1. "R.C.A. Records" National Fan Club Button,
1956. Black on pink. Litho. Variety - **$50 $75 $150**
Scarcer Cello. Variety - **$75 $150 $225**

ELV-2. Color Photo 3" Cello. Button,
1956. Vendor Item. - **$20 $40 $75**

ELV-3. "TV Guide", September 8,
1956. Issue has first part of three-part article. -
$35 $75 $150

ELV-5

ELV-4

ELV-4. Jeans Tag,
1956. Elvis Presley Enterprises store item. - **$25 $75 $125**

ELV-5. Song Title T-Shirt,
1956. Store item. Elvis Presley Enterprises copyright. -
$75 $175 $250

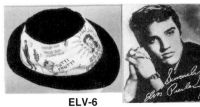

ELV-6

ELV-6. Fabric Hat,
1956. Store item by Magnet Hat & Cap Corp.
With Tag - **$60 $125 $200**
No Tag - **$40 $80 $125**

ELV-7

ELV-7. Brass Lipstick Tube,
1956. Store item by Teen-Ager Lipstick Corp. Available in six colors. - **$50 $75 $125**

ELV-8   **ELV-9**   **ELV-10**

ELV-8. Glass Tumbler,
1956. Store item. Copyright Elvis Presley Enterprises. -
$50 $80 $140

ELV-9. "Elvis Presley For President" Litho. Tin Tab,
1956. - **$20 $40 $75**

ELV-10. "Love Me Tender" Paper Photo,
1956. Theater hand-out. - **$5 $15 $25**

ELV-11

ELV-12

ELV-11. "Love Me Tender" Litho. Button,
1956. Elvis Presley Enterprises. From set of 10 with pictures, record titles or slogans. Each - **$5 $12 $20**

ELV-12. Metal Charm Bracelet,
1956. Store item. Elvis Presley Enterprises copyright. -
$35 $60 $90

ELV-13   **ELV-14**   **ELV-15**

ELV-13. Plastic Picture Frame Charm,
c. 1956. Vending machine item. - **$10 $25 $50**

ELV-14. Metal Ring With Photo Under Plastic Dome,
c. 1956. Elvis Presley Enterprises store item. Two different color photos. Each - **$50 $100 $200**

ELV-15. Gold Record Litho. Button,
c. 1956. Known with seven different record titles. Each - **$15 $25 $50**

ELV-16

ELV-17

ELV-16. "Elvis Presley Photo Folio",
1957. Elvis Presley Enterprises. From concert tour. - **$20 $40 $75**

ELV-17. "King Creole" Wallet Card,
1958. Movie promotion. - **$25 $50 $90**

ELV-18

ELV-18. Christmas Postcard,
1959. - **$15 $25 $50**

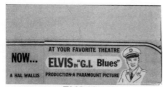

ELV-19

ELV-19. "G.I. Blues" Paper Army Hat,
1960. Advertises movie and record album. - **$15 $35 $75**

ELV-20

ELV-20. "Blue Hawaii" Movie Promotion Lei,
1961. Tissue paper lei with 5" cardboard disk. - **$25 $50 $100**

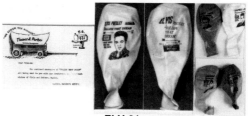

ELV-21

ELV-21. "Follow That Dream" Movie Balloons With Promotion Letter,
1962. Rubber balloons with cover form letter from Thomas A. Parker, Elvis' manager. Letter - **$15 $25 $50**
Each Balloon - **$3 $8 $15**

ELV-22

ELV-23

ELV-22. Movie Coloring Contest Sheet,
1962. Paramount Pictures for local stores. Promotion for "Girls! Girls! Girls!" movie. - **$20 $40 $75**

ELV-23. Girls! Girls! Girls! Album Insert,
1963. - **$10 $20 $30**

ELV-24

ELV-25

ELV-24. Fan Club Booklet,
1967. - **$10 $20 $35**

ELV-25. "Elvis' Gold Car On Tour" RCA Postcard,
1960s. - **$8 $12 $20**

FAWCETT COMICS

Fawcett Publications began with *Capt. Billy's Whiz Bang*, a digest-sized somewhat bawdy magazine of the 1920s. The mix of girlie photos, stories, and cartoons (later Donald Duck artist Carl Barks being a regular contributor) was successful enough that Fawcett would expand into a major magazine publisher in the 1930s. Titles included *True Confessions, Motion Picture,*and *Mechanix Illustrated*.

Late in 1939 Roscoe Fawcett announced the company's entry into the comic book field with *Whiz Comics*, dated February, 1940. Captain Marvel was the lead feature, ably drawn by C.C. Beck and his assistants Pete Costanza and Kurt Schaffenberger. The success of Captain Marvel spawned a number of spin-offs including Captain Marvel Jr., Mary Marvel, and Hoppy the Marvel Bunny.

By 1943 Fawcett was also publishing *Captain Midnight, Bulletman, Spy Smasher*, and *Don Winslow*. In the later 1940s the line was expanded to westerns (including *Hopalong Cassidy, Tom Mix Western*, and *Gabby Hayes Western*) as well as romance, humor, sports, horror, and science fiction titles. Fawcett had become a major comic book publisher, with a yearly circulation of 50 million copies in the mid 1940s which grew to over 70 million by 1949. A 1941 DC Comics lawsuit alleging Captain Marvel was an imitation of Superman was settled in DC's favor in 1953. This, combined with lost sales due to the popularity of TV, brought an end to the Fawcett comic book empire. They re-entered the field with *Dennis the Menace* in 1958 and published that title until 1980.

FAW-1

FAW-1. "American Alphabet" Song Book,
1944. Patriotism song pages with cover art of Hoppy the Marvel Bunny and other Fawcett characters. - **$15 $35 $50**

FAW-2

FAW-2. "Funny Animals Acrobats" Punch-Out,
1944. Store item and probable club issue.
Unpunched - **$35 $50 $75**

FAW-3   FAW-4

FAW-3. "Tippy Toy" Punch-Out Sheet With Envelope,
1945. Store item and club premium. For assembly of 3-D rocker toy featuring Hoppy the Marvel Bunny and Millie Bunny. Unused - **$5 $10 $15**

FAW-4. "Comic Stamps" Perforated Sheet,
c. 1945. Pictures 24 Fawcett comic book characters. - **$15 $35 $60**

FAW-5

FAW-5. "Funny Animals Coloring Book",
1946. Store item by Abbott Publishing Co. Features Hoppy the Marvel Bunny and other Fawcett characters. - **$25 $40 $65**

FAW-6

FAW-6. "Funny Animal Paint Books" With Box,
c. 1946. Store item by Abbott Publishing Co. Set of six including Hoppy the Marvel Bunny and five other Fawcett animals. Boxed - **$50 $90 $150**
Hoppy Book - **$10 $25 $50**
Others Each - **$5 $10 $15**

FAW-7

FAW-7. Coco-Wheats "Tattoo Transfers" Kit With Mailer Envelope,
1956. Transfer sheets picture 22 Fawcett characters.
Mailer - **$10 $15 $25**
Illustrated Inner Envelope With Two Sheets - **$25 $50 $75**

FELIX THE CAT

Felix has been called one of the great creations of comic art...a supercat...an animation superstar...the Charlie Chaplin of cartoon characters. Alienated, alone, a heroic and resourceful battler against fate, Felix was created by cartoonists Otto Messmer and Pat Sullivan shortly after World War I. His first animated appearance came in 1919 and by the mid-1920s he was an international star, most notably in England. Sullivan was quick to license the character and many early merchandised items were produced. A Sunday comic strip from King Features Syndicate debuted in August 1923 and a daily strip followed in May 1927. Comic book appearances began in the 1930s and Felix has had his own books from the 1940s into the 1990s. Hundreds of the silent shorts were distributed to television in 1953 by Pathe Films. New color episodes, produced for television by the Joe Oriolo Studios, appeared in 1960. Felix now had a magic bag of tricks to rely on in place of his talented and multifunctional tail.

FLX-1

FLX-1. English Cream Toffee Candy Tin,
c. 1920s. Scarce. Store item. - **$300 $800 $2000**

FLX-2   **FLX-3**   **FLX-4**

FLX-2. Tin Pull Toy,
1930s. Store item by Nifty Toys. - **$150 $300 $600**

FLX-3. "Herald & Examiner" Litho. Button,
1930s. Chicago newspaper. From "30 Comics" series featuring various characters. - **$10 $20 $40**

FLX-4. "Warner Bros. State" Theater Cello. Button,
1930s. Obvious Felix image although "Krazy Kat Klub" designation. - **$30 $75 $150**

FLX-5   **FLX-6**   **FLX-7**

FLX-5. "Evening Ledger Comics" Cello. Button,
1930s. Philadelphia newspaper. From set of 14 various characters. - **$60 $150 $300**

FLX-6. Aviation Shield Badge,
1940s. Scarce. - **$50 $90 $175**

FLX-7. "Felix The Cat" Litho. Button,
1950s. From set of various King Features Syndicate characters. - **$10 $20 $30**

FLX-8

FLX-8. "Felix The Cat Candy And Toy" Product Box,
1960. Phoenix Candy Co. - **$20 $50 $100**

FIBBER McGEE AND MOLLY

Jim and Marian Jordan were veterans of small-time vaudeville before they ventured into radio comedy in Chicago, first as The O'Henry Twins in 1924, then as The Smith Family in 1925, as The Air Scouts in 1927 and in Smackout from 1931 to 1935. Finally along with writer Don Quinn, they created Fibber McGee and Molly for Johnson's Wax. The show premiered on the NBC Blue network in April 1935 and developed into one of the most popular radio comedies of all time.

From their home at 79 Wistful Vista, McGee - the blundering windbag - and Molly - his long-suffering, forgiving wife presided over one domestic disaster after another. Listeners waited each week for Fibber to open his closet door, whereupon the stacked contents would crash to the floor. The show featured a number of regular supporting characters, their neighbor Gildersleeve, Beulah the maid, henpecked Wallace Wimple, the Old Timer, Mayor La Trivia and Myrt the telephone operator whose voice was never heard.

After Johnson's Wax dropped the show in 1950, Pet milk sponsored it until 1952, then Reynolds Aluminum until 1953 when the half-hour format was replaced by a 15-minute weekday series that ran until 1957. There was a comic book in 1949, the Jordans made some movies in the 1940s and a television series had a brief run on NBC in 1959-1960 but nothing equaled the McGee success on radio.

FIB-1   **FIB-2**   **FIB-3**

FIB-1. Cast Photo,
. 1935. Shown at "NBC" microphone. - $15 $30 $45

FIB-2. Fibber Cello. Spinner Top On Wood Peg,
936. Scarce. Johnson's Wax Polishes. - $75 $200 $500

FIB-3. Molly Cello. Spinner Top With Wood Peg,
936. Scarce. Johnson's Wax Polishes. - $60 $175 $450

FIB-4

FIB-5

FIB-4. "Johnson Glo-Coat Floor Polish" 8x14" Cardboard
Display Sign ,
937. - $50 $150 $250

FIB-5. Cardboard 9x15" Store Display Sign,
. 1937. Designed for holding sample can of Johnson's
Wax. - $75 $150 $300

FIB-6

FIB-7

FIB-6. Cardboard 11x16" Store Display Sign,
1937. Designed for holding sample can of Johnson's
Wax. - $60 $125 $250

FIB-7. Cast Photo,
930s. - $15 $30 $50

FIB-8

FIB-9

FIB-8. Cardboard Advertising Blotter,
930s. Prudential Insurance. - $15 $30 $50

FIB-9. Fan Photo,
1940s. - $15 $30 $50

FLASH GORDON

Flash Gordon first blasted into space in January 1934 in a Sunday comic strip created by Alex Raymond for King Features. Since then, along with his companions Dale Arden and Dr. Zarkov, Flash has done violent battle with Ming the Merciless on the planet Mongo and with an assortment of interplanetary menaces in every possible medium. The Sunday strip, an immediate success, generated many comic book appearances - the first in *King Comics* #1 of April 1936; a radio series on the Mutual network in 1935-1936; an original novel published in 1936; three chapter plays for Universal starring Buster Crabbe between 1936 and 1940; a daily comic strip that ran from 1940 to 1944 and was revived in 1951; a syndicated live-action television series in 1953-1954; hardback reprints of early strips in 1967 and 1971; a Filmation animated cartoon for NBC in 1979-1980 and a lavish Technicolor movie in 1980. "Steady, Dale!"

FGR-1   FGR-2

FGR-3

FGR-1. "Flash Gordon" Litho. Button,
1934. From set of seven showing various King Features
Syndicate characters. - $25 $50 $85

FGR-2. "Dale Arden" Litho. Button,
1934. From set of seven showing various King Features
Syndicate characters. - $25 $50 $85

FGR-3. Buster Crabbe Dixie Ice Cream Lid,
1936. - $12 $20 $40

FGR-4

FGR-4. "Flash Gordon Strange Adventure Magazine"
Vol. 1 #1,
1936. - $200 $400 $750

FGR-5   FGR-6

FGR-5. "Flash Gordon Adventure Club" Cello. Button,
1938. Rare. Universal Pictures. For 12-chapter movie serial "Flash Gordon Conquers The Universe" starring Buster Crabbe and Carol Hughes, both pictured. - **$250 $600 $1000**

FGR-6. Movie Serial Club Member Card,
c. 1938. Scarce. Buster Crabbe pictured as Flash Gordon. - **$200 $350 $750**

FGR-7

FGR-8

FGR-7. "Chicago Herald And Examiner" Club Litho. Button,
1930s. - **$75 $125 $250**

FGR-8. "World Battle Fronts" World War II Folder Map,
1943. Macy's department store "Flash Gordon Headquarters". Map opens to 20x27" sheet picturing global areas on both sides. - **$40 $75 $140**

FGR-9

FGR-10

FGR-9. "S.F. Call-Bulletin" Cardboard Disk,
c. 1940s. San Francisco newspaper. From series of contest disks, match number to win prize. - **$10 $25 $40**

FGR-10. "Flash Gordon Comics",
1951. Gordon Bread Give-Away. Two issues of strip reprints. Each - **$2 $5 $10**

FGR-11

FGR-12

FGR-11. "March Of Comics No. 133" Booklet,
1955. Poll-Parrot Shoes. From series by K.K. Publications. - **$12 $35 $80**

FGR-12. "Puck" 10x10" Paper Store Sign,
1950s. Puck The Comic Weekly and Sunday Comics. From series for drugstore use picturing various King Features characters. - **$25 $60 $100**

FGR-13

FGR-13. "Puck" 15x40" Paper Store Sign,
1950s. Puck The Comic Weekly and Sunday Comics. For drugstore use picturing King Features characters. - **$35 $75 $125**

FGR-14

FGR-15

FGR-14. Dale Arden Litho. Button,
1960s. From set of King Features characters marked only by copyright symbol. - **$10 $20 $35**

FGR-15. Candy Boxes,
1978. Phoenix Candy Co. Set of eight. Each - **$5 $10 $25**

THE FLASH

The fastest man alive, a superhero of the golden age of comic books, made his first appearance in *Flash Comics #* of January 1940. The book was discontinued in 1949 after 104 issues and was revived with issue #105 in March 195. The speedster also appeared in *All-Flash* comics from 194 to 1948 and showed up in early issues of *All-Star Comic* and *Comic Cavalcade* and in various DC Comics collection He was revived in *Showcase* #4 of October 1956. Among the colorful villains confronted by The Flash were The Fiddle and his magic Stradivarius, Mirror Master and Captain Col each with special evil powers. A 1946 giveaway comic boo was distributed taped to boxes of Wheaties and a comic club offered a membership card and button as premiums.

FLA-1

FLA-2

LA-1. "The Flash/Fastest Man Alive" Litho. Button, 943. Rare. Flash Comics. Only 1000 produced. - 300 $1000 $2800

LA-2. "Flash Comics" Wheaties Purchase Comic Book, 946. As taped to two-box purchase, highest grade is fine. ood - $300
ne - $900

THE FLINTSTONES

anna-Barbera's Flintstones started life as the first adult rime-time television cartoon, went on to become the longest inning such animated series in TV history and spawned umerous reruns, specials, spinoffs and adaptations - as well s a merchandising bonanza. The Flintstones premiered on BC in September 1960 and ran uninterrupted for six years, as rebroadcast on NBC Saturday mornings from 1967 to 70 and has been around in one form or another ever nce. A major film starring John Goodman was released in 94.

ed and Wilma Flintstone and their friends Barney and Betty ubble are a prehistoric parody of the Kramdens and ortons of The Honeymooners, complete with marital bicker- g, get-rich-quick schemes, bowling nights out and lodge embership. As added attractions, Dino, their pet dinosaur, as joined in 1963 by a baby daughter, Pebbles and by the ubbles' adopted son, Bamm-Bamm. The kids spun off on eir own show in 1971.

omic book appearances began in 1961 and continued into e 1990s. The characters have been merchandised exten- vely, with several thousand tie-in items licensed. Post's ebbles cereal and Flintstones chewable vitamins were pro- otional successes. "Yabba dabba doo!"

FLN-1

FLN-2

.N-1. "Stone Age Candy" Boxes,
62. Store item. Each - $5 $10 $15

.N-2. "March Of Comics" #243,
63. Various retail sponsors. - $10 $25 $55

FLN-3

FLN-3. 1964-1965 New York World's Fair Comic Book, 1964. Officially licensed souvenir published by JW Books With Hanna-Barbera copyright. - $5 $15 $40

FLN-4

FLN-5

FLN-4. "History Of Bedrock" 23x28" Poster,
1970. Miles Laboratories. - $25 $45 $75

FLN-5. Flintstone Jewelry Display With 36 Character Rings,
1972. Store item by Cartoon Celebrities Inc.
Complete - $150 $250 $350
Each Ring - $3 $5 $8

FLN-6

FLN-7

FLN-6. Fred Flintstone "Powell Valves" Pencil Eraser,
1972. Wm. Powell Co. - $15 $30 $50

FLN-7. Vending Machine Litho. Button Set,
1973. Set of 12, various color combinations.
Each - $3 $5 $15

FLN-8

FLN-8. Litho. Buttons,
1973. Store item. Set of 10. Each - $5 $10 $15

FLN-10

FLN-9

FLN-9. Vending Machine Header Card,
c. 1970s. Includes generic rings, generic Dino figure and rubber Flintstones figures. Complete - **$50**

FLN-10. "Flintstick" Plastic/Metal Miniature Cigarette Lighter,
c. 1970s. Flintstones Multiple Vitamins. - **$50 $100 $150**

FLN-11

FLN-11. Flintstones Brand Multiple Vitamins Plastic Mugs,
1970s. Each - **$5 $8 $15**

FLN-12

FLN-12. "Post" Plastic Cereal Box Banks,
1984. Cocoa Pebbles and Fruity Pebbles.
Each - **$8 $12 $20**

FLN-13

FLN-13. Fred & Barney Ceramic Figurines,
1990. Post Cereals. Boxed - **$15 $30 $50**
Loose Pair - **$5 $15 $25**

FLYING ACES CLUB

One of the many 1930s aviation-themed clubs inspired in part by the accomplishment of Charles Lindbergh. Sponsored by *Flying Aces Magazine*, most premiums carry the initials "FAC."

FAC-1

FAC-2

FAC-1. Club Membership Card,
1932. - **$10 $25 $50**

FAC-2. Gold Cadet Wings,
1932. - **$30 $60 $90**

FAC-3

FAC-3. "Cadet/FAC" Brass Wings Rank Badge,
1932. Propeller on top of wings.
Silver version. - **$15 $30 $50**
Gold version - **$30 $60 $90**

FAC-4

FAC-4. "Pilot/FAC" Silvered Brass Wings Badge,
1932. Propeller on top of wings.
Silver version. - **$10 $20 $30**
Gold version - **$30 $60 $90**

FAC-5

FAC-6

FAC-5. Silver Pilot Wings,
1932. - **$30 $60 $90**

FAC-6. "Ace/FAC" Star Badge,
1932. Scarce. - **$35 $70 $140**

FAC-7

AC-7. "Flying Aces" Silvered Brass Bracelet,
932. Link bands with top plate in wing and propeller design. - **$20 $45 $100**

FAC-9

FAC-8

AC-8. "F.A.C. Distinguished Service Medal" Brass edal With Ribbon ,
932. Rare. Back inscription "Awarded By Flying Aces ub". - **$50 $100 $200**

AC-9. FAC Propeller Pins,
932. Rare. For placement on "Service Medal" ribbon. ach - **$10 $20 $40**

FAC-10

AC-10. "FAC" Stitched Fabric Wings Patch,
932. Scarce. Flying Aces magazine. - **$20 $50 $75**

THE FLYING FAMILY

his children's adventure program aired briefly on NBC in 932-1933. The program dramatized the true-life story of olonel George Hutchinson, his wife Blanche, and their aughters Kathryn and Janet. Accompanied by Sunshine, eir lion cub mascot, the flying family found adventure in all arts of the country. Cocomalt sponsored the series, and oung listeners could obtain their Flight Commander wings ? drinking Cocomalt for at least 30 days and mailing in a atement witnessed and signed by a parent.

FLY-1

.Y-1. Puzzle, Flight Commander Folder And Envelope,
*32. Complete - **$10 $15 $25**

FLY-2

FLY-3

FLY-2. "Flight Commander/Flying Cubs" Brass Wings Rank Badge,
1932. Highest rank depicting tiger head. - **$15 $30 $50**

FLY-3. "Flying Cubs" Brass Wings Medal,
1932. Depicts tiger head. - **$15 $25 $40**

FLY-5

FLY-4

FLY-4. Family Picture Wheaties Box Back,
c. 1932. - **$10 $20 $30**

FLY-5. "Cub" Brass Wings Pin,
c. 1932. Association with this program is uncertain. - **$10 $30 $50**

FLY-6

FLY-6. "Cub" Silvered Brass Lapel Stud,
c. 1932. Association with this program is uncertain. - **$10 $30 $50**

FOODINI

They started out in 1948 as the bumbling villains of the *Lucky Pup* series on CBS but Foodini and his dimwit accomplice Pinhead eventually took over the show and by 1951 were starring in their own series, *Foodini the Great*, on ABC. The hand puppets, created by Hope and Morey Bunin, were fated never to accomplish their swindling schemes, defeated by the Pup's pal Jolo the clown as well as by their own ineptitude. Sponsors of the two series (1948-1951) included Ipana toothpaste, Good and Plenty candy, Sundial shoes and Bristol-Myers. Licensed items are normally copyrighted R. P. Cox.

FOO-1

FOO-1. Paper Portraits,
c. 1948. Scarce. CBS-TV. Set of four: Doris Brown with Lucky Pup, Foodini, Pinhead, Jolo. Each - **$15 $25 $35**

FOO-2

FOO-2. Plastic Microscope With Instructions,
1950. Ipana Toothpaste. Includes six slides for microscope.
Instruction Folder - **$10 $15 $25**
Microscope - **$15 $30 $50**
Slides Each - **$1 $3 $5**

FOO-3

FOO-4

FOO-5

FOO-3. Cardboard Mask,
c. 1950. Scarce. Punch-out from unknown source. -
$50 $150 $250

FOO-4. "Foodini" As Magician Dexterity Puzzle,
1951. Plastic over tin frame puzzle. - **$20 $50 $75**

FOO-5. "Jolo" Juggling Dexterity Puzzle,
1951. Plastic over tin frame puzzle. - **$20 $50 $75**

FOO-6

FOO-7

FOO-6. "Pinhead" Dexterity Puzzle,
1951. Plastic over tin frame puzzle. - **$20 $50 $75**

FOO-7. Cardboard Pop Gun,
c. 1951. Sundial Bonnie Laddie Shoes. - **$20 $40 $75**

FOO-8

FOO-8. "Television Studio" Cardboard Kit With Mailer,
c. 1951. Sundial Bonnie Laddie Shoes. Includes stage, figures and accessories. Near Mint In Mailer - **$200**

FOXY GRANDPA

Cartoonist C. E. Schultze created his *Foxy Grandpa* comic
strip for the Sunday New York Herald in 1900. The strip,
which showed Grandpa consistently outwitting a pair of
young tormentors, was an instant success with readers, but
its popularity waned over the years. It moved to the New
York American in 1902, then to the New York Press, where it
ran until 1918. A series of nature tales, *Foxy Grandpa
Stories*, ran in newspapers during the 1920s. Hardcover
reprints of the strip were published in the early years and a
musical comedy based on the strip opened on Broadway in
1902. Schultze typically signed his drawings Bunny, with an
appropriate sketch.

FOX-1

FOX-2

FOX-1. Comic Strip Announcement 15x20" Paper Poster,
1902. New York Sunday Journal. - **$75 $150 $250**

**FOX-2. "Foxy Grandpa's Grocery Store" Cut-Out
Supplement,**
1902. New York American & Journal newspaper.
Uncut - **$25 $50 $75**

FOX-3

FOX-4

FOX-3. "Six Months In New York" Cello. Button,
1902. For theater version based on comic strip. -
$20 $35 $65

FOX-4. "Foxy Grandpa" Cello. Button,
c. 1902. Hearst's Chicago American. Promotes start of comic
strip by that newspaper. - **$15 $25 $50**

FOX-5

FOX-5. Foxy Grandpa Song Sheet,
c. 1902. Scarce. Newspaper supplement. - **$20 $60 $120**

FOX-6

FOX-7

OX-6. Foxy Grandpa Song Sheet,
1902. Scarce. Newspaper supplement. - **$20 $60 $120**

OX-7. "Foxy Grandpa/Chicago American" Diecut White
etal Stickpin,
1902. Lightly tinted, depicts him and both boys. -
5 $40 $60

FOX-8

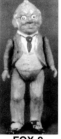
FOX-9

FOX-10

)X-8. Bisque Figure,
1905. Store item. - **$40 $75 $125**

)X-9. Composition Figure,
1905. Store item. Jointed arms and legs. - **$50 $80 $150**

)X-10. Flocked Composition Candy Container,
1905. Store item. - **$75 $150 $225**

FRANK BUCK

imal hunter and trapper Frank Buck (1884-1950) achieved
ernational fame after World War I as a jungle explorer
ose claim that he never intentionally harmed a wild animal
1 to his motto "Bring 'Em Back Alive." Buck went around
e world more than a dozen times collecting animals, giving
:tures, making movies and writing magazine articles and
oks, and at one point owned the world's largest private zoo
Amityville, New York. He appeared as himself in two brief
lio series: on NBC in 1932 sponsored by A. C. Gilbert toys
d on the Blue network in 1934 sponsored by Pepsodent
othpaste. Buck and his animals were featured at the 1933-
34 Century of Progress Exposition in Chicago and the
39-1940 New York World's Fair. A 1932 documentary film
owed him through the Malay jungles as he collected vari-
s animals and Buck played an adventurer in Columbia
:tures' first chapter play, Jungle Menace, in 1937. CBS-TV
ed a Bring 'Em Back Alive fiction series in 1982-1983 star-
g Bruce Boxleitner as the legendary hunter.

FRB-1

FRB-2

FRB-1. A.C. Gilbert Christmas Ad Photo,
1932. Frank Buck inscription "I Hope You Get An Erector Set
For Christmas". - **$20 $40 $60**

FRB-2. Club Manual,
1934. Pepsodent toothpaste. - **$35 $80 $150**

FRB-3

FRB-4

FRB-5

FRB-3. "A Century Of Progress" Chicago World's Fair
Litho. Button,
1934. From exhibit, dated for second year of fair. -
$35 $75 $125

FRB-4. "Adventurers Club-Member" Brass Button,
1934. Pepsodent toothpaste. - **$5 $12 $25**

FRB-5. "Frank Buck" Brass Lucky Piece,
1934. Pepsodent toothpaste. Back pictures leopard head
with inscription "Tidak Hilang Berani". Copy of Hindu hunter's
charm carried by Ali, Frank Buck's Number 1 Boy. -
$20 $50 $120

FRB-6

FRB-7

FRB-6. "Adventurers Club" Fabric Neckerchief,
1934. Pepsodent toothpaste. - **$40 $80 $150**

FRB-7. "Jungle Camp" Metal Letter Opener/Bookmark,
1939. From exhibit at New York World's Fair. - **$25 $50 $90**

FRB-8

FRB-9

FRB-10

FRB-8. "Frank Buck's Jungle Camp" Cello. Button,
1939. From exhibit at 1939-1940 New York World's Fair. - **$15 $30 $50**

FRB-9. "Bring 'Em Back Alive" Ivory Initial Ring,
1939. Ivory Soap. Brass with personalized initial ivory-colored insert. - **$150 $300 $450**

FRB-10. "Frank Buck's Jungleland" New York World's Fair Brass Ring,
1939. Rare. Tiny "NYWF" initials rather than traditional Frank Buck's Adventurers Club inscription. - **$1200 $3000 $6000**

FRB-11

FRB-11. Cello./Steel Pocketknife,
1939. Ivory Soap. White grips with facsimile signature on one. - **$50 $100 $160**

FRB-12

FRB-12. "Bring 'Em Back Alive" Map And Game 14x22",
1930s. Two versions: premium from "Scott's Emulsion" or store item by "Funland Books & Games". - **$50 $100 $200**

FRB-13

FRB-14

FRB-13. "Frank Buck Explorer's Sun Watch",
1949. Jack Armstrong/Wheaties. - **$20 $35 $65**

FRB-14. Wheaties Caribbean Cruise Contest And Sun Watch Leaflets,
1949. Contest Sheet - **$5 $15 $25**
Sun Watch Order Form - **$5 $10 $15**

FRANK MERRIWELL

Dime novels, the forerunner of pulp magazines, became popular in the 1880s. Colorful covers highlighted text stories embellished with daring deeds and the triumph of good over evil. Writer Gilbert Patten, under various pseudonyms, had been doing stories for several years when approached by the large publishing company Street & Smith to come up with a character for their new magazine *Tip Top Library*. Using

"Frank" for frankness, "Merri" for happy disposition and "Wel[l]" for good health, he came up with Frank Merriwell.

Written under the pen name Burt L. Standish, Frank's firs[t] adventure was published on April 18, 1896. Author Patte[n] imbued Frank Merriwell with a Yale education, a sharp min[d], physical fitness, an honest demeanor and a penchant f[or] hard work. Merriwell became an inspiration to boys and gir[ls] nationwide. He was not only a role model, but an imagina[ry] friend they could trust. Patten went on to author 208 Fra[nk] Merriwell books, which sold over 100 million copies.

Merriwell's adventures remained popular well in the 1940s [in] a comic strip, a Big Little Book title, a movie serial and [a] radio program with Lawson Zerbe in the title role. Fra[nk] Merriwell's adventures and personality set the tone for one [of] radio's most popular characters, the next "All-American Boy[,]" Jack Armstrong.

FRM-1

FRM-2

FRM-1. "Frank Merriwell At Yale" BLB,
1935. Store item. Whitman #1121. - **$12 $25 $50**

FRM-2. "Club Member/Follow The Adventures Of Frank Merriwell" Cello . Button,
1936. Scarce. Universal Pictures. For 12-chapter movie ser[i]al "The Adventures Of Frank Merriwell". - **$25 $75 $100**

FRED ALLEN

Fred Allen (1894-1956) was a vaudeville juggler and stand[up] comic who became one of the legendary radio comedians [of] the 1930s and 1940s. From his first show on CBS in 1932 [to] his last on NBC in 1949, hardly a week went by withou[t a] Fred Allen program of one sort or another. Allen wrote [his] own material and his "feud" with Jack Benny was a succes[s]ful running gag from 1936 to 1949. Also memorable w[as] Allen's Alley, a mythical street he developed in 1942, inhab[it]ed by Mrs. Nussbaum, Titus Moody, Ajax Cassidy a[nd] Senator Claghorn. Sponsors over the years included L[ux] bath oil, Hellmann's mayonnaise, Sal Hepatica, Ipana too[th]paste, Texaco gasoline, Tenderleaf tea and Ford autom[o]biles. Allen made a number of television appearances in [the] 1950s on comedy and quiz shows but his biting wit and lit[er]ate humor were better suited to radio.

FRD-1

FRD-2

RD-1. "Town Hall Tonight" Fan Postcard,
937. Radio show title on back. - $10 $15 $25

RD-2. Fred Allen & Portland Hoffa Fan Photo,
1937. Ipana toothpaste and Salhepatica Stomach Relief.
ack names "Town Hall Tonight" radio show. - $8 $15 $30

FRIENDS OF THE PHANTOM

etween 1933 and 1953 Richard Curtis Van Loan - alias the
hantom - solved over 150 crimes in the pages of the pulp
agazine *Phantom Detective*. Created by D.L. Champion
riting under the name Robert Wallace, the Phantom was a
enius of disguise and a physical marvel. During the 1930s,
aders who joined his crime-fighting club would receive a
iends of the Phantom badge.

FPH-1

FPH-2

H-1. "Friends Of The Phantom" Letter And
embership Card,
30s. Phantom Detective magazine.
rd - $50 $125 $200
tter - $50 $100 $150

H-2. "Friends Of The Phantom" Brass Shield Badge,
30s. Phantom Detective magazine. Phantom depicted in
ask and top hat. - $75 $175 $400

FU MANCHU

ster scientist and brilliant prince of evil, Fu Manchu was
eated by novelist Sax Rohmer in 1911. He appeared in a
ies of silent films in the 1920s and in talkies from 1929 to
30 played by Warner Oland, Boris Karloff, Henry Brandon,
ristopher Lee or Peter Sellers. The evil oriental, who was
her avenging the death of his wife and son or out to con-
er or destroy the world, starred in several radio serials: on
e *Collier Hour*, sponsored by Collier's magazine, on the
e network in 1927; on CBS in 1932-1933 sponsored by
mpana Balm and in *The Shadow of Fu Manchu*, a syndi-
ed 1939-1940 serial. A syndicated television series had a
ef run in 1956.

FUM-1

FUM-2

FUM-3

FUM-1. Paper Mask,
1932. Rare. Various theaters. - $50 $100 $150

FUM-2. "Shadow Of Fu Manchu" Radio Promo
Matchbook Cover,
1939. - $10 $20 $35

FUM-3. "The Shadow Of Fu Manchu" Radio Serial Cello.
Button,
1939. - $50 $100 $200

FUM-4

FUM-5

FUM-6

FUM-4. "Drums Of Fu Manchu" Movie Serial Cello.
Button,
1940. Scarce. - $50 $125 $350

FUM-5. "Drums Of Fu Manchu" 41x77" Three-Sheet
Poster,
1940. Republic Pictures. 15-chapter movie serial. -
$200 $400 $750

FUM-6. "Drums Of Fu Manchu" 27x41" Movie Serial
Poster,
1940. Republic Pictures. - $200 $400 $600

FUM-7

FUM-7. "Drums Of Fu Manchu" 14x22" Window Card,
1940. Republic Pictures. - $30 $50 $75

FURY

Fury was a black stallion and the star attraction on NBC-TV's
Saturday morning lineup from 1955 to 1966. His human co-
stars in this extremely popular series were Bobby Diamond
as a young orphan and Peter Graves as the rancher who
adopted the boy and gave him the horse as a means of
teaching him responsibility. The show received a number of
awards from various civic and service groups for its non-vio-

lent handling of problems of right and wrong. Post cereals was an early sponsor but merchandising was not extensive. Items are normally copyrighted Vision Productions Inc., Television Programs of America Inc. or Independent Television Corp. The show has been syndicated under the title *Brave Stallion*. Dell published a series of *Fury* comic books between 1957 and 1962.

FUR-1

FUR-1. "Fury's Western Roundup" Party Kit,
c. 1955. Borden Co. Extensive paper items including eight punch-out sheets. Unused - **$20 $40 $75**

FUR-2

FUR-2. "Fury Adventure Kit",
1960. Post Alpha-Bits. Multi-purpose plastic including weather indicator, flashlight, whistle, pen and miniature writing tablet. - **$75 $150 $250**

GABBY HAYES

George "Gabby" Hayes (1885-1969) acted in a traveling repertory company and played burlesque and vaudeville before he went to Hollywood for a film career that spanned more than 30 years. Known as Windy, then Gabby, the whiskered, ornery, toothless geezer played sidekick to Hopalong Cassidy, Roy Rogers, Gene Autry, Bill Elliott, Randolph Scott and John Wayne in well over 100 Westerns. Hayes was a regular on radio's *Roy Rogers Show* in the 1940s and had his own program on the Mutual network in 1951-1952, sponsored by Quaker cereals. Adventure and Western comic books appeared between 1948 and 1957. On television, two separate series - both called *The Gabby Hayes Show* - ran concurrently. One was a weekly educational program about episodes in American history (NBC 1950-1951), the other a fictional series of tall tales and Western film clips (NBC 1950-1954 and ABC 1956). Sponsors were Quaker cereals and Peter Paul candy.

GAB-1

GAB-2

GAB-1. "George 'Gabby' Hayes" Cello. Button,
c. 1948. - **$10 $20 $30**

GAB-2. Prospector's Hat 16x21" Paper Store Sign,
1951. Quaker Cereals. - **$50 $100 $175**

GAB-3

GAB-3. Prospector's Black Felt Hat,
1951. Quaker Cereals. - **$25 $50 $100**

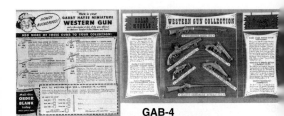

GAB-4

GAB-4. "Gabby Hayes Miniature Western Gun Collection",
1951. Quaker Cereals. Set of six: Buffalo Rifle, Colt Revolver, Flintlock Dueling Pistol, "Peacemaker" Pistol, Remington Breech-Loader Rifle, Winchester 1873 Rifle.
Gun Set - **$25 $40 $80**
Display Folder - **$20 $50 $75**
Order Sheet - **$5 $10 $20**

GAB-5

GAB-6

GAB-5. Quaker Cereal Comic Booklets With Mailing Envelopes,
1951. Set of five. Each Book Or Mailer - **$10 $30 $60**

GAB-6. Quaker Cannon Ring,
1951. Puffed Wheat & Puffed Rice. Large ring with brass base and spring-loaded barrel in either brass or aluminum. - **$100 $175 $250**

GAB-7

GAB-7. Quaker "Five Western Wagons" Cereal Box,
1952. Quaker Puffed Rice. Complete Box - **$50 $150 $250**

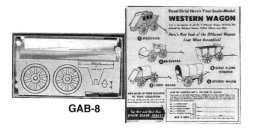
GAB-8

GAB-8. Gabby Hayes Western Wagon Kits,
1952. Quaker Cereals. Five different kits: Buckboard, Chuck Wagon, Covered Wagon, Great Plains Freighter, Stagecoach. Each Boxed - **$10 $20 $40**

GAB-9

GAB-9. Movie Viewer Set,
1952. Quaker Cereals. Filmstrip with five titles, instruction s, mailer. Near Mint Boxed - **$175**

GAB-10

GAB-10. Quaker "Pocket-Sized Movie Viewer" Newspaper Ad,
1952. - **$5 $10 $15**

GAB-11

GAB-11. Gabby Hayes Metal Automobiles,
1952. Quaker Cereals. Set of six.
Near Mint Boxed - **$140**
Each - **$5 $10 $20**

GANG BUSTERS

Marching against the underworld, proving each week that crime does not pay, *Gang Busters* was based on case files of the FBI and local police and proved so popular that it ran on network radio for 21 years. The show premiered on CBS in 1936 sponsored by Palmolive. Succeeding sponsors including Cue magazine (1939-1940), Sloan's liniment (1940-1945), Waterman pens (1945-1948), Tide soap (1948), Grape-Nuts cereal (1949-1954) and Wrigley's gum (1954-1955). The show was last aired in 1957. Descriptions of actual criminals, broadcast at the end of each program, apparently resulted in the capture of hundreds of fugitives. A television series with the same format had a nine-month run on NBC in 1952. *Gang Busters* comic books were published from 1938 to 1959.

GNG-1

GNG-1. "Stop Thief" 22x30" Paper Game Board Map,
1937. Palmolive. Came with nine metal cars.
Game - **$20 $50 $75**
Each Car - **$1 $3 $5**

GNG-2 GNG-3 GNG-4

GNG-2. Member's Badge,
c. 1937. - **$15 $30 $60**

GNG-3. "Green's Gang Busters Crime Crusaders"
Enameled Brass Badge,
c. 1937. "Phillips H. Lord's" copyright. - **$40 $75 $135**

GNG-4. Enameled Belt Buckle,
c. 1937. Rare. - **$50 $100 $200**

GNG-5

GNG-6

GNG-5. Tie,
1937. Scarce. - **$50 $100 $200**

GNG-6. "Gang Busters" Game,
1938. Store item by Lynco Inc. - **$75 $150 $300**

GNG-7

GNG-7. Whitman Boxed Board Game,
1939. Store item. - **$40 $75 $135**

GENE AUTRY

America's favorite singing cowboy was born in 1907 on a small ranch in Texas and grew up in Oklahoma, where he worked as a railroad telegraph operator and began his career singing and composing. Local performances as a yodeling cowboy led to national radio spots on the *National Barn Dance* and *National Farm and Home Hour* programs in the 1930s. Autry began recording cowboy songs in 1929 and had phenomenal success both as a composer and as a singer. He moved to Hollywood in 1934 and a year later starred in *Phantom Empire*, a 12-episode chapter play for Mascot. Over the years Autry was to write more than 250 songs and act in more than 100 Westerns.

Gene Autry's Melody Ranch, a program of Western songs and stories told around a campfire, premiered on CBS radio in 1940 and ran continually until 1956, interrupted only by

Autry's service in the Army Air Corps from 1942 to 1945. The program, sponsored by Wrigley's gum, featured bearded sidekick Pat Buttram for comic relief, along with a variety of musical groups.

On television, also sponsored by Wrigley's gum, *The Gene Autry Show* aired on CBS from 1950 to 1956. Filmed at his 125-acre Melody Ranch and produced by his Flying A Productions company, the program put Autry back in the saddle again each week to do battle with assorted villains. Riding his wonder horse Champion and accompanied by saddle-partner Buttram, Autry set a consistently high moral tone for his young fans. A spinoff series, *The Adventures of Champion*, which ran for a season (1955-1956) on CBS, featured young Barry Curtis and his dog Rebel along with the hero horse.

A *Gene Autry* Sunday comic strip from General Features Syndicate was begun in 1940 and revived from 1952 to 1955, and Autry comic books from Dell and Fawcett - including giveaways from Pillsbury (1947) and Quaker Oats (1950) - appeared from 1941 through the 1950s. Autry and Champion made countless personal appearances at fairs, parades, Wild West shows, and rodeos, and Flying A Productions did extensive merchandising of Autry-related items ranging from 10-cent club membership cards to complete buckskin outfits.

In the 1950s Autry began a career in business that mirrored his show-business success. He invested in oil and real estate, bought a radio-TV chain and a major league baseball team, served as chairman of the Cowboy Hall of Fame, and created a Western Heritage Museum in Los Angeles.

GAU-1

GAU-2

GAU-1. Movie Serial Club Member Button,
1935. Rare. Name of club formed by kids in Mascot serial *The Phantom Empire*. - **$200 $400 $600**

GAU-2. Wheaties Box Back,
c. 1937. For Republic Picture "The Big Show" released late 1936. - **$10 $20 $35**

GAU-3

GAU-4

GAU-3. Composition Statue,
c. 1930s. Rare. Store item. - **$100 $250 $400**

GAU-4. Fan Photo With Insert Sheet,
1940. Republic Studio. Near Mint In Mailer - **$35**
Photo Only - **$8 $12 $20**

GAU-6

GAU-5

AU-5. Rodeo Handbill,
1940. World Championship Rodeo, Boston Garden. -
$25 $50 $85

AU-6. "Boston Garden Rodeo" Litho. Button,
1940. Single event issue. - **$20 $40 $75**

GAU-7

GAU-8

AU-7. "Adventure Comics And Play-Fun Book",
1947. Pillsbury Pancake Mix. - **$25 $75 $190**

AU-8. Gene Autry Dixie Ice Cream Picture,
1948. - **$10 $25 $50**

GAU-9

GAU-10

AU-9. Clothing Manufacturer Photo And Cover Note,
1948. J. M. Wood Mfg. Co., maker of Autry shirts and jeans.
- **$20 $35 $50**

AU-10. Gene Autry/Lone Ranger Plastic Ring,
1948. Dell Comics. U.S. flag pictured under plastic dome,
offered for comic book subscription for each character. -
$100 $150 $200

GAU-11

GAU-12

GAU-11. Dell Publishing Co. Picture Strip,
1949. Folder strip of five color photos. - **$25 $50 $80**

GAU-12. Cello. Button,
1940s. Probably a rodeo souvenir. - **$15 $25 $45**

GAU-13 GAU-14 GAU-15

GAU-13. "Minneapolis Aquatennial Rodeo" Cello. Button,
1940s. Souvenir button. - **$50 $100 $150**

GAU-14. Official Club Badge Cello. Button,
1940s. - **$15 $25 $40**

GAU-15. "Republic's Singing Western Star"
Cello. Button,
1940s. - **$25 $50 $75**

GAU-16

GAU-17

GAU-16. Store Owner's 10x12" Cardboard Sign,
1940s. Wrigley Doublemint Gum. Signifies sponsorship of
"Doublemint Melody Ranch" radio show. - **$40 $60 $125**

GAU-17. "March Of Comics" #25,
1940s. Various sponsors. - **$25 $75 $170**

GAU-18

GAU-19

GAU-25

GAU-26

GAU-18. "Gene Autry" Ring,
1940s. Brass or silvered brass varieties. - **$75 $115 $150**

GAU-19. Quaker Comic Booklets,
1950. Puffed Wheat/Rice box inserts. Set of five.
Each - **$10 $35 $75**

GAU-25. "March Of Comics No. 120",
1954. Poll-Parrot Shoes. - **$10 $30 $70**

GAU-26. Rodeo Souvenir Photo,
1957. - **$5 $12 $20**

GAU-20

GAU-21

GAU-27

GAU-28

GAU-20. "Sunbeam Bread" Color Photo,
c. 1950. - **$10 $18 $30**

GAU-21. "Sunbeam Bread" Cardboard Gun,
c. 1950. - **$25 $40 $65**

GAU-27. Flying A Cardboard Wrist Cuffs,
1950s. Scarce. Probable premium. - **$50 $100 $200**

GAU-28. Medal Of Honor On Card,
1950s. Scarce. Medal - **$100 $200 $300**
Card - **$20 $40 $80**

GAU-22

GAU-23

GAU-24

GAU-30

GAU-29

GAU-22. Sunbeam Bread Litho. Button,
c. 1950. 1-3/8" size, also as 1-1/4" cello.
Each - **$10 $15 $20**

GAU-23. Sunbeam Bread "Gene Autry Show" 3-1/2"
Cello. Button,
c. 1950. - **$20 $40 $75**

GAU-24. Plastic Ring,
c. 1950. Store item. Gold finish with inset paper photo. -
$10 $15 $20

GAU-29. Horseshoe Nail Ring On Card,
1950s. Store item. Complete - **$250**
Ring Only - **$20 $30 $40**

GAU-30. Plastic Ring With Photo,
1950s. Store item, from card of rings featuring various personalities. Plastic cover over photo. - **$10 $20 $35**

GAU-31

GAU-32

GAU-37

GAU-37. Dell Picture Strip,
1950s. Unfolds with five photos. - **$25 $50 $75**

AU-31. School Tablet,
950s. Clothing stores. - **$15 $25 $50**

AU-32. "Adventure Story Trail Map",
950s. Stroehmann's Bread. Large folder to hold 16 color
photo bread end labels telling story of "Gene Autry And The
Black Hat Gang!". Folder - **$30 $60 $100**
Each Mounted Label - **$3 $6 $10**

GAU-38

GAU-39

GAU-38. Litho. Tin Club Tab,
1950s. - **$15 $30 $60**

GAU-39. "Gene Autry & Champion" Cello. Button,
1950s. Star design in gold or silver. - **$15 $25 $35**

GAU-33

GAU-34

GAU-40

GAU-41

AU-33. Bread Labels,
950s. Various bread companies. Numbered photos in at
ast five different series. Each - **$5 $10 $15**

AU-34. Publicity Photo,
950s. Columbia Records. - **$5 $10 $18**

GAU-40. Flying A Symbol Brass Wings Badge,
1950s. - **$20 $40 $75**

GAU-41. Ranch Symbol Cigarette Lighter,
1950s. Promotional item by Penguin. Chrome metal with
plastic wrapper, other side has "Melody Ranch". -
$25 $45 $80

GENERAL MILLS MISCELLANEOUS

This mammoth food and related products company, born and
still based in Minneapolis, was a mid-1920s pioneer in
national radio advertising via a powerful transmitter provided
jointly by an immediate preceding company, Washburn
Crosby Co. and other business interests in the Minneapolis-
St. Paul Twin Cities area. The first three programs - *Betty
Crocker, The Wheaties Quartet, The Gold Medal Fast Freight*
- were of homemaker nature and offered a few premiums in
like style. The premium heyday for youngsters, however,
began in the early 1930s through the *Skippy and His Pals*
program based on the Percy Crosby comic strip. Skippy was
followed in 1933 by *Jack Armstrong, The All-American Boy.*
Both offered premiums by sponsor Wheaties, a very popular
Depression era cereal that continues to the present. General
Mills through the years has offered hundreds of premiums for
purchase of food products, principally breakfast cereals.
Various General Mills brands are represented in this section
while Cheerios, Wheaties and major characters they sponsored are covered in separate sections.

GAU-35

GAU-36

AU-35. Rain Boots Merchandise Card,
950s. Servus Rubber Co. - **$10 $15 $25**

AU-36. English Fan Club Badge On Card,
950s. Gene Autry Comics, Silvered tin with insert photo.
ar Mint On Card - **$125**
ose - **$25 $50 $75**

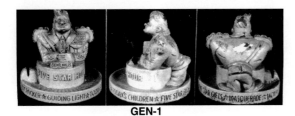

GEN-1

GEN-5

GEN-6

GEN-7

GEN-8

GEN-1. "Gen'l Mills/Five Star Hour" Plaster Figurine,
c. 1938. Rare. Probably issued to retailers, base lists six
radio programs. - **$250 $600 $1000**

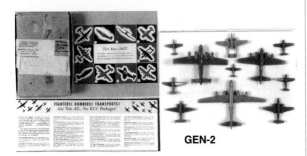

GEN-2

GEN-2. Kix Plastic Planes,
1946. 24 planes in set. Booklet - **$15 $25 $40**
Each Plane - **$3 $5 $8**

**GEN-5. Franken Berry 2-3/4" Tall Figural Plastic Pencil
Sharpener,**
1960s. - **$5 $10 $15**

GEN-6. "Franken Berry" Vinyl Doll With Box,
1975. Near Mint Boxed - **$150**
Loose - **$25 $40 $75**

GEN-7. "Count Chocula" Vinyl Doll With Box,
1975. Near Mint Boxed - **$150**
Loose - **$25 $40 $75**

GEN-8. "Fruit Brute" Vinyl Squeeze Doll,
1975. Near Mint Boxed - **$150**
Loose - **$25 $40 $75**

GEN-3

GEN-3. "General Mills Map Of The Old West" 20x28",
c. 1940s. - **$8 $20 $50**

GEN-9

GEN-10

GEN-9. "Boo Berry" Vinyl Squeeze Doll,
1975. Near Mint Boxed - **$150**
Loose - **$25 $40 $75**

GEN-10. Secret Compartment Plastic Ring Set,
1976. Four rings with Hasbro name in four colors depicting
Franken Berry, Boo Berry, Count Chocula, Fruit Brute.
Each - **$125 $190 $250**

GEN-4

GEN-4. General Mills Airplanes/Missile Launchers,
1950s. At least eight different planes in various colors and
missile launchers. Each - **$2 $4 $6**

GEN-11

GEN-11. "Stampos" Printing Kit,
1970s. Ink stampers with portraits of Franken Berry, Count Chocula, Boo Berry. Each - **$15 $30 $50**

GEN-12

GEN-12. Big Monster Flicker Rings,
1970s. Five of six shown: two feature the Count and Franken Berry, two feature the Count only, two feature Franken Berry only. Each - **$50 $75 $100**

GEN-13

GEN-13. Character Card Games,
1981. Two sets of cards featuring Lucky Charms, Cocoa Puffs, Trix, Franken Berry, Count Chocula, Boo Berry. Complete With Mailer - **$10 $15 $20**

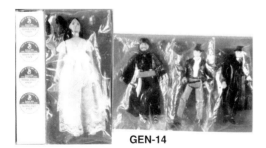

GEN-14

GEN-14. "Raiders Of The Lost Ark" Packaged Action Figures,
1982. Set of "Indiana Jones Four Pack" of him, Toht, Cairo Swordsman, Marian Ravenwood. Near Mint Complete - **$175**

GEN-15

GEN-15. "Count Chocula" Cereal Box And Disguise Stickers,
1987. Box art depicts necklace on Dracula's neck with design similar to Star of David. Box was quickly redesigned.
Box - **$25 $75 $150**
Stickers - **$5 $15 $30**

GEN-16

GEN-16. "Count Chocula" Cereal Box,
1987. Box art altered to remove Dracula's necklace that resembled Star of David. - **$25 $75 $150**

GEN-17

GEN-17. Franken Berry Cereal Box With Spooky Shape Maker Offer,
1987. Three different to emboss paper with images of Franken Berry, Count Chocula, Fruity Yummy Mummy.
Box - **$20 $35 $50**
Each Shape Maker - **$5 $10 $20**

GEN-18

GEN-18. Fruity Yummy Mummy Cereal Box,
1987. Packaging introduces the character and the cereal to the public while back panel introduces the new character to the established monsters. - **$100 $150 $250**

GEN-19

GEN-19. Boo Berry Cereal Box With Monster Poster And Crayons Offer,
1988. Last premium issued for monster cereals. Crayons shaped like monsters in their correct colors.
Box - **$10 $25 $50**
Poster And Crayons - **$20 $35 $60**

GI JOE

Hasbro's creative director of product development Don Levine was approached by independent toy designer Stanley Weston in March of 1962. Weston was selling merchandising rights to the TV show *"The Lieutenant,"* based on a Marine, and thought Hasbro would be interested in doing combat action figures for boys similar in design to what the Mattel Co. was doing with Barbie figures for girls. Levine and the people at Hasbro decided to go with a more universal appeal, basing the name on a 1945 Robert Mitchum war movie *The Story of G.I. Joe.* Hasbro claimed the trademark and christened the new product GI Joe.

Test marketing began in New York stores in August, 1964 and the figures sold out in one week. By early fall the figures were selling out nationwide. The GI Joe Club started in December and soon had 150,000 members. 1965 saw the introduction of a black action soldier into the line of American Army, Air Force, Navy and Marine figures.

1966 brought the introduction of Action Soldiers of the World, offering soldiers from six countries. In 1969 GI Joe's hard core military image was softened to an "Adventurer" concept which would expand the merchandising even further. 1975 saw the introduction of the 11-1/2" Atomic Man.

The oil shortage of 1976 halted production due to lack of petroleum used in manufacturing the figures. In 1982 Joe was re-introduced in a new 3 and 3/4" size. In 1991 Hasbro brought out the first original 12-inch action figure since 1976, master sergeant Duke, based on the *GI Joe, A Real American Hero* cartoon series.

Over the years, the company has sold hundreds of millions of the ever-popular GI Joe dolls and associated figures, vehicles and gear.

GIJ-1   GIJ-2

GIJ-1. "Command Post News" Newspaper. Vol. 1 #1, April, 1965. - **$25 $40 $75**

GIJ-2. "Command Post News" Newspaper #4, April, 1966. - **$5 $12 $25**

GIJ-3

GIJ-3. Catalogue,
1967. Came only with the 1967 series of talking GI Joe figures. - **$3 $8 $15**

GIJ-4

GIJ-4. "Command Post Yearbook",
1967. - **$20 $40 $75**

GIJ-5

GIJ-5. GI Joe Letter With Transfer,
1960s. Letter - **$3 $6 $12**
Transfer - **$5 $10 $20**

GIJ-6   GIJ-7

GIJ-6. Cello. Button,
c. 1970s. Probably Hasbro promotional button. - **$5 $10 $20**

GIJ-7. "Commando" Enameled Metal Badge,
1982. Possibly from membership kit. - **$8 $15 $25**

THE GOLDBERGS

The Goldbergs, the first memorable Jewish radio comedy, was the brainchild of Gertrude Berg, who wrote, produced, directed, and starred as Molly, the benevolent matriarch of a working-class family in the Bronx. With husband Jake, children Sammy and Rosalie, and Uncle David, Molly was a fixture on the NBC, CBS, or Mutual networks from 1929 to 1945 and again in 1949-1950. Sponsors included Pepsodent (1931-1934), Colgate (1936), Oxydol (1937-1945), and General Foods (1949-1950). A successful television series aired from 1949 to 1954, a Broadway play (*Molly and Me*) was produced in 1948, and a movie (*Molly*) was released in 1951. "Yoo-Hoo, Mrs. Bloom!"

GLD-1   GLD-2

GLD-1. Molly Goldberg Fan Photo,
1930s. - **$8 $15 $30**

GLD-2. Gertrude Berg 11x14" Frame Tray Jigsaw Puzzle,
1952. Store item by Jaymar. - **$12 $25 $40**

GONE WITH THE WIND

One of the most popular films of all time, *Gone with the Wind* premiered in Atlanta, Georgia, on December 15, 1939, won 10 Academy Awards, and remains a perennial smash in theaters, on television, and in video rentals. This Civil War saga, based on Margaret Mitchell's novel, starred Clark Gable, Vivien Leigh, an all-star cast - and the burning of Atlanta. Merchandising, including portrait dolls, collector plates, and porcelain figurines, continues to this day.

GON-1   GON-2

GON-1. Book Publishing House Summary Booklet,
1936. Macmillan Co. - **$35 $70 $125**

GON-2. Movie Theater Herald,
1940. Various theaters. - **$15 $30 $60**

GON-3

GON-4   GON-5

GON-3. "Scarlett O'Hara Perfume" Novelty Container,
1940. Store item. - **$50 $85 $150**

GON-4. Scarlett O'Hara "Yesteryear" Perfume Glass Vial,
1940. Babs Creations. Figure image within vertical dome. - **$60 $150 $250**

GON-5. Cardboard String Tag From Clothing Dress,
1940. Mae Delli's Originals. - **$40 $100 $150**

GON-7

GON-6   GON-8

GON-6. Cookbook Store Display From Pebeco Toothpaste,
1940. Scarce. - **$100 $150 $275**

GON-7. Brass Heart-Shaped Jewelry Pin,
1940. Store item. - **$35 $75 $125**

GON-8. "Gone With The Wind" Brass Charm Locket Designed In Book Image,
1940. Opens to hold two miniature pictures. - **$50 $100 $175**

GON-9

GON-10

GNT-1

GON-9. Gone With The Wind Brass/Cello. Cameo Brooch,
1940. Lux Toilet Soap. Replica of brooch worn by Scarlett in movie, offered originally for 15 cents and three soap wrappers. - **$40 $100 $200**

GON-10. Scarlett's Brooch,
1940. Lux Soap. Movie jewelry replica in brass accented by simulated pearls around single simulated turquoise stone. - **$40 $100 $200**

THE GREAT GILDERSLEEVE

Throckmorton P. Gildersleeve started life as a character on the *Fibber McGee and Molly* radio series in the 1930s. Created and played by actor Harold Peary, Gildy was a pompous windbag who was spun off successfully to his own program on NBC in 1941. He was a small-town water commissioner, but the show centered on his life as the bachelor uncle of Leroy and Marjorie and his romantic encounters as the town's most prominent eligible man. Willard Waterman stepped into the role in 1950, and the program ran until 1958. Kraft Foods was the sponsor. There was a brief television series and a 1942 RKO movie of the same name.

GIL-1

GIL-2

GIL-1. Litho. Tin 2-1/4" Jar Lid,
c. 1941. - **$15 $25 $45**

GIL-2. Radio Show Studio Audience Ticket,
1947. Parkay margarine. Pictured example for December 24 Christmas Eve broadcast. - **$10 $20 $35**

GREEN GIANT

The Green Giant was born in 1925 as the trademark for a new variety of peas by the Minnesota Valley Canning Company. The original illustration of a giant wrapped in fur, created to satisfy trademark requirements, was redesigned 10 years later into the character we now recognize - a smiling green giant clothed in leaves. Little Sprout was added in the early 1970s, and the company has merchandised both characters.

GNT-1. 20th Anniversary Birthday Record With Envelope
1949. In Mailer - **$5 $12 $20**
Loose - **$2 $5 $10**

GNT-2

GNT-3

GNT-2. Earliest Cloth Doll,
1966. - **$10 $20 $35**

GNT-3. Campaign Kit,
1968. Voter card, litho. badge, sticker, 26x38" poster. - **$12 $20 $35**

GNT-4

GNT-5

GNT-6

GNT-4. Little Sprout Cloth Doll,
c. 1970. - **$5 $10 $15**

GNT-5. "Speakin' Sprout" Talking Cloth Doll,
1971. Contains battery operated tape recorder. - **$25 $50 $75**

GNT-6. Little Sprout Vinyl Doll,
1970s. - **$10 $15 $30**

THE GREEN HORNET

Accompanied by his faithful valet Kato, the Green Hornet matched wits with the underworld on the radio from 1936 to 1952, first on WXYZ in Detroit, then on the Mutual network in 1938, on NBC in 1939, on the ABC Blue network in 1940, and finally back on Mutual in 1952. Sponsors included General Mills in 1948 and Orange Crush in 1952. Under his mask the Hornet was Britt Reid, crusading newspaper publisher

...sher and grand-nephew of the Lone Ranger, and his crime-fighting exploits in the big city resembled those of his relative in the West. (Both shows were created by George W. Trendle and written largely by Fran Striker.) Also featured was Miss Case, secretary and love interest, along with Black Beauty, the Hornet's supercharged limousine, and his non-lethal gas gun. Kato, originally Japanese, became a Filipino after Pearl Harbor.

Two Green Hornet chapter plays were released by Universal in 1940, with Keye Luke as Kato, and a souped-up television series aired for a season (1966-1967) on ABC, with Van Williams in the title role and Bruce Lee as Kato. Comic books appeared more or less regularly from 1940 to 1949, followed by a one-shot in 1953, three issues in 1966-1967 timed to coincide with the television series, and a revival in 1989.

GRN-1

GRN-1. Radio Fan Club Photo,
1938. Golden Jersey Milk. Pictures Britt Reid (Al Hodge) as Green Hornet with back ad text. - **$75 $150 $250**

GRN-2

GRN-3

GRN-2. Radio Fan Club Photo,
1938. Golden Jersey Milk. Pictures Miss Case (Lee Allman) with back ad text, from G-J-M Club photo series of several cast members. - **$60 $100 $150**

GRN-3. "Kato" Portrait Photo,
1938. Golden Jersey Milk. - **$50 $100 $150**

GRN-4

GRN-4. "Mike Oxford" Portrait Photo,
1938. Golden Jersey Milk. - **$50 $100 $150**

GRN-5

GRN-6

GRN-5. Membership Card,
1938. Golden Jersey Milk. - **$50 $100 $150**

GRN-6. Green Hornet Glass,
c. 1938. Scarce. Golden Jersey Milk. - **$40 $100 $250**

GRN-7

GRN-8

GRN-7. Kato And Black Beauty Glass,
c. 1938. Scarce. Golden Jersey Milk. - **$40 $100 $250**

GRN-8. Radio Show Postcard,
1939. - **$75 $125 $175**

GRN-9   GRN-10   GRN-11

GRN-9. "The Green Hornet Adventure Club" Cello. Button,
1940. Rare. Universal Pictures. For 13-chapter movie serial. - **$150 $300 $600**

GRN-10. "The Green Hornet Strikes Again" Movie Serial Cello. Button,
1940. Rare. Universal Serial/Adventure Club. For 13-chapter serial. - **$150 $300 $600**

GRN-11. Secret Compartment Glow-In-Dark Ring,
1947. General Mills. Brass with hinged lid over glow plastic compartment. - **$250 $600 $1000**

GRN-12

GRN-13

GRN-19

GRN-21

GRN-20

GRN-12. Green Hornet Sting Whistle,
1966. Scarce. Chicken Of The Sea Tuna (Required Two Labels). Two-piece plastic slide whistle with small name mark on handle. Newspaper Ad - **$25 $50 $100**
Whistle - **$200 $600 $1500**

GRN-13. Battery Operated "Signal Ray",
1966. Store item by Colorforms. Display card is 10x11".
Display With Toy - **$300 $600 $1000**

GRN-19. Rubber Figural Ring,
1966. Vending machine issue. - **$5 $7 $10**

GRN-20. Green Hornet Pez Dispenser,
c. 1966. Several hat variations, grey & brown hats worth more. - **$75 $150 $250**

GRN-21. 3-1/2" Cello. Button,
c. 1966. Store item by Button World Mfg. - **$10 $20 $30**

GRN-16

GRN-14

GRN-15

GRN-22

GRN-14. "The Green Hornet/Kato" Glass,
1966. Probable food product container. - **$40 $80 $125**

GRN-15. Vernors Plastic "Trick Or Treat Bag",
1966. Vernors Ginger Ale. - **$20 $40 $75**

GRN-16. "Agent" 4" Litho. Button,
1966. Store item. - **$10 $20 $35**

GRN-22. Flicker Button 3",
1967. Store item. - **$10 $25 $40**

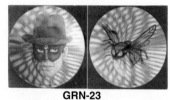

GRN-23

GRN-23. Flicker Disk 7",
1967. Store item. - **$15 $30 $50**

GRN-18

GRN-17

GRN-24

GRN-24. Flicker Picture Plastic Ruler,
1967. Store item by Vari-Vue. 6" length. - **$50 $100 $150**

GRN-17. Litho. Buttons,
1966. Vending machine set of nine. Two color styles, with or without yellow. Each - **$5 $10 $15**

GRN-18. Green Hornet Character Plastic Flicker Rings,
1966. Set of 12, each with double image when tilted.
Silver Base Each - **$10 $15 $20**
Blue Base Each - **$8 $12 $15**

THE GREEN LAMA

The first appearance of the Green Lama was in *Prize Comic* #7 in 1940. He then appeared in his own book for eig[ht] issues from 1944 to 1946. For a dime readers could join th[e] *Green Lama Club* and receive a membership card, the key [to] the Lama's secret code, and an Escapo folding trick th[at] showed victory over Fascist rats. The character was reviv[ed] on CBS radio for the summer of 1949 as a New York-based crime fighter with special powers acquired after 10 years of study in a Tibet monastery.

(instructions)

(variation 2)

(card and mailer)

GLM-1

GLM-1. Club Kit,
1945. Came with club kit.
Club Card - **$75 $100 $170**
Mailer - **$20 $40 $80**
Escape Trick with Instructions - **$50 $125 $250**

GLM-2

GLM-2. Radio Episode Script,
1949. For June 26 broadcast "Million Dollar Chopsticks". -
$50 $100 $150

THE GUMPS

The Gumps, one of the most popular comic strips of the 1920s, was created by Sidney Smith for the *Chicago Tribune*. The story of Andy and Min, son Chester, and rich Uncle Bim began as a daily strip in 1917 and as a Sunday feature in 1919, and lasted until 1959, some 24 years after Smith was killed in an automobile accident. Comic book reprints appeared from 1918 into the 1940s, and a radio series based on the strip and sponsored by Pebeco toothpaste was aired on CBS from 1934 to 1937. The popularity of the Gumps is reflected by the large variety of licensed items - figures, toys, games, books, buttons, etc. "Oh Min!"

GMP-1

GMP-1. "The Sunshine Twins" Book,
1925. Sunshine Andy Gump Biscuits by Loose-Wiles Biscuit Co. Pictured example is designated fourth edition. -
$20 $40 $70

GMP-2

GMP-3

GMP-4

GMP-2. "Chester Gump And His Friends" Booklet,
1934. Tarzan Ice Cream Cups. #5 from series of various character titles. - **$20 $40 $80**

GMP-3. "The Gumps In Radio Land" Booklet,
1937. Pebeco toothpaste. - **$20 $35 $65**

GMP-4. "Andy Gump" Wood Jointed Doll,
1930s. Store item. - **$50 $75 $150**

GMP-5

GMP-6

GMP-7

GMP-5. "Andy Gump For Congress" Cello. Button,
1930s. Various newspapers. - **$10 $15 $25**

GMP-6. "Investigator/Gump Charities/Use Solder Seal" Cello. Button,
1930s. - **$15 $25 $40**

GMP-7. "Andy Gump For President" Cello. Button,
1930s. Wonder Milk, various other food products.
$15 $25 $40

GMP-8

GMP-9

GMP-8. "Andy Gump For President" 2" Cello. Button,
1930s. Good Humor Ice Cream Suckers. - **$40 $85 $150**

GMP-9. "The Gumps/Friendly Refreshment" Metal Cap For Soda Bottle,
1930s. Bon-Ton Beverages, Chicago. - **$10 $20 $30**

GUNSMOKE

Dodge City, Kansas, in the 1880s was the site of this adult Western that premiered on CBS radio in 1952 and on CBS television in 1955 for 20 years until the program ended in 1975. Starring James Arness as Matt Dillon, other continuing characters included the saloon keeper Miss Kitty, old Doc Adams, and the Marshal's deputy Chester, replaced by Festus in 1964. Radio sponsors included Post Toasties (1953), Chesterfield cigarettes (1954), and Liggett & Myers (1954-1957). L & M cigarettes was also a television sponsor. Related comic books appeared from the 1950s to 1970, and two Gunsmoke movies starring James Arness were released in 1987 and 1990. Items usually carry a copyright of CBS Television Enterprises or Columbia Broadcasting System.

GUN-1

GUN-2

GUN-1. "L&M Cigarettes" 21x22" Cardboard Store Sign,
c. 1954. Liggett & Meyers. - **$35 $60 $125**

GUN-2. L&M Cigarettes Cast Card,
c. 1954. - **$8 $15 $30**

GUN-3

GUN-4

GUN-3. "James Arness Fan Club" Cello. Button,
c. 1958. - **$15 $25 $40**

GUN-4. "Matt Dillon/U.S. Marshal" Metal Badge,
1959. Store item. On Card - **$20 $30 $50**
Loose - **$10 $15 $25**

GUN-5

GUN-5. "U.S. Marshal" Metal Badge,
1959. Store item. Badge version omits "Matt Dillon" name.
On Card - **$20 $30 $50**
Loose - **$10 $15 $25**

GUN-6

GUN-6. Personal Appearance Souvenir Folder With Photo,
c. 1960. - **$15 $25 $50**

GUN-7

GUN-8

GUN-7. "All Star Dairies" Litho. Button,
c. 1960. - **$8 $15 $25**

GUN-8. Metal Cuff Links With Bw Photo Inserts,
1960s. Issuer unknown. - **$20 $40 $75**

GUN-9

GUN-9. "Matt Dillon's Favorite" Key Ring,
1960s. Reverse of plastic star reads "Sanders Dairy/All Star". - **$20 $35 $60**

HAPPY HOOLIGAN

Happy Hooligan, the ever-innocent optimist, was created by Frederick Opper for the Hearst Sunday comics in 1900 and continued, under a variety of titles, until 1932. The strip, considered a major classic comic, also involved Happy's pet dog Flip and his brothers Gloomy Gus and Lord Montmorency in a series of ill-fated adventures. Happy, with his tin-can hat, and Gus, with his battered top hat, were immensely popular characters, appearing in stage plays, silent animated cartoons, sheet music, and reprints of the strips in book form.

HAP-1   HAP-2

HAP-1. "How To Make Happy Hooligan Dance" Cut-Out Supplement,
1902. New York American & Journal newspaper.
Uncut - **$25 $50 $75**

HAP-2. "Shoemakers Fair" Cello. Button,
1905. Figure back view although frontal head for slogan "Are You Goin' Or Comin'?" - **$20 $40 $75**

HAP-3   HAP-4   HAP-5

HAP-3. Happy Hooligan Song Sheet,
c. 1905. Rare. Newspaper supplement. - **$50 $100 $200**

HAP-4. Composition Figure,
c. 1910. Store item. Jointed arms and legs. - **$50 $80 $150**

HAP-5. Papier Mache Roly-Poly,
c. 1910. Store item. - **$200 $300 $500**

HAP-6   HAP-7

HAP-6. Cello. Button,
c. 1915. - **$10 $18 $30**

HAP-7. Seated Bisque Nodder Figure,
1920s. Store item. - **$50 $100 $200**

HELEN TRENT

The Romance of Helen Trent reigned as the melodramatic queen of the daytime soap operas for over a quarter of a century on CBS radio from 1933 to 1960. Helen, remaining single and 35 through the years, was noble, pure, and pursued by dozens of suitors, most of whom came to a violent end. Sponsors included American Home Products, Affiliated Products, Whitehall Drugs, Pharmaco, Spry, Breeze, and Scott Waldorf tissue.

HLN-1   HLN-2

HLN-1. Radio Replica Mechanical Brass Badge,
1949. Five identified cast members are pictured in sequence through diecut opening by rear disk wheel. - **$20 $50 $75**

HLN-2. Silvered Brass Medallion,
1949. Kolynos dental product. Design motifs on both sides including Sphinx, pyramids, other abstract symbols. - **$10 $18 $30**

THE HERMIT'S CAVE

Produced at Los Angeles radio station KMPC, this syndicated horror show aired from 1940 to 1944, offering ghost stories, weird stories, and mayhem and murders galore. Scary sound effects and the voice of Mel Johnson as the old hermit distinguished these weekly tales of carnage. Olga Coal was the sponsor.

HER-1

HER-1. Cast Pictures,
1940s. Scarce. Each - **$10 $20 $40**

HER-2   HER-3

HER-2. Promo Brochure,
1940s. - **$30 $60 $120**

HER-3. Letter,
1940s. - **$20 $40 $80**

HOBBY LOBBY

From 1937 to 1949 on various networks this popular half-hour program highlighted listeners' unusual hobbies, everything from collecting elephant hairs to talking backwards. Dave Elman created the show, and each week a celebrity guest would show up to "lobby his hobby." Sponsors over the years included Hudson cars, Jell-O, Fels-Naptha soap, Colgate, and Anchor-Hocking glass. A television version with Cliff Arquette (Charley Weaver) as host was broadcast on ABC in 1959-60.

HOB-1   HOB-2

HOB-1. Promotional Ad,
c. 1940s. Rare. - **$30 $60 $100**

HOB-2. "Hobby Lobby" Rocking Horse Charm,
c. 1940s. - **$20 $40 $60**

HOOT GIBSON

Edmund R. Gibson (1892-1962), known as Hoot because as a boy he liked to hunt owls, was born in Nebraska and learned to rope and ride on his father's ranch. He left home as a teenager and worked as a cowboy on the trail and in Wild West shows before arriving in Hollywood in 1910. His first minor film role was in 1911, but he became a star in the 1920s, ultimately appearing in well over 200 silent and talk-

ing movies. Gibson's popularity in the late 1920s was second only to Tom Mix. He retired in 1944, then had a few cameo film roles and a brief run as the host of a local television show in Los Angeles. Hoot Gibson comic books appeared in 1950.

HGB-1   HGB-3

HGB-2

HGB-1. "Rope Spinning" Instruction Folder,
1929. Came with Hoot Gibson Rodeo Ropes by Mordt Co., Chicago. - **$10 $18 $30**

HGB-2. "Robbins Bros. Circus" 14x22" Cardboard Poster,
1930s. - **$50 $100 $150**

HGB-3. Movie Felt Patch,
1930s. - **$50 $100 $200**

HGB-4   HGB-5   HGB-6

HGB-4. Cello. Button,
1930s. Probably circus souvenir. - **$25 $60 $100**

HGB-5. Cello. Button,
1930s. Probably circus souvenir. - **$75 $150 $225**

HGB-6. Litho. Button From Movie Star Set,
1930s. - **$5 $8 $15**

HGB-7

HGB-7. "Ideal Moving Pictures" Flip Booklet,
1930s. Flip sequence pictures Gibson lassoing two fistfighters. - **$20 $35 $60**

HOPALONG CASSIDY

William Boyd (1898-1972) was born in Ohio, grew up in Oklahoma, and worked at odd jobs before he went to Hollywood in 1919 to look for work in the movies. By the mid-1920s he had become a major star of silent films. Boyd made his first cowboy movie in 1931, and his first as Hopalong Cassidy in 1935. (The original Cassidy character came from the pulp stories and novels of C.E. Mulford in the early 1900s). Dressed in black, with silver spurs and saddle, riding his white stallion Topper, with Andy Clyde or Gabby Hayes as sidekick, Hoppy battled outlaws in a series of movies among the most successful "B" Westerns ever made. Boyd became completely identified with the noble cowboy, and by the time he retired in 1959 he had made more than 100 theatrical and television Cassidy films.

Boyd bought the rights to the Hoppy character in 1948 and released edited versions of the films for syndication to Los Angeles television station KTLA, where they ran from 1948 to 1950. Barbara Ann bread and Wonder bread were sponsors. In 1950 the programs were leased to NBC, with General Foods as sponsor. *The Hopalong Cassidy Show* - the first major television Western series - was a sensation, airing on more than 60 stations and ranking consistently among the top three programs in the country. After two years a new series of half-hour made-for-TV films ran until 1954, with Edgar Buchanan in the sidekick role.

The television success spawned a radio series (1950-1952) on the Mutual and CBS networks, also sponsored by General Foods, and a comic strip drawn by Dan Spiegle that ran in more than 150 newspapers until 1955. Millions of Hoppy comic books appeared from 1943 through the 1950s, including giveaways by White Tower in 1946, Grape-Nuts Flakes in 1950, and several by Bond bread in 1951.

Hoppy's immense popularity with his young audience around the nation also generated an unprecedented merchandising cornucopia. Hundreds of endorsements and licensed products flooded the land, from roller skates to bicycles, watches, pocket knives, toy guns, cowboy outfits, pajamas, peanut butter, candy bars, cottage cheese, bread, cereal, cookies, milk, toothpaste, savings banks, wallpaper - even hair oil became part of the Hopalong Cassidy legend.

HOP-1

HOP-2

HOP-1. Dixie Ice Cream Picture,
1938. - **$20 $40 $85**

HOP-2. Pillsbury's Promotional 12x24" Sign,
1940. Scarce. Advertises punch-out gun and targets. - **$200 $400 $600**

HOP-3

HOP-3. Punch-Out Gun And Targets Sheet,
1940. Pillsbury's Farina. Boyd/Hoppy identified as "Paramount" star. Unpunched - **$35 $80 $175**

HOP-4

HOP-5

HOP-4. "Bill Boyd/For Democracy 100%" Cello. Button,
c. 1942. Rare. From patriotism series picturing various cowboys. - **$100 $200 $350**

HOP-5. Fan Club Form Letter With Envelope,
1946. Hopalong Cassidy Productions. Promotes new film series, photo on folder reverse.
With Envelope - **$50 $75 $150**
No Envelope - **$40 $60 $100**

HOP-6

HOP-7

HOP-6. Cole Bros. Circus Pennant,
c. 1948. - **$20 $50 $80**

HOP-7. Round-Up Club "Special Agent Pass" Card,
c. 1948. Probable movie theater give-away. - **$15 $30 $50**

HOP-8

HOP-8. Barclay Knitwear Co. Photo,
1949. Given with sweater purchase. - **$15 $25 $40**

HOP-9

HOP-9. Butter-Nut Bread "Troopers News" Vol. 1 #1,
1949. First issue of periodic newsletter. - **$75 $150 $250**

HOP-10

HOP-11

HOP-10. "Trooper's Club" Application Card,
1949. Various sponsors. - **$15 $25 $40**

HOP-11. "Hopalong Cassidy Official Bar 20 T-V Chair",
1949. Store item and Big Top Peanut Butter premium. Wood and canvas folding chair that opens to 16x16x22" tall. -
$250 $500 $1000

HOP-12

HOP-13

HOP-12. Adult Hat,
1950. Scarce. Premium and store item. Has white picture band and photo button. - **$100 $200 $400**

HOP-13. Child's Hat,
1950. Premium and store item. - **$50 $75 $150**

HOP-14

HOP-15

HOP-14. Bond Bread Loaf End Labels,
1950. Photo style pictures, unnumbered series.
Each - **$3 $6 $12**

HOP-15. Bond Bread Loaf End Labels,
1950. Numbered with perforation around illustration, 16 in se
(#17-32). Each - **$5 $8 $12**

HOP-16

HOP-16. Bond Bread "Hang-Up Album",
1950. Folder wall poster for bread loaf end pictures for story "Hoppy Captures The Bank Robbers." Unused -
$30 $50 $80

HOP-17
HOP-18

HOP-17. Bond Bread Label Flyer 6x9",
1950. - **$40 $75 $125**

HOP-18. "Bond Bread" Store Hanger Sign 6x7",
1950. - **$100 $175 $250**

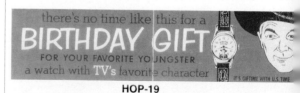

HOP-19

HOP-19. Watch Paper Sign 6x24",
1950. Scarce. US Time. - **$100 $225 $400**

HOP-21

HOP-20

HOP-20. "Timex" 16" Painted Latex Store Display,
1950. Rare. Timex Watches. English made. -
$750 $1500 $2500

HOP-21. Metal Pocketwatch,
1950. Store item by US Time. - $200 $400 $600

HOP-22

HOP-22. Savings Club Thrift Kit,
1950. Advertised in comic book and sponsored by various
banks. Includes certificate, cover letter, color photo, post-
card, folder showing club ranks.
Near Mint In Mailer - $300
Certificate - $30 $60 $100
Letter - $10 $20 $30
Photo - $5 $10 $15
Postcard - $5 $12 $20
Folder - $25 $50 $75

HOP-23

HOP-23. Savings Club Membership Card & Postcard
(separate items),
1950. Various sponsoring banks.
Membership Card - $35 $60 $90
Postcard - $15 $25 $40

HOP-24

HOP-25

HOP-26

HOP-24. Plastic Bank,
1950. Store item and Hopalong Cassidy Savings Club give-
away. Gold Plastic - $25 $50 $75
White Plastic (rare) - $50 $100 $200
Other Colors - $40 $75 $125

HOP-25. Bank Teller's 3" Litho. Button,
1950. - $15 $25 $40

HOP-26. Saving Rodeo "Tenderfoot" Canadian Version
Litho. Button,
1950. Various Canadian banks. Smaller size than U.S. versions, first five ranks are 1-1/8" litho. while Straw Boss and
Foreman versions are 1-3/8". Add 25% To U.S. Version -
$20 $40 $60

HOP-27   HOP-28   HOP-29

HOP-27. Saving Rodeo "Tenderfoot" Litho. Button,
1950. Various banks. Awarded for saving $2.00. -
$15 $30 $50

HOP-28. Saving Rodeo "Wrangler" Litho. Button,
1950. Various banks. Awarded for saving $10.00. -
$10 $18 $25

HOP-29. Saving Rodeo "Bulldogger" Litho. Button,
1950. Various banks. Awarded for saving $25.00. -
$12 $25 $35

HOP-30   HOP-31   HOP-32

HOP-30. Saving Rodeo "Bronc Buster" Litho. Button,
1950. Various banks. Awarded for saving $50.00. -
$15 $35 $50

HOP-31. Saving Rodeo "Trail Boss" Litho. Button,
1950. Fifth highest of seven ranks. - $20 $40 $75

HOP-32. Saving Rodeo "Straw Boss" 2-1/4" Litho.
Button,
1950. Scarce. Honor circle rating awarded for saving
$250.00, also Canadian issue in smaller cello. version. -
$75 $125 $225

HOP-33

HOP-34

HOP-33. Saving Rodeo"Foreman" 2-1/4" Litho. Button,
1950. Scarce. Highest rank Honor Circle rating awarded for saving $500, also Canadian issue in smaller cello. version. - **$75 $150 $250**

HOP-34. "Hoppy's Favorite" Litho. Button,
1950. Issued with names of various sponsors.
Each - **$10 $25 $50**

HOP-35

HOP-35. Premium Catalogue With Order Form,
1950. Big Top Peanut Butter. - **$50 $100 $200**

HOP-36

HOP-37

HOP-36. Metal Binoculars,
1950. Store item and Big Top Peanut Butter premium. - **$25 $60 $100**

HOP-37. Boxed Camera,
1950. Store item and Big Top Peanut Butter premium.
Boxed - **$100 $150 $225**
Loose - **$40 $80 $150**

HOP-38

(enlarged view)

HOP-39

HOP-38. "Junior Chow Set" Ad Sheet,
1950. Big Top Peanut Butter. - **$15 $25 $50**

HOP-39. Stainless Steel Table Utensils,
1950. Store item and Big Top Peanut Butter premium.
Each - **$10 $20 $30**

HOP-40

HOP-41

HOP-40. Plastic Wrist Compass,
1950. Store item and Big Top Peanut Butter premium. - **$25 $50 $75**

HOP-41. Glass Mugs,
1950. Big Top Peanut Butter. Set of four in black, green, blue, red on white. Each - **$10 $18 $30**

HOP-42

HOP-42. "Bar 20 Chow Set" Boxed Glassware,
1950. Store item and Big Top Peanut Butter premium. Set fo "Gun Totin' Buckaroos". Near Mint Boxed - **$350**
Each - **$30 $50 $75**

HOP-43

HOP-44

HOP-43. Silvered Brass Identification Bracelet,
1950. Big Top Peanut Butter. Center plate edges have "Hopalong Cassidy-XX Ranch", center is designed for engraving owner's name. - **$50 $100 $150**

HOP-44. Silvered Brass Hair Barrette,
1950. Store item and Big Top Peanut Butter premium. - **$20 $35 $60**

HOP-45

HOP-46

HOP-47

HOP-45. Metal Thermos,
1950. Store item by Aladdin Industries and Big Top Peanut Butter premium. - **$25 $70 $150**

HOP-46. Metal Lunch Box,
1950. Store item by Aladdin Industries and Big Top Peanut Butter premium. Rectangular decal. - **$60 $125 $300**

HOP-47. Metal Lunch Box,
1950. Store item by Aladdin Industries. Cloud-shaped decal. - **$60 $125 $300**

HOP-48

HOP-48. Wallet With Coin & Papers,
1950. Store item and Big Top Peanut Butter premium.
Complete - **$75 $125 $200**
Coin Only - **$5 $10 $15**

HOP-49

HOP-50

HOP-49. "Good Luck From Hoppy" Aluminum Medal,
1950. Came with Hoppy wallets, reverse pictures good luck symbols. - **$5 $10 $15**

HOP-50. Burry's Cookies Cut-Out Box Panel,
1950. #1 panel from 24 different packages with "The Continued Story Of Hopalong Cassidy's Bar-20 Ranch Adventures". Each Uncut Panel - **$20 $40 $60**

HOP-51

HOP-52

HOP-51. "Hopalong Cassidy Picture Card Gum" Waxed Paper Wrapper,
1950. Topps Chewing Gum. - **$20 $50 $100**

HOP-52. Candy Bag,
1950. Topps Candy Division. - **$25 $50 $75**

HOP-53

HOP-54

HOP-53. Litho. Tin Potato Chips Can,
1950. Kuehmann Foods Inc. - **$60 $125 $200**

HOP-54. Grape-Nuts Flakes Comic Book,
1950. - **$12 $35 $85**

HOP-55

HOP-56

HOP-55. Boxed Drinking Straws,
1950. Various pictures on reverse.
Complete - **$50 $80 $140**

HOP-56. Hard Plastic Figures,
1950. Store item by Ideal Corp.
Boxed - **$75 $150 $250**
Loose - **$30 $60 $100**

HOP-57

HOP-57. "Hair Trainer" 8x22" Paper Poster With Picture,
1950. Poster - **$75 $150 $250**
Picture - **$5 $12 $18**

HOP-60

HOP-58   HOP-59

HOP-58. Pocketknife,
1950. Store item by Hammer Brand. - **$30 $65 $125**

HOP-59. Vinyl Pocketknife Loop,
1950. Store item. - **$25 $50 $90**

HOP-60. Cardboard Noisemaker Gun,
1950. Capitol Records. - **$30 $60 $100**

HOP-63

HOP-61

HOP-62

HOP-61. "Hopalong Cassidy Bikes And Skates" Ad Card,
1950. Rollfast Co. - **$25 $60 $100**

HOP-62. New York Daily News 10x13" Cardboard Poster,
1950. Announces start of daily comic strip. - **$80 $175 $250**

HOP-63. "Hopalong Cassidy In The Daily News" 2" Cello. Button,
1950. - **$15 $30 $50**

HOP-64

HOP-65   HOP-66

HOP-64. Hopalong Cassidy Western Badge,
1950. Post's Raisin Bran. From set of 12 including titles Calamity Jane, General Custer, Wild Bill Hickok, Rodeo Trick Rider, Sheriff, Ranch Boss, Bull Dogging Champ, Annie Oakley, Chief Sitting Bull, Roping Champ, Indian Scout.
Hoppy Tab - **$12 $25 $50**
Others Each - **$5 $12 $20**

HOP-65. Radio Show 9x11" Handbill,
c. 1950. Grape-Nuts Flakes. Probable grocery bag insert. - **$40 $75 $125**

HOP-66. "Strawberry Preserves" Glass,
c. 1950. Ladies Choice Foods. With Label - **$35 $75 $120**

HOP-67

HOP-68

HOP-67. "Hoppy's Favorite" Bond Bread Cards,
c. 1950. Some fronts advertise bread loaf seals. Reverse caption "Ways Of The West." Unnumbered, set of 16.
Each - **$3 $6 $12**

HOP-68. Bond Bread Postcard,
c. 1950. - **$8 $15 $25**

HOP-69

HOP-69. Bond Bread Book Cover,
c. 1950. - **$12 $20 $35**

HOP-70

HOP-70. Bond Bread Book Cover,
c. 1950. - **$12 $20 $35**

HOP-71

HOP-71. "Ranch House Race" Game,
c. 1950. Stroehmann's Sunbeam Bread. - $35 $65 $100

HOP-72

HOP-73

HOP-72. TV Show "Special Guest" 11x16" Cardboard Store Sign,
c. 1950. Wonder Bread. - $40 $125 $200

HOP-73. Dairylea Milk 13x20" Paper Store Poster,
c. 1950. Various dairies. - $40 $100 $150

HOP-74

HOP-74. Dairylea Ice Cream Carton,
c. 1950. Offers neckerchief and t-shirt. - $40 $75 $150

HOP-76

HOP-75

HOP-75. "Dairylea Milk" Glass Inscribed "Do As Hoppy And Miss Dairylea Do/Drink Dairylea Milk",
c. 1950. - $75 $150 $300

HOP-76. "1 Cent Play Money" Cardboard Milk Bottle Cap,
c. 1950. - $8 $12 $20

HOP-77

HOP-77. Product Box And Premium Order Coupon,
c. 1950. Scarce. Honey Roll Sugar Cones.
Box - $200 $300 $450
Coupon - $20 $40 $75

HOP-78

HOP-79

HOP-78. Waxed Cardboard Ice Cream "Hoppy Cup",
c. 1950. - $15 $30 $60

HOP-79. "Hopalong Cassidy Bar 20" Vectograph Brass Clip,
c. 1950. Hopalong Cassidy Ice Cream Bar. Plastic mechanical insert reveals Hoppy picture, although image almost always gone. No Image - $15 $40 $75

HOP-80

Meadow Gold Butter

HOP-80. "Bob Atcher's Meadow Gold Song" TV Show Music Folder,
c. 1950. Meadow Gold Butter. - $20 $40 $75

HOP-82

HOP-81

HOP-81. "All-Star Milk" Pint Glass Bottle,
c. 1950. Local imprint for "McClellan's". - $30 $65 $100

HOP-82. Vinyl Tumbler,
c. 1950. Cloverlake Cottage Cheese.
With Lid - $25 $60 $100
No Lid - $20 $40 $70

HOP-85

HOP-84

HOP-83

HOP-83. Popsicle "Hopalong Cassidy" Silvered Tin Badge,
c. 1950. Various sponsors. Sold carded in stores. - $20 $40 $75

HOP-84. "HC" Silvered Metal Portrait Ring,
c. 1950. Popsicle and various sponsors. - **$20 $40 $60**

HOP-85. Miniature Plastic TV With Hoppy Film,
c. 1950. Hole on side for key chain, film has four color pictures of Hoppy. - **$35 $75 $110**

HOP-86

HOP-86. "Dudin'-Up Kit",
c. 1950. Fuller Brush Co. Hair treatment set with two trading cards on box back. Complete - **$200 $350 $550**

HOP-87

HOP-88

HOP-87. "Daily News" Cardboard Clicker Gun,
c. 1950. Various sponsors. - **$30 $60 $125**

HOP-88. Color Photo,
c. 1950. Came with gun to project filmstrips. - **$15 $25 $40**

HOP-89

HOP-90

HOP-91

HOP-89. "Hopalong Cassidy/Sheriff" Cello. Button,
c. 1950. From Arizona radio station. For Mutual Network broadcasts. - **$30 $60 $100**

HOP-90. Double Sponsor Cello. Button,
c. 1950. Filene's department store, Boston and Loew's State Theater. Dark red/black featuring Hoppy portrait. -
$100 $200 $300

HOP-91. Encased Penny With Coded Message,
1951. Reads "Member Hopalong Cassidy Savings Club/Security-First National Bank." Coded message and good luck symbols on rim. Code was printed on member's club card. - **$25 $60 $100**

HOP-92

HOP-93

HOP-92. Wild West Trading Cards,
1951. Post Cereals. Set of 36. Each - **$5 $10 $20**

HOP-93. Bond Bread "The Strange Legacy" Comic Booklet,
1951. 3-1/2x7" format. Titles also in series "The Mad Bomber" and "Meets The Brend Brothers, Bandits."
Each - **$12 $30 $60**

HOP-94

HOP-94. Concho/Branding Iron,
c. 1951. Post's Grape-Nuts Flakes. Plastic steer head with tie slide loop on back, used as ring or tie clip. Front has steer head cover over "HC" initials for printing paper. -
$100 $175 $250

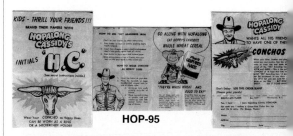

HOP-95

HOP-95. Concho/Branding Iron Instruction Leaflet,
c. 1951. Post's Grape-Nuts Flakes. - **$30 $40 $50**

HOP-96

HOP-96. "Western Badges" 9x20" Paper Sign,
1952. Not specified on sign but issued by Post's Raisin Bran. - **$40 $90 $175**

HOP-97

HOP-98

OP-97. "Hoppy Savings Club Honor Member" Litho. utton,
952. Rare. U.S. club folder doesn't show this button. ncertain if U.S. or Canadian. Rarest of all in series. - 00 $250 $400

OP-98. Hat/Compass Ring,
952. Post cereal. Brass bands, removable metal hat over astic magnetic compass. - **$100 $150 $200**

HOP-99

OP-99. All-Star Dairy Products Folder,
1956. Pictured premiums include those for Hoppy as well baseball stars Mickey Mantle and Stan Musial. - 0 $80 $125

HOP-100

HOP-101

OP-100. Autographed Photo,
50s. Pictured holding supplement to Philadelphia Sunday lletin. - **$50 $100 $150**

OP-101. Secretarial Autographed Photo,
50s. Signed by secretary or similar representative. - 5 $30 $50

HOP-102

OP-102. "Hoppy's Bunkhouse Clothes Corral" Wood ck,
50s. Northland Milk. - **$75 $150 $200**

HOP-103

HOP-103. Melville Milk 11x42" Cardboard Store Sign,
1950s. Various dairies. Simulated wood grain. - **$60 $150 $250**

HOP-104

HOP-104. "Hopalong Cassidy Fan Club" English Black And White Photo Postcards,
1950s. Each - **$10 $18 $30**

HOP-105

HOP-106

HOP-107

HOP-105. Portrait Photo,
1950s. Various sponsors. - **$12 $25 $40**

HOP-106. Restaurant Ad Postcard,
1950s. Sherman Skipalong Club, Hotel Sherman, Chicago. Also pictures manager "Skipalong Tattler". - **$25 $40 $65**

HOP-107. Milk Carton,
1950s. Various sponsors. - **$40 $75 $150**

HOP-108

HOP-108. Western Series Glass,
1950s. Probably held food product. At least four in the set. - **$30 $60 $90**

HOP-109

HOP-109. "Hopalong Cassidy" Silvered Metal Kerchief Slide,
1950s. Steer head has rhinestone eyes, his name is across the horns. - **$15 $30 $60**

HOP-110

HOP-111

HOP-110. Sterling Silver Ring,
1950s. Portrait framed by horseshoe, non-adjustable band. - **$50 $100 $200**

HOP-111. "Hopalong Cassidy Bar 20 Ranch" 2" Silvered Metal Badge,
1950s. English made store item with "Sheriff" under inset bw photo. - **$30 $50 $80**

HOP-112

HOP-112. "People and Places" Magazine,
1950s. Scarce. Car premium. - **$30 $60 $120**

HOP-113

HOP-114

HOP-113. Topper Bracelet,
1950s. Scarce. Anson Jewelry, gold finish. - **$30 $60 $120**

HOP-114. Bar 20 Bracelet,
1950s. Rare. Anson Jewelry, gold finish. - **$40 $80 $160**

HOP HARRIGAN

America's ace of the airways, Hop Harrigan made his debut in *All-American Comics* #1 in 1939, complete with Flying Club wings, patch, and other membership paraphernalia. On the ABC and Mutual radio networks from 1942 to 1948, Hop and his mechanical pal Tank Tinker conquered the Axis powers during the war years and fought assorted American villains once the war ended. The program was locally sponsored for much of its run; network sponsors included Grape Nuts Flakes (1944-1946) and Lever Brothers (1947-1948). Columbia Pictures released a 15-episode Hop Harrigan chapter play in 1946.

HPH-1

HPH-1. "Hop Harrigan All American Flying Club" Copper Finish Brass Wings Badge,
c. 1940. - **$25 $60 $100**

HPH-2

HPH-2. "All-American Flying Club" Kit.
c. 1942. Membership letter, card, stickers, fabric patch.
Near Mint In Mailer - **$150**
Patch - **$20 $30 $75**
Card - **$10 $20 $40**

HPH-3

HPH-4

PH-3. Club Fabric Patch,
, 1942. - **$20 $30 $75**

PH-4. Plastic Movie Viewer With Films,
, 1942. Includes three films. Near Mint Boxed - **$175**
iewer And Films - **$40 $80 $125**

HPH-5

HPH-6

PH-5. "Para-Plane With Parachutists" 15x16" Diecut ardboard Store Sign,
1944. Rare. Grape-Nuts Flakes. Sign is three-dimensional d has open center to display cereal box. -
250 $500 $1200

PH-6. Superfortress Grape Nuts Flakes Sign,
044. Scarce. - **$75 $150 $300**

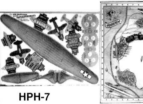

HPH-7

PH-7. "Boeing B-29 Superfortress Model Plane And rget Game",
1944. Scarce. Grape-Nuts Flakes. Includes target, two nch-out sheets, marbles. Complete - **$100 $200 $300**

HOWDY DOODY

aired on NBC-TV from 1947 to 1960, starting out as *The ppet Playhouse*, created and hosted by Buffalo Bob Smith. was one of television's all-time successes, winner of the st Peabody award, attracting millions of devoted young ewers and responsible for millions of dollars in licensed erchandise. It was *Howdy Doody Time*, a combination of ntasy, music, films, and slapstick played out by puppets d humans in front of a screaming studio audience of 40 ds for more than 2,300 performances.

wdy, with voice supplied by Buffalo Bob, consorted with a g list of characters, including Clarabell the clown (played ginally by Bob Keeshan); Mr. Bluster, the mayor of odyville; Flub-A-Dub, a fantastic animal crossbreed; Dilly-lly, a big-eared carpenter; Indian Princess Summerfall-nterspring; and many others. The original Howdy puppet s replaced with a new design in 1948.

nong the program's many sponsors: Wonder Bread, lgate tooth powder, Ovaltine, Poll-Parrot shoes, Mars ndy, Tootsie Rolls, Welch's grape juice, Marx and Ideal

toys, Kellogg's and Nabisco cereals, and Royal pudding. Character licensees were barely able to meet the huge demand for toys, dolls, lunch boxes, clothes, marionettes, wristwatches, mugs, piggy banks, figurines, records, T-shirts, even a musical rocking chair. Items were copyrighted Bob Smith (1948-1951), Kagran Corp. (1951-1959), or NBC (1960 on).

A Sunday *Howdy Doody* comic strip appeared from 1950 to 1953, and Dell published comic books from 1950 to 1957. A radio version of the show aired on NBC from 1952 to 1958, and the TV series was revived briefly on NBC in 1976, but, sadly, it was no longer *Howdy Doody Time.*

HOW-1

HOW-2

HOW-1. "I'm For Howdy Doody" Cello. Button,
1948. First item and premium offered March 23, 1948 as part of Howdy Doody for President campaign. Five stations carried the show and the offer was made seven times. NBC was astonished by 60,000 requests. Colgate, Continental Baking, Ovaltine and Mars candy quickly signed as sponsors. -
$20 $50 $85

HOW-2. "The Billboard" Magazine With Cover Photo,
November 27, 1948. Early item from first year of Howdy show. - **$20 $30 $50**

HOW-3

HOW-4

HOW-3. Howdy Doody Newspaper #1,
1950. Poll-Parrot. Scarce. - **$30 $75 $150**

HOW-4. Thank-You Letter,
1950. Rare. Recipient awarded box of Snickers for poem selected from a contest. - **$75 $150 $250**

HOW-5

HOW-6

HOW-7

HOW-5. Wood Jointed Doll,
c. 1950. Store item. Includes leather belt and fabric bandanna. - **$150 $275 $450**

HOW-6. Ovaltine Plastic Mug With Decal,
c. 1950. - **$20 $24 $75**

HOW-7. Ovaltine Plastic Shake-Up Mug,
c. 1950. - **$25 $50 $90**

HOW-8

HOW-9

HOW-8. Cardboard Store Sign,
c. 1950. Colgate Dental Cream. - **$12 $20 $35**

HOW-9. "Magic Trading Card" 14x21" Proof Sheet,
1951. Issued individually in boxes of Burry's Howdy Doody Cookies. Uncut - **$80 $200 $350**
Each Card - **$2 $5 $8**

HOW-10

HOW-11

HOW-10. "Howdy Doody Talkin' Tag",
1951. Wonder Bread/Hostess Cupcakes. Disk turns to form four mouth expressions. - **$20 $35 $60**

HOW-11. "Poll Parrot's" Comic Book #4,
1951. Series of four. Each - **$10 $30 $70**

HOW-12

HOW-12. Store Clerk Paper Cap,
c. 1951. Wonder Bread. - **$15 $30 $50**

HOW-13

HOW-14

HOW-13. "Circus Album" 5-1/2x8" Ad Sheet,
c. 1951. Wonder Bread. - **$35 $75 $125**

HOW-14. T.V.-Merrimat Paper Place Mat,
1952. Store item. Placematters, Inc. - **$15 $30 $60**

HOW-15

HOW-16

HOW-15. T.V.-Merrimat Plastic Place Mat,
1952. Store item. Placematters, Inc. - **$20 $40 $80**

HOW-16. "Howdy Doody For President" Cello. Button,
1952. Wonder Bread. - **$25 $50 $85**

HOW-17

HOW-18

HOW-17. "Campaign Cap",
c. 1952. Poll-Parrot Shoes. Paper punch-out assembled by slots and tabs. Unpunched - **$25 $60 $100**
Assembled - **$15 $50 $90**

HOW-18. Welch's Cookbook,
1952. Welch's Grape Juice. - **$15 $35 $60**

(bottom of bottle)
HOW-19

HOW-20

OW-19. Welch's Grape Juice Glass Bottle,
1952. Various character portraits embossed on bottom.
ach - **$10 $25 $40**

OW-20. Welch's Grape Juice Tin Cap From Bottle,
1952. - **$5 $10 $15**

HOW-21   **HOW-22**

OW-21. Welch's Grape Juice 3" Tin Lid From Glass
lly Jar,
)53. - **$8 $15 $25**

OW-22. Welch's Grape Jelly Glasses,
)53. Six designs, various colors, character faces on bottom.
ch - **$5 $10 $15**

HOW-23

)W-23. "Doodyville" Cardboard Houses,
53. Welch's Grape Juice. Set of eight.
ch Unused - **$20 $40 $75**
ch Assembled - **$10 $25 $40**

HOW-24   **HOW-25**   **HOW-26**

W-24. "Coloring Comics" Sheet #1,
53. Blue Bonnet Margarine. From numbered series of box
erts. Each - **$5 $10 $20**

W-25. "Snap-A-Wink" Target,
53. Poll-Parrot Shoes. - **$25 $45 $60**

W-26. "Comic Circus Animals" Picture Toy,
54. Poll-Parrot Shoes. - **$30 $75 $125**

HOW-27

HOW-27. "Big Prize Doodle List" Sheet,
1954. Howdy Doody Ice Cream Club. Premium listing for
1954-1955. - **$10 $20 $30**

HOW-28   **HOW-29**

HOW-28. Kellogg's Rice Krispies Box Panel Masks,
1954. One of a set: Howdy, Clarabell, Dilly Dally, The
Princess. Each Uncut Box Back - **$10 $25 $40**

HOW-29. Merchandise Manual,
1954. Rare. - **$100 $200 $400**
1955. Rare. - **$75 $150 $300**

HOW-30

HOW-31

HOW-30. Ice Cream Cup Lid,
1955. Doughnut Corp. of America. Lid and 25 cents used to
order "Howdy Doody Magic Talking Pin." - **$10 $20 $35**

HOW-31. "Clarabell Dangle-Dandy" Box Back,
c. 1955. Kellogg's. One of a series.
Uncut Each - **$20 $50 $75**
Assembled Each - **$10 $25 $50**

HOW-32

HOW-32. "Twin-Pop" 7x14" Paper Store Sign,
1956. - **$20 $50 $75**

HOW-33

HOW-34

HOW-33. "Jackpot Of Fun" Comic Book,
1957. DCA Food Industries. - **$15 $25 $45**

HOW-34. Ceramic Piggy Bank,
1950s. Store item. - **$75 $125 $200**

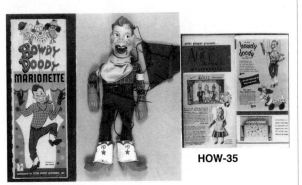

HOW-35

HOW-35. Composition Marionette,
1950s. Store item by Peter Puppet Playthings.
Boxed - **$75 $125 $200**
Loose - **$35 $60 $100**

HOW-37

HOW-38

HOW-36

HOW-36. Large Glazed Ceramic Bust Bank,
1950s. Store item. - **$200 $300 $600**

HOW-37. Photo Glow Ring,
1950s. Ring name implies image glows in dark but all examples seen do not glow. - **$125 $188 $250**

HOW-38. Flicker Picture Ring With Brass Base,
1950s. Portrait of Howdy alternates with image of Poll Parrot on a perch. - **$50 $75 $100**

...

HOW-39

HOW-40

HOW-41

HOW-39. Poll-Parrot TV Plastic Ring With Flicker Picture
1950s. Frame image of TV screen, image alternates between Howdy and parrot. - **$100 $150 $200**

HOW-40. Plastic Ring With Paper Insert Picture,
1950s. - **$75 $110 $150**

HOW-41. Illuminated Head Ring,
1950s. Brass bands holding plastic head lighted by bulb and battery. - **$75 $140 $200**

HOW-43

HOW-42

HOW-44

HOW-42. Jack-In-The-Box Plastic Ring,
1950s. Poll-Parrot Shoes. Lid lifts over miniature 3-D plastic Howdy head. - **$1725 $3450 $5500**

HOW-43. "Poll-Parrot" Plastic Ring,
1950s. Raised portrait. - **$75 $110 $150**

HOW-44. Clarabell's Horn Ring,
1950s. Scarce. Brass bands picture Clarabell and Howdy, top has aluminum horn that works by blowing. -
$150 $325 $500

HOW-45

HOW-46

HOW-47

HOW-45. Newspaper Comic Strip Litho. Button,
1950s. - **$20 $35 $75**

HOW-46. "Howdy Doody Safety Club/CBC" Cello. Butto
1950s. Canadian Broadcasting Company. Canadian issue Toronto maker. - **$35 $75 $125**

HOW-47. "Sunday Post-Dispatch" Litho. Button,
1950s. Issued for newspaper comic strip. - **$30 $60 $100**

HOW-48

HOW-48. "Poll-Parrot's Howdy Doody Photo Album",
1950s. Includes four blank pages to mount four photos.
Complete - **$75 $110 $160**

HOW-49

HOW-49. Tuk-A-Tab Mask,
1950s. Poll-Parrot. Masks of Howdy and Clarabell.
Each Unpunched - **$20 $30 $50**

HOW-50

HOW-51   HOW-52

HOW-50. Poll-Parrot Coloring Book,
1950s. - **$20 $40 $60**

HOW-51. Jointed Cardboard Puppet,
1950s. Wonder Bread. 13" tall. - **$10 $20 $40**

HOW-52. Jointed Cardboard Puppet,
1950s. Wonder Bread. 7-1/2" tall. - **$10 $20 $40**

HOW-53

HOW-54

HOW-55

HOW-53. Princess Cardboard Jointed Puppet,
1950s. Wonder Bread. - **$15 $25 $40**

HOW-54. Howdy Doody Periscope,
1950s. Rare. Wonder Bread. - **$75 $150 $375**

HOW-55. Bread Labels,
1950s. Wonder Bread. From two different sets.
Each - **$5 $8 $12**

HOW-56

HOW-56. "Wonder-Land Game" Sheet,
1950s. Wonder Bread. With spinner and 16 spaces for cut-
outs from bread end labels. Unused - **$20 $40 $75**
Complete - **$75 $100 $200**

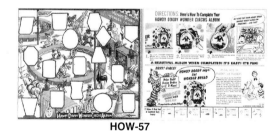

HOW-57

HOW-57. "Wonder Bread Circus Album" Label Sheet,
1950s. - **$30 $50 $80**

HOW-58

HOW-58. "Wonder Bread Balloon Parade" Label Sheet,
1950s. - **$30 $50 $80**

HOW-59   HOW-60   HOW-61

HOW-59. "Howdy Doody's Favorite Doughnuts" Cellophane Package,
1950s. Tom Thumb. - **$15 $35 $60**

HOW-60. "Wonder Bread Zoomascope",
1950s. Opens to 3-1/2x51". - **$25 $50 $85**

HOW-61. Cardboard Disk Flipper Badge,
1950s. Wonder Bread. Disk flips by pulling string to complete phrase "The Princess Says...Eat Wonder Bread". From set picturing various Howdy Doody characters.
Each - **$10 $20 $30**

HOW-62   HOW-63   HOW-64

HOW-62. "Hostess" Cupcake Package Tag,
1950s. Continental Baking Co. - **$50 $75 $100**

HOW-63. Litho. Tab,
1950s. Ten tabs were collected for free "Twin Pop Or Fudge Bar". - **$10 $20 $35**

HOW-64. Ice Cream Waxed Cardboard Cup,
1950s. - **$20 $35 $50**

HOW-65

HOW-65. Packaged Wood Ice Cream Spoon,
1950s. - **$5 $10 $15**

HOW-66

HOW-66. "Fudge Bar" Waxed Paper Bag,
1950s. Offers talking pin and ice cream club membership. - **$5 $12 $20**

HOW-67

HOW-67. Christmas Cards,
1950s. Mars Candy. At least seven known.
Each - **$8 $12 $20**

HOW-68   HOW-69

HOW-68. "Mason Candy Words To The 'Howdy Doody' Song" Sheet,
1950s. - **$10 $18 $30**

HOW-69. "Howdy Doody Animated Puppet" Punch-Out With Envelope,
1950s. Three Muskateers/Mars candy bars.
Near Mint In Mailer - **$75**

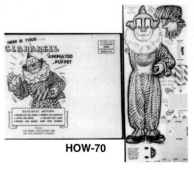

HOW-70

HOW-70. "Clarabell Animated Puppet" Punch-Out With Envelope,
1950s. Mars Coconut Bar. Near Mint In Mailer - **$90**

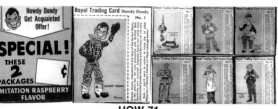

HOW-71

HOW-77

HOW-71. "Royal Trading Card",
1950s. Royal Pudding. Set of 14.
Each Complete Box - **$5 $12 $20**
Each Cut Card - **$3 $4 $12**

HOW-77. Blue Bonnet Margarine Box Panels,
1950s. Waxed cardboard set of 12 for "Play TV" stage
offered separately as mail premium.
Each Uncut Panel - **$10 $20 $35**

HOW-72

HOW-73

HOW-74

HOW-78

HOW-72. Princess Face Mask With Glassine Envelope,
1950s. Royal Desserts. Issued for additional characters.
With Envelope - **$15 $25 $50**
Loose - **$10 $20 $30**

HOW-78. Four-Sided Mask,
1950s. Philco TV depicting Howdy, Gabby Hayes and
National/American League baseball players to promote
World Series on Philco TV. - **$40 $75 $125**

HOW-73. Silver Plate Iced Tea Spoon,
1950s. Sponsor unknown. - **$8 $15 $30**

HOW-74. "Howdy Doody Climber" Cardboard Figure,
1950s. Luden's Wild Cherry Cough Drops.
Near Mint In Mailer - **$60**
Loose - **$10 $20 $35**

HOW-79

HOW-80

HOW-75

HOW-76

HOW-79. "Howdy Doody Napkins" Trading Card Sheet,
1950s. Colonial Paper Products Co. At least two different
sheets. Each Uncut - **$20 $40 $75**

HOW-80. "Princess Summerfall Winterspring" Photo,
1950s. Pictures Judy Tyler. - **$20 $40 $75**

HOW-75. "Magic Kit" With Envelope,
1950s. Luden's, makers of Fifth Avenue candy bar. Tricks on
punch-out sheets. Near Mint In Mailer - **$100**

HOW-76. Cereal Box Mask,
1950s. Wheaties. Cut Mask - **$15 $20 $40**
Complete Box - **$100 $300 $750**

HOW-81

HOW-81. Hat,
1950s. Store bought. - **$10 $20 $30**

HOW-82

HOW-82. Large Postcard,
1950s. - **$30 $60 $90**

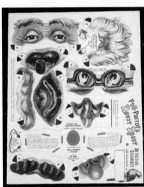

HOW-84

HOW-83

HOW-85

HOW-83. Detective Disguise Punch-Out Sheet,
1950s. Poll-Parrot Shoes - **$20 $40 $60**

HOW-84. "Howdy Doody For President" Litho. Tin Tab,
c. 1976. National Broadcasting Corp. - **$10 $20 $30**

HOW-85. "A 40-Year Celebration" 3" Cello. Button,
1987. National Broadcasting Co. - **$5 $12 $25**

HOWIE WING

The air adventures of ace Howie Wing were heard on CBS radio five times a week in 1938 and 1939, with William Janney battling evil as young Howie. Kellogg's cereals sponsored the program and issued a number of aviation-related premiums, including wings, a weather forecaster ring, decoder, model airplane kits, and membership paraphernalia for the Cadet Aviation Corps.

HWN-1   HWN-2

HWN-1. "Kellogg's Cadet Aviation Corps" Club Manual,
1938. - **$10 $20 $35**

HWN-2. Premium Order Sheet,
c. 1938. Offers Cadet Aviation Corp. button, Flying Guide and Pilot Test Card. - **$8 $12 $20**

HWN-3   HWN-4

HWN-3. "Kellogg's Rubber Band Pilot's Pistol And Targets",
c. 1938. Unpunched - **$50 $80 $150**

HWN-4. "Kellogg's Moving Picture Machine",
c. 1938. Unpunched - **$50 $80 $150**

HWN-5   HWN-6

HWN-5. "Official Handbook",
1939. Kellogg's. - **$25 $40 $75**

HWN-6. "Howie Wing/Cadet Aviation Corps" Club Membership Card,
1939. Kellogg's. - **$10 $15 $25**

HWN-7   HWN-8

HWN-7. "Kellogg's Cadet Aviation Corps" Club Member Certificate,
1930s. - $10 $20 $30

HWN-8. "Howie Wing's Adventures On The Canadian Lakes" Map,
1930s. Kellogg's of Canada. 11x16" opened. - $50 $125 $200

HWN-9

HWN-10

HWN-9. "Howie Wing/Kellogg's" Holed Aluminum Coin,
1930s. - $25 $50 $100

HWN-10. "Howie Wing Cadet" Silvered/Enameled Brass Badge,
1930s. - $5 $10 $15

HWN-11

HWN-12

HWN-11. Weather Forecast Ring,
1930s. Brass bands with metal clip holding slip of litmus paper. - $250 $400 $550

HWN-12. "Cadet" Cello. Button,
1930s. Distributed to Canadian members. - $10 $20 $35

HWN-13

HWN-13. "Pilot CAC" Aluminum Wings Badge,
1930s. For Howie Wing Cadet Aviation Corps. Probably Canadian issue. - $20 $35 $50

HWN-14

HWN-14. "Kellogg's Cadet Aviation Corps" Pamphlet Set,
1930s. Set of 17. Each - $3 $5 $8

H. R. PUFNSTUF

This Saturday morning children's television series, which used both live actors and puppets, aired on NBC from 1969 to 1971 and was repeated on ABC from 1972 to 1974. The program told, with songs and dances, the adventures of young Jimmy and his golden talking flute Freddie as they try to escape the clutches of the wicked Witchiepoo on Living Island. A movie version was released by Paramount in 1970, and comic books appeared from 1970 to 1972.

HPF-1

HPF-1. Soundtrack Record Album,
1970. Kellogg's. With Mailer - $40 $75 $125
No Mailer - $25 $50 $85

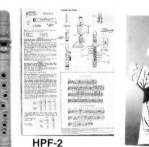
HPF-2

HPF-3

HPF-2. "Freddie The Flute" Musical Toy With Instructions,
1970. Kellogg's. Flute - $100 $250 $350
Instruction Sheet - $25 $50 $75

HPF-3. H.R. Pufnstuf Vinyl Hand Puppet,
1970. Store item by Remco. - $25 $50 $75

HPF-4

HPF-5

HPF-4. Jimmy Vinyl Hand Puppet,
1970. Store item by Remco. - $25 $50 $75

HPF-5. Cling Or Clang Vinyl Hand Puppet,
1970. Store item by Remco. - $25 $50 $75

HUCKLEBERRY HOUND

Huckleberry Hound, the first animated cartoon to win an Emmy, was Hanna-Barbera's first major television hit and the source of hundreds of licensed products. The syndicated series, sponsored by Kellogg's cereals, aired from 1958 to 1962 and was watched by millions of viewers all over the world. Huck was a noble-hearted bloodhound who remained untroubled no matter what misfortunes plagued him. Other cartoon segments on the show: Pixie and Dixie, a pair of carefree mice who tormented the affable tomcat Mr. Jinks ("I love those meeces to pieces!"); Yogi Bear, who debuted on the show and went on to his own major series in 1961; and Hokey Wolf, a Sgt. Bilko-like con artist whose pal was Ding-a-Ling, a fox. *Huckleberry Hound* comic books appeared from 1959 into the 1970s.

HUC-1   HUC-2

HUC-1. "Fun Cards" Box Back,
1959. Kellogg's Corn Flakes. Back Panel Only - **$10 $15 $25**

HUC-2. Plush Doll With Vinyl Face,
1960. Store item by Knickerbocker and Kellogg's premium. - **$25 $40 $65**

HUC-3

HUC-3. "Huck Hound Club" Kit,
1960. Kellogg's. Includes letter, member card, two color pictures, club button, Breakfast Score Card (not shown). Complete - **$75 $150 $250**

HUC-4

HUC-5

HUC-6

HUC-4. "Huckleberry Hound For President" 3" Litho. Button,
1960. - **$15 $30 $60**

HUC-5. "The Great Kellogg's TV Show" Record Album,
c. 1960. - **$8 $12 $20**

HUC-6. Plastic Bank,
c. 1960. Store item by Knickerbocker. - **$15 $25 $35**

HUC-7   HUC-8

HUC-7. "Huck Hound Club" Enameled Brass Ring,
c. 1960. Kellogg's. - **$30 $65 $100**

HUC-8. "Huck Hound Club" Brass Ring Copyrighted,
1961. Kellogg's. Variety without enamel paint accents. - **$30 $65 $100**

HUC-10

HUC-9

HUC-9. "Kellogg's Special K" 17x41" Cardboard Hange String Sign,
1960s. - **$75 $125 $200**

HUC-10. Huck Hound/Mr. Jinks Plastic Flicker Ring,
1960s. Sponsor unknown but probable premium. - **$30 $60 $125**

INNER SANCTUM

ne memorable squeaking door and the sinister voice of Raymond, your host" introduced the macabre *Inner anctum* mysteries on radio from 1941 to 1952, first on the ue network, then on CBS (1943-1950), and ABC. The orbid anthology featured such film veterans as Boris arloff, Peter Lorre, and Claude Raines in ghostly tales of urder and mayhem. Sponsors included Carter's Little Liver lls (1941-1943), Colgate-Palmolive shaving cream (1943-944), Lipton tea and soup (1945), Bromo-Seltzer (1946-950), and Mars candy (1950-1951). A number of second-ature Inner Sanctum movies were made in the 1940s by niversal, most starring Lon Chaney Jr.

INN-1

N-1. Cardboard Ink Blotter,
45. Scarce. Lipton tea and soup. - **$15 $30 $50**

INSPECTOR POST

eneral Foods created Post's Junior Detective Corps in 32-1933 to promote its line of cereals. The club was adver-ed in Sunday newspaper comic sections and on the cereal xes, offering its young members manuals edited by spector General Post and badges for detective ranks up to e level of Captain.

INS-1

INS-2

S-1. **"Inspector Post's Case Book" Manual,**
33. Post Toasties. Includes 10 mysteries solved by swers on back. - **$10 $20 $30**

S-2. **Junior Detective Corps" Club Manuals,**
33. Set of four. Each - **$10 $20 $35**

INS-3

INS-4

INS-3. "Detective/Post's J.D.C." Silvered Tin Badge,
1933. - **$15 $25 $40**

INS-4. "Detective Sergeant/Post's J.D.C." Brass Rank Badge,
1933. - **$10 $20 $35**

INS-5

INS-6

INS-5. "Lieutenant Post's J.D.C." Silvered Brass Rank Badge ,
1933. - **$15 $25 $40**

INS-6. "Captain/Post's J.D.C." Brass Rank Badge,
1933. Scarce. - **$20 $40 $80**

JACK ARMSTRONG

Jack Armstrong hit the air in July 1933 and ruled the late-afternoon airwaves until 1951, one of the most popular and longest-running radio adventure series ever — and, thanks to Wheaties' sponsorship, one of the most bountiful sources of premiums. Jack started as a sports hero at Hudson High School, but within a year he and cousins Billy and Betty were seeking adventure with Uncle Jim in exotic spots all over the world. They were still waving the flag for Hudson High, but the intrepid four were tackling Tibet, searching out the ele-phants' graveyard in darkest Africa, recovering sunken urani-um in the Sulu Sea, always looking for something lost or stolen or buried.

Jack Armstrong premiums were frequently linked to the pro-gram's story line - a Hike-O-Meter just like the one Jack used to measure how far he'd walked, a torpedo flashlight or explorer telescope, a signaling mirror or secret whistle ring to send messages, a bombsight, a bracelet just like Betty's, and, of course, club memberships. During World War II lis-teners were urged to buy war bonds, collect scrap, and write letters to servicemen, and to stay strong by eating their Wheaties. In 1950 the program was renamed *Armstrong of the SBI* and Jack, Billy, and Betty began working for the Scientific Bureau of Investigation. The series went off the air in 1951.

Jack Armstrong comic strips and a series of 13 comic books were published from 1947 to 1949, all drawn by Bob Schoenke. Also in 1947, Columbia Pictures released a 15-episode chapter play.

JAC-1

JAC-1. Wheaties Box With 1st Premium Offer On Back,
1933. Rare. Offers hand exercise grips. Complete -
$75 $150 $375

JAC-2

JAC-3

JAC-4

JAC-2. "Johnny (Tarzan) Weissmuller" Photo,
1933. Rare. One of earliest Jack Armstrong Wheaties premiums. - **$40 $80 $160**

JAC-3. Wheaties "How To Hit A Home Run" Flip Booklet,
1933. Scarce. Photo pages in sequence of batting stance, complete swing, follow-through. - **$50 $100 $300**

JAC-4. Armstrong On Horse Blackster Photo,
1933. - **$10 $15 $25**

JAC-5

JAC-5. "Shooting Plane" With Directions And Mailer,
1933. Made by Daisy Mfg. Co. Metal gun and two spinner wheels. Near Mint Boxed - **$175**
Gun - **$50 $75 $100**
Each Spinner - **$10 $20 $30**

JAC-6

JAC-6. "Wee-Gyro" Flying Ship, Instruction Paper,
1934. Sheet came with a balsa model similar to autogyro. -
$25 $75 $125

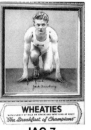

JAC-7

JAC-8

JAC-7. Box Back Panel,
1935. - **$10 $18 $25**

JAC-8. Box Back Panel,
1935. - **$5 $10 $15**

JAC-9

JAC-10

JAC-11

JAC-9. Box Back Panel,
1935. - **$8 $12 $20**

JAC-10. Betty Fairfield Box Back Panel,
1935. - **$5 $10 $15**

JAC-11. Betty Fairfield Box Back Panel,
1935. - **$8 $12 $20**

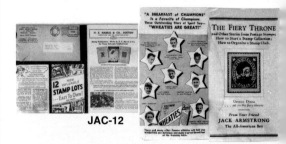

JAC-12

JAC-12. Stamp Collecting Items,
1935. Includes booklet and pamphlets about stamp collecting with offer of oriental stamps. Each - **$5 $8 $12**

JAC-13

JAC-13. "Jack Armstrong's Chart Game/Adventures With The Dragon Talisman" Map Game,
1936. Map Game Only - **$35 $75 $150**
Spinner and Game Markers (4) - **$10 $20 $40**
Dragon Talisman - **$20 $35 $75**

JAC-14

JAC-15

JAC-16

JAC-14. "Big Ten Football Game",
1936. Near Mint In Mailer - **$175**
Board Only - **$10 $18 $35**

JAC-15. Milk Glass Bowl,
1937. - **$10 $25 $35**

JAC-16. Movie Viewer With Filmstrip,
1937. Film title is "Graveyard Of Elephants".
Box - **$10 $20 $35**
Viewer And Film - **$40 $75 $125**

JAC-17

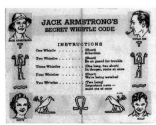
JAC-18

JAC-17. Secret Whistling Brass Ring,
1937. Egyptian symbols on sides. - **$40 $95 $150**

JAC-18. "Secret Whistle Code" Instruction Sheet,
1937. Paper (not cardboard). For Egyptian Whistle Ring. - **$10 $15 $25**

JAC-19

JAC-20

JAC-19. "Hike-O-Meter" Aluminum Pedometer,
1938. Blue painted rim. - **$20 $40 $75**

JAC-20. "Treasure Hunt" Instruction Booklet,
1938. Came with Hike-O-Meter pedometer. - **$15 $25 $35**

JAC-21

JAC-21. "Adventures Of Jack Armstrong" Box Backs,
1938. Wheaties. Set of six. Each Back Panel - **$15 $30 $50**

JAC-22

JAC-23

JAC-22. Explorer Telescope,
1938. Cardboard tube with metal caps holding glass lenses. - **$8 $15 $25**

JAC-23. Heliograph And Distance Finder,
1938. Scarce. Brass multi-function premium for land and water measurements, message sender, secret compartment, Morse Code. Scarce test premium. - **$200 $500 $1000**

JAC-24

JAC-24. "Jack Armstrong Magic Answer Box",
1938. Complete Boxed - **$50 $75 $150**
Answer Box Only - **$30 $50 $75**

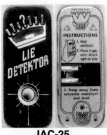

JAC-26

JAC-25

JAC-25. "Lie Detektor" Metal Answer Box,
c. 1938. Supposed first version of "Magic Answer Box" quick-ly redesigned because parents objected to children telling lies. - **$75 $150 $300**

JAC-26. All American Boy Ring Lead Proof,
1939. Unique - **$2000**

JAC-27   JAC-28   JAC-29

JAC-27. Decoder Lead Proof,
1939. Designed by Orin Armstrong for Robbins Company. Never produced. Unique - **$2000**

JAC-28. Pedometer,
1939. Version with unpainted aluminum rim. - **$15 $25 $40**

JAC-29. Torpedo Flashlight Set,
1939. Set of three in red, blue, or black cardboard barrels with metal nose and rear cap.
Blue - **$15 $25 $40**
Red - **$15 $30 $50**
Black - **$20 $35 $60**

JAC-30

JAC-30. Wheaties "Stampo" Game With Mailer Envelope
1930s. Two sheets to be cut and four leaflets for game devised by H. E. Harris Co., domestic and foreign postage stamps dealer of Boston. Uncut In Mailer - **$25 $50 $75**

JAC-31

JAC-31. How to Fly Promo Sign,
1930s. - **$20 $40 $80**

JAC-32

JAC-32. Sentinel Junior Ace First Aid Kit Complete with Mailer,
1930s. **$100 $200 $300**
Tin Box Only - **$30 $60 $120**

JAC-33

JAC-33. Windfair W. J. A. C. Club Lead Proof,
1930s. Unique. - **$300 $500 $1000**

JAC-34   JAC-35

JAC-34. Betty's Luminous Gardenia Bracelet,
1940. Rare. Glows in the dark. - **$75 $150 $350**

JAC-35. Glow-In-Dark Brooch 3" Plastic Pin,
1940. Known as "Betty's Gardenia Brooch." - **$50 $100 $150**

JAC-36

JAC-37

JAC-44

JAC-45

JAC-36. Sky Ranger Plane,
1940. - **$50 $125 $200**

JAC-37. Listening Squad Membership Card,
1940. Rare. Test premium. - **$100 $200 $300**

JAC-44. Dragon's Eye Ring With Instruction Paper,
1940. White glow plastic ring topped by dark green stone.
Ring - **$300 $750 $1200**

JAC-45. "Sound Effects Kit" Sheet,
1941. "Spy Hunt" mystery script utilizing sound effects. -
$20 $35 $50

JAC-38

JAC-40

JAC-39

JAC-41

JAC-47

JAC-46

JAC-38. "Lieutenant/Listening Squad" Brass Whistle Badge,
1940. Scarce. Test premium, small quantity distributed. -
$125 $300 $750

JAC-39. Lieutenant/Listening Squad Whistle Lead Proof,
1940. Unique - **$1000**

JAC-40. "Captain/Listening Squad" Sample Brass Whistle Badge,
1940. Rare. Test premium, even scarcer than Lieutenant version. - **$300 $600 $1200**

JAC-41. Captain/Listening Squad Whistle Lead Proof,
1940. Unique - **$1500**

JAC-46. "Write A Fighter Corps" Kit,
1942. Includes manual, stencils (6), star sticker sheets (6),
insignia patches (6). Near Mint In Mailer - **$250**
Manual Only - **$25 $50 $75**

JAC-47. Press Release Photo Picturing Wood Bombsight,
1942. Mutual Broadcasting System. Pictures radio cast members Uncle Jim and Jack Armstrong holding Wheaties premium. - **$20 $40 $85**

JAC-43

JAC-42

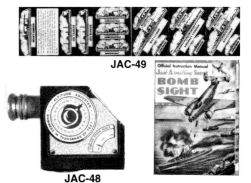

JAC-49

JAC-48

JAC-42. Crocodile Glow in the Dark Plastic Whistle,
1940. Rare. Test premium with two known. -
$1000 $2000 $4000

JAC-43. "Dragon's Eye Ring" Instructions/Order Blank Sheet,
1940. Order coupon for additional rings expired January 2,
1941. - **$125 $150 $175**

JAC-48. Wheaties Secret Bombsight,
1942. Wood/litho. paper bomb release holding three wooden
bombs. Bombsight Only - **$50 $100 $200**
Each Bomb - **$20 $30 $40**

JAC-49. "Secret Bomb Sight Instruction Manual",
1942. Scarce. Includes cut-out ships for use with bomb sight.
Uncut - **$60 $150 $300**

JAC-50

JAC-51

JAC-50. "Future Champions Of America" Club Manual,
1943. - **$20 $40 $75**

JAC-51. "Future Champions Of America" Fabric Patch,
1943. - **$5 $12 $20**

JAC-52

JAC-53

JAC-52. Tru-Flite News Vol. 1 #1 Newspaper,
Sept. 1944. - **$15 $35 $60**

JAC-53. Tru-Flite News Vol. 1 #2 Newspaper,
Oct. 1944. - **$15 $30 $55**

JAC-54

JAC-54. Model Planes 16x36" Paper Store Sign,
1944. - **$50 $100 $150**

JAC-55

**JAC-55. Wheaties Tru-Flite Warplane Paper Model Kit
With Envelope,**
1944. Seven sets (A-G), each with two cut-out airplanes and
instructions. Each Uncut Set In Mailer - **$25 $60 $90**

JAC-56

**JAC-56. "Cub Pilot Corps News" Vol. 1 #1 Newsletter
With Mail Envelope,**
1945. Includes punch-out Pre-Flight Training Kit. Near Mint
In Mailer - **$150**
Newsletter - **$15 $35 $50**
Punch-Out - **$20 $40 $60**

JAC-57

**JAC-57. "Cub Pilot Corps" Contest Newspaper With I.D.
Tag And Envelope,**
1945. Includes newspaper #3 and metal "G.I. Identification
Tag". Near Mint In Mailer- **$150**
Newspaper - **$15 $35 $50**
Tag - **$20 $40 $75**

JAC-58

JAC-58. "Parachute Ball" With Instructions And Mailer,
1946. Aluminum ball with paper parachute.
Near Mint Boxed - **$200**
Ball And Parachute Only - **$35 $60 $100**

JAC-60

JAC-59

AC-59. Jack Armstrong #1 Comic,
947. Odd size. - **$35 $110 $250**

AC-60. "Explorer's Sun Watch" With Glow-In-Dark Dial,
948. Version without "Frank Buck" name with insert com-
ass and movable pointer. - **$20 $30 $50**

JAC-61   JAC-62

AC-61. Armstrong & Betty Fairfield Photo Cards,
1940s. Each - **$20 $40 $75**

AC-62. Pictorial Pedometer,
940s. Metal with lt. green rim picturing six golfers. -
50 **$100 $150**

JACK BENNY

ack Benny (1894-1974) started in show business at the age
eight as a combination usher and violinist in a theater in
aukegan, Illinois. Thirty years later, when his program
ebuted on radio, he was a major star of stage and vaude-
le. For 23 years on radio (1932-1955) and for 15 years on
levision (1950-1965) Benny was a Sunday night comic
stitution. His long-running feud with Fred Allen, his penny-
nching, his blue eyes, his ancient Maxwell car, his vault in
e basement, his violin, his age - always 39 - became part of
e country's pop culture. Also featured over the years were
s wife Mary Livingston, Rochester the valet, Don Wilson,
ennis Day, Phil Harris, Mel Blanc, and a host of others.
ong-term radio sponsors were Jell-O (1934-1942) and
ucky Strike cigarettes (1944-1955); others included Canada
ry ginger ale (1932-1933), Chevrolet (1933-1934), General
re (1934), and Grape-Nuts Flakes (1942-1944). Benny
so appeared on numerous other television shows and
ade a number of movies.

JBE-1

JBE-2

BE-1. Fan Photo,
1934. Jell-O. - **$5 $12 $25**

BE-2. Jell-O Recipe Book,
937. Inside covers have Jack Benny and Mary Livingston
mic strips. - **$10 $20 $35**

JBE-3

JBE-4

JBE-3. "Benny Buck" Movie Theater Play Money,
1939. Local theaters. For film "Buck Benny Rides Again" picturing supporting stars Ellen Drew and Andy Devine on
back. - **$10 $20 $30**

JBE-4. Dixie Ice Cream Picture,
1930s. - **$5 $10 $15**

JBE-5

JBE-5. Radio Show Program,
c. 1944. Lucky Strike cigarettes. - **$20 $40 $60**

JBE-6   JBE-7

JBE-6. "Rochester" Fan Photo,
c. 1940s. Store item, probable sample from dime store picture frame. Pictured is Jack Benny's long-time valet on radio
show, played by Eddie Anderson. - **$8 $12 $20**

JBE-7. "Friars Luncheon/Jack Benny" Gold Luster Metal
Money Clip,
c. 1950s. Dinner event souvenir. Raised design of his
violin. - **$15 $25 $45**

THE JACK PEARL SHOW

A veteran comic of vaudeville and burlesque, Jack Pearl
(1895-1982) brought his dialect character Baron
Munchausen to radio in 1932. When straight man Cliff Hall
expressed doubts about one of the Baron's tall tales, the
inevitable response, "Vas you dere, Sharlie?" brought down
the house. Sponsors of *The Jack Pearl Show* included
Chrysler (1932), Lucky Strike cigarettes (1932-1933), Royal
gelatin (1934), Frigidaire (1935), and Raleigh and Kool cigarettes (1936-1937). Comeback attempts in 1942 and 1948
were not successful.

JPL-1

JPL-2

JPL-1. "Baron Munchasen" Map Of Radioland 19x24",
c. 1932. Scarce. - **$50 $100 $200**

JPL-2. "Jack Pearl As Detective Baron Munchausen"
Book,
1934. Store item published by Goldsmith Co. with endorsement of Juvenile Educators League. - **$10 $20 $30**

JACK WESTAWAY UNDER SEA ADVENTURE CLUB

Membership in Jack Westaway's U.S.A.C. entitled young fans of the 1930s to wear the club badge (shaped like a diving helmet) and to a member's identification card that spelled out the club rules - including, whenever possible, eating a breakfast of Malt-O-Meal hot puffed wheat and puffed rice cereal.

(front)

JWS-2

(back)

JWS-1

JWS-1. "Under Sea Adventure Club News" Vol. 1 #1
Newspaper With Envelope,
1930s. Malt-O-Meal. Newspaper - **$15 $40 $60**
Mailer - **$3 $5 $10**

JWS-2. Club Membership Card,
1930s. Malt-O-Meal. - **$20 $40 $75**

JWS-3

JWS-3. "Jack Westaway Under The Sea/U.S.A.C." Brass
Diver's Helmet Badge,
1930s. - **$3 $15 $25**

JAMES DEAN

The untimely and tragic death of this young actor in 195□ evoked an international outpouring of anguish and disbelie□ by his fandom. His brief acting career epitomized the moody□ brooding, casual restlessness of young adulthood. Due t□ this brevity, related memorabilia from the 1950s is scarce. □ few buttons were produced before his death but the most fre□ quently encountered 1950s item is a memorial brass medale□ offered by *Modern Screen Magazine* in October 1956.

JDN-2

JDN-1

JDN-1. "James Dean's" Denim Jeans,
1955. Store item by J.S.B. Adult sized, likened to those worn□ in his movies Rebel Without a Cause, East of Eden, Giant. With Tag - **$40 $65 $100**

JDN-2. Cello. 3-1/2" Photo Button,
c. 1955. Store item. Issued before his death. - **$15 $35 $7□**

JDN-3

JDN-4

JDN-3. Cello. 3-1/2" Button,
c. 1955. Store item. Issued before his death. - **$15 $35 $75**

JDN-4. Commemorative Brass Necklace Medallion,
c. 1955. "Modern Screen" magazine. Inscription "In Memory Of James Dean 1931-1955". - **$5 $12 $25**

JDN-5

JDN-6

JDN-5. Commemorative China Plate,
c. 1956. Store item. - **$30 $50 $85**

JDN-6. "I, James Dean" Paperback Biography,
1957. Store item published by Popular Library. First published biography after his death. - **$8 $15 $30**

JIMMIE ALLEN

The Air Adventures of Jimmie Allen thrilled its young radio listeners from 1933 to 1943. Jimmie was a 16-year-old messenger at the Kansas City airport, taught to fly by veteran pilot Speed Robertson. Together they courted danger, searched for lost treasure, and competed in international air races. The series was syndicated, sponsored initially by the Skelly Oil company in the Midwest, then by Richfield Oil on the West Coast and by bakeries and many other companies eager to share in the show's large audience.

Premiums were an integral part of the program from the beginning, starting with a free jigsaw puzzle offer during the third week of broadcasting and available only at Skelly gas stations. The Jimmie Allen Flying Club and the Weather-Bird Flying Club attracted thousands of applicants, all of whom received membership cards, wings, emblems, patches, flight charts, and personal letters from Jimmie. Members could pick up weekly flying lessons and model airplane kits at their local gas stations.

Other promotional items followed in great profusion: photo albums, stamp albums, road maps, whistles, ID bracelets, model planes, Flying Cadet wings. Since sponsors were free to design and mark their own premiums, many varieties were produced. Jimmie Allen Air Races were held throughout the Midwest, with thousands of fans gathering to watch the young contestants piloting their model planes.

Paramount Pictures released a Jimmie Allen movie, The Sky Parade, in 1936. Transcriptions of the original broadcasts were re-released in 1942-1943.

JMA-1

JMA-1. "Map Of Countries Visited In 'Air Adventures Of Jimmie Allen ' 11x25",
1934. Skelly Oil Co. - **$50 $100 $150**

JMA-2

JMA-2. Skelly Oil Holiday Newsletter,
1934. - **$20 $40 $60**

JMA-3

JMA-4

JMA-3. "Flight Lesson" Sheet,
1934. Various sponsors. Five lessons in set.
Each - **$5 $8 $12**

JMA-4. "Merry Christmas" Photo,
1934. Skelly Oil Co. - **$10 $20 $30**

JMA-5

JMA-6

JMA-5. "What's On The Air" Pacific Coast Schedule Book,
1934. Richfield Oil Co. - **$15 $30 $60**

JMA-6. Skelly "Jimmie Allen Flying Cadet" Brass Airplane Badge,
1934. - **$10 $20 $35**

JMA-7

JMA-7. Richfield Flight Wings,
1934. - **$12 $20 $45**

JMA-8

JMA-8. Richfield I.D. Bracelet,
1934. - **$15 $25 $50**

JMA-9

JMA-10

JMA-9. Skelly Club Membership Card,
c. 1934. - **$8 $15 $25**

JMA-10. "Speed Robertson" Photo,
c. 1934. Skelly Oil Co. - **$10 $20 $30**

JMA-11   JMA-12

JMA-11. Skelly "Jimmie Allen Flying Cadet" Bronze Luster Brass Wings Badge,
c. 1934. - **$15 $25 $35**

JMA-12. "Jimmie Allen/Skelly Flying Cadet" Brass Wings Badge,
c. 1934. - **$15 $25 $50**

JMA-13

JMA-14

JMA-13. Membership Card,
c. 1934. Richfield Oil Co. - **$10 $15 $25**

JMA-14. Club Creed Certificate,
c. 1934. Richfield Oil. - **$10 $20 $30**

JMA-16

JMA-15

JMA-15. Photo,
c. 1934. Richfield Oil. - **$5 $12 $20**

JMA-16. Felt Fabric Aviator Cap,
c. 1934. Scarce. Richfield Oil. - **$35 $70 $125**

JMA-17

JMA-17. Postcard,
c. 1934. Log Cabin Bread. - **$10 $20 $40**

JMA-18

JMA-19

JMA-18. "Jimmie Allen Flying Cadet/Log Cabin" Brass Wings Badge,
c. 1934. Log Cabin Syrup. - **$15 $30 $50**

JMA-19. "Speed Robertson" Photo Card,
c. 1934. Hi-Speed Gasoline of Hickok Oil Corp. Pictured is comrade aviator of Jimmie Allen. - **$12 $20 $30**

JMA-21

JMA-20

JMA-20. "Jimmie Allen Cadet/Fairmont Air Corps" Brass Wings Badge,
c. 1934. - **$40 $85 $150**

JMA-21. "B A Flying Cadet" Canadian Flight Wings,
c. 1934. - **$25 $60 $100**

JMA-22

JMA-22. Richfield Oil Travel Map,
1935. Paper folder that opens to 18x24" map of California with panel ad for Jimmie Allen radio show. - **$10 $20 $30**

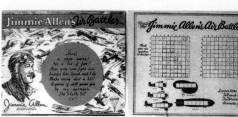

JMA-23

JMA-23. Skelly "Jimmie Allen's Air Battles" Booklet,
1935. Contents include game pages plus comic strips. - **$20 $40 $60**

JMA-24

JMA-25

JMA-24. "Jimmie Allen Air Races" Silvered Brass Bracelet,
1935. Skelly Oil. - **$60 $100 $150**

JMA-25. Kansas City Air Races Enameled Bracelet,
1935. Rare. Skelly Oil. - **$75 $200 $450**

JMA-26

JMA-27

JMA-26. "Jimmie Allen Air Races" Sterling Silver Bracelet With Silvered Brass Chain,
c. 1935. Skelly Oil. - **$60 $100 $150**

JMA-27. "Jimmie Allen/Pilot" Silvered Brass Bracelet,
c. 1935. Skelly Oil. - **$60 $100 $150**

JMA-28

JMA-28. Browntone Photos,
1936. Skelly Oil Co. Numbered set of six. Each - **$3 $6 $12**

JMA-29

JMA-30

JMA-29. "Flying Club Stamp Album",
1936. Richfield Oil Co. Near Mint With Stamps - **$75**
Album Only - **$15 $25 $50**

JMA-30. Richfield Gasoline Cardboard Ink Blotter,
1936. - **$8 $15 $25**

JMA-31   JMA-32

JMA-33

JMA-31. "Official Jimmie Allen Secret Signal" Brass Whistle,
1936. - **$50 $85 $150**

JMA-32. Movie Cast Photo,
1936. For movie "The Sky Parade" picturing Jimmie Allen, Grant Withers, Katherine DeMille, Kent Taylor. - **$15 $25 $40**

JMA-33. "Jimmie Allen" Bone Handle Pocketknife,
1930s. Sponsor unknown. Grip has silvered metal club symbol. - **$35 $75 $125**

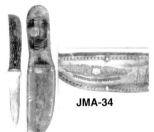

JMA-34

JMA-35

JMA-34. "Official Outing Knife" With Sheath,
1930s. Sponsor unknown. - **$75 $150 $250**

JMA-35. "Jimmie Allen Model Builder Merit Award" Brass Badge,
1930s. Scarce. Richfield Oil. Also designated "Richfield Hi-Octane Flying Cadet". - **$75 $140 $200**

JMA-37

JMA-36

JMA-36. Cloth "Mail Pouch",
1930s. Cleo Cola. For saving bottle caps. - **$35 $75 $125**

JMA-37. Club Membership Card,
1930s. Hi-Speed Gasoline. - **$10 $18 $30**

JMA-38

JMA-38. Gummed Paper Sticker,
1930s. Hi-Speed Gasoline. - **$15 $30 $60**

JMA-39

JMA-40

JMA-39. "Jimmie Allen Hi-Speed Flying Cadet" Brass Wings Badge,
1930s. - **$10 $15 $25**

JMA-40. Hi-Speed Photo Card,
1930s. Hickok Oil Co. - **$10 $20 $35**

JMA-41

JMA-41. Flying Club Aviation Lesson Newspapers,
1930s. Republic Motor Oil. Map inside lesson #1.
Each - **$10 $20 $35**

JMA-42

JMA-43

JMA-42. "Certificate In Aviation",
1930s. Republic (Oil) Air Corps. Awarded for completion of advanced aviation course. - **$20 $30 $50**

JMA-43. "Jimmie Allen/Republic Pilot" Brass Wings Badge,
1930s. - **$20 $35 $65**

JMA-44

JMA-44. Skelly Oil Club Album,
1930s. Booklet of photo pages.
Album Only - **$10 $15 $25**
Each Photo Page - **$2 $4 $6**

JMA-46

JMA-45

JMA-45. Jimmie & Barbara Photo,
1930s. Skelly Oil. - **$10 $15 $25**

JMA-46. "Yellow Jacket" Model Airplane Construction Kit,
1930s. Skelly Oil. Balsa parts with instructions and insignia cut-outs. - **$40 $75 $125**

JMA-47

JMA-48

JMA-47. "Thunderbolt" Model Airplane Construction Kit,
1930s. Skelly Oil. Balsa parts with instruction sheet and insignia cut-outs. - **$40 $75 $125**

JMA-48. "J.A. Air Cadets" Cello. Button,
1930s. Canadian issue. - **$40 $75 $125**

JMA-50

JMA-49

JMA-49. "J.A. Air Cadets" Brass Ring,
1930s. Rare. Canadian issue. - **$100 $200 $350**

JMA-50. "J.A. Air Cadets" Brass Wings Badge,
1930s. Canadian issue. - **$20 $50 $85**

JMA-51

JMA-51. "Jimmie Allen Listening Post" Member Kit,
1944. Re-broadcast of shows sponsored by Bamby Bread,
Atlanta, Georgia. Includes cover letter, photo, member card,
charter, song sheet, application, "Listening Post" tag.
Each Item - **$5 $10 $15**

JIMMIE MATTERN

An actual aviator in the early 1930s era of personal and
mechanical endurance flying, Mattern is best remembered
for his June 3 to August 3, 1933 solo flight around the world
begun in his "Century of Progress" single engine aircraft
(crashed enroute) and finished by other borrowed planes.
Premiums were typically aviation theme booklets and photo
albums by sponsor Pure Oil.

JMT-1

JMT-1. "The Diary Of Jimmie Mattern" Paper Folder,
1935. Pure Oil Co. "Diary Sheet" insert pages issued separately, probably weekly. Folder Only - **$10 $20 $35**
Each Insert Page - **$3 $5 $10**

JMT-2

JMT-3

JMT-2. "Book 2 'Hawaii To Hollywood'",
1936. Pure Oil Co. Hardcover. - **$5 $15 $25**

JMT-3. "Air-E-Racer" Figural Rubber Eraser,
c. 1936. Pure Oil Co., also marked "Tiolene Motor Oil". -
$20 $35 $60

JIMMY DURANTE

At the age of 17 Jimmy Durante (1893-1980) was playing
piano in a Coney Island beer garden. By his mid-thirties,
after years in vaudeville and burlesque, he was playing
Broadway and making movies. In 1943, when he and Gary
Moore appeared together on NBC in the *Camel Comedy
Caravan*, Durante was on the road to national stardom. With
his joyful mangling of the language, his legendary nose, his
mythical friends Umbriago and Mrs. Calabash, Durante
charmed his radio audience for seven years, first for Camel
cigarettes (1943-1945), then for Rexall drugs (1945-1948),
then again for Camel (1948-1950). A couple of Durante
comic books appeared in the late 1940s, and from 1950 to
1957 Durante was a regular on television for such sponsors
as Buick, Colgate, and Texaco.

JIM-1

JIM-2

JIM-3

JIM-1. "Schnozzle Durante/Vice-President" Cello. Button,
1932. Paramount Pictures. Based on movie "Phantom
President" that year. - **$15 $30 $50**

JIM-2. "My Friend Umbriago" Litho. Button,
c. 1940s. Durante holds hand puppet. - **$8 $15 $25**

JIM-3. "The Candidate" Book,
1952. Publisher Simon & Schuster. - **$8 $12 $18**

JIM-4

JIM-5

JIM-6

JIM-4. "Gimme Jimmy! The Candidate" Cello. Button,
1952. Issued with booklet of same title. - **$5 $10 $15**

JIM-5. Rubber/Fabric Hand Puppet,
1950s. Store item. - **$15 $25 $ 50**

JIM-6. "Children's Fund" Metal Portrait Pin On Card,
1950s. - **$8 $15 $25**

(front)   **JIM-7**   (back)

JIM-7. Corn Flakes Testimonial,
1965. Gary Lewis and the Playboys record offer. -
$30 $60 $100

JOE E. BROWN

Show-business veteran Joe E. Brown (1892-1973), noted for
the contortions of his big mouth, started out as a circus acro-
bat at the age of 10, was a featured comedian in burlesque
and vaudeville in his mid-twenties, graduated to musical
comedies, and started making movies in 1927. He made
dozens of films, with memorable roles in *You Said a Mouthful*
(1932), *Alibi Ike* (1935), and *Some Like It Hot* (1959).
Quaker Oats issued the *Joe E. Brown Bike Club* premiums in
1934. In 1936, Post cereal sponsored the *Joe E. Brown Club*
through newspapers and packaging offers. On radio, the *Joe
E. Brown Show*, a musical variety program, ran for a season
(1938-1939) on CBS, sponsored by Post Toasties cereal.

JOE-1   **JOE-2**

JOE-1. "Joe E. Brown's Funny Bike Book",
1934. Quaker Oats. - **$10 $20 $35**

JOE-2. "Member/Joe E. Brown Bike Club" Cello. Button,
1934. Quaker Oats. - **$5 $15 $25**

JOE-3   **JOE-4**   **JOE-5**

JOE-3. Premium Folder Sheet,
1936. Grape-Nuts Flakes. Offers about 30 premiums with
expiration date December 31. - **$10 $20 $35**

**JOE-4. Club Member Brass Badge With Three Award
Bars,**
1936. Grape-Nuts Flakes. Bars in different colors individually
marked by 1, 2, 3 stars denoting club ranks.
Portrait Badge Only - **$5 $12 $20**
For Each Bar Add - **$5 $10 $20**

JOE-5. Brass Club Member Ring,
1936. Grape-Nuts Flakes. Features small portrait. -
$50 $100 $150

JOE-6   **JOE-7**

JOE-6. Radio Fan Photo,
c. 1936. Probable Grape-Nuts Flakes. - **$8 $15 $25**

JOE-7. "You Said A Mouthful" Booklet,
1944. Doughnut Corp. of America with local dealer imprint.
Contents include World War II tour photos plus mention of
radio quiz show "Stop Or Go". - **$8 $15 $20**

JOE-8

**JOE-8. Joe E. Brown "How To Play Baseball" Record
Album,**
1940s. Store item by RCA Victor. - **$20 $30 $50**

JOE PENNER

"Wanna buy a duck?" Perhaps no other comedian is so we
remembered for such a single phrase as Joe Penner
Penner's trademark prop, of course, from vaudeville day
into radio and 1930s to early 1940s films, was the inevitabl
live duck carried in a basket. His wacky repartee style ende
with his death in 1941 at the early age of 37 years with hi
duck remaining unbought.

JOP-1

JOP-1. "Wise Quacks" Fan Newsletter Vol. 1 #4, November 1934. - **$10 $15 $25**

JOP-2

JOP-3

JOP-4

JOP-2. "Cocomalt Big Book Of Comics", 1938. Featuring Joe Penner, various comic characters. - **$140 $430 $1400**

JOP-3. "Raisin Bread/Radio Special" Cello. Button, 1930s. Unknown bakery or bakeries. From series listing various types of breads or rolls. - **$3 $6 $12**

JOP-4. "I'm A Joe Penner Quacker" Cello. Button, 1930s. - **$5 $10 $15**

JOP-5

JOP-6

JOP-5. First Issue "Joe Penner Songs" Folio, 1941. - **$5 $15 $25**

JOP-6. Photo/Dexterity Game Brass Ring, c. 1940s. Scarce. - **$300 $475 $650**

JONNY QUEST

Jonny Quest, a prime-time animated adventure series from the Hanna-Barbera studios, premiered on ABC in 1964 and aired for a year. The series was repeated on Saturday mornings on CBS (1967-1970), on ABC (1970-1972), and on NBC, first as part of the Godzilla Power Hour (1978), then on its own (1979-1981). Created by comic book artist Doug Wildey, Jonny and his scientist father traveled to exotic places in their supersonic plane, fought mythical beasts, confronted unsolved mysteries, and triumphed over danger wherever they found it.

JNY-1

JNY-1. Boxed Card Game, 1965. Store item by Milton Bradley. - **$20 $25 $75**

JNY-2

JNY-2. "Magic Ring" 21x22" Cardboard Store Sign, 1960s. P.F. footwear of B.F. Goodrich. Shows gold plastic decoder ring (Pictured in Rings, Miscellaneous section). - **$30 $75 $150**

JUNIOR BIRDMEN OF AMERICA

Hearst newspapers sponsored this club for young aviation enthusiasts in the 1930s, offering membership cards and manuals along with pins and patches. Club activities included flying model airplanes, with medals awarded to contest winners.

JRB-1

JRB-2

JRB-3

JRB-1. Champion Award Medal In Presentation Box, 1934. Rare. Near Mint Boxed - **$300**
Unboxed - **$35 $100 $200**

JRB-2. Second Place Award Medal In Presentation Box, 1934. Scarce. Near Mint Boxed - **$150**
Unboxed - **$35 $60 $90**

JRB-3. Hearst Newspapers Club Card, 1930s. For various newspapers of Hearst Syndicate with facsimile signature of George Hearst, National Commander. - **$15 $25 $40**

JRB-4

JRB-5

JRB-4. "Field Day" Felt Fabric Pennant,
1930s. 22" long. - **$25 $60 $100**

JRB-5. Hearst Newspapers "Flight Squadron" Charter Certificate,
1930s. For various newspapers of Hearst Syndicate with facsimile signature of George Hearst, National Commander. - **$25 $50 $75**

JRB-6

JRB-7

JRB-6. Felt Fabric Emblem,
1930s. Large 2-1/2x8" size. - **$35 $100 $200**

JRB-7. "Jr. Birdmen Of America" Enameled Brass Wings Badge,
1930s. - **$15 $30 $50**

JRB-8

JRB-8. "Eagle" Enameled Brass Wings Badge With Rank Bar,
1930s. Scarce. - **$25 $60 $100**

JUNIOR JUSTICE SOCIETY OF AMERICA

The Justice Society of America began in the DC Comics publication *All Star* #3 published in the fall of 1940. During its existence members included the Flash, the Spectre, Hawkman, Sandman, the Green Lantern and Hourman. Wonder Woman was club secretary as well as a member. The December 1942 *All Star* #14 announced the formation of the *Junior Justice Society of America*, a comic book club for readers. The 15¢ membership fee included: a welcome letter from Wonder Woman, a silver plated membership badge (later replaced by a cloth sew-on patch), a cardboard decoder, a four-page war bond comic *The Minute Man Answers the Call*, and a four color membership certificate which encouraged the recipient to keep the country united despite differences in cultural or ethnic backgrounds.

JUN-1

JUN-2

JUN-1. Solid Brass Badge,
1942. Rare. In-house prototype with tie-tac fastener. - **$500 $1000 $2000**

JUN-2. Club Member Fabric Patch,
1942. Replaced large letter badge because of metal shortage. - **$100 $250 $600**

JUN-3

(back view)

(back view)

JUN-4

JUN-3
(close-up)

JUN-4
(close-up)

JUN-3. Silver Finish Club Badge,
1942. Scarce. Large letter style only offered for two months. **$100 $300 $900**

JUN-4. Silver Finish Club Badge,
1948. Small letter style. - **$75 $175 $350**

JUN-5

JUN-5. Club Kit Envelope,
1942. - **$20 $30 $50**

JUN-6

JUN-6. Club Kit Envelope,
1945. - **$30 $60 $90**

JUN-7

JUN-7. Club Kit Envelope,
1948. - **$30 $60 $90**

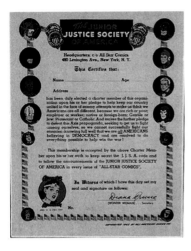

has been duly elected a charter member of this organization upon his or her pledge to help keep our country
united in the face of enemy attempts to make us think we
Americans are all different, because we are rich or poor;
employer or worker; native or foreign-born; Gentile or
Jew; Protestant or Catholic. And makes the further pledge
to defeat this Axis propaganda, seeking to get us to fight
among ourselves, so we cannot successfully fight our
enemies—knowing full well that we are all AMERICANS
believing in DEMOCRACY and are resolved to do
everything possible to help win the war!

(close-up)

JUN-8

JUN-8. Club Kit Certificate,
1942. Type 1. - **$75 $250 $400**

JUN-9

has been duly elected a Charter Member of The Junior
Justice Society of America upon his pledge: (1) to help
keep our country united in the face of enemy attempts to
make us think we Americans are all different because
we are rich or poor, employer or worker. White or Negro,
native or foreign born, Gentile or Jew, Protestant or Catholic; (2) to help defeat Axis propaganda which seeks to
cause us to fight among ourselves instead of successfully
fighting our enemies.

(close-up)

JUN-9

JUN-9. Club Kit Certificate,
1942. Type 2. - **$50 $200 $300**

JUN-10

JUN-10. Club Kit Certificate,
1945. Note Wildcat photo. - **$175 $300 $500**

JUN-11

JUN-11. Club Kit Certificate,
1948. Note Black Canary & Atom pictured. - **$75 $250 $400**

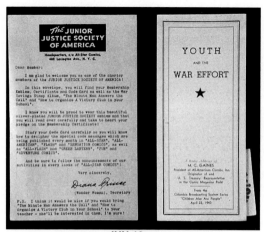

JUN-12

JUN-12. Club Kit Letter,
1942. - **$50 $75 $100**

JUN-13

JUN-13. Club Kit Letter,
1948. - **$70 $100 $150**

JUN-14

JUN-14. Club Kit Decoder,
1942. - **$50 $100 $200**

(close-up)

JUN-15

JUN-15. Club Kit Decoder,
1945. Note Wildcat in window. - **$75 $150 $300**

JUN-16

JUN-16. Club Kit Decoder,
1948. Black rectangle design. - **$60 $120 $240**

JUN-17

JUN-17. Comic Book Ad for Club,
1948. Original art. - **$200**

KATE SMITH

Kate Smith (1909-1986) had a brief stage career on Broadway before she moved to radio and became a beloved American institution. Guided throughout by her partner and friend Ted Collins, she broadcast continually from 1931 to 1959, mainly on CBS. Known as the Songbird of the South, she was a large woman, with voice and personality to match. She made her opening theme, *When the Moon Comes Over the Mountain*, practically her own, and for a time she had exclusive rights to Irving Berlin's *God Bless America*. Audiences loved her, and sponsors followed: La Palina cigars (1931-1933), Hudson cars (1934-1935), Philip Morris (1947-1951), and Reader's Digest (1958-1959). During World War II her patriotic efforts sold millions of dollars in war bonds. On television, she had an afternoon show (1950-1954) and two evening variety programs, in 1951-1952 on NBC and in 1960 on CBS.

KAT-1

KAT-2

AT-1. Fan Photo,
1931. La Palina Cigars. - **$10 $15 $25**

AT-2. "Kate Smith La Palina Club" Litho. Button,
1931. La Palina cigars. - **$12 $20 $35**

KAT-3

AT-3. "Philadelphia A & P Party" 2-1/2" Cello. Button,
1935. Great Atlantic & Pacific Tea Co. (grocery chain). Single day issue for November 4. - **$20 $35 $60**

KAYO

Frank Willard's *Moon Mullins*, one of the most successful comic strips of all time, first appeared in 1923. Four years later Moon was joined by kid brother Kayo, a brat in a derby hat. Together with Lord Plushbottom, Emmy, Uncle Willie, and Mamie, the Mullins boys were to hang out at carnivals and in pool rooms for decades. The Kayo name and character were licensed to promote a chocolate-flavored drink in the 1930s and 1940s. *Moon Mullins* comic books appeared from 1927 to 1933 and through the 1940s. After Willard's death in 1958 the strip was continued by long-time assistant Ferd Johnson.

KAY-1

KAY-1. "Kayo And Moon Mullins-'Way Down South" Booklet,
1934. Lemix & Corlix Desserts. Book #7 from Whitman series. - **$15 $30 $60**

KAY-2

KAY-2. Club Member Cello. Button,
1930s. Kayo Chocolate. - **$10 $20 $35**

KAY-3   KAY-4

KAY-3. "Kayo Comics Club" Litho. Button,
1930s. San Francisco Chronicle newspaper. - **$15 $25 $40**

KAY-4. "Park Theater Kayo Club" Cello. Button,
1930s. - **$20 $30 $65**

(front)   **KAY-5**   (back)

KAY-5. Cloth Doll,
1930s. - **$30 $60 $90**

(bottom view showing dice)

KAY-6

KAY-6. Statue with Dice Salesman's Premium,
1930s. - **$200 $400 $800**

KAY-7

KAY-7. "Drink Kayo Chocolate" Transfer Picture,
c. 1940s. Kayo Chocolate Drink. Image is reversed in unused
condition. - **$20 $40 $75**

KAY-8

KAY-8. Promo Chocolate Drink Sign,
1940s. Holed for display on bottle. - **$30 $60 $120**

KELLOGG'S CEREAL MISCELLANEOUS

Dr. John Harvey Kellogg was at the center of a vegetaria
health-food craze in Battle Creek, Michigan, in the late 19
century. The experimental kitchen at his Battle Cree
Sanitarium created a number of meat substitutes for h
patients, including Protose, Nuttose, Nuttolene, Granola, ar
Caramel Coffee. With his brother, W.K. Kellogg, he devised
wheat flake cereal in 1894 and, four years later, a varie
made from corn, which he sold by mail as Sanitas Co
Flakes.

W.K. Kellogg struck out on his own in 1903, adding flavoring
to the cereal, naming it Kellogg's Toasted Corn Flakes, ar
promoting it heavily with advertising and free samples. Th
cereal became, and remains, a breakfast staple in millions
homes. Over the years the company has used a variety
promotional symbols, starting with the Sweetheart of th
Corn in 1907. With new cereals came the need for new pe
sonalities: Snap, Crackle, and Pop in 1933 to promo
Kellogg's Rice Krispies, Tony the Tiger in 1953 for Kellogg
Sugar Frosted Flakes, and Toucan Sam in 1964.

Kellogg's sponsored many programs such as *Tom Corbe
Howdy Doody, Superman,* and *Huckleberry Hound* but th
items in this section focus on characters specifically create
for Kellogg's advertising and a sampling of the many no
character premiums they offered over the years. See sep
rate sections devoted to Snap, Crackle, and Pop, as well
Tony the Tiger.

KEL-1

KEL-7

KEL-6

KEL-1. "Kellogg's Funny Jungleland Moving-Pictures" Booklet,
1909. Among the earliest premium booklets (3-1/2x4-3/4") but re-issued in 6x8" and available for many years.
Earliest Version - **$20 $40 $75**
Later Version - **$12 $20 $50**

KEL-6. Fairy Tales Wall Plaques Premium Sign 12x18",
1930s. Rare. Designed by Vernon Grant, picturing six plaques. Sign - **$200 $400 $600**
Each Plaque - **$25 $50 $100**

KEL-7. Baseball Hat with Mailer,
1930s. - **$15 $30 $45**

KEL-3

KEL-2

KEL-8

KEL-2. "My Visit To Kellogg's" Factory Visit Souvenir Book,
1924. - **$12 $20 $35**

KEL-3. "Kellogg's Toasted Corn Flakes" Cello. Button,
1920s. - **$10 $20 $35**

KEL-8. Beamy Beanie with Mailer,
1942. Scarce. - **$20 $40 $60**

KEL-4

KEL-5

KEL-9

KEL-9. "Kellogg's Pep Model Warplanes" 16x43" Advertising Poster,
c. 1942. Scarce. - **$75 $200 $400**

KEL-4. "Junior Texas Ranger Force" Member Certificate,
1933. Facsimile signatures of commanding officer Colonel Louis and W. K. Kellogg. - **$20 $35 $50**

KEL-5. "Junior Texas Ranger" Club Kit,
1936. Five paper items: Two premium folders, card that held badge, survey postcard, leaflet promoting Mother Goose stories by Kellogg's Singing Lady plus mailer.
Each - **$5 $10 $20**

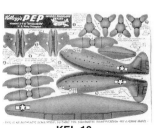
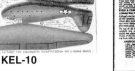

KEL-10

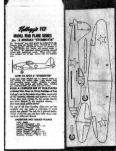

KEL-11

KEL-10. "Kellogg's Pep Model Warplane" Punch-Out,
c. 1942. About 20 different. Each Unpunched - **$10 $15 $25**

KEL-11. "Pep Model Warplane" Balsa Sheet In Envelope,
c. 1942. Numbered series, some envelopes mention
Superman radio show. Each In Envelope - **$10 $15 $25**

KEL-12

KEL-12. "Kellogg's Pep" Felt Beanie,
1943. Orange and white. With Tag - **$25 $50 $75**
Missing Tag - **$15 $25 $50**

KEL-13

**KEL-13. Pep Beany/Military Insignia Buttons 16x44"
Paper Store Poster,**
1943. Scarce. - **$100 $200 $400**

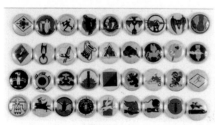

KEL-14

KEL-14. Pep Military Insignia Litho. Buttons,
1943. Set of 36. Paint very susceptible to aging and wear,
most examples grade fine or worse. Each - **$3 $8 $15**

KEL-15

KEL-16

KEL-15. Pep Airplane Litho. Buttons,
1943. Set of 12. Four planes in green, four planes in brown
with photo-style artwork and same four planes in brown with
hand illustrated style artwork. Paint very susceptible to wear.
Each - **$25 $60 $95**

KEL-16. Pep "Plane Spotter" Box Card,
c. 1944. Two cards on each back, at least 42 cards in set.
Uncut Back - **$10 $15 $25**

KEL-17

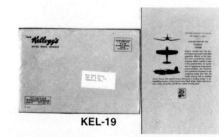

KEL-18

KEL-17. Pep Large Diecut Cardboard Sign,
1945. 38" x 26". Features Pep buttons and boy wearing Pep
beanie. Three known. - **$750 $2000 $5000**

KEL-18. Pep Comic Character Litho. Button Set,
1945. Complete set of 86.
Most Characters - **$5 $10 $15**
Felix - **$15 $30 $50**
Phantom - **$25 $50 $75**

KEL-19

**KEL-19. Pep Punch-Out Warplane Pictures With
Envelope,**
c. 1945. Set of six. Near Mint In Mailer - **$250**

KEL-20

KEL-20. "Kellogg's Walky Talky" Punch-Out,
c. 1945. Near Mint In Mailer - **$350**
Complete Assembled Pair - **$50 $125 $200**
Promotional Sign - **$75 $150 $300**

KEL-21

KEL-21. Pep Beanie,
1945. Black and white. - **$20 $40 $60**

KEL-22

KEL-22. Pep Comic Character Buttons Ad Sheet,
1947. Canadian issue. - **$75 $125 $200**

(close-up)

KEL-23

KEL-23. "Flight Control Sabre Jet Plane",
1948. Unused In Mailer - **$20 $40 $60**

KEL-24

KEL-24. Punch-Out Airport in Mailer,
1940s. - **$30 $60 $90**

KEL-25

KEL-25. Kellogg's Pep "Photo Album",
1940s. 10 pages for mounting miniature premium photos of sports and entertainment stars. Near Mint With Mailer - **$150** Album Only - **$35 $60 $100**

KEL-26

KEL-26. "Kellogg's Pep" Box With Ring Ads,
1950. Complete Box - **$75 $125 $200**

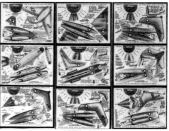

KEL-27

KEL-27. "Flying Model Jet Planes" Punch-Outs,
1951. Ten in the set. Unpunched Each - **$3 $5 $10**

KEL-28

KEL-29

KEL-28. Sugar Smacks Flat,
1951. Soldier premium offer. Maxie the seal on front. - **$50 $100 $250**

KEL-29. Soldiers in Mailer,
1951. Rare. 12 total. - **$20 $40 $80**

KEL-30   KEL-31   KEL-32

KEL-30. Baking Soda Frogman 3-1/2" Size,
1954. Obstacles Scout. Depicts scuba diver holding knife. Various colors. - **$10 $25 $40**

KEL-31. Baking Soda Frogman 3-1/2" Size,
1954. Demolitions Expert. Depicts diver holding mine. Various colors. - **$10 $25 $40**

KEL-32. Baking Soda Frogman 3-1/2" Size,
1954. Torch Man. Depicts diver holding cutting torch. Various colors. - **$10 $25 $40**

KEL-33   KEL-34

KEL-33. Jumbly Jungle Book with Mailer,
1950s. - **$20 $30 $40**

KEL-34. Kellogg's Presidents,
1950s. Stamps, booklet, and mailer. - **$20 $40 $80**

KEL-35

KEL-35. Rocket Beanie with Mailer,
1950s. Rare. Kellogg's Rice Krispies premium. - **$20 $40 $80**

KEL-36

KEL-36. Pep Whirl-Erang,
1950s. Scarce. Discontinued because children were injured. - **$10 $20 $40**
Box Back with Ad - **$50**

KEL-37

KEL-37. "U.S. Navy PT Boat",
c. 1960s. Includes boat, jet race way, package of propellant and instruction sheet. Near Mint Boxed - **$125**
Boat Only - **$15 $30 $50**

KEL-38

KEL-38. Cereal Box With "Pin-Me-Ups" Back,
1960s. Set of eight featuring Hanna-Barbera characters.
Complete Box - **$20 $40 $75**

KEL-39

KEL-39. "U.S.S. Nautilus" Plastic Atomic Sub,
c. 1960s. Near Mint In Box - **$125**
Sub Only - **$15 $25 $40**

KEL-40   KEL-41

KEL-40. "Dig 'Em" Metal Wind-Up Alarm Clock,
1979. - **$15 $25 $35**

KEL-41. "Toucan Sam" Plastic Secret Decoder,
1983. Movable disk code wheel. - **$5 $12 $20**

KEN MAYNARD

n all-around sagebrush hero, cowboy actor Maynard was rst an accomplished trick rider and rodeo championship der. Pre-movie years included performances at King anch, Texas; Buffalo Bill's Wild West Show, Ringling Bros. Vild West Show, Tex Rickard's World's Champion Cowboy ompetition (first place in 1920). He was introduced into lent movies by Tom Mix and best remembered for his First ational films of the mid-1920s and following decade, also eaturing his talented horse Tarzan. He is credited by many s the first to introduce song to the western movie. His 938-1948 years were mostly a return to live performances nd he continued to draw audiences even into his fifties. Maynard died March 23, 1973 at 87 years of age.

KEN-1   KEN-2

EN-1. "First National Films" Studio Matchbook,
)29. Reverse lists six film titles from that year. -
12 $20 $30

EN-2. "Ken Maynard Club/First National Pictures"
ello. Button,
1929. - $10 $20 $30

KEN-4

KEN-3

EN-3. Paper Mask,
33. Einson-Freeman movie promo. - $50 $100 $250

EN-4. "Round Up/Buckaroo Club" Card,
30s. Various radio stations. - $15 $30 $50

KEN-5   KEN-6

EN-5. Portrait Cello. Button,
30s. Probably circus souvenir. - $30 $60 $100

EN-6. "Cole Bros. Circus" Cello. Button,
30s. - $50 $100 $150

KING FEATURES MISCELLANEOUS

King Features Syndicate, the country's largest newspaper comic-strip syndicator, has been the agency of such legendary giants as Popeye, Flash Gordon, Felix the Cat, Krazy Kat, Beetle Bailey, Henry, Skippy, Betty Boop, Barney Google, and dozens of other major comic characters. In 1915 King Features became the sales agent for all the combined Hearst Newspapers syndicate operations. Over the years it has issued a number of items promoting various combinations of its comic characters.

KIN-2

KIN-1

KIN-1. "Polar Lark" Metal Paperweight,
1926. 10 King Features character heads form North Pole in homage to Commander Byrd's flight over pole. -
$150 $300 $600

KIN-2. The Comic Club Stamps,
1934. Wrigley's Gum. 18 stamps on sheet. - $60 $125 $175

KIN-3

KIN-4

KIN-3. "Sunday Examiner" Newspaper Contest Litho.
Button,
1930s. Part of a set. - $10 $20 $30

KIN-4. "Sing With King At Christmas" Book,
1949. Pictures numerous Christmas caroles sung by various syndicate characters. - $20 $40 $60

KIN-5

KIN-5. "King Features Syndicate Famous Artists &
Writers" Book,
1949. Biographies of those represented by K.F.S. -
$50 $85 $140

KIN-6

KIN-6. "Popular Comics" Boxed Christmas Cards,
1951. Set of 16. - **$35 $90 $150**

KIN-7

KIN-7. "King Features Syndicate Blue Book",
1955. Full color sample pages of strips represented by
K.F.S. - **$75 $150 $225**

KIN-8

KIN-8. Plastic Ornament Set Showing 12 Characters,
c. 1950s. Boxed - **$50 $125 $175**

KIN-9

KIN-10

KIN-9. Glass Ashtray,
1950s. Pictures 14 comic strip characters. - **$15 $30 $50**

KIN-10. Plastic Pen Holder,
1964. - **$15 $25 $35**

KUKLA, FRAN AND OLLIE

Puppeteer Burr Tillstrom created Kukla, a chronic worrier
and Ollie, a one-tooth dragon, in Chicago in the late 1930s.
Along with singer-actress Fran Allison, the Kuklapolitan
were to produce one of early television's most beloved long
running successes, first as *Junior Jamboree* on WBKB
(1947-1948), then as *Kukla, Fran & Ollie* on NBC (1948-
1954), on ABC (1954-1957), again on NBC (1961-1962), on
public television (1970-1971), and in syndication (1975-
1976). Sponsors included RCA Victor, Sealtest, Ford and
Pontiac automobiles, National Biscuit, Life magazine, Procter
& Gamble, and Miles Laboratories. Promotional items are
normally copyrighted Burr Tillstrom. A radio version aired on
NBC in 1952-1953.

KUK-1

**KUK-1. "Kuklapolitan Courier" Newsletter With
Envelope,**
1949. One of series sent to fans.
With Envelope - **$10 $30 $50**
Without Envelope - **$5 $15 $25**

KUK-2

KUK-2. Fan Postcard,
1950. Announces August 8 starting day for third season of
TV show. - **$15 $30 $50**

KUK-3

KUK-3. "Kuklapolitan Courier Year Book",
1951. - **$25 $50 $100**

KUK-4

KUK-5

JK-4. Vinyl On Cardboard Postcard Record,
1957. Curtiss Candy Co. Several versions. - **$15 $30 $55**

JK-5. Curtiss Candy Co. Vinyl Cardboard Record,
50s. - **$15 $30 $55**

KUK-6

JK-6. Spoon Set,
50s. Rare. - **$75 $150 $300**

LASSIE

e story of the courageous, intelligent collie first appeared in
ck Knight's 1938 short story and 1940 best-selling novel
ssie Come Home - the start of an odyssey that was to con-
ue for some 35 years: the 1943 MGM movie, followed by a
f-dozen sequels over eight years; the radio serial spon-
red by Red Heart dog food on ABC (1947-1948) and NBC
948-1950); three decades of comic books beginning in
49; and ultimately the CBS television saga, from 1954 to
71, followed by three years of syndication under various
es (1972-1975), all sponsored by Campbell's soup.
ssie's human companions were played by Tommy Rettig
954-1957) and Jon Provost (1957-1964), and by Robert
y (1964-1969) as an adventurous forest ranger. *Lassie's*
scue Rangers, an animated series, ran on ABC from 1973
1975. The 50th anniversary of the original movie was cele-
ted in 1994 with the release of a new movie (*Lassie*), a TV
gram, a new book (*Lassie: A Dog's Life*), and numerous
als for spinoff products. Items bear the copyright of
ather Corp., Rankin & Bass Productions, or Jack Wrather
ductions.

LAS-1

LAS-2

LAS-1. Color Premium Picture - Red Heart, Large,
1949. Scarce. - **$20 $40 $60**

LAS-2. Comic Book Premium - Red Heart,
1949. Scarce. - **$20 $60 $140**

LAS-3

LAS-4

LAS-3. "Jeff's Collie Club" Member Card,
c. 1954. Virginia Dairy Co., probable others. No direct Lassie
reference but obviously based on early version of TV
series. - **$10 $20 $35**

LAS-4. Lassie Friendship Silvered Brass Ring,
c. 1955. Campbell Soup Company. Initial "L" on each side
with high relief portrait on top. - **$90 $135 $180**

LAS-5

LAS-5. "Lassie Club" Savings Bond Certificate,
1956. - **$20 $30 $50**

LAS-6

LAS-7

LAS-6. "Have You Voted For Lassie?" Cello. Button,
1950s. 1-3/4" size. - **$10 $15 $30**

LAS-7. "I Voted For Lassie" Cello. Button,
1950s. 1" version. - **$8 $12 $20**

LAS-8

LAS-8. Wallet With Membership Card,
c. 1950s. Campbell's Soups. Card reads "Lassie-Get-Up-And-Go Club". - **$15 $25 $40**

LAS-9

LAS-9. "Lassie Forest Ranger" Vinyl Wallet With Contents,
1964. Campbell's Soups. Includes white metal badge and Lassie photo. Complete - **$20 $40 $60**

LAS-10

LAS-10. "Forest Ranger Handbook",
1967. Authored by "Corey Stewart And Lassie." - **$10 $20 $35**

LAS-11

LAS-12

LAS-11. TV Patch,
1960s. - **$20 $40 $60**

LAS-12. Lassie/Corey Stuart TV Photo,
1960s. - **$20 $40 $60**

LAS-13

LAS-14

LAS-13. Fan Card,
1960s. Recipe Brand Dinners. Back has facsimile paw print of Lassie and signature of trainer Rudd Weatherwax. - **$10 $20 $30**

LAS-14. "A Friend Of Lassie" Brass Dog Tag,
c. 1970s. Probable dog food sponsor. Back identification inscription to be completed by dog owner. - **$10 $20 $35**

LIGHTNING JIM

U.S. Marshal Lightning Jim Whipple was the hero of Western adventure radio series broadcast on the West Coast in the 1940s and syndicated in the 1950s. Meadow Gold dairy products sponsored the program. Membership in Lightning Jim's Special Reserve entitled the young listener to wear the Meadow Gold Round-Up Badge. Whitey Larson served as Jim's sidekick and deputy.

LGH-1

LGH-1. "Meadow Gold Round-Up" Photo,
1940s. - **$10 $20 $35**

LGH-2

LGH-3

LGH-2. Membership Card,
1940s. Scarce. - **$10 $30 $60**

LGH-3. Membership Brass Badge,
1940s. Scarce. - **$20 $50 $100**

LGH-4

LGH-5

LGH-4. Mailer,
1940s. Scarce. - **$10 $20 $40**

LGH-5. Drinking Glass,
1940s. Rare. - **$30 $60 $120**

LI'L ABNER

Capp created *Li'l Abner* for United Features as a daily comic strip in 1934 and as a Sunday page in 1935. Along with the handsome hillbilly from Dogpatch has come a string of unforgettable characters: Daisy Mae, Mammy and Pappy Yokum, Marryin' Sam, Sadie Hawkins, Sir Cecil and Lady Cesspool, Hairless Joe, Lonesome Polecat, Fearless Fosdick, the bountiful Shmoos, the Kigmys, Kickapoo Joy Juice, and many others. Comic books appeared from the 1930s into the 1950s. A *Li'l Abner* radio show on NBC in 1939-1940 featured John Hodiak as Abner; a brief run of five animated shorts was released in 1944-1945; a musical comedy ran on Broadway for almost 700 performances in 1956-1957; and a Paramount film was released in 1959.

LIL-1   LIL-2

LIL-1. "Tip Top Comics" 11x14" Store Sign,
1938. - **$50 $75 $125**

LIL-2. "Buy War Stamps" 14x18" Poster,
1944. U.S. Government. - **$40 $75 $125**

LIL-3   LIL-4   LIL-5

LIL-3. Li'l Abner Beanie with Tag,
1948. Cereal premium. - **$30 $60 $90**

LIL-4. High Relief Brass Badge,
1948. - **$20 $35 $60**

LIL-5. "Shmoo Club Member" Litho. Button,
1948. - **$15 $35 $60**

LIL-6   LIL-7

LIL-6. Shmoo Paddle Ball,
1948. Scarce. - **$50 $100 $200**

LIL-7. Shmoo Plastic Wall Clock,
c. 1948. Store item by Lux Clock Co.
Near Mint Boxed - **$350**
Loose - **$50 $100 $150**

LIL-8   LIL-9

LIL-8. Shmoos Savings Bond Certificate,
1949. - **$25 $50 $75**

LIL-9. Shmoo "Snow Week" Cello. Button,
1949. University of Minnesota. Rim curl has 1948 copyright. - **$35 $75 $150**

LIL-10

LIL-10. Decal Sheet With Envelope,
1940s. Orange-Crush. - **$10 $20 $35**

LIL-11   LIL-12   LIL-13

LIL-11. "Tangle Comics" Cello. Button,
1940s. Philadelphia Sunday Bulletin. - **$10 $20 $35**

LIL-12. "Shmoo Lucky Rings" 12x13" Cardboard Store Display Sign,
c. 1950. Store item by Jarco Metal Products.
Empty Card - **$50 $125 $200**
Brass Ring - **$30 $45 $60**

LIL-13. "Li'l Abner" Cello. Button,
c. 1950. - **$15 $30 $50**

LIL-14   LIL-15

LIL-14. Civil Defense Comic Book,
1956. Features Civil Defense comic figure created by Al Capp. - **$5 $12 $20**

LIL-15. Kigmy Plastic Charm,
1950s. Scarce. - **$30 $60 $90**

LITTLE LULU

Mischievous Little Lulu(Moppet), the brainchild of Marjorie H. Buell (Marge), started life as a single-panel cartoon in the *Saturday Evening Post* in 1935. She began her comic book career as a one-shot in 1945 and as a regular series in 1948, scripted by John Stanley. A newspaper strip ran from 1955 to 1967, and from 1944 to 1960 Lulu was featured in advertising campaigns for Kleenex tissues. She also appeared, along with boyfriend Tubby Tompkins and little Alvin, in an animated cartoon series from Paramount Pictures in 1944-1948. The series was syndicated on television in 1956, and other series were produced in the 1970s. A new series with Tracey Ullman as the voice of Little Lulu debuted on HBO in 1995.

LUL-1   LUL-2

LUL-1. "Tubby Tom And Flipper" Glass,
1940s. Dairy product container, from set of six. -
$30 $60 $125

LUL-2. Annie And Mops Glass,
1940s. Dairy product container, from set of six. -
$25 $50 $85

LUL-3

LUL-3. Kleenex Cut-Out Doll 11x14" Cardboard Store Sign,
1952. - **$20 $40 $60**

LUL-4   LUL-5

LUL-4. Little Lulu Mask,
1952. Kleenex. - **$20 $40 $60**

LUL-5. Tubby Mask,
1952. Kleenex. - **$25 $50 $75**

LUL-6

LUL-6. March of Comics Booklet,
1964. Various retail stores. - **$10 $35 $80**

LITTLE ORPHAN ANNIE

Orphan Annie was the life work of cartoonist/storyteller Harold Gray. From her comic strip debut in the *New York Daily News* in 1924 until Gray's death in 1968, the curly-haired pre-teen with blank eyes survived one thrilling adventure after another, accompanied by her faithful dog Sandy (Arf!), saved when necessary by billionaire Daddy Warbucks and his enforcers the Asp and Punjab.

The strip, consistently among the most popular of its time, gave rise to the classic radio serial that captivated its young fans on NBC from 1931 to 1942, sponsored by Ovaltine (1931-1940), then by Quaker Puffed Wheat and Rice Sparkies (1941-1942). With the new sponsor, Annie's pal Joe Corntassel was replaced by heroic combat pilot Captain Sparks, but the program could not survive the change and was soon dropped.

Merchandising of Annie premiums during the Ovaltine years was extensive, producing a seemingly endless stream of mugs, masks, decoders, games, books, pins, dolls, toys, dishes, rings, photos, whistles, and membership gear for *Radio Orphan Annie's Secret Society*. Premiums during the Puffed Wheat years included membership in the Secret Guard and the Safety Guard, along with aviation-related items.

A string of artists and writers continued the Annie comic strip after Gray's death, with little success, and in 1974 the strip was replaced by reprints of the original strip. Comic book hardcover reprints of the newspaper strips, and giveaway books proliferated from 1926 through the 1940s.

wo movies added to the legend: the 1932 *Little Orphan Annie* from RKO and the 1982 *Annie* from Columbia ictures, the latter based on the successful 1977 Broadway usical. In 1995 an animated series, *Annie & the Tomorrow eam*, was announced by Tribune Media Services.

LAN-1

LAN-2

LAN-3

LAN-7

LAN-8

LAN-7. Joe Corntassel "Voters Button" Card,
1931. Also issued for Annie. Each - **$40 $100 $175**

LAN-8. Beetleware Shake-Up Mug,
1931. - **$20 $40 $75**

LAN-9

LAN-9. "Shake-Up Game" Instruction Folder,
1931. Came with Shake-Up mug. - **$20 $40 $60**

AN-1. "Little Orphan Annie/Her Story By Harold Gray" onvention Booklet,
J27. Chicago Tribune Newspaper Syndicate. 32 pages of ler Adventures To Date" given away at convention of merican Newspapers Publishers Association. -
'5 $175 $350

AN-2. "Some Swell Sweater" Cello. Button,
J28. Given with sweater purchase. - **$25 $75 $150**

AN-3. Song Sheet Giveaway,
J28. Scarce. Chicago Tribune. - **$50 $100 $200**

LAN-10

LAN-11

LAN-10. Ceramic Mug,
1932. - **$25 $50 $75**

LAN-11. "Mitzi Green As Little Orphan Annie" Movie Photo,
1932. Imprinted for local theaters. - **$25 $60 $100**

LAN-4

LAN-5

LAN-6

N-4. "Little Orphan Annie's Song" Sheet Music,
31. Probably 1st Ovaltine Annie premium. - **$15 $25 $50**

N-5. "Orphan Annie" Cello. Button,
31. Scarce. Known as Voter's Button issued as companion r with Joe Corntassel version, awarded respectively for te preferring Ovaltine with ice or Ovaltine with ice cream. -
00 $400 $800

N-6. "Joe Corntassel" Cello. Button,
31. Known as Voter's Button with companion Orphan nie button issued respectively for voters preferring altine with ice cream or simply ice. - **$100 $250 $500**

LAN-12

LAN-13

LAN-12. "Shirley Bell" Radio Show Photo,
1932. Pictured is Radio Orphan Annie portrayer. -
$20 $30 $50

LAN-13. "Joe Corntassel/Allan Baruck" Radio Show Photo,
1932. - **$15 $25 $40**

LAN-14

LAN-14. "Tucker County Fair" Jigsaw Puzzle With Mailer Box,
1933. Near Mint In Mailer - **$75**
Loose - **$15 $30 $60**

LAN-15

LAN-16

LAN-15. Paper Face Mask,
1933. - **$20 $40 $60**

LAN-16. Beetleware Plastic Cup,
1933. - **$15 $25 $50**

LAN-17

LAN-17. "Treasure Hunt" Game With Paper Boats,
1933. With Four Sailboats. Brown & yellow cover variations.
Set - **$60 $125 $250**
Board Only - **$20 $30 $75**
Mailer - **$20 $40 $60**

LAN-18

LAN-19

LAN-20

LAN-18. "Secret Society" Manual,
1934. - **$20 $40 $75**

LAN-19. Secret Society Bronze Badge,
1934. - **$10 $15 $25**

LAN-20. Bandanna Ring Slide Offer Sheet,
1934. "Face" ring also used as bandanna holder. - **$20 $50 $80**

LAN-21

LAN-22

LAN-23

LAN-21. Annie Portrait Ring and Bandanna Slide,
1934. - **$50 $75 $100**

LAN-22. "Flying W" Bandanna,
1934. - **$20 $50 $75**

LAN-23. "Flying W" Bandanna Explanation Card,
1934. Explains the 26 brands pictured on bandanna. - **$25 $50 $75**

LAN-24

LAN-24. "Identification Bureau" Bracelet With Mailer Envelope,
1934. Silver finish, personalized with initial.
Near Mint In Mailer - **$150**
Bracelet Only - **$20 $30 $60**

LAN-25

LAN-26

LAN-27

LAN-25. "Good Luck" Brass Medal,
1934. Includes "Ovaltine 3 Times A Day" with back "Good Luck" in several languages. - **$10 $20 $35**

LAN-26. Silver Star Club Badge,
1934. Silvered brass. - **$15 $30 $45**

AN-27. "Silver Star Member" Manual,
934. Near Mint In Mailer - **$85**
ɔose - **$20 $40 $60**

LAN-28

AN-28. Adventure Books & Contest Winner Sheet,
934. One side lists winners of "Shake-Up Naming
ɔntest". - **$15 $30 $50**

LAN-30

LAN-29

AN-29. Club Manual,
)35. - **$25 $60 $100**

AN-30. Brass Decoder,
)35. Silver flashing often worn off outer rim. -
5 **$35 $100**

LAN-31

AN-31. Premium Catalogue Folder With Envelope,
35. Opens to 4x22" with May 15 expiration date, envelope
s NRA symbol of Depression era.
ar Mint In Mailer - **$325**
lder - **$75 $150 $275**

LAN-34

LAN-32

LAN-33

LAN-32. Beetleware Cup,
1935. Green circle background. - **$15 $30 $75**

LAN-33. Beetleware Plastic Shake-Up Mug,
1935. Orange lid. Shows Annie from waist up. -
$25 $50 $80

LAN-34. Ovaltine Apology Postcard,
1935. Form message for delay in shipment of Orphan Annie
Identification Disk postmarked January 5. - **$15 $35 $60**

LAN-35   LAN-36

LAN-35. Magic Transfers and Instruction Sheet,
1935 Scarce. - **$50 $100 $200**

LAN-36. Club Manual,
1936. - **$15 $30 $65**

LAN-37   LAN-38

LAN-39

LAN-37. Secret Compartment Brass Decoder,
1936. - **$15 $25 $75**

LAN-38. Dog-Naming Contest Notice,
1936. Thank you notice for entering contest to name Bob
Bond's new dog. - **$10 $25 $50**

LAN-39. "Book About Dogs",
1936. Contents include Annie characters in various activities
plus photo descriptions of various dog breeds. -
$15 $30 $65

LAN-41

LAN-40

LAN-40. "Silver Star Member" Secrets Folder,
1936. For Silver Star Ring, shown on cover. - **$25 $50 $75**

LAN-41. Silver Star Ring,
1936. Silvered brass design of crossed keys over star. -
$200 $325 $450

LAN-42

LAN-42. "Birthday Ring" With Folder And Envelope,
1936. Birthstones in various colors.
Near Mint In Mailer - **$400**
Ring - **$75 $150 $250**
Folder - **$20 $40 $75**

LAN-43

LAN-43. "Welcome To Simmons Corners" 19x24"
Paper Map,
1936. - **$25 $75 $125**

LAN-44

LAN-45

LAN-44. "Little Orphan Annie Circus" Punch-Out Book,
1936. Six pages including more than 30 punch-outs.
Unpunched - **$150 $300 $500**

LAN-45. Glassips Package In Mailer,
1936. Rare. Contents are cellophane drinking straws. -
$100 $200 $400

LAN-46

LAN-46. Club Manual with Mailer and Silver Star Ring
Order Form,
1937. Manual - **$20 $35 $60**
Other Items - **$5 $10 $20**

LAN-47

LAN-49

LAN-48

LAN-47. Sunburst Brass Decoder Badge,
1937. - **$15 $35 $90**

LAN-48. "Silver Star Members" Folder With Mailer
Envelope,
1937. Includes code for Silver Star Ring.
Folder - **$65 $140 $225**
Envelope - **$10 $20 $30**

LAN-49. Silver Star Member Secret Message Ring,
1937. Silvered brass with coded message to be decoded by
that year's decoder. - **$150 $225 $300**

LAN-50

LAN-51

LAN-50. Two Initial Signet Brass Ring,
1937. Ring was customized with recipient's initials. -
$110 $180 $250

LAN-51. Foreign "Coin Collection" Folder,
1937. - **$15 $30 $50**

LAN-52

LAN-52. "Talking Stationery",
1937. Diecut paper mouths open and close, came with 12
letter sheets and envelopes. Near Mint Complete - **$200**
Each Sheet - **$5 $10 $15**

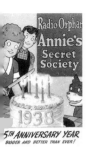

LAN-53

LAN-54

LAN-55

LAN-61

LAN-53. Club Manual,
1938. - **$20 $50 $75**

LAN-54. Telematic Brass Decoder Badge,
1938. - **$25 $60 $100**

LAN-55. Silver Star Manual,
1938. - **$90 $200 $350**

LAN-61. "Snow White And The Seven Dwarfs Cut-Out Book" With Envelope ,
1938. Scarce. Ovaltine as Radio Orphan Annie premium, also store item. Published by Whitman with six punch-out sheets. Near Mint In Mailer - **$600**
No Mailer, Unpunched - **$150 $300 $450**

LAN-56

LAN-57

LAN-58

LAN-62

LAN-63

LAN-56. Silver Star Triple Mystery Secret Compartment Ring,
1938. Silvered brass with removable cap covering member's serial number. - **$300 $600 $1200**

LAN-57. Miracle Compass Sun-Watch,
1938. - **$20 $50 $100**

LAN-58. School Brass Badge,
1938. Customized with two initials. - **$15 $30 $60**

LAN-62. Silver Plated Foto-Frame,
1938. Scarce. Metal base inscribed on front "To My Best Friend". - **$100 $250 $400**

LAN-63. "Shadowettes" Mechanical Paper Portraits,
1938. Set of six. Sandy, Annie, Warbucks, Joe Corntassel, Mr. Silo, Mrs. Silo. Near Mint In Mailer - **$250**
Each Assembled - **$10 $20 $30**

LAN-59

LAN-60

LAN-64

LAN-65

LAN-66

LAN-59. Beetleware Shake-Up Mug,
1938. Light blue with orange top, dancing scene. -
35 $80 $175

LAN-60. "Little Orphan Annie Gets Into Trouble" Booklet,
1938. J. C. Penney Co. - **$12 $25 $40**

LAN-64. Ann Gillis Photo,
c. 1938. Little Orphan Annie radio portrayer of late 1930s. -
$20 $30 $50

LAN-65. Manual with Mailer,
1939. Manual - **$20 $40 $75**
Mailer - **$5 $10 $20**

LAN-66. Mysto-Matic Brass Decoder Badge,
1939. - **$25 $50 $100**

LAN-67

LAN-68

LAN-67. Code Captain Secret Compartment Badge,
1939. Silvered finish. Sometimes found with link chain on back to fasten to that year's decoder badge. - **$35 $60 $100**

LAN-68. "Code Captain Secrets" Folder,
1939. - **$50 $85 $175**

LAN-69

LAN-70

LAN-69. Mystic-Eye Detective (Look-Around) Ring,
1939. Brass ring with American eagle cover cap over look-in mirror. Also issued for Captain Midnight and The Lone Ranger. - **$75 $115 $150**

LAN-70. "Mystic-Eye Detective Ring" Instruction Sheet,
1939. - **$15 $30 $60**

LAN-72

LAN-71

LAN-71. "Initial Identification Disc And Chain" Order Sheet,
1939. Back explains how Identification Bureau works above order coupon. Brass finish. - **$20 $40 $60**

LAN-72. Identification Bracelet,
1939. Brass version with American flag in bow design, personalized by single initial designated by orderer. -
$20 $40 $75

LAN-73

LAN-74

LAN-73. Beetleware Plastic Shake-Up Mug,
1939. Brown mug with orange lid. - **$50 $100 $175**

LAN-74. "Goofy Gazette" Newspaper #3 With Envelope,
1939. Three issues. Each Newspaper - **$35 $60 $100**
Each Mailer - **$5 $15 $25**

LAN-75

LAN-75. "Goofy Circus" Punch-Out Kit With Mailer Envelope,
1939. Mailer - **$15 $30 $50**
Unpunched - **$200 $350 $700**

LAN-77

LAN-78

LAN-76

LAN-76. Little Orphan Annie Oilcloth Doll,
1930s. Premium, unknown sponsor. - **$100 $200 $300**

LAN-77. Sandy Oilcloth Doll,
1930s. Premium, unknown sponsor. - **$75 $150 $225**

LAN-78. Cello. Button,
1930s. Cunningham Ice Cream. - **$75 $125 $200**

LAN-79

LAN-80

LAN-79. "Pittsburgh Post-Gazette" Newspaper Contest Cello. Button,
1930s. Part of a set showing other characters in the newspaper. - **$40 $75 $150**

LAN-80. "Funy Frostys Club" Cello. Button,
1930s. Two styles: "Member" in straight or curved type. - **$75 $150 $250**

LAN-81

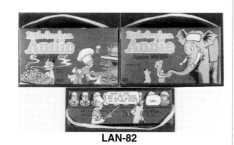

LAN-82

LAN-81. "Funy Frostys" Waxed Paper Wrapper,
1930s. Funy Frostys Ice Cream. Bottom has cardboard finger hole card for holding ice confection bar. - **$25 $50 $80**

LAN-82. "Sunshine Biscuits" Box,
1930s. Loose-Wiles Biscuit Co. - **$100 $250 $400**

LAN-83

LAN-84

LAN-85

LAN-83. "Word Building Contest" Acknowledgement Letter,
1930s. Response to entrant in contest to see how many different words can be made from single word Ovaltine plus Christmas greeting from Shirley Bell, ROA portrayer. - **$20 $50 $90**

LAN-84. "Los Angeles Evening Express" Cello. Button,
1930s. From set of newspaper characters, match number to win prize. - **$30 $50 $75**

LAN-85. Bisque Toothbrush Holder,
1930s. Store item. - **$60 $90 $175**

LAN-86

LAN-87

LAN-88

LAN-86. Club Manual,
1940. - **$50 $80 $150**

LAN-87. Speed-O-Matic Brass Decoder Badge,
1940. - **$30 $60 $125**

LAN-88. Beetleware Plastic Shake-Up Mug,
1940. Green with red lid. - **$40 $80 $150**

LAN-89

LAN-91

LAN-90

LAN-89. Shake-Up Mug Leaflet,
1940. Came with green mug. - **$25 $50 $75**

LAN-90. Sandy 3-Way Dog Whistle,
1940. 3-1/4" brass tube whistle that extends to 5-1/4" length. - **$20 $35 $75**

LAN-91. "3 Way Mystery Dog-Whistle" Instruction Leaflet,
1940. - **$20 $30 $50**

LAN-92

LAN-93

LAN-92. "Code Captain" Brass Buckle With Fabric Belt,
1940. Complete - **$100 $225 $350**
Buckle Ony - **$50 $125 $200**

LAN-93. Club Manual,
1941. Quaker Cereals. - **$50 $125 $200**

LAN-94

LAN-95

LAN-94. "Slidomatic Radio Decoder",
1941. Quaker Cereals. Cardboard slide with instructions on back. - **$25 $60 $100**

LAN-95. "Safety Guard" Application Blank for Captain's Commission,
1941. Quaker Cereals. Also see item LAN-105-
$10 $20 $35

LAN-86

LAN-96   **LAN-97**

LAN-96. Secret Guard Mysto-Snapper,
1941. Quaker Cereals. Litho. tin clicker. - **$15** **$60** **$100**

LAN-97. "Captain's Secrets" Folder Manual,
1941. Quaker Sparkies. - **$50** **$175** **$300**

LAN-98

LAN-98. Secret Guard Member Letter With Quaker Cereal Leaflet,
1941. Both explain "Vitamin Rain" additives to Quaker cereals. Each - **$10** **$20** **$35**

LAN-99   **LAN-100**

LAN-99. Secret Guard Wood Handle Rubber Stamp With Mailer,
1941. Rare. Quaker Cereals. Stamp Only - **$150** **$300** **$400**
Mailer - **$50** **$100** **$200**

LAN-100. Brass Slide Dog Whistle,
1941. Scarce. Quaker Cereals. End has Orphan Annie head. - **$100** **$200** **$300**

LAN-101

LAN-101. "The Adventures Of Little Orphan Annie" Comic Book,
1941. Quaker Puffed Wheat & Rice Sparkies. "...Kidnappers/Magic Morro..." stories. - **$15** **$30** **$75**

LAN-102   **LAN-103**

LAN-102. "The Adventures Of Little Orphan Annie" Comic Book,
1941. Quaker Puffed Wheat & Rice Sparkies. "...Rescue/Magic Morro..." stories. - **$15** **$45** **$105**

LAN-103. Quaker "How To Fly" Manual,
1941. - **$30** **$75** **$125**

LAN-104

LAN-105

LAN-104. "Captain Sparks Airplane Cockpit" Cardboard Assembly Kit,
1941. Quaker Cereals. 6x27" assembled with him pictured at center. Unassembled - **$150** **$250** **$400**
Assembled - **$100** **$200** **$300**

LAN-105. "SG/Captain" Glow-In-Dark Plastic Badge,
1941. Quaker Cereals. Also see item LAN-95. - **$65** **$150** **$350**

LAN-106   **LAN-107**

LAN-106. Secret Guard Magnifying Ring,
1941. Quaker Cereals. Offered briefly in 1941 with 8/31/41 expiration date "before Orphan Annie comes back on the air next Fall". - **$1125** **$2250** **$4500**

LAN-107. "SG" Secret Guard Brass Ring,
1941. Scarce. Quaker Cereals. Also inscribed "Bravery/Health/Justice" and personalized with initial. - **$1250** **$2500** **$5500**

LAN-108

LAN-108. "S.G." Secret Guard 3" Metal Flashlight,
1941. Scarce. Quaker Cereals. - **$100 $175 $250**

LAN-109

LAN-109. "Little Orphan Annie Scribbler" Canadian Booklet,
1941. Quaker Puffed Wheat And Puffed Rice. Canadian issue. - **$35 $60 $100**

LAN-110

LAN-110. Captain Sparks Box Cut-Outs,
1941. Quaker Sparkies cereal. From "Home Defense Series" set of 12. Each Panel Cut-Out - **$5 $10 $15**

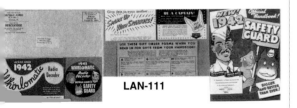

LAN-111

LAN-111. "Safety Guard" Membership Kit,
1942. Quaker Cereals. Included tin whistle not shown (see item LAN-113). Set Near Mint - **$600**
Decoder - **$50 $100 $150**
Whistle - **$20 $40 $75**
Handbook - **$60 $150 $300**

LAN-112

LAN-113

LAN-112. "Safety Guard" Captain Application Blank,
1942. Quaker Cereals. Also see item LAN-117. -
$10 $20 $35

LAN-113. "Safety Guard" Tri-Tone Signaler Badge,
1942. Quaker Cereals. Litho. tin whistle from member's kit (see item LAN-111). - **$20 $40 $75**

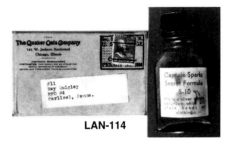

LAN-114

LAN-114. Quaker "Detector-Kit" With Mailer Box,
1942. Many items for photo printing, "Captain Sparks Secret Formula S-10" on bottle label. Boxed - **$100 $150 $300**

LAN-115

LAN-115. "3 In 1 Periscope",
1942. Scarce. Quaker Cereals. No Annie name but offered in 1942 Safety Guard handbook. - **$60 $150 $250**

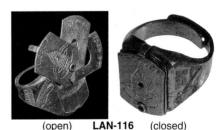

(open)   **LAN-116**   (closed)

LAN-116. Altascope Ring,
1942. Rare. Quaker Cereals. Several moveable brass plates for sighting airplanes and estimating their altitudes. -
$3000 $8000 $21000

LAN-117   **LAN-118**

LAN-119

LAN-117. "SG Captain" Safety Guard Magic Glow Bird Badge,
1942. Rare. Quaker Cereals. Also see item LAN-112. - **$100 $250 $750**

LAN-118. "SG Captain" Glow-In-Dark Canadian Club Brass Badge,
1942. Rare. Quaker Cereals. Design includes Canadian maple leaf symbol. - **$150 $250 $500**

LAN-119. "Super Book Of Comics-Little Orphan Annie",
c. 1943. Pan-Am gasoline. Book #7 from numbered series featuring various characters. - **$10 $35 $75**

LAN-120

LAN-121

LAN-120. "Super-Book Of Comics Featuring Little Orphan Annie",
1946. Omar Bread. Book #23 from numbered series featuring various characters. - **$10 $25 $45**

LAN-121. Quaker Puffed Wheat Comic Book,
1947. - **$2 $4 $8**

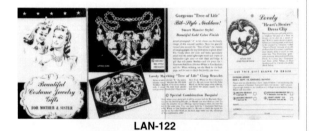
LAN-122

LAN-122. "Beautiful Costume Jewelry Gifts" Folder,
1940s. Annie name on order coupon. - **$50 $125 $175**

LAN-123

LAN-124

LAN-123. "Orphan Annie's Parents Smoked" Litho. Tin Tab,
1968. "Truth About Smoking" group. - **$10 $20 $40**

LAN-124. Plastic Cup,
1980. Ovaltine. - **$15 $25 $40**

LAN-125

LAN-126

LAN-125. Ceramic Anniversary Mug,
1981. Ovaltine. - **$10 $20 $30**

LAN-126. Movie Plastic Shake-Up Mug,
1982. Ovaltine. - **$10 $20 $30**

LAN-127

LAN-127. Plastic 50-Year Anniversary Shake-Up Mug,
1982. Ovaltine. - **$15 $30 $60**

LAN-128

LAN-128. "Annie" Cloth Doll With Order Form,
1982. Ivory, Zest, Camay soaps and others. Offered April 15 to September 30. Doll - **$5 $10 $25**
Order Form - **$2 $4 $6**

LAN-129

LAN-129. "In Person At Kennedy Center" Litho. Button,
1980s. Related to stage play. - **$10 $20 $35**

THE LONE RANGER

The legend of the Lone Ranger was born on Detroit radio station WXYZ in January 1933, the product of station owner George W. Trendle and writer Fran Striker. The program was a success from the start, and within a year was also being heard on WGN in Chicago and WOR in New York - in effect forming the nucleus of the new Mutual network. By 1937, "Hi-Yo Silver!" was echoing nationwide. Initially sustained by the station, the program was sponsored by Silver Cup bread starting in November 1933. Bond bread took over as sponsor in 1939 except in the Southeast states, where Merita bread retained its franchise. General Mills became the sponsor in 1941, tying the masked rider to such cereals as Kix and Wheaties until the radio series went off the air in 1955. Cheerios sponsored rebroadcasts until 1956, ending some 23 years and over 3,000 episodes of Western radio thrills and adventure.

Jack Deeds was the first actor to play the Lone Ranger, followed within weeks by George Seaton, and then in May 1933 by Earl Graser, who kept the role until his death in 1941. Probably best remembered is Brace Beemer, who played the part from 1941 to 1955.

On television, the Lone Ranger rode for more than 30 years on the networks and in syndication. The series, sponsored by General Mills (and Merita bread), premiered on ABC in 1949 and aired in prime time until 1957. Reruns were shown on all three networks: CBS (1953-1960 and 1966-1969), ABC (1957-1961 and 1965), and NBC (1960-1961). Syndication began in 1961. Clayton Moore played the lead for most of the series (John Hart covered the years 1952-1954) and Jay Silverheels, a Mohawk Indian, was Tonto, his faithful companion.

Republic Pictures released two 15-episode chapter plays, *The Lone Ranger* (1938), with Lee Powell as the lead, and *The Lone Ranger Rides Again* (1939), with Robert Livingston. Wrather Productions made three full-length films, *The Lone Ranger* (1955) and *The Lone Ranger and the Lost City of Gold* (1958), both with Clayton Moore and Jay Silverheels, and *The Legend of the Lone Ranger* (1981), with Klinton Spilsbury and Michael Horse.

A Saturday morning animated Lone Ranger series aired on CBS from 1966 to 1969, with the Ranger and Tonto battling mad scientists as well as conventional Western villains. The animated defenders of law and order surfaced again on CBS in 1980-1981 as part of *The Tarzan/Lone Ranger Adventure Hour*.

A Sunday comic strip distributed by King Features appeared from 1938 to 1971 and was revived from 1981 to 1984 - one of the longest running of the Western strips. Comic books, including giveaways, novels, coloring books, photo albums, and scrapbooks appeared in great numbers from the 1940s on.

It would be hard to overestimate the number of items licensed and merchandised in the name of the Lone Ranger, especially during the years the program ruled the air on radio and television. Items may be copyrighted by Lone Ranger Inc., Lone Ranger Television Inc., or, starting in 1954, Wrather Corp.

LON-1   LON-2   LON-3

LON-1. Safety Scout Member's Badge,
1934. Silvercup Bread. - **$10 $20 $50**

LON-2. Silvercup Bread "Chief Scout" Enameled Brass Badge,
1934. Also inscribed "Lone Ranger Safety Scout/Silvercup". - **$100 $200 $325**

LON-3. "Oke Tonto" Photo Card,
1934. Various bread company radio sponsors. - **$15 $25 $50**

LON-4

LON-4. Silvercup Bread "Chief Scout" Qualification Cards Set,
1934. Scarce. Fifth card (shown first) came with "Chief Scout" brass badge, others denoted "Degree" rank advancements to the badge.
1st - **$30 $60 $100**
2nd - **$30 $60 $100**
3rd - **$40 $80 $160**
4th - **$50 $90 $200**
5th - **$60 $100 $250**

LON-5   LON-6

LON-5. Silvercup Bread Safety Club Folder,
c. 1934. - **$30 $65 $100**

LON-6. Radio Sponsorship Brochure Opens To 19x25",
c. 1934. Silvercup Bread. - **$50 $100 $150**

LON-7

LON-8

LON-7. "How The Lone Ranger Captured Silver" Booklet,
1936. Silvercup Bread. - **$25 $60 $100**

LON-8. "Lone Ranger Safety Sentinel" Brass Badge,
1936. Miami Maid Bread. - **$60 $150 $250**

LON-9

LON-9. "Lone Ranger Target Game",
1936. Morton's Salt. Punch-out cardboard parts include gun
and six targets. Near Mint Unpunched - **$400**
Loose - **$100 $200 $300**

LON-10

LON-11

LON-10. Silvercup Bread Picture,
1936. - **$12 $20 $30**

LON-11. Cobakco Bread Story Booklet,
c. 1936. "How The Lone Ranger Captured Silver" seven-
page story collected over seven weeks. - **$60 $125 $200**

LON-12

LON-13

LON-12. "The Lone Ranger Magazine" Vol. 1 #1,
1937. Trojan Publishing Corp., Chicago. - **$100 $250 $450**

LON-13. Composition/Cloth Doll With Fabric Outfit,
1938. Store item as well as premium. 16" tall.
Lone Ranger - **$500 $1000 $1800**
Matching Tonto - **$400 $800 $1600**

LON-14

LON-15

LON-16

LON-14. Strong Box Bank,
1938. Sun Life Insurance. - **$40 $80 $160**

LON-15. Bat-O-Ball,
1938. Scarce. Pure Oil premium. WOR Radio. -
$30 $60 $120

LON-16. Bond Bread Promo,
1938. Scarce. WOR Radio. - **$30 $60 $120**

LON-17

LON-18

LON-19

LON-20

LON-21

LON-17. Glass,
1938. - **$20 $50 $100**

LON-18. Republic Serial Promo,
1938. Scarce. 15 episodes. - **$30 $60 $90**

**LON-19. Detroit Sunday Times Comic Strip
Announcement,**
1938. Strip began September 11. - **$20 $40 $75**

LON-20. Star Badge Used On Large Composition Doll,
1938. Rare. Dollcraft Novelty Doll Co. - **$25 $60 $150**

LON-21. Radio WOR Promo,
1938. - **$20 $40 $60**

LON-22

LON-23

LON-22. Republic Serial Club Brass Badge,
1938. Republic Pictures. Badges are serially numbered. -
$40 $75 $125

LON-23. Movie Discount Card,
1938. Republic Pictures. Admits child for 5 cents to Saturday
matinee. - **$40 $75 $100**

LON-24

LON-24. Wright Bread Picture,
1938. - **$20 $40 $60**

LON-25

LON-25. "White Cross" First Aid Booklet,
1938. - **$25 $50 $100**

LON-26

LON-27

LON-26. Tin Litho. Wind-Up,
1938. Store item by Marx Toys.
"Silver" In White - **$100 $250 $400**
"Silver" In Silver - **$150 $300 $500**

LON-27. Gum Wrappers Mail Picture,
1938. Scarce. Lone Ranger Bubble Gum. One of five collected by sending wrappers. 8x10" size.
Each - **$100 $200 $350**

LON-28

LON-28. "Lone Ranger Safety Club" Membership Card,
1938. Merita Bread. - **$15 $30 $50**

LON-29

LON-30

LON-29. Silvercup Bread Picture,
1938. - **$10 $20 $35**

LON-30. Cardboard Mask,
1938. Schultz Butter-Nut Bread and Dolly Madison Cakes. -
$35 $75 $125

LON-31

LON-32

LON-31. Bond Bread 9x13" Paper Poster,
1938. Scarce. Announces local radio broadcast times. -
$50 $110 $175

**LON-32. "Bond Bread Lone Ranger Safety Club"
Enameled Brass Star Badge,**
1938. - **$10 $25 $40**

LON-33

LON-34

LON-33. "Lone Ranger Cones" Paper Wrapper,
1938. Offers comic book, bracelet, Lone Ranger Ring, Tonto
Ring with October 31, 1940 expiration date. - **$20 $50 $75**

LON-34. "Lone Ranger Cones" Matchbook,
1938. - **$10 $20 $40**

LON-35

LON-36

**LON-35. Lone Ranger Ice Cream Cones
Enameled/Silvered Metal Picture Bracelet,**
1938. Rare. - **$300 $600 $1200**

LON-36. Tonto Lucky Ring,
1938. Rare. Lone Ranger Ice Cream Cones. Green plastic to
simulate onyx with paper portrait, also issued for Lone
Ranger. Tonto - **$800 $1600 $3000**
Lone Ranger - **$1000 $2000 $4000**

LON-37

LON-38

LON-37. Blue Beanie With Red Trim,
1938. Rare. Lone Ranger Ice Cream Cones. -
$100 $200 $400

LON-38. Silvercup Bread Photo,
c. 1938. - **$15 $30 $75**

LON-39

**LON-39. Silvercup Bread 13x17" "Lone Ranger Hunt
Map" With Envelope,**
c. 1938. With Envelope - **$75 $150 $250**
Map Only - **$50 $100 $175**

LON-40   **LON-41**   **LON-42**

LON-40. Cobakco Bread Picture Card,
c. 1938. - **$15 $30 $50**

LON-41. "Friend Of The Lone Ranger" Photo Card,
c. 1938. Cobaco Bread. Pictured is "Your Friend, U.S.
Marshal" from radio series. - **$15 $30 $50**

**LON-42. Cobakco Bread "Chuck Livingston" Picture
Card,**
c. 1938. Pictures "Outlaw On Lone Ranger Dramas". -
$15 $30 $50

LON-43

LON-44

LON-43. "Cobakco Safety Club" Enameled Brass Badge,
c. 1938. Cobakco Bread. - **$30 $60 $100**

LON-44. 7up Personalized Picture,
c. 1938. Black/white print personalized in white ink "To" recipient's first name. - **$15 $30 $50**

LON-46   **LON-47**

LON-45

LON-45. Merita Bread Photo,
c. 1938. - **$20 $50 $75**

LON-46. "Dr. West's Tooth Paste" Cello. Club Button,
c. 1938. - **$35 $65 $110**

LON-47. "Silver's Lucky Horseshoe" Enameled Brass Badge,
c. 1938. Smaller 1-1/4" size. - **$20 $40 $75**

LON-48   **LON-49**   **LON-50**

LON-48. "Silver's Lucky Horseshoe" Enameled Brass Badge,
c. 1938. Larger 1-3/4" size. - **$20 $40 $75**

LON-49. "Lone Ranger/Hi-Yo Silver" Brass Good Luck Medal,
c. 1938. Reverse design and inscription "Silver's Lucky Horseshoe". - **$15 $25 $50**

LON-50. "WFIL/Daily News Safety Club" Cello. Button,
c. 1938. Philadelphia radio station. - **$40 $75 $135**

LON-51   **LON-52**   **LON-53**

LON-51. "Lee Powell/Original Motion Picture" Cello. Button,
c. 1938. Scarce. Republic Pictures. -
$75 $175 $300

LON-52. "Supplee Lone Ranger Club" Enameled Brass Badge,
c. 1938. - **$25 $60 $100**

LON-53. Merita Enameled Brass Star Badge,
c. 1938. Merita Bread. - **$20 $50 $75**

LON-54   **LON-55**   **LON-56**

LON-54. "The Lone Ranger" Cello. Button,
c. 1938. Possibly Merita Bread Safety Club. - **$20 $50 $75**

LON-55. Rath's Enameled Brass Star Badge,
c. 1938. Rath's Bread. - **$35 $75 $125**

LON-56. Bestyett Enameled Brass Star Badge,
c. 1938. Bestyett Bread. - **$35 $75 $125**

LON-57   **LON-58**   **LON-59**

LON-57. A. B. Poe Enameled Brass Star Badge,
c. 1938. Poe Bread. - **$35 $75 $125**

LON-58. "The Lone Ranger Radio Station" Cello. Button,
c. 1938. WCSC, Charleston, South Carolina. - **$20 $40 $75**

LON-59. "Sunday Herald And Examiner" Litho. Button,
c. 1938. - **$15 $25 $40**

LON-60

LON-60. Movie Serial Ticket With Sears Offer,
c. 1938. Scarce. Ticket for 15-episode serial, reverse promotes cowboy suits at Sears, Roebuck. - **$35 $60 $100**

LON-61

LON-61. "The Lone Ranger Comic Book No. 1",
1939. Rare. Lone Ranger Ice Cream Cones. -
$580 $1750 $3500

LON-62

LON-62. "Ice Cream Cone Coupons" Envelope To Merchant,
1939. Lone Ranger Cones. Originally held 100 mail coupons expiring Jan. 1, 1940. Envelope Only - **$25 $60 $100**
Each Coupon - **$1 $2 $4**

LON-64

LON-63

LON-63. "Lone Ranger Cake Cones" Matchbook,
c. 1939. - **$10 $20 $40**

LON-64. "Lone Ranger Cones" Matchbook Cover,
c. 1939. Inscribed "Lone Ranger Ice Cream Cone Campaign." - **$10 $15 $30**

LON-66

LON-65

LON-65. Bond Bread Safety Club "Lone Ranger Roundup" Vol. 1 #1 Newspaper,
August 1939. Rare. At least seven issues through Vol. 2 #1.
First Issue - **$50 $100 $150**
Other Issues - **$25 $50 $75**

LON-66. World's Fair Bond Bread Premium,
1939. Rolled penny. - **$20 $40 $60**

LON-67

LON-67. Weber's Bread Club Manual,
1939. - **$50 $85 $175**

LON-69

LON-68

LON-68. Calendar,
1939. Cobakco Bread. - **$75 $150 $200**

LON-69. Pony Contest 11x14" Cardboard Poster,
c. 1939. Cobakco Bread. - **$50 $100 $200**

LON-70

LON-70. "Lapel Watch" Boxed Pocketwatch,
1939. Store item by New Haven Time Co. as well as premium. Near Mint Boxed - **$800**
Watch Only - **$100 $200 $400**

LON-71

LON-72

LON-71. Leather Watch Fob Holster With Miniature Gun,
1939. Came with some issues of New Haven pocketwatches. - **$35 $50 $100**

LON-72. Horlick's Malted Milk Picture,
1939. "Over Station WGN-Chicago". - **$15 $30 $50**

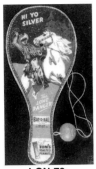

LON-73

LON-74

LON-73. "Bat-O-Ball" Toy,
1939. Scarce. Tom's Toasted Peanuts. Cardboard paddle with rubber band and ball. With Ball - **$40 $90 $150**
No Ball - **$20 $60 $100**

LON-74. Bond Bread Color Cellophane Picture Sheet,
c. 1939. 6x9" probably for window display. - **$35 $75 $125**

LON-75

LON-75. "Safety Club" Application Postcard,
1939. Bond Bread. - **$10 $20 $35**

LON-76

LON-76. "Bond Bread Safety Club" Letter And Membership Card,
1939. Card - **$15 $30 $50**
Letter - **$20 $40 $60**

LON-78

LON-79

LON-77. Bond Bread Contest Card Stub,
c. 1939. - **$15 $30 $65**

LON-78. May Co. Activity Booklet,
1939. May department store. Christmas issue. -
$20 $50 $100

LON-79. Bond Bread 8x12" Cardboard Store Sign,
1940. Scarce. - **$100 $200 $300**

LON-80

LON-81

LON-80. Bond Bread Wrapper,
1940. - **$20 $40 $65**

LON-81. Color Photo,
c. 1940. Bond Bread. - **$15 $25 $50**

LON-82

LON-83

LON-77

LON-82. "Hi-Yo Supplee Lone Rangers" Newsletter,
1940. Supplee Milk. First anniversary issue. - **$25 $50 $75**

LON-83. "Orange Pops" 6x12" Cardboard Store Sign,
1940. Scarce. - **$100 $300 $500**

LON-84

LON-84. "Cloverine Salve" Premium Catalogue With Watch Ads,
c. 1940. - **$10 $25 $40**

LON-85

LON-86

LON-85. "Lone Ranger Cones" Paper Wrapper,
c. 1940. Offers same premiums as 1938 wrapper without expiration date. - **$20 $50 $75**

LON-86. Kix Cereal "Name Silver's Son" 16x20" Contest Poster,
1941. Rare. - **$1000 $2000 $3000**

LON-87

LON-87. Photo With Insert And Envelope,
1941. Came with insert announcing Kix as new radio sponsor. Complete - **$40 $80 $150**
Photo Only - **$10 $15 $30**

LON-88

LON-88. "National Defenders Secret Portfolio" Manual,
1941. - **$75 $150 $250**
Mailer - **$20 $40 $60**

LON-89

LON-89. "Silver Bullet Defender" Leaflet With 45-Caliber Silver Bullet,
1941. Contains silver ore. Bullet - **$20 $40 $75**
Folder - **$15 $35 $65**

LON-90

LON-90. Kix Luminous Blackout Plastic Belt,
1941. Near Mint Boxed With Insert Folder - **$200**
Belt Only - **$50 $75 $150**

LON-91

LON-92

LON-91. National Defenders Danger-Warning Siren,
1941. Scarce. Came with carrying cord. Offered as bounce back premium with Gardenia Brooch. - **$200 $500 $1000**
Tube Mailer - **$20 $40 $60**

LON-92. National Defenders Look-Around Brass Ring,
1941. No inscription but offered in Lone Ranger premium advertisements. Also issued for Captain Midnight and Radio Orphan Annie. - **$75 $115 $150**

LON-93   LON-94

LON-99

LON-93. Victory Bread Wrapper,
1942. Weber's White Bread. - **$20 $40 $60**

LON-94. Victory Corps Club Promo,
1942. - **$50 $100 $200**

LON-99. "Victory Corps" Membership Kit,
1942. Cheerios/Kix. Includes cover letter with
membership/I.D. folder plus brass tab (see item LON-98).
Envelope - **$20 $50 $75**
Letter - **$15 $40 $60**
Folder - **$30 $60 $90**

LON-95   LON-96

LON-95. "War Album Of Victory Battles" With Mailer
Envelope,
1942. General Mills. No Lone Ranger mention but offered on
radio show, came with battle scene stamps.
Complete With Mailer - **$35 $60 $100**
Complete Album - **$25 $40 $60**
Album No Stamps - **$10 $20 $30**

LON-96. Sailor Hat,
1942. - **$50 $75 $100**

LON-100   LON-101

LON-100. "Lone Ranger VC" Victory Corps Cello. Button,
1942. - **$30 $60 $100**

LON-101. Secret Compartment Ring Instruction Paper,
1942. Leaflet opens to four panels with other Lone Ranger
radio and club notes. - **$40 $75 $150**

LON-97

LON-98

LON-97. Military Hat with Metal Button,
1942. Rare. - **$100 $200 $400**

LON-98. "Lone Ranger Victory Corps" Brass Tab,
1942. - **$15 $30 $60**

LON-102

LON-102. Kix Air Force Ring With Envelope,
1942. Interior ring photos of Lone Ranger and Silver often
missing. Ring Complete - **$375 $590 $800**
Ring, No Photos - **$100 $210 $320**
Envelope - **$10 $25 $50**

LON-104   LON-105

LON-99

LON-103

LON-103. Marine Corps Brass Ring,
1942. Two inside photos of Lone Ranger and Silver often
missing. Complete - **$400 $625 $850**
No Photos - **$110 $225 $340**

→

LON-104. Army Insignia Secret Compartment Brass Ring,
1942. Two inside photos of Lone Ranger and Silver often missing. Complete - **$400 $625 $850**
No Photos - **$110 $225 $340**

LON-105. "USN" Navy Photo Ring,
1942. Brass, two inside photos of Lone Ranger and Silver often missing. Complete - **$500 $750 $1000**
No Photos - **$135 $270 $400**

LON-106

LON-107

LON-106. Kix "Blackout Kit" With Envelope,
1942. Contents include luminous paper items.
Near Mint In Mailer - **$300**

LON-107. Meteorite Ring,
1942. Scarce. Kix bounce back offer with Lone Ranger military rings April, 1942. Company recorded 85 requests. Brass with plastic dome over tiny "meteorite" granules. -
$1175 $2350 $5000

LON-108

LON-109

LON-110

LON-108. Decoder,
1943. Rare. - **$100 $200 $325**

LON-109. Kix Decal Sheet,
1944. Set #5 sheet from series with water transfer decals of Lone Ranger and other western subjects. - **$15 $30 $50**

LON-110. "Kix Airbase" 27x27" Play Sheet Map With Envelope,
1945. No Lone Ranger inscription but offered on his show. Used with 32 warplane cut-outs from four Kix cereal boxes.
With Envelope - **$50 $100 $200**
No Envelope - **$25 $50 $100**

LON-111

LON-112

LON-111. Weather Forecasting Ring,
1946. Brass with clear lucite cover over small litmus paper. -
$60 $90 $125

LON-112. Portrait Picture,
1946. Artist signature appears to be Frederic Myer. -
$75 $125 $225

LON-113

LON-113. Punch-Out Sheet,
1947. American Bakeries Co. - **$35 $75 $110**

LON-114

LON-115

LON-116

LON-114. Atomic Bomb Ring,
1947. Kix cereal. Brass with plastic bomb cap. -
$50 $100 $150

LON-115. Six-Gun Ring,
1947. Brass with plastic gun holding flint. - **$60 $90 $125**

LON-116. "Lone Ranger 6-Shooter Ring" 17x22" Store Poster,
1947. - **$50 $90 $150**

LON-117

LON-118

ON-117. "Lone Ranger .45" Secret Compartment Bullet,
947. Aluminum with removable cap. - **$25 $50 $90**

ON-118. Merita Bread Safety Club Calendar,
948. Rare. 16"x24". With calendar tablet pages and club
pplication forms. - **$300 $750 $1600**
maller version without calendar - **$100 $200 $400**

LON-119

LON-120

ON-119. Tonto Set Of Two Metal Bracelets,
948. Scarce. No character name on the bracelets, each has
ndian symbols. Complete With Mailer - **$50 $100 $200**

ON-120. Gift Subscription Christmas Card With
nvelope,
948. Dell Comics. - **$15 $30 $60**

(map) LON-121 (building section)

ON-121. "Lone Ranger Frontier Town" Punch-Outs
nd Maps,
948. Four separate maps and four separate unpunched
uilding sections.
ach Unpunched Section With Mailer - **$400**
omplete Punched Section - **$250**
ach Map - **$75 $125 $200**

LON-123

LON-122

ON-122. "Frontier Town" Cheerios Box,
948. Set of nine. Complete Box Each - **$100 $350 $500**
ach Back Panel Used to Complete Lone Ranger Town -
5 **$50 $75**

ON-123. Flashlight Ring,
948. Brass with lightbulb and battery. - **$30 $60 $125**

LON-124

LON-124. Cheerios Aluminum Pedometer With Fabric Strap,
1948. Near Mint Boxed - **$75**
Loose - **$15 $30 $50**

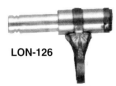

LON-126

LON-125

LON-125. Lone Ranger/Gene Autry Flag Ring,
c. 1948. Dell Comics. Plastic with dome over flag image, for
one-year subscription to comic book for either. -
$100 $150 $200

LON-126. Filmstrip Ring,
1949. Brass bands with aluminum viewing tube, came with
25-frame 8mm color filmstrip titled "U.S. Marines".
Ring - **$50 $90 $125**
Film - **$35 $50 $85**

LON-127

LON-128

LON-127. Flashlight Gun With Secret Compartment Handle and Lenses,
1949. Battery operated with clear, red and green lenses. -
$50 $150 $200

LON-128. General Mills Outfit,
1949. Rare. Includes shirt, mask, neckerchief, cardboard tag
with official seal. Set - **$100 $200 $400**

LON-130

LON-129

LON-129. Cheerios "Deputy Secret Folder",
1949. - **$15 $30 $50**

LON-130. "Lone Ranger Deputy" 2" Brass Badge With Secret Compartment,
1949. - **$25 $50 $100**

LON-131

LON-132

LON-133

LON-131. Schmidt's Bread Wrapper,
1940s. - **$30 $60 $90**

LON-132. "Lone Ranger" Waxed Paper Bread Loaf Liner,
1940s. Harris-Boyer Bakeries. - **$25 $50 $90**

LON-133. Child Labor Law Folder,
1940s. New York State Department of Labor. Lone Ranger endorsement for labor laws affecting boys and girls aged 14-17. - **$20 $35 $60**

LON-134

LON-135

LON-134. Pocketknife,
1940s. Store item with grips in black, red or white. -
$35 $75 $110

LON-135. Buchan's Bread Cello. Button,
c. 1940s. 12 known in either 7/8" or 1-1/4" size, various Lone Ranger slogans. Each - **$15 $30 $50**

LON-136

LON-137

LON-138

LON-136. Seal Print Face Ring,
1940s. Unmarked believed Lone Ranger premium tin ring designed to press face image into soft material. -
$150 $225 $300

LON-137. Merita Bread Safety Club 8x15" Cardboard Wall Calendar,
1950. Scarce. - **$75 $150 $250**

LON-138. "Lone Ranger Lucky Piece" Silvered Brass 17th Anniversary Key Ring Fob Medal,
1950. Cheerios. - **$15 $25 $40**

LON-139

LON-140

LON-139. Fabric Bandanna,
1950. Offered by Betty Crocker Soups. - **$25 $60 $90**

LON-140. Cheerios Contest Postcard,
1951. Back text for coloring contest. - **$8 $15 $30**

LON-141

LON-142

LON-141. Cheerios Crayon Offer Box Back,
1951. #1 from set of four. - **$10 $20 $30**

LON-142. Cheerios Crayon Offer Box Backs,
1951. #2 and #4 shown, from set of four offering free crayon set for crayoned box picture sent to General Mills. -
$10 $20 $30

LON-143

LON-143. Cheerios Saddle Ring With Filmstrip, Paper and Box,
1951. Near Mint Boxed - **$400**
Ring Only - **$75 $125 $200**
Film Only - **$30 $50 $75**

LON-144

LON-144. Cheerios Paper Mask,
1951. Back text "See The Lone Ranger And Silver In Person At Minneapolis Aquatennial". - **$25 $60 $100**

LON-145

LON-145. Cheerios Box With Comic Book Advertising,
1954. - **$100 $250 $400**

LON-146

LON-146. "The Lone Ranger And The Story Of Silver" Comic,
1954. Cheerios. - **$15 $45 $105**

LON-147

LON-147. Merita Bread Coloring Book,
1955. - **$10 $20 $35**

LON-148

LON-148. Merita Bread Safety Club "Branding" Booklet,
1956. Cattle branding explained by Lone Ranger. - **$20 $50 $85**

LON-149

LON-149. "Lone Ranger Ranch Fun Book",
1956. Cheerios. - **$20 $40 $75**

LON-150   LON-151

LON-150. Cheerios "Lone Ranger Fun Kit" Sign,
1956. Diecut 6x8" paper display sign. - **$30 $60 $100**

LON-151. Wheaties "Lone Ranger Hike-O-Meter" Sign,
1956. Diecut 6x8" paper display sign. - **$25 $40 $60**

LON-152   LON-153

LON-152. Sugar Jets "Lone Ranger Six-Shooter Ring" Sign,
1956. Diecut 6x8" paper display sign. - **$25 $40 $60**

LON-153. Trix "Tonto Belt" Sign,
1956. Diecut 6x8" paper display sign. - **$25 $40 $60**
Belt with Mailer - **$30 $60 $120**

LON-154   LON-155

LON-154. Kix "Lone Ranger Branding Iron" Sign,
1956. Diecut 6x8" paper display sign. - **$30 $50 $75**

LON-155. Lone Ranger With Guns 6' Standee,
1957. Rare. General Mills. - **$1000 $2000 $3000**

LON-156

LON-157

LON-156. Wheaties Box With Posters Offer,
1957. Complete Box - **$200 $300 $500**
Box Back - **$20 $40 $60**

LON-157. Wheaties Life-Sized Posters,
1957. Set of two 25x75" paper posters.
Lone Ranger - **$80 $175 $300**
Tonto - **$75 $150 $250**

LON-158

LON-159

LON-158. Life-Sized Uncut Poster Sheet (not separated),
1957. Used in lobby at General Mills headquarters.
Unique - **$1250**

LON-159. Cheerios "Wild West Town" Figures With Sheet And Box,
1957. Scarce. Set of 22 figures including Lone Ranger, Tonto, three horses, nine cowboys, eight Indians.
Near Mint Complete - **$400**

LON-160

LON-161

LON-160. Cheerios "Movie Ranch Wild West Town" Ad Sheet,
1957. Box insert 3x4". - Set Complete - **$100 $200 $400**
Sheet - **$15 $40 $60**

LON-161. Merita Bread "Lone Ranger Peace Patrol" Aluminum Token,
1959. Sponsored in conjunction with U.S. Treasury Department. Promotion for savings bonds. - **$40 $75 $125**

LON-162

LON-164

LON-163

LON-162. "Peace Patrol" Member Card,
c. 1959. U.S. Treasury Department. Encourages savings bond purchase, back has creed and pledge. - **$5 $15 $25**

LON-163. "Join The Peace Patrol" 11x14" Paper Poster
c. 1959. U.S. Treasury Department. Encourages savings bond purchase. - **$60 $150 $250**

LON-164. Full Color Cello. Button,
c. 1959. Unmarked but probably related to Treasury Department campaign to promote sales of U.S. Savings Bonds. - **$10 $20 $35**

LON-165

NOW! HERE'S HOW TO ORGANIZE A LONE RANGER CLUB AND BECOME A DEPUTY CHIEF!
As a trusted Lone Ranger Deputy you have the power to swear-in any one (or more) boys and girls as Deputies and form a Lone Ranger secret club. When you do this you automatically become a DEPUTY CHIEF.

LON-166

LON-165. Litho. Button With Bw Photo On Lt. Blue,
c. 1959. Same design as full color 1-1/4" cello. button but rare 1-3/8" litho. - **$100 $300 $600**

LON-166. Deputy Chief Badge,
1950s. Rare. Detail of paper also shown. - **$100 $200 $30**

LON-167

LON-168

LON-167. "Merita Bread" Color Picture,
1950s. - $15 $30 $60

LON-168. Merita Bread Aluminum Silver Bullet Pencil Sharpener,
1950s. - $20 $50 $75

LON-169

LON-169. Dell Comics Picture Strip,
1950s. Strip folio of five pictures. - $50 $80 $150

LON-170

LON-170. Smoking Click Plastic Pistol,
1950s. Store item by Marx Toys.
Boxed - $75 $125 $200
Loose - $50 $80 $150

LON-171

LON-171. "Magic Lasso" With Brass Badge,
1950s. Store item by Round-Up Products.
Near Mint Boxed - $400
Badge Only - $60 $150 $250

LON-172   LON-173   LON-174

LON-172. Litho. Tin Tab Star Badge,
1950s. Pictures Clayton Moore. - $15 $30 $50

LON-173. "Lone Ranger Deputy" 2-1/4" Silvered Metal Badge,
1950s. Red and black painted versions. Store Item.
Card with 12 Badges - $500
Each - $10 $20 $30

LON-174. "Lone Ranger Deputy" Gold Finish Metal Badge,
1950s. Store item. - $15 $25 $40

LON-175

LON-176

LON-175. "Lone Ranger Junior Deputy" Gold Luster Tin Star Badge,
1950s. From Junior Deputy kit. - $20 $30 $45

LON-176. English Cookie Tin,
1961. Huntley & Palmers Biscuits. - $40 $65 $125

LON-177

LON-178

LON-177. English Cookie Tin,
1961. Huntley & Palmers Biscuits. Version pictures Tonto only. - $40 $65 $125

LON-178. "The Legend Of The Lone Ranger" Comic Book,
1969. Chain restaurant promotion. Identifies him as "The Good Food Guy". - $5 $8 $12

LON-179

LON-180

LON-181

LON-179. "The Good Food Guy" Cello. Button,
c. 1969. Chain restaurant promotion. - **$10 $18 $25**

LON-180. Autographed Clayton Moore Photograph,
1977. Lynn Wilson's Convenient Fun Food. Design includes
Lone Ranger Creed. Signed - **$15 $30 $60**
Unsigned - **$8 $15 $25**

**LON-181. Amoco Gas Station "Ride With Silver" 44x70"
Vinyl Sign,**
1970s. "Amoco Silver" lead-free gasoline. - **$35 $60 $125**

LON-182

LON-182. "Lone Ranger Deputy Kit",
1980. Cheerios. Contains Deputy certificate, "Legend" story
folder, punch-out mask, 2-1/2" plastic Deputy badge and
17x22" color poster. Complete - **$10 $20 $35**

LON-183

LON-184

LON-183. Cheerios Box Back "Deputy Kit" Offer,
1980. Complete Box - **$15 $25 $40**
Back Only - **$5 $8 $15**

LON-184. Movie Press Kit,
1981. Contains saddle bag mailer with 14 photos & script. -
$20 $40 $80

LON-185

LON-185. Movie Lone Ranger Rocking Book,
1981. Lone Ranger on front cover, Tonto on back cover. -
$10 $20 $30

LONE WOLF TRIBE

Wrigley's gum sponsored this children's program on CBS
1932-1933. The series offered dramatized versions of the
American Indian way of life, told by Chief Wolf Paw to the
tribe members "with the voice that flies (radio)." Listeners
could obtain premiums by sending in "wampum" (Wrigley
wrappers). Most premiums were marked with the imprint of a
wolf paw. The club ring, sterling silver and non-adjustable,
considered the earliest issued premium ring.

LWF-1

LWF-2

LWF-1. Wrigley's Chewing Gum Samples Folder,
1932. Held three sticks of gum, reverse lists radio times and
offers Lone Wolf Tribe Book.
With Gum - **$25 $50 $100**
Folder Only - **$15 $30 $75**

LWF-2. Club Manual,
1932. Wrigley Gum. - **$15 $25 $75**

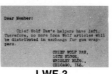

LWF-3

LWF-4

WF-3. New Member Letter,
932. Wrigley Gum. - **$15 $25 $40**

WF-4. "Treasure Of The Lone Wolf" 11x17" Paper Map,
932. Scarce. Wrigley Gum. - **$50 $100 $150**

LWF-5

LWF-6

LWF-7

WF-5. Chief Wolf Paw Sterling Ring,
932. Wrigley's Gum. Considered the first radio premium
ng. - **$100 $150 $200**

WF-6. Arrowhead Silvered Brass Member's Badge,
932. On Card - **$20 $40 $60**
oose - **$15 $25 $40**

WF-7. Tribe Bracelet,
932. Wrigley Gum. Silvered metal expansion bracelet with
bal code symbols. - **$30 $60 $100**

LWF-8

LWF-9

WF-8. Tribe Necklace,
32. Scarce. - **$100 $200 $300**

WF-9. Chief Wolf Paw Arrowhead Fob,
32. Wrigley Gum. Thin silvered brass picturing paw and
row designs. - **$12 $20 $35**

LWF-10

LWF-11

WF-10. Cow Head Tie Holder,
32. Actual bone tie slide from "Vertebra Of A Range
imal". - **$20 $40 $60**

WF-11. "Sitting Bull" Picture,
1932. Lone Wolf Tribe premium with back text "How Sitting
ll Got His Name". - **$10 $20 $40**

LWF-12

LWF-12. "Lone Wolf Tribe Tom-Tom" Leather And Thin
Rubber Drum With Beater Stick,
c. 1932. Rare. Wrigley's Gum. Boxed - **$50 $100 $150**
Loose - **$25 $50 $75**

LWF-13

LWF-13. Out Of Business Paper,
c. 1933. Wrigley Gum. Paper reads "Dear Member: Chief
Wolf Paw's Helpers Have Left. Therefore, No More Lone
Wolf Articles Will Be Distributed In Exchange For Gum
Wrappers." - **$25 $50 $100**

LUM AND ABNER

For 22 years on various radio networks and for a long list of
sponsors, Lum Edwards and Abner Peabody ran the Jot 'Em
Down Store in the mythical town of Pine Ridge, Arkansas.
The show was conceived by Chester Lauck and Norris Goff,
boyhood friends in rural Arkansas who played not only the
title roles but also most of the other characters in a continuing mixture of dialect comedy and rustic soap opera. The
program premiered on Hot Springs station KTHS in 1931 and
soon moved to Chicago and went national. Sponsors included Quaker Oats (1931), Ford automobiles (1933), Horlick's
malted milk (1934-1938), Postum (1938-1940), Alka-Seltzer
(1941-1948), and Frigidaire (1948-1949). The final broadcast was in 1953. (In 1936, in honor of the show, the town of
Waters, Arkansas, officially changed its name to Pine Ridge).

LUM-1 **LUM-2**

LUM-1. "Pine Ridge News" Vol. 1 #1 Newspaper, November
1933. Ford Motor Co. - **$25 $50 $80**

LUM-2. "The Pine Ridge News" Newspaper With Envelope,
1936, Spring. Horlick's Malted Milk.
Near Mint In Mailer- **$75**
Loose - **$15 $25 $50**

LUM-3

LUM-4

LUM-5

LUM-3. "Lum And Abner's Almanac",
1936. Horlick's Malted Milk. - **$5 $10 $25**

LUM-4. "Walkin' Weather Prophet" Brass Badge,
1936. Horlick's Malted Milk. Litmus paper insert changes color with humidity but almost always inactive due to age. - **$10 $20 $35**

LUM-5. Lum Edwards For President Cello. Button,
1936. Horlick's Malted Milk. - **$5 $10 $15**

LUM-6

LUM-7

LUM-8

LUM-6. Glass Shake-Up Decanter With Aluminum Lid,
c. 1936. For preparing Horlick's Malted Milk. Lid has pouring spout. - **$40 $75 $150**
With Metal Top, No Spout - **$35 $70 $140**

LUM-7. "Family Almanac",
1937. Horlick's Malted Milk. - **$10 $15 $25**

LUM-8. "Lum And Abner's Family Almanac",
1938. Horlick's Malted Milk. - **$10 $20 $35**

LUM-9

LUM-10

LUM-9. Fan Photo,
1930s. Inset photo of radio portrayers Chester Lauck and Norris Goff. - **$20 $35 $60**

LUM-10. Movie Postcard,
1946. Various theaters. Announces upcoming movie "Partners In Time". - **$5 $15 $25**

MAD COMICS

What started as an irreverent little comic book in August 1952 has grown into probably the nation's leading humor magazine. Early issues, edited by Harvey Kurtzman, satirized popular comic strips with features such as *Little Orphan Melvin* and *Batboy and Rubin*. With issue #24 in 1955 publisher Bill Gaines changed the format from comic book to magazine. Alfred E. Neuman, a cartoon rendering of a 19th century icon, made his debut on the cover of issue #21 and has become the magazine's (What - Me Worry?) trademark. Annual issues of *More Trash from Mad* and *The Worst from Mad* appeared from 1958 to 1969, *Mad Follies* from 1963 to 1969, and *Mad Specials* from 1970 on. Licensed merchandise includes clothing, food products, games, trading cards and greeting cards. *Mad TV*, a late-night comedy show debuted on the Fox television network in October 1995.

MAD-1

MAD-2

MAD-3

MAD-1. "Comfort Soap" Cello. Button,
c. 1901. Very strong early character resemblance to later Alfred E. Neuman. - **$125 $250 $500**

MAD-2. Birthday Card,
c. 1930s. - **$50 $125 $200**

MAD-3. "Me Worry?" Cello. Button,
1941. "Superior" unknown sponsor. - **$100 $250 $400**

MAD-4

MAD-4. Get Well Card,
c. 1940s. - **$25 $60 $100**

MAD-5

MAD-6

MAD-12

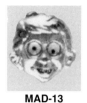

MAD-13

MAD-5. "EC Fan-Addict Club" Patch And Bronze Badge,
1953. Part of membership kit. Re-issue patch includes copyright symbol. Original Patch - **$50 $100 $150**
Re-issue Patch - **$25 $50 $75**
Badge - **$75 $125 $200**

MAD-6. Figurine,
1960. Glazed base with unglazed white bust to be painted by recipient. Small 3-3/4" Size - **$100 $250 $500**
Large 5-1/2" Size - **$200 $400 $600**

MAD-12. "Alfred E. Neuman" Aurora Plastics Model Kit,
1965. Store item. Boxed And Unbuilt - **$150 $200 $250**

MAD-13. Alfred E. Neuman Plastic Portrait Pin,
c. 1960s. Store item. Vending machine issue, unlicensed, marked "Hong Kong". - **$10 $25 $40**

MAD-7   **MAD-8**

MAD-14   **MAD-15**

MAD-7. "For President" 2-1/2" Cello. Button,
1960. - **$40 $75 $140**

MAD-8. "Me Worry??" Composition Bust Figure,
1960. Unlicensed. With Tag - **$75 $150 $250**
No Tag - **$50 $125 $200**

MAD-14. "What Me Worry?" Dark Gold Luster Metal Necklace Pendant,
c. 1960s. Store item. Depicts Alfred E. Neuman riding bomb. - **$40 $75 $125**

MAD-15. Movie Promotion 3" Cello Button,
1980. Warner Brothers. - **$8 $12 $20**

MAD-10

MAD-9

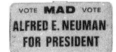

MAD-11

MAD-9. "What Me Worry?" Doll,
1961. Unlicensed store item by Baby Barry. -
$400 $800 $1500

MAD-10. "For President" 2-1/2" Cello. Button,
1964. - **$20 $40 $75**

MAD-11. "Alfred E. Neuman For President" Litho. Tin Tab,
1964. - **$10 $20 $35**

MAJOR BOWES ORIGINAL AMATEUR HOUR

Edward Bowes (1874-1946), a major in U.S. Army intelligence in World War I and a show-business veteran, introduced his amateur hour on New York radio station WHN in 1934. The following year, sponsored by Chase & Sanborn coffee, it aired on the NBC network, and from 1936 to 1946, sponsored by Chrysler automobiles, it was a Thursday night institution on CBS. 'Round and 'round she goes, and where she stops nobody knows - so went the wheel of fortune, each week drawing thousands of amateur performers looking for the big break. For most, it was a dream that didn't come true.

MJB-1   **MJB-2**

MJB-1. First Fan Newsletter #1,
1935. Chase & Sanborn Coffee. - **$15 $30 $50**

MJB-2. Second Fan Newsletter #2,
1935. Chase & Sanborn Coffee. - **$12 $20 $30**

MJB-3

MJB-4

MJB-3. Fan Photo,
1936. Chrysler Corp. Radio show title on back. -
$10 $15 $25

MJB-4. "Major Bowes Amateur Parade" Photo Newsletter,
June 1937. Chrysler Corp. - **$8 $12 $20**

MJB-5

MJB-6

MJB-5. Gong Alarm Clock,
c. 1930s. Made by Ingersoll. - **$75 $125 $200**

MJB-6. Home Broadcasting Microphone With Box,
1930s. Store item by Pilgrim Electric Corp. Metal actual working device for household radio set.
Boxed - **$100 $200 $300**
Loose - **$50 $125 $200**

MJB-7

MJB-8

MJB-7. "Capitol Theatre Family" Fan Photo Card,
1930s. Pictures Capitol Radio orchestra of radio broadcasts. - **$5 $12 $20**

MJB-8. Fan Postcards,
1930s. Each - **$5 $8 $12**

MAJOR JET

A mid-1950s character created to promote Sugar Jets cere of General Mills, Major Jet was an otherwise unidentifie individual although always appearing in his jet-age flight he met snappily accented by voltage bolt symbols centered by "J" symbol denoting speed. His resemblance to an esta lished comic strip jetting hero of the era, Milton Caniff's *Ste Canyon*, may have been more than coincidental. Act Roger Pace portrayed Major Jet in TV commercials. H motto, "Jet Up And Go With Sugar Jets," accompanied pr mium offers—notably a mail premium Rocket-Glider kit styrofoam and plastic but "made for high, jet-speed flying The Rocket-Glider was offered by a May 1, 1955 Sunda comic section ad "while supplies last" and probably by cere box as well.

MAJ-1

MAJ-1. Magic Paint Set Booklet,
1954. Sugar Jets cereal. #1 from set of three.
Each - **$8 $15 $25**

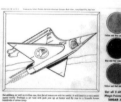

MAJ-2

MAJ-2. "Magic Paint Set" Book #2,
1954. Sugar Jets cereal. From set of three.
Each - **$8 $15 $25**

MAJ-3

MAJ-4

AJ-3. Sugar Jets "Filmo Vision" Box Back,
954. Cut-out parts for assembly of spaceship viewer for atching two cut-out films. Uncut Back - **$10 $20 $30**

AJ-4. Rocket-Glider With Launcher,
955. Sugar Jets cereal. Near Mint Boxed - **$50**
ose - **$10 $15 $20**

MANDRAKE THE MAGICIAN

reated by writer Lee Falk and artist Phil Davis, Mandrake ebuted as a daily comic strip in 1934 and as a Sunday page 1935. Distributed by King Features, the adventures of the p-hatted magician with supernatural and hypnotic powers as an immediate success. Assisted by his faithful compan- n Lothar, an African king with enormous strength, and rincess Narda, Mandrake triumphed over earthly enemies d extraterrestrial invaders. He made his first comic book ppearance in *King Comics* #1 in 1936 and has appeared in merous collections in the decades since. Columbia ctures released a 12-episode chapter play in 1939 with arren Hull as Mandrake, and a syndicated radio series red on the Mutual network from 1940 to 1942. A pilot ade-for-TV movie was broadcast in 1979.

MAN-1   MAN-2

MAN-3

N-1. "Member Mandrake's Magic Club" Litho. Button,
34. - **$50 $100 $175**

N-2. "Mandrake Magicians' Club/Taystee Bread" ameled Brass Pin,
34. - **$40 $100 $175**

N-3. "New Magic Tricks" Sheet,
1940. Taystee Bread and WOR (New York City). Sheet s earlier 1934 King Features copyright. - **$20 $40 $65**

MAN-6

MAN-4   MAN-5

N-4. Magic Kit Leaflet,
48. Suchard Chocolate Bars. Offers trick premiums with iration date of January 31, 1949. - **$10 $15 $25**

N-5. Christmas Card,
0s. King Features Syndicate. From series featuring vari- s syndicate characters. - **$10 $20 $35**

MAN-6. Plastic Gumball Charm,
c. 1950s. Store item. Clear plastic with insert paper picture, from vending machine series. Second character on reverse. - **$8 $12 $20**

MAN-7

MAN-7. Sponge,
c. 1960s. Store item. - **$5 $12 $20**

MA PERKINS

Beginning in 1933, Oxydol's own Ma Perkins solved her neighbors' problems and dished out her homespun philoso- phy from her lumber yard in Rushville Center for a total of 27 years. The program, first heard on Cincinnati radio station WLW, went national on NBC four months after its debut. From 1942 to 1948 it was broadcast on both the NBC and CBS networks, and from 1948 until it went off the air in 1960 it aired exclusively on CBS. Virginia Payne played the part of the widowed Ma for the entire run of over 7,000 episodes, and Proctor & Gamble's Oxydol was the long-term sponsor.

MPK-2

MPK-1

MPK-1. Oxydol Fan Photo,
1930s. - **$12 $25 $35**

MPK-2. "Ma Perkins-Your Radio Friend" Photo,
1930s. Oxydol. - **$8 $20 $30**

MARVEL COMICS

Marvel began in 1939 with a firm known as Timely Publications operated by Martin Goodman who began pub- lishing pulp magazines in 1932. Science fiction, western, crime and horror were steady sellers and Goodman became very astute at publishing and distribution. Superman had created quite a splash in 1938 and Goodman took notice. Funnies Inc. was a comic book shop, a business with artists, writers and editors who would produce comic books for oth- ers to publish. Their art director, Bill Everett, had created Prince Namor, The Sub-Mariner for another title and co- worker Carl Burgos came up with the Human Torch. Both characters made their debut in Goodman's Marvel Comics #1, October 1939. Martin Goodman was in the comic book business.

Joe Simon was Goodman's first editor and he and fellow artist Jack Kirby came up with Captain America Comics, the company's biggest seller. Super heroes waned in the 1950s but Goodman told editor Stan Lee that they should consider a revival in 1961. Shortly thereafter Jack Kirby's Fantastic Four appeared followed by Steve Ditko's Spider-Man, The Hulk, Daredevil and others. A risky venture into a new field in 1939 formed the foundation for what is today the best selling comic book company in the world.

Items in this section promote Marvel Comics in general and a variety of their superhero characters. Captain America and Spider-Man are in separate sections.

MAR-1

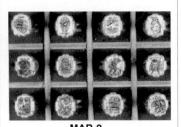

MAR-2

MAR-1. "Marvel Action Rings" Vending Machine Display Card,
1966. Promotes set of 12 flicker rings and features Jack Kirby signed art. - **$50 $75 $150**

MAR-2. Vending Machine Flicker Rings,
1966. Set of 12. Each Gold Base - **$10 $15 $20**
Each Blue Base - **$10 $12 $15**

MAR-3

MAR-4

MAR-5

MAR-3. "Daredevil" 3-1/2" Cello. Button,
1966. Store item. #4 from numbered series.
Near Mint Bagged - **$35**
Loose - **$10 $15 $25**

MAR-4. "The Incredible Hulk" 3-1/2" Cello. Button,
1966. Store item. #5 from numbered series.
Near Mint Bagged - **$35**
Loose - **$10 $15 $25**

MAR-5. "The Invincible Iron Man" 3-1/2" Cello. Button,
1966. Store item. #7 from series.
Near Mint Bagged - **$35**
Loose - **$10 $15 $25**

MAR-6

MAR-7

MAR-8

MAR-6. "Sub-Mariner" 3-1/2" Cello. Button,
1966. Store item. #8 from series.
Near Mint Bagged - **$35**
Loose - **$10 $15 $25**

MAR-7. "The Mighty Thor" 3-1/2" Cello. Button,
1966. Store item. #9 from series.
Near Mint Bagged - **$35**
Loose - **$10 $15 $25**

MAR-8. "The Avengers" 3-1/2" Cello. Button,
1966. Store item. #10 from series.
Near Mint Bagged - **$35**
Loose - **$10 $15 $25**

MAR-9

MAR-10

MAR-9. "Mini-Books" Vending Machine Insert Paper,
1966. Advertises tiny 1" tall, 48 page books for Captain America, Incredible Hulk, Millie the Model, Sgt. Fury, Spider Man, Thor. Each Book - **$4 $12 $30**
Paper - **$8 $15 $30**

MAR-10. "Merry Marvel Marching Society" Membership Kit,
1967. Envelope with letter, card, record, etc.
Complete Near Mint - **$180**
Each Paper Piece - **$5 $20 $40**
Record - **$10 $40 $60**

MAR-11

MAR-12

MAR-11. Club Member 3" Cello. Button,
1967. - **$10 $20 $30**

MAR-12. "Convention '75" 3" Cello. Button,
1975. - **$10 $20 $30**

McDONALD'S

What began as a simple hamburger joint in southern California has become an international symbol of American initiative and drive. At last count there were more than 8,000 McDonald's fast-food restaurants in some 89 countries - the busiest of all in Pushkin Square, Moscow. It all started in 1937 when the McDonald brothers, Maurice and Richard, opened a small stand near Pasadena. Two years later they opened a second spot, fine-tuning their fast-food philosophy in a building with two yellow arches poking through the roof. A character called Speedee, with a hamburger for a head, courted drive-in customers atop another arch. Franchising the successful operation began in 1953, and Ray Kroc opened his first franchise in 1955. Six years later, with more than 200 stores licensed, Kroc bought out the entire operation. Speedee was retired in 1962 and replaced by the Ronald McDonald character in 1963. Other characters - Big Mac, the Hamburglar, Grimace, Mayor McCheese, Captain Crook, and the Professor - were introduced in the 1970s. Toys, games, premiums, licensed products, and promotional items continue to proliferate.

McD-1

McD-2

McD-1. "Speedee" Litho. Button,
1955. Pictures trademark character used from beginnings until his retirement c. 1962. - **$25 $60 $100**

McD-2. Cardboard Drive-In Punch-Out Sheet,
1962. Design intent of coin bank. Unpunched - **$25 $50 $100**

McD-3

McD-4

McD-3. "Let's Go To McDonald's" Plastic/Tin Palm Puzzle,
1964. Pictured is "Archie" serving character. - **$20 $40 $75**

McD-4. "Let's Eat Out!" Storybook,
1965. Issued for 10th anniversary, stiff covers. - **$35 $75 $150**

McD-5

McD-6

McD-5. Model Kit,
c. late 1960s. Store item made by Life-Like Products (H.O. scale). - **$50 $125 $200**

McD-6. Ronald Cloth Doll,
1971. - **$3 $8 $12**

McD-7

McD-8

McD-9

McD-7. Ronald Litho. Tin Tab,
c. 1970s. - **$3 $8 $15**

McD-8. Mayor McCheese Litho. Tin Tab,
c. 1970s. - **$3 $8 $15**

McD-9. Employee Doll,
c. 1970s. Jointed vinyl 11" doll in brown uniform. - **$20 $35 $50**

McD-10

McD-11

McD-12

McD-10. Ronald Wristwatch,
1970s. - **$15 $25 $40**

McD-11. Employees Glasses Promotion 3-1/2" Cello. Button,
c. 1970s. McDonald's and Coca-Cola Canadian issue. - **$8 $12 $20**

McD-12. Captain Crook Orange Vinyl Ring,
c. 1980. - **$5 $7 $10**

McD-13   McD-14   McD-15

McD-13. Big Mac Yellow Vinyl Ring,
c. 1980. - **$5 $7 $10**

McD-14. Grimace Purple Vinyl Ring,
c. 1980. - **$5 $7 $10**

McD-15. Hamburglar Plastic Siren Whistle,
1986. - **$5 $8 $12**

MELVIN PURVIS

The story of FBI agent Melvin Purvis (1903-1960) is a mixture of fact and legend. Purvis, a South Carolina lawyer, joined the FBI in 1927 and chased minor criminals in Texas and Oklahoma, eventually ending up in the Bureau's Chicago office. In 1934, with the help of a "woman in red," Purvis and other agents ambushed and killed the notorious John Dillinger as he left the Biograph movie theater in Chicago. Three months later Purvis, again acting on a tip, led a raid on an Ohio farm that ended in the killing of Pretty Boy Floyd. Purvis left the FBI in 1935, wrote a book about his experiences, and worked in law and broadcasting. In 1960, in poor health, he committed suicide.

As the embodiment of law and order and the implacable enemy of criminals, Purvis was heavily promoted in the 1930s by Post cereals in newspapers, on cereal boxes, and in magazine advertising. His *Junior G-Man Corps* and *Law and Order Patrol* enlisted kids by the thousands with a profusion of premiums — a variety of badges, ID cards, rings, flashlights, knives, fingerprint kits, manuals, pen and pencil sets, even separate badges for members of the Girls Division. Dale Robertson played Purvis in a 1974 television movie.

MLV-1

MLV-2

MLV-3

MLV-1. Club Manual Of Instructions,
1936. - **$20 $30 $50**

MLV-2. Junior G-Man Corps "Chief Operative" Certificate,
1936. - **$25 $40 $65**

MLV-3. Premium Folder,
1936. - **$15 $25 $40**

MLV-4

MLV-5   MLV-6

MLV-4. "Melvin Purvis Junior G-Man Corps" Brass Ring,
1936. - **$25 $50 $75**

MLV-5. "Junior G-Man Corps" Brass Badge,
1936. - **$15 $25 $40**

MLV-6. "Roving Operative" Brass Badge,
1936. - **$20 $40 $75**

MLV-7

MLV-8

MLV-7. "Chief Operative" Brass Shield Badge,
1936. - **$20 $40 $75**

MLV-8. "Girls Division" Brass Club Badge,
1936. - **$15 $30 $50**

MLV-9

MLV-10

MLV-9. "Special Agent" Metal Flashlight Gun,
1936. Battery operated. - **$35 $75 $125**

MLV-10. "Junior G-Man Corps" Member Card In Leather Wallet,
1936. Wallet - **$20 $50 $75**
Card - **$10 $25 $40**

MLV-11

MLV-12

MLV-11. "Junior G-Men Secret Passport",
1936. Envelope - **$5 $10 $15**
Card - **$20 $40 $75**

MLV-12. Junior G-Men Fingerprint Set With Mailer Envelope,
1936. Cardboard folder containing fingerprint powder, ink pad, instruction booklet. Mailer - **$10 $20 $30**
Set - **$20 $50 $100**

MLV-13

MLV-14

MLV-15

MLV-16

MLV-13. Wood Pencil With "G-Man" Metal Clip,
1936. Scarce. Pencil - **$20 $40 $60**
Clip - **$20 $40 $60**

MLV-14. "G-Men" Brass Watch Fob,
1936. Unmarked for Purvis but pictured in his premium catalogues. Came with unmarked dark brown leather strap.
Fob Only - **$25 $50 $80**
With Correct Strap - **$50 $100 $175**

MLV-15. Club Manual,
1937. Pictures 33 premiums. - **$15 $30 $60**

MLV-16. Premium Catalogue Folder Sheet,
1937. Pictures 12 premiums. - **$15 $30 $50**

MLV-17

MLV-18

MLV-19

MLV-17. Scarab Ring,
1937. Scarab in green. Also issued for Captain Frank Hawks. - **$250 $500 $1200**

MLV-18. Secret Operator/Law & Order Patrol Brass Ring,
1937. - **$75 $112 $175**

MLV-19. "Secret Operator" Brass Badge,
1937. - **$20 $40 $60**

MLV-20

MLV-21

MLV-22

MLV-20. "Lieutenant" Brass Rank Badge,
1937. - **$20 $40 $75**

MLV-21. "Captain" Brass Rank Badge,
1937. - **$20 $40 $75**

MLV-22. "Secret Operators/Girls Division" Brass Badge,
1937. - **$20 $35 $60**

MLV-23

MLV-24

MLV-23. "Secret Operator" Grained Leather Wallet,
1937. Inside has two slot pockets and small note pad. -
$20 $40 $80

MLV-24. "Inter-District Pass" Club Card,
1937. - **$15 $30 $60**

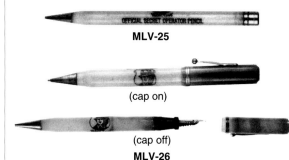

MLV-25

(cap on)

(cap off)
MLV-26

MLV-25. "Melvin Purvis Official Secret Operator Pencil",
1937. Scarce. 5-1/2" bakelite mechanical pencil with inscription plus portrait. - **$50 $100 $200**

MLV-26. "Melvin Purvis Official Secret Operator Combination" Bakelite Pen/Mechanical Pencil,
1937. Rare. - **$100 $400 $750**

MLV-27

MLV-27. G-Man Tin Whistle,
1930s. - **$20 $40 $60**

MICKEY MOUSE

Mickey Mouse has been called a legend, a national symbol, a worldwide celebrity, a work of art, a merchandising monarch, the successor to Charlie Chaplin, the keystone of the Walt Disney empire. Mickey's career took off in 1928 with *Steamboat Willie*, the first animated cartoon with sychronized sound. Ub Iwerks did the animation, Walt Disney did the voice of Mickey, and success was immediate.

Over the next 25 years the studio turned out some 120 cartoons starring Mickey. Supporting characters included Minnie Mouse, Pluto the Pup, Donald Duck, Goofy, Horace Horsecollar, and Clarabelle Cow. The Mickey daily comic strip, distributed by King Features, began in 1930 and the Sunday pages in 1932, scripted and drawn by Floyd Gottfredson for the next 45 years.

1930 also saw the first Mickey book published by Bibo and Lang followed by a continuing flood of magazines, collections, reprints, albums, specials, and hardbacks, along with feature appearances in other Disney books.

Mickey and his pals had a brief run on NBC radio in 1938, sponsored by Pepsodent toothpaste. *The Mickey Mouse Club* - the most popular afternoon children's network television series ever - was broadcast on ABC from 1955 to 1959, with reruns syndicated in 1962-1965, 1975-1976, and as *The New Mickey Mouse Club* in 1977-1978. The series, hosted by the Mouseketeers, was a mix of music, cartoons, serialized adventures, children's news features, and visits by guest celebrities. In 1995 *Runaway Brain*, the first Mickey cartoon short in more than 40 years, was released to theaters.

Mickey's popularity continues undiminished, as does the merchandising and licensing of Mickey Mouse items of all shapes and sizes.

MCK-1

MCK-1. First "Mickey Mouse Book",
1930. Published by Bibo & Lang, several printings. The first Disney publication, pages 9-10 often missing due to cut-out puzzle. Complete - **$1400 $7100 $10000**
Missing Pages 9-10 - **$200 $1300 $2000**

MCK-2

MCK-3   MCK-4

MCK-2. "Theme Song" Music Sheet,
1930. Movie theater hand-out. Song title "Minnie's Yoo Hoo." - **$25 $50 $75**

MCK-3. Movie Club Cello. Button,
1930. Inscribed "Copy. 1928-1930 By W. E. Disney". - **$60 $100 $175**

MCK-4. "Mickey Mouse Club" Cello. Button,
1930. 1928-1930 W. E. Disney copyright. - **$50 $90 $150**

MCK-5   MCK-7

MCK-6

MCK-5. "Meets Every Saturday" Club Member Cello. Button,
1930. Standard image with 1930 Disney copyright and name on bottom edge but uncommon imprint. - **$75 $150 $200**

MCK-6. "Mickey Mouse" Wood Jointed Figure,
1930. Scarce. Store item. 4-1/2" tall with flat disk hands to allow balancing in various positions. - **$200 $400 $800**

MCK-7. Mickey In Santa Outfit Cello. Button,
c. 1930. Several imprints but usually "Meet Me At Hank's Toyland." - **$150 $350 $800**

MCK-8

MCK-9   MCK-10

MCK-8. First Newspaper Premium Picture Card,
May 1931. Various newspapers. 3-1/2x5-1/2" bw. - $100 $400 $750

MCK-9. Mickey Mouse Paper Face Mask,
1933. Store and theater give-away, published by Einson-Freeman Co. - $25 $50 $75

MCK-10. Minnie Mouse Paper Mask,
1933. Store and theater give-away. - $15 $25 $50

MCK-11

MCK-11. "Mickey Mouse Magazine" Vol. 1 #1,
January 1933. Rare #1. Various dairies, stores. "Published by Kamen-Blair, Inc." on front cover. Nine issues, first few had 5 cents on cover. First Issue - $350 $1050 $3000
Other Issues - $115 $350 $900

MCK-12

MCK-13

MCK-12. "Mickey Mouse Magazine",
1933. #1 Rare. Various dairies, Nov. 1933-Oct. 1935. "Edited by Hal Horne" on cover. 1st Issue - $85 $250 $650

MCK-13. "Mickey Mouse Magazine",
1933. Various dairies, Nov. 1933-Oct. 1935.
Nos. 2-12 Each - $45 $130 $330

MCK-14

MCK-14. "Mickey Mouse Bubble Gum" Example Cards,
1933. Gum Inc. #1-96 first series plus #97-120 titled "Mickey Mouse With The Movie Stars".
First Series Each - $5 $12 $25
Movie Stars Each - $35 $75 $150

MCK-15

MCK-15. Picture Card Album Vol. 2,
1933. For cards #49-96. Volume 1 holds cards #1-48.
Unused #1 - $50 $200 $200
Unused #2 - $75 $150 $250

MCK-16

MCK-17

MCK-16. "Mickey Mouse Bubble Gum" Waxed Paper Wrapper,
1933. Store item, used for cards #1-96 of Gum Inc. card set. - $60 $150 $200

MCK-17. "Mickey Mouse With The Movie Stars" Gum Wrapper,
1933. Gum Inc. Wrapper for cards #97-120. - $150 $300 $600

MCK-18

MCK-19

MCK-18. "Mickey Mouse The Mail Pilot" BLB,
1933. American Oil Co. Softcover version. - $40 $90 $150

MCK-19. Cello. Button 3-1/2",
c. 1933. Worn by store employees. - $250 $1000 $2000

MCK-20

MCK-20. "Mickie Mouse Animal Crackers" Box,
c. 1933. Rare. Apparent unauthorized item (or printing error) with misspelled name. Near Mint Flat - $1500
Folded - $150 $400 $750

MCK-21

MCK-21. "Mickey Maus" 17x24" German Film Poster,
1934. Rare. - **$500 $2000 $3500**

MCK-22

MCK-22. Post Toasties Box,
1934. Rare. Mickey pictured on front. Several versions.
Each Complete - **$750 $1500 $2500**

MCK-23

MCK-23. Post Toasties Box,
1935. Scarce. Mickey pictured on front. Several versions.
Each Complete - **$500 $1000 $2000**

MCK-24

MCK-24. First "Mickey Mouse Magazine" Vol. 1 #1,
1935. Later became "Walt Disney's Comics & Stories". Kay
Kamen Publications/Western Publishing Co., size 10-1/4x
13-1/4". - **$1100 $3300 $11000**

MCK-25

MCK-25. "Mickey Mouse And The Magic Carpet" Book,
1935. Various sponsors. - **$150 $250 $400**

MCK-27   MCK-28
MCK-26

**MCK-26. "Mickey Mouse And Minnie March To Macy's"
Booklet,**
1935. Rare. Macy's department store. Published by Whitman
in format of Big Little Book. - **$300 $750 $1000**

MCK-27. "Mickey Mouse Hose" Cello. Button,
c. 1935. - **$60 $100 $175**

MCK-28. Litho. Button,
c. 1935. Comes with back paper reading "Mickey Mouse
Gloves And Mittens". - **$75 $150 $350**

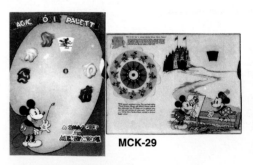
MCK-29

MCK-29. "Magic Movie Palette",
1935. Store give-away. Mechanical paper. - **$75 $150 $300**

MCK-31

MCK-30

MCK-30. Glazed Ceramic Toothbrush Holder,
c. 1936. Store item by S. Maw & Son, London.-
$250 $450 $700

MCK-31. "The Atlanta Georgian's Silver Anniversary"
Litho. Button,
1937. Named newspaper. From set of various characters. -
$150 $350 $750

MCK-32

MCK-32. Pepsodent 10x40" Paper Poster,
1937. For NBC radio show. - $125 $250 $400

MCK-33

MCK-33. Post Toasties Mickey Box,
1937. - $100 $200 $300

MCK-34

MCK-34. "The Mickey Mouse Globe Trotter Weekly" Vol.
1 No. 3 Example ,
1937. Various bakeries and dairies. Each - $20 $40 $60

MCK-35   MCK-36

MCK-35. "Globe Trotter Club" Membership Card,
1937. Various sponsors. - $20 $40 $75

MCK-36. "Mickey Mouse Globe Trotters/Member" Cello.
Button,
1937. Imprints of various bakeries and dairies. -
$20 $40 $75

MCK-37

MCK-37. "Round The World" Map,
1937. Issued by various bread companies. Opens to 20x27"
for mounting 24 "Globe Trotters" picture cards.
Without Pictures - $50 $125 $250

MCK-38

MCK-38. Sunoco Oil Advertising Booklet,
1938. - $40 $60 $125

MCK-39

MCK-39. "Mickey Mouse Magazine" Gift Subscription
Card With Envelope ,
1938. With Envelope - $50 $125 $175
Loose - $35 $75 $125

MCK-40

MCK-40. Dental Appointment Envelope, Card And Certificate,
c. 1938. Envelope - **$5 $10 $15**
Card - **$15 $25 $40**
Certificate - **$25 $60 $90**

MCK-41

MCK-42

MCK-41. "Mickey Mouse-Good Teeth" Cello. Button,
c. 1938. Back paper for Bureau of Public Relations/American Dental Association. - **$50 $80 $150**

MCK-42. Christmas Giveaway for Shoes,
1939. Rare. - **$140 $420 $1400**

MCK-43

MCK-43. Cereal Box,
1939. Mickey not on front. - **$100 $200 $300**

MCK-44

MCK-44. "All-Star Parade Glasses" Brochure,
1939. Includes order blank for cottage cheese filled glasses. - **$40 $75 $125**

MCK-45

MCK-45. "Mickey's And Donald's Race To Treasure Island" 20x27" Paper Map.
1939. Standard Oil of California. Pictures from "Travel Tykes" weekly newspapers go around border.
Unused - **$100 $200 $450**

MCK-46

MCK-46. Sunoco Winter Oil Postcard,
1939. Pictures Mickey as pilgrim. - **$20 $30 $50**

MCK-47

MCK-48

MCK-47. Blue Sunoco Cardboard Ink Blotter,
1939. Pictures Minnie and Mickey as bride and groom. - **$25 $50 $75**

MCK-48. Pocket Mirror,
1930s. Black/white/red printed on ribbed paper with satin-like finish. Only authentic 1930s design known, fantasy mirrors include Chicago 1933 and New York 1939 World's Fair reference. - **$75 $150 $300**

MCK-49

MCK-50

MCK-49. "Mickey Mouse Scrapbook",
1930s. Various bakery imprints. The first bread card book. Designed to hold 24 large sized cards, see next item. - $75 $125 $250

MCK-50. Large Recipe Cards,
1930s. Photo shows 16 of 24 in set for previous item. Each - $8 $12 $20

MCK-51

MCK-51. "Mickey Mouse Recipe Scrapbook",
1930s. Various bakery and dairy company imprints. Designed to hold 48 cards, see next item. - $40 $75 $125

MCK-52

MCK-52. Small Recipe Cards,
1930s. Photo shows 35 of 48 in set for previous item. Each - $5 $10 $15

MCK-53

MCK-54

MCK-55

MCK-53. Bread Loaf Waxed Paper Insert Band,
1930s. Various breads. Offers free Recipe Scrapbook for bread pictures. - $50 $125 $200

MCK-54. Mickey Mouse 7-1/2" Bavarian China Plate,
1930s. Used as movie theater give-aways, various designs.
7-1/2" Size - $150 $300 $600
6" Size - $100 $200 $400

MCK-55. Mickey Mouse Bavarian China Cream Pitcher,
1930s. Used as movie theater give-aways, various designs. - $100 $200 $400

MCK-56

MCK-57

MCK-58

MCK-56. German Bisque Figures,
1930s. Store item. Pair - $150 $300 $600

MCK-57. Hard Rubber Figure,
1930s. Store item by Seiberling Rubber Co. Thin rubber tail usually gone. No Tail - $35 $75 $150
With Tail - $75 $150 $300

MCK-58. Cardboard String Climbing Toy,
1930s. Store item by Dolly Toy Co. - $200 $400 $650

MCK-59

MCK-60

MCK-59. Cardboard Figural Pencil Case,
1930s. Store item by Dixon Pencil Co. - $125 $225 $350

MCK-60. "Dixon's Mickey Mouse Map Of The United States" 10x14",
1930s. Came in pencil boxes. - $25 $60 $100

MCK-61

MCK-62

MCK-61. Mickey & Minnie Bisque Toothbrush Holder,
1930s. Store item. - $75 $150 $250

MCK-62. Paper Hat,
1930s. Mickey Mouse Comic Cookies. - $35 $75 $125

MCK-63

MCK-64

MCK-63. Toasted Nut Chocolate Candy Wrapper,
1930s. Wilbur-Suchard Chocolate Co. - **$30 $60 $100**

MCK-64. Dixie Ice Cream Cup Lid,
1930s. Southern Dairies. - **$25 $60 $100**

MCK-65

MCK-65. Post Cereal Spoon,
1930s. Near Mint In Mailer - **$200**
Spoon Only - **$8 $15 $30**

MCK-66

MCK-67

MCK-66. Mickey Mouse Bottle Cap Set Of Six,
1930s. Stores supplied a purple felt hat for bottle caps that
had brass pins for mounting. Usually found without the spring
pins. Hat - **$35 $85 $150**
Each - **$15 $30 $60**

**MCK-67. "Mickey And Oswald Shake Hands" Department
Store Card,**
1930s. Boston store. Christmas "Toytown" give-away with
unauthorized art. - **$25 $50 $80**

MCK-68

MCK-68. "Mickey Mouse's Midnight Adventure" Folder,
1930s. Accompanied "USA Lites" flashlights. -
$35 $75 $125

MCK-69

MCK-69. Dodge Motors Advertising Flip Booklet,
1930s. Story title "Mickey Takes Minnie For A Ride". -
$35 $75 $150

MCK-70

MCK-71

MCK-70. Movie Theater Club Card,
1930s. Back has club creed. - **$40 $85 $150**

**MCK-71. "Penney's For Back To School Needs" Cello.
Button,**
1930s. - **$35 $65 $100**

MCK-72

MCK-73

MCK-74

MCK-72. Minnie Mouse "Good Teeth" Cello. Button,
1930s. Kern County Health Department, California. -
$300 $800 $1750

MCK-73. "Southern Dairies Ice Cream" Cello. Button,
1930s. Scarce. - **$300 $700 $1500**

MCK-74. "California Mickey Mouse Club" Cello. Button,
1930s. - **$60 $100 $175**

MCK-75

MCK-76

MCK-77

MCK-75. "Evening Ledger Comics" Cello. Button,
1930s. Philadelphia newspaper. From set of 14 various characters. - **$200 $400 $700**

MCK-76. "Evening Ledger Comics" Cello. Button,
1930s. Philadelphia newspaper. From set of 14 various characters. - **$150 $300 $600**

MCK-77. "Mickey Mouse Undies" Cello. Button,
1930s. - **$50 $90 $150**

MCK-78

MCK-79

MCK-78. "Ask For Mickey Mouse Undies" Paper Tag,
1930s. Stamp nature but example seen had ungummed back, other inscriptions "Make Children Happier" and "Undergarments Of Quality". - **$35 $60 $100**

MCK-79. Goodyear Tires Mailing Brochure,
1940. Canadian issue, opens to 11x20". - **$35 $75 $125**

MCK-80

MCK-81

MCK-80. Mickey Mouse "Nu-Blue Sunoco" Cardboard Ink Blotter,
1940. Example pictures him in speeding car. - **$20 $40 $60**

MCK-81. "Sunheat Furnace Oil" Cardboard Ink Blotter,
c. 1940. Sun Oil Co. Mickey hanging wall plaque. - **$12 $25 $40**

MCK-82

MCK-83

MCK-82. Sunoco Oil Cardboard Ink Blotter,
c. 1940. Pictures Donald listening for motor knocks. - **$20 $40 $60**

MCK-83. Sunoco Oil Ink Blotter,
1941. Depicts Mickey and Donald in military outfits. - **$50 $100 $150**

MCK-84

MCK-84. Sunoco Oil Ink Blotter,
1942. Mickey by artillery gun with oil bottle body. - **$10 $20 $45**

MCK-85

MCK-86

MCK-85. "Mickey Mouse...On The Home Front" Newspaper,
April 1944. Beechcraft Aviation Corp. - **$35 $75 $150**

MCK-86. "Mickey Mouse" Weekly English Newspaper,
1945. Long running publication, seldom better than Fine condition. 1930s Each - **$10 $20 $30**
1940s Each - **$8 $15 $25**

MCK-87

MCK-87. "US Time" Comic With Mickey Watch Ad,
c. 1947. - **$25 $50 $80**

MCK-88

MCK-89

MCK-88. Beanie,
1940s. Scarce. - **$100 $200 $300**

MCK-89. "March Of Comics" #60,
1950. Various sponsors. - **$35 $105 $245**

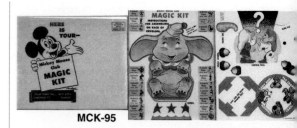

MCK-95

MCK-90

MCK-90. 78 RPM Record,
1956. General Mills, Inc. #3 from series of four.
Each With Sleeve - **$10 $15 $25**

MCK-95. "Mickey Mouse Club Magic Kit" Punch-Out Set,
1950s. Mars candy. Near Mint In Mailer - **$75**

MCK-96

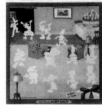

MCK-91

MCK-92

MCK-96. "Mars/Mickey Mouse Club Magic Manual" Booklet,
1950s. - **$10 $20 $30**

MCK-91. Mickey Mouse And His Pals Plastic Rings,
1956. Sugar Jets cereal. Peter Pan example from set of eight: Mickey, Minnie, Donald, Pluto, Snow White, Pinocchio, Dumbo, Peter Pan. Each - **$40 $60 $80**

MCK-92. Picture Sheet For Bread Label Cut-Outs,
1950s. NBC Bread. Blank - **$15 $30 $75**

MCK-97

MCK-93

MCK-94

MCK-97. Pillsbury "Mickey Mouse Club" Ring Offer Box,
1950s. Offered set of five aluminum rings: Donald, Goofy, Jiminy, Bambi, Cinderella. Box - **$25 $50 $75**
Each Ring - **$10 $20 $35**

MCK-98

MCK-99

MCK-93. Mouseketeer Doll,
1950s. Scarce. Mickey Mouse Club. Store bought marionette on roller skates. - **$50 $150 $300**

MCK-94. Punch-Out Paper Puppet,
1950s. Donald Duck Bread. Unpunched - **$10 $20 $35**

MCK-98. "KVOS-TV 12" Cello. Club Button,
1950s. Unidentified but TV station of Bellingham, Washington. - **$15 $25 $40**

MCK-99. "Member Mickey Mouse Club" Litho. Tin Tab,
1950s. - **$8 $15 $25**

MCK-101

MCK-100

MCK-100. "Mickey Mouse Explorers Club Coloring Book",
1965. Kroger food stores. - **$8 $12 $20**

MCK-101. "Seed Shop" 3" Cello. Button,
1976. Promotion for garden seeds in packages featuring Disney characters. - **$35 $85 $150**

MCK-102

MCK-103

MCK-102. "Around The World In 80 Days" Hardcover Book,
1978. Crest Toothpaste. - **$5 $10 $20**

MCK-103. "Mickey And Goofy Explore The Universe Of Energy" Comic Book ,
1985. Exxon. - **$1 $2 $3**

MIGHTY MOUSE

The rodent equivalent of Superman, Captain Marvel and other humanoid cloaked flying heroes, Mighty Mouse was probably the best-known Terrytoons character and certainly one of the most prolific in animated episodes. Originally dubbed Supermouse in his 1942 creation year by Paul Terry, the battler of villainous cats was renamed Mighty Mouse in 1944. He starred in about 80 television episodes between 1955 and 1967, frequently saving girlfriend Pearl Pureheart from her perils. In addition to animated adventures, Mighty Mouse starred also in numerous comic books by various publishers, including Gold Key and Dell, from the mid-1940s into the early 1990s.

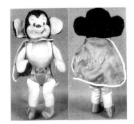

MGH-1

MGH-2

MGH-1. Mighty Mouse 12" Stuffed Oilcloth Doll,
1942. Rare. Rubber head, star designs on cape. - **$200 $400 $600**

MGH-2. Vinyl/Plush/Fabric Doll,
c. 1950. Store item by Ideal Toys. Tag inscriptions include "CBS". - **$50 $100 $150**

MGH-3

MGH-4

MGH-3. Post Cereals "Merry-Pack" Punch-Outs With Envelope,
1956. Post Treat-Pak and Post Alpha-Bits. Consists of three sheets to form about 20 items. Unpunched - **$15 $35 $60**

MGH-4. Club Member Paper Wallet,
1956. Part of previous punch-out set. - **$3 $7 $12**

MGH-5

MGH-5. "Post Cereals Mighty Mouse Mystery Color Picture" Cards,
1957. Set of six. Water makes invisible character appear.
Unused Set - **$30 $50 $75**
Used Set - **$20 $35 $50**

MGH-6

MGH-7

MGH-8

MGH-6. Rubber Squeaker Figure,
1950s. Store item. Comes with red felt cape. - **$20 $50 $75**

MGH-7. Terrytoons Fabric Scarf,
1950s. Store item. - **$15 $25 $40**

MGH-8. "Mighty Mouse In Toyland" Record,
1960. Store item by Peter Pan Records. - **$10 $20 $35**

THE MONKEES

Four "insane" boys, picked from hundreds of hopefuls who answered an audition call, comprised the Monkees, a fictional rock group that nevertheless enjoyed considerable success on records and on network television. The show, inspired stylistically by the Beatles' 1964 film *A Hard Day's Night*, featured surrealistic camera work and comic or melodramatic story lines. The series ran on the three television networks, originally on NBC (1966-1968), and repeated on CBS (1969-1972) and ABC (1972-1973). *Monkees* comic books appeared from 1967 to 1969. Merchandising was extensive, and a custom-built Monkeemobile was created for appearances at automobile shows and shopping centers. Items are usually copyrighted by Raybert Productions or Screen Gems.

MON-1

MON-2

MON-1. Celluloid 3-1/2" Button,
1966. Vendor item. - **$10 $20 $35**

MON-2. Fan Club Postcard,
1967. - **$5 $8 $12**

MON-3

MON-4

MON-5

MON-3. Official Fan Club Button,
1967. Litho. 2-1/4". - **$5 $10 $15**

MON-4. Kellogg's "Mike" Flicker Ring,
1967. Set of 12 silvered plastic with insert alternating picture of individual for group. Each - **$10 $20 $45**

MON-5. Monkees Litho. Button,
1967. Vending machine issue set of six. Four with single portraits, two with group portraits. Each - **$3 $5 $10**

MON-6

MON-6. "Monkee Coins",
1967. Kellogg's. Set of 12 color photos in yellow plastic frames. Canadian issue with reverse text in English and French. Each - **$3 $6 $12**

MON-7

MON-7. Photo Flip Booklets,
1967. Store item. Set of 16. Each - **$3 $8 $12**

MON-8

MON-8. "Monkees" Cereal Box Cut-Out Record,
c. 1970. Kellogg's. Series of four box backs. Each - **$5 $8 $12**

MOVIE MISCELLANEOUS

The first known moving pictures on a public screen were shown at Koster and Bial's Music Hall in New York City April 23, 1896. The program included films of two blonde girls performing an umbrella dance, a comic boxing exhibition and a view of surf breaking on a beach. Movies remained only a novelty until shortly after the turn of the century. 1903 released two pioneer efforts, *The Passion Play* and *The Great Train Robbery* and movies as mass entertainment were born.

The 1920s added dimensions of sound plus color experimentation; full-length features were soon followed by the popular episode serial or "chapter play" that remained popular to the mid-1950s. Premiums followed a few individual stars of universal acclaim such as Charlie Chaplin, Our Gang, Shirley Temple.

Generally, movies produced souvenirs of only non-premium original purpose, e.g., heralds and programs, lobby cards, posters and similar that since have matured to status paralleling premiums. Notable exceptions, of course, are classic films such as *Gone With The Wind*, Disney creations from the early 1930s Mickey Mouse to the 1990s *Dick Tracy* version, other animated cartoons plus premiums resulting from the most popular of the adventure hero serials.

Movie premiums after the advent of television were very limited for a time but recent years have seen frequent tie-ins between movies aimed at family audiences and fast food restaurants.

MOV-1   MOV-2   MOV-3

MOV-1. "Chas. Chaplin" Plaster Figurine,
1915. Includes wire cane. Store item. - **$50 $75 $125**

MOV-2. Charlie Chaplin Composition/Cloth Doll,
. 1915. Scarce. Store item by Louis Amberg & Son. -
100 $250 $500

MOV-3. Charlie Chaplin Candy Container Bank,
920s. Store item. Glass plus metal lid. - **$75 $150 $250**

MOV-4   MOV-5   MOV-6

OV-4. Charlie Chaplin Cello. Button,
920s. Sampeck Suits. - **$15 $30 $50**

MOV-5. "Jackie Coogan Club" Cello. Button,
920s. - **$10 $20 $35**

MOV-6. Roscoe "Fatty" Arbuckle Cello. Button,
920s. - **$15 $30 $50**

MOV-7   MOV-8

MOV-9

**MOV-7. "'Freaks' Metro-Goldwyn-Mayer's Amazing
Picture" Cello. Button,**
932. Scarce. Movie was quickly withdrawn from
distribution. - **$200 $500 $900**

**MOV-8. "Tom Tyler/Clancy Of The Mounted" Movie Club
Cello. Button,**
1933. Universal Pictures. For 12-chapter serial. -
$75 $175 $250**

**MOV-9. Laurel & Hardy "Old Gold Cigarettes" 31x42"
Cardboard Sign,**
1934. - **$500 $800 $1500**

MOV-11

MOV-10

MOV-10. "Mae West" 17x30" Cardboard Store Sign,
1934. Old Gold cigarettes. Text includes "Goin' To Town"
movie title. - **$350 $600 $1200**

MOV-11. Mae West-Inspired China Ashtray,
c. 1934. Store item. - **$30 $50 $75**

MOV-12

MOV-12. Rio Theatre Photo Folder,
1938. Theatre premium. 16 photos (folder & two photos
shown). Photos - **$2 $4 $10**
Folder - **$5 $10 $20**

MOV-13

MOV-13. "Gulliver's Travels" Booklet,
1939. Macy's department store. - **$20 $40 $75**

MOV-14

MOV-14. "The Black Falcon Of The Flying G-Men" Game,
1939. Store item by Ruckelshaus Game Corp. Based on
Columbia Pictures movie serial. - **$100 $250 $350**

MOV-15

MOV-16

MOV-15. Laurel & Hardy Salt & Pepper Set,
1930s. Store item. By Beswick China - **$75 $125 $200**
Japanese Version - **$60 $100 $150**

MOV-16. Junior Cagney Club Litho. Buttons,
1930s. Theater patrons collected set of 11, each with single
letter of James Cagney name, to gain free admission.
Each - **$5 $10 $15**

MOV-17

MOV-18

MOV-19

**MOV-17. "The Terrytooners Music And Fun Club" Cello.
Button,**
1930s. Pictures Farmer Alfalfa and Little Wilbur. -
$20 $45 $75

MOV-18. "George O'Brien Outdoor Club" Cello. Button,
1930s. - **$20 $35 $65**

MOV-19. "Sabu Club" Cello. Button,
1940. Inscribed for "The Thief Of Baghdad" movie of that
year. - **$8 $5 $25**

MOV-20

MOV-21

MOV-20. "Perils Of Nyoka" 27x41" Movie Serial Poster,
1942. Republic Pictures. Poster is for Chapter 1. -
$200 $400 $750

MOV-21. "Perils Of Nyoka" 27x41" Movie Serial Poster,
1942. Republic Pictures. Same art for Chapters 2-15.
Each - **$100 $250 $ 400**

MOV-22

MOV-23

**MOV-22. "Secret Service In Darkest Africa" 27x41" Movie
Serial Poster,**
1943. Republic Pictures. - **$40 $75 $125**

**MOV-23. "International Reno Browne Fan Club"
Newsletter And Membership Card,**
c. 1946. Issued by Canadian headquarters.
Near Mint In Mailer - **$35**
Newsletter - **$5 $10 $15**
Card - **$5 $10 $15**

MOV-25

MOV-24

MOV-24. "The Black Widow" 27x41" Movie Serial Poster,
1947. Republic Pictures. - **$75 $250 $500**

MOV-25. "The Sea Hound Club" Movie Serial Card,
1947. For admission to 15-episode Columbia Pictures serial
starring Buster Crabbe. - **$50 $100 $150**

MOV-26

**MOV-26. Martin & Lewis Fan Club Member Card And
Cello. Button,**
1949. Card - **$10 $15 $25**
Button - **$10 $20 $35**

MOV-32. "The Day The Earth Stood Still" 5' Standee,
1951. Rare. - **$1500** **$2500** **$5000**

MOV-27   MOV-28

MOV-27. "Ginger Rogers" Cigarette Ad Paper Standup,
1940s. Lucky Strike Cigarettes. Lunch place card holder also
designed to hold two cigarettes, one of a series. -
$15 **$25** **$40**

**MOV-28. "Reno Browne/Queen Of The Westerns" Cello.
Button,**
1940s. - **$15** **$25** **$40**

MOV-33

MOV-34

MOV-33. Martin & Lewis 21x22" Cardboard Sign,
1951. Chesterfield cigarettes. - **$50** **$90** **$150**

**MOV-34. "Jungle Drums Of Africa" Republic Serial,
27x41",**
1952. Starred Clayton Moore. - **$15** **$25** **$50**

MOV-29

**MOV-29. Little Women Movie Premium Plastic Jewel Box
with Mailer,**
1940s. Scarce. - **$40** **$80** **$120**

MOV-36

**MOV-35. "Radar Men From The Moon" 27x41" Movie
Serial Poster,**
1952. Republic Pictures. - **$150** **$275** **$400**

MOV-30

MOV-30. "Glance" Magazine With Monroe,
May 1950. Features Marilyn Monroe by her original name,
Norma Jean Dougherty. - **$50** **$100** **$175**

MOV-35

MOV-36. Marilyn Monroe Movie Postcard,
1953. For movie "Niagara." - **$25** **$60** **$125**

MOV-38

MOV-31

MOV-39

MOV-32

**MOV-31. "John Wayne/The Cowboy Troubleshooter"
Comic Booklet,**
1950. Procter & Gamble wrappers or boxtops from Dreft,
Oxydol or Ivory Soap. - **$15** **$45** **$100**

MOV-37

**MOV-37. "The Seven Year Itch" 39" By 6'8" Theater
Lobby Standee,**
1955. - **$750** **$1500** **$3000**

MOV-38. Martin & Lewis Ceramic Salt & Pepper Set,
1950s. Store item by Napco Ceramic Japan. -
$125 $250 $400

MOV-39. Jerry Lewis Watch,
1950s. Store item. - **$30 $60 $85**

MOV-40

MOV-41

MOV-40. Marilyn Monroe Pocket Mirror,
1950s. Store item. Full color paper photo with cello. rim. -
$30 $65 $85

MOV-41. Sunbeam Bread Movie Star Loaf End Labels,
1950s. Each - **$5 $10 $15**

MOV-42

MOV-43

MOV-42. "Walkie-Talkie Set" Offer Folder,
1950s. Campbell's tomato products. Promotional folder for
distributors or retailers featuring endorsements of Abbott &
Costello, Howdy Doody TV shows. - **$10 $20 $30**

MOV-43. Melody Time Promotional Brochure (Disney),
1950s. - **$20 $40 $80**

MOV-44

MOV-45

MOV-44. "Alfred Hitchcock's The Birds" Movie Theater Mask,
1963. - **$10 $20 $30**

MOV-45. Dell "James Bond 007" Magazine,
1964. - **$20 $35 $60**

MOV-46

MOV-46. James Bond Attache Case,
1965. Store item by Multiple Products. Often missing bullets
or rubber knife. - **$150 $300 $500**

MOV-47   MOV-48

MOV-47. Sean Connery Fan Photo,
1960s. - **$5 $10 $15**

MOV-48. "007" Replica Pistol Ring in Package,
1960s. Store item, unauthorized. Gold luster or aluminum.
Packaged - **$10 $20 $30**
Loose - **$5 $15 $20**

MOV-49   MOV-50   MOV-51

MOV-49. James Bond Plastic Snow Dome,
1960s. Store item. - **$50 $125 $200**

MOV-50. James Bond "Agent 007 Espionage" Litho. Button,
1960s. Vending machine issue. - **$5 $10 $15**

MOV-51. James Bond "Goldfinger's Death Derby" Litho. Button,
1960s. Vending machine issue. - **$5 $10 $15**

MOV-52   MOV-53   MOV-54

MOV-52. James Bond "Laser Beam/Goldfinger's Ray Machine" Litho. Button,
1960s. Vending machine issue. - **$3 $8 $12**

MOV-53. James Bond "Calling Agent 007" Litho. Button,
1960s. Vending machine issue. - **$5 $10 $15**

MOV-54. James Bond "Agent 007" Plastic Ring,
1960s. Vending machine issue. - **$8 $15 $22**

MOV-55

MOV-55. Tom Thumb Standee,
1960s - **$20 $50 $100**

MOV-56

MOV-57

MOV-56. "Join The Laurel And Hardy Laff Club!" 3-1/2" Button,
1960s. Larry Harmon's Pictures Corp. - **$15 $25 $45**

MOV-57. Donuts 9x13" Diecut Cardboard Store Signs,
1960s. Various users. Depict Laurel and Hardy.
Each - **$30 $50 $90**

MOV-58

MOV-59

MOV-58. Alien Poseable Plastic Figure,
1979. Store item by Kenner. Came with poster in box. Often missing fangs from mouth. Near Mint Boxed - **$450**
Figure Only - **$100 $200 $300**

MOV-59. Ghostbusters "Ectomobile" Die-Cast Vehicle,
1988. Carded offer with two film rolls from Fuji Film.
Carded - **$40 $75 $125**
Loose - **$10 $20 $30**

MR. MAGOO

Near-sighted, stubborn, crotchety Mr. Magoo first stumbled into view in 1949 in the UPA animated cartoon *Ragtime Bear*, and over the next 10 years he starred in more than 50 theatrical cartoons. He went to television on Los Angeles station KTTV in 1960 and to prime-time network television on NBC in *The Famous Adventures of Mr. Magoo* in 1964-1965. Other televised specials followed, and in 1977-1979 the old-timer reappeared in *What's New, Mister Magoo?* on CBS. A theatrical film, *1001 Arabian Nights*, was released by UPA in 1959. Jim Backus (1913-1989) was the voice of Magoo from the beginning. Comic books appeared between 1953 and 1965. General Electric has featured Mr. Magoo in various promotions, and Magoo films have been made for the National Heart Association, Timex, General Foods, Rheingold beer, Ideal toys, Dell Publishing, Colgate-Palmolive, and other advertisers.

MGO-2

MGO-3

MGO-1

MGO-1. Figural Metal Badge,
1960. GE Lightbulbs. On Card - **$15 $25 $35**
Badge Only - **$8 $15 $20**

MGO-2. General Electric Flicker Plastic Keychain Tag,
1961. - **$10 $18 $25**

MGO-3. Vinyl/Cloth Doll,
1962. Store item. - **$40 $80 $150**

MGO-5

MGO-4

MGO-4. Glass Ashtray,
1960s. General Electric. - **$10 $20 $35**

MGO-5. Plastic Ring Kit,
1960s. Store item. Comes with attachment heads of Magoo, Waldo or Charlie. Near Mint Bagged - **$25**
Each Complete Ring - **$4 $6 $8**

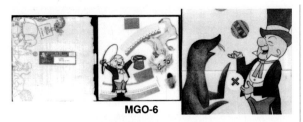

MGO-6

MGO-6. "Big Pop Birthday Bash" Party Kit,
1960s. GE/Hershey's numerous paper items of circus theme.
Near Mint In Mailer - **$90**

MR. PEANUT

The corporate symbol for the Planters Nut and Chocolate
Company was the inspiration of a 13-year-old schoolboy in a
1916 company-sponsored contest. Decked out in top hat,
monocle, and cane, Mr. Peanut has been promoting the
products of this Suffolk, Virginia, company ever since. The
design has been refined from the original figure, first in 1927
and again in 1962. Mr. Peanut has appeared in the form of a
wide variety of promotional items, from lamps to salt and
pepper sets, peanut dishes, banks, buttons, pins, book-
marks, figures and dolls of wood, plastic, bisque, and cloth,
silverware, cigarette lighters, and mechanical pencils, as well
as in a series of children's story and paint books first published in 1928 and available from the company in exchange
for product wrappers.

MRP-1

**MRP-1. "Mr. Peanut Book No. 1" Canadian Version
Coloring Book,**
c. 1928. Pictured example shows cover and sample coloring
page. - **$40 $75 $150**

MRP-2

MRP-3

MRP-4

MRP-5

MRP-2. New York World's Fair Cardboard Bookmark,
1939. - **$5 $12 $20**

MRP-3. Laminated Wooden Pin As Santa,
c. 1939. - **$35 $60 $115**

MRP-4. Laminated Wood Pin,
c. 1939. - **$20 $40 $75**

MRP-5. Wood Jointed Figure,
1930s. Frequently missing his cane. - **$125 $225 $350**

MRP-6

MRP-7

MRP-8

MRP-9

MRP-6. Bisque Ashtray,
1930s. - **$35 $70 $100**

MRP-7. New York World's Fair Wood Figure Pin,
1940. Dated for second year of 1939-1940 NYWF. -
$25 $50 $85

MRP-8. "Spooky Picture" Optical Illusion Card,
c. 1940. Believed insert for Planter's Jumbo Block Bar. -
$5 $15 $25

MRP-9. "The People's Choice" Litho. Button,
c. 1940s. - **$10 $20 $35**

MRP-10

MRP-11

MRP-12

MRP-10. 50th Anniversary Metal Tray,
1956. - **$20 $40 $60**

MRP-11. Composition Bobbing Body Figure,
1960s. - **$60 $90 $150**

MRP-12. Mr. Peanut Metal Ring,
c. 1960s. Gold luster with raised image of him. -
$15 $22 $30

MUSIC MISCELLANEOUS

Great vocalists, instrumentalists or instruments do not necessarily great premiums make. Vocalists, other than Elvis and the Beatles, have created little furor in premiums throughout the years, other than a small flurry of pin-back buttons picturing crooner stars of the 1940s-1950s. Rock music groups beginning in the 1960s have inspired some very attractively designed buttons, although mainly of retail nature. Music instruments and premiums seldom mingle. Possibly a kazoo here, a harmonica there and - by considerable leeway - bird calls, sirens, etc. Still, music in its broadest sense has produced a modest assortment of premiums such as songbooks, records and novelty items.

MUS-1

MUS-2

MUS-3

MUS-1. "Lucky Strike Presents Your Hit Parade Starring Frank Sinatra" Cardboard Fan,
1943. Scarce. Lucky Strike cigarettes. 12" tall diecut tobacco leaf replica inscribed on back "A Fan For My Fans-Frank Sinatra". - **$25 $60 $100**

MUS-2. "Four Aces" Cello. Button,
1940s. Philadelphia Fan Club. - **$10 $15 $25**

MUS-3. Tony Bennett "Bennett Tones Fan Club" Litho. Button,
1940s. - **$10 $20 $35**

MUS-4

MUS-5

MUS-4. "Liberace" Gold Luster Metal Link Charm Bracelet,
1956. Store item. Miniature framed photo plus charms depicting hands on keyboard, grand piano, candleabra, piano lid. - **$15 $35 $60**

MUS-5. "Pat Boone/4th Anniversary" Litho. Button,
1959. Dot Records. - **$5 $10 $15**

MUS-6

MUS-7

MUS-6. "Pat Boone Fan" Litho. Button,
c. 1959. - **$5 $10 $15**

MUS-7. "Picture Patches",
1950s. Store item. Probable set of eight. Includes Dick Clark, Ricky Nelson, Dave Nelson, Bobby Darin, Frankie Avalon, Tommy Sands, Jimmie Rodgers, Fabian.
Each Packaged - **$3 $6 $10**

MUS-8

MUS-9

MUS-8. Fabian And Frankie Avalon 3-1/2" Cello. Buttons,
1950s. Store item. Matching designs, possibly issued for others. Each - **$8 $15 $25**

MUS-9. "Everly Brothers Fan Club" Litho. Button,
1950s. - **$12 $20 $35**

MUS-10

MUS-11

MUS-12

MUS-10. "Herman's Hermits" 3-1/2" Cello. Button,
c. 1965. Store item. - **$8 $15 $25**

MUS-11. "The Rolling Stones" 3-1/2" Cello. Button,
c. 1966. Probably sold at concerts. - **$20 $35 $60**

MUS-12. "Woodstock" Celebration Litho. Button,
1969. Issued for 1970 live-action movie filmed during four-day concert. - **$10 $15 $25**

MUTT AND JEFF

Bud Fisher's *Mutt and Jeff*, the first continually published six-day-a-week comic strip, was to become one of the best known, funniest, and most popular strips in America. It started as a horseracing cartoon called *A. Mutt* in the *San Francisco Chronicle* in 1907. Jeff showed up the following year but it wasn't until 1916 that the strip was titled *Mutt and*

Jeff. A Sunday color strip was added in 1918. There were many early collections of reprints starting around 1910, hardback books, and comic books into the 1960s. A series of *Mutt and Jeff* musicals toured the country from about 1911 to 1915, and from 1918 to 1923 Bud Fisher Productions turned out animated cartoons, typically at a pace of one a week.

MUT-1

MUT-2

MUT-1. Stage Show Cardboard Ink Blotter,
1912. - **$10 $20 $35**

MUT-2. "Mutt And Jeff In Mexico" Cardboard Blotter,
c. 1912. For musical comedy stage production. -
$10 $20 $30

MUT-3

MUT-4

MUT-3. "Mutt And Jeff In College" Cardboard Blotter,
c. 1913. For musical comedy stage production. -
$10 $20 $30

MUT-4. Cast Iron Bank,
c. 1915. Store item. - **$60 $100 $175**

MUT-5

MUT-6

MUT-7

MUT-5. "Join The Evening Telegraph" Cello. Button,
c. 1915. Promotion for strip beginning and "Mutt & Jeff Club". - **$20 $35 $70**

MUT-6. "Cut That Stuff" Cartoon Litho. Button,
c. 1916. Various cigarette sponsors. Example from set featuring art by Bud Fisher and other cartoonists. Paint easily worn. Fisher Cartoons - **$5 $12 $20**
Other Artists - **$3 $8 $15**

MUT-7. Composition/Steel Jointed Flexible Figures,
1920s. Store item. With fabric outfits.
Each - **$100 $225 $400**

MUT-8

MUT-9

MUT-10

MUT-8. "Meet Us At Forest Park" Cello. Button,
c. 1920s. - **$25 $50 $85**

MUT-9. "Buffalo Evening News" Cello. Button,
1930s. From series of newspaper contest buttons, match number to win prize. - **$10 $20 $35**

MUT-10. "Tangle Comics" Cello. Button,
1940s. Philadelphia Sunday Bulletin. - **$10 $20 $35**

NABISCO MISCELLANEOUS

The giant National Biscuit Company was formed in 1898 b the merger of a number of smaller companies and indepen dent bakers. The following year its sales totaled 70% of a the crackers and cookies sold in America. Adolphus Green company chairman, set about to create a new product and national brand. He named it the Uneeda biscuit, developed carton (In-er-Seal) to keep it fresh, chose a picture of a bo wrapped in rain gear as a symbol, and invested heavily i advertising. In 1900 the company sold 100 million boxes Uneeda biscuits. Then quickly came Oysterettes, Zu Zu gir ger snaps, Fig Newtons, sugar wafers, and Barnum's Anima Crackers. Nabisco, always a heavy advertiser, issued number of promotional items over the years and has spor sored such children's television classics as *The Adventure of Rin-Tin-Tin, Jabberwocky, Kukla, Fran & Ollie*, and *Sk King*. In the mid-1980s the company was acquired by R. Reynolds and became part of RJR Nabisco.

NAB-1

NAB-1. Plastic Dinosaurs With Guide Folder And Box,
1957. Near Mint In Mailer - **$150**

NAB-2

NAB-2

AB-2. Wheat Honeys Store Promotional Kit With Plastic Dinosaurs,
957. Set of 10. Box Only - **$50 $125 $200**
ach Figure - **$3 $5 $10**

NAB-3   NAB-4   NAB-5

AB-3. "Munchy" Vinyl Attachment For Spoon Handle,
959. One of three Nabisco Spoon Men. Three rows of buttons. - **$15 $25 $50**

AB-4. "Crunchy" Vinyl Attachment For Spoon Handle,
959. Two rows of buttons. - **$15 $25 $50**

AB-5. "Spoon Size" Vinyl Attachment for Spoon Handle,
959. One row of buttons and smaller size than Munchy and runchy. - **$25 $35 $60**

NAB-6

NAB-7   NAB-8

AB-6. "Rocket Man" Paper Mask,
950s. - **$15 $30 $60**

AB-7. Rice Honey Bee,
961. Designed to perch on edge of cereal bowl. -
$12 $20

AB-8. Rice Honey Clown,
1961. Vinyl figure designed to perch on edge of cereal wl. - **$5 $12 $20**

NANCY AND SLUGGO

ancy, a stubby little girl with a perpetual hair arrangement sembling black steel wool held by a white bow, was creat- in 1933 by cartoonist Ernie Bushmiller, originally as a

niece and periodic visitor to her aunt, the established Fritzi Ritz. By the late 1930s, niece and aunt had reversed their featured roles. Nancy's equally-stubby platonic boyfriend & sidekick, Sluggo, came into her life and the pair remains an inseparable cartoon strip duo to this day.

NAN-1

NAN-2

NAN-3

NAN-1. "Fritzi Ritz Spinner",
1930s. United Features Syndicate. Cello. over metal disk that has underside center bump for spinning. - **$50 $100 $150**

NAN-2. "Journal-Transcript Funnies Club" Litho. Button,
c. 1930s. From set of various characters, also has radio call letters for station in Peoria, Illinois. - **$10 $25 $45**

NAN-3. Nancy 7-1/2" Hard Plastic Doll,
1940s (late). Rare. Post Grape-Nuts Flakes. -
$500 $1000 $1600

NAN-5

NAN-4

NAN-4. Sluggo 7-1/2" Hard Plastic Doll,
1940s (late). Rare. Post Grape-Nuts Flakes. -
$400 $900 $1450

NAN-5. "Comic Capers Club" 2-1/8" Cello. Button,
1940s. Sun-Times (newspaper). - **$250 $500 $1000**

NAN-6   NAN-7

NAN-6. Nancy Rubber/Vinyl Doll,
1954. Store item by S&P Doll and Toy Co.
Near Mint Boxed - **$500**
Loose - **$75 $150 $300**

NAN-7. Sluggo Rubber/Vinyl Doll,
1954. Store item by S&P Doll and Toy Co.
Near Mint Boxed - **$500**
Loose - **$75 $150 $300**

NEW FUN COMICS

Former pulp magazine writer and cavalry officer Major Malcolm Wheeler-Nicholson came up with the idea of a comic book containing all original material in late 1934. The 10x15" tabloid size magazine *New Fun*, with color covers and black and white interiors, appeared on newsstands with a cover date of February 1935. Pages were laid out in a Sunday comic page format with continuing stories, humor pages, text stories and games. Subsequent issues were titled *More Fun*. The magazine added more color and adapted to the standard comic book size and format by 1936. Historically, *More Fun* not only was one of the first comic books with original material but also the first to publish work by Walt Kelly of later *Pogo* fame and Siegel and Shuster of *Superman* fame. *New Fun* formed the cornerstone of the DC Comics publishing empire. The title ran through issue #127 dated November-December 1947.

NEW-1

NEW-1. "New Fun Club" Cello. Button,
1935. Rare. - **$100 $300 $750**

NICK CARTER, MASTER DETECTIVE

Nick Carter, hero of hundreds of dime novels, began life in 1886 in the pages of Street & Smith's *New York Weekly*. The stories, signed by "Nicholas Carter," were written by a number of different authors. Following decades of pulp magazine appearances, the master detective came to the Mutual radio network in 1943 and was broadcast until 1955. Sponsors included Lin-X Home Brighteners (1944-1945), Cudahy meats (1946-1951), and Old Dutch cleanser (1946-1952). Walter Pidgeon played Carter in a 1939 MGM movie. *The Nick Carter Club* was a 1930s Street & Smith promotion.

NCK-1

NCK-2

NCK-1. "Nick Carter Magazine" Pulp Vol. 1 #3,
May 1933. Published by Street & Smith. - **$20 $40 $85**

NCK-2. Club Shield Badge,
c. 1934. - **$40 $75 $125**

NCK-3

NCK-3. "Nick Carter Fingerprint Set",
1934. Store item by New York Toy & Game Co. Includes "Nick Carter 999 Club" instruction book with Street & Smith club enrollment form. Complete - **$35 $75 $125**

NCK-4

NCK-5

NCK-4. Club Card,
c. 1934. Nick Carter Magazine. Came with badge. - **$25 $60 $100**

NCK-5. "Nick Carter Magazine" Gummed Envelope Sticker,
1930s. Street & Smith Publications. -**$20 $40 $75**

OG, SON OF FIRE

The prehistoric adventures of Og and his companions - R Nada and Big Tooth - were broadcast for a year (1934-193 on CBS radio, sponsored by Libby. Alfred Brown played t primeval hero of the series, written by Irving Crump, t author of the original Og stories.

OGS-1

OGS-1. "Adventures Of Og, Son Of Fire" 15x20" Map,
1935. Rare. Libby. - **$150 $200 $400**

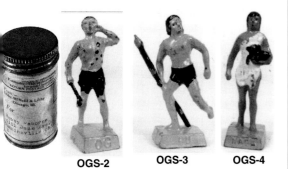

OGS-2   OGS-3   OGS-4

OGS-2. "Og" 2-1/4" Painted Metal Figure,
. 1935. Marked under base "Made For Libby's Milk By
incoln Logs USA." Six figures in set. For each mailing canis-
er with metal lid add $10-20-30. - **$40 $60 $100**

OGS-3. "Ru" Metal Figure,
. 1935. Part of Og set. - **$40 $60 $100**

OGS-4. "Nada" Metal Figure,
. 1935. Part of Og set. - **$40 $60 $100**

OGS-6

OGS-5   OGS-7

GS-5. "Big Tooth" Metal Figure,
1935. Part of Og set. - **$40 $60 $100**

GS-6. "Three Horn" Metal Figure,
1935. Part of Og set. - **$50 $75 $125**

GS-7. "Rex" Metal Figure,
1935. Part of Og set. - **$50 $75 $125**

OMAR THE MYSTIC

so known as *Omar the Wizard*, this radio series ran for a
ear (1935-1936) on the Mutual radio network, sponsored by
aystee bread. M.H. Joachim played Omar.

OMR-1

OMR-1. "The Secrets Of Omar The Mystic" Book,
1936. Scarce. Taystee Bread. - **$35 $50 $100**

OMR-2

OMR-2. Taystee Bread Code Card,
1936. Back has instructions for using "Mystic Wheel". -
$20 $40 $75

ONE MAN'S FAMILY

The saga of the Barbour family, written lovingly by Carlton E.
Morse, was the longest running serial drama in the history of
radio. The program debuted in 1932 on NBC's San
Francisco station KGO and a year later went to the NBC network, where it continued until 1959. The family tree series
told the stories of Henry and Fanny Barbour, their five children (Paul, Hazel, the twins Claudia and Clifford, and Jack),
and succeeding generations of Barbours as they lived and
died, married, had children, and faced family crises against
the backdrop of a changing world. Sponsors included
Wesson Oil (1932-1933), Kentucky Winner tobacco (1933-
1935), Royal gelatin (1935-1936), Tenderleaf tea (1936-
1949), Miles Laboratories (1950-1954), and Toni Home
Permanents (1954-1955). A television version ran on NBC
prime time from 1949 to 1952 and as a daytime serial in
1954-1955.

ONE-2

ONE-1

ONE-1. "One Man's Family History In Words And
Pictures" Folder,
1935. Standard Brands Foods. - **$12 $20 $35**

ONE-2. "Scrapbook" Yearbook,
1936. Tenderleaf Tea. Published in graphic style of personally kept album. - **$10 $20 $30**

ONE-4

ONE-3

ONE-3. Teddy Barbour "Diary" Book,
1937. Standard Brands Foods. Family events in simulated handwriting. - **$5 $12 $20**

ONE-4. Fanny Barbour "Memory Book",
1940. Standard Brands Foods. Family photos, notes, etc. in simulated scrapbook form. - **$5 $12 $20**

ONE-5

ONE-5. "I Believe In America" Album,
1941. Standard Brands Foods. Style of family scrapbook heavily emphasizing early war years. - **$20 $30 $60**

ONE-6

ONE-7

ONE-6. Barbour Family Scrapbook,
1946. Standard Brands Foods. Format of simulated family photos, news clippings, telegrams, etc. - **$8 $15 $30**

ONE-7. TV Cast Photo,
c. 1949. - **$20 $30 $40**

ONE-8

ONE-9

ONE-8. "Barbour Family Album",
1951. Miles Laboratories. - **$5 $12 $20**

ONE-9. "Mother Barbour's Favorite Recipes" Booklet,
c. 1951. Miles Laboratories. 20th anniversary souvenir picturing cast members over the years. - **$5 $15 $25**

OPERATOR #5

America's Undercover Ace, handsome young Jimm Christopher, fought spies and foreign agents from 1934 un the outbreak of World War II as Secret Service Operator # in the pages of the pulp magazine of the same name. H task, month after month, was to save the United States fro destruction. A 1934 offer of a replica Operator #5 skull rin must have been short-lived as the ring is quite scarce.

OPR-1

OPR-2

OPR-1. Enameled Silvered Metal Club Ring,
1934. Rare. Operator 5 Magazine. Silvering easily worn off. **$3500 $8500 $22000**

OPR-2. "Secret Service Operator #5" Pulp Magazine,
June-July 1936. Published by Popular Publications. - **$20 $40 $100**

OUR GANG

Between 1922 and 1944 the Hal Roach Studios and MG produced 221 *Our Gang* comedies. The short films, one two-reelers, were immensely successful, with the little ra cals - Alfalfa, Farina, Buckwheat, Spanky, Darla Hood, Ba Jean, Mickey, Waldo, and their dogs Pete the Pup, Pal, a Von - joyfully getting into and out of mischief, playing hook putting on musicals, and generally doing no harm and havi lots of fun. The films were syndicated on television as *T Little Rascals* (1955-1965), as *Our Gang Comedies* (195 1965), and as *Mischief Makers* (1960-1970). The *Lit Rascals* series was re-edited and televised again in t 1970s. A prime-time animated cartoon, *The Little Rasca Christmas Show*, aired on NBC in 1979. *Our Gang* con books were published in the 1940s.

OUR-1

OUR-2

OUR-1. "Pete" With Child Photo,
c. 1920s. Child's souvenir of Steel Pier, Atlantic City. - **$15 $25 $40**

OUR-2. Cardboard Ad Blotter,
1920s. Various sponsors. - **$15 $25 $40**

OUR-4　　　　OUR-5

OUR-3

OUR-3. "Hal Roach's Rascals" Photo,
920s. - **$20 $40 $75**

OUR-4. Joe Cobb China Mug,
920s. Store item by Sebring Pottery Co. - **$60 $125 $175**

OUR-5. Scooter Lowry China Mug,
920s. Store item by Sebring Pottery Co. - **$75 $125 $250**

OUR-6

OUR-7

OUR-6. "Majestic Electric Radio" Cardboard Ink Blotter,
920s. - **$12 $25 $40**

OUR-7. Dickie Moore Mask,
1932. U.S. Caramel Co. One of a set. - **$10 $25 $40**

OUR-8　　　　OUR-9　　　　OUR-10

OUR-8. "Pete" Cello. Button,
1932. From "Member Spanky Safety Club" series with Hal
Roach copyright. - **$40 $85 $140**

OUR-9. "Buckwheat" Cello. Button,
1932. From "Member Spanky Safety Club" series with Hal
Roach copyright. - **$40 $90 $150**

OUR-10. "Alfalfa" Cello. Button,
1932. From "Member Spanky Safety Club" series with Hal
Roach copyright. - **$35 $75 $125**

OUR-11

OUR-12

OUR-11. "Darla Hood" Cello. Button,
c. 1932. From "Member Spanky Safety Club" series with Hal
Roach copyright. - **$30 $65 $115**

OUR-12. Fan Photo,
1934. Hal Roach Studios. - **$10 $20 $45**

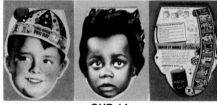

OUR-13

OUR-13. Fan Photo,
1937. Hal Roach Studios. - **$10 $20 $45**

OUR-14

OUR-14. "Fun Kit" Diecut Booklet,
1937. Morton's Salt. Features colored mask-like photos,
activity pages, rules for their "Eagles Club". - **$35 $75 $150**

OUR-15

OUR-16

OUR-17

OUR-15. "Our Gang Painting Book",
1937. Sears, Roebuck. Copyright by Hal Roach Studios. -
$30 $60 $100

OUR-16. Spanky Fan Photo,
c. 1937. Hal Roach Studios. - **$10 $18 $35**

OUR-17. Our Gang Calendar,
1939. Tastee bread. Cardboard sheet issued monthly.
Each - **$20 $40 $80**

OUR-19

OUR-18

OUR-20

OUR-18. Our Gang Comedy Blatz Gum,
1930s. - **$20 $40 $60**

OUR-19. "Contestant" Cello. Button,
1930s. Probable theater or newspaper contest. -
$15 $35 $60

OUR-20. "Our Gang Club" Cello. Button,
1930s. Superba Theatre by Chicago button maker. Matinee
inscription plus "Watch For Your Color". - **$25 $50 $75**

OUR-21

OUR-21. Figure Mold Play Kit,
1930s. Store item by Jem Clay Forming Co. for Louis Wolf
Co. Eight hollow plaster figures for painting plus backdrop
panel. Near Mint Boxed - **$350**
Each Painted Figure - **$8 $20 $30**

OUR-22

OUR-22. Bisque Nodders,
1930s. German made store item. Set of six as shown: Pete,
Chubby Chaney, Wheezer, Jackie Cooper, Farina, Mary Ann
Jackson. Each - **$75 $125 $200**

OUR-23   **OUR-24**   **OUR-25**

OUR-23. "Safety First" Cello. Button,
1930s. Probable Our Gang member club button, rim curl
copyright "Hal Roach Studios". - **$12 $25 $40**

**OUR-24. "King Carl 'Alfalfa' Switzer" 2-1/2" Cello.
Button,**
1930s. National Ice Cream Week. His name is followed by
"Of Hal Roach's Our Gang-A MGM Release". -
$75 $150 $300

OUR-25. "The Little Rascals' Club" Member Card,
c. 1955. WHUM-TV Channel 61. - **$10 $20 $35**

OVALTINE MISCELLANEOUS

Ovaltine was created in 1904 by Swiss physician Dr. Georg
Wander as a flavored milk additive, and the original combination of malt, eggs, vitamins, and minerals is still in use
Europe. The Wander Company brought Ovaltine to the
United States in 1905, using the same mix of ingredien
except for the addition of sugar. Ovaltine found wide use a
a tasty health food for children and adults. (The Red Cros
shipped Ovaltine to Allied prisoner-of-war camps as a nut
tional supplement during both World Wars.) The Sande
Pharmaceutical Company acquired the Wander Company
1967 and Ovaltine is now sold in "chocolate malt" (introduce
in the 1960s) and "rich chocolate" (introduced in the 1980
flavors, as well as the "original malt" version. In addition
the many premiums the company issued as the sponsor
such classic radio programs as *Radio Orphan Annie* an
Captain Midnight, Ovaltine has produced promotional item
not related to specific programs.

OVL-1

OVL-2

**OVL-1. "Lecture On Nutrition And Digestion By The
Wonder Robot" Booklet,**
1934. Issued at Century of Progress Hall of Science. -
$40 $80 $150

OVL-2. Litho. Tin Canister,
1939. 9" tall "Hospital Size". - **$15 $25 $40**

OVL-3   OVL-4   OVL-5

VL-3. Glass Shaker with Mixer,
)30s. - **$20 $40 $80**

VL-4. English "Delicious Ovaltine" China Mug,
)30s. - **$15 $25 $45**

**VL-5. English "Delicious Ovaltine" China Mug
esigned Without Handle,**
30s. - **$15 $25 $40**

OVL-6   OVL-7

VL-6. Sample Size Tin Container,
'30s. Miniature 2-1/4" diameter by 2" tall.
ith Lid - **$15 $30 $55**

VL-7. "School Size" Sample Tin Container,
30s. English issue miniature 1-1/2" diameter by 1-3/4" tall.
ctures Johnnie, Winnie, Elsie.
mplete - **$20 $35 $55**
)ened - **$15 $25 $40**

OVL-8   OVL-9

'L-8. Plastic Mug,
40s. Sandy Strong. - **$20 $40 $60**

'L-9. "Ding Dong School" Plastic Mug,
50s. Decal pictures "Miss Frances," the teacher on 1952-
56 TV educational series. - **$15 $30 $50**

PEANUTS

Probably the most successful comic strip of all time, Charles Schulz's *Peanuts* appeared for a couple of years as *Li'l Folks* in the St. Paul *Pioneer Press* before it was syndicated under its new name by United Features in 1950. The antics of Charlie Brown, the strip's unlikely hero, Snoopy the wonder dog, Lucy van Pelt, Linus, Schroeder, and Pigpen have become part of American culture. There have been numerous reprint books, feature-length animated films, prime-time television specials, a musical comedy, and extensive merchandising and licensing of the major characters. Items are usually copyrighted Charles M. Schulz or United Features Syndicate. Copyright dates on items relate to character designs and are usually unrelated to the date an item was issued.

PEA-1   PEA-2   PEA-3

PEA-1. Charlie Brown Composition Bobbing Head,
1960s. Store item. Other characters also issued. -
$15 $60 $100

PEA-2. Lucy Composition Bobbing Head,
1960s. Store item, other characters also issued.
Each - **$15 $50 $100**

PEA-3. Charlie Brown Enameled Metal Necklace Charm,
1960s. Store item. United Features Syndicate copyright.
From character series. - **$12 $25 $50**

PEA-4   PEA-5   PEA-6

PEA-4. Plastic Clip-On Badge,
1970. Millbrook Bread. Five or more characters in set.
Carded - **$5 $8 $12**
Loose - **$3 $5 $8**

PEA-5. "Snoopy's Spotters Club" 2" Litho. Tab,
c. 1970. Millbrook Bread. - **$5 $10 $15**

PEA-6. Litho. Tab,
c. 1970. Restaurant issue. - **$3 $5 $8**

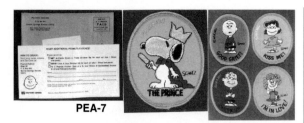

PEA-7

PEA-7. "Peanuts Patches",
1971. Interstate Brands. Set of five with envelope and order coupon. Set With Mailer - **$10 $20 $50**

PEA-8

PEA-9

PEA-10

PEA-8. "Colonial Capers Cartoon Comics" 2-1/2" Cello. Button,
1971. Probable newspaper issue. - **$5 $12 $20**

PEA-9. "Red Baron's Albatross" Punch-Out,
1973. Coca-Cola. - **$25 $50 $75**

PEA-10. "Happy Birthday, America!" Cello. Button,
1976. Bicentennial issue. - **$8 $12 $20**

PEP BOYS

The Pep Boys - Manny, Moe and Jack - were three pals who opened an auto supply store in Philadelphia in 1921. The store prospered and eventually grew into a chain of operations in the Eastern states, watched over through the years by the smiling cartoon faces of the founders.

PEP-1

PEP-2

PEP-1. Catalogue,
1938. - **$20 $40 $60**

PEP-2. Catalogue,
1939. - **$20 $40 $60**

PEP-3

PEP-3. Boxed Playing Cards,
1940s. - **$25 $50 $90**

PEP-4

PEP-5

PEP-4. Mail Catalogue May,
1954 - **$10 $15 $30**

PEP-5. Plastic Cigarette Holder,
c. 1950s. - **$25 $40 $80**

PETE RICE

Pistol Pete Rice was the sheriff of Buzzard Gap, Arizona, i series of Street and Smith pulp westerns. Written by E Conlon under the name Austin Gridley, *Pete Rice West Adventures* appeared From November 1933 to June 19: For a dime, readers could get a *Pete Rice Club* dep badge and a members' pledge card.

PTR-1

PTR-2

PTR-1. "Pete Rice" Gummed Paper Envelope Sticker,
c. 1934. Street & Smith Co., publishers of Pete Rice pulp magazine. - **$15 $30 $50**

PTR-2. Deputy Club Metal Badge,
c. 1934. Badge - **$25 $50 $100**
Envelope - **$5 $10 $15**

PETER PAN

he story of Peter Pan, the boy who lived in Never-Never and and refused to grow up, was created in 1904 by British ovelist and playwright Sir James M. Barrie (1860-1937). he fantasy of Peter, Wendy, Tinker Bell, and the evil aptain Hook was given new life in 1953 with the release of he full-length Disney animated feature, and in 1991 Tri-Star ictures released *Hook*, a revised version of the beloved tale rected by Steven Spielberg and starring Dustin Hoffman nd Robin Williams.

PAN-1

AN-1. "Animated Coloring Book",
943. Derby Foods. Non-Disney with punch-out sheet to ani-ate the pictures. - **$15 $25 $40**

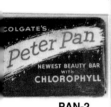

PAN-2

AN-2. Soap Bar With 18x24" Paper Map,
1953. Colgate-Palmolive. Map - **$35 $75 $150**
ap Bar - **$5 $12 $20**

PAN-3

PAN-5

PAN-5. Bread Labels,
c. 1953. Various bread companies. Examples from set of 12.
Each - **$3 $6 $10**

PAN-6

PAN-6. "Hallmark Pirate Ship" Kit With Mailer Envelope,
c. 1953. Store item, Hallmark Cards. Includes 21x29" map and four punch-out sheets to assemble pirate ship.
Near Mint In Envelope - **$85**
Map Only - **$15 $25 $45**

PAN-7

PAN-8

PAN-7. Litho. Button,
1950s. Hudson's department store, Detroit. No Disney copy-right. - **$10 $17 $39**

PAN-8. Coloring Book,
1963. Peter Pan Peanut Butter, non-Disney. - **$5 $15 $25**

PEZ

This peppermint candy originated in Austria in 1927. Edward Haas, the inventor, shortened the German word for pepper-mint, *pfeffermintz*, to Pez. Sales were slow until the compa-ny, Pez Candy Inc., entered the United States in 1952 target-ing the children's market with a figural head on the dispenser and a cherry flavored candy. Collectors are now willing to spend four-figure amounts for a rare example. In addition to the classic dispensers featuring cartoon figures, animals, superheroes, and Disney characters, PEZ watches, jewelry, keychains, and clip-ons have been produced.

PAN-4

N-3. Coasters 11x14" Paper Store Sign,
953. Peter Pan Peanut Butter. - **$30 $60 $90**

N-4. "Peter Pan Peanut Butter" Tin Lids,
953. Examples from set. Each - **$3 $8 $15**

PEZ-1

PEZ-2   (enlarged view)

PEZ-1. Litho. Tin Clicker,
c. 1948. - **$150 $300 $450**

PEZ-2. Tin Rotating Store Rack,
1950s. 16" tall. - **$100 $175 $250**

PEZ-3

PEZ-4

PEZ-3. Space Gun,
1950s. Candy shooter gun. - **$40 $75 $100**

PEZ-4. Litho. Tin Yo-Yo,
1950s. - **$60 $130 $200**

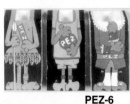

PEZ-5

PEZ-6

PEZ-5. Tin Clicker,
c. 1960s. - **$15 $30 $50**

PEZ-6. Dispenser Cardboard Costumes,
c. 1960s Three examples and one back panel from 12 in series "A". Each - **$5 $10 $20**

PEZ-7

PEZ-7. Disney Pez Dispenser Display Card,
c. 1960s. Card fits into the back of a display box. - **$10 $18 $30**

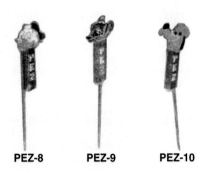

PEZ-8   PEZ-9   PEZ-10

PEZ-8. Donald Duck Miniature Plastic Dispenser Replica On Brass Stickpin,
c. 1960s. From European made Disney character series. - **$10 $20 $35**

PEZ-9. Bambi Miniature Plastic Dispenser Replica On Brass Stickpin,
c. 1960s. From European made Disney character series. - **$10 $25 $40**

PEZ-10. Pluto Miniature Plastic Dispenser On Brass Stickpin,
c. 1960s. From European made Disney character series. - **$10 $20 $30**

PEZ-11

PEZ-11. "Pez Premium Club" Paper,
1970s. - **$8 $12 $20**

PEZ-12   PEZ-13

PEZ-12. Spider-Man Cardboard Mask,
1970s. - **$20 $40 $60**

PEZ-13. Hulk Cardboard Mask,
1970s. - **$15 $35 $50**

PHANTOM PILOT PATROL

angendorf baked goods sponsored this regionally broadcast
dio adventure series on the West Coast in the 1930s. The
ass and black enamel paint membership badge is the only
emium known.

PLT-1

LT-1. Black Enamel On Brass Member's Badge,
030s. - **$10 $25 $75**

THE PHANTOM

e legendary ghost-who-walks was created by writer Lee
lk and artist Ray Moore as a daily comic strip for King
atures in 1936. A Sunday page was added in 1939.
ded by Guran, the leader of the Bandar pygmies, and by
wolf Devil, the masked crime fighter with the sign of the
ull has been battling evil and pursuing his fiancee Diana
lmer in comic strips in the U.S. and overseas ever since.
mic book reprints were first published in 1939, with new
aterial added starting in 1951. A 15-episode chapter play
arring Tom Tyler was released by Columbia Pictures in
43.

PHN-1

PHN-3

PHN-2

PHN-4

N-1. Portrait Ring,
948. Gold plastic bands with clear cover over color pic-
e. - **$25 $50 $75**

N-2. "The Phantom Club Member" Australian Cello.
tton,
0s. Scarce. - **$150 $350 $750**

N-3. "S.F. Call-Bulletin" Cardboard Disk,
940s. San Francisco newspaper. From series of contest
ks, match number to win prize. - **$8 $20 $35**

N-4. Three-Sheet,
0s. Columbia Pictures. 80" by 40". - **$2000 $4000 $6000**

PHN-5

PHN-6

PHN-7

PHN-5. China Portrait Mug,
1950s. Store item. - **$35 $75 $125**

PHN-6. Litho. Tab,
1950s. - **$20 $40 $75**

PHN-7. "The Phantom" Litho. Button,
1950s. From set of various King Features Syndicate characters. - **$10 $20 $30**

PHN-8

PHN-9

PHN-8. Plastic Frame Picture Charm,
1950s. Store item. Gumball vending machine issue. -
$8 $15 $25

PHN-9. Board Game With Plastic Skull Ring,
1966. Store item by Transogram.
Near Mint Boxed With Ring - **$250**
Ring Only - **$50 $100 $150**

PHN-10

PHN-11

PHN-12

PHN-10. Australian Ink Stamp Ring,
1960s. Rubber with raised skull symbol as ink stamp,
"Phantom" name on ring band. - **$50 $100 $150**

PHN-11. Australian Brass Ring,
1960s. Depicts raised skull symbol with red eye sockets. -
$60 $120 $175

PHN-12. Sticker,
1975. King Features. - **$5 $10 $20**

PILLSBURY

The Pillsbury Company was formed in 1869 when 27-year-old Charles Alfred Pillsbury bought a flour mill in Minneapolis and set about improving the milling process and producing a finer flour. Pillsbury's Best XXXX, a conversion of the historic bakers' XXX symbol for premium bread, was adopted as a company trademark in 1872. The Pillsbury Doughboy, created by animator Hal Mason, was introduced in television commercials in 1966 and named Poppin' Fresh in 1971. He was soon joined by Poppie Fresh, and the two characters have been successfully merchandised as corporate symbols.

In 1964, Pillsbury introduced the Funny Face products, a sugar-free drink mix for children. There were six flavors originally. The line went national in 1965 and more flavors were added throughout the 1970s. The brand faded in the late 1970s with stiff competition from market leader Kool-Aid. Pillsbury sold the line in 1980 to Brady Enterprises. The new owners test marketed Chug A Lug Chocolate in 1983 and offered the final plastic cup premium. Limited distribution makes this the scarcest of the nine cups in the Funny Face series.

PLS-1.   PLS-2

PLS-1. "Poppin' Fresh Doughboy",
c. 1971. Full figure color label on plastic can holding vinyl figure. - **$30 $60 $100**

PLS-2. "Poppin' Fresh Doughboy",
c. 1971. Closeup portrait label on plastic can holding vinyl figure. - **$30 $60 $100**

PLS-3   PLS-5
PLS-4

PLS-3. "Poppin' Fresh" & "Poppie" Plastic Salt & Pepper Shakers,
1974. - **$12 $18 $25**

PLS-4. "Poppin' Fresh" Vinyl Playhouse,
1974. Complete with four figures. - **$60 $100 $150**

PLS-5. "Pillsbury" Cloth Doll,
c. 1970s. - **$5 $10 $18**

PLS-6   PLS-7

PLS-6. "How Freckle Face Strawberry Got His Freckles" Book,
1965. - **$15 $25 $40**

PLS-7. "Crash Orange" Book,
1967. - **$20 $40 $70**

PLS-8

PLS-8. Funny Face Mugs,
1969. First three of nine in set. Chug A Lug Chocolate introduced in 1983.
First Eight Each - **$5 $12 $20**
Chug A Lug - **$10 $20 $40**

PLS-9   PLS-10

PLS-9. Choo Choo Cherry Cloth Pillow Doll,
1970. Pillsbury Co. - **$10 $25 $40**

PLS-10. Lefty Lemon Cloth Pillow Doll,
1970. Grape and Strawberry also issued.
Each - **$10 $25 $40**

PLS-11

PLS-11. Funny Face Plastic Walkers,
1971. Set of four, each with plastic weight.
Each - **$50 $75 $125**

PLS-13

PLS-12

PNK-5

PNK-4

PLS-12. Goofy Grape Plastic Pitcher,
1974. Pillsbury Co. Two versions: Single face or face on each side of pitcher. - **$20 $40 $70**

PLS-13. "Goofy Grape Sings" Record,
1970s. - **$10 $20 $35**

THE PINK PANTHER

This slinky, bulgy-eyed pantomime creature first appeared in the opening credits of the 1964 live-action feature film of the same title starring actors David Niven and Peter Sellers. The catchy animated antics, abetted by Henry Mancini theme music, prompted a spin-off single cartoon short that evolved into a career of other performances in theaters, TV cartoons and comic books. Creators were animators DePatie-Freleng enterprises. Early adventures typically pitted Pink Panther against his traditional inept, dim-witted foil Inspector Clouseau. Later animations added other characters and the 1985 *Pink Panther And Sons* (Pinky, Panky, Punkin) TV series was produced in association with Hanna-Barbera studios.

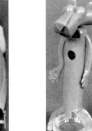

PNK-1

PNK-2

PNK-3

PNK-1. Inspector Clouseau 3" Cello. Button,
1965. Issued following original 1964 Pink Panther film starring Peter Sellers as Clouseau. - **$5 $12 $20**

PNK-2. RPX Race Car,
1973. Pink Panther Cereal. Styled after George Barris car. - **$0 $80 $150**

PNK-3. 5-1 Spy Kit,
1973. Pink Panther Cereal. - **$50 $75 $125**

PNK-4. "One Man Band" Battery Toy With Box,
c. 1980. Store item by Illco Toys. Plush/vinyl/metal action movement toy. Boxed - **$40 $75 $100**
Loose - **$25 $50 $75**

PNK-5. Albertson's 3-1/2" Cello. Button,
1984. - **$5 $10 $15**

PINOCCHIO

Italian author Carlo Collodi wrote the children's tale *Pinocchio: the Story of a Puppet* in 1880. The classic adventure of a wooden marionette who wants to become a real boy was first translated into English in 1892 and given new life as a full-length animated feature by the Disney studio in 1940. The film was a huge success, and the characters were merchandised extensively. Pinocchio, his tiny conscience Jiminy Cricket, Figaro the cat, Cleo the goldfish, the Blue Fairy, Monstro the whale, and the other creations were produced in a great variety of materials and formats, and Pinocchio was licensed to a long list of manufacturers of foods, candy, gum, paint, salt, razors, mouthwash, clothing, watches, etc. Comic book appearances began in 1939, animated sequels were released in 1964 and 1987, and a television special using a stop-motion process was aired on ABC in 1980.

PCC-1

PCC-2

PCC-1. "Walt Disney's Pinocchio" Book,
1939. Store item and Cocomalt premium.
Premium Edition - **$15 $40 $75**
Store Edition - **$10 $30 $60**

PCC-2. Cocomalt "Walt Disney's Pinocchio" 10x16" Book Ad Poster,
1939. - **$40 $75 $125**

PCC-3

PCC-3. Post Toasties Box,
1939. Various boxes with cut-outs.
Each Complete - **$150 $300 $600**

PCC-4

**PCC-4. "Save Pinocchio Lids From Ice Cream Cups"
6x18" Paper Sign,**
1939. - **$60 $100 $150**

PCC-5

PCC-6

PCC-5. "Pinocchio Circus" 32x51" Linen Sign,
1939. Various sponsors. - **$300 $1200 $2000**

PCC-6. "Pinocchio's Circus" Cut-Out Sheet,
1939. Various bread companies. Came with 60 cards.
Uncut Tent - **$50 $75 $100**
Each Uncut Card - **$1 $3 $5**

PCC-7

PCC-8

PCC-7. "Pinocchio Masks Free" Newspaper Ad,
1939. Gillette Blue Blades. - **$10 $20 $35**

PCC-8. Pinocchio Paper Mask,
1939. Gillette Blue Blades. From set of five characters:
Pinocchio, Jiminy Cricket, Geppetto, Figaro, Cleo.
Each - **$5 $12 $18**

PCC-9

**PCC-9. "Pinocchio's Christmas Party" Department Store
Give-Away Book,**
1939. Various stores. - **$15 $25 $50**

PCC-10

PCC-11

PCC-10. "Good Teeth Certificate",
1939. American Dental Association. - **$25 $60 $100**

PCC-11. "Good Teeth" Cello. Button,
1939. Back paper for Bureau of Public Relations/American
Dental Association. - **$75 $150 $275**

PCC-13

PCC-12

CC-12. Catalin Plastic Thermometer,
939. Store item. - **$40 $80 $150**

CC-13. Studio Issued Fan Card,
940. - **$30 $50 $75**

PCC-14

CC-14. Theater Give-Away Sheet,
40. - **$35 $60 $125**

PCC-15

C-15. "Poster Stamps" Booklet,
40. Independent Grocers Alliance of America. Holds 32
amps. Booklet - **$15 $35 $60**
ch Stamp - **$10 $20 $30**

PCC-16   **PCC-17**

C-16. "Pinocchio Candy Bar" Box,
40. Schutter Candy Co. Originally held 24 bars. -
0 **$150 $250**

PCC-17. "Pinocchio Chewing Gum" Paper Wrapper,
1940. Store item by Dietz Gum Co. - **$15 $30 $60**

PCC-18   **PCC-19**   **PCC-20**

**PCC-18. "Jiminy Cricket Official Conscience Medal"
Brass Badge,**
1940. - **$40 $85 $150**

PCC-19. "Walt Disney's Pinocchio" Cello. Button,
1940. Back paper has Kay Kamen distributorship name.
Used by toy stores and others as giveaway. - **$10 $20 $35**

PCC-20. Victor Records Cello. Button,
1940. Phonograph record design inscribed "Pinocchio
Comes To Town On Victor Records". - **$200 $500 $1000**

PCC-21   **PCC-22**
                              PCC-23

PCC-21. Jiminy Cricket Wood Jointed Doll,
c. 1940. Store item by Ideal. - **$150 $250 $450**

PCC-22. Figaro 6" Figure,
1945. Store item by Multi Products, Chicago. -
$40 $110 $175

PCC-23. Geppetto Sitting 6" Figure,
1945. Store item by Multi Products, Chicago. -
$60 $150 $275

PCC-24   **PCC-25**
                              PCC-26

PCC-24. Geppetto Standing 6" Figure,
1945. Store item by Multi Products, Chicago. -
$40 $110 $175

PCC-25. Giddy 6" Figure,
1945. Store item by Multi Products, Chicago. -
$40 $80 $200

PCC-26. Jiminy Cricket 6" Figure,
1945. Store item by Multi Products, Chicago. -
$40 $110 $175

PCC-27

PCC-28

PCC-29

PCC-27. Jiminy Cricket United Fund 6" Figure,
1945. Store item by Multi Products, Chicago. -
$40 $125 $250

PCC-28. Lampwick 6" Figure,
1945. Store item by Multi Products, Chicago. -
$30 $100 $150

PCC-29. Pinocchio 6" Figure With Hands Down,
1945. Store item by Multi Products, Chicago. -
$40 $80 $200

PCC-30

PCC-31

PCC-32

PCC-30. Figaro 2" Figure,
1945. Store item by Multi Products, Chicago. -
$40 $125 $250

PCC-31. Geppetto 2" Figure,
1945. Store item by Multi Products, Chicago. -
$40 $110 $175

PCC-32. Giddy 2" Figure,
1945. Store item by Multi Products, Chicago. -
$40 $110 $175

PCC-33

PCC-34

PCC-33. Lampwick 2" Figure,
1945. Store item by Multi Products, Chicago. -
$40 $110 $175

PCC-34. Pinocchio 2" Figure,
1945. Store item by Multi Products, Chicago. -
$40 $80 $200

PCC-35

PCC-37

PCC-36

PCC-35. Pinocchio Silver Spoon Premium,
1940s. - **$20 $40 $75**

PCC-36. Tell The Truth Ring,
1954. Weather-Bird Shoes. Brass with rubber nose. -
$250 $375 $500

PCC-37. "Tell The Truth Club" Membership Card,
1954. Weather-Bird Shoes. - **$15 $25 $40**

PCC-38

PCC-39

PCC-40

PCC-38. Cardboard Punch-Out Puppet Sheets With Envelope,
1950s. Campbell's Pork and Beans plus "Rex Allen" names on mailer. Near Mint In Mailer - **$50**

PCC-39. "I've Seen Pinocchio At Hudson's" Cello. Button,
1950s. Sponsored by Detroit department store. -
$35 $75 $100

PCC-40. "United/Official Conscience" Litho. Button,
c. 1950s. United Way. - **$20 $40 $75**

POGO

Walt Kelly chose the Okefenokee Swamp as home for his characters making their debut in Animal Comics, which ran briefly in the early 1940s. The strip then ran in the New York Star in 1948 and moved to the New York Post and syndication in 1949. Pogo the wise possum and his contrary pal Albert the alligator thrived for more than 25 years, dealing with the eccentricities of a cast of characters that included such creatures as Howland Owl, Churchy-la-Femme the turtle, Beauregard the retired veteran bloodhound, Porky Pine, and P.T. Bridgeport the scheming bear. Comic books appeared in the 1940s and 1950s and Simon & Schuster published more than 30 Pogo books between 1951 and 1976. An animated cartoon aired on NBC in 1969 and an animated puppet film was produced by Warner Brothers in 1980. The strip was discontinued in 1975.

POG-1

POG-1. "Peter Wheat" Cut-Out Circus,
1951. Bakers Associates. Designed by Walt Kelly.
Near Mint Uncut - **$250**
Cut - **$40 $100 $150**

POG-2

POG-3

POG-2. "I Go Pogo" Litho. Button,
1952. 7/8" version, similar button issued for 1956. -
$5 $10 $18

POG-3. Pogomobile Kit,
1954. Store item published by Simon and Schuster. Cardboard assembly parts for ceiling mobile.
Near Mint In Envelope - **$250**

POG-4

POG-5

POG-4. 4" Diameter Litho. Button,
1956. Probably sent by Post-Hall Syndicate to newspapers carrying the strip. - **$35 $60 $100**

POG-5. "I Go Pogo" Litho. Button,
1956. 7/8" version. - **$8 $15 $25**

POG-6

POG-7

POG-8

POG-6. Walt Kelly Christmas Card,
1958. His own personal issue. Unsigned. - **$35 $75 $125**

POG-7. Walt Kelly Christmas Card,
1960. His own personal issue. Unsigned - **$35 $75 $125**

POG-8. Walt Kelly Christmas Card,
1961. His own personal issue. Unsigned - **$35 $75 $125**

POG-9

POG-10

POG-9. Cello. Button,
1968. One of 30 known designs with Walt Kelly facsimile signature on each. - **$10 $20 $40**

POG-10. Vinyl Figures,
1968. Poynter Products, distribution method unknown. Includes Beauregard, Albert, Churchy, Howland, Hepzibah, Pogo. Often missing are Pogo's hat and flowers, Churchy's fish on end of string. Each - **$50 $100 $150**

POG-11

POG-11. Vinyl Figures,
1969. Procter & Gamble. Six in set: Pogo, Beauregard Hound, Churchy La Femme, Howland Owl, Albert Alligator, Porky Pine. Each - **$5 $10 $15**

POG-13

POG-12

POG-12. Pogo Characters Plastic Mug Set,
1969. Procter & Gamble. Set of six: Pogo, Albert, Churchy, Porky Pine, Howland, Beauregard. Each - **$5 $10 $15**

POG-13. "Sunday Newsday" 2-1/2" Cello. Button,
1972. Long Island newspaper promotion. Further inscribed "Try It/You'll Like It". - **$35 $75 $150**

POLL-PARROT SHOES

Paul Parrot, owner of the Parrot Shoe Company, decided to christen his products Poll-Parrot Shoes in 1925. Extensive use of advertising and appropriate giveaways for boy and girl customers - carrying the parrot trademark - were successful marketing tools for the company's shoes and replacement parts. From 1947 to 1950 the company sponsored the *Howdy Doody* program on NBC television, resulting in a number of paper premiums and rings linking the puppet and the parrot.

POL-1

POL-2

POL-1. Litho. Tin Spinner Top With Wood Peg,
c. 1920s. - **$12 $20 $35**

POL-2. Litho. Tin Top with Wood Peg,
1930s. - **$8 $15 $25**

POL-3

POL-4   **POL-5**

POL-3. "Poll Parrot Shoe Money",
1930s. Various denominations and colors. - **$3 $5 $10**

POL-4. Litho. Tin Whistle,
1930s. - $**10 $20 $30**

POL-5. Litho. Tin Clicker,
1930s. - **$10 $15 $25**

POL-6   **POL-7**

POL-6. Litho. Tin Disk Spinner,
c. 1930s. - **$10 $18 $30**

POL-7. "Uncle Sam" Paper Over Tin Bank,
c. 1945. - **$25 $50 $75**

POL-9   **POL-10**

POL-8

POL-8. Flying Parrot Plastic Flicker Ring,
1950s. - **$20 $35 $50**

POL-9. "Poll-Parrot Shoes" Symbol Brass Ring,
c. 1950s. - **$20 $30 $40**

POL-10. "Poll-Parrot Shoes" Symbol Aluminum Ring,
c. 1950s. - **$20 $30 $40**

POPEYE

Popeye was introduced to the world in E.C. Segar's *Thimble Theatre* comic strip in 1929 and within a year was the strip's most popular character. The adventures of the spinach-chomping sailor, Olive Oyl, the hamburger-mooching Wimpy, Jeep, Swee'pea, and a host of other characters proved to be a phenomenal success. Comic book reprints appeared as early as 1931, and in 1933 the Fleischer Studios released the first of what would eventually add up to more than 450 animated cartoon shorts for theaters and television. A Popeye radio series aired on NBC and CBS from 1935 to 1938, sponsored by Wheatena (1935-1937) and Popsicles (1938). Early cartoon shorts were syndicated on television starting in 1956, new films were added in 1961, plus a further series from Hanna-Barbera on CBS in 1978. Robin Williams and Shelley Duvall starred in the 1980 Paramount film. The Popeye characters have been merchandised extensively since the 1930s.

PPY-1

PY-1. Character Painted Cast Iron Figurines,
1929. Store items. Each - **$60 $125 $200**

PPY-2

PY-2. "Popeye Comic" Gum Folders,
1933. Tattoo Gum by Orbit Gum Co. From numbered set.
Each - **$8 $15 $30**

PPY-3

PPY-4

PY-3. Pipe Toss Game,
1935. Store item by Rosebud Art Co. Also used as Popsicle premium. - **$30 $65 $100**

PY-4. "Penney's 'Back To School Days' With Popeye" Cello. Button,
1935. J. C. Penney Co. - **$10 $20 $30**

PPY-5

PPY-5. "Popeye The Sailor Man" 9x13" Cardboard Book Sign,
c. 1937. Grosset & Dunlap. - **$100 $200 $400**

PPY-6. Popsicle-Fudgsicle-Creamsicle 13x18" Cardboard Store Sign,
1938. Scarce. Pictures premiums and announces Popeye "On The Radio After May 1st". - **$100 $250 $400**

PPY-7

PPY-8

PPY-9

PPY-7. Bisque Toothbrush Holder,
1930s. Store item. Has moveable arm. - **$75 $150 $250**

PPY-8. Painted White Metal Lamp With Pipe,
1930s. Store item. - **$75 $150 $300**

PPY-9. Poll Parrot Shoes Photo Ad Card,
c. 1930s. Probable unauthorized use of Popeye character by local store owner. - **$12 $20 $30**

PPY-10

PPY-10. Enameled Metal Pin,
1930s. Wheatena cereal. Set of three: Popeye, Olive Oyl, Wimpy. Each On Card (Two Varieties) - **$75 $150 $300**
Popeye Pin - **$20 $40 $80**
Olive Pin - **$30 $60 $100**
Wimpy Pin - **$30 $60 $100**

PPY-11

PPY-12

PPY-13

PPY-18

PPY-19

PPY-11. Olive Oyl Enamel On Silvered Brass Pin,
1930s. Wheatena cereal.
On Card - **$75 $150 $300**
Pin Only - **$30 $60 $100**

PPY-12. Jeep Enamel On Brass Pin,
1930s. Apparent store item, similar to Wheatena giveaways
and used as premium by Popsicle. - **$75 $150 $250**

PPY-13. "New York Evening Journal" Club Card,
1930s. - **$8 $15 $30**

PPY-14

PPY-14. Theatre Club Card And Cello. Button,
1930s. Various theaters.
Button - **$10 $20 $35**
Card - **$15 $30 $50**

PPY-15

PPY-16

PPY-17

PPY-15. "I Yam Strong For King Comics" Cello. Button,
1930s. One of earliest buttons to advertise comic books. -
$15 $25 $40

PPY-16. "Sunday Examiner" Litho. Button,
1930s. From "50 Comics" set of various newspaper characters, match number to win prize. - **$20 $30 $60**

PPY-17. "S. F. Examiner" Litho. Button,
1930s. San Francisco newspaper. From set of various characters, match number to win prize. - **$20 $35 $65**

PPY-18. Wimpy Color Picture Silvered Brass Ring,
1930s. - **$25 $50 $75**

PPY-19. Coca-Cola Postcards With Wrapper,
1942. Set of four. Near Mint With Wrapper - **$90**
Each Card - **$5 $10 $15**

PPY-20

PPY-21

PPY-20. "Buy War Stamps" 14x18" Poster,
c. 1944. U.S. Government. - **$50 $100 $150**

PPY-21. Popeye Sailor's Cap,
1940s. Probable premium. - **$75 $125 $250**

PPY-22

PPY-23

PPY-22. Popeye 8x14" Diecut Cardboard Display,
1940s. Glows in dark and holds 12 Magic Nite Glo flashlights with whistles. Display Card - **$50 $100 $200**
Each Glow In Dark Flashlight - **$20 $40 $60**

PPY-23. "Sunshine Popeye Cookies" Cardboard Tab,
c. 1940s. - **$20 $45 $75**

PPY-24

PPY-25

PPY-24. Popeye Cello. Button,
1950s. Comes in 3-1/2" size and scarcer 1-3/4" size.
Larger Size - **$10 $20 $35**
Smaller Size - **$25 $50 $75**

PPY-25. Cloth/Vinyl Doll,
1950s. Store item by Gund Mfg. Co. - **$50 $80 $150**

PPY-26

PPY-26. "Crew Club" 16-Page Comic Booklets,
1989. Instant Quaker Oatmeal. Photo shows set of four
different plus one back. Each - **$3 $6 $12**

POPSICLE

Add some flavor and coloring to water, freeze it around a pair
of flat sticks, and the result is a Popsicle, a popular alterna-
tive to ice cream promoted as a frozen drink on-a-stick. In
addition to flavored ice, the producers created Popsicle Pete,
a comic book character that started on a long run in *All-
American Comics* in 1939. *The Popsicle Pete Fun Book*
(1947) and *Adventure Book* (1948) contained stories, games,
and cut-outs, and the company sponsored two short-lived
television variety shows: *The Popsicle Parade of Stars* on
CBS in 1950 and *Popsicle Five-Star Comedy* on ABC in
1957.

PSC-1

PSC-1. "Popsicle" Premium Sheet,
1937. - **$5 $12 $20**

PSC-2

PSC-3

PSC-2. "Jo-Lo Creamsicles" Waxed Paper Bag,
1930s. Popsicles with Joe Lowe Corp. copyright for various
local retailers. Bags were saved for gifts. - **$8 $12 $20**

PSC-3. "Adventurer's Popsicle Club" Litho. Button,
1930s. - **$8 $15 $25**

PSC-4

PSC-5

PSC-4. Paper Store Sign 9x19",
1946. - **$20 $35 $60**

PSC-5. Paper Store Sign 11x14",
1946. - **$30 $50 $75**

PSC-6

PSC-6. "Popsicle Pete Free Gift News",
1947. - **$15 $20 $35**

PSC-7

PSC-8

PSC-7. "Giant Gift List" Catalogue,
1949. - **$15 $25 $45**

PSC-8. "Popsicle Pete Jo-Lo-Fone",
1940s. Assembled Pair - **$15 $25 $40**

PSC-9

PSC-10

PSC-9. Popsicle Pete's "Mystery Box With Mystery Prize",
c. 1940s. Held prize and stick good for free Popsicle.
Complete - **$15 $30 $50**
Empty - **$8 $20 $30**

PSC-10. Cowboy Boot Plastic Ring,
1951. Popsicle. Top has magnifier lens, compass, secret compartment. Boot holds "Cowboy Ring Secret Code" symbols paper. - **$25 $50 $100**

PSC-11

PSC-12

PSC-11. "Giant Gift List" Sheet,
1953. For 1953-1954 premium offers. - **$15 $25 $45**

PSC-12. Abbott And Costello Paper Sign,
1954. 11x15". - **$20 $50 $100**

PSC-13

PSC-14

PSC-13. "Giant Gift List" Sheet,
1954. For 1954-1955 premium offers. - **$15 $25 $45**

PSC-14. "5 Star Comedy Party" 8x15" Paper Poster,
1957. For short-lived May-July ABC-TV program. -
$25 $50 $75

PORKY PIG

Porky Pig, one of the star cartoon characters created by the Warner Brothers studio in the 1930s, made his screen debut in 1935 and had his first feature role the following year. From then until the mid-1960s the stuttering little porker appeared in more than 100 cartoon shorts, frequently paired with Daffy Duck, Sylvester the cat, or his girlfriend Petunia. Porky went through several early design changes, and from 1937 on was given voice by Mel Blanc. Porky made his comic book debut in issue #1 of *Looney Tunes & Merrie Melodies* in 1941, had his own book by 1943, and over the years has appeared in numerous special issues and as a guest star in other Warner character books. On television the *Porky Pig Show* aired on ABC from 1964 to 1967 and *Porky Pig and His Friends* was syndicated to local stations starting in 1971. "Tha- Tha- That's All Folks!"

PRK-1

PRK-2

PRK-3

PRK-1. Bisque Bank,
c. 1936. Store Item - **$30 $75 $150**

PRK-2. "Porky's Book Of Tricks" Activity Booklet,
1942. K. K. Publications. - **$40 $120 $300**

PRK-3. "Petunia" Wood Jointed Doll,
1940s. Store item. - **$40 $75 $140**

PRK-4

PRK-4. Warner Bros. Character Place Mats,
c. 1940s. Probable store item. "Rhyme-A-Day Series" set of seven. Each - **$15 $30 $50**

PRK-5

PRK-5. Dell Comic Pictures,
1940s. Version in top hat with Warner Bros. copyright, second version Leon Schlesinger copyright.
Each - **$15 $30 $50**

PRK-6

PRK-6. "March Of Comics" #175,
1958. Various sponsors. - $3 $8 $15

POST CEREALS MISCELLANEOUS

Charles W. Post, a patient at Dr. John Kellogg's Battle Creek Sanitarium, was introduced to the benefits of a vegetarian diet in 1891. His enthusiasm for Kellogg's Caramel Coffee led him to develop his own formula and by 1895 he was marketing Postum Cereal Food Drink, a coffee substitute that "Makes Red Blood." Within two years he had created Grape-Nuts, a cold breakfast cereal that was also promoted as a health food. Post advertised his products as if they were medicines under the theme "There's a Reason." The company flourished, expanded, and took the name of General Foods in the late 1920s.

PST-1

PST-2

PST-1. Andy Gump Litho. Tin Ring,
1948. This and the next 11 rings are from the 1948 Post Raisin Bran set. The Near Mint price is for unbent examples with no rust. - $5 $15 $25

PST-2. Dick Tracy Litho. Tin Ring,
1948. - $20 $60 $100

PST-3

PST-4

PST-3. Harold Teen Litho. Tin Ring,
1948. - $5 $15 $25

PST-4. Herby Litho. Tin Ring,
1948. - $5 $15 $25

PST-5

PST-6

PST-5. Lillums Litho. Tin Ring,
1948. - $5 $15 $25

PST-6. Orphan Annie Litho. Tin Ring,
1948. - $10 $30 $50

PST-7

PST-8

PST-7. Perry Winkle Litho. Tin Ring,
1948. - $5 $15 $25

PST-8. Skeezix Litho. Tin Ring,
1948. - $5 $15 $25

PST-9

PST-10

PST-9. Smilin' Jack Litho. Tin Ring,
1948. - $10 $30 $50

PST-10. Smitty Litho. Tin Ring,
1948. - $5 $15 $25

PST-11

PST-12

PST-11. Smokey Stover Litho. Tin Ring,
1948. - $5 $15 $25

PST-12. Winnie Winkle Litho. Tin Ring,
1948. - $5 $15 $25

PST-13

PST-14

PST-13. Alexander Litho. Tin Ring,
1949. This and the next 23 rings are from the 1949 Post Toasties set. The Near Mint price is for unbent examples with no rust. - $5 $15 $25

PST-14. Blondie Litho. Tin Ring,
1949. - $5 $15 $25

PST-15

PST-16

PST-15. Captain Litho. Tin Ring,
1949. - $5 $15 $25

PST-16. Casper Litho. Tin Ring,
1949. - $5 $15 $25

PST-17

PST-18

PST-17. Dagwood Litho. Tin Ring,
1949. - $10 $30 $50

PST-18. Felix The Cat Litho. Tin Ring,
1949. - $20 $60 $100

PST-19

PST-20

PST-19. Flash Gordon Litho. Tin Ring,
1949. - **$20 $60 $100**

PST-20. Fritz Litho. Tin Ring,
1949. - **$5 $15 $25**

PST-21

PST-22

PST-21. Hans Litho. Tin Ring,
1949. - **$5 $15 $25**

PST-22. Henry Litho. Tin Ring,
1949. - **$5 $15 $25**

PST-23

PST-24

PST-23. Inspector Litho. Tin Ring,
1949. - **$5 $15 $25**

PST-24. Jiggs Litho. Tin Ring,
1949. - **$5 $15 $25**

PST-25

PST-26

PST-25. Little King Litho. Tin Ring,
1949. - **$10 $30 $50**

PST-26. Mac Litho. Tin Ring,
1949. - **$5 $15 $25**

PST-27

PST-28

PST-27. Maggie Litho. Tin Ring,
1949. - **$5 $15 $25**

PST-28. Mama Litho. Tin Ring,
1949. - **$5 $15 $25**

PST-29

PST-30

PST-29. Olive Oyl Litho. Tin Ring,
1949. - **$10 $30 $50**

PST-30. The Phantom Litho. Tin Ring,
1949. - **$20 $60 $100**

PST-31

PST-32

PST-31. Popeye Litho. Tin Ring,
1949. - **$20 $60 $100**

PST-32. Snuffy Smith Litho. Tin Ring,
1949. - **$10 $30 $50**

PST-33

PST-34

PST-33. Swee' Pea Litho. Tin Ring,
1949. - **$10 $30 $50**

PST-34. Tillie The Toiler Litho. Tin Ring,
1949. - **$5 $15 $25**

PST-35

PST-36

PST-35. Toots Litho. Tin Ring,
1949. - **$10 $30 $50**

PST-36. Wimpy Litho. Tin Ring,
1949. - **$10 $30 $50**

PST-37

PST-38

PST-37. "Turbo Jet Pilot" 3-1/2" Plastic Badge,
1949. Center has built-in siren whistle. - **$10 $30 $75**

PST-38. Sugar Crisp Order Form for Puppets (Handy, Dandy, Candy),
1953. Post Cereal. - **$10 $20 $30**

PST-39

ST-39 Sugar Crisp Puppets,
953. Cereal premium. Post Cereal. With accesories add
20 each. - **$10 $20 $40**

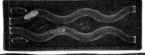

PST-40   **PST-41**

ST-40. Sugar Crisp Bears Mug & Bowl Set,
954. With instructions & mailer. Blue & Pink. Post Cereal. -
30 $50 $100

ST-41. Post Race Car Premium (Speed Town) with
Mailer,
950s. - **$30 $60 $90**

PST-42

ST-42. Football Booklet Set,
962. Each - **$2 $4 $8**

PST-43

ST-43. "Linus The Lion Fun Book" With Play Scene
Card,
964. Near Mint In Mailer - **$100**
Book Only - **$20 $40 $75**

POT O' GOLD

A thinly-disguised lottery radio show hosted by Horace Heidt and sponsored by Tums from 1939-1941 on NBC, although briefly revived for one season by ABC in 1946. A "Wheel of Fortune" was spun three times during each broadcast to determine: (1) a telephone directory from a random city, (2) a page from it, and (3) a specific home telephone number from that page. The number, then called by Heidt, rewarded the answerer $1,000 by Western Union. Obviously people listened in hopes of being selected, probably with no concept of the millions-to-one odds against it. The wheel selections were interspersed by musical entertainment by Heidt's Musical Knights. The show left the air as a result of a ruling by the Federal Communications Commission.

PGL-2

PGL-1

PGL-1. "Pot O' Gold" Game,
1939. Store item. Large 13x20 box reading "America's Newest Radio Game Craze As Played Over NBC Network". - **$40 $60 $100**

PGL-2. "Tums Pot-O-Gold" 3" Metal Pocket Flashlight,
c. 1939. Inscription continues "With Horace Heidt On Your Radio Thursday Night". - **$30 $60 $100**

(front)

(back)

PGL-3   **PGL-4**

PGL-3. Tums Metal Container With Show Logo,
c. 1939. Rare. - **$50 $100 $200**

PGL-4. Metal Pencil With Logo On Attached Cello.
Pencil Clip,
c. 1939. - **$25 $50 $100**

PRETTY KITTY KELLY

The story of a young Irish immigrant girl who arrived in New York with amnesia, no friends, and charged with murder, aired on CBS radio from 1937 to 1940. Kitty managed to make friends and had a number of spirited adventures during her three-year run. Continental Baking Company's Wonder bread and Hostess cupcakes were sponsors.

PKK-1   **PKK-2**

PKK-1. "Pretty Kitty Kelly" 12x17-1/2" Paper Store Sign,
c. 1937. Wonder Bread. - **$10 $15 $25**

PKK-2. "Pretty Kitty Kelly Balloon" 11x15" Paper Store
Sign,
c. 1937. Wonder Bread. - **$5 $8 $15**

PKK-3   PKK-4

PKK-3. "Kitty Kelly" Enameled Brass "Perfume Pin" On Card,
c. 1937. Wonder Bread. Complete - **$25 $40 $60**
Pin Only - **$10 $25 $40**

PPK-4. Cello. Button,
c. 1937. Columbia Broadcasting System. - **$3 $5 $8**

PULP MAGAZINE MISCELLANEOUS

Pictured is sampling of 1930s to 1940s membership cards. "Pulps" derived the name from inexpensive paper used for publication of fantasy and adventure magazines produced at low cost; very few pulps made the leap to producing a badge, ring or other premiums.

PUL-1   PUL-2

PUL-1. "Weird Tales Club" Member Card,
1930s. - **$50 $75 $150**

PUL-2. "Black Arts Club" Member Card,
1930s. - **$20 $40 $60**

PUL-3   PUL-4

PUL-3. "The Futuremen" Club Card,
1930s. Captain Future magazine. - **$20 $40 $60**

PUL-4. "The Lone Eagles Of America" Member Card,
1930s. Lone Eagle magazine. Back has club Ten Commandments. - **$20 $50 $75**

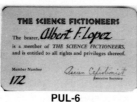

PUL-5   PUL-6

PUL-5. "Science Fiction League" Club Card With Metal Lapel Stud,
1930s. Thrilling Wonder Stories magazine.
Card - **$10 $25 $50**
Lapel Stud - **$15 $25 $50**

PUL-6. "The Science Fictioneers" Club Card,
1930s. Facsimile signature of executive secretary "Ascien Cefictionist". - **$10 $20 $30**

PUL-7

PUL-7. "Globe Trotters Club" Member Card,
1930s. Thrilling Adventures magazine. - **$15 $40 $70**

QUAKER CEREALS MISCELLANEOUS

The Quaker Oats Company got its start in 1877 when an oat meal processor named Henry D. Seymour opened his Quaker Mills Company in Ravenna, Ohio, and registered likeness of a somber Quaker as his trademark. The company was sold in 1879 and by 1890 was part of the giant American Cereal Company. With the Quaker as the symbol of its principal product, the company sold its rolled oats in cardboard boxes rather than in bulk, making it one of the first packaged foods. Heavy advertising and promotion - including cross-country trains distributing free samples - made Quaker Oats a national success. The company entered the cold cereal market with Puffed Wheat and Puffed Rice, "shot from guns." The Quaker logo was revised in 1945 and further modernized in 1971. This section shows Quaker premiums not associated with the many major characters they sponsored over the years.

QKR-1   QKR-2

QKR-1. Trade Card,
1883. - **$20 $40 $60**

QKR-2. "Quaker Rolled White Oats" Cello. Button,
c. 1905. - **$10 $20 $35**

QKR-3

**KR-3. Muffets Biscuits Humming Rocket Premium Sign
2x15",
**930s. - $40 $80 $160

QKR-4

**QKR-4. Muffets Biscuits Humming Rocket,
**930s. - $20 $40 $60

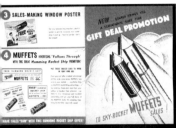

QKR-6

QKR-5

**QKR-5. Humming Rocket Ship Promo Manual,
**930s. - $30 $60 $90

**QKR-6. "Milton Berle's Jumbo Fun Book",
**940. Pre-TV era. - $5 $10 $20

QKR-7   QKR-8
                            QKR-9

**QKR-7. "Veronia Lake" Litho. Button,
**1948. Quaker Puffed Wheat & Rice. From set of 20 movie
stars, each including studio name in inscription.
Each - $5 $10 $15

**QKR-8. Lizabeth Scott Litho. Button,
**c. 1948. Similar to photographic set of 20 distributed in
America by Quaker Puffed Wheat & Rice but this is
Canadian version with line drawings and back inscription
"Quaker Puffed Wheat And Rice Sparkies." Eleven different
known, all marked "A PARAMOUNT STAR".
Each - $10 $20 $35

QKR-9. Plastic Mug,
c. 1950. - $5 $10 $15

QKR-10

QKR-10. "Space Flight To The Moon" Box Backs #1-5,
1953. Quaker Puffed Rice. From set of eight.
Each Complete Box - $35 $75 $150
Each Uncut Back - $10 $25 $40

QKR-11

QKR-12

QKR-11. Indian Picture Cards (18) & Mailer,
1950s. - $50 $90 $180

QKR-12. Indian Bead Rings with Mailer,
1962. Frosty-O's cereal premium. Rare. - $30 $60 $90

QUISP AND QUAKE

Quaker Oats Company introduced a pair of competing new
cereals in 1965 - Quisp, for quazy energy, and earthquake-
powered Quake. The Quisp character was a propeller-head-
ed pink alien who promoted "the biggest selling cereal from
Saturn to Alpha Centauri," and Quake was a spelunking
superhero in a hard hat and logging boots who could swim
through bedrock. Initial promotions included battery-operat-
ed helmets as premiums for grocers. Though the two cereals were virtually identical, Quake was dropped in the early
1970s, while Quisp still survives in selected areas.

QSP-1

QSP-2

QSP-1. "Adventures Of Quake And Quisp" Comic Book,
1965. - **$2** **$5** **$10**

QSP-2. Quisp Cloth Doll,
1965. - **$25** **$60** **$120**

QSP-3

QSP-4

QSP-3. Quake Cloth Doll,
1965. - **$25** **$60** **$100**

QSP-4. "Quisp Flying Saucer" With Instruction Sheet,
1966. Battery operated plastic toy.
Near Mint In Generic Box - **$300**
Saucer Only - **$50** **$125** **$200**

QSP-5

QSP-6

QSP-7

QSP-8

QSP-5. "Quisp Beanie",
1966. Battery operated plastic with turning propeller. -
$75 **$150** **$300**

QSP-6. Quisp Friendship Figural Plastic Ring,
1960s. Rare. - **$1000** **$1500** **$2000**

QSP-7. Space Disk Whistle Plastic Ring,
1960s. - **$250** **$375** **$500**

QSP-8. Meteorite Plastic Ring,
1960s. - **$250** **$375** **$500**

QSP-9

QSP-10

QSP-11

QSP-9. Space Gun Plastic Ring,
1960s. - **$250** **$375** **$500**

QSP-10. Quake Figural Plastic Ring,
1960s. - **$250** **$425** **$600**

QSP-11. Quake Volcano Plastic Ring,
1960s. - **$250** **$400** **$550**

QSP-12

QSP-13

QSP-12. Quake World Plastic Ring,
1960s. - **$750** **$1075** **$1400**

QSP-13. "Quazy Moon Mobile" Punch-Out Assembly Sheet,
c. 1960s. Assembly parts glow in the dark.
Complete/Unpunched - **$50** **$90** **$135**

QSP-14

QSP-15

QSP-14. Quisp Gyro Trail Blazer,
c. 1960s. - **$20** **$40** **$75**

QSP-15. Smoke Gun,
1960s. Plastic inscribed "Quisp" on each side. -
$75 **$175** **$300**

QSP-16

QSP-16. Cereal Box,
1985. Two panels have "Space Trivia" game parts.
Complete Box - **$10** **$15** **$30**

QUIZ KIDS

A panel of juvenile experts (from as young as 4 to as old as 16) answering questions submitted by listeners, the *Quiz Kids* had a successful 13-year run on network radio from 1940 to 1953. The program was heard initially on NBC, then on the Blue Network (1942-1946), and again on NBC (1946-1951) - sponsored throughout by Alka-Seltzer. For its final season it was sustained on CBS. The show was simulcast on television starting in 1949 and continued on NBC or CBS until 1953, sponsored by Alka-Seltzer (1949-1951) and Cat's Paws Soles (1952-1953). Show-business veteran Joe Kelly served as moderator and quizmaster. A brief television revival in 1956 was hosted by Clifton Fadiman.

QIZ-1

QIZ-1. "Quiz Kids" Game,
1940. Store item by Parker Brothers. - **$10 $15 $20**

QIZ-2

QIZ-3

QIZ-2. Photo Postcard,
c. 1949. Alka-Seltzer. - **$3 $6 $10**

QIZ-3. Photo Postcard,
c. 1949. Alka-Seltzer. - **$3 $6 $10**

QIZ-4

QIZ-5

QIZ-6

QIZ-4. Tin Badge,
1940s. - **$5 $12 $25**

QIZ-5. "Quiz Kids" Cello. Button,
1940s. - **$5 $8 $12**

QIZ-6. "Quiz Kids" Gold Finish Metal Figural Badge,
1940s. Quiz Kid figure suspends miniature metal book that
opens to pull-out paper listing questions and answers. -
$20 $40 $60

RADIO MISCELLANEOUS

Radio of the 1930s to early 1950s has little resemblance to the typical formats offered today's listeners. Newspapers and other periodicals could be perused as time or leisure allowed but radio program timing was firm if "live" household entertainment was desired. There was little casual listening, no lengthy spans of similar format. Program nature differed distinctively from one time slot to the next and the intervening commercial breaks could be as creative as the program itself. The earliest and infrequently offered radio premiums were usually tailored to adult listeners. The early 1930s ushered in premiums for youngsters - ever mindful that mom or other adult was still necessary for product purchase - and the subsequent flourishing of club badges, manuals, secret devices, etc. is a matter of record. This section is a sampling of shows, some admittedly obscure, whose sponsors issued at least one imaginative premium.

RAD-1

RAD-1. "Just Plain Bill" Puzzle With Mailer Envelope,
1933. Koloynos toothpaste. Puzzle pictures the three major
radio cast members.
Envelope - **$3 $5 $10**
Puzzle - **$10 $15 $25**

RAD-2

RAD-3

RAD-2. Congo Bartlett's "Ethiopia" 21x29" Paper Map,
1935. Karl's White Bread. - **$40 $75 $150**

RAD-3. Radio Explorers Club Kit,
1935. American-Bosch radios. Contents of certificate and
folder sheet that opens to 17x22" including picture of Captain
James P. Barker, master mariner and club commander.
Folder - **$15 $25 $35**
Certificate - **$10 $18 $30**

RAD-5

RAD-6

RAD-4

RAD-4. "Radio Explorers Club" Metal Globe,
c. 1935. American-Bosch, made by J. Chein Co. -
$25 $60 $90

RAD-5. "Mary Marlin" Cast Member Photo,
c. 1935. Pictured are Mary, Joe, Sally from "The Story Of
Mary Marlin" radio serial drama. - **$5 $10 $15**

RAD-6. Roi-Tan Cigars Contest Novelty,
1939. Miniature metal car with mounted litho. tin sign for contest offering 1939 Chevrolet daily prize with added inscription
for Sophie Tucker CBS radio show. - **$35 $100 $200**

RAD-7

RAD-7. "Voodoo Eye" Metal Pendant With Envelope,
1930s. Wheato-Nuts. Pendant designed as look-around
device. Envelope - **$50 $100 $125**
Pendant - **$75 $200 $300**

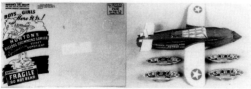

RAD-8

RAD-8. "Horton's Bulldog Drummond Bomber",
c. 1941. Cardboard punch-out that releases marble bombs
onto four small battleships.
Unused In Mailer - **$75 $150 $250**

RAD-10

RAD-9

RAD-9. "The Sea Hound" Paper Map,
1942. Blue Network. Pictures "Captain Silver's Sea Chart". -
$20 $40 $75

RAD-10. "David Harum" Seed Packets,
1943. Jermin Seed & Plant Co., Los Angeles. Contents are
actual flower seeds "Packed For Season Of 1943".
Each - **$5 $10 $15**

RAD-11

RAD-11. Big Brother Radio Kit with Mailer,
1945. KMBC radio, Kansas City, Kansas. - **$30 $60 $120**

RAD-12

RAD-12. "David Harum Handprint" Folder,
c. 1940s. Bab-o Cleanser. Cover pictures "Homeville" community and cast members, inside "Handprint" is apparent
clue to ongoing serial mystery. - **$10 $15 $25**

RAD-13

RAD-13. Big Jon Arthur & Sparkie Fan Card,
1950s. American Broadcasting Corp. - **$15** **$25** **$50**

THE RANGE RIDER

An early 1950s television weekly series, *The Range Rider* starred Jock Mahoney in the title role and Dick Jones as his youthful sidekick Dick West. The two wandered the West, apparently for the sole purpose of correcting local injustices. Both actors were accomplished stuntmen, a skill well displayed in each episode. The show was produced by Gene Autry's Flying A Productions and ran 1951-1953 on CBS-TV before syndication. Premiums were issued by bread companies in addition to non-premium coloring books and Dell comic books.

RAN-1

RAN-2

RAN-1. Langendorf Bread Photo,
. 1951. - **$8** **$15** **$30**

RAN-2. Sunbeam Bread "Range Rider's Brand" Cello. Button,
. 1951. Pictures Jock Mahoney. - **$20** **$50** **$75**

RAN-3

RAN-4

RAN-3. "TV Guide Cowboy Album" Celluloid Covered Wall Plaque,
953. From series of TV Guide promotional plaques sent to stations. - **$50** **$75** **$125**

RAN-4. Cello. Button 2-1/4",
950s. Peter Pan Bread. - **$25** **$65** **$90**

RAN-5

RAN-6

RAN-5. Philadelphia TV Program Promotion Card,
1950s. Pictures Jock Mahoney, Sally Starr and Gene Autry. Back has an offer for Oldsmobile "Wild West Fun And Game Booklet". - **$8** **$15** **$25**

RAN-6. ButterKrust Bread Label Folder,
1950s. Opens to 11x17" for mounting 16 labels. -
$25 **$50** **$75**

RANGER JOE

Ranger Joe Honnies began in 1939, a creation of Jim Rex for the Philadelphia area. A new owner extended distribution throughout the east and south, operating as Ranger Joe, Inc. from Chester, Pennsylvania, a suburb southwest of Philadelphia. Despite this limited Western exposure, the cereal box depicted him as an authentic cowboy with horse; glassware premiums of "Ranch Mug" and cereal bowl repeated his image plus cowboy scenes. The other known Ranger Joe premium is a wood and cardboard gun designed for shooting rubber bands. Product and premiums were apparently tied into local telecasts of *Ranger Joe*, a 1951-1952 NBC-TV Saturday morning adventure show for youngsters.

Rice Honnies joined the original Wheat Honnies product in 1951. Nabisco bought the company in 1954 replacing Ranger Joe with Buffalo Bee, changing Honnies to Honeys and initiating national distribution.

RJO-1

RJO-2

RJO-1. Rubber Band Cardboard Gun,
c. 1940s. - **$25** **$50** **$75**

RJO-2. Fan Card,
c. 1951. - **$8** **$12** **$20**

RJO-3

RJO-4

RJO-3. Glass Cup,
c. 1951. Blue & red. - **$5 $10 $15**

RJO-4. Glass Cereal Bowl,
c. 1951. Blue & red. - **$8 $15 $25**

RJO-5

RJO-6

RJO-5. Free Gift Coupon,
1952. - **$5 $8 $12**

RJO-6. "Wheat Honnies" Cereal Box,
1950s. Complete Box - **$35 $65 $100**

REDDY KILOWATT

The friendly little fellow with a lightbulb for a nose and a lightning-bolt torso was created in 1926 by A.B. Collins of the Alabama Power Company. Designed to personify the electric power industry, Reddy was licensed freely to local power companies for promotional use, and his image has adorned a wide variety of items from ashtrays to soap, pinback buttons to comic books. A competing figure, Willie Wiredhand, was created in 1950 by the National Rural Electric Cooperative.

RKL-1

RKL-2

RKL-3

RKL-1. Early Silvered Metal Badge With Red Accent,
c. 1938. - **$75 $150 $200**

RKL-2. Translucent Plastic Figure,
1940s. Earliest design style. Pink - **$85 $150 $250**
1950s-60s design style. Red - **$75 $125 $200**

RKL-3. "25th Anniversary Public Service" Cello. Button,
1951. Public Service Co. of New Hampshire. - **$20 $40 $75**

RKL-4

RKL-4. "Your Favorite Pin-Up" Enameled Brass Pin On Card,
1952. On Card - **$10 $15 $20**
Loose - **$3 $5 $10**

RKL-5

RKL-6

RKL-5. "Light's Diamond Jubilee" Cello. Button,
1954. - **$35 $75 $120**

RKL-6. Cuff Links,
c. 1950s. Color image under glass dome with brass frame and shaft. - **$20 $40 $75**

RKL-7

RKL-8

RKL-7. Cello. Button,
c. 1950s. Canadian. - **$20 $50 $80**

RKL-8. Plastic Cookie Cutter With Card,
c. 1950s. Boxed - **$10 $20 $35**
Loose - **$5 $15 $20**

RKL-9

RKL-10

KL-9. Glow-In-The-Dark Plastic Figure,
61. 1961 copyright on base. - **$50 $75 $125**

KL-10. "The Mighty Atom" Comic Book,
66. Back cover may designate sponsoring electric utility
mpany. - **$5 $15 $35**

RKL-13

RKL-11   **RKL-12**

KL-11. "Reddy" Composition Bobbing Head,
60s. - **$250 $400 $750**

KL-12. Employee Bowling Trophy,
60s. Metal figure and award plate on wood base. -
00 $1200 $2000

KL-13. "Courteous Personal Attention To Every
astomer" Litho. Button,
60s. - **$15 $25 $50**

RKL-14

KL-14. "Inspectors Club Big Rock Point Nuclear Plant",
70s. Consumers Power Company. - **$10 $15 $25**

RED RYDER

tist Fred Harman created the *Red Ryder* comic strip as a
nday feature in 1938 and added a daily version the follow-
 year. The strip, which ran until the late 1960s, told the
ry of rancher Ryder and his Navajo ward Little Beaver as
y ranged the West of the 1890s, battling bandits and
stlers and settling frontier quarrels. Comic book reprints
st appeared in 1939 and continued through most of the
50s, and more than 20 "B" Westerns from Hollywood
ronicled the popular hero's adventures. A radio series
ed on the Mutual network - primarily on the West Coast -
m early 1942 to 1949, sponsored by Langendorf bread
d other bakeries. A television adaptation was syndicated
1956. The Red Ryder character was used extensively for
any years to promote Daisy air rifles.

RYD-1

RYD-1. Red Ryder Target Game with Box,
1939. Store item. - **$100 $200 $400**

RYD-2

RYD-2. "Daisy Air Rifles" Catalogue,
1940. Near Mint In Mailer - **$250**
Loose - **$50 $125 $175**

RYD-4

RYD-3

RYD-3. Victory Patrol Member Card,
1943. Back has Red Ryder radio listings. - **$20 $40 $60**

RYD-4. Victory Patrol Cardboard Luminous Badge,
1943. Scarce. Design glows in dark. - **$50 $150 $300**

RYD-5

RYD-5. Instructions for Glow-in-Dark Victory Patrol Badge,
1943. Scarce. - **$30 $60 $120**

RYD-6

RYD-6. "Rodeomatic Radio Decoder",
c. 1943. Rare. From "Victory Patrol" kit.
Unpunched - **$100 $300 $600**
Punched - **$100 $300 $500**

RYD-7

RYD-7. Victory Patrol Comic Book Kit,
1944. Scarce. Includes membership card, map, comic book, code card and regular cards. Complete - **$350 $1075 $3200**

RYD-8

RYD-9

RYD-8. "Victory Patrol" Paper Store Signs,
1944. Scarce. Langendorf Bread. Larger sign 7x15", smaller oval 4x5". Picture Sign - **$50 $125 $200**
Oval Sign - **$20 $40 $75**

RYD-9. "Red Ryder Victory Patrol" Copper Luster Metal Badge,
1944. - **$35 $65 $125**

RYD-10   RYD-11

RYD-10. "Bobby Blake/Little Beaver" Dixie Ice Cream Picture,
1945. - **$15 $25 $40**

RYD-11. Plastic Horse Statue,
c. 1947. Saddle inscribed "Red Ryder" on each side. Believed to be one of 100 second place prizes in glove selling contest sponsored by Wells Lamont Corp., maker of Red Ryder gloves. - **$50 $90 $175**

RYD-12

RYD-12. "Daisy Handbook No. 2",
1948. - **$35 $100 $250**

RYD-14

RYD-13

RYD-13. Salesman's Fiberboard Glove Case,
1940s. Wells-Lamont Co. - **$100 $200 $300**

RYD-14. Pocketknife,
1940s. Store item by Camco USA. Steel with plastic grips.
$75 $150 $250

RYD-15

RYD-16   RYD-17

YD-15. Radio Sponsor Handbill,
940s. N.B.C. Bread, probably others. Imprint includes local
roadcast times. - **$35 $60 $100**

YD-16. "Red Ryder" Cello. Button,
940s. - **$15 $30 $50**

YD-17. "Little Beaver" Cello. Button,
940s. - **$15 $30 $50**

RYD-18   RYD-19   RYD-20

YD-18. "Red Ryder Patrol" Silvered Metal Badge,
940s. - **$30 $50 $100**

YD-19. "I Have Entered The Red Ryder Pony Contest"
tho. Button,
940s. - **$8 $15 $25**

YD-20. Penney's "Red Ryder Lucky Coin",
940s. J. C. Penney Co. Brass, holed for keychain. Back
ogan "Penney's For Super Value". - **$8 $12 $20**

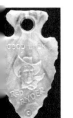

RYD-21   RYD-22   RYD-23

YD-21. "Good Luck/Red Ryder" Plastic Arrowhead
eychain Charm,
940s. Daisy Mfg. Co. - **$35 $80 $160**

YD-22. "Red Ryder Gloves" Silvered Tin Whistle,
940s. Wells-Lamont Co. - **$35 $75 $135**

YD-23. "Red Ryder Gloves/Red Ryder Sheriff" Silvered
etal Star Badge,
940s. Probable Wells-Lamont Co. - **$50 $100 $165**

RYD-24   RYD-25

RYD-24. Red Ryder/Little Beaver Fan Card,
c. 1950. Fred Harman art. - **$10 $20 $35**

RYD-25. Trading Cards Sheet,
1952. Wells-Lamont Corp. Uncut. - **$15 $25 $40**

RYD-26

RYD-26. "Daisy Gun Book",
1955. Daisy Mfg. Co. - **$20 $40 $75**

RENFREW OF THE MOUNTED

Inspector Douglas Renfrew of the Royal Canadian Mounties, the hero of a dozen adventure novels by Laurie York Erskine, came to CBS radio in 1936. Sponsored by Wonder bread for two years, the series then moved to the Blue network, where it was sustained until it went off the air in 1940. Renfrew movies, produced by Grand National Pictures and Monogram in the late 1930s and early 1940s, were edited into 30-minute tales for television syndication in 1953. While he lasted, the strong, silent Renfrew always got his man.

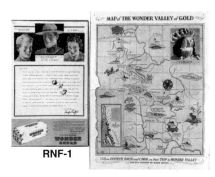

RNF-1

RNF-1. "Renfrew Of The Mounted" 17x22" Premium Map,
1936. Wonder Bread. - **$40 $75 $125**

RNF-2
RNF-3

RNF-2. "Lost Wonder Valley Of Gold" Map Order Postcard,
1936. Wonder Bread. Used to order previous item. - **$10 $20 $30**

RNF-3. "Around The Camp Fire With Carol And David" Leaflet,
c. 1936. Wonder Bread. Illustrated magic tricks including "Tricks That Fooled Renfrew". - **$12 $20 $30**

RNF-4

RNF-4. Fan Postcard,
c. 1936. Wonder Bread. - **$20 $40 $65**

RNF-5

RNF-6

RNF-5. Wonder Bread Radio Show Paper Sign 10x17",
c. 1936. - **$50 $100 $200**

RNF-6. "Renfrew Of The Mounted" Cello. Button,
c. 1936. Wonder Bread. - **$3 $6 $10**

RIN-TIN-TIN

The Wonder Dog was introduced to the world by Warner Brothers in 1923 and the talented German shepherd, an instant success, proved to be the studio's first major film star. There were a number of Rintys over the years, but the canine hero consistently battled villains and the elements, rescued those in danger, preserved his good name, turned into a noteworthy "actor" - and saved the studio from bankruptcy. Rinty starred in 19 films for Warner Brothers between 1923 and 1930, and went on to make a series of chapter plays for the Mascot studios.

On radio, *Rin-Tin-Tin* aired on the Blue network (1930-1933) and CBS (1933-1934), sponsored by Ken-L-Ration, and returned for a season on the Mutual network in 1955, sponsored by Milk Bone.

On television, Rinty joined young Corporal Rusty and the troopers of the 101st Cavalry, the Fighting Blue Devils, in maintaining law and order in the West of the 1880s. The hit series, sponsored by the National Biscuit Company, aired in

prime time on ABC from 1954 to 1959 and was the source of a wide variety of premiums and licensed products. Reruns were broadcast on ABC (1959 to 1961) and CBS (1962 to 1964), and sepia-tinted episodes were offered briefly for syndication in 1976. Comic books appeared during most of the 1950s and early 1960s.

RIN-1

RIN-2

RIN-3

RIN-1. "The Lone Defender" Cello. Button,
1930. For Mascot Pictures 12-chapter movie serial. - **$15 $25 $40**

RIN-2. "The Lightning Warrior" Movie Serial Cello. Button,
1931. Mascot Pictures. Comes in 7/8" or 1-1/4" sizes. - **$15 $25 $40**

RIN-3. Ken-L-Ration Photo,
1931. - **$8 $12 $20**

RIN-4

RIN-5

RIN-4. "What Every Dog Should Know" Booklet,
c. 1931. Ken-L-Ration. - **$12 $20 $35**

RIN-5. Advertising Litho. Button,
1930s. Atwater Kent Radios. - **$25 $50 $75**

RIN-6

RIN-6. Club Membership Kit,
1954. Nabisco. Includes fabric banner, membership card, white metal badge.
Complete Near Mint - **$400**
Banner - **$60 $100 $200**
Card - **$10 $25 $50**
Badge - **$20 $50 $75**

RIN-7

IN-7. Stereo Cards With Viewer,
954. Nabisco. Set of 24 cards.
iewer - **$10 $20 $35**
ard Set - **$30 $50 $80**

RIN-9

RIN-8

RIN-10

IN-8. Nabisco "Wonda-Scope",
1954. Components include compass, mirror, magnifying
nses. Dial marked "Rin-Tin-Tin". - **$20 $40 $75**

IN-9. "Bugle Calls" Vinyl Cardboard Record,
1954. Nabisco. Came with plastic bugle premium. -
5 **$25 $40**

IN-10. Felt Cavalry Hat,
1954. Nabisco. Fabric patch on brim front. -
0 **$100 $150**

RIN-11

RIN-12

RIN-13

N-11. Magic Brass Ring,
1954. Nabisco. Portrait cover opens over two miniature felt
ds. Came with magic pencil and chemically treated paper
ps. Complete - **$250 $500 $750**
g Only - **$115 $230 $350**

N-12. Nabisco Plastic Rings,
55. Set of 12, various characters. Each - **$10 $15 $20**

N-13. Nabisco Cast Photo,
1955. - **$10 $18 $25**

RIN-14

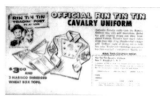

RIN-15

RIN-14. English Postcard,
c. 1955. - **$10 $20 $30**

RIN-15. Nabisco Box Insert Cards,
1956. At least 12 different examples. Each - **$3 $6 $12**

RIN-16

RIN-17

RIN-16. "Rusty" Tin/Plastic Palm Puzzle,
1956. From "Nabisco Juniors" set of 12. - **$5 $10 $15**

RIN-17. Gun And Holster,
1956. Nabisco. Includes gun and leather holster with belt and
buckle. Belt - **$20 $40 $75**
Holster - **$30 $60 $150**
Gun - **$50 $100 $200**

RIN-18

RIN-18. Leather Belt With Metal Buckle,
1956. Complete - **$20 $40 $75**
Buckle Only - **$10 $20 $35**

RIN-19

RIN-20

RIN-19. Plastic Mug,
1956. - **$15 $25 $40**

RIN-20. Plastic Cup,
1956. - **$15 $25 $40**

RIN-21

RIN-22

RIN-23

RIN-21. Cavalry Rifle Ballpoint Pen,
1956. Nabisco. Near Mint In Mailer - **$50**
Rifle Pen Only - **$8 $15 $25**

RIN-22. Cast Member Photo,
c. 1956. - **$8 $12 $20**

RIN-23. Color Litho. Button,
c. 1956. Sent to participants in Nabisco's 'Name The Puppy
Contest.' - **$5 $12 $20**

RIN-24

RIN-25

RIN-26

RIN-24. Miniature Plastic Telegraph Set,
c. 1956. Nabisco. Tapper key makes clicking sound. -
$10 $15 $25

RIN-25. "101st Cavalry" Plastic Canteen With Strap,
1957. Nabisco. - **$10 $20 $35**

RIN-26. Plastic On Steel Pocketknife,
c. 1957. Store item. - **$25 $60 $100**

RIN-27

RIN-27. Totem Pole Plastic Punch-Outs,
1958. Nabisco. Set of eight. Each Unpunched - **$5 $10 $15**

RIN-28

RIN-28. Insignia Patch,
1958. Nabisco, paper peel-off stickers. Set of seven.
Each Unused - **$3 $5 $10**

RIN-29

RIN-29. Plush And Vinyl Toy Dog,
1959. Smile Novelty Co. Store item, about 15" long. -
$40 $80 $160

RINGS MISCELLANEOUS

...ds love to wear rings, and the sponsors of radio programs ...nd their merchandisers, particularly cereal makers, learned ...at offering a ring related to their heroes was sure to bring in ...flood of box tops. Hardly a radio character in the 1930s ...nd 1940s could get through a season without a special ring ...emium offer. There were rings with secret compartments, ...ow-in-the-dark rings, flashlight rings, magnifying-glass ...ngs, whistle rings, saddle rings, compass rings, magnet ...ngs, rocket rings, decoder rings, baseball rings, movie ...ngs, microscope rings, treasure rings, cannon rings, weath-...rings, and membership rings, along with rings bearing ...otos, faces, and logos. Collecting premium rings has ...come a specialty of its own.

RGS-1   RGS-2   RGS-3

...GS-1. "Kewpie" Sterling Silver Ring,
...1920s. Store item. Depicts single Kewpie with raised ...nds and kicking one foot. - $75 $110 $150

...GS-2. "Rosalie Gimple" Brass Ring,
...36. Rare. Pabst-ett cheese food. Depicts air hostess. -
...25 $210 $300

...GS-3. "Huskies Club" Brass Ring,
...37. Post's Huskies Cereal. Top depicts discus thrower,
...nds picture various sports equipment. - $300 $450 $600

 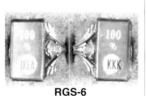

RGS-5   RGS-6

RGS-4

...S-4. "Murray-Go-Round Ring" Folder,
...37. Radio sponsor Fleischmann's Yeast. - $20 $40 $60

...S-5. "Murray-Go-Round" Brass Spinner Ring,
...37. Fleischmann's Yeast for Arthur Murray Dance Studios.
...k pictures male dancer on one side, female on other.
...ey appear to unite in dance when disk is spun. -
...0 $150 $200

...S-6. Ku Klux Klan,
...0s. Organizational ring, not radio related. Moving the ring
...nges letters in cut-out window from "USA" to "KKK". -
...0 $350 $500

RGS-7   RGS-8   RGS-9

RGS-7. Kool-Aid "Treasure Hunt" Brass Ring,
1930s. - $100 $150 $200

RGS-8. Chicago "Cubs" Gold Luster Metal Ring,
1930s. Cubs name accented in blue, bands have baseball motifs. - $100 $175 $250

RGS-9. Lucky Sheik Brass Ring,
1930s. Catalogue item from Johnson & Smith Novelty Co. Coiled snake design around Pharoh's head plus tiny accent stones. - $75 $110 $150

RGS-10   RGS-11   RGS-12

RGS-10. "Junior Broadcasters Club" Brass Ring,
1930s. Top depicts radio microphone, bands depict radio transmission towers. - $50 $100 $150

RGS-11. Viking Magnifying Ring,
1941. Rare. Kellogg's All Rye Flakes. Brass with magnifying glass to view Prince "Valric Of The Vikings". Very limited distribution. - $1750 $3500 $7500

RGS-12. Pirate's Gold Ore Detector Ring,
1947. Quaker Cereals. Brass with aluminum/plastic telescope viewer holding tiny gold flakes. Documentation associating this ring with Terry and the Pirates has not been seen. - $50 $100 $150

RGS-13   RGS-14

RGS-13. "His Nibs Compass Ring" On Card,
1947. Nabisco. Ring - $15 $25 $60
Card - $20 $40 $60

RGS-14. Roger Wilco Rescue Ring,
1948. Power House Candy. Brass base with glow-in-dark plastic top over brass whistle. - $115 $190 $250

RGS-15   RGS-16

RGS-15. Roger Wilco Magni-Ray Brass Ring,
1948. Power House candy bar. Paper insert under hinged cover glows in dark. - $30 $50 $75

RGS-16. F-87 Super Jet Plane Ring.
1948. Kellogg's Corn Flakes. Black plastic plane on nickel-plated ring. Advertised on Superman radio program but no other association. Ring - $125 $190 $250
Instructions - $125 $135 $150

RGS-17 **RGS-18** **RGS-19**

RGS-17. Jet Plane Ring,
1948. Kellogg's Pep. Brass bands, metal airplane shoots off ring by spring lever. Advertised on Superman radio program but no other association. - **$125 $190 $250**

RGS-18. Fireball Twigg Explorer's Ring,
1948. Post Cereals. Brass bands hold glow-in-dark plastic sundial under clear plastic dome. - **$50 $100 $150**

RGS-19. "Ted Williams Baseball Ring" Newspaper Ad,
1948. Nabisco Shredded Wheat. - **$10 $20 $30**

RGS-21 **RGS-23**

RGS-20 **RGS-22**

RGS-20. "Ted Williams" Mechanical Ring,
1948. Nabisco. Plastic batter figure moves by spring in brass base. - **$300 $610 $925**

RGS-21. "Andy Pafko" Baseball Scorer Brass Ring,
1949. Muffetts cereal. Named for Chicago Cubs star, top has three turning wheels for counting balls, outs, strikes. - **$75 $155 $235**

RGS-22. "Scorekeeper Baseball Ring" Order Blank,
1949. Mechanical ring featuring Andy Pafko of Chicago Cubs. - **$15 $25 $40**

RGS-23. Baseball Game Mechanical Ring,
1949. Kellogg's. Silvered metal capped by diamond-shaped plastic compartment with lever action for game of miniature palm puzzle nature. - **$75 $155 $235**

RGS-24 **RGS-25** **RGS-27**

RGS-26

RGS-24. Your Name Ring,
1949. Kellogg's Rice Krispies. Brass bands with good luck symbols hold plastic dome over paper with personalized first name designated by orderer. - **$20 $35 $50**

RGS-25. Glow-In-Dark "Flying Tigers Rescue Ring",
c. 1949. Red plastic base with glow-in-dark top featuring secret compartment holding tiny brass whistle. - **$75 $110 $150**

RGS-26. "Flying Tiger Rescue Ring" Leaflet,
c. 1949. Power House candy bar. - **$20 $40 $60**

RGS-27. Bazooka Joe Brass Initial Ink Stamp Ring,
1940s. Bazooka Joe Gum. Personalized by rubber stamp single initial designated by orderer. - **$60 $100 $150**

RGS-28 **RGS-29** **RGS-30** **RGS-31**

RGS-28. "Billy West Club" Silvered Brass Ring,
1940s. Depicts cowboy on horseback. - **$50 $110 $175**

RGS-29. (Buffalo) Bill Jr. Brass Ring,
1940s. Depicts bucking horse, holster gun, buffalo on top. - **$30 $45 $60**

RGS-30. Cap-Firing Brass Ring,
1940s. Store item. Cover snaps down to fire single cap. - On Card - **$65**
Loose - **$12 $15 $20**

RGS-31. Glow-In-Dark Whistle Ring,
c. 1940s. Rare. Probable candy sponsor. Very similar to Ki. atom bomb ring but varies by glow white plastic cap, whist element is aluminum. - **$300 $800 1500**

RGS-32 **RGS-33** **RGS-34**

RGS-32. Basketball Action Brass Ring,
1940s. Scarce. Holds back board with tiny hoop and chain basketball to throw through it. - **$75 $150 $300**

RGS-33. "Joe DiMaggio Sports Club" Member Card,
1940s. M&M's Candies. Probably came with club ring. - **$25 $40 $75**

RGS-34. "Joe DiMaggio Sports Club" Brass Ring,
1940s. Scarce. M & M's candies. Bands have club name a picture sports equipment. - **$200 $300 $400**

RGS-35 **RGS-37** **RGS-38**

RGS-36

RGS-35. Knights Of Columbus Secret Compartment Glow-In-Dark Metal Ring,
1940s. Rare. Same base as Green Hornet version except initials "GH" altered to "HG" (Holy Ghost). - **$750 $2000 $3750**

RGS-36. "Red Goose Shoes" Glow-In-Dark Secret Compartment Ring,
c. 1940s. Metal and plastic with swing-out disk over paper label in glow compartment. - **$115 $170 $225**

RGS-37. Skelly Oil Co. Red Checkmark Brass Ring,
1940s. Top has stamped-in red enameled checkmark, possible Captain Midnight association but no documentation seen. - **$75 $135 $200**

RGS-38. Sundial Brass Ring,
c. 1950. Sundial Shoes. Top has plastic dome over sundial. - **$30 $45 $60**

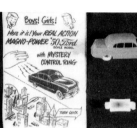

RGS-39   RGS-40

RGS-39. "Magno-Power '50 Ford Mystery Control" Ring With Instruction Slip,
1950. Kellogg's Pep. Magnetized plastic ring and car.
Ring - **$200 $250 $300**
Instructions - **$75 $90 $100**

RGS-40. Ralston Wheat Chex "Magic Pup" Ring,
1951. Magnet ring moves pup's magnetized head.
Complete - **$60 $90 $120**

RGS-41

RGS-42   RGS-43

RGS-41. Rocket-To-The-Moon Ring,
1951. Kix cereal. Brass bands with plastic top for launching three glow-in-dark rockets.
Ring Only - **$200 $400 $600**
Each Rocket Near Mint - **$200**

RGS-42. "The Range Rider" Aluminum Ring With Paper Tag,
c. 1951. Tag names TV show title produced by Autry Flying A Productions. Near Mint With Tag - **$550**
No Tag - **$75 $135 $200**

RGS-43. Quaker Cereals "Crazy Rings" Set,
1957. Set of 10 plastic rings of assorted nature.
Near Mint In Mailer - **$350**
Each - **$12 $20 $30**

RGS-46

RGS-44

RGS-45

RGS-44. "Jets Super Space Ring",
c. 1950s. Ball-Band. One of the few rings that actually decodes. Near Mint In Package - **$40**
Assembled - **$12 $20 $30**

RGS-45. "U.S. Keds" Space Symbols Silvered Brass Ring,
c. 1962. Keds footwear. Depicts "K" space capsule, band has atomic symbol. - **$50 $80 $110**

RGS-46. Old West Trail Club Kit,
1968. Old West Trail Foundation. Includes map, member card, ring. Complete Near Mint - **$125**
Ring Only - **$25 $50 $80**

RGS-47   RGS-48   RGS-49

RGS-47. "Cousin Eerie" Brass Ring,
1969. Warren Publishing Co., publisher of Eerie Comics. - **$30 $45 $60**

RGS-48. "Uncle Creepy" Gold Finish Metal Ring,
1969. Warren Publishing Co., publisher of Eerie Comics. - **$100 $150 $200**

RGS-49. P.F. Magic Decoder Ring With Card,
1960s. P.F. footwear. Also used as Jonny Quest premium. Gold plastic ring with several functions.
Card - **$10 $20 $30**
Ring - **$20 $30 $40**

RGS-50   RGS-51

RGS-50. Ralston "Chex's Agent" Decoder Ring,
c. 1960s. Plastic base topped by two cardboard dials. -
$5 $7 $10

RGS-51. "Wonder" Bread Loaf Plastic Ring,
c. 1970s. - **$5 $7 $10**

RIPLEY'S BELIEVE IT OR NOT!

Robert L. Ripley's Believe It or Not! started life as a newspaper cartoon for the New York Globe in 1919 and was ultimately syndicated in as many as 300 newspapers. The focus was on bizarre or freakish events and people and human oddities, all of which, Ripley claimed, could be substantiated. In 1930 he took the show to radio, where it aired in various formats on NBC or CBS for 18 years. Sponsors included Colonial Oil, Esso, General Foods, Royal Crown Cola and Pall Mall cigarettes. A television version ran on NBC in 1949-1950, with other hosts after Ripley's death in 1949 and resurfaced on CBS in 1982 with Jack Palance as host. Collections were published in book form around 1930 and as comic books in the 1960s.

RPY-1

RPY-1. "Disk-O-Knowledge" Cardboard Diecut Mechanical Wheel,
1932. Oddities appear in diecut openings on both sides. -
$10 $20 $30

RPY-2

RPY-2. "Electronic Flash" Quiz Game,
1933. Store item by Meccano Co. Battery operated. -
$20 $40 $60

RPY-3

RPY-3. "Odditorium" Exhibit Souvenir,
1936. From Texas Centennial exposition. Booklet and 12 postcards. Set - **$25 $50 $90**

RPY-4   RPY-5

RPY-4. Oddities Fabric Bandanna,
1930s. - **$8 $15 $25**

RPY-5. "Believe It Or Not/Ripley" Diecut Metal Miniature Charm,
1930s. Usually in green antiqued copper finish. -
$10 $20 $35

RPY-6

RPY-7

RPY-6. Oddities Fold-Out Card,
1940. Various local sponsors as Christmas premium. Opens to 13x19" sheet illustrated on both sides. - **$15 $35 $60**

RPY-7. Cardboard Ink Blotters,
1948. Various local sponsors. Examples from monthly series dated October, November, December. Each - **$5 $10 $15**

ROCKY JONES, SPACE RANGER

his early television space opera was two years in preparation and survived only one season of 39 episodes before it as syndicated. The series premiered in December 1953 on NXT in Los Angeles, in February 1954 on WNBT in New ork, and late in 1954 on WBKB in Chicago. Richard Crane 'ayed Rocky, chief of a 21st century security patrol force harged with maintaining peace in the galaxies. Silvercup read was a sponsor, and Space Ranger toys, uniforms, and omic books were licensed to promote the series.

RKJ-1

RKJ-2

KJ-1. Two Stills,
1954. Each - **$5** **$12** **$25**

KJ-2. Color Photo,
1954. Possible school tablet cover. - **$10** **$20** **$30**

RKJ-4

RKJ-3

KJ-3. "Official Space-Ranger" Metal Wings Pin On rd,
1954. Space Rangers Enterprises.
Card - **$12** **$20** **$30**
ose - **$8** **$12** **$20**

KJ-4. Cardboard Rubber Band Gun,
1954. Johnston Cookies And Crackers. - **$15** **$30** **$75**

RKJ-5

RKJ-6

J-5. "Johnston Cookies" Litho. Button,
954. Also comes with "Silvercup Bread" imprint. -
D **$20** **$35**

J-6. Silvercup Bread Litho. Button,
954. - **$10** **$20** **$35**

ROCKY LANE

Harold Albershart (1904-1973), as Allan Rocky Lane, was a longtime actor in adventure films. He made dozens of "B" Westerns, Royal Mountie serials, and jungle epics for Republic Pictures between 1938 and 1961. Lane took over the film role of Red Ryder around 1944 and continued as a star for the studio into the 1950s. *Rocky Lane* comic books were published between 1949 and 1959, and Lane was the television voice of Mr. Ed, the talking horse, from 1961 to 1965.

RLN-1

RLN-2

RLN-1. "Allan 'Rocky' Lane" Cello. Button,
c. 1950. Store item. - **$10** **$20** **$30**

RLN-2. "Member 'Rocky' Lane Posse" Decal Club Patch,
c. 1950. Rare. Patch - **$50** **$150** **$300**
Mailer - **$25** **$50** **$100**

RLN-3

RLN-4

RLN-3. "Rocky Lane Posse" Cello. Button,
c. 1950. - **$50** **$100** **$150**

RLN-4. Dixie Ice Cream Picture,
c. 1952. - **$8** **$15** **$25**

ROOTIE KAZOOTIE

Who is the lad who makes you feel so glad? He was Rootie Kazootie, the little puppet hero who became a giant hit in children's television. The series, known initially as *The Rootie Tootie Club* when it debuted locally in New York in 1950, changed its name to *The Rootie Kazootie Club* and was broadcast nationally on NBC (1951-1952) and ABC (1952-1954). Other puppet charcters were Polka Dottie, El Squeako Mouse, the villainous Poison Zoomack, and the pup Little Nipper, who became Gala Poochie when RCA dropped out as a sponsor. Todd Russell served as host, and Mr. Deetle Doodle, the silent policeman, was the only other human to appear. Sponsors, in addition to RCA, included Coca-Cola, Power House candy, and Silvercup bread. *Rootie Kazootie* comic books were published in the early 1950s.

ROO-1   ROO-2

ROO-1. "Rootie Kazootie Stars" Puppet Punch-Outs,
c. 1952. Coca-Cola. Set of five. Each Unpunched -
$12 $20 $40

ROO-2. "Rootie Kazootie Stars" Animated Punch-Outs,
c. 1952. Coca-Cola. Set of five. Each Unpunched -
$12 $20 $40

ROO-3

ROO-3. "Rootie Kazootie Rooters Club" Membership Card,
c. 1952. - **$10 $20 $35**

ROO-4   ROO-5

ROO-6

ROO-4. Club Member Litho. Button,
c. 1952. Color (6 characters) or black/white (5 characters) versions. Each - **$5 $12 $20**

ROO-5. "Rootie Kazootie's Lucky Spot" Embossing Ring,
c. 1952. Designed to emboss title and four-leaf clover image on paper. - **$250 $500 $750**

ROO-6. "Rootie Kazootie Rooter" Glow-In-Dark Plastic Disk,
c. 1952. Back has pin fastener. - **$20 $35 $60**

ROSCOE TURNER

A real-life aviator hero and successful aviation entrepeneur, Col. Roscoe Turner was idolized in the 1930s much like cowboy fans adored Tom Mix. Turner was a barnstormer flyer and stunt performer of the 1920s following the start of his air career in the Balloon Service during World War I. He was the major test pilot for the DC-2 (Douglas Commercial) first passenger transport aircraft in 1934. In the latter 1930s, his frequent winning of the Thompson Trophy and Bendix Trophy for speed events at annual National Air Races enthralled a nation of speed fans. His enterprises included a passenger run from Los Angeles to Reno to Las Vegas and

return, called by some the "Alimony Special" circuit due to frequent use by movie stars. Turner's popularity promoted premiums by several sponsors, notably Gilmore Oil, H. J. Heinz and Wonder Bread (see Sky Blazers). Probably his best remembered gimmick was for Gilmore Oil Co. An actual African lion - a Gilmore trademark lookalike - was acquired and flew with Turner throughout the United States, Canada and Mexico. Despite insistence by humane agencies that the lion be equipped with a parachute, Turner and his lion were welcomed everywhere until the lion died of old age and natural causes.

RTU-1

RTU-1. Flying Corps Certificate,
1934. Heinz Rice Flakes. - **$20 $30 $50**

RTU-2

RTU-2. Membership Card with Mailer,
c. 1934. Heinz Rice Flakes. - **$20 $40 $80**
Mailer - **$15 $30 $50**

RTU-3   RTU-4

RTU-3. "Flying Corps" Bronze Wings Badge On Card,
1935. Heinz Co. "Lieutenant" version.
Card - **$10 $15 $25**
Badge - **$10 $15 $20**

RTU-4. "Flying Corps" Silver Wings Badge On Card,
1935. Heinz Co. "Captain" version.
Card - **$15 $20 $30**
Badge - **$15 $20 $25**

RTU-5   RTU-6

TU-5. **"Flying Corps" Gold Wings Badge On Card,**
935. Heinz Co. "Major" version.
ard - **$20 $25 $35**
adge - **$20 $25 $30**

TU-6. **"Roscoe Turner" Photo,**
)30s. Heinz Rice Flakes. - **$10 $ 25 $40**

HEINZ RICE FLAKES
RTU-7

RTU-8

TU-7. **"I Want You To Join My Flying Corps" 20x23"
ardboard Store Sign,**
)30s. Heinz Rice Flakes. - **$100 $200 $300**

TU-8. **"Col. Roscoe Turner" Cello. Button,**
1930s. For "Corinth Airport Dedication". - **$10 $18 $30**

ROY ROGERS

nging, movies, radio, records, comic books, comic strips,
evision, rodeos, personal appearances, merchandising -
)y Rogers has done it all, with style and huge success.
rn Leonard Slye in Ohio in 1912, he started out organizing
wboy bands and singing in a hillbilly group, and made his
st movies - in bit roles or as a member of the Sons of the
)neers - as Slye or as Dick Weston in the mid-1930s.

s first film as Rogers was Republic Pictures' *Under
estern Stars* (1938). He changed his name legally to Roy
)gers in 1942, and went on to make more than 80
esterns for Republic, pursuing the Happy Trails to stardom
"King of the Cowboys," riding his palomino Trigger ("The
nartest Horse in the Movies") and accompanied by wife
ile Evans ("Queen of the West") on her steed Buttermilk.

1 radio, *The Roy Rogers Show* aired on the Mutual or NBC
tworks from 1944 to 1955, initially as a musical variety
ow with Dale, the Sons of the Pioneers, and a movie side-
k Gabby Hayes, later as a Western thriller with Pat Brady
)lacing Hayes. The show was sponsored by Goodyear
e (1944-1945), Miles Laboratories (1946-1947), Quaker
its and Mother's Oats (1948-1951), Post Sugar Crisp
)51-1953), and Dodge automobiles (1954-1955).

)y Rogers comic books were first published in 1944 and
ntinued well into the 1960s, and daily and Sunday strips
ndicated by King Features appeared from 1949 to 1961.

television, *The Roy Rogers Show* was seen on NBC from
51 to 1957, sponsored by Post cereals. The series was
en syndicated for six years, sponsored by Nestle's from
58 to 1964 and co-sponsored by Ideal Novelty & Toy Corp.
m 1961 to 1964. Further syndication followed in 1976.
e programs continued the successful mix of adventure,
Isic, and comedy of the Rogers movies, with the usual
st, including Pat Brady and his trick jeep Nellybelle, and
llet the Wonder Dog. *The Roy Rogers & Dale Evans*

Show, a musical variety hour, had a brief run on ABC in
1962.

Merchandising of the Roy Rogers empire and sponsor premiums peaked during the radio and television years. At one
point some 400 products were franchised by Roy Rogers
Enterprises, earning millions for manufacturers and for the
endorsers. A chain of family restaurants opened in the
1960s.

The Roy Rogers Museum in California displays the stuffed
remains of Trigger, Buttermilk, Bullet; plus Nellybelle and
other relics and memorabilia.

ROY-1

ROY-1. Sons Of Pioneers Photo Card With Roy,
1935. One of earliest items to picture Roy. Text on reverse. -
$50 $125 $200

ROY-2

ROY-3

ROY-4

ROY-2. Dixie Ice Cream Picture,
1938. - **$20 $40 $75**

ROY-3. "Broadway Journal" 12x16" Publicity Newspaper,
1938. Republic Studios. "Special Roy Rogers Edition" for July
16 appearances in New York City. - **$75 $135 $200**

ROY-4. Dixie Ice Cream Picture,
1940. - **$20 $40 $75**

ROY-5

ROY-6

ROY-5. "My Pal Trigger" 13x19" Contest Paper Poster,
1946. Republic Pictures for local theaters. - **$50 $150 $250**

ROY-6. "Roy Rogers And His Trick Lasso" Photo,
1947. Store item packaged with trick lasso. - **$15 $25 $40**

ROY-7

ROY-7. "Roy Rogers Trick Lasso",
1947. Store item. Came with photo (see item ROY-6) and game book. Cellophane wrapper very fragile.
Wrapper - **$10 $25 $50**
Lasso - **$10 $15 $25**
Game Book - **$25 $60 $100**

ROY-8

ROY-9

ROY-8. Contest Card,
1948. Quaker Oats. - **$10 $20 $40**

ROY-9. "Roy Rogers And His World Championship Rodeo" Program,
1948. - **$25 $60 $125**

ROY-10

ROY-11

ROY-10. Dixie Ice Cream Picture,
1948. - **$35 $75 $100**

ROY-11. Branding Iron/Initial Brass Ring,
1948. Quaker Cereals. Plastic stamper under brass cover with ink pad was personalized with any requested initial. - **$100 $160 $225**

ROY-12

ROY-12. Product Box With "Branding Iron" Ring Offer,
1948. - **$30 $50 $90**

ROY-13   ROY-14

ROY-13. Sterling Silver Saddle Ring,
1948. Store item by W. G. Simpson Co., Phoenix, Az. Facsimile signature on saddle seat. - **$250 $385 $525**

ROY-14. "Roy Rogers Riders Club" Membership Card,
c. 1948. - **$15 $30 $50**

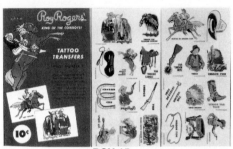
ROY-15

ROY-15. "Tattoo Transfers" Kit,
c. 1948. Pack #7 with Fawcett Publications copyright, two sheets with 22 transfers. - **$30 $70 $125**

ROY-16

ROY-16. Quaker Contest Postcard,
1949. - **$10 $15 $25**

ROY-17

ROY-17. Quaker Contest Prize 19x26" Poster With Mail
1949. Rare. Near Mint With Label On Tube - **$1700**
Poster Only - **$250 $750 $1500**

ROY-18

ROY-18. "March Of Comics" #47,
1949. Various sponsors. Pictured example for Sears merchandise. - **$20 $65 $150**

ROY-19   ROY-20

ROY-19. Microscope Ring/Saddle Ring Newspaper Ad,
1949. Quaker Oats. - **$15 $30 $50**

ROY-20. Quaker Microscope Ring,
1949. - **$50 $80 $110**

ROY-22

ROY-23

ROY-21

ROY-21. Rodeo Souvenir Cello. Button,
1940s. Various attachments. - **$15 $30 $60**

ROY-22. Republic Studios Photo,
1940s. - **$10 $20 $30**

ROY-23. Republic Studios Photo,
1940s. Includes facsimile signature. - **$10 $25 $40**

ROY-25

ROY-24

ROY-24. RCA Victor 18x24" Cardboard Store Sign,
c. 1940s. - **$200 $350 $500**

ROY-25. Fan Club Membership Card,
1940s. - **$20 $35 $50**

ROY-26

ROY-26. Movie Serial Club Card/Ticket With Metal Badge,
1940s. Badge designated "Roy Rogers Deputy".
Card - **$20 $50 $75**
Badge - **$15 $30 $50**

ROY-27

ROY-28

ROY-29

ROY-27. "Roy Rogers" Sterling Silver Child's Ring,
c. 1940s. Store item. Image of Roy on rearing Trigger, bands
have branding iron design. - **$125 $210 $300**

ROY-28. "Dale Evans Fan Club" Cello. Button,
1940s. - **$35 $60 $100**

ROY-29. Plastic Mug,
1950. Quaker Oats. - **$10 $18 $30**

ROY-30

ROY-30. "Roy Rogers Riders Club" Member's Pack,
1950. Package includes two cover letters, six cards, litho.
button on card. Near Mint In Mailer - **$800**
Each Card - **$10 $20 $30**
Loose Button - **$8 $12 $20**

ROY-31

ROY-32

ROY-31. "Souvenir Cup" 15x20" Paper Store Sign,
1950. Quaker Oats. - **$100 $250 $400**

ROY-32. Quaker Canister With "Souvenir Cup" Offer,
1950. - **$35 $60 $125**

ROY-33

ROY-33. Quaker Brass Badge With Sheet And Mailer,
1950. Near Mint Boxed - **$150**
Badge Only - **$25 $60 $100**

ROY-34

ROY-35

ROY-34. Record Album 12x12" Cardboard Store Sign,
c. 1950. RCA Victor. - **$50 $100 $150**

ROY-35. "Thrill Circus" Felt Pennant,
c. 1950. - **$25 $40 $75**

ROY-36

ROY-36. Newspaper Strips Promo,
1951. Rare. Large and colorful. - **$75 $150 $300**

ROY-37

ROY-38

ROY-37. Quaker "Roy Rogers Cookies" Box,
1951. One side panel pictures his gun belt.
Complete - **$200 $400 $600**

ROY-38. Quaker "Roy Rogers Cookies" Newspaper Ad,
1951. Offers Humming Lariat premium. - **$15 $35 $60**

ROY-39

ROY-39. Roy Rogers' Cookies "Crackin' Good" Paper Pop Gun,
1951. - **$15 $30 $50**

ROY-40

ROY-40. Quaker Cereal Box Puzzle Panel,
1951. Back Panel Uncut - **$15 $30 $50**

ROY-41

ROY-41. Bubble Gum Album,
1951. Designed to hold two sets of 24 cards for movies "In
Old Amarillo" and "South Of Caliente." Album
Complete - **$75 $150 $250**
Album Empty - **$25 $50 $75**
Each Card Set - **$25 $50 $75**

ROY-42

ROY-49

ROY-43

ROY-48

ROY-50

ROY-42. "March Of Comics" Sears Christmas Book #77,
1951. - **$15 $45 $105**

ROY-43. "Trick Lasso Contestant" Transfer Sheet,
1952. Issued for national lasso contest. - **$25 $50 $75**

ROY-48. Post Cardboard Sign 13x18",
1953. Scarce. Pictures all 12 Raisin Bran rings. -
$200 $400 $600

ROY-49. "Bullet" Post's Raisin Bran Litho. Tin Ring,
1953. This and the next 11 rings comprise a set of 12. The
Near Mint price is for unbent examples with no rust. -
$8 $30 $50

**ROY-50. "Dale Evans" Post's Raisin Bran Litho. Tin
Ring,**
1953. - **$10 $35 $60**

ROY-44 ROY-45 ROY-46

ROY-51 ROY-52

ROY-44. "Roy Rogers Riders Club Comics",
1952. From membership kit. - **$12 $35 $180**

ROY-45. Litho. Tin Tab,
1952. Roy Rogers Riders Club. Came with club comic
book. - **$20 $40 $65**

ROY-46. Post Cereals Pop-Out Card #22,
1952. From numbered set of 36 issued into 1955.
Each Unpunched - **$8 $15 $25**

**ROY-51. "Dale's Brand" Post's Raisin Bran Litho. Tin
Ring,**
1953. - **$8 $24 $40**

**ROY-52. "Deputy Sheriff" Post's Raisin Bran Litho. Tin
Ring,**
1953. - **$8 $24 $40**

ROY-53 ROY-54

**ROY-53. "Roy Rogers" Post's Raisin Bran Litho. Tin
Ring,**
1953. - **$10 $35 $60**

**ROY-54. "Roy's Boots" Post's Raisin Bran Litho. Tin
Ring,**
1953. - **$8 $24 $40**

ROY-47

ROY-55 ROY-56

**ROY-55. "Roy's Brand" Post's Raisin Bran Litho. Tin
Ring,**
1953. - **$8 $24 $40**

ROY-56. "Roy's Gun" Post's Raisin Bran Litho. Tin Ring,
1953. - **$8 $24 $40**

ROY-47. Post Cereals "RR Bar Ranch" Set,
1953. Punch-outs, metal Nellybelle, plastic figures of Roy,
Dale, Pat, Trigger, Buttermilk and Bullet.
Complete - **$100 $200 $300**

ROY-57 ROY-58

ROY-57. "Roy's Holster" Post's Raisin Bran Litho. Tin Ring,
1953. - **$8 $24 $40**

ROY-58. "Roy's Saddle" Post's Raisin Bran Litho. Tin Ring,
1953. - **$8 $24 $40**

ROY-59   ROY-60

ROY-59. "Sheriff" Post's Raisin Bran Litho. Tin Ring,
1953. - **$8 $24 $40**

ROY-60. "Trigger" Post's Raisin Bran Litho. Tin Ring,
1953. - **$8 $24 $40**

ROY-62

ROY-61

ROY-61. Litho. Tin Button Set,
1953. Post's Grape-Nuts Flakes and Rogers copyright text appears on reverse but also issued with blank reverses.
Each - **$5 $10 $15**

ROY-62. Grape-Nuts Flakes Litho. Buttons,
1953. Post's Canadian version of American set. Slightly smaller 3/4" size, 13 seen, probable 15 in set.
Each - **$15 $30 $50**

ROY-64

ROY-63

ROY-63. Roy Rogers Western Medal Litho. Tin Tab,
1953. Post's Raisin Bran. From set of 27.
Each - **$5 $12 $20**

ROY-64. 3-D Photos,
1953. Post's Sugar Crisp. Four photo folder with 3-D glasses, numbered series. Intact - **$8 $15 $25**

ROY-65

ROY-65. "March Of Comics" #105,
1953. Various sponsors. Pictured example for Sears Christmas give-away. - **$10 $30 $70**

ROY-66

ROY-66. Post Grape-Nut Flakes Box With Roy Billboard,
c. 1953. - **$40 $75 $150**

ROY-67

ROY-67. "Double R Bar Ranch" Cut-Outs,
c. 1953. Post Grape-Nuts Flakes. Canadian Box, three in set.
Each Box - **$100 $200 $400**

ROY-68

ROY-68. Merchandise Manuals (all rare),
1953 - **$125 $250 $500**
1954-1955 - **$100 $200 $400**
1955-1956 - **$75 $150 $300**

ROY-69

ROY-70

ROY-69. Paint By Number Set,
1954. Post's Sugar Crisp. Three sets, each with two pictures.
Each - **$25 $50 $80**

ROY-70. "Roy Rogers Ranch Set" 21x22" Store Poster,
1955. Post Cereals. - **$50 $150 $250**

ROY-71

ROY-72

ROY-71. "Roy Rogers Ranch",
1955. Post Cereals. All cardboard parts. - **$40 $75 $125**

ROY-72. Roy & Dale Golden Records Set With Mail Envelope,
1955. Post's Sugar Crisp "Special Premium" offer not available at retail. Set of two. Near Mint In Mailer - **$150** Each Record - **$15 $30 $50**

ROY-73

ROY-73. Dodge Motors Comic Booklet,
1955. Ad story "Roy Rogers And The Man From Dodge City". - **$10 $30 $75**

ROY-74　　　　**ROY-75**

ROY-74. March of Comics #136,
1955. Various sponsors. - **$10 $30 $65**

ROY-75. "San Antonio World Championship Rodeo" Cello. Button,
1955. Admittance serial number. - **$60 $90 $135**

ROY-76

ROY-77

ROY-76. "Tracard" Photo Cards #2-3,
c. 1955. American Tract Society. Examples from Christian message set. Each - **$3 $5 $10**

ROY-77. "March Of Comics" #146 Booklet,
1956. Printed for Sears, Roebuck. - **$10 $30 $70**

ROY-78

ROY-78. Post Cereal Puzzles,
1957. Set of six. Each - **$8 $15 $25**

ROY-79

ROY-79. "Flash-Draw" Flip Booklet,
1958. Classy Products Corp. Sequence photo "Movies" pages, came with cap gun set. - **$30 $60 $100**

ROY-80

ROY-80. "Roy Rogers Ranch Calendar",
1959. Unmarked probably Nestle Quik. - **$50 $100 $150**

ROY-81　　　　**ROY-82**

ROY-81. "Roy Rogers Trick Lasso" 15x24" Cardboard Store Display,
1950s. Scarce. Equipped with rope lasso on spring wire at center. - **$300 $750 $1800**

ROY-82. Lariat Flashlight On Store Display Card,
1950s. Bantamlite Inc. Carded - **$75 $150 $275**
Light Only - **$15 $35 $75**

ROY-83

ROY-83. Promo with Premium Record,
1950s. Scarce. Sugar Crisp Cereal. - **$100 $200 $300**

ROY-84

ROY-85

ROY-84. Yellow Records in Mailer,
1950s. - **$20 $40 $80**

ROY-85. Grape Nuts Flakes Flat,
1950s. Promotes pop-out cards. - **$150 $300 $600**

ROY-86

ROY-87

ROY-86. "Roy Rogers Riders" Metal/Plastic Harmonica,
1950s. Store item by Harmonic Reed Corp. Also inscribed "King Of The Cowboys".
Boxed - **$40 $75 $100**
Loose - **$10 $20 $35**

ROY-87. Frosted Glass Tumbler With Gold Image,
c. 1950s. Probable store item. On old glass, Trigger's front legs overlap. On Roy Rogers Museum new glass, Trigger's front legs each show without overlap.
Old - **$25 $50 $100**
New - **$3 $5 $8**

ROY-88

ROY-88. Flash Camera With Papers And Box,
1950s. Includes camera club card, press pass card.
Near Mint Boxed - **$250**
Unboxed With Flash - **$40 $75 $100**
Unboxed, No Flash - **$20 $50 $75**
Each Card - **$10 $20 $30**

ROY-89

ROY-90

ROY-91

ROY-89. "Riders Club" Membership Card,
1950s. Back has club rules. - **$5 $20 $50**

ROY-90. "Roy Rogers Riders" Cello. Club Button,
1950s. - **$15 $35 $60**

ROY-91. "Roy Rogers Riders Lucky Piece",
1950s. 1" version brass medalet with Roy portrait on side, Trigger other side with slogan "Good Luck Forever". - **$5 $15 $25**

ROY-92

ROY-93

ROY-92. "Roy Rogers Riders Lucky Piece",
1950s. 1-1/4" version brass medalet picturing Roy one side, Trigger on other with slogan "Good Luck Forever". - $10 $18 $30

ROY-93. "Double R Bar Ranch News" Club Newspaper,
1950s. Issued bi-monthly. - $25 $50 $75

ROY-94   **ROY-95**   **ROY-96**

ROY-94. Fan Club Response Card,
1950s. Club Headquarters. Back includes offer for View-master reels plus name of TV sponsor Post Cereals. - $15 $30 $50

ROY-95. Fan Club Response Card,
1950s. Club Headquarters. Back includes ad for store item decals plus name of TV sponsor Post Cereals. - $15 $30 $50

ROY-96. English Candy Cigarette Box,
1950s. - $40 $75 $150

ROY-97

ROY-97. "Wild West Action Toy" Punch-Out Sheet,
1950s. Roy Rogers Cookies. Unpunched - $60 $125 $200

ROY-98

ROY-99

ROY-98. Deputy Tin Star Badge,
1950s. Issued by Popsicle and probably others. Comes in copper finish or silver finish. - $10 $20 $30

ROY-99. Glass,
1950s. Probably held dairy product. - $50 $80 $150

ROY-100   **ROY-101**

ROY-100. "Roy Rogers Rodeo" 13x21" Cardboard Poster,
1950s. - $75 $150 $250

ROY-101. "Roy Rogers Sweaters" Store Postcard,
1950s. - $10 $20 $30

ROY-102

ROY-102. Dell Comics Photo Strip Folder,
1950s. - $40 $75 $135

ROY-103

ROY-103. Sears Toy Town Cards,
1950s. Two Christmas premium cards with holiday verse on back. Each - $8 $15 $25

ROY-104   **ROY-105**

ROY-104. "King Of The Cowboys/Roy Rogers" Litho. Button,
1950s. Comes in 1-1/8" or 1-3/4" sizes. Each - $10 $20 $30

ROY-105. "Queen Of The West/Dale Evans" Litho. Button,
1950s. 1-1/8" size only. - $15 $25 $40

ROY-106

ROY-106. "Nestle's Quik" Canister With Premium Offer,
1960. Back offers 3-D plastic plaque set with expiration date June 30. - **$50 $125 $200**

ROY-107

ROY-107. "Roy Rogers Ranch Calendar",
1960. Nestle's Quik. - **$50 $100 $150**

ROY-108

ROY-108. "Roy Rogers Ranch Calendar",
1961. Nestle's Quik. - **$50 $100 $150**

ROY-109

ROY-109. Nestle's Candy Coupon,
1961. - **$15 $30 $50**

ROY-110

ROY-111

ROY-110. Litho. Soda Can,
c. 1960s. Continental Beverage Corp., La Jolla, California. - **$60 $130 $200**

ROY-111. Paper Hat,
c. 1970s. Roy Rogers Restaurants. - **$3 $6 $15**

ROY-112

ROY-113

ROY-112. Life-Sized 75" Tall Cardboard Standee,
c. 1980. Thousand Trails Campgrounds. - **$100 $225 $400**

ROY-113. "Roy Rogers Family Restaurants" 2" Litho. Button,
1980s. Various locations, pictured example from Maryland. - **$3 $6 $10**

SCOOP WARD

Laddie Seaman, alias Scoop Ward, narrated dramatization of the news for his teenage audience in News of Youth o CBS radio from late 1935 to 1937. The program was spor sored by Ward's Soft Bun bread and Silver Queen poun cake.

SCW-1

SCW-2

SCW-1. Club Newsletter With Envelope,
1936. Ward's Bread and Silver Queen Pound Cake.
Mailer - **$3 $5 $10**
Newsletter - **$10 $20 $30**

SCW-2. "Official Reporter" Brass Shield Badge,
1936. Ward's Soft Bun Bread. - **$5 $12 $25**

SECKATARY HAWKINS

This children's program was developed from a comic strip of the same name by Robert F. Schulkers. Hawkins was the leader of a boys' club that spent its time helping to round up bad boys. The club's motto was "Fair and Square." The radio series, sponsored by Ralston Purina, was broadcast on NBC in 1932-1933.

SKH-1

SKH-1. Club Kit,
1929. With pin, card, and mailer. - **$30 $60 $120**

SKH-2   SKH-3   SKH-4

SKH-2. "Fair And Square" Member's Cello. Button,
1932. 7/8" size. Red rim. - **$5 $8 $12**

SKH-3. "Fair And Square" Cello. Club Button,
1932. 7/8" size. Blue rim. - **$3 $5 $8**

SKH-4. "Fair And Square" Litho. Club Button,
1932. 3/4" size. - **$3 $5 $8**

SKH-6

SKH-5

SKH-5. "Fair And Square" Ralston Club Enameled Brass Spinner,
1932. Spinner disk forms club slogan with spun. - **$20 $50 $75**

SKH-6. "Sunday Baltimore American" Cello. Club Button,
c. 1932. - **$8 $12 $20**

SECRET AGENT X-9

Written by Dashiell Hammett and drawn by Alex Raymond, *Secret Agent X-9* was introduced by King Features in January 1934. X-9 is a loner who fights urban criminals by seeming to become part of their evil world. Hammett and Raymond went on to other things in 1935, and the strip was continued by an assortment of writers and artists, evolving in 1967 to *Secret Agent Corrigan*. Comic book reprints of the first eight months of the strip were published in 1934. There was a short-lived radio program, and Universal Pictures made two *Secret Agent X-9* chapter plays, one in 1937 starring Scott Kolk; the other, with Lloyd Bridges starring, in 1945.

SCX-1

SCX-1. Daily Comic Strip Book,
1934. Store item. - **$40 $120 $300**

SCX-2   SCX-3

SCX-2. Club Membership Card With Envelope,
1930s. With Envelope - **$12 $20 $35**
Card Only - **$8 $12 $20**

SCX-3. "Secret Agent X-9/Chicago Herald And Examiner" Silvered Metal Badge,
1930s. - **$15 $25 $40**

SCX-4

SCX-5

SCX-4. Cello. Button,
1940s. - **$10 $20 $30**

SCX-5. Water Gun,
1950s. Irwin. Store item. Billy club serves as water tank. - **$15 $30 $50**

THE SECRET 3

Murray McLean starred in this serial detective drama sponsored by 3-Minute Oat Flakes and apparently broadcast only regionally in the 1930s. Premiums included a membership badge, a Confidential Code Book, and a variety of generic crime-fighting paraphernalia. The show's main characters were: Ben Potter, Chief of Detectives; Jack Williams, 1st Lieutenant; Mary Lou Davis; 2nd Lieutenant.

SCT-1

SCT-1. Silvered Brass Badge,
1929. Rare. - **$50 $100 $150**

SCT-2

SCT-3

SCT-2. Club Member Code/Rule Book,
1930s. Rare. 3-Minute Oat Flakes. Includes two pages of detective premiums. - **$25 $75 $150**

SCT-3. Club Headquarters Cover Letter,
1930s. Scarce. P.S. notation on letter is "Burn this letter after you read it." - **$10 $20 $30**

SCT-4

SCT-4. Secret 3 "Detective Bureau" Curved Brass Badge,
1930s. Rare. - **$15 $50 $75**

SERGEANT PRESTON OF THE YUKON

Under its original title, *Challenge of the Yukon*, this adventure series of the Royal Canadian Mounties during the gold-rush days of the 1890s was heard initially on Detroit radio station WXYZ from 1938 to 1947. Created by George W. Trendle and Fran Striker after their success with *The Lone Ranger* and *The Green Hornet*, the program centered on the crime-fighting exploits of Sgt. Frank Preston and his malamute partner Yukon King, "the swiftest and strongest lead dog of the Northwest." The series moved to the ABC network in 1947 and then to Mutual in 1950, where it remained until 1955. Quaker Puffed Wheat and Rice were the long-

term sponsors. In 1951 the program changed its name officially to *Sergeant Preston of the Yukon*, although it was also popularly known as Yukon King, a reflection of the dog's central role in Preston's always getting his man.

On television, the series was broadcast on CBS from 1955 to 1958, sponsored by Quaker Oats and Mother's Oats. Richard Simmons starred in the title role, riding his black stallion Rex and assisted, as always by Yukon King. Reruns were seen on NBC during the 1963-1964 season.

Sergeant Preston comic books were published between 1951 and 1959, including a set of four giveaways in two sizes from Quaker cereals in 1956. The cereal company also offered a great variety of other premiums, notably a 1955 in-package deed to a one-square-inch tract of land in the Yukon.

SGT-1

SGT-2

SGT-3

SGT-1. Autographed Photo,
c. 1947. Believed to picture Paul Sutton radio voice of Sgt. Preston. - **$75 $125 $200**

SGT-2. Fan Photo,
1947. - **$20 $30 $60**

SGT-3. 2-Way Signal Flashlight,
1949. Plastic disk produces red or green light. - **$25 $60 $90**

SGT-4

SGT-4. Dog Cards,
1949. Set of 35. Each - **$1 $2 $3**

SGT-5

SGT-5. "Sergeant Preston Gets His Man" Game,
1949. Game board and playing pieces from Quaker cereal boxes. Cut But Complete - **$20 $40 $65**

SGT-6

SGT-7

SGT-6. "Dog Sled Race" Quaker Box Back,
1949. From series of three games offered.
Complete Box - **$75 $150 $250**
Uncut Box Back With Side Parts Panel - **$20 $40 $65**

SGT-7. "Great Yukon River Canoe Race" Quaker Box Back,
1949. From series of three games offered.
Complete With Markers - **$20 $40 $65**

SGT-8

SGT-9

SGT-8. "Official Seal" Litho. Button,
1949. Rare. 1-3/8" black and red on yellow background. - **$600 $2000 $5000**

SGT-9. "Yukon Trail" Quaker Puffed Wheat Box Back,
1950. Set of eight. Complete Box - **$100 $200 $350**
Each Uncut Box Back - **$25 $50 $80**

SGT-10

SGT-11

SGT-10. Police Whistle 17x22" Paper Store Sign,
1950. - **$100 $250 $400**

SGT-11. Brass Whistle,
1950. Facsimile signature on side. - **$20 $30 $50**

SGT-12

SGT-13

SGT-12. "Sergeant Preston Yukon Adventure Picture Cards",
1950. Set of 36. Each - **$1 $3 $5**

SGT-13. Quaker Contest Entrant Acknowledgement Postcard,
1950. - **$15 $25 $40**

SGT-15

SGT-14

SGT-16

SGT-14. Dog-Naming Contest 16x22" Award Poster,
1950. Scarce. - **$200 $400 $800**

SGT-15. Mailing Tube For Dog-Naming Contest Award Poster,
1950. Rare. - **$25 $50 $100**

SGT-16. Award Poster Small Version,
1950. - **$20 $35 $60**

SGT-17

SGT-18

SGT-17. Portrait Photo,
c. 1950 Probably a Quaker premium. - **$20 $35 $60**

SGT-18. "Quaker Camp Stove" With Folder,
1952. Scarce. Metal items are firebox & cover, oven, tongs.
Set - **$35 $100 $250**
Tent - **$250 $500 $750**

SGT-19

SGT-20

SGT-19. Aluminum Pedometer,
1952. - **$20 $40 $75**

**SGT-20. "The Case That Made Preston A Sergeant"
Decca Record #1,**
1952. - **$20 $40 $75**

SGT-22

SGT-21

**SGT-21. "The Case Of The Indian Rebellion" Decca
Record #3,**
1952. - **$20 $40 $75**

**SGT-22. "Sgt. Preston Trail Goggles" Quaker Cereal Box
Cut-Out,**
1952. - Complete Box - **$75 $150 $250**
Cut-out - **$10 $20 $40**

SGT-23

**SGT-23. "Electronic Ore Detector" With Instructions And
Box,**
1952. Plastic battery operated detector.
Near Mint Boxed - **$200**
Detector Only - **$50 $80 $150**

SGT-24

SGT-24. Wood Totem Poles,
1952. Set of five. Each - **$10 $18 $30**

SGT-26

SGT-25

SGT-25. "Distance Finder",
1954. Metal and paper insert distance gauge. - **$20 $35 $5**

**SGT-26. "Klondike Big Inch Land Deed" Certificate With
Cover Sheet,**
1955. Deed - **$10 $15 $20**
Sheet - **$5 $10 $15**
Mailer (rare) - **$30 $60 $120**

SGT-27

SGT-28

SGT-27. "Map Of Yukon Territory" 8x10",
1955. Quaker Cereals box insert. - **$8 $25 $50**

SGT-28. "Prospector's Pouch Order Blank",
1955. - **$15 $30 $60**

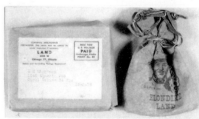

SGT-29

SGT-29. "Klondike Land" Pouch,
1955.
Near Mint Boxed With Klondike Dirt Still In Pouch - **$300**
Pouch Only (pouch is generally cracked) - **$50 $100 $175**

SGT-30

GT-30. "How He Found Yukon King" Comic Booklet, 956. Quaker box insert. Set of four, each 5" or 7" long. - 8 $25 $50

SGT-31

GT-31. "How Yukon King Saved Him From The Wolves" omic Booklet, 956. Quaker box insert. Set of four, each 5" or 7" long. - 8 $25 $50

SGT-32

GT-32. "How He Became A Mountie" Comic Booklet, 956. Quaker box insert. Set of four, each 5" or 7" long. - 8 $25 $50

SGT-33

SGT-34

GT-33. "The Case That Made Him A Sergeant" Comic ooklet, 956. Quaker box insert. Set of four, each 5" or 7" long. - 8 $25 $50

GT-34. Official Seal Cello. Button, 956. Full color 1-1/4". White rim. Scarce. - 500 $1000 $2000

SGT-35

SGT-36

GT-35. Quaker Cereals T-Shirt, . 1956. Scarce. - $75 $150 $300

GT-36. Official Seal Tin Badge, . 1956. Seen in copper, silver or matte silver luster, all are. - $300 $700 $1200

SGT-37

SGT-38

SGT-37. Official Seal White Metal Badge With Insert Paper Photo, c. 1956. Photo is yellow/black. - $200 $350 $600

SGT-38. Quaker Cereals Coloring Contest Letter And Photo, 1957. Near Mint In Envelope - $175 Photo Only - $35 $75 $100

SGT-39

SGT-39. "Richard Simmons" Pencil Tablet, 1950s. Store item. - $10 $30 $50

SETH PARKER

Seth Parker was an early radio creation of Phillips H. Lord, who was later to create Gang Busters and other adventure programs. In contrast, Seth Parker combined the story of a gentle, kindly Maine philosopher with lots of hymn singing, and it was immensely successful. Also know as Sunday at Seth Parker and Sunday Evenings at Seth Parker, the series was sustained on NBC from 1929 to 1933, and sponsored by Frigidaire as Cruise of the Seth Parker in 1933-1934. It later aired from 1935 to 1939, sponsored by Vick Chemical for its final three years.

SET-1

SET-2

SET-3

SET-1. "Aboard The Seth Parker" Booklet, 1934. Frigidaire Corp. Includes drawings of the various rooms of global sailing boat. - $5 $10 $15

SET-2. Schooner 11x15" Paper Print,
c. 1934. Frigidaire Corp. Pictures world cruise ship used by
Phillips H. Lord, creator and radio voice of Seth Parker. -
$8 $12 $20

**SET-3. "Seth Parker's Two-Year Almanac And Party
Book",**
1939. Vicks Chemical Co. Hardcover edition for 1939-1940. -
$5 $10 $15

SET-4

SET-5

SET-4. "Seth Parker's Scrapbook",
1930s. Collection of folksy, small-town humor and wisdom. -
$10 $20 $30

SET-5. Cast Member Fan Photo,
1930s. Pictures family in a parlor hymn sing. - **$5 $8 $15**

THE SHADOW

The Shadow, alias Lamont Cranston, was born in the 1930s,
both as a character in Street & Smith publications and by
radio sponsor Blue Coal. Written by Walter B. Gibson under
the pen name Maxwell Grant, the Shadow fought crime and
clouded men's minds not only in the pulps and on the radio
but also, along with the lovely Margot Lane, in the movies, in
comic books, and in a comic strip.

On the radio, the *Shadow* aired on CBS, NBC, or Mutual
from 1932 to 1954, and the programs were resurrected and
syndicated in the 1960s and 1970s. There were a number of
regional or national sponsors: Blue Coal for most of the
years between 1932 and 1949, along with Perfect-O-Lite
(1932), Goodrich tires (1938-1939), Grove Laboratories
(1949-1950), the Army Air Force (1950-1951), Wildroot
Cream Oil (1951-1953), Carey Salt Company, and Bromo
Quinine cold tablets. Both Blue Coal (in 1941) and Carey
Salt (in 1945) offered glow-in-the-dark premium rings, and
The Shadow Magazine offered a club membership lapel
emblem and other items.

A *Shadow* comic strip appeared in newspapers from 1938 to
1942, and comic books were published from 1940 to 1950, in
1964-1965 (with the Shadow as costumed superhero), and in
1973-1975. The Shadow made a number of low-budget film
appearances in the 1930s and 1940s, notably in a 15-
episode chapter play from Columbia Pictures in 1940 with
Victor Jory in the title role. In 1994 Alec Baldwin played the
lead in a Universal film. "Who knows what evil lurks in the
hearts of men?"

SHA-1   SHA-2

SHA-3

SHA-1. "Eyes Of The Shadow" 7x11" Ad Card,
c. 1931. For Maxwell Grant novel. - **$30 $75 $150**

**SHA-2. Perfect-O-Lite Radio Broadcast Promotion
Folder,**
1932. For Perfect-O-Lite sales people. 11x17" folder that
opens to 17x22" promoting new radio sponsorship over 29
stations of Columbia network. - **$60 $150 $300**

SHA-3. "The Shadow" 11x14" Cardboard Window Poster
c. 1934. Blue Coal, Shadow magazine. Promotes Monday
and Wednesday radio broadcasts on Columbia network. -
$400 $800 $1500

SHA-5

SHA-4   SHA-6

SHA-4. "Secret Society Of The Shadow" Club Card,
1939. Pledge card originally holding glow-in-dark "Magic
Button". - **$75 $150 $250**

SHA-5. "The Shadow" Glow-In-Dark Cello. Magic Button
1939. Rare not cracked or stained. - **$200 $450 $1000**

SHA-6. Blue Coal Portrait Photo,
1930s. - **$75 $150 $250**

SHA-8

SHA-7

SHA-7. The Shadow Unmasked Photo,
1930s. Blue Coal. - **$60 $120 $180**

SHA-8. The Shadow Club Card,
1930s. Street & Smith Publishers. Originally held Shadow
lapel stud. Card - **$100 $200 $300**
Mailer (Pictures The Shadow) - **$75 $150 $275**

SHA-9

SHA-10

SHA-9. "The Shadow Club" Silvered Brass Lapel Emblem,
1930s. Lapel Stud - **$100 $200 $300**
Pin - **$125 $250 $350**

SHA-10. "The Shadow Strikes Again" Paper Folder,
1930s. Blue Coal. Includes listing of radio stations and broadcast times. - **$75 $150 $300**

SHA-11

SHA-12

SHA-11. "Member/The Shadow Club" Rubber On Wood Stamp Block,
1930s. Picture example includes ink stamp image from the block. - **$250 $500 $800**

SHA-12. "Tune In On-The Shadow" Paper Gummed Back Sticker,
1930s. - **$40 $70 $120**

SHA-13

SHA-13. "The Shadow On The Air" Gummed Back Paper Sticker,
1930s. - **$35 $75 $125**

SHA-14

SHA-15

SHA-14. "The Shadow Is Back On The Air" Paper Gummed Back Sticker,
1930s. - **$40 $75 $135**

SHA-15. Pulp Magazine Ad Sticker,
1930s. - **$50 $90 $150**

SHA-16

SHA-16. Boxed Board Game,
1940. Store item by Toy Creations. - **$250 $600 $1000**

SHA-17

SHA-17. "The Shadow" Brown Felt Fabric Hat,
1940. Adult size, offered by The Shadow Magazine. - **$150 $250 $400**

SHA-18

SHA-18. Blue Coal Ink Blotter,
1940. - **$15 $25 $50**

SHA-19

SHA-20

SHA-19. "Blue Coal" Ring Instruction Sheet With Mailer Envelope,
1941. Rare. Envelope - **$300 $350 $400**
Instruction Sheet - **$500 $575 $650**

SHA-20. Blue Coal Ring,
1941. Glows in the dark. - **$200 $400 $600**

SHA-21

SHA-21. Cardboard 11x16" Ad Wall Calendar,
1942. Picture example shows calendar and corner detail from it. - **$100 $175 $ 300**

SHA-22

SHA-23

SHA-22. Magic Ring,
1945. Carey Salt. Black plastic stone, base glows in dark. - **$500 $850 $1200**

SHA-23. Blue Coal Sticker,
1940s. - **$50 $90 $150**

SHA-24

SHA-24. Matchbook Cover,
1940s. Inside cover has diecut hinged tab that lowers to expose jail cell view.
With Matches - **$40 $80 $150**
Empty - **$30 $60 $100**

SHA-25

SHA-25. Blotter,
1940s. Blue Coal. - **$10 $25 $50**

SHA-26

SHA-26. Blotter,
1940s. Blue Coal. - **$10 $20 $40**

SHA-27

SHA-27. Blotter,
1940s. Blue Coal. - **$10 $20 $40**

SHA-28

SHA-29

SHA-28. Blotter,
1940s. Blue Coal. - **$15 $35 $75**

SHA-29. Blotter,
1940s. Blue Coal. - **$20 $40 $85**

SHA-30

SHA-31

SHA-30. Blotter,
1940s. Blue Coal. - **$30 $60 $125**

SHA-31. Canadian Ink Blotter,
1940s. Various coal companies. - **$30 $60 $125**

SHERLOCK HOLMES

The world's most famous detective made his debut in 1887 Arthur Conan Doyle's story *A Study in Scarlet*. Since the millions of fans have followed the adventures of the brillia Holmes and his trusted chronicler Dr. John Watson in book on stage, on the radio, on television, and in numerous film Holmes solved cases in radio series from 1930 to 1936 ar from 1939 to 1950, on various networks, with different spo sors, and through multiple cast changes. Best remembere are Basil Rathbone and Nigel Bruce, who played the rad leads from 1939 to 1946. G. Washington coffee was an ear sponsor (1930-1935), followed by Household Financ Corporation (1936), Bromo-Quinine cold tablets (1939-194 Petri wine (1943-1946 and 1949-1950), and others. Holme also made scattered comic book appearances from th 1940s to the 1970s. "Elementary, my dear Watson."

SHL-1

SHL-1. Sherlock Holmes Game,
1904. Store item by Parker Brothers. - **$40 $80 $150**

SHL-2

SHL-2. Sherlock Holmes Map,
1930s. Rare. Household Finance. - **$80 $160 $320**

SHIELD G-MAN CLUB

Joe Higgins, alias the Shield, was one of the most popular comic book heroes of the 1940s, fighting to protect the American way of life with truth, justice, patriotism, and courage - and a costume that made him invulnerable. He debuted in *Pep Comics* #1 in 1940 and, despite some changes in character, lasted until *Pep* #65 in 1948. Between 1940 and 1944 he also appeared in *Shield-Wizard Comics*. The *Shield G-Man Club*, which offered pins and a membership card, had a short life before becoming the *Archie Club*.

SGM-1

SGM-2

SGM-1. Club Member Card,
1940. Pep Comics, M.L.J. Magazines.
Card - **$50 $90 $175**
Mailer - **$10 $20 $30**

SGM-2. "Shield G-Man Club" Cello. Button (blue border),
c. 1940. Rare. 1-3/4" version. - **$200 $600 $1000**

SGM-3

SGM-4

SGM-3. "The Shield" Cardboard Movie Projector,
c. 1941. Shield Wizard Comics. Filmstrips cut from comic book page by reader to produce "film." Pictured example has replaced viewing tube. - **$200 $400 $800**

SGM-4. Club Member's Cello. Badge,
c. 1943. Bar pin behind top folded edge. Also issued as 1-1/4" circular cello. button.
Button (no border) - **$75 $250 $500**
Badge - **$15 $30 $60**

SHIRLEY TEMPLE

America's dimpled sweetheart, the world's darling, Shirley Temple was probably the most popular child prodigy actress ever to come out of Hollywood. Born in 1928, she sang, danced, and acted in 30 movies by the age of 13, was a top box-office star, and charmed the nation. Merchandising during the 1930s was extensive, including Shirley Temple dresses, hats, underwear, mugs, soap, and an estimated 1.5 million Shirley Temple dolls from Ideal Novelty & Toy Corp. She made further films as a teen and as an adult, but could not sustain her immense popularity. There were several short-lived ventures on CBS radio: *Shirley Temple Time* (1939), the *Shirley Temple Variety Show*, sponsored by Elgin watches (1941), and *Junior Miss* (1942). On television, *Shirley Temple's Story Book* was seen in 1958-1959 and *The Shirley Temple Show* aired in 1960-1961. In 1967, as Shirley Temple Black, she lost a primary race for a California Congressional seat; in 1974 she was appointed U.S. Ambassador to Ghana.

SHR-1

SHR-1. "The Americal Girl" Scout Magazine With Doll Ad,
1936. Doll offered as premium for four subscriptions. - **$8 $10 $20**

SHR-2

SHR-2. Doll Contest Newspaper Advertisement,
1936. - **$15 $30 $50**

SHR-4

SHR-3

SHR-11

SHR-12

SHR-3. 15" Tall Composition Doll,
c. 1936. Store item by Ideal Toy Co. Dress based on 1934 "Bright Eyes" movie costume. - **$200 $350 $650**

SHR-4. Wheaties Box Back Panels,
c. 1936. Set of 12. Each - **$5 $10 $15**

SHR-11. Swimsuit Cardboard String Tag,
1930s. Forest Mills. Various photos. - **$20 $40 $60**

SHR-12. Portrait Picture,
1930s. Probably store or theater give-away. - **$8 $12 $20**

SHR-6

SHR-7

SHR-8

SHR-5

SHR-13

SHR-14

SHR-5. Enameled Brass Figural Pin,
c. 1936. Probable store item. - **$50 $90 $150**

SHR-6. "Shirley Temple's Pet/Rowdy" Enameled Brass Pin,
c. 1936. Pictures her pet dog. Probably store item. - **$60 $100 $175**

SHR-7. "Chicago Times Shirley Temple Club" Litho. Button,
c. 1936. - **$30 $60 $125**

SHR-8. Cello. Button Off Doll,
c. 1936. Ideal Novelty And Toy Co. - **$15 $25 $50**

SHR-13. "A Movie Of Me" Flip Book,
1930s. Probably Quaker Cereals. - **$35 $75 $150**

SHR-14. Diecut 12x16" Cardboard Hanger Sign For Theater Lobby,
1930s. Color portrait each side. - **$40 $90 $150**

SHR-10

SHR-9

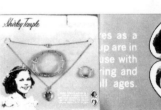

SHR-16

SHR-15

SHR-9. "Shirley Temple League" Enameled Brass English Pin,
c. 1937. Sunday Referee newspaper. - **$35 $50 $100**

SHR-10. Photo Portrait European Ring,
c. 1937. Store item, "Made In Czechoslovakia". Thin metal band with brass bracket holding black/white photo. - **$75 $150 $250**

SHR-15. Cardboard Advertising Fan,
1944. Royal Crown Cola. Inscribed for her 1944 movie "I'll B Seeing You". - **$25 $50 $80**

SHR-16. "Picture Locket Jewelry" On Card,
1940s. Store item. Heart-shaped symbol on ring, bracelet, locket. Set - **$75 $150 $250**

SHOCK GIBSON

Speed Comics began in October 1939 with the origin and first appearance of Shock Gibson in issue #1. Gibson was the cover feature and lead character of the first 15 issues. *Speed Comics* continued through issue #44 in 1947.

SHK-1   SHK-2

SHK-1. Volunteers Club Membership Card,
1939. Brookwood Publishing/Speed Publishing. -
25 $50 $75

SHK-2. Volunteers Club Cello. Button,
1939. - $75 $150 $300

SILVER DOLLAR BRADY

Silver Dollar Brady was a character created to promote Seagram's alcohol. Hoppy, Roy and Gene refused to support projects that used alcohol or cigarettes as sponsors. As a result of this dilemma, these companies had to create their own cowboy heroes. Silver Dollar Brady is a classic example of using in-house characters for this type of advertising. The premium listed was designed to test whether or not you had too much to drink and were off on your own "happy trails."

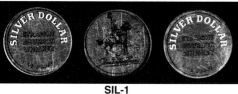

SIL-1

SIL-1. Test Your Eye Card,
40s. Includes three different thin metal silver dollar sized play coins with Brady pictured on obverse.
Filler - $20 $40 $60
Card - $15 $30 $45
Each Play Dollar - $10 $20 $30

SILVER STREAK

Magazine publisher Arthur Bernhard entered the comic book market with *Silver Streak Comics* #1 in December 1939. Jack Cole, later the creator of Plastic Man and a popular Playboy cartoonist, was brought in as artist/editor and drew the first Silver Streak story for issue #3, March 1940. Silver Streak became the second super-speed hero introduced that year, following the debut of The Flash just weeks earlier. The title is notable not only for Silver Streak but for the first appearance of Daredevil and the villainous Claw in issue #6. With issue #22 the title was changed to *Crime Does Not Pay*. Arthur Bernhard sold out to Lev Gleason shortly afterwards and Gleason continued to build a modest success based on the crime comics genre.

SLV-1

SLV-1. Photo,
c. 1941. Rare. - $100 $200 $300

THE SINGING LADY

Ireene Wicker was the Singing Lady, and for 13 years (1932-1945) she told fairy tales and sang to the nation's children on a highly popular network radio program called *The Singing Story Lady*. The show, loved by parents as well as children, won many major broadcasting awards, including a Peabody. Kellogg's cereals, the long-term sponsor, offered a number of premiums, mostly song and story booklets designed by Vernon Grant. *The Singing Lady* moved to ABC television (1948-1950) with a similar format, using puppets to illustrate fairy tales and historical sketches. In 1953-1954, with Kellogg's again sponsoring, the program returned as *Story Time*.

SNG-1

SNG-2

SNG-1. "Singing Lady Song Book",
c. 1932. Art by Vernon Grant. - $15 $20 $30

SNG-2. Kellogg's "Mother Goose" Booklet,
1933. Cover art by Vernon Grant. - $15 $25 $40

SNG-3

SNG-3. Punch-Out Paper "Party Kit",
1936. Near Mint With Mailer - $75
Book Only - **$20 $40 $60**

SNG-4

SNG-4. "Mother Goose Action Circus" Punch-Out Book With Mailer Envelope,
1936. Six sheets of Vernon Grant illustrations.
Mailer - **$10 $20 $30**
Punch-Out Book - **$60 $150 $300**

SNG-5

SNG-5. "Ireene Wicker" Fan Postcard,
1940. National Broadcasting Co. for her "Musical Stories" radio broadcasts on Blue Network. - **$5 $12 $20**

SKEEZIX

The central character of the meandering continuity comic strip *Gasoline Alley*, Skeezix was an exception to the traditional comic style in that he aged accordingly as the strip continued over the years. Skeezix was a doorstep infant foundling left by unknown parents in 1921. He served in World War II and returned to continue his small town, middle-class life so readily identifiable to mass readership. Skeezix was an adult and father in the 1960s but the vast majority of related premiums are from his 1930s happy childhood years with guardian Uncle Walt surrounded by the extensive assortment of relatives, friends and neighbors created by cartoonist Frank King.

SKX-1

SKX-2

SKX-1. Club Letter,
1930s. Wonder Bread. - **$10 $20 $30**

SKX-2. Skeezix Badge,
1930s. Wonder Bread. - **$20 $40 $80**

SKX-3

SKX-4

SKX-3. Litho. Tin Toothbrush Holder,
1930s. Pro-phy-lac-tic Listerine. - **$40 $100 $200**

SKX-4. Birthstone Design "I Wear Skeezix Shoes" 2-1/4" Cello. Pocket Mirror,
1930s. - **$12 $20 $40**

SKX-5

SKX-6

SKX-7

SKX-5. "I Like Skeezix Sweaters" Cello. Button,
1930s. - **$10 $20 $35**

SKX-6. "Skeezix Loves Red Cross Macaroni" Cello. Button,
1930s. - **$10 $20 $35**

SKX-7. "Buffalo Evening News" Cello. Button,
1930s. From series of newspaper contest buttons, match number to win prize. - **$10 $20 $35**

SKIPPY

Artist Percy Crosby created the cartoon Skippy Skinner for the old *Life* humor magazine in the early 1920s and began syndicating the strip in 1925. Dressed in shorts, long jacket, and a checked hat, Skippy was the neighborhood pessimist, with a cynical view of the adult world, his humor shadowed by sadness and defeat. Even so, the strip was a popular one and ran until 1943, when Crosby became too ill to continue it. Comic book collections and illustrated Skippy novels appeared in the 1920s and 1930s, and there were two 1931 movies, *Skippy* and *Sooky*, both starring Jackie Cooper. A radio series aired on NBC (1932) and CBS (1932-1935), sponsored first by Wheaties (1932-1933), then by Phillips Magnesia toothpaste (1933-1935). Premiums included membership in *Skippy's Secret Service Society* and the *Skippy Mystic Circle Club*.

SKP-1

SKP-2

SKP-1. Wheaties 9x15" Sign For Club Membership,
1932. Rare. Three perforated pieces. - **$200 $400 $600**

SKP-2. Wheaties Skippy Letter,
c. 1932. "Dear Friend" form letter in simulated Skippy hand-writing urging club membership after proof of Wheaties eaten for 15 days. - **$5 $12 $20**

SKP-3

SKP-4

SKP-3. Wheaties Ceramic Bowl (Sooky),
1932. Rare. Same side view shown for both. Sooky pictured in bottom. - **$75 $150 $300**

SKP-4. Wheaties Ceramic Bowl (Skippy),
1932. Rare. Skippy pictured in bottom. - **$50 $100 $200**

SKP-5

SKP-6

SKP-5. Wheaties Cello. Club Button,
1932. Initialed for Skippy's Secret Service Society. - **$5 $10 $15**

SKP-6. Captain Application Form,
c. 1932. Wheaties. - **$5 $10 $15**

SKP-7

SKP-8

SKP-7. Wheaties "Captain" Cello. Rank Button,
1932. For highest club rank. - **$20 $40 $65**

SKP-8. Wheaties Skippy Letter,
c. 1932. "Dear Captain" form letter in simulated Skippy hand-writing certifying rank attained by eating Wheaties "According To The Regulations And Rules". - **$8 $15 $25**

SKP-9

SKP-9. Wheaties "Captain's Commission" Certificate,
c. 1932. Paper award for proven Wheaties consumption. - **$15 $40 $60**

SKP-10

SKP-10. Wheaties "Skippy Racer Club" Cello. Button,
c. 1932. - **$15 $30 $60**

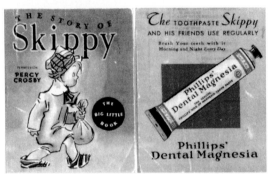

SKP-11

SKP-11. "The Story Of Skippy" BLB,
1934. Phillips' Dental Magnesia Toothpaste. - **$10 $25 $60**

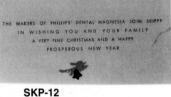

SKP-12

SKP-12. Christmas Card,
c. 1935. Phillips Dental Magnesia. - **$10 $25 $40**

SKP-13

SKP-13. Mystic Circle Club Folder,
c. 1935. Phillips Toothpaste. Folder opens to 16" length. -
$20 $40 $75

SKP-14

SKP-15

SKP-14. "Skippy Mystic Circle Club" Member Card,
c. 1935. Phillips Dental Magnesia. - **$10 $20 $30**

SKP-15. "Skippy Mystic Circle" Felt Fabric Beanie,
c. 1935. Phillips Dental Magnesia. - **$25 $50 $100**

SKP-16

SKP-17

**SKP-16. "The Atlanta Georgian's Silver Anniversary"
Litho. Button,**
1937. Named newspaper. From set of various characters. -
$15 $40 $60

**SKP-17. "Stories Of Interesting People Who Wear
Glasses Booklet,**
1937. Manual for "Skippy Good Eyesight Brigade". -
$10 $15 $20

SKP-18

SKP-19

SKP-18. Skippy Good Eyes Brigade Silvered Badge,
1937. Scarce. - **$30 $60 $120**

SKP-19. Bisque Figure,
1930s. Store item, several versions.
Movable Arms, No Base - **$60 $125 $250**
One Arm Moves, Green Base - **$50 $90 $185**
Celluloid Figure - **$75 $200 $400**

SKP-20   SKP-21

KP-20. Skippy Mazda Lamps Sign,
930s. 15" by 26". - **$150 $300 $600**

KP-21. "Fro-Joy Ice Cream" 24x36" Cardboard Store ign,
930s. - **$100 $200 $300**

SKP-24

SKP-22

SKP-23

KP-22. Paper Mask,
930s. Socony Oil. From set of "Five Free Funny Faces". - **0 $20 $30**

KP-23. Fabric Patch,
930s. Probably Wheaties. Orange/blue/white stitched esign. - **$20 $40 $60**

KP-24. Skippy Cello. Button From Effanbee Doll,
930s. - **$20 $35 $60**

SKP-25   SKP-26   SKP-27

KP-25. Cello. Button,
930s. Includes artst's name "P. L. Crosby". - **$20 $30 $50**

KP-26. "Saturday Chicago American" Litho. Button,
930s. From newspaper "16 Pages Of Comics" series of 10 own characters including two Skippy versions. - **0 $20 $30**

SKP-27. "Sunday Examiner" Litho. Button,
1930s. From "50 Comics" set of various newspaper characters, match number to win prize. - **$10 $20 $35**

THE SKY BLAZERS

The Sky Blazers, a radio series that dramatized episodes in the history of aviation, aired on CBS for a season (1939-1940), sponsored by Wonder bread. The show was created by Phillips H. Lord and hosted and narrated by Colonel Roscoe Turner, an early aviation hero and holder of various speed records. Each show closed with Turner interviewing the subject of that night's episode. Two issues of a *Sky Blazers* comic book appeared in 1940.

SBZ-1

SBZ-2

SBZ-1. "'Sky Blazers' Wonder Bread" Brass Wings Pin,
c. 1939. - **$15 $20 $35**

SBZ-2. Balsa Airplane In Tube,
c. 1939. - **$60 $120 $240**

SBZ-3

SBZ-4

SBZ-3. Wonder Bread 8x12" Diecut Paper Sign,
1940. Scarce. Promotes 7:00 P.M. CBS radio show. - **$50 $100 $200**

SBZ-4. Comic Book #1,
Sept. 1940. **$45 $135 $365**

SBZ-5

SBZ-6

SBZ-5. "Sky Blazers/Roscoe Turner" Photo,
1940. Wonder Bread. From Sponsor Day Kit at New York World's Fair. - **$15 $25 $35**

SBZ-6. "Sky Blazers Model Aircraft Exposition/Roscoe Turner" Contest Registration Folder,
1940. Wonder Bread. For Sponsor Day at New York World's Fair. - **$10 $15 $25**

SBZ-7

SBZ-7. "Sky Blazers/Roscoe Turner" Waxed Paper Bread Loaf Inserts,
c. 1940. Wonder Bread. Each - **$10 $15 $25**

SKY CLIMBERS

The Sky Climbers of America was an aviation-related club sponsored by boys' clothing stores around 1929. Members could qualify as Oiler, Mechanic, Pilot, Ace, or Flight Leader. The symbol of the club was a youthful aviator type known as Pete Weet.

SCL-1

SCL-2

SCL-1. "Sky Climbers Of America" Club Manual,
1929. - **$20 $40 $80**

SCL-2. Fabric Patch,
1929. - **$20 $35 $60**

SCL-3

SCL-4

SCL-3. Club Member Card,
1929. - **$20 $40 $60**

SCL-4. Club Water Transfer Paper Picture,
1929. Rare. - **$30 $60 $120**

SCL-5

SCL-6

SCL-5. "The Sky Climbers" Cello. Button,
1929. - **$10 $20 $30**

SCL-6. Rules And Regulations Book,
c. 1929. - **$30 $60 $90**

SCL-7

SCL-7. "Secret Manual For Sky Climbers Only!",
c. 1930. - **$20 $40 $80**

SCL-8

SCL-9

SKY-1

SKY-2

**CL-8. "Ace/The Sky Climbers Of America" Brass Bar
d Pendant Badge,**
1930. "Ace" designation on pendant is one of higher club
nks. - **$40 $80 $160**

**CL-9. "The Sky Climbers Of America/Flight Leader"
ass Award Bar Badge,**
1930. Denotes high rank in club. - **$30 $60 $120**

SKY-1. Radar Signal Ring,
1946. Top glows in dark. - **$75 $110 $150**

SKY-2. "Secret Signalscope",
1947. Whistle/magnifier held in scope tube.
Near Mint In Mailer - **$175**
Scope - **$35 $75 $100**

SCL-10

SKY-3

SKY-3. Sky King Secret Compartment Belt Buckle,
1948. Prototype designed by Orin Armstrong for Robbins Co.
Unique - **$5000**

L-10. Last Club Manual,
930. - **$20 $40 $80**

SKY-4

SKY-5

SKY-6

SKY KING

erica's favorite flying cowboy, Sky King aired on ABC
o from 1946 to 1950 and on Mutual from 1950 to 1954,
nsored starting in 1947 by Peter Pan peanut butter. The
es centered on the crime-fighting exploits of rancher-pilot
uyler King and his niece Penny and nephew Clipper.
g's Flying Crown Ranch had an airstrip from which he and
young sidekicks flew off in his plane The Songbird to
g criminals to justice. The program made a successful
sition to television as *Sky King Theater*, airing on NBC
51-1952) and ABC (1952-1954), with Peter Pan again
nsoring. A new television series titled *Sky King* was syn-
ted from 1956 to 1958, then aired on CBS from 1959 to
6, sponsored by Nabisco. Kirby Grant played King and
ria Winters was Penny. Both Peter Pan and Nabisco
ed program-related premiums, usually copyrighted by
k Chertok Productions.

SKY-4. "Mystery Picture Ring" Instruction Sheet,
1948. - **$75 $90 $100**

SKY-5. Mystery Picture Ring,
1948. Faint image on rectangular plastic sheet under gray
plastic top has almost always disappeared.
Complete No Image - **$125 $250 $400**
Near Mint With Image - **$900**

SKY-6. Magni-Glo Writing Ring,
1949. - **$50 $75 $100**

SKY-7

SKY-8

SKY-7. "Spy Detecto Writer",
1949. Elaborate premium that includes decoder. Comes in all brass or brass/aluminum versions. - **$40 $85 $125**

SKY-8. Electronic Television Picture Ring,
1949. Brass and plastic, came with photo strip to be developed and cut showing Jim, Penny, Clipper, Martha.
Ring Only - **$50 $90 $125**
Photo Set - **$75 $90 $100**

SKY-10

SKY-9

SKY-11

SKY-9. "2-Way Tele-Blinker Ring" Instruction Sheet,
1949. Peter Pan Peanut Butter. Sheet includes ring order coupon expiring March 13, 1950. - **$15 $30 $60**

SKY-10. Tele-Blinker Ring,
1949. Brass and other metals signal ring. - **$75 $120 $160**

SKY-11. Navajo Treasure Ring,
1950. - **$75 $110 $150**

SKY-12

SKY-13

SKY-12. "Safety Is No Accident" Litho. Button,
c. 1950. - **$30 $50 $80**

SKY-13. Kaleidoscope Prototype Ring,
c. 1950. Large brass and other metals viewer ring developed in prototype design by Orin Armstrong but never actually offered as premium.
Unique - **$9500**

SKY-14

SKY-14. "Aztec Emerald Calendar Ring" With Instruction Sheet,
1951. Mint Boxed With Instructions - **$1100**
Ring - **$300 $625 $950**
Instructions - **$125 $135 $150**

SKY-15

SKY-15. "Detecto-Microscope" With Accessories,
1952. Cardboard stand and four specimens not shown, ma glows in dark. Near Mint Complete - **$500**
Plastic Tube Only - **$25 $50 $75**
Map - **$20 $40 $60**

SKY-16

SKY-16. "Mystery Picture Ring" Newspaper Ad,
1953. - **$5 $10 $15**

SKY-18

SKY-17

SKY-17. "Stamping Kit" Order Blank,
1953. - **$15 $25 $40**

SKY-18. Stamping Kit,
1953. Tin container holding ink pad and personalized rubb stamp. Ink often rusts the tin. - **$20 $40 $75**

SKY-19

SKY-19. Figure Set,
1956. Nabisco Wheat & Rice Honeys. Soft plastic in various colors. Sky King, Clipper, Penny, Sheriff, Song Bird (plane), Yellow Fury (horse). Each - **$15 $20 $35**

SKY-20

SKY-21

SKY-20. Nabisco Fan Postcard,
c. 1956. - **$10 $20 $35**

SKY-21. Kirby Grant Contest Photo,
1957. McGowan Studios. Note on back about search for look-alike to play Kirby's twin in upcoming film. - **$15 $30 $50**

SKY-22

SKY-22. Fan Club Nabisco Contest Postcard,
1959. Oversized 5-1/2x7" card. - **$20 $40 $75**

SKY-24

SKY-23

SKY-25

SKY-23. Nabisco Fan Club Member Kit,
1959. Includes cut-out Sky King neckerchief ring plus membership card. - **$35 $70 $150**

SKY-24. Nabisco "Sky King Fan Club" Litho. Tin Tab Wings,
c. 1959. - **$40 $75 $125**

SKY-25. Autographed Photo,
1950s. - **$20 $40 $75**

SKY-26

SKY-27

SKY-26. "Cook Out With Sky King" Recipe Folder,
1950s. Nabisco. - **$30 $60 $100**

SKY-27. Cowboy Tie With Envelope,
1950s. Near Mint In Mailer - **$75**
Tie Only - **$15 $25 $35**

SKY RIDERS

Spelled either Sky Riders or Skyriders, this 1930s aviation related club issued celluloid buttons, brass wings badges and lithographed tin wings. The items don't specify a sponsor and research efforts yielded no information.

SRD-1

SRD-2

SRD-1. Club Knife,
1930. Scarce. - **$30 $60 $120**

SRD-2. "Skyrider Pilot's Club/Certified Pilot" Cello. Button,
1930s. - **$20 $40 $75**

SRD-3

SRD-4

SRD-3. "Sky Riders Club" Member Cello. Button,
1930s. - **$20 $40 $75**

SRD-4. "Lieutenant/Member Skyriders Club" Brass Wings Badge,
1930s. Bronze luster. - **$10 $20 $30**

SRD-5   SRD-6

SRD-5. "Captain/Member Skyriders Club" Brass Wings Badge,
1930s. Dark gold luster. - **$15 $30 $50**

SRD-6. "Colonel/Member Skyriders Club" Brass Wings Badge,
1930s. Bronze luster. - **$15 $30 $50**

SRD-7   SRD-8

SRD-7. "General" Brass Wings Badge,
1930s. Highest rank club badge. - **$20 $40 $100**

SRD-8. "Lieutenant" Litho. Tin Rank Badge,
1930s. - **$10 $20 $30**

SRD-9

SRD-9. "Captain" Litho. Tin Rank Badge,
1930s. - **$10 $20 $30**

SMILIN' ED McCONNELL

Ed McConnell (1892-1954), singer and banjo picker, moved from vaudeville to local radio in 1922, then to the networks from 1932 to 1941, doing his musical variety shows for a number of sponsors. In 1944 McConnell teamed with Buster Brown shoes to create a children's program combining dramatic tales, music, and listeners' letters. Known variously as *Smilin' Ed's Buster Brown Gang, The Smilin' Ed McConnell Show, The Buster Brown Gang*, or *The Buster Brown Show*, the program aired on NBC radio until 1953 and meantime made a successful move to television in 1950, appearing on all three networks: NBC (1950-1951), CBS (1951-1953), and ABC (1953-1955). The imaginary cast starred Froggy the Gremlin, along with Squeeky the Mouse, Midnight the Cat, and Old Grandie the Piano. Items are normally copyrighted J. Ed. McConnell. After McConnell's death Andy Devine took over and the show was renamed *Andy's Gang*.

SMI-1   SMI-2   SMI-3

SMI-1. "Smilin' Ed McConnell" Autographed Photo,
1932. First year of CBS radio show. - **$25 $50 $75**

SMI-2. "Under His Wing" Theme Song Folder,
1939. Taystee Bread. - **$20 $40 $75**

SMI-3. "Smilin' Ed McConnell/Bill Stewart" Fan Card,
1930s. - **$8 $12 $20**

SMI-4

SMI-4. Froggy Paper Mask,
1946. - **$15 $25 $50**

SMI-5   SMI-6   SMI-7

SMI-5. "Member Buster Brown Gang" Litho. Tin Tab,
1946. From radio show. - **$15 $30 $50**

SMI-6. "Member Buster Brown Gang/Squeeky" Litho. Ti Tab,
1946. From radio show. - **$10 $20 $30**

SMI-7. "Froggy" Litho. Tin Tab,
1946. From radio show. - **$20 $45 $75**

SMI-8

SMI-9

MI-8. "Midnight" Litho. Tin Tab,
946. From radio show. - **$15 $30 $50**

MI-9. Squeeze Toy,
948. Store item by Rempel Mfg. Co.
mall 5" Size - **$60 $125 $200**
arge 9-1/2" Size - **$75 $150 $250**

SMI-10

SMI-11

MI-10. "Smilin' Ed's Buster Brown Comics" #13,
48. Buster Brown Shoes. Issued between 1945 and 1959.
rst Issue - **$60 $190 $500**
econd Issue - **$20 $60 $135**
hers - **$8 $22 $45**

MI-11. Buster Brown Paddle Ball Game,
1948. - **$30 $60 $120**

SMI-12

SMI-13

MI-12. "Buster Brown Gang" Card With Brass Badge,
1948. Card - **$15 $25 $50**
dge - **$8 $15 $25**

MI-13. Buster Brown Gang Brass Ring,
1948. Pictures him and Tige with Froggy and Squeeky on
nds. - **$25 $50 $75**

SMI-14

SMI-15

**SMI-14. "Smilin' Ed McConnell's Buster Brown Gang"
Bandanna,**
c. 1948. - **$25 $50 $80**

SMI-15. "Buster Brown T.V. Theatre" Flicker Card,
c. 1950. Screen area has movement image of Froggy jumping up and down. - **$30 $65 $100**

SMI-16

SMI-17

SMI-16. "Buster Brown Gang" Card With Litho. Button,
1953. Card - **$10 $20 $40**
Button - **$8 $12 $20**

SMI-17. "Treasure Hunt Game" Shoe Box,
c. 1950s. - **$25 $50 $75**

SMOKEY BEAR

Smokey was created for a U.S. Forest Service poster in 1944 to warn of the dangers - and the threat to the country's wartime lumber supply - of forest fires. Since then the brown bear with the ranger hat has become the beloved symbol of the Forest Service and spokesbear for the nation's trees. Smokey has been given special trademark status, had his own zip code, appeared on a postage stamp in 1984, and in balloon form has floated in Macy's Thanksgiving Day Parade since 1968. "Remember - only you can prevent forest fires!" dates from 1947. In 1950 a four-pound black bear cub that survived a forest fire in New Mexico was given the name Smokey, nursed back to health, and sent to live at the National Zoo in Washington, D.C. That Smokey died in 1976 but he was promptly replaced to continue as a symbol of conservation.

The Smokey Bear Show, a half-hour animated cartoon series, was broadcast on ABC from 1969 to 1971, stressing the importance of saving natural resources and protecting wildlife. Smokey comic books appeared from 1950 into the 1970s, and in 1994 a traveling exhibition and party on the Mall in Washington celebrated Smokey's golden anniversary.

SMO-1

SMO-7

SMO-8

SMO-9

SMO-1. "Prevent Woods Fires" 12x14" Cardboard Sign,
1955. - **$15 $30 $50**

SMO-2. Calendar,
1956. - **$5 $8 $15**

SMO-7. "Soaky" Plastic Soap Bottle,
c. 1965. Colgate-Palmolive Co. - **$5 $12 $20**

SMO-8. Ceramic Salt & Pepper Shakers,
c. 1960s. Store item. - **$12 $20 $30**

SMO-9. Wristwatch,
c. 1960s. Store item. Boxed - **$60 $90 $125**
Loose - **$25 $40 $75**

SMO-3

SMO-4

SMO-10

SMO-11

SMO-12

SMO-3. "Forest Fire Prevention" Award Certificate,
1950s. - **$10 $20 $35**

SMO-4. Cloth Doll With Plastic Hat And Badge,
c. 1950s. Store item by Ideal Toy Corp. - **$25 $50 $75**

SMO-10. Plastic Bank,
c. 1960s. Store item. - **$15 $30 $50**

SMO-11. Composition Bobbing Head,
1960s. Store item. - **$60 $100 $150**

SMO-12. "Junior Forest Ranger/Prevent Forest Fires" T Badge,
1960s. Either silver, brass or copper luster. - **$5 $10 $15**

SMO-5

SMO-6

SMO-13

SMO-14

SMO-5. "Join Smokey Ranger Club" Litho. Tin Tab,
1950s. - **$15 $25 $40**

SMO-6. Biographical Card,
1965. U.S. Department Of Agriculture-Forest Service. -
$3 $5 $10

SMO-13. "March Of Comics",
1973. Various Advertisers. - **$2 $4 $8**

SMO-14. Fabric Patch,
c. 1970s. - **$5 $10 $15**

SNAP, CRACKLE, POP

The Kellogg Company introduced Snap, Crackle, and Pop in 1933 to personify the lively sounds made when a bowl of its Rice Krispies meets cold milk. Originally drawn by Vernon Grant, the cartoon trio has survived to this day on cereal boxes and in advertising, singing and dancing and crackling and popping for kids everywhere.

SNP-1

SNP-1. Paper Masks,
1933. Kellogg's copyright with unsigned Vernon Grant art.
Each - **$30 $60 $90**

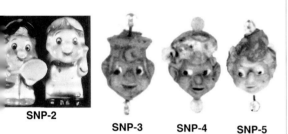

SNP-2   SNP-3   SNP-4   SNP-5

SNP-2. "Snap/Pop" China Salt & Pepper Shakers,
1930s. - **$8 $15 $25**

SNP-3. "Pop" Face Ring,
1952. Brass bands holding soft rubber head that changes expressions by turning small knobs. - **$250 $450 $650**

SNP-4. "Snap" Face Ring,
1952. Brass bands holding soft rubber head that changes expressions by turning small knobs. - **$200 $375 $550**

SNP-5. "Crackle" Face Ring,
1952. Brass bands holding soft rubber head that changes expressions by turning small knobs. - **$100 $200 $300**

SNP-6

SNP-7

SNP-6. Cloth Pattern Doll,
1954. Uncut - **$20 $40 $60**
Mailer - **$10 $20 $40**

SNP-7. Cloth Pattern Doll,
1954. Uncut - **$20 $40 $60**
Mailer - **$10 $20 $40**

SNP-8

SNP-8. Cloth Pattern Doll,
1954. Uncut - **$20 $40 $60**
Mailer - **$10 $20 $40**

SNP-9. Friendly Folk Wood & Fabric Figure Set,
1972. Frosted Mini-Wheats. Accent by simulated hair or fur.
Each - **$3 $5 $8**

SNP-9

SNP-10   SNP-11

SNP-10. Vinyl Figure Set,
1975. Each - **$8 $15 $25**

SNP-11. Glow Plastic Figures,
c. 1980. Snap, Crackle, Pop, Tony, Tony Jr., Toucan Sam, Dig 'Em, Tusk (elephant). Each - **$2 $3 $5**

SNOW WHITE AND THE SEVEN DWARFS

Disney's first full-length animated feature, *Snow White and the Seven Dwarfs* was both a cinematic masterpiece and a box office smash. The film, a retelling of the Grimm brothers' 19th century fairy tale, premiered in December 1937 and went on to break attendance records in the U.S. and throughout the world. Manufacturers rushed to jump on the bandwagon, producing a wealth of licensed items that elevated Dopey, Grumpy, Doc, Bashful, Sleepy, Happy, and Sneezy, as well as Snow White, to the level of Mickey and other earlier Disney characters as merchandising phenomena. Toys, dolls, games, costumes, storybooks, comic books, clothing, umbrellas, food and drink, watches and clocks, lamps and radios, jewelry, furniture - the list of Snow White items is virtually endless.

SNO-1   **SNO-2**

SNO-1. Mask,
1937. Procter And Gamble. Set of eight including Dwarfs issued by Proctor And Gamble and others. Each -
$15 $25 $40

SNO-2. Board Game,
1937. Johnson & Johnson Tek Toothbrushes. Board edge held perforated playing pieces.
Complete With Slip Case Wrapper - **$35 $75 $125**
Board Only - **$15 $30 $50**

SNO-3

SNO-3. Movie Herald,
1938. Various theaters. - **$10 $15 $30**

SNO-4   **SNO-5**

SNO-4. Gum Wrapper,
1938. Dietz Gum Co. Also see item SNO-7. - **$30 $50 $80**

SNO-5. Dairy Glasses,
1938. Various sponsors. Set of eight. Each - **$10 $15 $25**

SNO-6

SNO-6. "Moving Picture Machine",
1938. Pepsodent toothpaste.
Assembled With All 56 Pictures - **$125 $200 $300**
Unpunched - **$150 $300 $450**

SNO-7

SNO-7. Dietz Gum Co. Box,
1938. Held 100 packages. Also see item SNO-4. -
$75 $175 $300

SNO-8

SNO-9

SNO-8. "Jingle Club" Membership Request Card,
1938. Various retailers. Offers Jingle Book and membership button. - **$20 $40 $75**

SNO-9. "Jingle Book" With Mailer Envelope,
1938. Various retailers. Album for bread company pictures.
Envelope - **$8 $15 $25**
Book - **$25 $50 $90**

SNO-10   **SNO-11**

SNO-10. "Snow White Jingle Club Member" Cello. Button,
1938. 1-1/4" size, widely distributed by toy stores and others. - **$10 $20 $30**

SNO-11. "Snow White Jingle Club" 3-1/2" Cello. Button
1938. Large version for employee of store participating in club advertising promotion. - **$175 $300 $700**

SNO-12

NO-12. Milk Glass Cereal Bowl,
938. Post's Huskies Whole Wheat Flakes. - **$20 $40 $70**

SNO-13

SNO-14

NO-13. Sleepy Beanie,
938. - **$30 $60 $90**

NO-14. Grape-Nuts Cereal Sign,
938. Scarce. - **$75 $150 $300**

SNO-15

NO-15. Palmolive Cut-Out Sheets,
1938. European issue, set of 12 sheets.
ncut Set - **$100 $200 $300**

SNO-16

SNO-17

NO-16. Post Toasties Box Back With Cut-Outs,
1938. Back Panel - **$10 $20 $30**

NO-17. "Dopey's Christmas Tree" Book,
1938. Various department stores. - **$25 $50 $75**

SNO-18

SNO-19

SNO-18. Department Store 18x25" Paper Hanger Sign,
c. 1938. Various stores. Same image both sides for
Christmas toy departments. - **$75 $175 $300**

**SNO-19. "Guards Of The Magic Forest" 18x20" Paper
Mounting Chart For Bread Premium Pictures,**
c. 1938. Unidentified bread company. Holds 36 cut-out pictures completing forest scene. Unused - **$100 $200 $300**
Completed - **$150 $300 $450**

SNO-20

SNO-21

SNO-20. "All Star Parade" Glass,
1939. From a set of dairy product containers picturing various
Disney characters. - **$10 $20 $40**

SNO-21. Dopey Studio Fan Card,
c. 1939. - **$20 $40 $75**

SNO-22

SNO-22. "Dopey Bubble Gum Club" Secret Code Folder,
1940s. Yankee Doodle Gum Co. - **$20 $40 $75**

SNO-23

SNO-23 Bendix Washing Machines Comic,
1952. - **$10** **$30** **$75**

SNO-24

SNO-25

SNO-24. "The Milky Way" Comic Booklet,
1955. American Dairy Association. - **$10** **$30** **$75**

SNO-25. "Dairy Recipes" Booklet,
1955. American Dairy Association. - **$10** **$20** **$35**

SNO-26

SNO-27

SNO-26. "Mystery Of The Missing Magic" Comic,
1958. Various advertisers. - **$10** **$20** **$40**

SNO-27. Bread Labels,
1950s. Eight designs shown from probable set of sixteen.
Each - **$2** **$4** **$6**

SNO-28

SNO-28. Bread Label Picture,
1950s. Various sponsors. Holds 16 label cut-outs.
Completed - **$30** **$60** **$100**
Blank - **$20** **$35** **$75**

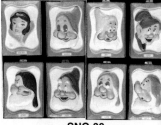

SNO-30

SNO-29

SNO-31

SNO-29. "Snow White" Paper Game,
1960s. Royal Gelatin. - **$15** **$25** **$40**

SNO-30. Thin Plastic Wall Plaques,
1960s. Reynolds Wrap. Set. - **$10** **$20** **$40**

SNO-31. McDonald's Acrylic On Metal Pin,
1980s. - **$8** **$15** **$25**

SPACE PATROL

High adventure in the wild, vast reaches of space! Mission
of daring in the name of interplanetary justice! Led b
Commander Buzz Corry, the crew of the spaceship Ter
policed the galaxies for the United Planets of the 30th cent
ry, traveling through time and battling crazed scientist
space pirates, and weird creatures.

Space Patrol was first broadcast locally on KECA-TV in L
Angeles in March 1950. Six months later it went national
the ABC television and radio networks, where it aired un
1955. Corry, played by Ed Kemmer, was accompanied I
young Cadet Happy (Smokin' rockets!), played by Ly
Osborne, and lovely Carol Karlyle, played by Virginia Hewi
as they triumphed over such villains as Mr. Proteus, Capta
Dagger, the Space Spider, and the evil Black Falcon, alia
Prince Baccarratti.

The shows were sponsored by Ralston cereals (1951-195
and Nestle foods (1954-1955), and dozens of program-rela
ed items were created for premium use and retail sale

pace suits, helmets, communicators, signal flashlights, a miniature spaceport, a rocket cockpit, Paralyzer Ray Gun, Cosmic Smoke Gun, trading cards, comic books and club membership material were among the available merchandise.

Many licensed items were sold by the May Stores on the West coast, but national distribution was limited. In 1952-1953, a wide variety of merchandise could be purchased through catalog flier order blanks from "Space Headquarters" Hollywood, California. In 1954 Ralston awarded a $30,000 replica of Buzz's spaceship to a young contest winner. Items are normally copyrighted Mike Moser Enterprises.

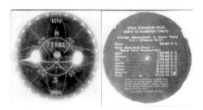

SPC-1

PC-1. Plastic Dome Compass,
1951. Store item. Came with boxed wristwatch by US Time. - $25 $50 $75

SPC-2

SPC-3

PC-2. "Space Patrol" Metal Buckle On "Jet-Glow" Belt,
1951. Decoder on back of buckle, belts usually no longer low. Complete - $75 $125 $200
Buckle Only - $40 $75 $125

PC-3. Ralston Club Membership Kit,
1952. Letter, handbook, photo, envelope.
Complete Near Mint - $250
Handbook - $50 $75 $125
Others, Each - $10 $20 $35

SPC-4

SPC-5

SPC-4. Membership Card,
1952. - $15 $30 $60

SPC-5. Official Catalogue,
1952. Shows 22 items priced for sale. - $35 $75 $125

SPC-6

SPC-6. "Chart Of The Universe" 8x11",
1952. - $50 $80 $150

SPC-7

SPC-7. "Space Patrol" Comic Book Vol. 1 #1,
1952. Back cover premium ad. - $70 $210 $565

SPC-9

SPC-8

SPC-8. "Space Patrol" Vol. 1 #2 Comic Book,
Oct.-Nov. 1952. Store item by Approved Comics. - $50 $150 $415

SPC-9. Cosmic Smoke Gun,
1952. Smaller 4-1/2" size in red plastic. - $75 $125 $240

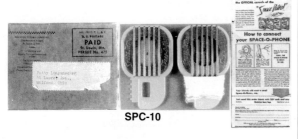

SPC-10. Space-O-Phone Set,
1952. Boxed - **$50 $75 $150**
Phones Only - **$25 $50 $75**

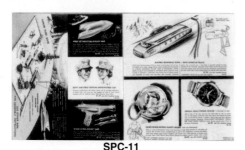

SPC-11. "Lunar Fleet Base" Instruction Sheet/Premium Catalogue,
1952. - **$35 $75 $125**

SPC-12. Ralston "Lunar Fleet Base",
1952. Rare. Plastic parts shown, set also includes cardboard buildings, etc. Near Mint In Mailer - **$2500**
Complete Used - **$300 $750 $1500**

SPC-13. Plastic Badge,
1952. Metallic red, blue, and silver finish. - **$75 $150 $300**

SPC-14. Cosmic Glow Rocket Ring,
1952. Unmarked Space Patrol premium plastic holding glow-in-dark powder in viewer. - **$400 $625 $850**

SPC-15. "Space Patrol Blood Boosters" Litho. Tin Tab,
1952. - **$35 $70 $125**

SPC-16. "Outer Space Plastic Helmet",
1952. Store item and also used as a contest prize. Includes inflatable vinyl piece that fits around neck.
Near Mint Boxed - **$1000**
Helmet Only - **$150 $250 $400**

SPC-17. Rice Chex Cardboard Hanging Mobile Store Display,
1953. Scarce. Each part printed identically on both sides, largest part is 27" wide. - **$300 $750 $1200**

SPC-18. "Magic Space Pictures" Five-Part Diecut Cardboard Store Ceiling Mobile,
1953. Scarce. Ralston Wheat Chex. Hanger display with 20" wide upper title part. - **$300 $750 $1200**

SPC-19. Plastic Microscope,
1953. Came with plastic slides. Complete - **$60 $100 $160**

SPC-20. Ralston Cardboard "Outer Space Helmet",
1953. Includes one-way viewing panel.
Near Mint With Mailer - **$200**
Complete Helmet - **$60 $80 $150**

SPC-22

SPC-21

SPC-23

SPC-26. Christmas Catalogue Mailing Folder,
c. 1953. Shows 13 items priced for sale. - **$35 $75 $125**

SPC-27. "Ralston Rocket" Card,
c. 1953. - **$25 $50 $100**

SPC-29

SPC-28

SPC-21. Magic Space Picture,
1953. Set of 24. Each - **$12 $20 $30**

SPC-22. Binoculars,
1953. Green plastic premium issue, black plastic store item.
Each - **$50 $85 $150**

SPC-23. "Terra V" Rocket Film Projector,
1953. Includes 20 frame filmstrip.
Projector - **$75 $150 $200**
Film - **$25 $60 $100**

SPC-28. Ralston "Buzz Corry Color Book",
c. 1953. Example picture shows both covers. -
$30 $70 $100

SPC-29. Smoke Gun,
c. 1953. 6" green metallic. Came on card with smoke packets "Good For 10,000 Safe Shots".
Gun Only - **$100 $250 $300**
On Card - **$200 $375 $500**

SPC-30

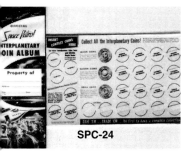

SPC-24

SPC-25

SPC-31

SPC-24. "Interplanetary Coin Album",
1953. Schwinn Bicycles, others. Slotted for 24-coin set plus supplemental Schwinn coins. - **$60 $125 $200**

SPC-25. "Interplanetary Space Patrol Credits" Plastic Coin,
1953. Four denominations each for Moon, Saturn, Terra in gold, blue, black or silver (most common).
Silver - **$3 $8 $12**
Other Colors - **$5 $12 $20**

SPC-30. Man-From-Mars Totem Head,
1954. Includes silvered one-way plastic sheet for viewing.
In Envelope - **$40 $75 $150**
Assembled - **$25 $50 $75**

SPC-31. Periscope Cardboard Assembly Kit In Mailer Envelope,
1954. Near Mint In Envelope - **$400**
Assembled - **$50 $125 $200**

SPC-26

SPC-27

SPC-32

SPC-33

SPC-32. Hydrogen Ray Gun Ring,
1954. - **$150 $240 $325**

SPC-33. Ralston Trading Card,
1950s. Wheat and Rice Chex. One card insert per box, set of 40. Star And Planets Series (13) - **$5 $10 $25**
Rockets, Jets And Weapons Series (14) - **$5 $10 $25**
Space Heroes Series (13) - **$5 $10 $25**
Except Buzz Corey-Cadet Happy Each - **$8 $16 $40**

SPC-34

SPC-35

SPC-34. Cast Photos Folder,
1950s. Dr. Ross dog & cat food. Front cover has photo, back cover facsimile signatures. - **$50 $80 $150**

SPC-35. Plastic Frame Character Charms,
1950s. Unsure if Ralston premium or vending machine issue.
Each - **$10 $20 $35**

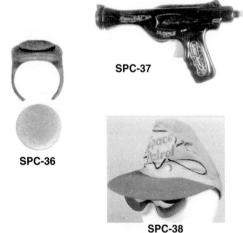

SPC-37

SPC-36

SPC-38

SPC-36. "Space Patrol" Title Printer Plastic Ring,
1950s. Top has "Space Patrol" printed backwards for correct stamped image after inking from included tiny ink pad.
Complete - **$300 $400 $500**
Missing Ink Pad - **$125 $175 $225**

SPC-37. Plastic Dart Gun,
1950s. Store item. Sold with two darts.
Complete - **$50 $75 $125**
Gun Only - **$30 $50 $75**

SPC-38. Fabric "Cosmic Cap",
1950s. Store item by Bailey of Hollywood. - **$75 $150 $250**

SPC-39   SPC-40

SPC-39. Plastic Rocketship Barrette,
1950s. Store item by Ben-Hur. On Card - **$35 $75 $125**

SPC-40. Plastic Gun Barrette,
1950s. Store item by Ben-Hur. On Card - **$35 $75 $125**

SPC-41

SPC-41. Plastic "Emergency Kit",
1950s. Store item by Regis Space Toys. Handle contains flashlight. Complete - **$300 $600 $1200**
Empty - **$200 $400 $600**

SPC-42   SPC-43

SPC-42. "Commander" Vinyl Rain Hat With Cardboard Tag,
1950s. Store item by Marketon Co. with license of Space Patrol Enterprises. Hat - **$50 $100 $175**
Tag - **$20 $50 $75**

SPC-43. "Space Patrol Cadet" Silvered Metal Badge,
1950s. Made in Japan. Near Mint On Card - **$450**
Badge Only - **$75 $150 $300**

SPEED GIBSON OF THE I. S. P.

Young Speed Gibson, at the age of 15, was an ace pilot and member of the International Secret Police in this radio adventure series that was syndicated briefly in 1937-1938. Speed along with his uncle, top agent Clint Barlow, and pilot Barney Dunlap, circled the globe in their ship The Flying Clipper on the trail of the criminal Octopus gang. "Suffering whang-doodles, Speed."

SGB-1

SGB-5   SGB-6

SGB-5. "Rocket-Gyro X-3" Balsa/Cardboard Flying Toy With Mailer,
c. 1937. "Hikes" chocolate-coated wheat cereal. Assembled toy flown by rubber band.
Near Mint With Mailer - $150
Without Mailer - $25 $50 $100

SGB-6. Stroehmann's Bread "Prize Winner" Cello. Badge,
c. 1937. Various sponsors. - $10 $18 $30

GB-1. Code Book Manual,
. 1937. Dreikorn's Orange Wrap Bread. Includes member-hip card and oath to sign. - $35 $75 $150

SGB-2

SGB-7   SGB-8   SGB-9

SGB-2. Adventure Map With Promotion Record And Envelope,
. 1937. Peter Pan Bakery and others.
Map - $50 $100 $150
Promotion Record - $15 $25 $35
Envelope - $5 $10 $15

SGB-7. "Secret Police I.S.P." Litho. Club Member Button,
c. 1937. - $10 $25 $35

SGB-8. Member's Small Blue/Silvered Brass Button,
c. 1937. Phil A. Halle. - $12 $25 $40

SGB-9. Gorman's Bread "Speed Gibson Flying Police" Enameled Brass Badge,
c. 1937. - $20 $35 $60

SGB-3

SGB-4

SGB-10   SGB-11

SGB-3. "African Adventure And Clue Hunt" Map,
. 1937. Brown's Bread Ltd. (Canada). - $65 $150 $250

SGB-4. "Wings" Newspaper #1,
. 1937. Cote's Master Loaf Bread. - $20 $40 $75

SGB-10. "Speed Gibson Flying Corps I.S.P." Brass Badge,
c. 1937. Pictures him in aviator helmet above airplane. - $50 $100 $150

SGB-11. I.S.P. "Canadian Division" Club Card,
c. 1937. Back has code used during Speed Gibson African adventures. - $25 $50 $75

SGB-12

SGB-13

SAS-4

SAS-5

SAS-6

SGB-12. "Speed Gibson/Secret Police I.S.P." Canadian Cello. Button,
c. 1937. Made by Shaw Mfg. Co., Toronto. - **$15 $30 $50**

SGB-13. "Speed Gibson's Great Clue Hunt" Paper Sheet,
1938. Unidentified bread company. Pencil activity sheet for following radio broadcasts. Rare. - **$40 $140 $300**

SAS-4. Store Display 8" Vinyl Figure,
1960s. - **$200 $350 $600**

SAS-5. "Pron-Tito" Spanish Litho. Tray,
1960s. - **$50 $100 $150**

SAS-6. Small Flicker Sheet,
1960s. About 1-1/2" square with "Pron Tito" name on his hat. He holds magician's wand and when tilted, a glass of the product appears. - **$15 $30 $50**

SPEEDY ALKA-SELTZER

Alka-Seltzer, an antacid/analgesic combination tablet, was first marketed in 1931 by Miles Laboratories of Elkhart, Indiana. From 1951 to 1964 product promotion featured a perky little fellow with a prominent forelock and a tablet for a hat. Originally called Sparky, Speedy evolved into a popular spokesfigure in television commercials and in promotional items issued by the manufacturer. Speedy is translated as Pron-Tito in Spanish.

THE SPIDER

Created by pulp author R.T.M. Scott in the 1930s, the Spider was actually Richard Wentworth, a wealthy New York crime fighter who divided his time between battling master criminals and hiding his true identity from the police. In the 1930s tale *Spider Strikes* and in the pulps into the 1940s, Wentworth's symbol, the drawing of a red spider, marked the foreheads of his vanquished and deceased criminal opponents. The same symbol appears on the pulp magazine club ring.

SPD-1

SPD-2

SPD-1. Movie Theater Club Member Card,
1938. Columbia Pictures. Rare. For 15-episode serial "The Spider Web" based on "The Spider Magazine" stories. - **$50 $125 $200**

SPD-2. Spider Enameled Metal Ring,
1939. Scarce. Spider Magazine and theater give-away. - **$2000 $4750 $9000**

SAS-1

SAS-2

SAS-3

SAS-1. Bank 5-1/2" Rubber Figure,
1950s. Earliest version with word "Bank" below coin slot on top of hat, later version without word.
First Version - **$75 $200 $400**
Later Version - **$65 $175 $300**

SAS-2. Cardboard Store Display,
1950s. - **$75 $100 $125**

SAS-3. "Speedy Alka-Seltzer" Enameled Brass Figural Pin,
c. 1950s. Back has threaded post fastener for lapel or button hole. - **$20 $30 $50**

SPD-3

SPD-4

D-3. "The Spider Returns" Movie Serial 9x12"
ndbill,
41. Columbia Pictures for local theater imprint. -
5 $50 $85

D-4. "The Spider Returns" Movie Pressbook,
41. Columbia Pictures. Contents show ring, example of
p cover, club card, mask. -
00 $200 $350

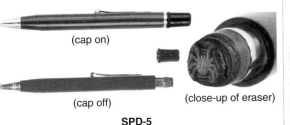

(cap on)

(cap off)

(close-up of eraser)

SPD-5

PD-5. Cello. Mechanical Pencil With "The Spider"
aser,
1942. Rare. The Spider pulp magazine. End cap covers
bber eraser with image on top surface. Succeeded Spider
ng as premium, produced in very limited quantity. -
:00 $1000 $2000

SPIDER-MAN

Vriter Stan Lee and artist Steve Ditko created *Spider-Man*
or the Marvel Comics Group in the 1960s and the superhero
as been battling for justice ever since. *Spider-Man* debuted
Amazing Fantasy #15 in August 1962. Six months later he
ppeared in his own comic book, the start of a series that
ontinues to this day. (A syndicated newspaper strip started
ublication in 1979.) Teenage Peter Parker, who acquired
is superhuman powers after being bitten by a radioactive
pider, takes on a variety of villains and criminals, all the
vhile working as a photographer for the New York *Daily*
Bugle and struggling with the problems of a typical 1962 ado-
escent. On television an animated *Spider-Man* series aired
n ABC from 1967 to 1970, and *Spider-Man and His*
Amazing Friends appeared on NBC in 1981. A 1977 live-
ction CBS special with Nicholas Hammond was followed by
brief prime-time series in 1978 and scattered repeats for a
ear. In 1995 Ralston Foods introduced Spider-Man sweet-
ned rice cereal, complete with trading cards inside specially
narked boxes. Merchandised items are usually copyrighted
Marvel Comics.

SPM-1

SPM-2

SPM-3

SPM-1. "The Amazing Spider-Man" 3-1/2" Cello. Button,
1966. Store item. #6 from numbered series.
Near Mint Bagged - $35
Loose - $10 $15 $25

SPM-2. Litho. Metal Bicycle Attachment Plate,
1967. Store item by Marx Toys. - $12 $25 $50

SPM-3. "Hong Kong" Vending Machine Aluminum Ring,
1960s. - $15 $25 $50

SPM-4

SPM-5

SPM-6

SPM-4. Spider-Man Vitamins Ring,
1976. Hudson Pharmaceutical Co. - $30 $45 $60

SPM-5. Plastic Magnetic Compass,
1978. - $5 $10 $15

SPM-6. "Spider-Man" 2-1/4" Cello. Button,
1978. Store item by Rainbow Designs. - $3 $8 $12

THE SPIRIT

The Spirit was created by Will Eisner in 1940 in the unusual
form of a comic book insert to be included with the comic
sections of Sunday newspapers. The feature, distributed by
the Register and Tribune Syndicate, survived until 1952,
accompanied by a daily strip from 1941 to 1944. *The Spirit* -
actually Denny Colt, a Central City crime fighter in a meager
eye mask - has become a strip classic. There have been
numerous comic book reprints from the 1940s into the
1990s, and a TV series pilot was broadcast in 1987.

SPR-1

SPR-1. "Paper Mask",
c. 1942. Various newspapers for Sunday comic book supplement beginning June 1940. - $75 $200 $400

SPR-2   SPR-3

SPR-2. "Star Journal" Cello. Button,
c. 1942. Various newspapers. For Sunday comic book supplement. - **$40 $80 $150**

SPR-3. "Minneapolis Morning Tribune" Cello. Button,
c. 1942. Announcement for daily comic strip. -
$50 $100 $ 175

SPR-4

**SPR-4. "The Spirit" Example Of Weekly Newspaper
Comic Insert,**
1940s. Various newspapers 1940-1952. Prices vary widely
by issue date, artist, condition. Consult "Overstreet Comic
Book Price Guide".

SPY SMASHER

Playboy Alan Armstrong took on the identity of *Spy Smasher*
to battle America's domestic enemies for Fawcett
Publications during World War II. The caped crusader made
his debut in *Whiz Comics* #1 in 1940, had his own comic
book from 1941 to 1943, made a brief appearance as *Crime
Smasher* in 1948, and finally was allowed to expire in 1953.
Republic Pictures released a 12-episode chapter play in
1942 starring Kane Richmond in a life-and-death struggle
against Nazi agents.

SPY-1

SPY-3

SPY-2

SPY-1. Fawcett Picture,
c. 1941. Title inscription "Hero Of Whiz Comics And Spy
Smasher Comics". - **$75 $125 $200**

SPY-2. "I Am A Spy Smasher" Litho. Button,
c. 1941. For comic book club member. - **$15 $25 $50**

**SPY-3. "Spy Smasher" Argentine 27x41" Movie Serial
Paper Poster,**
1942. - **$50 $125 $200**

SPY-4

SPY-5

SPY-4. "Spy Smasher" 27x41" Movie Serial Poster,
1942. Republic Pictures. - **$200 $400 $750**

SPY-5. Movie Three-Sheet,
1942. Republic Pictures serial. - **$2000 $4000 $6000**

STAR TREK

The *Star Trek* phenomenon, originating in the futuristic Gene
Roddenberry TV series that aired on NBC from 1966 to
1969, has grown over the years into an international community of devoted fans, generating four additional TV series,
eight movies, dozens of books, comic books, an animated
cartoon, countless Trekkie conventions, and millions of dollars in licensed merchandise. On television *Star Trek* was
followed by *Star Trek: The Animated Series* (1973), *Star
Trek: The Next Generation* (1987), *Star Trek: Deep Space
Nine* (1993), and *Star Trek: Voyager* (1995). The first movie
- *Star Trek-The Motion Picture* (1979) - was followed by *Star
Trek II: The Wrath of Khan* (1982), *Star Trek III: The Search
for Spock* (1984), *Star Trek IV: The Voyage Home* (1986),
Star Trek V: The Final Frontier (1989), *Star Trek VI: The
Undiscovered Country* (1991), *Star Trek: Generation*
(1994), and *Star Trek: First Contact* (1996). Captain Kirk
(William Shatner) has been succeeded by Captain Picard
(Patrick Stewart), Captain Sisko (Avery Brooks), and Captain
Janeway (Kate Mulgrew). Spock (Leonard Nimoy) and the
rest of the original crew may be gone, but the U.S.S.
Enterprise and the U.S.S. Voyager continue to boldly cruise
the galaxies, where no man has gone before, well into the
future. Paramount Pictures holds the copyright.

STR-1

STR-1. Action Fleet Punch-Out Mobile,
1978. M&M/Mars Inc. Includes six punch-out sheets,
instruction sheet, poster. In Envelope - **$20 $35 $50**

STR-2   STR-3

STR-2. "The Bridge" McDonald's Meal Box,
1979. Two versions: Reverse panel pictures Mr. Spock or Dr. McCoy. Unused/Flat - **$5 $12 $25**

STR-3. "Spacesuit" McDonald's Meal Box,
1979. Unused/Flat - **$5 $12 $25**

STR-4   STR-5

STR-4. "Klingons" McDonald's Meal Box,
1979. Unused/Flat - **$5 $12 $25**

STR-5. "Transporter" McDonald's Meal Box,
1979. Unused Flat - **$5 $12 $25**

STR-6   STR-7

STR-6. "United Federation Of Planets" McDonald's Meal Box,
1979. Unused/Flat - **$5 $12 $25**

STR-7. McDonald's Plastic Secret Compartment Ring,
1979. Set of four: Kirk, Spock, U.S.S. Enterprise, insignia. Each - **$25 $50 $75**

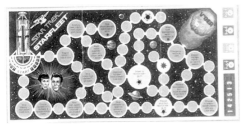

STR-8

STR-8. Star Fleet Game,
1979. McDonald's. - **$5 $8 $12**

STR-9

STR-9. Spoon Premium,
1970s. - **$30 $40 $60**

STR-10   STR-11

STR-10. Twentieth Anniversary 3" Plastic Badge,
1986. - **$5 $10 $15**

STR-11. Pocket Books 2-1/4" Tin Tab,
1986. - **$10 $15 $25**

STR-12

STR-12. Cheerios Box With First Promotion For Star Trek The Next Generation,
1987. Boxes contained six different sticker portraits to determine winners of 75,000 replicas of Enterprise (4" pale blue vinyl) by Galoob. Box - **$30 $75 $150**
Each Sticker - **$5 $10 $20**
Replica - **$75 $150 $250**

STAR WARS

George Lucas' movie trilogy - Star Wars (1977), The Empire Strikes Back (1980), and Return of the Jedi (1983) - chronicles the battle between good and evil a long time ago in a galaxy far, far away. Luke Skywalker (Mark Hamill), Princess Leia (Carrie Fisher), and Han Solo (Harrison Ford), along with Chewbacca the Wookiee and the droids C-3PO and R2D2, lead the Rebel Alliance in their epic struggle against Darth Vader and the Imperial Forces of the Empire. The phenomenal success of the films has spawned a world of merchandised items - action figures, comic books, novels, video games, trading cards, etc. An audio adaptation was broadcast on National Public Radio in 1980. The movies were digitally remastered for home video in 1995, and enhanced versions of the films will be re-released theatrically as "Special Editions" in 1997. Lucas is also planning to film further episodes of the saga.

STW-1

STW-1. Lucky Charms Box,
1977. General Mills. Offers four "Character Stick-ons". - **$5 $10 $20**

STW-2

STW-2. Cocoa Puffs Box,
1977. General Mills. Offers four "Robot" stick-ons. - **$5 $10 $20**

STW-3

STW-3. Trix Box,
1977. General Mills. Offers four "Creature" stick-ons. - **$5 $10 $20**

STW-4

STW-4. Cantina Adventure Set,
1977. Store item by Kenner. Sears Exclusive with blue Snaggletooth figure. - **$100 $200 $300**

STW-5

STW-5. Lucky Charms Cereal Box With Hang Gliders Offer,
1978. Boxes included four different punch-outs.
Box - **$50 $75 $150**
Punch-Outs Each - **$10 $20 $40**

STW-6

STW-7

STW-6. "Star Wars Weekly" Vol. 1 #1,
February 8, 1978. English edition by Marvel Comics International. - **$5 $10 $15**

STW-7. Cello. Button,
1978. From 14-button set depicting the characters. Each - **$5 $12 $20**

STW-8

STW-8. Procter & Gamble 19x20" Paper Posters,
1978. Set of three. Set - **$10 $20 $35**

STW-9

STW-10

STW-9. "The Empire Strikes Back" Cards,
1980. Burger King. Set of 36. Set - **$10 $20 $30**

STW-10. Cookie Box,
1983 Pepperidge Farms. Complete - **$10 $20 $35**

STEVE CANYON

Following his success with *Terry and the Pirates*, Milton Caniff created his *Steve Canyon* comic strip for distribution by Field Enterprises in 1947. Canyon, who runs a small airline, finds adventure and exotic women in all corners of the globe as he fights criminals and international spies. As the Cold War progresses, he sees service in Korea, Vietnam, and other hot spots, frequently doing battle with dangerous women. Comic books appeared in the late 1940s and 1950s, a radio adaptation with Barry Sullivan was syndicated in 1948, and a TV series with Dean Fredericks aired on NBC in 1958-1959 and was rerun on ABC in 1960. The newspaper strip ended publication in 1988. Items are copyrighted Field Enterprises Inc.

STV-1

STV-2

STV-1. "P.I." Cello. Button,
c. 1947. - **$40 $75 $125**

STV-2. "Daily Record/Sunday Advertiser" Cello. Button,
c. 1950. Various newspapers. - **$50 $115 $175**

STV-3

STV-4

STV-3. "Steve Canyon's Airagers" Wings Litho. Tab,
1950s. - **$15 $25 $40**

STV-4. Space Goggles On Picture Card,
1950s. Store item by Rock Industries. Gold finish slitted plastic goggles of similar nature to sunglasses.
Carded - **$15 $30 $50**

STV-5

STV-5. Chesterfield Cigarettes "Meet Steve Canyon-NBC TV" 21x22" Cardboard Store Poster,
1950s. - **$35 $60 $100**

STRAIGHT ARROW

Straight Arrow was a Western adventure radio series that was broadcast from 1948 to 1951, first on the Don Lee network on the West Coast, and starting in 1949 on the Mutual network nationally. The series was created for the National Biscuit Company as a means of promoting Nabisco shredded wheat. Boxtop premiums, on-package items, and retail products were offered in impressive quantities, all related to his scripted adventures.

Straight Arrow was actually young Steve Adams, owner of the Broken Bow Ranch, until innocent people were threatened or evil-doers plotted against justice. Then Adams would ride to his secret cave, mount his golden palomino Fury, and gallop out of the darkness as Straight Arrow, a Comanche warrior ready to fight for law and order. Howard Culver played Adams, and Fred Howard was his sidekick Packy McCloud.

Among the *Straight Arrow* premiums were several rings, a Mystic Wrist Kit containing an arrowhead and cowrie shell, an arrowhead flashlight, Indian war drum, bandanna, patch, and feathered headband. Sets of Injun-Uity cards, originally packaged in the cereal boxes, were later reissued as bound volumes.

Straight Arrow comic books with sales reaching one million per month, were published from 1950 to 1956, many of them containing advertisements for the program's premiums and other merchandise. A daily newspaper strip distributed by the Bell Syndicate appeared from 1950 to 1952. "Kaneewah, Fury!"

STA-2

STA-5

STA-6

STA-7

STA-1

STA-1. Large 20x36" Diecut Cardboard Store Sign,
c. 1948. Promotes radio series on Mutual Network. -
$400 $1000 $2500

STA-2. Two-Red Feathered Headband With Mailer,
1948. Includes two feathers.
Near Mint In Mailer - **$175**
Headband Only - **$30 $50 $100**

STA-5. "Book One" Box Insert Cards,
1949. Set of 36. Each - **$1 $2 $3**

STA-6. Bandanna,
1949. - **$20 $30 $50**

STA-7. Bandanna Gold Plastic Slide,
1949. - **$20 $35 $50**

STA-8

STA-9

STA-8. Gold Luster Metal Spring Tie Clip,
1949. Bar image of arrow. - **$40 $125 $250**

STA-9. War Drum,
1949. Complete Boxed - **$75 $125 $250**
Drum Only - **$50 $75 $125**

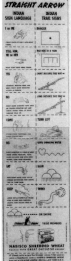

STA-3

STA-4

STA-3. "Indian Sign Language/Indian Trail Signs" Paper,
1948. Came with headband. - **$25 $50 $100**

STA-4. Radio Broadcast Reminder 12x15" Cardboard Store Sign,
1949. Diecut to extend feathers at top edge. -
$125 $250 $400

STA-10

STA-11

STA-12

STA-10. War Drum,
1949. 12" tall cardboard/thin rubber with beater stick.
Complete - **$65 $125 $200**

STA-11. Jigsaw Puzzle,
1949. Set of 12. Each In Envelope - **$15 $25 $40**
Loose - **$5 $15 $15**
Box For 10 Puzzles (Rare) - **$50 $100 $200**

STA-12. Nabisco Shredded Wheat 4x10" Cardboard
Display Sign,
. 1949. - **$150 $250 $400**

STA-13

STA-14

STA-13. Radio/Comic Strip Pressbook,
1950. Rare. Contains comic strips, list of premiums, sales
information. - **$200 $400 $750**

STA-14. Straight Arrow Coloring Book,
1950. Premium and store item. - **$25 $75 $150**

STA-16

STA-15

STA-17

STA-15. "Book 2" Box Insert Cards,
1950. Set of 36. Each - **$1 $2 $3**

STA-16. Mystic Wrist Kit,
1950. Plastic bracelet and arrowhead. Cowrie shell of set not
pictured. Complete - **$60 $125 $175**

STA-17. Plastic Powder Horn With String Cord,
1950. - **$40 $100 $250**

STA-19

STA-18

STA-20

STA-18. Tribal Shoulder Patch,
1950. - **$10 $20 $35**

STA-19. Brass Portrait Ring,
1950. - **$20 $35 $50**

STA-20. Golden Nugget Picture Ring,
1950. Gold plastic with view lens holding picture scene within
cave interior, also known as "Cave Ring". Shows Straight
Arrow, his horse Fury and his assistant Packy McCloud. -
$100 $175 $250

STA-21

STA-21. Target Game with Box,
1950. Store item. Metal target with bow-like launcher to fire
"magnetic arrows." - **$75 $200 $350**

STA-23

STA-22

STA-22. "Injun-Uities" 21x27" Store Announcement
Poster,
1951. Scarce. Pictures 12 "Injun-Uities" Nabisco cards from
first series. - **$100 $375 $750**

STA-23. "Straight Arrow Injun-Uities Manual",
1951. Series 1 and 2 box inserts in book format. -
$15 $25 $40

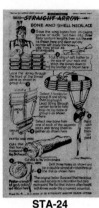

STA-24

STA-25

STA-26

STA-24. "Book Three" Box Insert Cards,
1951. Set of 36. Each - **$1 $2 $3**

STA-25. "Rite-A-Lite" Order Form,
1951. - **$10 $20 $30**

STA-26. Rite-A-Lite Arrowhead With Cap On Bottom,
1951. Scarce. Gold heavy plastic battery operated light.
Discontinued because of use of material for Korean War. -
$150 $400 $1000
Incomplete Arrowhead - **$60 $90 $120**

STA-27

STA-28

STA-27. Rite-A-Lite Arrowhead Cancellation Letter,
1951. Rare. - **$100 $150 $200**

STA-28. Glow-In-Dark Membership Card,
1951. - **$35 $100 $200**

STA-29

STA-30

STA-29. "Book Four" Box Insert Cards,
1952. Set of 36. Each - **$2 $3 $4**

STA-30. Punch-Out Puppets Sheet,
c. 1953. - **$8 $12 $20**

STROMBECKER MODELS CLUB

A model kit maker (principally aviation) from the 1930
onward, Strombecker Co. sponsored a model building club
with a code book and series of badges to denote club rank
based on model building expertise. A similar club was sponsored by competitor Megow Co.

SMC-1

SMC-2   SMC-3

SMC-1. Club Manual,
1930s. Includes secret code, photos of famous adult club
members, photos of airplane and locomotive models. -
$15 $25 $40

SMC-2. "Apprentice" Bronze Finish Badge,
1930s. - **$8 $15 $25**

SMC-3. "First Class" Bronze Finish Badge,
1930s. Awarded for building four models in four categories.
$12 $20 $35

SMC-4

SMC-5

**SMC-4. "Airman 1st Class" Club Rank 3" Metal Wings
Badge,**
1930s. Silver finish with red shield, one star. - **$10 $20 $30**

SMC-5. "Wing Loader" Club Rank 3" Metal Wings Badge,
1930s. Gold finish, blue shield, two stars. - **$10 $20 $30**

SMC-6

SMC-7

MC-6. "Captain" Club Rank Metal Wings Badge,
930s. Brass finish, green shield, three stars for highest
ank. - **$15 $25 $40**

MC-7. Club Application Folder,
late 1940s. Features "Captain 'Jet'" and pictures "Air Man
st Class" tin badge to be received.
older - **$5 $12 $20**
adge - **$8 $15 $25**

SUPER CIRCUS

'hat started out as a kids' radio quiz program in Chicago
ecame one of television's highest-rated children's shows.
uper Circus, a weekly variety spectacular, aired on ABC-TV
om 1949 to 1956. Claude Kirchner acted as ringmaster,
ary Hartline - with dazzling blonde hair and miniskirt -
virled her baton, and clowns Cliffy, Nicky, and Scampy took
re of the slapstick. Among the sponsors were Weather Bird
oes, Canada Dry, Kellogg's cereals, Quaker Oats, Mars
andy, and Sunkist. Also, Mary Hartline Enterprises market-
d a line of dolls, toys, children's clothes, food products,
cords, and books. The show moved to New York in 1955,
d Jerry Colonna and Sandy Wirth replaced Kirchner and
artline for the final season. Super Circus comic books
ppeared between 1951 and 1956.

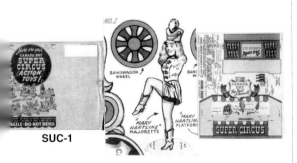

SUC-1

**UC-1. "Super Circus Action Toy" Punch-Out Kit With
nvelope,**
950. Canada Dry. Set of 10 punch-out sheets.
nused In Mailer - **$40 $75 $150**

SUC-2

SUC-3

SUC-2. "Weather-Bird Shoes" Photos,
c. 1950. From a set. Each - **$5 $10 $12**

SUC-3. "Mary Hartline" Hand Puppet,
c. 1950. Three Musketeers. - **$15 $25 $40**

SUC-4

**SUC-4. "Super Circus Side Show" Punch-Out Kit With
Envelope,**
c. 1950. Milky Way candy bars. Punch-out sheet opens to
11x34". Complete In Mailer - **$50 $100 $150**

SUC-5

SUC-6

SUC-5. "Super Circus Club" Member's Litho. Button,
1951. Canada Dry. - **$5 $10 $20**

SUC-6. Spiral-Bound Photo Book,
1951. - **$25 $50 $75**

SUC-7

SUC-8

SUC-7. Weather Bird Shoes Comic Book Vol. 1 #1,
1951. - **$10 $30 $60**

SUC-8. Iron-On Transfer Sheets,
1951. Weather-Bird shoes. Four tissue sheets in reverse
image picturing Mary, Scampy, Nicky, Cliffy.
Each - **$3 $6 $10**

SUC-10

SUC-9

SUC-9. Hard Plastic Doll,
1950s. Sponsor unknown, marked "Lingerie Lou Doll." -
$35 $75 $150
Picture Box - **$20 $40 $60**

SUC-10. Punch-Out Puppets With Envelope,
1950s. Snickers Candy Bars. Unused In Mailer -
$20 $40 $100

SUPERMAN

Writer Jerry Siegel and artist Joe Shuster created Superman in the early 1930s but it wasn't until 1938 that the Man of Steel made his first appearance, in *Action Comics* #1. The feature was an immediate success, and the character's popularity has never ceased. The story of Superman's arrival from the planet Krypton, his disguise as mild-mannered Clark Kent, reporter for the *Daily Planet*, love interest Lois Lane, young Jimmy Olsen, editor Perry White, and the citizens of Metropolis, have become a permanent part of American popular mythology.

There have been hundreds of Superman comic books, and daily and Sunday comic strips appeared from 1939 to 1967. On radio *The Adventures of Superman* aired from 1938 to 1951, on the Mutual network from 1940 to 1949, then on ABC. Bud Collyer starred as Superman from 1940 to 1949, and Kellogg's Pep sponsored from 1943 to 1947. The series moved successfully to prime-time television syndication (1953-1958), mainly on ABC outlets, with George Reeves in the lead and Kellogg's Sugar Frosted Flakes as sponsor.

The first Superman cartoons were 17 six-minute theatrical shorts made by the Fleischer Studios for Paramount Pictures in 1941-1943. Television cartoons, with Bud Collyer returning as the voice of Superman, aired on CBS in the late 1960s under various titles: *The New Adventures of Superman* (1966-1967), *The Superman/Aquaman Hour of Adventure* (1967-1968), and *The Batman/Superman Hour* (1968-1969). Superman was also part of the *Superfriends* animated series on ABC in the 1970s, and a musical show, *It's a Bird...It's a Plane...It's Superman*, had a brief run on Broadway in 1966 and was shown on ABC-TV in 1975.

Superman's movie career began with two 15-episode chapter plays from Columbia Pictures, *Superman* (1948) and *Atom Man vs. Superman* (1950), with Kirk Alyn in the lead roles. *Superman and the Mole Men*, with George Reeves starring, was released in 1951 and later served as a pilot for the TV series. *Superman - The Movie* (1978), with Christopher Reeve and Margot Kidder - a box office smash -

was followed by *Superman II* (1981), *Superman III* (1983) and *Superman IV: The Quest for Peace* (1987).

In 1993 a new prime-time television series, *Lois and Clark: The New Adventures of Superman*, premiered on ABC-TV, another indication that only Kryptonite may finally put an end to the comics' first costumed superhero. There have been countless Superman premiums and promotional items issued over the years, typically copyrighted by National Comic Publication Inc., National Periodical Publications Inc., or DC Comics.

SUP-1   SUP-2

SUP-1. "Action Comics" Flier,
1939. Sent to magazine wholesalers requesting they inform retailers Superman strip appears only in "Action Comics". -
$300 $750 $1200

SUP-2. "Action Comics" Cover Letter,
1939. Came with flier above. - **$250 $500 $750**

SUP-3

SUP-3. Action Comics "Superman" Litho. Button,
1939. Back inscription "Read Superman/Action Comics Magazine". - **$40 $75 $125**

SUP-4

SUP-5

SUP-4. Letter,
1939. N. Y. World's Fair. - **$100 $200 $500**

SUP-5. Candy Patch,
1940. - **$500 $2000 $4000**

SUP-6

SUP-7

SUP-6. Handkerchief,
1940. - **$500 $1000 $2000**

SUP-7. Letter,
1940. Came with Action Comics Patch. -
$200 $400 $1000

SUP-8

SUP-9

SUP-8. Patch,
1940. Scarce. Has "Action Comics" at bottom of front side. -
$2500 $5000 $10000

SUP-9. Patch,
1940. Rare. Prize same as the above Supermen of America patch except has word "Leader" at bottom. -
$5000 $7500 $15000

SUP-10

SUP-11

SUP-10. Action Comics "Superman" Litho. Button,
1940. Back inscription "Read Superman Action Comics magazine". - **$35 $65 $100**

SUP-11. Superman Contest Prize Ring,
1940. Rare. 12 known. Inscribed "Supermen Of America, Member." Issued by DC Comics promoted in Superman and Action Comics. 1600 issued. Silver base, gold luster image, red accent on logo and around lettering. -
$10000 $35000 $100000 (price varies widely)

SUP-12

SUP-13

SUP-14

SUP-12. Large Candy Box,
1940. - **$250 $500 $1000**

SUP-13. "Superman's Magic Flight" Cardboard Mechanical Toy,
1940. - **$250 $500 $1000**

SUP-14. "Superman's Christmas Adventure" Comic Book,
1940. First issue, various stores. - **$375 $1125 $3400**

SUP-15

SUP-15. Marx Wind-Up Tin Tank,
1940. Store item. - **$200 $400 $1000**

SUP-16

SUP-17

SUP-18

SUP-16. Candy & Surprise Cut-Out Panels,
1940. Set of 36. Candy company ring offered for 10 coupons and 10 cents or 75 coupons.
Cut Box Front With Coupon - **$25 $37 $50**
Cut Back With Card - **$25 $37 $50**

SUP-17. Superman Candy Secret Compartment Initial Brass Ring,
1940. Leader Novelty Candy Co. Recipient's inital on top cover. First version with red/white/blue image of Superman glued on inside surface of removable top. -
$5000 $15000 $40000 (price varies widely)

SUP-18. Superman Gum Secret Compartment Brass Ring,
1940. Rare. Pictures Superman, lightning bolt and letter "S". Top snaps off. No Superman image under top. -
$7500 $20000 $50000 (price varies widely)

SUP-19

SUP-20

SUP-21

SUP-19. Gum, Inc. "Superman" Enameled Brass Badge,
1940. Offered on wrappers holding Superman gum cards. -
$750 $1800 $4000

SUP-20. Rectangular Fabric Patch,
1940. Scarce. - **$750 $2500 $5000**

SUP-21. "Macy's Superman Adventure" Gummed Sticker,
1940. Macy's department store, applied to purchased items. -
$30 $60 $90

SUP-22

SUP-23

SUP-22. "Krypto-Raygun" With Box,
1940. Store item by Daisy Mfg. Co. Came with seven film-strips. Complete Boxed - **$300 $600 $1200**
Gun Only - **$100 $200 $300**
Filmstrip - **$5 $15 $25**

SUP-23. Wood And Composition Jointed Doll,
1940. Store item by Ideal Toys. Includes cloth cape. -
$300 $900 $1800

SUP-25

SUP-24

SUP-26

SUP-24. Plaster "Carnival" Statue,
c. 1940. Various colors. - **$50 $100 $250**

SUP-25. "Superman/American" Brass Figural Badge,
c. 1940. - **$75 $125 $250**

SUP-26. Cartoon Movie 6' Standee,
1941. From Fleischer cartoon film. - **$8000 $15000 $25000**

SUP-27   **SUP-28**   **SUP-29**

SUP-27. Syroco-Style 5-1/2" Figure,
1942. Wood composition in brown with red accents on logo and red cape. Promotional item from DC Comics for Superman comic books to distributors and retailers. 100 made. - **$1000 $3000 $5000**

SUP-28. Syroco-Style 5-1/2" Painted Figure,
1942. Full color, made of cellulose nitrate. See previous item 25 made. - **$1500 $4000 $6000**

SUP-29. Junior Defense League Brass Badge,
1942. - **$50 $80 $150**

SUP-30

SUP-30. "Junior Defense League Of America" Card or Pin,
1942. Various bread companies. Example shown has "Pledge" stickers on reverse. Unused Card - **$50 $100 $200**

SUP-31

SUP-32

SUP-31. "The Adventures Of Superman/Armed Services Edition" Book,
1942. Superman Inc. Paperback edition. - **$50 $100 $200**

SUP-32. DC Comics Portrait Sheet,
1942. Reverse shows covers of "Superman" #14, "World's Finest" #5, "Action Comics" #47. - **$75 $150 $300**

SUP-33

SUP-34

SUP-35

SUP-33. Cardboard Shield Badge,
1942. Rare. Superman Bread. - **$200 $400 $800**

SUP-34. "Superman-Tim Club" Litho. Button,
1942. Back slogan "Member In Good Standing". - **$15 $25 $50**

SUP-35. "Superman-Tim Club" Litho. Button,
1942. - **$15 $25 $50**

SUP-36

SUP-36. Decoder Folder,
1943. Scarce. Similar to one used in club kit. Pictures comics on the reverse. Given away at theaters. - **$100 $200 $300**

SUP-37

SUP-37. Kellogg's Pep Box Back,
1943. #3 from series from first year of Superman radio sponsorship. - **$20 $40 $75**

SUP-38

SUP-38. Superman-Tim Birthday Postcards,
1943. Various designs. Each - **$20 $35 $75**

SUP-39

SUP-39. "Superman's Christmas Adventure" Comic Book,
1944. Various stores. Example photo shows both covers. - **$100 $300 $775**

SUP-40

SUP-41

SUP-42

SUP-40. "Superman's Christmas Play Book" Comic Book,
1944. Various stores. Candy cane and Superman cover. - **$80 $250 $675**

SUP-41. "Sincerely, Superman" Charity Reply Postcard,
1944. Response card for March of Dimes contribution. -
$75 $150 $250

SUP-42. "Superman-Tim Club" Felt Patch,
1945. Various stores. Six different known.
Each - **$200 $500 $1000**

SUP-43

SUP-43. "Superman-Tim Press Card",
c. 1946. Opens to 9" to hold 12 poster stamps.
No Stamps - **$50 $90 $150**
Each Stamp Add $10

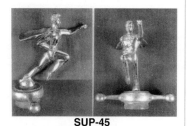

SUP-44   **SUP-45**

SUP-44. Superman Glow-In-The-Dark Picture,
c. 1945. Probable store item, at least four different known. -
$75 $150 $250

SUP-45. Metal Hood Ornament,
c. 1946. Store item by L. W. Lee Mfg. Co.
6-1/2" Chrome Finish - **$1300 $2600 $4000**
4-1/2" Chrome Or Gold Finish - **$1800 $3600 $5000**

SUP-46

SUP-46. Pep Calendar Sign,
1946. - **$100 $250 $500**

SUP-47

SUP-48

SUP-49

SUP-47. Sterling Silver Full-Dimensional Charm,
1947. Del Weston. Only 1-1/8" tall with red enamel painted
cape. - **$100 $200 $300**

SUP-48. "Superman-Tim Club Membership Card",
1947. Various clothing stores. - **$30 $55 $90**

SUP-49. "Superman-Tim" Gummed Album Stamp,
May 1947. Various participating stores. Issued monthly
1947-1950 to mount in club magazine. Each - **$12 $25 $4**

SUP-50

SUP-50. Membership Kit Version,
1948. DC Comics. Includes envelope, letter, certificate, coc
folder, cello. button.
Complete With Envelope - **$150 $225 $400**
Letter - **$20 $40 $60**
Certificate - **$60 $80 $120**
Code Folder - **$20 $30 $60**
Button - **$20 $35 $60**

SUP-51

SUP-51. "Gilbert Hall Of Science" Catalogue, 1948. A. C. Gilbert Co. - **$75 $150 $250**

SUP-52

SUP-53

SUP-52. DC Comics Picture, 1948. Back pictures comic book covers. - **$50 $125 $200**

SUP-53. "Radio Quiz Master Games With Model Microphone" With Mailer Envelope, 1948. National Comics. Superman name on envelope and game but no picture. Includes punch-out cardboard microphone.
Mailer - **$10 $25 $50**
Game - **$30 $60 $150**

SUP-54

SUP-55

SUP-56

SUP-54. "Superman-Tim" Magazine, 1940s. One of two examples shown. Issued monthly August 1942-May 1950. See next item for prices.

SUP-55. "Superman-Tim Magazine, 1940s. Issued monthly August 1942-May 1950.
First Issue - **$75 $225 $600**
Typical Other Issues - **$20 $55 $130**

SUP-56. War Savings Bond Poster, 1940s. 12-1/2" by 19-1/2". **$3000 $6000 $10000**

SUP-57

SUP-58

SUP-57. Sunny Boy Cereal Code Premium, 1940s. Scarce. Canadian issue. - **$100 $250 $500**

SUP-58. Superman-Tim Bracelet, 1940s. Scarce. - **$300 $600 $1000**

SUP-59

SUP-60

SUP-59. Superman-Tim Celluloid Pin, 1940s. - **$500 $1000 $1500**

SUP-60. Superman-Tim "Press Card", 1940s. Reverse blocks for 12 code stamps.
Card - **$75 $125 $200**
Each Stamp Mounted - **$5 $8 $12**

SUP-61

SUP-62

SUP-61. "Superman-Tim" Felt Pennant, 1940s. Scarce. Various clothing stores. Seen in yellow or red. Each - **$100 $500 $750**

SUP-62. Superman-Tim "Redback" Currency Bills, 1940s. Each - **$5 $8 $15**

SUP-63

SUP-64

SUP-63. "Superman-Tim Club" Bat Toy, 1940s. Various participating stores imprinted on back. Diecut masonite with litho. paper art from set that included rubber darts to strike at. - **$35 $75 $125**

SUP-64. "Superman-Tim Club" Bat Toy, 1940s. Various participating department stores imprinted on back. Diecut masonite with litho. paper design. - **$35 $75 $125**

SUP-65

SUP-66

SUP-65. Superman-Tim Silvered Brass Store Ring,
1940s. Depicts Superman flying above initials "S T". -
$1500 $6000 $14000 (price varies widely)

SUP-66. Kellogg's "Superman Crusader" Silvered Brass Ring,
1940s. - **$100 $200 $300**

SUP-67

SUP-68

SUP-69

SUP-67. "Supermen Of America" Color Variety Cello. Button,
1940s. DC Comics. Pictures him in white shirt with red/yellow chest symbol, rare variety from DC files, apparently for test purposes. - **$200 $500 $800**

SUP-68. "Supermen Of America" Club Cello. Button,
1940s. Scarce 7/8" size in full color. - **$150 $300 $500**

SUP-69. "Atom Man Vs. Superman" 6' Movie Standee,
1950. Columbia serial. - **$2000 $4000 $7500**

SUP-70

SUP-71

SUP-72

SUP-70. "Superman Muscle Building Club" Litho. Button,
1954. Store item. Came with child's exercise set. -
$25 $60 $100

SUP-71. Kellogg's Stereo-Pix Box Back,
1954. Sugar Frosted Flakes. #3 from series of 3-D assembly panels. Uncut Box Back - **$30 $60 $100**

SUP-72. "The Superman Time Capsule" Comic Book,
1955. Kellogg's Sugar Smacks. From set of three. -
$50 $150 $380

SUP-73

SUP-74

SUP-73. "Duel In Space" Comic Book,
1955. Kellogg's Sugar Smacks. From set of three. -
$40 $115 $290

SUP-74. "The Supershow Of Metropolis" Comic Booklet,
1955. Kellogg's Sugar Smacks. From set of three. -
$40 $115 $290

SUP-75

SUP-75. Kellogg's "Flying Superman" Toy Offer Box,
1955. Complete Box - **$75 $200 $500**

SUP-76

SUP-76. Kellogg's "Flying Superman" Thin Plastic Toy With Instruction Leaflet,
1955. Fragile premium flown by rubber band.
Instructions - **$40 $75 $100**
Figure And Plastic Stick - **$100 $200 $300**

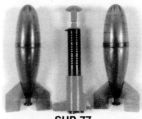

SUP-77

SUP-78

SUP-77. "Krypton Rocket" Plastic Set With Launcher,
1955. Kellogg's. Rockets in red, blue, or green plastic with Superman logo. Each Rocket - **$10 $40 $60**
Launcher - **$25 $75 $150**

SUP-78. Kellogg's Belt And Buckle,
1955. Aluminum buckle with plastic belt.
Buckle - **$40 $75 $150**
With Belt - **$75 $125 $200**

SUP-79

SUP-80

SUP-85

UP-79. Kellogg's Dangle-Dandy Box Back,
955. Uncut Box Back - **$25 $50 $80**
rimmed Out Figure - **$15 $30 $60**

UP-80. "Sports Club" Membership Card,
1955. Store item. Came with swim fins or goggles. -
0 $20 $35

SUP-81

SUP-82

SUP-83

JP-81. Rubber Swim Fins,
1955. Store item. - **$25 $50 $75**

JP-82. Kellogg's "Space Satellite Launcher Set",
56. Came with two plastic spinners.
mplete With Spinners - **$200 $500 $750**
x And Instructions - **$25 $50 $100**

IP-83. Life-Size Cardboard Store Display,
56. Kellogg's Corn Flakes. Top diecut to hold jumbo dis-
ay box. Promotes Superman TV series. -
00 $750 $1500
splay Box - **$100 $200 $400**

SUP-84

P-84. "Kellogg's Fun Catalog",
50s. - **$25 $50 $85**

SUP-85. Playsuit Mailing Folder,
1950s. Promotion to retailers from Funtime Playwear, Inc. -
$25 $60 $125

SUP-86

SUP-88

SUP-87

SUP-86. Fan Club Card,
1950s. Probably came with playsuit by Funtime Playwear. -
$20 $35 $70

SUP-87. Toy Watch,
1950s. Store item by Esco, West Germany. -
$50 $125 $200

SUP-88. George Reeves Fan Card,
1950s. DC Comics. - **$35 $75 $150**

SUP-89   SUP-90   SUP-91

SUP-89. "Supermen Of America" Cello. Button,
1950s. DC Comics. - **$20 $40 $60**

**SUP-90. "Supermen Of America" Color Variety Cello.
Button,**
1950s. DC Comics. Pictured in white shirt rather than blue
with red/yellow chest symbol. Rare variety from DC files,
apparently for test purposes. - **$200 $500 $800**

SUP-91. "Supermen Of America" Cello. Button,
1961. National Periodical Publications. Final version of series
with 1961 copyright on rim edge. - **$15 $25 $50**

SUP-92

SUP-93

SUP-92. "Initiative Award" Poster 11x14",
c. 1963. Independent News Co. Inc. given to comic book
retailers. - **$40 $75 $100**

SUP-93. Superman Litho. Button,
1966. N.P.P. Inc. Vending machine issue, set of eight.
Each - **$5 $10 $15**

SUP-94

**SUP-94. Superman Club 3-1/2" Cello. Button With
Retail Box,**
1966. Store item. Box originally held quantity of buttons.
Button - **$5 $10 $20**
Empty Box - **$25 $50 $75**

SUP-95

SUP-96

SUP-95. "Superman Golden Records" Boxed Set,
1966. N.P.P. Inc. Includes comic book, LP record, iron-on
patch, membership card with secret code, Supermen Of
America litho. button. Complete - **$20 $40 $75**

**SUP-96. "New Adventures Of Superman" Gummed Paper
Sticker,**
1966. CBS-TV. For introduction of Saturday morning animated series beginning September 10. Unused - **$10 $20 $35**

SUP-97

SUP-98

SUP-97. "All Star Dairy Foods" Plastic Truck Bank,
1960s. - **$35 $60 $100**

SUP-98. Vending Machine Header Card,
c. 1971. Includes Marvel and DC characters in form of magnet, sticker, rubber figures and Wonder Woman/Diana Princ
flicker picture. - **$50 $100 $175**

SUP-100

SUP-99

SUP-101

SUP-99. "Original Radio Broadcast" Cereal Box Offer,
1974. Kellogg's Corn Flakes. Clipped back panel offering
four-volume record album set with expiration date March 31
1976. - **$5 $10 $15**

**SUP-100. "Original Radio Broadcast" Vol. 1 Record
Album,**
1974. Kellogg's Corn Flakes. Issued as set of four.
Each - **$5 $10 $20**

SUP-101. "I Saw Superman" 3-1/2" Cello. Button,
1976. Issued for Albright-Knox Art Gallery exhibit. -
$15 $30 $60

SUP-102

SUP-103

SUP-102. Nestle's Domed Plastic Ring With Mailer,
1976. Near Mint With Mailer - **$65**
Ring Only - **$25 $37 $50**

SUP-103. Drake's Trading Cards 23x32" Store Sign,
1978. - **$15 $30 $50**

SUP-104

UP-104. "Super Heroes Fun Book And Check List",
78. Various bread companies. Check list for sticker set. -
5 $30 $50

SUP-105

SUP-106

JP-105. Super Hero Stickers,
78. Various bread companies. Set of 30.
ch Unused - **$1 $2 $3**

JP-106. "Superbank" 3-1/2" Cello. Button,
70s. Garden State National Bank, probably others. -
5 $25 $45

SUP-107

SUP-108

JP-107. "Superman Peanut Butter" 7x11"
per Store Sign,
81. Includes pad of t-shirt order forms. - **$25 $40 $60**

JP-108. Clark Kent Super Powers Figure,
1984. Kenner mail order premium.
xed - **$40 $60 $100**
ose - **$25 $40 $75**

SUP-110

SUP-111

SUP-109

SUP-109. Super Powers Standee,
1984. 1st standee to promote Superboy. - **$30 $60 $90**

SUP-110. Kryptonite Ring,
1990. Toy Biz. Came packaged with Superman action
figure. - **$10 $20 $30**

SUP-111. Syroco-Style Limited Edition Figure,
1995. 4" tall, 250 made. Mint - **$200**

SYROCO FIGURES

Adolph Holstein, a skilled European immigrant woodcarver, founded the Syracuse Ornamental Company in 1890, specializing in making hand-carved decorative components for the furniture industry. Demand for the company's intricate products soon exceeded production capacity, so Holstein developed a process to mass-produce replicas of the carvings by compressing a mixture of wood flour, waxes, and resins into molds. In the 1930s and 1940s the company changed its name to Syroco Inc. and manufactured a line of novelty items - cigarette boxes, pipe racks, plates, serving trays, and figurines of popular entertainers, comic strip characters and public personalities, for sale in roadside souvenir shops. Syroco Inc. continues in business to this day, but production of the figures was discontinued by about 1950.

Syroco products of greatest interest to premium collectors are the 1941 Great American Series of historic personalities (about 6" tall) and the 1944 series of King Features Syndicate comic strip characters (about 4-5" tall). There are 24 known characters. Pillsbury Mills, Inc. offered the following 12 as premiums in 1944 each for 25¢ and a Pillsbury Enriched Farina box top: Alexander, Annie Rooney, Archie, Barney Google, Blondie, Cookie, Dagwood, Jiggs, Little King, Popeye, Tim Tyler, Wimpy.

Similar wood composition figures are pictured in sections on Captain Marvel, Pinocchio and Superman. While these are also generically known as "syroco" figures, the 1945 Captain Marvel figure and the Pinocchio character figures are attributed to Multi Products, Chicago. This inscription appears on the Pinocchio figures.

SYR-1

SYR-2

SYR-3

SYR-1. Ben Franklin,
1941. Great American Series. - **$40 $80 $200**

SYR-2. George Washington,
1941. Great American Series. - **$40 $80 $200**

SYR-3. Will Rogers,
1941. Great American Series. - **$50 $120 $275**

SYR-12   SYR-13   SYR-14   SYR-15

SYR-4   SYR-5   SYR-6   SYR-7

SYR-12. Dagwood,
1944. - **$30 $100 $150**

SYR-13. Flash Gordon,
1944. Scarce. - **$200 $500 $825**

SYR-14. Fritz,
1944. - **$25 $75 $125**

SYR-4. Alexander Syroco Figure,
1944. This and the following 23 figures comprise a set of 24
King Features Syndicate characters, all from 1944. -
$20 $40 $100

SYR-15. Hans,
1944. - **$25 $75 $125**

SYR-5. Annie Rooney,
1944. - **$30 $100 $150**

SYR-6. Archie In Uniform,
1944. - **$30 $100 $150**

SYR-7. Barney Google In Navy Uniform,
1944. - **$25 $75 $125**

SYR-16   SYR-17   SYR-18   SYR-

SYR-16. Jiggs,
1944. - **$40 $110 $175**

SYR-8   SYR-9   SYR-10   SYR-11

SYR-17. Little King,
1944. - **$40 $150 $250**

SYR-18. Maggie,
1944. Scarce. - **$200 $300 $425**

SYR-19. Rosie,
1944. Rare. - **$200 $300 $450**

SYR-8. Blondie,
1944. Scarce. - **$60 $150 $350**

SYR-9. Captain,
1944. - **$30 $100 $150**

SYR-10. Casper,
1944. - **$20 $85 $125**

SYR-11. Cookie,
1944. - **$20 $40 $100**

SYR-20   SYR-22   SYR

SYR-21

YR-20. Olive Oyl,
1944. - **$200 $300 $400**

YR-21. Phantom,
1944. Scarce. Brown Costume - **$300 $900 $1200**
Purple Costume - **$250 $700 $1000**

YR-22. Popeye,
1944. - **$50 $120 $275**

YR-23. Prince Valiant,
1944. - **$75 $160 $375**

SYR-24   **SYR-25**   **SYR-26**   **SYR-27**

YR-24. Tillie In Uniform,
1944. Scarce. - **$200 $300 $425**

YR-25. Tim Tyler In Navy Uniform,
1944. - **$20 $75 $125**

YR-26. Toots,
1944. Scarce. - **$200 $300 $425**

YR-27. Wimpy,
1944. - **$40 $80 $200**

TALES OF THE TEXAS RANGERS

With stories said to be based on the files of the Texas Rangers between the 1830s and the 1950s, this series aired on NBC radio from 1950 to 1952, with Joel McCrea as Ranger Jace Pearson. A television version was broadcast from 1955 to 1957 on CBS and from 1957 to 1959 on ABC, with Willard Parker and Harry Lauter as the leading lawmen. General Mills sponsored the radio series and Tootsie Rolls candy joined the cereal company in sponsoring the TV version. Texas Ranger and Jace Pearson comic books appeared in the 1950s. Items may be copyrighted Screen Gems Inc.

TXS-1

TXS-1. Membership Kit,
1955. Curtiss Candy. Box Or Card - **$10 $15 $25**
Lettered Metal Badge - **$20 $30 $45**
Ring - **$20 $35 $60**

TXS-2   **TXS-3**

TXS-2. Candy Display Card,
c. 1955. Curtiss Candy Co. - **$25 $50 $75**

TXS-3. Jace Pearson Fan Photo,
c. 1955. - **$8 $12 $20**

TARZAN

Between 1911 and 1944 Edgar Rice Burroughs (1875-1950) wrote some 26 Tarzan novels, creating a world of adventure where justice and fair play triumph in the hands of an English orphan raised by apes in the African jungle. One of the most popular fictional characters of all time, Tarzan has thrilled readers and viewers throughout the world in print, in comics, in feature films and chapter plays, on radio, and on television. Tarzan's first appearance was in *All Story Magazine* in October, 1912.

The first Tarzan movie was the 1918 silent *Tarzan of the Apes*, starring Elmo Lincoln, but the best remembered ape-man is undoubtedly Olympic hero Johnny Weissmuller, who originated the abiding victory cry and made a dozen Tarzan films between 1932 and 1948. Notable among the many other cinema Tarzans: Buster Crabbe (1933), Lex Barker (1949-1953), and Gordon Scott (1955-1966). Including the silents and chapter plays, there have been more than 40 Lord of the Jungle movies.

The *Tarzan* comic strip, distributed by Metropolitan Newspaper Service, debuted in 1929 and lasted until 1973. A Sunday version from United Feature Syndicate appeared in 1931. There have been numerous *Tarzan* comic books, with reprints of the strips starting in 1929 and original material starting in the late 1940s.

There have been two series of *Tarzan* radio programs, the first (1932-1936) syndicated by WOR in New York with the Signal Oil Company as a sponsor until 1934, the second (1952-1953) on CBS, sponsored by Post Toasties. Premiums from the 1930s series include membership material in a Tarzan Club and a number of items from such sponsors as Foulds macaroni, Kolynos toothpaste, Bursley coffee, Hormel foods, and the dairy industry.

A live-action TV adaptation starring Ron Ely was aired on NBC in 1966-1968 and rerun on CBS in 1969, and animated versions from Filmation studios were broadcast on CBS from 1976 to 1981. The University of Louisville in Kentucky maintains an extensive Burroughs Memorial Collection of printed material and memorabilia.

TRZ-1

TRZ-1. "Elmo Lincoln In Adventures Of Tarzan" Movie Serial Paper Mask,
1921. Great Western Producing Co. 15-chapter serial imprinted on back for local theaters. - **$75 $175 $275**

TRZ-2

TRZ-3

TRZ-2. "The Tarzan Twins" Book,
1927. Store item. - **$60 $175 $400**

TRZ-3. Cardboard Bookmark,
c. 1920s. Grosset & Dunlap, publisher of Edgar Rice Burroughs novels. - **$15 $25 $50**

TRZ-4

TRZ-5

TRZ-4. Plaster Statues,
1932. Fould's Products. Set of 12 includes Tarzan, Kala, Numa, three monkeys, Sheeta, Jane, D'Arnot Fr. Lt., pirate, cannibal, witch doctor.
Set Painted - **$60 $125 $250**
Set Unpainted - **$80 $160 $325**

TRZ-5. Fould's Background For Plaster Statues,
1932. Scarce. - **$75 $150 $350**
Offer Blank - **$20 $40 $60**

TRZ-6

TRZ-6. "Signal Tarzan Club" Member Card,
1932. Signal gasoline. Qualifies recipient as "Charter Member Of The Tribe Of Tarzan". - **$100 $225 $400**

TRZ-7

TRZ-8

TRZ-7. "Signal Tarzan Club" Cello. Button,
1932. Signal Oil Co. - **$20 $40 $65**

TRZ-8. "Tarzan Of The Apes" Jigsaw Puzzle,
c. 1932. Screen Book Magazine.
In Envelope, Sealed - **$600**
Near Mint With Envelope - **$400**
Loose - **$25 $60 $150**

TRZ-9

TRZ-10

TRZ-9. "Tarzan The Fearless" 9x14" Cardboard Sign,
1933. Rare. - **$75 $150 $300**

TRZ-10. Northern Paper Mills Color Poster For Masks,
1933. - **$250 $500 $1000**

TRZ-11

RZ-11. Paper Masks,
933. Northern Paper Mills. Set of three picturing Tarzan, uma the Lion, Akut the Ape. Tarzan - **$25 $60 $100** ach Animal - **$15 $40 $75**

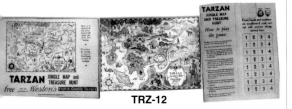

TRZ-12

RZ-12. "Tarzan Jungle Map And Treasure Hunt" Game /ith Mailer Envelope,
933. Rare. Canadian version has "W" above logo for /eston's English Quality Biscuits. U.S. version has "T" bove logo. Playing pieces printed on envelope back. anada Near Mint In Mailer - **$400** anada Map Only - **$100 $200 $300** .S. Near Mint In Mailer - **$600** .S. Map Only - **$125 $250 $500**

TRZ-13

RZ-13. Paper Film,
933. Scarce. Hormel Soups. - **$75 $150 $375**

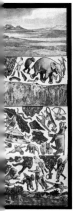

TRZ-15

TRZ-14

RZ-14. Tarzan Cup Magic Picture Cutouts,
•33. Rare. Complete Uncut - **$100 $200 $400**

RZ-15. Johnny Weissmuller Picture,
•33. Rare. Wheaties premium for Jack Armstrong ogram. - **$40 $80 $160**

TRZ-16

TRZ-16. "Notebook Filler" Paper Wrapper Band,
c. 1933. Store item. Reverse pictures Mickey Mouse Ingersoll watch offered for saved bands. - **$10 $25 $40**

TRZ-17

TRZ-17. "Tarzan 'Rescue'" Puzzle Game,
1934. Store item by Einson-Freeman Co. - **$150 $300 $600**

TRZ-18

TRZ-18. Tarzan of the Air Promo with Mailer,
1934. - **$60 $120 $180**

TRZ-19

TRZ-20

TRZ-19. "Tarzan Of The Apes" Book,
1935. Various advertisers. - **$25 $60 $100**

TRZ-20. "The New Adventures Of Tarzan" Cardboard Knife Movie Give-Away,
c. 1935. Various theaters. - **$12 $25 $50**

TRZ-21

TRZ-22

TRZ-21. "Tarzan And His Jungle Friends" Booklet #1,
1936. Tarzan Ice Cream Cup. First of listed series of 12. -
$60 $125 $225

TRZ-22. "Tarzan: Gift Picture No. 1 Of A Series",
1937. "Tarzan Appears Each Month In Tip Top Comics Magazine Copyright 1937 By United Feature Syndicate Inc." Art by Rex Maxon. - **$75 $150 $300**

TRZ-23

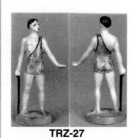

TRZ-24

TRZ-30

TRZ-23. "Tarzan And A Daring Rescue" Booklet,
1938. Pan-Am gasoline and motor oils. Title page offers bow and arrow set plus school bag premiums. - **$75 $150 $250**

TRZ-24. "Tip Top Comics" 11x14" Store Sign,
c. 1938. - **$125 $200 $300**

TRZ-31

TRZ-32

TRZ-30. "Tarzan Ice Cream Cup" 10x20" Paper Store Poster,
1930s. - **$100 $200 $300**

TRZ-31. "Tarzan Cups" 6x19" Paper Store Poster,
1930s. Offers premiums for lids saved. - **$60 $125 $200**

TRZ-32. "Tarzan And The Crystal Vault Of Isis" Card #18
1930s. Schutter-Johnson Candies. Card title "The Electric Menace" from numbered set of 50. Each - **$10 $20 $35**

TRZ-25

TRZ-26

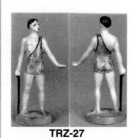

TRZ-27

TRZ-25. Clans Manual,
1939. Tarzan Clans of America, Tarzana, California. Complete procedures and rituals for organizing and running a clan. - **$150 $350 $600**

TRZ-26. Celluloid Pocketknife With Steel Blades,
1930s. Store item made by Imperial. - **$150 $400 $900**

TRZ-27. French Cello. Figure,
1930s. 2-1/2" tall marked "F Clairet". - **$250 $500 $1000**

TRZ-33

TRZ-33. "Myles Salt Cut-Outs" Boxes,
1930s. Panels picture Tarzan, Dan Dunn, Ella Cinders. Tarzan Box Uncut - **$35 $75 $150**
Others Uncut Each - **$10 $25 $40**

TRZ-34

TRZ-34. Safety Club Cards,
1930s. Various radio sponsors. Two cards printed each side originally joined by perforation. One card to order badge, on card of safety pledges. Pair - **$100 $250 $500**

TRZ-28

TRZ-29

TRZ-28. School Paper Supplies 10x14" Cardboard Store Sign,
1930s. Birmingham Paper Co. - **$100 $200 $300**

TRZ-29. "Tarzan Cups" 12x18" Paper Store Poster,
1930s. - **$100 $200 $300**

TRZ-35

TRZ-36

TRZ-35. "The Son Of Tarzan" Movie Serial Cardboard Ad Blotter,
1930s. Scarce. - **$30 $65 $100**

TRZ-36. "Tarzan The Tiger" Movie Serial Cello. Button,
1930s. Universal. Four known with this title, four known with "Tarzan the Mighty" title. Each depicts animal or bird. Each - **$20 $40 $75**

| TRZ-37 | TRZ-38 | TRZ-39 |

TRZ-37. "Tarzan Radio Club/Drink More Milk" Enameled Brass Badge,
1930s. Scarce. - **$100 $300 $750**

TRZ-38. "Tarzan Radio Club/Bursley Coffees" Enameled Brass Badge,
1930s. Scarce. - **$100 $300 $750**

TRZ-39. "Vita Hearts" Litho. Club Button,
1930s. - **$100 $175 $300**

TRZ-40

TRZ-41

TRZ-42

TRZ-40. "Tarzan Safety Club" Cello. Button,
1930s. 7/8" version. - **$80 $175 $350**

TRZ-41. "Feldman's Tarzan Safety Club" Cello. Button,
1930s. 1-1/4" version of previous button. - **$100 $250 $500**

TRZ-42. "The Nielen Tarzan Club" Member's Cello. Button,
1930s. - **$125 $250 $500**

TRZ-43

TRZ-44

TRZ-45

TRZ-43. Club Member Cello. Button,
1930s. Gano Downs Boys & Girls Shops. - **$125 $250 $500**

TRZ-44. "Sons Of Tarzan Club" Cello. Button,
1930s. Facsimile Johnny Weissmuller signature. Theater contest issue, match number to win prize. - **$50 $80 $125**

TRZ-45. "Tarzan's Grip" Australian Cello. Button,
1930s. - **$100 $200 $400**

TRZ-46

TRZ-47

TRZ-46. Advertising Flip Booklet,
c. 1940s. Thom McAn shoes. Pages flipped one direction show Tarzan spearing an ape, reverse page sequence shows grateful child getting Thom McAn shoes from dad. - **$50 $100 $150**

TRZ-47. Dell Publishing Co. Pictures,
1950. One sheet consisting of five photos.
Near Mint In Mailer - **$125**
Loose - **$25 $50 $80**

TRZ-48

TRZ-48. Plastic Flicker Picture Rings,
1960s. Set of six. Gold plastic bases. Each - **$10 $15 $20**

TEENAGE MUTANT NINJA TURTLES

Donatello, Leonardo, Michaelangelo, and Raphael burst upon the scene in 1984 in issue #1 of *Teenage Mutant Ninja Turtles*. Since then the pizza-loving sewer dwellers and their ninja master have thrived not only in comic books but in a 1988 animated TV series, movies in 1990, 1991, and 1993, millions of premiums from Burger King, a concert tour sponsored by Pizza Hut, merchandising, and licensing to promote hundreds of products. "Cowabunga!"

TMT-1

TMT-1. Fan Club Kit Ad and Coupon,
1988. Playmates Toy Co. - **$10 $20 $30**

TMT-2

TMT-2. Fan Club Kit,
1988. Playmates Toy Co. Envelope with bandanna, letter, story comic, sticker, charter member certificate with perforated membership card. Set - **$40 $65 $90**

TMT-3

TMT-4

TMT-3. Movie Promotion 2-1/8" Cello. Button,
1990. Mirage Studios. - **$3 $5 $10**

TMT-4. Nabisco Shreddies Canadian Cereal Box,
1990. Box offers first four of eight "Power Rings".
Complete Box - **$200**
Turtles Rings - **$5 $15 $25**
Other Character Rings - **$10 $25 $35**

TMT-5

TMT-5. Nabisco Shreddies Canadian Cereal Box,
1991. Box offers last four of eight rings.
Complete Box - **$200**
Turtles Rings - **$5 $15 $25**
Other Character Rings - **$10 $25 $35**

TELEVISION MISCELLANEOUS

Television, only an experimental and isolated technical dream through the 1930s, would likely have erupted sooner not for the World War II years. But erupt it did in the late 1940s to present day norm of scarcely any household in the United States without at least one TV set. Early TV programming could be much more easily sponsored by a single sponsor per show. It has been estimated that an early sponsor could well finance an entire season or more for the current cost, in equal dollars, of a 30-second advertising spot during recent Super Bowl telecasts. The basic cost of TV advertising, of course, is a prior consideration to the supplement cost of premiums; thus the noticeable lack of mail premium offers so prevalent in the radio and earliest TV eras. Premiums associated to TV characters or shows are now most likely found as part of a retail item if indeed offered at all. This book section depicts a sampling of premium collectibles from a wide variety of shows.

TEL-1

TEL-2

TEL-1. Dumont "Small Fry Club" Cello. Button,
1947. Dumont television network, hosted by Big Brother Bob Emory. - **$10 $15 $25**

TEL-2. "Crosley's House Of Fun" Comic Booklet,
1950. Crosley Appliances. - **$5 $8 $12**

TEL-3

TEL-4

TEL-3. Early Version Beany Hand Puppet,
c. 1950. Sears store item. From era of KTLA-TV (Los Angeles) show "Time For Beany". - **$75 $200 $350**

TEL-4. "4 Norge TV Comic Masks" With Envelope,
1951. Norge Appliances. Paper masks of Ed Wynn, Jack Carson, Danny Thomas, Jimmy Durante. Unpunched In Envelope - **$30 $50 $80**

TEL-5

TEL-6

TEL-5. "TV Guide" 8x11" Vending Rack Insert Card,
c. 1952. Design based on Sgt. Joe Friday of Dragnet police
TV series. - **$15 $30 $50**

TEL-6. Nelson Family Fan Photo,
c. 1952. Pictures Ozzie, Harriet, Ricky, David with facsimile
signatures. - **$10 $25 $40**

TEL-7

TEL-7. "Jerry Lester 'Bean Bag' Club" Kit,
1953. Genesee Beer & Ale. Includes membership card, button, message card. Complete - **$10 $20 $30**

TEL-8

TEL-8. This is Your Life - Book Shaped Locket,
1953. With coupon and ad. - **$50 $75 $150**

TEL-9

TEL-10

TEL-9. "TV Guide" Vol. 1 #1,
April 3, 1953. First national issue with cover article "Lucy's
Fifty Million Dollar Baby". - **$200 $500 $1000**

TEL-10. "Rocket Ranger March" Record,
c. 1953. Store item. From 1953-1954 CBS-TV show "Rod
Brown Of The Rocket Rangers" on Columbia label. -
$10 $20 $35

TEL-11

TEL-12

TEL-11. "Groucho Marx" Fan Postcard,
1954. Back ad for "You Bet Your Life" NBC-TV show. -
$20 $40 $65

TEL-12. "Father Knows Best" Cast Photo Postcard,
c. 1954. Oversized 5-1/2x7" card picturing Anderson family of
TV series. - **$5 $12 $20**

TEL-13

TEL-14

TEL-13. "Jack Webb Fan Club" Membership Card,
1954. For star of Dragnet TV series. - **$8 $12 $20**

TEL-14. "Dragnet Code Chart" Cardboard Decoder,
1955. Sponsor unknown. - **$10 $15 $25**

TEL-15

TEL-16

TEL-15. "Dragnet 714 Club" Metal Badge, Card and Case,
1955. Store item. - **$15 $25 $35**

TEL-16. "Dragnet Whistle" 20x20" Cardboard Store Sign,
1955. Kellogg's Corn Flakes.
Sign - **$50 $100 $150**
Whistle - **$1 $3 $5**

TEL-17

TEL-18

TEL-17. Lucy & Desi Ad Postcard,
1955. Pontiac Motors. - **$12 $20 $40**

TEL-18. "Chester A. Riley" Fan Postcard,
c. 1955. Cast photo of "Life Of Riley" series. - **$8 $15 $25**

TEL-19

TEL-20

TEL-19. Sgt. Bilko Cardboard Ad Fan,
c. 1955. Amana Refrigeration. - **$10 $20 $50**

TEL-20. "Win A Sgt. Bilko Money Tree" Contest Folder,
1957. Joy liquid dishwashing soap. Contest expired October 15. - **$8 $15 $30**

TEL-21

TEL-22

TEL-21. "The Adventures Of Ozzie & Harriet" Candy Box,
c. 1958. Almond Joy candy bars of Peter Paul Candies. TV sponsorship also indicated for "Maverick" series. - **$35 $60 $80**

TEL-22. Jack Paar 12" Cardboard Standee,
1950s. Schrafft's. - **$60 $90 $120**

TEL-23

TEL-24

TEL-23. Jack Paar Beech-Nut Gum Container,
1950s. Held small free sample boxes. - **$30 $60 $90**

TEL-24. TV Cameraman Plastic Pull Toy,
1950s. Kraft Foods. - **$40 $90 $150**

TEL-25

TEL-25. "RCA TV Coloring Book",
1950s. - **$8 $15 $30**

TEL-26

TEL-27

TEL-26. "Crusader Rabbit Club" Member's Cello. Button,
1950s. - **$20 $40 $80**

TEL-27. Television Bread Loaf End Label,
1950s. Pictured example from set depicts "Television Demonstrated" in 1927. Each - **$8 $15 $30**

TEL-28

TEL-28. Buffalo Bill Belt Buckle and Plastic Belt with Instructions,
1950s. sponsor Milky Way. - **$20 $40 $80**

TEL-29   **TEL-30**   **TEL-31**

TEL-29. Ding Dong School Bell,
1950s. - **$20 $40 $60**

TEL-30. "Hollywood Off-Beat" TV Show Starring Melvin Douglas - Dixie Cup Promo,
1950s. - **$20 $40 $60**

TEL-31. Flying Turtle Club Beany TV,
1950s. - **$20 $40 $80**

TEL-32   **TEL-33**

TEL-32. I Led Three Lives Promo,
1950s. Small cardboard tag. - **$20 $40 $60**

TEL-33. "Winky Dink And You" TV Art Kit,
1950s. Includes erasable "magic" window, crayons and erasing cloth. - **$40 $60 $125**

TEL-34   **TEL-35**   **TEL-36**

TEL-34. "Desi's Conga Drum",
1950s. Store item by A&A American Metal Toy Co. Came with wooden beater. - **$250 $450 $800**

TEL-35. "I Love Lucy" Doll With Apron,
1950s. Store item. - **$150 $300 $450**

TEL-36. "Lucy's Notebook",
1950s. Philip Morris cigarettes. 40-page recipe booklet with Lucy/Desi photos. - **$20 $40 $60**

TEL-37

TEL-37. "Pinky Lee Party Pack",
1950s. Includes booklet, place mats, napkins, party hats, cardboard figures, "Pin The Hat On Pinky" poster with paper hats. Near Mint In Envelope - **$100**

TEL-38   **TEL-39**

TEL-38. "TV Bank" Litho. Bank,
1950s. Various companies. - **$10 $20 $30**

TEL-39. "Farfel" Ceramic Mug,
1950s. - **$15 $25 $40**

TEL-40   **TEL-41**

TEL-42

TEL-40. "Gene London Club" 3" Cello. Button,
1950s. Channel 10, Philadelphia TV station. - **$5 $10 $15**

TEL-41. "Soupy Sales Society" 3-1/2" Cello. Button,
1950s. - **$8 $15 $25**

TEL-42. Arthur Godfrey Sponsor Ad Photo,
1950s. Snow Crop Frozen Foods. Pictured are Godfrey and Teddy Snowcrop symbol character. - **$8 $15 $30**

TEL-43   **TEL-44**   **TEL-45**

TEL-43. "Jackie Gleason Fan Club" Cello. Button,
1950s. - **$30 $50 $90**

TEL-44. "Winky Dink" Litho. Button,
1950s. - **$10 $20 $35**

TEL-45. "The Ghost Rider" Cello. Button,
1950s. WCAU-TV (Philadelphia). - **$8 $15 $25**

TEL-46

TEL-47

TEL-46. Annie Oakley Hat,
1950s. Store bought. - **$20 $40 $80**

TEL-47. Robin Hood Hat,
1950s. Store bought. - **$20 $40 $80**

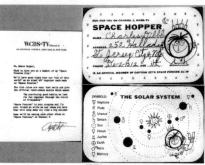

TEL-48

TEL-48. "Space Hopper" Club Letter And Card,
c. 1960. WCBS-TV, New York City. Items for "Captain Jet"
club. Letter - **$8 $15 $20**
Card - **$10 $15 $25**

TEL-49

TEL-50

TEL-51

TEL-49. "New! Beany & Cecil In '62!" Cello. Button,
1962. Mattel Toys with Bob Clampett copyright. Probably
from industry toy show. - **$30 $100 $200**

TEL-50. "The Munsters Theatre" Gum Card Box,
1964. Leaf Gum. - **$60 $100 $150**

TEL-51. "Chipmunks/Soaky" Cardboard Record,
1964. Colgate-Palmolive. - **$5 $8 $12**

TEL-52

TEL-53

TEL-52. "Mr. Ed March Of Comics" #260,
1964. Various sponsors. - **$5 $15 $30**

**TEL-53. "Jimmy Nelson's Instant Ventriloquism" Record
Album,**
1964. Album also pictures Danny O'Day and Farfel. -
$8 $12 $20

TEL-54

TEL-55

TEL-54. "March Of Comics" Booklet #352,
1964. Various sponsors. "Space Family Robinson/Lost In
Space" story. - **$15 $40 $90**

TEL-55. "Soupy Sales" 3" Litho. Button,
1965. - **$20 $35 $60**

TEL-56-58

**TEL-56. Man From U.N.C.L.E. Membership Kit
Instructions,**
1965. Premium, sponsor unknown. - **$10 $20 $30**

TEL-57. Man From U.N.C.L.E. Membership Kit Card,
1965. Premium, sponsor unknown. - **$30 $60 $100**

TEL-58. Man From U.N.C.L.E. Membership Kit Photo,
1965. Premium, sponsor unknown. - **$20 $40 $60**

TEL-59

TEL-60

TEL-61

TEL-59. Man From U.N.C.L.E. Plastic Badge,
1965 Store item that came with various sets by Ideal Toy Corp. - **$10 $20 $35**

TEL-60. "Napoleon Solo" 3-1/2" Cello. Button,
1965. Store item. From "The Man From U.N.C.L.E." - **$5 $12 $20**

TEL-61. "The Men From U.N.C.L.E." 6" Cello. Button,
1966. - **$20 $30 $50**

TEL-62

TEL-63

TEL-62. "Mrs. Beasley" Talking Doll,
1966. Store item by Mattel. Includes plastic glasses.
Talking - **$75 $150 $250**
Not Talking - **$40 $80 $150**

TEL-63. "Lost In Space" Battery Operated Robot,
1966. Store item by Remco. Boxed - **$200 $400 $600**
Loose - **$100 $200 $400**

TEL-64

TEL-65

TEL-64. "Lost In Space" Cast Photo,
. 1966. CBS-TV fan card. - **$20 $40 $75**

TEL-65. Munsters Flicker Picture Rings,
. 1966. Vending machine issue. Set of four plastic rings in either silver or blue base.
Silver Base Each - **$35 $55 $75**
Blue Base Each - **$25 $35 $50**

TEL-66

TEL-66. Flipper "Magic Whistle" 5"x24" Paper Store Sign,
c. 1966. P.F. Flyers footwear of B.F. Goodrich. - **$15 $25 $50**

TEL-67

TEL-67. Dolphin "Magic Whistle" Plastic Assembly Parts On Card,
c. 1966. P.F. footwear of B.F. Goodrich. "Flipper" not named but card pictures dolphin, assembled whistle is to produce tone "That Sounds Like A Dolphin".
Unassembled With Card - **$15 $30 $50**
Assembled - **$8 $15 $25**

TEL-68

TEL-69

TEL-70

TEL-68. Addams Family Plastic Ring Figures,
1960s. Store item. Set of four, originally on card also holding attachment ring. Near Mint Carded - **$160**
Each Ring With Base - **$2 $3 $4**

TEL-69. "Maynard" G. Krebs Composition Bobbing Head,
1960s. Store item. - **$125 $300 $500**

TEL-70. "Dr. Ben Casey M.D." Composition Bobbing Head,
1960s. - **$50 $80 $140**

TEL-71

TEL-72

TEL-73

TEL-71. "Dr. Kildare" Composition Bobbing Head,
1960s. - **$75 $125 $250**

TEL-72. Gumby Flexible Plastic Ring,
1960s. - **$4 $6 $10**

TEL-73. Danny Thomas Flicker Sign,
1960s. Post Corn Flakes. - **$50 $75 $100**

TEL-75

TEL-74

TEL-74. Laugh-In Vending Machine Display,
c. 1970. Paper insert on styrofoam with two plastic rings with
Laugh-In slogans, other generic rings and novelties. -
$35 $60 $125

TEL-75. "Flipper" Fan Postcard,
1975. - **$10 $20 $35**

TEL-77

TEL-76

TEL-76. "I Dream Of Jeannie" Doll,
1977. Store item by Remco. 6-1/2" tall version.
Boxed - **$75 $150 $250**
Loose - **$50 $125 $200**

TEL-77. "6 Million Dollar Man Club" Cello. Button,
1977. - **$5 $12 $20**

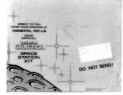

TEL-78

TEL-79

TEL-78. "Lost In Space" Battery Operated Robot,
1977. Store item by Ahi. Boxed - **$75 $175 $250**
Loose - **$50 $125 $175**

TEL-79. "Battlestar Galactica Space Station Kit",
1978. General Mills. Includes manual, punch-out control center and headset, activator card, patch, 11 mission cards,
poster, four iron-on transfers. Near Mint In Mailer - **$100**

TENNESSEE JED

The frontier adventures of Jed Sloan aired on ABC rad
from 1945 to 1947. Acting as an undercover agent f
General Grant in the period just after the Civil War, Sloa
was a deadly marksman who daily did away with cattl
rustlers and other villains of the Western Plains. Tip-To
bread and cakes was the sponsor. A single issue of a give
away comic book was published in 1945.

TEN-1

**TEN-1. Exhibit Card And Cardboard Dexterity Puzzle
With Envelope,**
1945. Tip-Top Bread.
Near Mint In Mailer - **$75**
Card - **$5 $10 $15**
Puzzle - **$10 $20 $30**

TEN-2

TEN-3

TEN-2. Oversized Cardboard Ear For Radio Broadcasts,
1945. Tip-Top Bread. 3x5" with attachment tabs. -
$12 $25 $40

TEN-3. Tip-Top Bread Comic Book,
1945. Inside has adventure map keyed to radio broadcasts.
$15 $45 $100

TEN-4

TEN-4. Tip-Top "Horse Puzzle" Cards With Envelope,
c. 1945. Three-card picture placement puzzle with solution
on envelope back. - **$20 $40 $65**

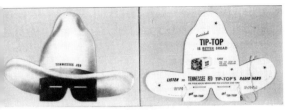

TEN-5

TEN-5. Paper Mask,
1946. - **$15 $20 $35**

TEN-6

TEN-7

TEN-6. "Atom Gun" Cardboard Clicker,
1946. Ward's Tip-Top Bread. - **$15 $30 $50**

TEN-7. Cardboard Ink Blotter,
c. 1946. - **$10 $20 $35**

TEN-8

TEN-9

TEN-8. Magnet Ring,
c. 1946. Brass base with diecut arrowhead designs holding top magnet. - **$125 $225 $450**

TEN-9. Look-Around Brass Ring,
c. 1946. - **$150 $325 $500**

TEN-10

TEN-10. "Catch The Ring" Toy,
1947. Cardboard with attached string and metal ring. -
$10 $20 $30

TERRY AND THE PIRATES

Milton Caniff created his *Terry and the Pirates* adventure comic strip in 1934 for the Chicago Tribune-New York News Syndicate. The scene of the action was China, and young Terry Lee and his pal Pat Ryan were to come up against a variety of evil-doers and exotic women, notably the infamous Dragon Lady. During World War II Terry became an air force pilot and, along with Colonel Flip Corkin, battled the Axis. The strip ceased publication in 1973. A number of *Terry and the Pirates* comic books were published between 1939 and 1955, including giveaways from Sears & Roebuck, Buster

Brown, Canada Dry, Libby Foods, Weather Bird shoes and others.

Radio adaptations aired on NBC from 1937 to 1939, sponsored by Dari-Rich chocolate drink, and on ABC from 1943 to 1948, sponsored by Quaker Oats, Puffed Wheat, and Puffed Rice. A 15-episode chapter play was released by Columbia Pictures in 1940 with William Tracy as Terry, and a syndicated television series aired in New York in 1952-1953 and had continued distribution through the 1950s.

TER-1

TER-2

TER-3

TER-1. "Terry And The Pirates Meet Again",
1936. Tarzan Ice Cream Cups. Booklet #10 from series of various character titles. - **$20 $45 $85**

TER-2. Quaker Puffed Wheat Comic Book,
1938. - **$1 $2 $5**

TER-3. "Adventures Of Terry And The Pirates" Booklet,
1938. From Whitman Penny Books series with inside ad for "Super-Comics" and "Crackajack Funnies" comic books. -
$15 $25 $35

TER-4

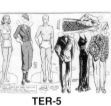

TER-5

TER-4. "Treasure Hunter's Guide" Booklet,
1938. Dari-Rich Chocolate Drink. Contents basically about stamp collecting. - **$20 $40 $60**

TER-5. "Ruby Of Genghis Khan" Comic Activity Book,
1941. Rare. Libby's fruit and vegetable juices. Contents include pencil puzzles, games, coloring pages, magic tricks, cut-out dolls. - **$200 $600 $1600**

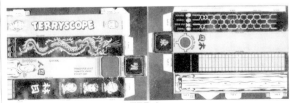

TER-6

TER-6. "Terryscope" Cardboard Assembly Kit,
1941. Rare. Libby, McNeill & Libby. Pictures six characters,
one side features secret code.
Near Mint Unassembled - **$600**
Assembled - **$100 $200 $400**

TER-7

TER-8

**TER-7. "Victory Airplane Spotter" Cardboard Mechanical
Disk With Envelope,**
1942. Libby, McNeill & Libby. Pictures Terry, Pat, April,
Burma, Connie plus identifies 16 warplane silhouettes. -
$50 $125 $300

TER-8. Quaker Oats B-25 Mascot Plane Photo,
1943. - **$15 $25 $40**

TER-9

TER-10

TER-9. "Pilot's Mascot" Wooden Button,
1943. Wire loop reverse for wearing with a safety pin. Came
with Quaker Cereals B-25 airplane picture. - **$10 $20 $35**

TER-10. Quaker Oats Pictures,
c. 1944. Set of six. Pat Ryan, Burma, Terry, Phil Corkin,
Dragon Lady, Connie. Near Mint In Mailer - **$400**
Each - **$20 $40 $60**

TER-11

TER-11. Quaker "Wings Of Victory" Box,
c. 1945. Set of 12 warplane back pictures.
Each Complete Box - **$50 $100 $200**
Each Cut Picture Panel - **$5 $10 $15**

TER-12

**TER-12. Quaker Cereals "Sparkies Jingle Contest"
Postcard,**
1946. - **$8 $15 $30**

TER-13

TER-13. "Tattoo Transfers" Set In Envelope,
c. 1948. Coco-Wheats cereal. 22 water transfer pictures on
two sheets, "Pack No. 9". - **$25 $50 $75**

TER-14

TER-15

TER-16

TER-14. "Canada Dry" 13x17" Cardboard Ad Sign,
1953. (Has 1952 copyright.) Offered a comic book with purchase of every carton of soda. - **$100 $150 $250**

**TER-15. "Hot Shot Charlie Flies Again" No. 1 Comic
Book,**
1953. Canada Dry. From set of three. - **$15 $40 $95**

**TER-16. "Terry And The Pirates In Forced Landing"
Comic Book #2,**
1953. Canada Dry. Third book in set "Dragon Lady In
Distress". Each - **$15 $40 $95**

TER-17

TER-18

ER-17. Canada Dry "Chop-Stick-Joe" Litho. Button,
953. From set of five also including Terry, Burma, Dragon
ady, Hot Shot Charlie. Each - **$10 $20 $30**

ER-18. "See Terry On TV" 3" Flicker Button,
. 1953. Canada Dry. - **$30 $50 $75**

TER-19

ER-19. Comic Book Ad,
950s. Canada Day. - **$10 $20 $30**

THREE LITTLE PIGS

Disney's *The Three Little Pigs*, based on a Grimm brothers
airy tale, premiered in New York in 1933 and went on to
ecome one of the most successful animated cartoons ever
roduced. The story of the pigs - Fifer, Fiddler, and
Drummer - defending their homes and defying the wolf at the
oor, entranced children and adults alike. The merry theme,
Who's Afraid of the Big Bad Wolf, became one of the most
popular songs of the 1930s. Merchandising was extensive,
nd many Disney licensees added pig and wolf items to their
product lines.

TLP-1

TLP-1. Three Little Pigs Paper Mask,
1933. Lord & Taylor (and others), publisher is Einson-
Freeman Co. - **$15 $25 $40**

TLP-2

TLP-2. Walt Disney Studio Christmas Card,
1933. - **$200 $350 $750**

TLP-3

TLP-3. Ingersoll Animated Pocketwatch With Box,
1934. Store item. Wolf's eye winks, red color on dial often
faded. Near Mint Boxed - **$1800**
Watch - **$300 $600 $1000**

TLP-4

TLP-5

**TLP-4. "Who's Afraid Of The Big Bad Wolf" Cello.
Button,**
c. 1935. Pictured as give-away in Disney merchandise catalogues of the time. - **$50 $75 $150**

TLP-5. Three Little Pigs Ceramic Ashtray,
1930s. Store item. - **$40 $65 $90**

TLP-6

**TLP-6. Three Little Pigs Enameled Brass Matchbox
Holder,**
1930s. Store item. - **$15 $25 $40**

TLP-7. China Compartment Dish,
1930s. Store item also used as premium. - **$50 $100 $150**

TLP-8

TLP-8. Bab-O Folder With Three Pigs Picture,
1930s. - **$25 $50 $75**

TLP-9

TLP-10

TLP-9. "Who's Afraid Of The Big Bad Wolf" Pocketknife,
1930s. Scarce. Store item by Geo. Schrade Co. Steel with
silvered brass and enamel paint grips. - **$50 $100 $150**

**TLP-10. "Who's Afraid Of The Big Bad Wolf" Enameled
Brass Badge,**
1930s. Pig at piano. - **$40 $85 $150**

TLP-11

TLP-12

TLP-13

**TLP-11. "Three Little Pigs/Who's Afraid Of The Big Bad
Wolf" Enameled Brass Badge,**
1930s. Version pictures Fiddler Pig. - **$40 $85 $150**

**TLP-12. "Who's Afraid Of The Big Bad Wolf" Tin Toy
Watch With Moving Hands,**
1930s. Store item. Finished in four colors. - **$75 $125 $20**

TLP-13. Lil Bad Wolf Glass Tumbler,
1985. Fanta soda. For German distribution with inscriptions
mostly in German. - **$8 $12 $20**

THREE STOOGES

Slapstick and comic mayhem were the wacky hallmarks
the Three Stooges in their two dozen feature films a
almost 200 two-reelers made between 1930 and 1965. T
original trio - Moe Howard, his brother Curly, and Larry Fine
went from success in vaudeville to cult status in Hollywo
and later to enduring popularity via television reruns in t
late 1950s. (Another brother, Shemp, took over when Cu
died; Joe Besser replaced Shemp on his death; and J
DeRita later replaced Besser.) Animated cartoon series pr
duced by Hanna-Barbera were syndicated on television, T
Three Stooges in 1965 and *The Three Robonic Stooges*
1978. Comic books appeared from the late 1940s to t
1970s. Will the Stooges' brand of comedy continue into t
future? "Soitenly!"

THR-1

THR-1. "Moving Picture Machine" Newspaper Ad,
1937. Pillsbury's Farina. - **$25 $60 $100**

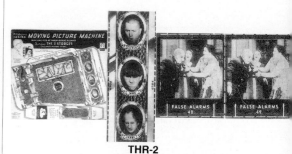

THR-2

THE THREE STOOGES 495

THR-2. "Moving Picture Machine" Cardboard Punch-Out Kit,
1937. Pillsbury's Farina. Came with films #5 and #6 based on actual movie "False Alarms," others available by purchasing more Farina. Scarce. Unpunched - **$250 $500 $1000** Assembled - **$150 $250 $400**

THR-6

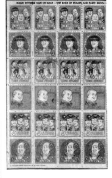

THR-7

THR-3

THR-3. Photo With Ad Reverse,
c. 1937. Pillsbury's Farina. Back offer is tied to Columbia Pictures promotion. - **$50 $125 $200**

THR-6. "Fan Club Of America" Membership Kit,
1959. Includes cover letter, sheet of stamps, membership cards (2), 8x10" photo. Complete - **$50 $100 $200**

THR-7. "Three Stooges/I'm Curly" Ring,
1959. Gold plastic base with two flicker portraits. Also issued with Moe and Larry. Each - **$10 $15 $20**

THR-4

THR-4. "Three Stooges" 3-D Comic Vol. 1 #2,
1953. St. John Publishing Co. - **$40 $120 $300**

THR-8

THR-8. Triple Image Ceramic Bank,
c. 1960s. Store item. - **$150 $300 $600**

THR-5

THR-5. Vending Machine Display Paper For Picture Rings,
1959. - **$20 $30 $40**

THR-9

THR-10

THR-9. Happy Birthday Record,
1960s. Possible premium, personalized to individual first name. - **$10 $20 $30**

THR-10. "Clark/Collector Cups" 3" Cello. Button,
1993. - **$5 $10 $18**

THURSTON, THE MAGICIAN

Howard Thurston (1869-1936) was a master magician who made a triumphant world tour in the early years of the 20th century, performing before royalty and notables. Thurston's exploits and adventures were dramatized in a short-lived radio series on the NBC Blue network in 1932-1933. The program, known as *Thurston, the Magician* or *Howard Thurston, the Magician*, was sponsored by Swift & Co.

THU-1

THU-2

THU-1. "Good Luck/Thurston" Cello. Button,
c. 1920. - **$15 $35 $75**

THU-2. "Good Luck" Card,
c. 1920s. - **$5 $10 $15**

THU-3

THU-3. "Thurston's Book Of Magic",
c. 1932. Swift's Premium Hams. One of a series. Each - **$8 $12 $25**

THU-4

THU 4. Trick Packets,
c. 1932. Swift & Co. At least 10 in set. Each - **$3 $5 $8**

TIM CLUB

This club, headed by "Tim," a cartoon image lad with no sur name, existed as early as 1929. Membership loosely con sisted of youngsters that patronized clothing stores electin to join the "Tim" endorsement theme. Premiums include code books, stamp albums and pin-backs related to "Pi Eater" activities. Tim's merchandising clout was revitalize beginning in the early 1940s by addition of a super partne Superman to be exact. Tim carried on his tradition bu became the second banana in the new "Superman-Tin Store" promotion. Premiums continued, apparently free including a monthly mailer newsletter/clothin catalogue/activities manual imprinted by local store name Superman was prominently featured in each. Additional pre miums were pin-back buttons, pennants, album stamps Secret Code and other membership items. Superman-Tin currency was also available. The Club was still officially licensed to Tim Promotions, Inc. of New York City.

TIM-1

TIM-1. Code Books,
c. 1930. Participating Tim stores. Pictured examples are for 1929, 1930, 1933. Each - **$8 $12 $20**

TIM-2

TIM-3

TIM-2. Pie-Eater Club Member Happy Birthday Letter,
1930s. Metropolitan (clothing) store. Invites recipient to pick up free pie. - **$10 $15 $25**

TIM-3. "Tim's Official Stamps",
1930s. Participating stores. For mounting in album supplied by store. Each - **$3 $5 $10**

TIM-4

TIM-5

IM-4. Cello. Club Button,
930s. Red, white, blue and gold. - **$8 $12 $20**

IM-5. Silvered Metal Portrait Ring,
930s. Raised portrait with dog portrait on each band, possi-
ly sterling. - **$150 $400 $650**

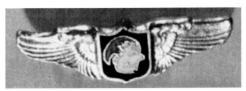

TIM-6

M-6. Tim Wings,
930s. Scarce. Store premium. - **$30 $60 $120**

TIM-7

M-7. "Tim's Magazine",
940. Participating stores. Issued monthly. Each -
$10 $15

TIM-8

TIM-9

M-8. Tim's "Redback" Currency,
940s. Various stores. Various denominations. Each -
$5 $8

M-9. "Pie Eaters Club/Tim" Litho. Button,
1940s. - **$3 $6 $10**

TIM-10   TIM-11   TIM-12

TIM-10. "Tim's Store For Boys" Cello. Button,
c. 1940s. - **$5 $8 $12**

TIM-11. "Tim's Official Pie Eaters Club" Cello. Button,
c. 1940s. - **$3 $6 $10**

TIM-12. "Pie Eaters Club/Tim" Cello. Button,
c. 1940s. - **$3 $6 $10**

TIM-13

TIM-13. "Tim's Lucky Coin",
c. 1940s. Front portrait, back inscription "From Tim's Official
Store". Brass. - **$5 $12 $20**

TIM TYLER

Cartoonist Lyman Young created *Tim Tyler's Luck* for the
King Features Syndicate as a daily strip in 1928 and as a
Sunday page in 1931. Tim's adventures took him to Africa,
where he joined the Ivory Patrol to help maintain law and
order. A syndicated radio program aired in 1936-1937, a
series of comic books appeared in the 1940s, and Universal
Pictures released a 12-episode chapter play, also called *Tim
Tyler's Luck*, in 1937, with Frankie Thomas as Tim.

TYL-1   TYL-2

TYL-1. "Tim Tyler's Luck/Ivory Patrol Club" Cello.
Button,
1937. Universal Pictures. For 12-chapter movie serial. -
$30 $60 $100

TYL-2. "Tim Tyler Ivory Patrol Club/Viva" Cello. Button,
c. 1937. - **$40 $75 $140**

TOM CORBETT, SPACE CADET

Set in the 24th century, this television space adventure followed the exploits of three young cadets as they trained in their spaceship Polaris to become officers of the Solar Guards. The series, based on Robert Heinlein's 1948 novel *Space Cadet* and scripted with the technical advice of rocket scientist Willy Ley, was distinguished by scientific accuracy and innovative camera effects. Corbett's unit at the Space Academy included Roger Manning (So what happens now, space heroes?) and Astro, a quick-tempered Venusian youth. Veteran actor Frankie Thomas played the part of Corbett.

Tom Corbett, Space Cadet was one of the few series to appear on all four commercial TV networks, and on two of them simultaneously. The show, which was broadcast live, debuted on CBS in 1950, moved to ABC in 1951-1952, appeared on NBC in the summer of 1951, on the Dumont network in 1953-1954, and again on NBC in 1954-1955. Sponsors were Kellogg's cereals (1950-1952), Red Goose shoes (1953-1954), and Kraft Foods (1954-1955). The series also ran on ABC radio for six months in 1952, featuring the same cast as sponsored by Kellogg, and as a simulcast on NBC in 1954-1955, sponsored by Kraft.

In print, a Corbett comic strip distributed by the Field Newspaper Syndicate appeared from 1951 to 1953, comic books between 1952 and 1955, and a series of Corbett novels from Grosset & Dunlap between 1952 and 1956.

Merchandising of Tom Corbett material was extensive, including toys, a watch, lunch boxes, space goggles, and helmets. Kellogg promoted a Space Academy membership club that offered badges, rings, patches, a cardboard decoder, ID cards, and autographed photos. Items are normally copyrighted Rockhill Productions.

TCO-2

TCO-1　　　　TCO-3

TCO-1. Membership Kit Cast Photo,
1951. - **$15 $25 $50**

TCO-2. "Space Cadet" 2-1/8" Cello. Button,
1951. Part of club membership kit. - **$50 $125 $200**

TCO-3. Fabric Patch,
1951. Part of member's kit. - **$20 $40 $75**

TCO-4

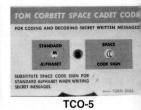

TCO-5

TCO-4. Certificate,
1951. Part of member's kit. - **$20 $45 $75**

TCO-5. Kellogg's Cardboard Decoder,
1951. Came with membership kit. - **$35 $65 $120**

TCO-6

TCO-6. "Tom Corbett Space Cadet News" Vol. 1 #1,
1951. Kellogg's. Part of member's kit. - **$35 $75 $125**

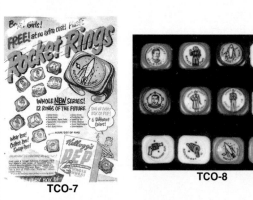

TCO-7　　　　　　TCO-8

TCO-7. "Rocket Rings" Comic Book Page Ad,
1951. Kellogg's Pep cereal. - **$2 $4 $6**

TCO-8. Kellogg's Plastic Rings With Insert Pictures,
1951. Set of 12. Near Mint Set - **$400**
Each - **$10 $15 $25**

TCO-9

TCO-9. Cereal Box With "Tom Corbett Space Cadet Squadron" Back,
1951. Also pictures "Rocket Launching Plane Catapulting Aircraft Carrier". Complete Box - **$150 $250 $350**

TCO-10

TCO-10. Butter-Nut Bread End Label Album #1,
1952. Complete with 24 bread labels.
Near Mint Complete - **$350**
Album Only - **$30 $80 $125**
Each Label - **$3 $5 $10**

TCO-11

TCO-12

TCO-13

TCO-11. "Tom Corbett/Space Cadet" Silvered Metal Ring,
1952. - **$50 $75 $100**

TCO-12. Rocket Ring,
1952. Silvered brass and white gold luster metal inscribed on underside "Space Cadet/Tom Corbett Unit". -
$175 $260 $350

TCO-13. Metal Badge,
1952. - **$15 $35 $75**

TCO-14

TCO-14. View-Master Set,
1954. Store item. - **$15 $25 $35**

TCO-15

TCO-16

TCO-15. Die-cut Metal Pin,
1954. In Sears catalogue, came with purchase of Corbett flashlight. - **$20 $50 $100**

TCO-16. Metallic Silver Fabric Cap with Sunglasses,
1950s. Scarce. Probable premium. - **$50 $75 $150**

TCO-17

TCO-18

TCO-17. Official Hat,
1950s. Scarce. Probable store item. Includes plastic badge on front. - **$75 $150 $300**

TCO-18. Fiberboard Helmet,
1950s. Scarce. Probable store item. Includes plastic badge on front. - **$75 $150 $200**

TCO-19

TCO-19. Litho. Clicker Gun,
1950s. Store item by Marx. - **$50 $125 $200**

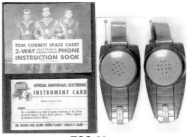
TCO-20

TCO-20. "Two-Way Electronic Walkie-Talkie Phone" Set,
1950s. Store item by Remco. Phone Set - **$30 $60 $100**
Instructions - **$15 $30 $50**
Code Card - **$15 $30 $50**

TCO-21

TCO-22

TCO-21. Rocket-Lite Squadron Club Card,
1950s. Reverse instructions for Space Cadet pin-on rocket light. - **$10 $15 $25**

TCO-22. Kellogg's "Space Cadet Rocketship" Plastic Flicker Disk,
1950s. From series picturing various Tom Corbett (and other) scenes. - **$8 $12 $25**

TOM MIX

Tom Mix (1880-1940), the greatest Western film star of the silent era, was born and grew up in rural DuBois, Pennsylvania. He enlisted in the Army at the outbreak of the Spanish-American war in 1898 and achieved the rank of first sergeant. His overseas military adventures are part of the legend, not reality, as he never left the United States. After leaving the Army in 1902 he moved to Oklahoma and found work as a drum major, bartender, and part-time ranch hand. In 1904 he attended the St. Louis World's Fair as a member of the Oklahoma Cavalry Band. In 1905 he went to work as a "cowboy" for the Miller Brothers' 101 Real Wild West Ranch, barnstormed in other Wild West shows, and served as a deputy sheriff and night marshal.

Tom Mix's movie career began in 1909 for the Selig Polyscope Company, first as an advisor and troubleshooter, then doubling as a stunt man, and ultimately starring in, writing, and directing some 64 silent shorts. By 1917, when he was hired by William Fox Productions, he was a star, and by 1921 he was one of the country's 10 top box office attractions. Over a period of 10 years he made 78 silent features for Fox, most of them as an idealized Western hero, doing his own stunts and riding his chestnut steed, Tony the Wonder Horse, to fame and fortune. He made another six silent features in 1928-1929 for the Film Booking Office, then left Hollywood to tour and star in Sells Floto Circus from 1929 to 1931.

Returning to films, he and Tony Jr. made his first talkies, nine features for Universal Pictures in 1931-1932, and his last movie, *The Miracle Rider*, a 15-episode chapter play, for Mascot Pictures in 1935. That same year he bought a circus, and from 1935 to 1938 the Tom Mix Circus toured the country and performed for crowds of admirers. In 1940 he was killed in an automobile accident in Arizona.

The Tom Mix radio program aired from 1933 to 1950, on NBC until 1944, then on the Mutual network. Ralston cereal was the exclusive radio program sponsor. Various actors played Tom in what was billed as a Western detective program. Tom and the Ralston Straight Shooters operated out of the T-M Bar Ranch, solving mysteries, crusading for justice, finding water for the cattle, even fighting saboteurs during the war years. Helping out, along with Tony, were young Jimmy and Jane, the Old Wrangler, Sheriff Mike Shaw, Wash the cook, and Pecos Williams, a singing sidekick played by Joe "Curley" Bradley until he took over the role of Tom in 1940.

Ralston offered hundreds of Tom Mix premiums - rings, flashlights, magnifiers, whistles, sirens, spurs, telescopes, wooden guns, comic books, photo albums, badges, anything that could carry the familiar Ralston checkerboard design or the T-M Bar brand. Tom's first comic book appearance was in issue #1 of *The Comics* in 1937, and he had his own books in the 1940s and 1950s. Ralston briefly revived the Straight Shooters in 1982-1983 as a 50th anniversary tribute, offering a comic book, patch, cereal bowl and watch in exchange for box tops. The Tom Mix Museum in Dewey, Oklahoma, opened in 1968.

TMX-1   TMX-2   TMX-3

TMX-1. "Sells Floto Circus" Cello. Button,
c. 1929. Word "Sells" is part of circus proper name. Mix toured with circus 1929-1931. - **$20 $40 $75**

TMX-2. "Tom Mix For Sheriff" Cello. Button,
c. 1930. - **$200 $400 $800**

TMX-3. "Tom Mix With Tony/Universal Pictures" Cello. Button,
1932. From his 1932-1933 years at Universal. -
$65 $125 $200

TMX-4

TMX-5

TMX-4. Chewing Gum Wrapper With Deputy Ring Offer,
1933. National Chicle Co. Product copyright is 1933. Ring offer expired June 30, 1935. - **$75 $90 $100**

TMX-5. "The Life Of Tom Mix" First Club Manual,
1933. - **$40 $80 $150**

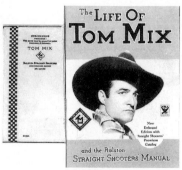

TMX-6

TMX-6. Club Manual "Enlarged Edition",
1933. Near Mint With Mailer - **$150**
Loose - **$40 $75 $125**

TMX-7

MX-7. Premium Catalogue Sheet,
33. - **$20 $40 $65**

TMX-8

MX-8. Tom Mix & Tony Photo,
33. - **$15 $25 $40**

TMX-9

MX-9. Paper Lario With Tricks And Stunts Sheet,
33. Tricks Sheet - **$35 $80 $125**
rio - **$50 $125 $200**

TMX-10   TMX-11
                      TMX-12

MX-10. Cigar Box Label,
33. - **$20 $40 $80**

MX-11. Cigar Box Label,
33. - **$20 $40 $80**

MX-12. Postcard,
33. - **$10 $20 $40**

TMX-13
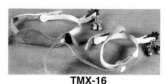

TMX-14

TMX-13. Revolver,
1933. Earliest gun, opens and cylinder revolves. -
$40 $80 $150

TMX-14. Cowboy Hat,
1933. Rare premium. Name on inner head band. -
$150 $300 $900

TMX-16

TMX-15

TMX-15. Leather Wrist Cuffs,
1933. No Mix identification, depict cowboy with lariat. -
$60 $125 $200

TMX-16. Metal Spurs With Leather Straps,
1933. No Mix identification, horse head on top strap. Rubber
rowels each have two metal jangle weights. -
$100 $175 $250

TMX-18

TMX-17

TMX-17. Fabric Bandanna,
1933. - **$30 $60 $125**

TMX-18. "Straight Shooters" Fabric Patch,
1933. - **$15 $25 $50**

TMX-20

TMX-21

TMX-19

TMX-19. "Good Luck/TM" Spinner,
1933. - **$20 $40 $65**

TMX-20. Horseshoe Nail Ring,
1933. Generic horseshoe nail with silver luster. No Tom Mix markings. - **$20 $30 $40**

TMX-21. "TM" Spinner Ring,
1933. Rare. Possibly a circus souvenir. - **$600 $1200 $2500**

TMX-22

TMX-23

TMX-22. "Lucky Pocket Piece" Brass Medalet,
c. 1933 "Exhibit Supply Company/Chicago" on reverse inside with horseshoe design. - **$25 $50 $90**

TMX-23. Radio Program 15x24" Cardboard Sign,
c. 1933. Printed both sides. - **$100 $200 $400**

TMX-24

TMX-25

TMX-24. "Tom Mix" Bisque 5" Figurine,
c. 1933. Rare. Store item. Only figural Mix item known. Made in Germany, marked #3509. - **$800 $1500 $5000**

TMX-25. Rodeorope And Full Color Box,
1934. Store item. - **$100 $200 $400**

TMX-26

TMX-27

TMX-26. National Chicle Co. Gum Booklet #2 Example,
1934. 48 numbered booklets. Each - **$10 $20 $35**

TMX-27. Premiums Catalogue Folder Sheet,
1934. Catalogue designated C 135 G. - **$20 $35 $50**

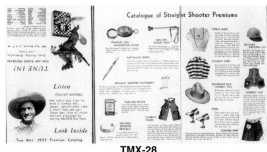

TMX-28

TMX-28. Premiums Catalogue Folder Sheet,
1934. Catalogue designated C 135 O. - **$15 $30 $45**

TMX-29

TMX-29. Paper Mask,
1934. Scarce. - **$250 $500 $750**

TMX-30

TMX-30. "Series A" Photo Set,
1934. Set of five. Each Photo Or Mailer - **$10 $25 $50**

TMX-31

TMX-31. "Series B" Photo Set With Envelope,
1934. Set of five photos. Each Photo Or Mailer -
$10 $25 $50

TMX-33

TMX-32

TMX-32. Zyp Gun With Mailer Envelope,
1934. Scarce. Metal spring gun with rubber cup dart. Also known as Tom Mix Target Gun.
Gun With Dart - **$150 $350 $600**
Mailer - **$15 $25 $40**

TMX-33. "Tom Mix Deputy" Gold And Silver Finish Brass Ring,
1935. National Chicle Gum. Required 75 certificates clipped from gum wrappers. - **$1375 $2750 $6000**

TMX-35

TMX-34

TMX-34. Tom Mix Big Little Book Puzzles (Boxed),
1935. Store item. - **$100 $200 $400**

TMX-35. Paint Book,
1935. Store item. - **$100 $200 $400**

TMX-36

TMX-37

TMX-36

TMX-36. "Miracle Riders" Picture Folio,
1935. Holds 15 bw numbered photo pages apparently corresponding to 15 serial chapters. Distributed by theaters, sponsored by Tootsie Rolls. Set - **$125 $250 $400**

TMX-37. "Miracle Rider" Serial Club Cello. Button,
1935. Mascot. - **$100 $250 $500**

TMX-38

TMX-38. "Shooting Gallery" Cardboard Target With Box,
1935. Store item by Parker Brothers. Includes rubber band gun. - **$75 $175 $300**

TMX-39

TMX-40

TMX-39. Litho. Portrait Button,
1935. Canvas Products Co., St. Louis. Five buttons given with purchase of Tom Mix tent. - **$35 $75 $150**

TMX-40. "The Trail Of The Terrible 6" Booklet,
1935. - **$15 $30 $75**

TMX-41

TMX-41. "Western Movie" Cardboard Mechanical Viewer,
1935. Film scenes from "The Miracle Rider" Mascot Pictures serial. - **$60 $135 $200**

TMX-42

TMX-43

TMX-42. "Western Movie" Cardboard Box Viewer,
1935. Film scenes from "Rustlers Roundup". - **$50 $125 $175**

TMX-43. "Miracle Rider" Dixie Ice Cream Lid,
1935. - **$5 $12 $25**

TMX-44

TMX-45

(enlarged view)

TMX-44. Spinning Rope,
1935. Red, white and blue twine with Mix Ralston endorsement on wooden grip. - **$40 $80 $140**

TMX-45. Suede Leather Chaps,
1935. - **$50 $125 $250**

TMX-46

(enlarged view)

TMX-46. Suede Leather Cowgirl Skirt,
1935. - **$60 $150 $250**

TMX-47

TMX-48

TMX-47. Metal Spurs With Leather Straps,
1935. Straps have TM Bar Ranch symbol. - **$75 $140 $225**

TMX-48. Leather Wrist Cuffs,
1935. - **$60 $150 $250**

TMX-49

TMX-50

TMX-51

TMX-49. Suede Vest,
1935. - **$60 $120 $175**

TMX-50. Brown Leather Holster,
1935. Cover panel has Tom Mix markings. - **$75 $175 $250**

TMX-51. Leather Bracelet With Foil On Brass Title Plate,
1935. Tom Mix or Ralston markings on both front and back. Named in ads "Lucky Wrist Band".
Complete - **$25 $60 $100**
No Strap - **$15 $30 $60**

TMX-52

TMX-53

TMX-54

TMX-52. Straight Shooter Bracelet With Checkerboard Logo,
1935. Silvered brass. - **$150 $250 $400**

TMX-53. Sun Watch,
1935. - **$20 $40 $85**

TMX-54. Bar Brand Branding Iron With Ink Pad Tin,
1935. Brass stamper has TM initials and checkerboard design. Branding Iron - **$25 $50 $85**
Ink Tin - **$10 $20 $35**

TMX-55

TMX-56

TMX-57

MX-55. Compass With Magnifier,
935. Unmarked Ralston premium. Aluminum case with eye-
et. - **$15 $25 $40**

MX-56. Lucky Charm Sterling Silver Horseshoe,
935. - **$90 $150 $250**

MX-57. "TM" Ralston Logo Brass Ring,
935. Named in ads "Tom Mix Lucky Ring". - **$60 $90 $125**

TMX-58

MX-58. Premium Catalogue Folder,
936. - **$15 $30 $50**

TMX-59

TMX-60

MX-59. Wood Gun With Cardboard Handles,
936. Cylinder revolves but gun doesn't open. -
0 $90 $150

MX-60. Championship Cowboy Belt Buckle,
936. Brass with foil paper insert, also came with belt.
uckle Only - **$35 $75 $125**
uckle And Belt - **$50 $100 $165**

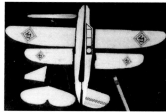

TMX-61

MX-61. Flying Model Airplane Kit,
36. Scarce. Balsa wood with Ralston logo decals. -
50 $300 $500

TMX-62

TMX-62. "Rocket Parachute",
1936. Consists of balsa and cardboard launcher, wood stick
with rubber band, metal figure string joined to paper parachute. Boxed - **$50 $100 $175**
Loose - **$35 $60 $100**

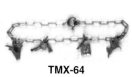

TMX-63

TMX-64

TMX-63. Fountain Pen With Mailer Envelope,
1936. Pen cap has Tom Mix ranch brand symbol decal.
Pen - **$40 $80 $150**
Mailer - **$8 $12 $20**

TMX-64. Girl's Brass Dangle Charm Bracelet,
1936. Scarce. Charms depict ranch symbol, Tom on Tony,
steer head, six-shooter. Also called "Championship Cowgirl
Bracelet". - **$200 $500 $1000**

TMX-66

TMX-65

TMX-67

TMX-65. Signet Ring Newspaper Advertisement,
1936. - **$10 $20 $30**

TMX-66. Lucky Signet Ring,
1936. Brass bands topped by raised personalized single initial designated by orderer. - **$100 $175 $250**

TMX-67. "Marlin Guns" Brass Target Ring,
1937. Marlin Firearms Co. For his endorsed Tom Mix Special
.22 caliber rifle. - **$100 $175 $250**

TMX-68

TMX-68. Premium Catalogue Folder,
1937. Pictured premiums include Signet Ring. -
$15 **$25** **$40**

TMX-69   **TMX-70**

**TMX-69. "Ralston Straight Shooter News" Vol. 1 #1
Issue,**
1937. - **$35** **$60** **$125**

TMX-70. "Ralston Straight Shooter News" #2,
1937. - **$20** **$50** **$80**

TMX-71

TMX-71. Baby Turtle Newspaper Advertisement,
1937. Premium was a real live baby turtle with Mix decal on
its shell. - **$10** **$15** **$30**

TMX-72

TMX-72. Movie Make-Up Kit With Paper,
1937. Five tins with TM brand and words Clown, Indian,
Chink, Mexican, Negro. Complete - **$50** **$75** **$150**
Each Tin - **$3** **$5** **$8**

TMX-73

TMX-74

TMX-73. "Postal Telegraph Signal Set",
1937. Cardboard box with metal tapper key. - **$35** **$75** **$12**

TMX-74. Silver Frame Photo,
1937. Photo is personalized by recipient first name. -
$35 **$50** **$90**

TMX-75   **TMX-76**   **TMX-77**

**TMX-75. Straight Shooter Metal Badge With Foil
Paper Insert,**
1937. Silver luster. - **$25** **$50** **$100**

TMX-76. Straight Shooter Brass Badge,
1937. Foil paper symbol. - **$35** **$75** **$125**

TMX-77. Straight Shooter Badge Lead Proof,
c. 1937. Unique - **$750**

TMX-78   **TMX-79**

**TMX-78. Prototype "Ranch Boss" Enameled
Brass Badge,**
c. 1937. Trial design for Ralston approval by Robbins Co.,
Massachusetts with enamel emblem rather than foil paper.
Unique - **$3000**

**TMX-79. Prototype "Tom Mix Ralston Straight Shooters
Star Brass Badge,**
c. 1937. Trial design for Ralston approval by Robbins Co.,
Massachusetts. Unique - **$3000**

TMX-80

MX-80. Premium Catalogue Sheet,
938. - **$15 $25 $45**

TMX-82

TMX-81

1X-81. Metal Telescope,
38. Near Mint With Mailer - **$150**
ose - **$35 $60 $100**

1X-82. Secret Ink Writing Kit,
38. Includes: manual, cardboard decoder, two glass vials
ink and developer. Manual - **$50 $150 $400**
coder - **$15 $50 $100**
ch Vial - **$10 $40 $60**

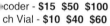

TMX-83

TMX-84

1X-83. Telephone Set,
38. Litho. tin transmitter and receiver units joined by
ng. - **$30 $60 $90**

1X-84. Bullet Flashlight,
38. 3" silvered brass tube with plastic end cap holding
b. - **$50 $75 $125**

TMX-85

TMX-85. Wrangler Badge Folder,
1938. - **$40 $85 $150**

TMX-86

TMX-87

TMX-88

TMX-86. "Wrangler" Brass Badge,
1938. - **$40 $80 $160**

TMX-87. Wrangler Badge Lead Proof,
c. 1938. Unique - **$750**

TMX-88. "Wrangler" Metal Badge With Foil Paper Insert,
1938. Version pictures him frontally rather than partial profile.
Issued in either silver or gold luster.
Either Version - **$50 $125 $250**

TMX-89

TMX-91

TMX-90

TMX-89. "Ranch Boss" Brass Rank Badge,
1938. Centered by foil paper emblem. - **$100 $200 $500**

TMX-90. Ranch Boss Badge Lead Proof,
c. 1938. Unique - **$1500**

TMX-91. Look-In Mystery Ring,
1938. Brass with tiny view hole for inside portrait photo of
Tom with Tony. - **$75 $125 $175**

TMX-92

TMX-92. Premium Catalogue Folder Sheet,
1939. - **$20 $30 $45**

TMX-93

TMX-94

TMX-93. Wood Gun,
1939. No moving parts. - **$50 $85 $150**

TMX-94. Streamline Parachute Plane,
1939. Scarce. Balsa wood with designs in red and blue.
Metal hinged wings. Came with parachutist and parachute,
see next item. Plane Only - **$125 $250 $400**

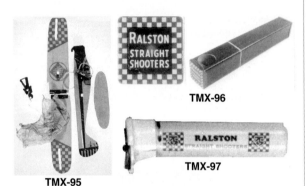

TMX-96

TMX-97

TMX-95

TMX-95. Streamline Plane Parachutist And Parachute,
1939. Rare. Came with previous item. Metal figure smaller
than 1936 Rocket Parachute and parachute is green. -
$25 $100 $200

TMX-96. Cardboard Periscope,
1939. Blue Tube - **$25 $40 $75**
Black Tube - **$35 $60 $100**

TMX-97. Signal Flashlight,
1939. 3" metal tube with lens disk for red, green or clear light.
Lens often missing and plastic end cap often cracked.
Complete - **$30 $60 $125**

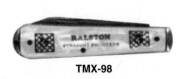

TMX-98

TMX-99

TMX-98. "Straight Shooters" Pocketknife,
1939. - **$30 $60 $90**

TMX-99. Brass Compass And Magnifier,
1939. Magnifying lens swings out. - **$20 $35 $75**

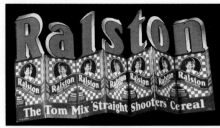

TMX-100

TMX-100. Ralston Diecut Accordion Fold Display Sign,
1930s. Rare. - **$400 $800 $1600**

TMX-103

TMX-101

TMX-102

TMX-101. Cinema Star Card #7,
1930s. England. Wills Cigarettes premium. - **$20 $40 $60**

TMX-102. Dixie Cup Lid,
1930s. Promotes Miracle Rider movie. - **$20 $30 $50**

TMX-103. Hollywood Gum Card,
1930s. - **$20 $40 $60**

TMX-104

TMX-105

TMX-106

TMX-104. "Wild West Club" Member Cello. Button,
1930s. Rare. - **$200 $400 $800**

**TMX-105. "Toledo Paramount Theater" Movie Cello.
Button,**
1930s. Scarce issue from a single theater in Ohio. -
$100 $300 $450

TMX-106. "Yankiboy Play Clothes" Cello. Button,
1930s. Yellow rim 1-3/4" size. - **$35 $60 $100**

TMX-107

TMX-107. Rexall Toothpaste Puzzle,
1930s. In Envelope - **$35 $60 $100**
Loose - **$20 $40 $60**

TMX-108

TMX-108. Pocketknife 6x24" Paper Store Sign,
1930s. Scarce. - **$150 $250 $400**

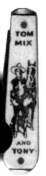

TMX-110

TMX-111

TMX-109

TMX-109. Cello./Steel Pocketknife,
1930s. Store item by Imperial. - **$40 $75 $150**

TMX-110. "Yankiboy Play Clothes" 2" Cello. Button,
1930s. Orange rim. - **$25 $40 $75**

TMX-111. "Capturing Outlaws In The Bad Lands",
1930s. Compliments Ralston Corn Flakes. Paper photo with
facsimile Mix inscription and signature. Reverse has short
story "As Told By The Old Wrangler". - **$50 $90 $150**

TMX-112

TMX-112. Humming Lariat
1930s. Store item. - **$40 $85 $150**

TMX-113

TMX-113. "Purina Bread" Handbill,
1930s. For various groceries. - **$35 $70 $100**

TMX-114

TMX-115

TMX-114. "Tom Mix Comics Book 1",
1940. Ralston premium sent via mail so rarely found in top
condition. Eleven additional issued between 1940-1942. -
$275 $825 $2200

TMX-115. "Tom Mix Comics Book 2",
1940. - **$90 $260 $700**

TMX-116

TMX-117

TMX-116. "Stars Of Our Radio Program" Fan Card,
1940. Back has form message for sending verses to contest
song. - **$30 $75 $150**

TMX-117. Gold Ore Assayer's Certificate,
1940. Came with watch fob. - **$15 $30 $65**

TMX-119

TMX-118

TMX-120

TMX-118. Gold Ore Watch Fob,
1940. - **$20 $50 $75**

TMX-119. Make-Up Kit Tin Canister,
1940. Red or black checkerboard design, came in disguise kit including false mustache, goatee, teeth and two canisters. - **$8 $12 $20**

TMX-120. Indian Blow Gun Target Printer's Engraving Plate,
1940. Unique - **$1000**

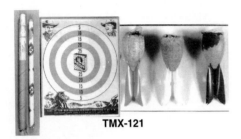

TMX-121

TMX-121. Indian Blow Gun Set,
1940. Scarce. With paper target, four darts, mailer tube.
Near Mint With Mailer - **$500**
Target - **$50 $100 $150**
Blow Gun - **$50 $100 $150**
Each Dart - **$10 $20 $30**

TMX-122

TMX-122. Telegraph Set With Box Mailer,
1940. Cardboard with metal tapper key.
Telegraph - **$35 $60 $100**
Box - **$10 $20 $35**

TMX-123

TMX-124

TMX-125

TMX-123. Straight Shooters Manual,
1941. - **$20 $35 $75**

TMX-124. "Tom Mix Comics" #3,
1941. - **$60 $170 $450**

TMX-125. "Tom Mix Comics" #4,
1941. - **$60 $170 $450**

TMX-126

TMX-127

TMX-128

TMX-126. "Tom Mix Comics" #5,
1941. - **$60 $170 $450**

TMX-127. "Tom Mix Comics" #6,
1941. - **$60 $170 $450**

TMX-128. "Tom Mix Comics" #7,
1941. - **$60 $170 $450**

TMX-129

TMX-130

TMX-129. Six-Gun Brass Decoder Badge,
1941. Gun turns brass pointer on reverse to one of nine code words. - **$40 $75 $150**

TMX-130. "Captain" Silvered Brass Spur Badge,
1941. - **$65 $125 $250**

TMX-131

TMX-132

TMX-131. "Tom Mix Comics" #8,
1942. - **$60 $170 $450**

TMX-132. "Tom Mix Comics" #9,
1942. - **$60 $170 $450**

TMX-133

TMX-134

TMX-135

TMX-133. "Tom Mix Commandos Comics" Book 10,
1942. - **$45 $130 $350**

TMX-134. "Tom Mix Commandos" Comic Book #11,
1942. - **$45 $130 $350**

TMX-135. "Tom Mix Commandos" Comic Book #12,
1942. - **$45 $130 $350**

TMX-136

TMX-137

TMX-138

TMX-136. "Tom Mix" Signature Ring,
1942. Brass with sterling silver top plate. - **$100 $175 $250**

TMX-137. "Secret Manual",
1944. - **$25 $60 $100**

TMX-138. Siren Ring,
1944. Brass with enclosed siren disk wheel for blowing. -
$100 $150 $200

TMX-139

TMX-140

TMX-139. "Tom Mix Straight Shooters Album" Manual,
1945. Near Mint With Envelope - **$125**
Manual Only - **$25 $50 $75**

TMX-140. "One-Act Play" Offer Sheet,
1945. Offered script for play titled "The Straight Shooters
Secret," issued with 1945 manual. No copy of the script is
known. - **$15 $25 $40**

TMX-141

TMX-142

TMX-141. Cloth Patch,
1945. Issued with 1945 club manual. - **$20 $35 $60**

TMX-142. Straight Shooters Service Ribbon And Medal,
1945. Fabric over metal bar pin suspending glow-in-dark
plastic medal. - **$25 $75 $150**

TMX-143

**TMX-143. "Curley Bradley The Tom Mix Of Radio" 78
RPM Three-Record Album,**
c. 1945. Universal Recording Corp. - **$50 $100 $200**

TMX-144

TMX-145

TMX-144. Curley Bradley Fan Photo Card,
1946. Radio portrayer of Tom Mix, back has Safety Code. -
$20 $50 $75

TMX-145. Glow Belt With Secret Compartment Buckle,
1946. Complete - **$50 $80 $150**
Buckle Only - **$25 $50 $75**

TMX-146

TMX-146. Decoder Buttons With Card,
1946. Set of five litho. buttons. Complete Near Mint - **$125**
Each Button - **$8 $12 $20**

TMX-147   TMX-148

TMX-147. "Luminous Compass-Magnifying Glass",
1946. Near Mint In Mailer - **$250**
Loose - **$20 $60 $100**

TMX-148. Dobie County Sheriff Siren Badge,
1946. - **$20 $50 $100**

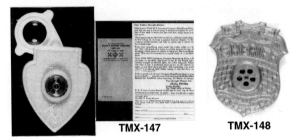

TMX-149
TMX-150

TMX-149. Folder Mailed With Siren Badge,
1946. - **$15 $30 $65**

TMX-150. "Look-Around" Ring,
1946. Near Mint In Mailer - **$250**
Ring Only - **$75 $110 $150**

TMX-151
TMX-152

TMX-151. "Rocket Parachute" Version #2 Re-issue With Box,
1947. Similar to original 1936 item with portrait added on
mailer box. Boxed - **$75 $125 $200**

TMX-152. "Tom Mix Bureau Of Identification File Card",
1947. Scarce as card was meant to be returned with member's fingerprints and ID bracelet number. - **$35 $60 $90**

TMX-153

TMX-154   TMX-155

TMX-153. Identification Bracelet,
1947. Personalized by single initial designated by orderer. -
$15 $25 $50

TMX-154. Magnet Ring,
1947. Brass with silver finish magnet. - **$45 $70 $100**

TMX-155. "Magnet Ring" Paper Slip,
1947. - **$30 $35 $40**

TMX-156
TMX-157

TMX-156. Super Magnetic Compass Gun And Whistle,
1948. Both gun and arrowhead whistle glow in dark. -
$50 $100 $175

TMX-157. "Tom Mix Safety Story" Poster,
1948. Yankee Network Station. Opens to 17x22". -
$35 $75 $125

TMX-158

TMX-158. Premiums Catalogue Sheet,
'49. - **$10 $20 $30**

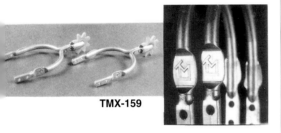

TMX-159

TMX-159. Cowboy Spurs,
'49. Aluminum with glow in dark rowels. - **$40 $75 $125**

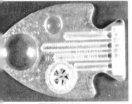

TMX-160

TMX-161

TMX-160. "Signal Arrowhead" Plastic Whistle/Siren/ Magnifier,
'49. - **$20 $40 $75**

TMX-161. Sliding Whistle Brass/Aluminum Ring,
'49. - **$50 $75 $100**

TMX-162   **TMX-163**   **TMX-164**

TMX-162. Miniature Gold-Plated TV Viewer,
'49. Scarce. Only 200 made for executives. -
$75 $150 $300

TMX-163. "RCA Victor" Miniature TV Film Viewer,
'49. Brass back includes Tom Mix name. - **$20 $30 $50**
Add $10 Per Mix Film Disk

TMX-164. "RCA Victor" Miniature TV Film Viewer,
'50. Version without Mix name on reverse. - **$20 $35 $50**
Add $10 Per Mix Film Disk

TMX-165

TMX-165. Ray O Print Outfit,
1940s. With tin holder for negative and photo paper with
envelope. - **$50 $100 $150**

TMX-166

TMX-166. "Tom Mix Color Book",
1950. - **$10 $20 $35**

TMX-167

TMX-168

TMX-167. Magic-Light Tiger-Eye Ring,
1950. Plastic with glow in the dark top. - **$100 $200 $300**

TMX-168. Golden Plastic Bullet Telescope & Birdcall,
1950. Gold plastic holding inside bird call whistle.
Complete - **$25 $50 $75**
Without Whistle - **$10 $20 $40**

TMX-169

TMX-169. "Tom Mix Ralston Straight Shooters Club" Revival Membership Kit,
1982. 50-year membership card, fabric patch, comic booklet,
early years photo reprint, current premium photo sheet.
Each - **$3 $5 $10**

TMX-170

TMX-171

TMX-170. "Tom Mix Ralston Straight Shooters" Revival Cereal Bowl,
1982. - **$10 $15 $25**

TMX-171. Revival Wristwatch,
1982. - **$50 $100 $300**

TONY THE TIGER

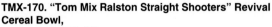

The Kellogg Company adopted Tony the Tiger in 1952 to speak for the company's Sugar Frosted Flakes. Tony was originally created by Martin Provensen, a children's book illustrator. The robust, smiling cartoon tiger is anything but shy, constantly reminding us that his cereal is Gr-r-reat!

TNY-1

TNY-2

TNY-1. Vinyl Inflated Figure,
1953. - **$10 $25 $40**

TNY-2. Plastic Bank,
1967. - **$30 $45 $70**

TNY-3

TNY-4

TNY-3. Hard Plastic Cookie Jar With Box,
1968. Jar Only - **$25 $50 $80**
Boxed - **$40 $75 $150**

TNY-4. "Astronaut Breakfast Game" Litho. Button,
1960s. White or blue background. - **$3 $8 $12**

TNY-5

TNY-6

TNY-5. Plush And Cloth Doll,
1970. - **$15 $25 $40**

TNY-6. Vinyl Doll With Movable Head,
c. 1974. - **$20 $35 $60**

TNY-7

TNY-8

TNY-7. Plastic Radio,
1980. Battery operated. Boxed - **$30 $40 $60**
Loose - **$10 $20 $35**

TNY-8. Stainless Steel Cereal Spoon,
1983. - **$5 $10 $15**

TNY-9

TNY-9. Frosted Flakes Canadian Issue Box,
1990. Offers Spider-Man and Tony The Tiger comic in English/French. Box - **$25 $40 $85**
Comic - **$10 $20 $40**

TOONERVILLE FOLKS

ntaine Fox's comic cartoon panels apparently began pearing in newspapers in 1915. The following year the oonerville Trolley was introduced, and in 1920 the Bell yndicate began distributing Fox's Sunday page as oonerville Folks. The ramshackle trolley and its Skipper, ong with such Toonerville denizens as Mickey (Himself) cGuire, the Powerful Katrinka, and the Terrible-Tempered r. Bang, delighted millions of readers for 40 years. Several llections of reprints were published in the early years, a ries of two-reel live-action film comedies were released in e 1920s, and Burt Gillett produced Toonerville animated orts in 1936. The strip survived until 1955.

TOO-1   TOO-2

DO-1. Cartoon Book,
21. Store item published by Cupples & Leon Co. -
0 $115 $265

OO-2. Coca-Cola Ad Folder,
31. - $20 $40 $65

TOO-3

OO-3. Cracker Box,
31. Uneeda Crackers by Nabisco. - $100 $200 $300

TOO-4

OO-4. Paper Masks,
930s. Westinghouse Mazda Lamps. Examples from set.
ach - $15 $25 $40

TOO-5

TOO-6

TOO-5. Mickey McGuire Bisque,
1930s. Store item, German made. - $25 $60 $100

TOO-6. Vaseline Petroleum Jelly Cut-Out Sheet,
1930s. Uncut - $40 $85 $150

TRIX

General Mills introduced Trix fruit-flavored corn puffs around 1955, and the distinctive Trix-loving rabbit made his debut on the cereal boxes and in animated television comercials in 1959. The original rabbit was a hand puppet that appeared in the introduction to Rocky and His Friends, Captain Kangaroo, and other General Mills-sponsored programs. "Silly rabbit, Trix are for kids."

TRX-1   TRX-3

TRX-2

TRX-1. Tiddly Wink Miniature Plastic Game,
c. 1960s. Lidded container holding small dexterity game featuring disks picturing Trix Rabbit. - $8 $15 $20

TRX-2. Vinyl Squeaker Figure,
1978. - $15 $25 $35

TRX-3. Club Stickers,
c. 1970s. Set Of Five - $5 $10 $25

TRX-4

TRX-4. "Walky Squawky Talky" Cardboard Units In Envelope,
1970s. With Envelope - **$15 $25 $50**
Loose - **$10 $20 $30**

TRX-5   TRX-6

TRX-5. "Yes! Let The Rabbit Eat Trix!" 2-1/4" Litho. Button,
1970s. For affirmative voter in contest, back has metal clip. - **$5 $15 $25**

TRX-6. "No! Trix Are For Kids!" 2-1/4" Litho. Button,
1970s. For negative voter in contest, back has metal clip. - **$5 $15 $25**

UNCLE DON

Between 1928 and 1949, broadcasting regionally from New York radio station WOR, Uncle Don Carney entertained kids with stories, poems, jokes, songs, birthday announcements, and advice on health and behavior. Carney, whose real name was Howard Rice, started in vaudeville as a trick pianist and turned his air time into a classic children's program. Along with nonsense syllables, pig latin, and made-up words, Uncle Don promoted a number of "clubs" related to the products of his many commercial sponsors. The show was aired on the Mutual network for one season (1939-1940), sponsored by Maltex cereal. Uncle Don also read the comics on the air on Sunday mornings, and narrated *The Adventures of Terry and Ted* on CBS radio in 1935-1936. The often-told tale that Carney, after signing off one night, said "I guess that'll hold the little bastards" with the microphone still on, apparently never happened.

UDN-1

UDN-3

UDN-2

UDN-1. Uncle Don Bank,
1920s. Two types. - **$10 $20 $40**

UDN-2. "Lionel Engineers Club" Cello. Button,
1930. - **$35 $75 $150**

UDN-3. Uncle Don's "Earnest Saver Club" Tin Bank,
c. 1938. Various banks. Wrapper design of character with "Bank Book" body. - **$10 $40 $60**

UDN-4

UDN-5

UDN-6

UDN-4. "Maltex 100% Breakfast Club" Litho. Button,
c. 1939. - **$3 $5 $10**

UDN-5. Uncle Don Letter and Mailer,
1930s. Savings Club. - **$20 $40 $60**

UDN-6. Uncle Don's "Terry And Ted And Major Campbell" 12x19" Map,
1930s. Bond Bread. Map follows route of trio in their "Land Cruiser" pictured at bottom. - **$40 $80 $160**

UDN-7   UDN-8   UDN-9

UDN-7. "Terry And Ted On The Trail Of The Secret Formula" Booklet,
1930s. Bond Bread. Story told by Uncle Don with color pictures. - **$5 $12 $20**

UDN-8. Autogiro Theme Photo,
1930s. Popsicles. Pictures Uncle Don as aviator with facsimile signature inscription for Popsicles. - **$5 $10 $15**

UDN-9. "Borden Health Club" Cello. Button,
1930s. - **$8 $12 $20**

UDN-10   UDN-12

UDN-11

JDN-10. "Ice Cream Club/Borden" Cello. Button,
930s. - **$5 $8 $12**

JDN-11. "Borden's Health Club Honor Prize",
930s. "Uncle Don" brass bar holding cloth ribbon suspend-
ng cello. pendant with reverse image of Borden milk bottle. -
10 **$20 $30**

JDN-12. "Bosco Club" Cello. Button,
930s. Pictured holding jar of chocolate drink syrup
roduct. - **$10 $15 $25**

UDN-13   UDN-14   UDN-15

DN-13. "Good Humor/G.H.H.C." Cello. Button,
930s. Pictured in Good Humor Ice Cream uniform. -
12 **$20 $35**

DN-14. "I.V.C. Club" Cello. Button,
930s. - **$3 $6 $10**

DN-15. "Mutual Grocery Club" Cello. Button,
930s. - **$5 $8 $12**

UDN-16   UDN-17

DN-16. "Remitypers" Cello. Button,
930s. Remington Typewriters. - **$10 $15 $25**

DN-17. "Taystee Bread Club" Cello. Button,
930s. - **$8 $15 $25**

UNCLE WIGGILY

ncle Wiggily Longears, an elderly rabbit in a tailcoat, was
eated by writer Howard R. Garis for a nationally syndicated
ewspaper column of bedtime stories that began appearing
1910. Drawings were added for a Sunday page that ran
om 1919 through the 1920s, and a daily comic strip
ppeared in the mid-1920s, illustrated by various artists.
iggily comic books were published between 1942 and
954, and there have been dozens of Uncle Wiggily story
ooks. On radio, Albert Goris was Wiggily, telling bedtime
ories to his young audience.

UWG-1

UWG-1. "Put A Hat On Uncle Wiggily" Party Game Kit,
1919. Store item by Milton Bradley. Game sheet is 22x27".
Uncut In Envelope - **$40 $80 $125**

UWG-2   UWG-3

UWG-2. China Mug,
Copyright 1924. House named "Ovaltine House". Also came
without name. With Name - **$20 $60 $125**
No Name - **$15 $50 $100**

UWG-3. China Plate,
Copyright 1924. Scarce. Store item by Sebring Pottery Co.
Design matches mug. - **$50 $125 $250**

UNCLE WIP

Philadelphia radio station WIP, owned and operated by
Gimbel's department store, started broadcasting in March
1922. Uncle Wip's Kiddie Club was a late-afternoon children's program organized by the store in the 1930s, probably
as early as 1936.

UWP-2

UWP-1

UWP-1. "Uncle Wip And His Friends/Their Bed-Time
Stories" Book,
1923. - **$10 $20 $50**

UWP-2. "Uncle Wip's Kiddie Club" Certificate,
1930s. Rare. - **$30 $75 $100**

UWP-3

UWP-4

UWP-3. "See Me At Gimbels" Cello. Button,
1930s. Gimbels department store, Philadelphia. -
$20 $40 $75

UWP-4. "Uncle Wip's Kiddie Club At Gimbels" Cello. Button,
1930s. Gimbels department store, Philadelphia. -
$10 $20 $35

UWP-5

UWP-6

UWP-5. "Uncle Wip's Kiddie Club/Listen In 6.45 P.M." Cello. Button,
1930s. Gimbels department store, Philadelphia. -
$10 $20 $30

UWP-6. "Kiddie Klub/Gimbels" Cello. Button,
1930s. Gimbels department store, Philadelphia. - **$3 $6 $10**

UNDERDOG

Loveable, humble canine Shoeshine Boy was in actuality plucky superhero Underdog, whose magic cape and energy pills gave him the power to overcome mad scientists and villains, such as Simon Bar Sinister and Riff Raff, and rescue Sweet Polly Purebred, ace TV reporter. This animated series, with Wally Cox providing the voice of Underdog, aired on NBC from 1964 to 1966, moved to CBS from 1966 to 1968, then went back to NBC from 1968 to 1973. *Underdog* comic books appeared in the early 1970s. Items are normally copyrighted Leonardo Productions.

UND-1

UND-2

UND-1. Dakin Co. Vinyl Figure,
1960s. Store item. Comes with blue felt cape. -
$35 $75 $125

UND-2. Underdog Mug,
1960s. Rare. Parents Magazine premium. - **$50 $100 $200**

UND-3

UND-4

UND-3. Premium Offer Poster,
1974. Pacific Gas and Electric. 16x21". - **$20 $45 $75**

UND-4. "Kite Fun Book",
1974. Pacific Gas and Electric. - **$5 $12 $20**

UND-5

UND-6

UND-5. Simon Barsinister Plastic Ring,
1975. Vending machine. - **$50 $75 $125**

UND-6. "Saturday Cartoon Magnets",
1975. Breaker Confections, Division of Sunline Inc., St. Louis. Set of four including Rocky, Bullwinkle, Speedy Gonzales, Underdog. Order Folder - **$5 $12 $25**
Each Magnet - **$3 $8 $18**

UND-7

UND-8

UND-7. Pepsi Glass,
c. 1970s. One of 5 Leonardo TTV characters in 16 oz. size. This one comes with and without Pepsi logo. - **$5 $10 $20**

UND-8. Plastic Cup And Bowl,
1970s. Store item. Each - **$5 $10 $20**

U. S. JONES

Defender of democracy in the all-American way, U.S. Jones had a brief comic book life at the outset of World War II. Jones made his first appearance in issue #28 of *Wonderworld Comics* in August 1941, and two issues of his own book appeared in 1941 and 1942. U.S. Jones Cadets received a decoder, a pinback button, and other membership material.

USJ-2

USJ-1

USJ-1. Secret Code Card,
1941. Rare. Part of member's kit. Has instructions for use of 6 different code keys. - **$100 $300 $500**

USJ-2. Cadets Membership Card,
1941. Rare. Part of member's kit. - **$50 $125 $250**

USJ-3

USJ-4

USJ-3. Cadet Cover Letter And Cadet Civil Defense Sheet,
1941. Rare. Part of member's kit. Explains kit and duties with pledge text. Each - **$25 $50 $100**

USJ-4. "U.S. Jones Cadets" Comic Book Club Cello. Button,
1941. Rare. Part of member's kit. - **$600 $2500 $4500**

VIC AND SADE

Considered by many to be one of the greatest radio shows ever, *Vic and Sade* has been called a true original and the best American humor of its day. The series told of events in the daily lives of radio's home folks - Victor Gook, his wife Sade, their son Rush, and Sade's Uncle Fletcher - who lived in the little house halfway up in the next block in the town of Crooper, Illinois. Written by Paul Rhyer, *Vic and Sade* aired on the NBC, CBS, and Mutual networks from 1932 to 1946. The program was supported by local advertisers the first two years until Crisco took over as longterm sponsor. Fitch's Coconut Shampoo sponsored in 1946.

VAS-1

VAS-1. Hometown Paper Map With Mailer Envelope,
c. 1942. Rare. Procter & Gamble. 14x16" map of "Crooper, Illinois/40 Miles From Peoria" with cast member pictures at lower corner. Also issued on cardboard.
Envelope - **$5 $10 $15**
Map - **$50 $100 $175**

WHEATIES MISCELLANEOUS

Wheaties, the Breakfast of Champions, was the result of a kitchen accident in 1921 when some gruel spilled on a hot stove and turned into crispy flakes. The Washburn Crosby Company in Minneapolis developed the cereal and began marketing it regionally in 1924. Advertising on radio, including the world's first singing commercial, proved successful and by 1928, when Washburn Crosby joined with other grain millers to form General Mills, Wheaties was an established product. Over the years sponsorship of such popular radio programs as *Jack Armstrong* and *Skippy*, as well as continuing promotion that linked the product to major figures in sports and the movies, has kept Wheaties an all-American favorite breakfast food. This section shows an assortment of their baseball and non-character premiums.

WHE-2

WHE-1

WHE-1. "Earl Averill" Box Back,
1937. From a series of baseball stars described by their 1936 season statistics. - **$15 $25 $40**
Complete Box - **$80 $160 $320**

WHE-2. Knothole Drilling Insect 2-1/2" Cello. Button,
c. 1930s. - **$15 $30 $50**

WHE-3

WHE-3. "Funny Stuff" Comic,
1946. Books were taped to boxes.
Good - **$70**
Fine - **$200**

WHE-4   **WHE-5**

WHE-4. Miniature Metal License Plates With Mailer,
1953. Offered in four sets of 12 plus bonus District of
Columbia if all ordered at same time.
Each License - **$2 $5 $8**

WHE-5. "Auto Emblems" Box,
1950s. Shows all 31 emblems offered.
Complete - **$25 $50 $75**

WHE-6

WHE-7

WHE-6. British Auto Metal Emblems,
1950s. Set of 10, Bentley and MG not shown.
Each - **$3 $6 $10**

WHE-7. Continental Auto Metal Emblems,
1950s. Set of 10. Volkswagen, Citroen, Bugati not shown.
Each - **$3 $6 $10**

WHE-8

WHE-9

WHE-8. Hike-O-Meter,
1950s. Pedometer with aluminum rim. - **$10 $18 $30**

WHE-9. Red Records,
1950s. Cereal premiums. Various popular folk, sea & traditional songs on labels. Each - **$20 $40 $60**

WHE-10

WHE-11

WHE-10. Rare Rock Card,
1950s. With 11 different rocks in descriptive mailers.
Display Card with Mailer - **$10 $20 $40**
Rocks in Mailer each - **$10**

**WHE-11. Miniature Reflective Paper License Plates With
Mailer,**
1963. Wheaties Bran With Raisin Flakes. Probable set of 25
for scattered states in reflective flocked surface with peel-off
back. Each License - **$2 $4 $6**

WILD BILL HICKOK

James Butler "Wild Bill" Hickok (1837-1876) was a U.
Marshal in Kansas after the Civil War with a reputation as
marksman and a deadly lawman. Hollywood produced
number of fictionalized versions of the Hickok legend as po
trayed by such stars as William S. Hart, Bill Elliott, R
Rogers, Bruce Cabot, and Gary Cooper. In 1951, with G
Madison as Hickok and Andy Devine as his sidekick Jingle
The Adventures of Wild Bill Hickok came to television a
radio. The television series, sponsored by Kellogg's Sug
Corn Pops, aired until 1958, first in syndication, then on CB
(1955-1958), and on ABC (1957-1958). The radio versi
lasted until 1956, with Kellogg also sponsoring until 195
Hickok comic books appeared from the late 1940s to the la
1950s. "Hey, Wild Bill, wait for me!"

WLD-1

WLD-1. "Secret Treasure Guide" And Treasure Map
5x36",
952. Kellogg's Sugar Corn Pops.
Near Mint In Mailer - $125
Treasure Guide Booklet - $10 $20 $35
Treasure Map - $20 $40 $75

WLD-2

WLD-3

LD-2. Cereal Display Box,
1952. Kellogg Co. of Canada. - $50 $175 $450

LD-3. Hickok/Guy Madison Fan Postcard,
954. - $5 $12 $18

WLD-5

WLD-4

LD-4. "Jingles" Cello. Button With Attachment,
1954. Fabric ribbon holds miniature metal six-shooter. -
0 $15 $25

LD-5. Deputy Marshal Certificate,
55. Probably a Kellogg's Sugar Corn Pops premium. -
2 $20 $35

WLD-6

WLD-7

WLD-6. Deputy Marshal Certificate,
1955. Wild Bill & Jingles pictured. - $20 $40 $80

WLD-7. "Special Deputy" Copper Luster Tin Star Badge,
1956. Kellogg's. Set of six. Others without Hickok/Jingles
name are: Deputy Sheriff, Junior Ranger, Sheriff.
Each - $5 $10 $20

WLD-8

WLD-9

WLD-8. Kellogg's "Wild Bill Hickok/Deputy Marshal"
2-1/4" Silvered Tin Star Badge,
1956. Set of six, see previous and following item. -
$8 $12 $25

WLD-9. Kellogg's "Jingles/Deputy" 2-1/4" Gold Luster
Tin Badge,
1956. Set of six, see previous items. - $8 $12 $25

WLD-10

WLD-11

WLD-10. Hickok/Jingles Waxed Cardboard Milk Carton,
1950s. Various dairies. - $20 $40 $75

WLD-11. "Drink Milk" Vinyl Tumbler,
1950s. Various sponsors. -$20 $50 $75

WLD-12

WLD-12. Promo Press Kit & 10 Photos,
1950s. Rare. - **$30 $60 $120**

WLD-13

WLD-14

WLD-13. "Kellogg's Sugar Corn Pops" Cereal Box,
1950s. 16 "Famous Indian" drawings on back panels.
Complete Box - **$50 $125 $200**

WLD-14. Color Photo Litho. Button,
1950s. - **$15 $40 $60**

WLD-15

WLD-16

WLD-17

**WLD-15. Hickok & Jingles "We're Pardners" Litho.
Button,**
1950s. - **$12 $20 $35**

**WLD-16. "Wild Bill Hickok/Marshal" 2-1/4" Silvered Brass
Badge,**
1950s. With insert paper photo, came with wallet and club
member card. - **$15 $35 $70**

**WLD-17. "Marshal Wild Bill Hickok" Silvered Brass
Badge On Metal Clip,**
1950s. Came with related wallet. - **$15 $30 $50**

WINNIE THE POOH

A.A. Milne (1882-1956) published his classic children's stories *Winnie-the-Pooh* in 1926 and *The House at Pooh Corner*
in 1928. A short-lived radio adaptation aired on NBC in
1935, but the Disney Studios gave new life to the beloved
characters in a series of 30-minute animated films. *Winnie
the Pooh and the Honey Tree* (1965), *Winnie the Pooh and
the Blustery Day* (1968), and *Winnie the Pooh and Tigger
Too* (1974) were produced for theatrical release and later
telecast as prime-time specials on NBC, sponsored by
Sears, Roebuck & Company. A fourth short, *Winnie the
Pooh and a Day for Eeyore*, was broadcast on the Disney
Channel in 1986. The cartoons were true to the Milne originals, with Pooh, Eeyore, Kanga and Baby Roo, Wol the Owl,
Tigger, Piglet, and the other characters joining Christopher
Robin in a variety of woodland adventures. Disney also
released a number of Pooh comic books between 1977 and
1984.

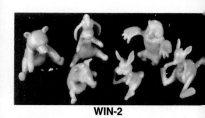

WIN-1

WIN-2

WIN-1. "Puppets Wheat Puffs Cereal" Plastic Container,
1966. Nabisco. Metal lid bottom. With Lid - **$20 $40 $60**

WIN-2. Spoon Sitter Vinyl Figures,
1966. Nabisco. Seven in set, Christopher Robin not shown.
Each - **$3 $8 $12**

WIN-3

WIN-4

WIN-5

WIN-3. "Winnie-The-Pooh And Friends" Glass Tumbler,
1970s. Sears, Roebuck & Co. Set of three.
Each - **$3 $6 $10**

**WIN-4. "Wardrobe Gets My Vote!" 3x4" Cello. Rectangle
Button,**
1980. - **$10 $20 $40**

WIN-5. "Grad Nite '81" 3-1/2" Cello. Button,
1981. From Disneyland graduation series of early 1980s pic
turing various characters. - **$3 $5 $8**

THE WIZARD OF OZ

L. Frank Baum (1856-1919) wrote 14 Oz books, but it w
the first, *The Wonderful Wizard of Oz*, published in 1900, th
served as the basis of MGM's 1939 Technicolor spectacula
The Wizard of Oz. (A musical theatrical adaptation ran
Broadway in 1903, a silent film was made in 1925, and
radio version sponsored by Jell-O aired on NBC in 193
1934.) The 1939 film, with an all-star cast headed by Ju
Garland, has proved to be an enduring classic, repeate
annually on television for millions of viewers since the 195C
There have also been Oz theme parks and resorts, an exhi
at the Smithsonian, appearances in Macy's Thanksgivi
Day parade, comic books, and extensive licensing in doze
of categories.

WIZ-1

WIZ-2

WIZ-3

WIZ-1. "What Did The Woggle Bug Say?" Cello. Button,
1904. Book advertising button. - **$20 $60 $140**

WIZ-2. Woggle Bug Cello. Button,
1904. Book advertising button. Colors on coat vary from yellow to green. - **$20 $60 $140**

WIZ-3. Magazine Story Poster 13x22",
1905. For issue of St. Nickolas magazine with art by F. Richardson for Baum serial story "Queen Zixi Of Ix". - **$150 $250 $400**

WIZ-4

WIZ-5

WIZ-4. "Read The New Baum Book/The Scarecrow Of Oz" Cello. Button,
1915. Early and rare book advertising release. - **$600 $1200 $2500**

WIZ-5. "Wonderland Of Oz" Map 16x22",
1932. Philadelphia Evening Bulletin newspaper. - **$150 $400 $800**

WIZ-6 (front) WIZ-7 (back)

WIZ-6. Jackpumpkinhead And The Sawhorse,
1933. Jell-O softbound book. - **$40 $75 $150**

WIZ-7. Ozma And The Little Wizard,
1933. Jell-O softbound book. - **$40 $75 $150**

WIZ-8 (front)

WIZ-9 (back)

WIZ-8. Tik Tok And The Nome King,
1933. Jell-O softbound book. - **$40 $75 $150**

WIZ-9. The Scarecrow And The Tin Woodman,
1933. Jell-O softbound book. - **$40 $75 $150**

WIZ-10

WIZ-11

WIZ-12

WIZ-10. Movie Advertising Cello. Button,
1939. Scarce. Seen with "Loew's" (theater) and "Hecht's" (Baltimore department store) imprints. - **$200 $400 $750**

WIZ-11. Dorothy Mask,
1939. Distributed by department stores and others. - **$15 $30 $50**

WIZ-12. Scarecrow Mask,
1939. Distributed by department stores and others. - **$15 $30 $50**

WIZ-13

WIZ-14

WIZ-15

WIZ-13. Cowardly Lion Mask,
1939. Distributed by department stores and others. - **$15 $30 $50**

WIZ-14. Tin Woodman Mask,
1939. Distributed by department stores and others. - **$15 $30 $50**

WIZ-15. Wizard Mask,
1939. Distributed by department stores and others. - **$15 $30 $50**

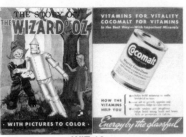

WIZ-16   **WIZ-17**

WIZ-16. "The Story Of The Wizard Of Oz" Coloring Book,
1939. Cocomalt. Premium Version - **$15 $30 $60**
Store Version Without Cocomalt Ad - **$12 $25 $50**

WIZ-17. Dorothy Glass,
1939. Sealtest Cottage Cheese. Seven known: Dorothy, Toto, Scarecrow, Tin Woodman, The Cowardly Lion, The Good Witch, The Bad Witch. The Wizard is unknown.
Each - **$50 $80 $125**

WIZ-22   **WIZ-23**

WIZ-24

WIZ-22. Scarecrow Valentine,
1940 Store item. From set of 12 picturing various characters by American Colortype Co. Each - **$20 $50 $75**

WIZ-23. "Magic Sand" Packet Envelope,
c. 1940. Various theaters. Contains sand "From Along The Yellow Brick Road.." - **$100 $250 $500**

WIZ-24. "S & Co." Glass Tumblers,
1953. Swift Peanut Butter. Six designs with wavy, plain or fluted bases. Characters depicted are Dorothy, Toto, Scarecrow, Cowardly Lion, Tinman, and the Wizard.
Each - **$5 $10 $15**

WIZ-18   **WIZ-19**   **WIZ-20**

WIZ-18. Movie 3" Cello. Button,
1939. M-G-M Studio. - **$50 $150 $300**

WIZ-19. "Frank Morgan" Movie Contest Cello. Button,
1939. M-G-M Studios. 1-1/4" size, set of five also includes Judy Garland, Ray Bolger, Jack Haley, Bert Lahr. This size has serial number to match for winning prize.
Each - **$100 $200 $400**

WIZ-20. "Jack Haley" Cello. Button,
1939. From 7/8" series of five characters with Oz film title in Spanish. Each - **$50 $125 $250**

WIZ-25

WIZ-25. Vinyl Hand Puppets,
1965. Procter & Gamble. Eight in set. Cardboard theater also issued. Each Puppet - **$5 $12 $25**
Theater - **$20 $45 $75**

WIZ-21

WIZ-26

WIZ-21. Pictorial Fabric Scarf,
1939. Store item. Two different designs with numerous color variations. - **$75 $150 $300**

WIZ-26. Set Of 12 Litho. Buttons,
1967. Samson Products. Vending machine distribution.
Each - **$3 $6 $10**

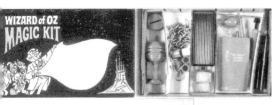

WIZ-27

WIZ-27. "Magic Kit",
1967. Store item by Fun Inc. - **$25 $40 $75**

WONDER WOMAN

Wonder Woman was created by psychologist/writer William Moulton Marston (pen name: Charles Moulton). The comics' first major female superhero debuted in issue #8 of *All Star Comics* in December 1941 and had her own comic book by the next summer. Wonder Woman came from mysterious Paradise Island (no men allowed) to America as Diana Prince to help fight World War II. Over the years she has also battled aliens and terrorists, lost her flag-like costume and superpowers, regained them, dabbled in I Ching, and fallen in and out of love. A comic strip appearance in 1944 had a short life, and a hardback anthology was published in 1972. There have been two TV movies - *Wonder Woman* (1974) with Cathy Lee Crosby, and *The New, Original Wonder Woman* (1975) with Lynda Carter - and a TV series, also starring Carter, that aired on ABC (1976-1977) and CBS (1977-1979). Items are usually copyrighted DC Comics or Warner Bros. TV.

WON-1

WON-2

WON-1. "Sensation Comics" Litho. Button,
1942. Rare. Offered in May issue of Sensation Comics. -
$600 $1250 $2500

WON-2. WWII Infantile Paralysis Comic Book Postcard Premium,
1940s. Rare. - **$100 $200 $500**

WON-3

WON-4

WON-3. "Wonder Woman" 3-1/2" Cello. Button,
1966. Store item. #14 from series.
Near Mint Bagged - **$40**
Loose - **$12 $20 $30**

WON-4. Boxed Board Game,
1967. Store item by Hasbro. Also features other Justice League of America characters. - **$25 $75 $150**

WON-6

WON-5

WON-5. "Wonder Woman" 2-1/4" Cello. Button,
1975. Store item by Rainbow Designs. DC Comics copyright. - **$3 $8 $12**

WON-6. Metal Ring With Cello. Portrait,
1976. N.P.P. Inc. Brass finish with copyright on underside. -
$35 $50 $70

WON-7

WON-7. Watch,
1977. Store item by Dabs.
Near Mint Boxed - **$175**
Loose - **$35 $75 $125**

WON-8

WON-9

WON-8. Pepsi Glass,
1978. - **$5 $10 $15**

WON-9. "See The Superheroes At Sea World" Photo,
1970s. Sea World appearance souvenir. Batman and
Wonder Woman pictured with facsimile signatures. -
$10 $20 $30

WOODY WOODPECKER

Between 1940 and 1972 Walter Lantz created more than 200
animated shorts featuring the hyperactive woodpecker with
the raucous laugh. Over the years Woody evolved from a
multicolored lunatic into an appealing red-haired imp. His
musical theme, *The Woody Woodpecker Song,* was nominat-
ed for an Academy Award in 1948. *The Woody Woodpecker
Show* aired on the Mutual radio network in 1952-1954 and
came to ABC television for the 1957-1958 season, then to
NBC in 1971-1972 and 1976-1977. Woody made a number
of comic book appearances starting in 1942. Items are normally copyrighted Walter Lantz Productions.

WDY-1   WDY-2

WDY-1. Promo,
1951. Scarce. 6 pages (4 pages of comics). -
$100 $200 $300

WDY-2. "Hi Pal!" Cello. Button,
1957. Came on store bought doll. - **$8 $15 $30**

WDY-3

WDY-4

WDY-5

WDY-3. Premium Comic Chevrolet,
1950s. - **$15 $50 $110**

WDY-4. Spoon,
1950s. Cereal premium. - **$10 $20 $30**

WDY-5. Comic,
1950s. Scotch Tape sponsor. - **$15 $50 $110**

WDY-6

WDY-7

WDY-6. Movie Label,
1950s. - **$10 $20 $30**

WDY-7. Parking Pass,
c. 1963. Lantz Studios. - **$30 $60 $90**

WDY-8

WDY-8. Kellogg's Plastic Mug And Cereal Bowl,
1965. Bowl image of log trough. Set - **$25 $40 $70**

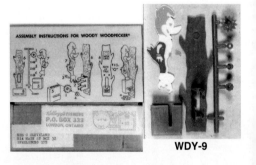

WDY-9

WDY-9. Kellogg's Plastic Door Knocker Assembly Kit,
1966. Canadian issue. Boxed - **$20 $40 $60**
Built - **$15 $25 $40**

(front)   WDY-10   (back)

WDY-10. Rice Krispies Stuffed Toy Offer,
1966. Cereal box flat. - **$40 $80 $120**

(front)   **WDY-11**   (back)

WDY-11. Stars Cereal Swimmer Offer,
1967. Cereal box flat. - **$40 $80 $120**

WDY-13

WDY-12

WDY-14

WDY-12. Gum Box Display Card,
1968. Fleer Gum. - **$8 $12 $25**

WDY-13. Plastic Portrait Ring,
. 1970s. - **$5 $8 $12**

WDY-14. Spoon,
1970s. Store bought. - **$10 $20 $30**

WORLD WAR II

American involvement in World War II was intense on the home front as well as the war zones. With millions of young men and women in uniform and far from home between early 1942 and 1945, family members and loved ones wanted to follow events as they occurred in Europe and in the Pacific. A number of advertisers answered the call by offering war maps and atlases and other print material that brought home details of the military movements and battles.

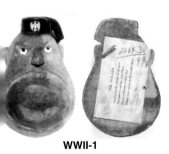 

WWII-1   **WWII-2**

WWII-1. Anti-Mussolini Plaster Ashtray With Sticker Label,
1943. - **$60 $100 $150**

WWII-2. "Radio At War Picture Book",
c. 1943. Various sponsors. Depicts programs and stars of "Blue Network." - **$15 $25 $45**

WWII-3

WWII-3. "Capt. Ben Dix" Comic Book,
1943. Bendix Aviation Corp. - **$10 $20 $40**

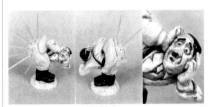 

WWII-4

WWII-5

WWII-4. Anti-Hitler Plaster Toothpick Holder,
c. 1943. - **$85 $150 $300**

WWII-5. Hitler Plaster Pin Cushion,
c. 1943. Large Size - **$75 $150 $250**
Smaller "Hotzi Notzi" Size - **$50 $80 $125**

WWII-6

WWII-6. "The Fighting Seabees" Movie Postcard,
1944. Republic Pictures. - **$8 $12 $20**

WWII-7

WWII-8

WWII-7. "Target Tokyo" Cardboard Wheel Game,
1944. Tip-Top Bread. - **$15 $25 $50**

WWII-8. "Sky Heroes" Stamp Album,
c. 1944. Sinclair Oil Corp. Twenty stamps in set.
Complete - **$25 $50 $100**

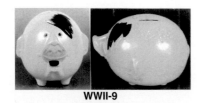

WWII-9

WWII-9. Anti-Hitler Composition Pig Bank,
c. 1944. Squeaking mechanism rarely works.
Not Working - **$75 $125 $200**

WWII-10

WWII-10. "Victory Star Tumblers" Glasses Set,
c. 1944. Pillsbury's Flour. Set - **$25 $60 $80**

WWII-11

WWII-11. "Exide Batteries At War" Book,
1946. Illustrations similar to Dixie Ice Cream series. -
$20 $50 $90

WWII-12

WWII-12. Esso War Maps,
1940s. Periodic revisions in war years. Each - **$5 $10 $15**

WYATT EARP

Legendary gunfighter and lawman Wyatt Earp (1848-1929)
has been portrayed in at least two dozen Hollywood
Westerns by such stars as George O'Brien, Randolph Scott,
Richard Dix, Henry Fonda, Joel McCrea, Burt Lancaster and
Kevin Costner. On television *The Life and Legend of Wyatt
Earp* starred Hugh O'Brian in a serial drama that aired on
ABC from 1955 to 1961. The series followed the romanti-
cized adventures of Earp as a frontier marshal in Ellsworth
and Dodge City, Kansas, and Tombstone, Arizona. Comic
books appeared from 1955 on. Most licensed items came
from the TV series and are copyrighted Wyatt Earp Ent. Inc.

(front)   WYT-1   (back)

WYT-1. Cheerios Box,
1955. Back panel has cut-out parts for "Peacemaker" gun on
10-1/2 oz. box; "Paterson" gun on 7 oz. box.
Each Complete Box - **$75 $150 $250**

WYT-2

WYT-3

WYT-2. "Marshal Wyatt Earp" Sterling Silver Initial Ring,
1958. Cheerios. Engraved personal initial, TV show
copyright. - **$40 $60 $80**

WYT-3. "Marshal Wyatt Earp" Metal Badge On Card,
c. 1958. Store item. On Card - **$15 $25 $40**
Loose - **$8 $10 $20**

X-MEN

Stan Lee and Jack Kirby created the X-Men, a band of
superpower teenage mutant fighters for good. Introduced in
issue #1 of *X-Men* in 1963, Cyclops, The Angel, The Beast
and Marvel Girl joined with Professor X to foil the evil
schemes of arch-enemy Magneto. The book was suspended
briefly in 1970, then revived with reprints and, starting in
1975, new adventures and new characters. Including
Specials and Annuals, Marvel has published well over 300 X-
Men comic books. An animated version debuted on the Fox
Children's Network in 1992.

XMN-1

XMN-1. X-Men #1,
Sept. 1963. Marvel Comics. Origin and first appearance of
the X-Men. - **$375 $1125 $4500**

XMN-2

XMN-2. Plastic Badge With Reverse Needle Post/Clutch,
1988. Marvel. - **$2 $4 $6**

XMN-3   **XMN-4**

XMN-3. Gold Ring,
1993. Diamond Comics Distribution seminar giveaway. 25
made. - **$750**

XMN-4. Silver Ring,
1993. Diamond Comics Distribution seminar
giveaway. - **$100**

(in display case)

(side view)   **XMN-5**   (top view)

XMN-5. Xavier Institute Class Ring,
1994. 10k gold. - **$400**
Sterling Silver Version - **$75**
Bronze Finished Pewter Version - **$20**

THE YELLOW KID

Richard F. Outcault's *Yellow Kid* is generally considered to
be the first true comic strip. After appearances as a minor
character in the *Hogan's Alley* gag panels in the *New York
World* in 1895, the bald, jug-eared kid in a nightshirt grew in
popularity and, by the beginning of 1896, his nightshirt was
yellow. Outcault never gave him a name, so readers referred
to him as the yellow kid. William Randolph Hearst hired
Outcault for his *New York Journal* later that year and titled
his panels *The Yellow Kid*. Outcault dropped the strip in
1898 and went on to other work, but the Kid made licensing
history in promoting a wide range of products such as chewing gum, candy, cookies, games, puzzles, cigarettes, soap,
bicycles, highchairs, and whiskey.

YLW-1

YLW-1. Yellow Kid And Lady 18x24" Paper Announcement Poster For New York Journal's Colored Sunday Supplement,
1896. Scarce. Also reads "Wait For It-It Is Coming" including artists' names Archie Gunn and R. F. Outcault. -
$1000 $2000 $3500

YLW-2

YLW-2. Wooden Cigar Box,
1896. - **$200 $400 $750**

YLW-3   **YLW-4**

YLW-3. Advertising Card,
1896. Sweet Wheat Chewing Gum. - **$75 $150 $250**

YLW-4. Gum Card #11 Example,
1896. Adams' Yellow Kid Chewing Gum. Set of 25, two styles: small number or large number (see next item). Small Numbers Each - **$10 $15 $40**

YLW-5

YLW-5. Gum Cards #6 and #21,
1896. Adams' Yellow Kid Chewing Gum. Examples from set of 25 with large numbers. Each - **$10 $15 $40**

YLW-6   **YLW-7**

YLW-6. Yellow Kid First Button In Set,
1896. High Admiral cigarettes. The first 35 buttons in the set are the most frequently found. Each - **$10 $25 $40**

YLW-7. Cello. Button #35,
1896. Buttons #35-94 become scarcer as the button number becomes higher. #90-94 are the scarcest. #95-100 were never issued. - **$25 $40 $65**

YLW-8   **YLW-9**   **YLW-10**

YLW-8. Yellow Kid With Various Flags Cello. Button,
1896. High Admiral Cigarette. Buttons numbered 101-160 depict him holding some type of flag, usually with the name of a country. Each - **$20 $40 $65**

YLW-9. Theatrical Production Cello. Button,
1896. - **$10 $20 $40**

YLW-10. Yellow Kid For President McKinley Enameled Brass Lapel Stud,
1896. Small figure inscribed "Hogan's Alley Is Out Fer McKinley". - **$125 $300 $500**

YLW-11

YLW-11. "The Latest And The Greatest" Sheet Music Clipping From Newspaper,
c. 1896. Rare. - **$75 $150 $300**

YLW-12

YLW-13

YLW-14

YLW-12. Trade Card,
. 1896. Various advertisers. - **$30 $60 $125**

YLW-13. Chocolate Ad Paper Bookmark,
. 1896. Hawley & Hoops Breakfast Cocoa. Pictured are enny chocolate pieces in figural images including Yellow Kid. - **$20 $60 $125**

YLW-14. Soap Figure,
. 1896. Store item by D. S. Brown & Co.
Near Mint Boxed - **$500**
Loose - **$100 $200 $300**

YLW-15

YLW-16

YLW-17

YLW-15. "The Original Yell-er Kid" Cello. Button,
. 1896. - **$50 $100 $175**

YLW-16. Miniature Painted White Metal Figure Stickpin,
. 1896. - **$20 $40 $75**

YLW-17. Pewter Candy Mold,
. 1896. - **$50 $100 $175**

YLW-18

YLW-19

YLW-18. "Big Bubble Chewing Gum" Cello. Button,
. 1910. Full inscription "There Is Only One Yellow Kid Big Bubble Chewing Gum". - **$15 $30 $60**

YLW-19. Calendar Postcard,
January 1914. Various advertisers. Series of monthly calendar cards with 1911 Outcault copyright. Each - **$25 $50 $75**

YLW-20

YLW-20. Ink Blotter,
Early 1900s. Rare. - **$75 $150 $300**

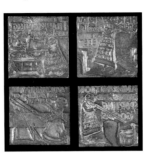

YLW-21

YLW-21. Ad Dies in Box,
1920s. Box with four dies & four ad flyers. - **$100 $200 $400**
Box - **$20 $30 $40**
Each Die - **$25 $50 $70**
Each Ad - **$5 $10 $20**

YOGI BEAR

Hanna-Barbera's Yogi Bear, a TV cartoon and merchandising superstar, was introduced in 1959 on The Huckleberry Hound Show and two years later was starring in his own series. The genial bear in a pork-pie hat, trailed by his diminutive pal Boo Boo, spent his time panhandling and swiping picnic baskets from visitors to Jellystone Park. Yogi's love interest was Cindy Bear (Ah do declare!). The Yogi Bear Show was syndicated from 1961 to 1963, sponsored by Kellogg cereals; Yogi's Gang with Yogi leaving the Park to crusade for the environment, was broadcast on ABC from 1973 to 1975; and Yogi's Space Race appeared on NBC from 1978 to 1979. Yogi has also appeared teamed with other Hanna-Barbera characters and in several TV specials. Yogi comic books began publication in 1959. His popularity continues to this day. Items are normally copyrighted Hanna-Barbera Productions.

YOG-1

YOG-2

YOG-1. Vinyl And Plush Doll,
1960. Store item and Kellogg's premium. 19" tall. -
$20 $50 $75

YOG-2. Ceramic Figurine,
c. 1960. Store item. - **$20 $40 $75**

YOG-3

YOG-4

YOG-3. "Hey There, It's Yogi Bear" Litho. Button,
c. 1960. - **$10 $20 $35**

YOG-4. Plastic Bank,
c. 1960. Store item by Knickerbocker. - **$20 $30 $50**

YOG-5

YOG-5. Yogi Bear Game Cloth,
1962. Kellogg's Corn Flakes. 35x45" vinyl sheet; markers of
Yogi, Huck, Quick Draw, Mr. Jinks; spinner; instructions; 24
red or black checkers picturing Yogi or Huck.
Near Mint In Mailer - **$50**
Complete/Loose - **$10 $20 $35**

YOG-6

YOG-7

YOG-8

YOG-6. "Yogi Bear For President" 3" Litho. Button,
1964. - **$15 $30 $60**

YOG-7. Purex Bottle Bank With Wrapper,
1967. Near Mint With Wrapper - **$75**
Bottle Only - **$15 $30 $55**

**YOG-8. "Procter & Gamble Dividend Day '85" 2-1/4"
Cello. Button,**
1985. Used by employees at amusement park outing. -
$5 $10 $20

YOG-9

YOG-9. Yogi Bear Hat,
1960s. Kellogg's premium. - **$20 $30 $40**

YOG-10

YOG-10. Yogi Bear Cereal Box,
1960s. - **$100 $200 $300**

YOUNG FORTY-NINERS

Colgate's Ribbon Dental Cream sponsored this radio serial i
the early 1930s, relating adventures in the California Gol
Rush of 1849. Premiums included a map of the gold territo
and punch-out versions of an Indian encampment and
wagon train. The program was apparently broadcast on
regionally.

YFN-1

YFN-1. United States Adventure Map With Envelope,
c. 1932. Colgate-Palmolive-Peet. Map opens to 20x31".
Envelope - **$10 $15 $20**
Map - **$40 $75 $125**

YFN-2

YFN-2. Capt. Sam's Wagon Cardboard Punch-Out Folder
c. 1932. Rare. Colgate-Palmolive-Peet. Sheet opens to
19x37". Unpunched - **$40 $75 $150**

YFN-3

YFN-3. Indian Village,
c. 1932. Rare. Colgate-Palmolive-Peet. Sheet opens to 19"x37". Unpunched - **$60 $100 $250**

ZORRO

Don Diego de la Vega, alter ego of Zorro, the fox, was created by author Johnston McCulley in serialized magazine stories around 1919. In the tradition of *The Scarlet Pimpernel*, Don Diego posed as an effete dandy until it was time to defend the oppressed. Then out came the black cape, mask, and sword. Zorro has a long film history, ranging from the 1920 silent *The Mark of Zorro*, starring Douglas Fairbanks Sr., to the 1981 spoof *Zorro, the Gay Blade,* with George Hamilton. On television Guy Williams played the flashy 19th century fencer in the popular Disney series that aired on ABC from 1957 to 1959. Some 24 years later Disney produced a comic version, *Zorro and Son,* that lasted less than two months on CBS in 1983. Zorro comic books appeared from 1949 to 1961, 1966 to 1968, and 1990-1991. The original TV series generated a wide variety of related merchandise, copyrighted by Walt Disney Productions.

ZOR-1

ZOR-1. "Don Q/Son Of Zorro" Cello. Button,
1925. Pictures movie title star Douglas Fairbanks, Sr. -
$60 $140 $225

ZOR-2

ZOR-3

ZOR-2. 7up Litho. Ad Button,
1957. 1-3/8" size. The 1-1/8" litho. variety appeared about 1990. Unsure if reproduction or quantity find-it is extremely common.
1-3/8" Size - **$8 $15 $30**
1-1/8" Size - **$1 $2 $3**

ZOR-3. 7up Litho. Tin Advertising Tab,
1957. Also marked "ABC/TV". - **$12 $20 $40**

ZOR-4

ZOR-4. Fan Postcard,
c. 1958. - **$10 $15 $25**

ZOR-5

ZOR-5. TV Station Litho. Tin Tab,
c. 1950s. - **$15 $25 $60**

ZOR-6

ZOR-6. "Zorro Candy" Display Box,
1950s. Super Novelty Candy Co. Held multiple packages. -
$20 $60 $125

ZOR-7

**ZOR-7. Paper 23x36" Dry Cleaning Bag Cut-Out
Costume,**
1950s. Various sponsors. - **$20 $30 $50**

ZOR-8

ZOR-9

ZOR-8. "Official Ring" Ad Paper,
1950s. - **$20 $30 $35**

ZOR-9. Plastic Ring,
1950s. Silver band with black top and name in gold. -
$30 $45 $60

ZOR-10

ZOR-11

ZOR-10. Plastic Ring,
1950s. Entirely black except name in gold. - **$30 $45 $60**

ZOR-11. English Plastic Lapel Stud,
1950s. Quaker Puffed Wheat. - **$20 $40 $60**

ZOR-12

ZOR-12. Hat with Mask,
1960s. Store item. - **$30 $60 $80**

PUBLISHER'S *note*

Hello Collectors!

I'm sure you've been pleased with *Hake's Price Guide to Character Toy Premiums and Related Store Bought Items*. This book represents the most extensive price guide ever published for premiums and toys. I'm especially proud that my company, Gemstone Publishing, had the honor of producing this book.

I'm also proud of this price guide because it represents the first collaboration between Bob Overstreet and Ted Hake, both of whom are extremely knowledgeable about the collectibles market. What a great way to start a new tradition - a work produced by two of the most respected scholars in the field of collecting!

This is one of the most professional books I've ever seen, and I'd like to extend my congratulations to Ted Hake for his many hours of research, documentation, and old-fashioned hard work. I'm sure you'll agree with me that all of Ted's time and work have paid off.

Hake's Price Guide to Character Toy Premiums and Related Store Bought Items comes at an excellent time. The comic collectible market is continually growing and attracting more collectors and investors, and this is a great time to become involved with a new hobby that's rooted in the past and promises to have a great future. If this marks your entry into collecting, may I offer a hearty "Welcome aboard!"

Regardless of whether you're a novice or seasoned veteran in the collecting hobby, you'll be happy to know that, for the first time, you now have a comprehensive guide containing thousands of these collectible items.

But that's not all! I am pleased to present one more section that's sure to be a feast for your eyes! Immediately following are more than sixty pages of full color photographs of some of the items listed in the price guide. This is the first time many of these collectibles have ever been seen in color!

Gemstone Publishing hopes you enjoy this reference book and find it useful.

Best,

Steve Geppi

Early Cereal Promotional Booklets

Classic examples of how children were used to promote cereal before the use of comic characters

Late 1800s Friends Oats Promo

Reverse of a Friends Oats Promo

1890s Friends Oats Promo

1902 Mapl-Flake promo

1899 Roasted Oats promo

537

1890's Brownies Cut Outs
(Lion's Coffee)

Ozma and the Little Wizard

Jack Pumpkinhead and the
Sawhorse

1933 Jell-O
Premium *Wizard*
of Oz Books

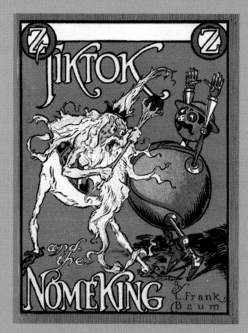

Tiktok and the Nome King

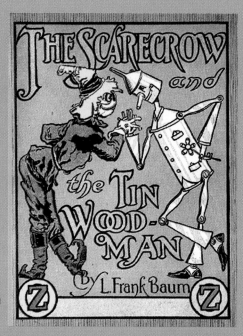

The Scarecrow and the Tin Woodman

Character Whistles

"G"Man   1930s

"DICK STEEL"
SPECIAL POLICE REPORTERS WHISTLE
**EDUCATOR HAMMERED
WHEAT THINSIES**

Dick Steel Radio Whistle 1934

Jack Armstrong
Glow in the Dark
Crocodile 1934

Red Goose Shoes 1930s

Radio Orphan Annie 1942

Buster Brown 1930s

Character Premium Maps

1933 Byrd Expedition

1930s Sherlock Holmes

1933 Tarzan U.S. Map
(Only difference "T" logo)

1933 Tarzan Canadian Map
(Only difference "W" logo)

**Buck Rogers
Repeller Ray**

The Spider Pulp

Knights of Columbus
with secret compartment
& seal

Rare Comic & Pulp Premium Rings

**Frank Buck
World's Fair**

**Radio Orphan Annie
Altascope**

Superman Prize

Gold Spiderman

**Howdy Doody
Jack in the Box**

**Captain Marvel
Compass**

**Buck Rogers
Sylvania**

Superman-Tim

Operator 5 Pulp

**Sky King
Kaleidoscope**

**Radio Orphan
Annie Magnifying**

**Radio Orphan
Annie Initial**

Character Clock & Watches

Buster Brown Pocket Watch with promo contest card

Red Goose Shoes Pocket Watch with fob

Donald Duck 60th Anniversary Watch in holder

Red Goose Shoes Alarm Clock

Promotional Items

Dick Tracy Hat Promo-1949 Dick Tracy Tommy Gun with Rubber Band Bullets

Ed Wynn Texaco Mask with Autograph

544

Character Premium Photos

Wild Bill Hickock shares his Corn Pops with a fan

1933 Shadow Unmasked

Lassie & Corey Stuart

Johnny (Tarzan) Weissmuller
(Jack Armstrong premium)

Don Winslow checks the equipment

Balsa Wood Rocket-Gyros

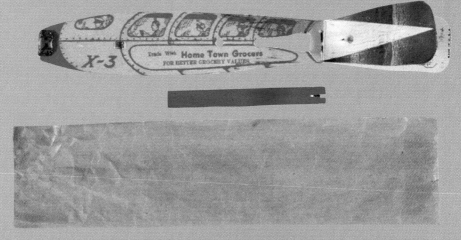

1938 Dick Tracy Rocket-Gyro X-3 with Mailer

1940s Rocket-Gyro X-3 with Mailer
(Sponsored by Home Town Grocers)

1937 Speed Gibson Rocket-Gyro X-3 with Mailer

Airplane Related Signs & Premiums

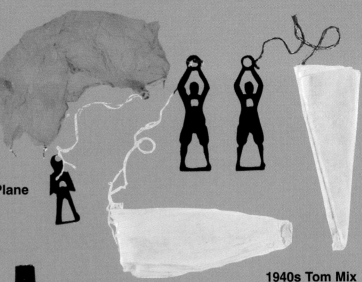

Parachute for Tom Mix's Plane
(green pararchute)
note figure smaller

1930s Tom Mix Rocket Parachute
(note white string)

1940s Tom Mix Rocket Parachute
(note dark string)

Tom Mix 1930s Rocket Parachute
(complete with type I box)

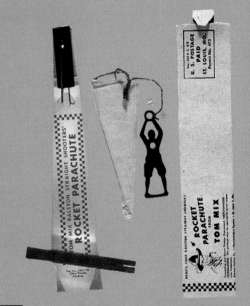

Tom Mix 1940s Rocket Parachute
(complete with type II box)

14"x 20" Cardboard Movie Sign for "Devil Dogs of the Air"
(premium offers pictured)

Great example of a movie star tie-in promoting Quaker Oats

Comic Character Ads

Free Badge Offer for Dick Tracy
with purchase of a Tommy Gun

Wonder Woman Picture Offer
March of Dimes ad

Tom Mix Ring Offer for Ralston Cereal

Tom Mix Ralston
Cereal Ad for
Compass
Arrowhead

Sergeant
Preston's Yukon
Trail Offer for
Quaker Puffed
Wheat & Puffed
Rice

Tom Mix Premium Badges

Straight Shooters
(star prototype)

Ranch Boss
(eagle prototype)

Ranch Boss

Silver Wrangler Badge
(front view)

Gold Wrangler Badge
(front view)

Silver Badge Straight Shooter

Gold Wrangler Badge
(three quarter view)

Silver Wrangler Badge
(three quarter view)

Gold Badge Straight Shooter

Tom Mix Memorabilia

1933 Cigar Box Label

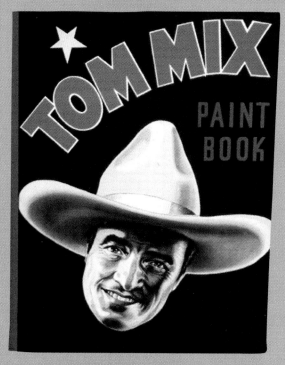

1935 Paint Book

1930's Cinema Star Card #7
England-Wills
Cigarette Premium

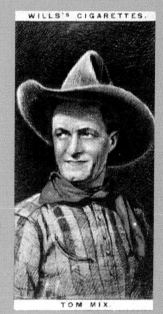

1933 Cigar Badge Label

1940's Ray-O-Print Outfit
(film negative in tin holder)

Comic Character Paddles

1948 Smilin' Ed McConnell Buster Brown Paddle Ball Game
(Froggy pictured)

1948 Shmoo Paddle Ball

Harold Teen

1938 Morton Salt Premiums

Lillums

1938 Lone Ranger Bat-O-Ball

Shadow

1941 Fleischer Studio 5' Standee for Superman Color Cartoon

1945 Pep Sign

1945 Kellogg's Pep Cereal Button Display 26"x 38," Wonderful example of Forties art using food and premiums to put a big smile on the face of the All-American Kid. This project was promoted on the Superman radio show and was featured in several comics using the Superman logo.

1940 Action Comics Patch
(given away for signing up subscribers)

1940 Action Comics Patch
(contest prize)

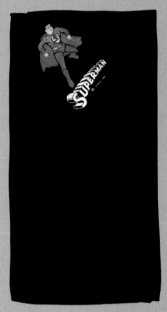

1940 Shield Style Badge

Folded Handkerchief 1940s

**Decoder Cereal Premium
(Canada) 1940s**

1940 Candy Box

1940s Brown & Red Paint Version Figure

1940s Magic Flight toy premium

1944 Christmas Comic Book Giveaway

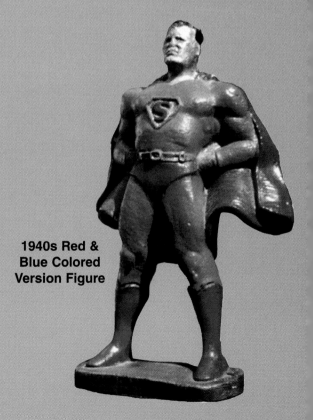

1940s Red & Blue Colored Version Figure

Junior Justice Society Items

1942 Silver Badge
(Junior in large letters)

1942 Gold Badge

1948 Silver Badge
(Junior in small letters)

**1942 Comic Book Ad Offer
for Patch Type (2) Kit**

**1945 Ad from
Comic Book**

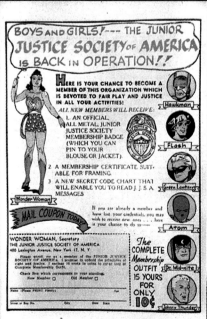

1948 Ad from Comic Book

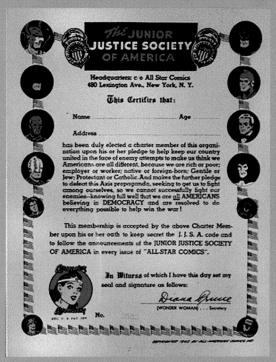

**Charter Membership Certificates
1942 type (1)**

Note changes in text and character drawings on each certificate

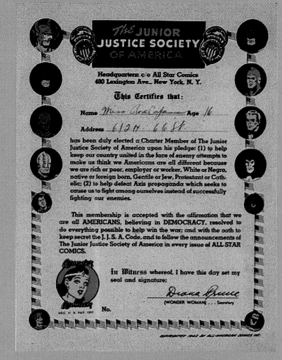

**Charter Membership Certificates
1942 type (2)**

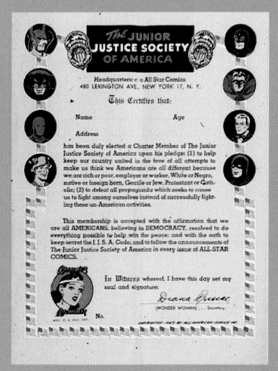

**Charter Membership Certificates
1945**

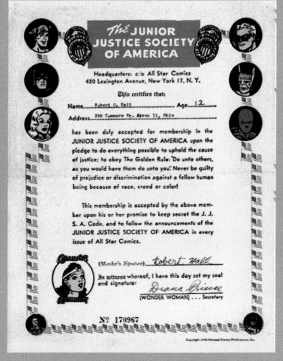

**Charter Membership Certificates
1948**

1942 Yellow Letter & Pamphlet (type 1)

Flyer & Stamps 1942 kit
(type 1)

1948 Mailer

1942 Mailer
(type 1)

**1942 Mailer & Letter on School
Defense Clubs for Victory**
(type 2)

1942 Decoder

1948 Letter white

1945 Decoder
Note Wildcat printed
only in 1945 decoder

**E.C. Giveaway comic offered
in both 1942 Junior Justice
Society Kits**
(type 1 and 2)

U.S. Jones Cadets Comic Ad with
Club Card and Decoder from 1941
Club Kit

Superhero Memorabilia

Captain America 50th Anniversary Pin
Set-1991
50 years and still going strong

1941 Captain America Sentinels of Liberty
Comic Ad

Captain Marvel Memorabilia

Chapter One Title Card 1941 Serial

Fawcett Club Letters

Club Kit

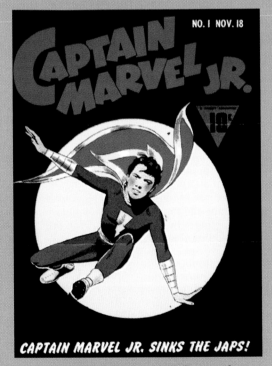

Captain Marvel Jr. 1942 Promotion Flyer for his first comic

Club Mailer
Note Remember Pearl Harbor postal cancellation

Captain Marvel Memorabilia

Christmas Greeting Letter from Captain Marvel

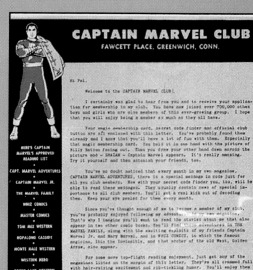

1940s Update Letter

Yellow Rectangular Patch

Envelope for Club Letter

Blue Rectangular Patch

1946 Statuettes Sign
art by C.C. Beck

Captain Marvel Family

**1946 Captain Marvel 5"
type 2**
(Capt. abbreviated on
base)

**1946 Mary
Marvel 5"**

1946 Mary Marvel 5"
(Solid red dress variety)

**1946 Captain
Marvel Jr. 5"**

**1945 Captain
Marvel 5" type 1**
(Syroco style; word
"Captain" spelled out
on base)

**1946 Plastic Mary
Marvel 6.5"**

**1946 Plastic Captain
Marvel 6.5"**

**1946 Plastic Marvel
Bunny 5.5"**

**1946 Plastic
Captain Marvel Jr.
6.5"**

562

Captain Marvel Premium Comics

1950 "Captain Marvel and the
Lieutenants of Safety" #1
Fawcett Publications/Ebasco Services

1950 "Captain Marvel and the
Lieutenants of Safety" #2
Fawcett Publications/Ebasco Services

1950 "Captain Marvel and the
Lieutenants of Safety" #3
Fawcett Publications/Ebasco Services

1945 Wheaties Cereal Giveaway
(taped to box)

Superhero Pinbacks

1941 Captain Battle

Shield Club (first version)

1941 Eagle Defenders

1942 Sensation Comics Premium (Wonder Woman)

Early 1940s Shock Gibson Volunteers

1941 U.S. Jones Cadets

1942 The Flash (offered in All Flash Comics)

Shield Club (second version)

Character Memorabilia

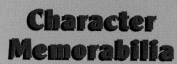

Donald Duck Movie Pinback
(contest)

**Captain America
Brass Badge**

**Melvin Purvis
Pen & Pencil
Combination**

**Radio Orphan Annie Secret
Guard Stamp**

**Donald Duck
Jackets Pinback**

Reverse
side of
Melvin
Purvis pen
& pencil

**Sky King Belt Buckle Secret
Compartment**
(Orin Armstrong prototype)

**Sergeant Preston
Full Color/White Rim**

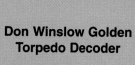

**Don Winslow Golden
Torpedo Decoder**

**Sergeant Preston
Red & Black on Yellow**

Dick Tracy Member Kit 1944

Manual including the "Recognizing Japanese" section

Member Certificate   no symbol

Saboteur Suspect Card

Manual Inside

Type I Mailer and Manual cover

Decoder with no symbol by the badge

Ruler goes to 18"

Dick Tracy Member Kit 1945

Member Certificate with symbol

Manual without the "Recognizing Japanese" section

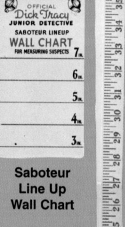

Saboteur Line Up Wall Chart

Ruler goes to 36"

Manual Inside

Decoder with the symbol by the badge

Type II Mailer

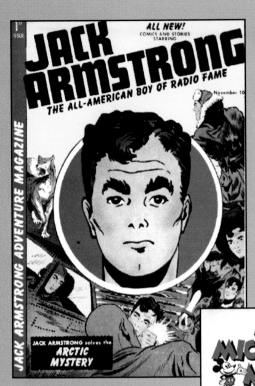

Jack Armstrong Comic #1
1947

Sky Blazers #1 1940

Buster Brown #1 1945
Giveaway

1940 Superman Giveaway

Mickey
Mouse #1
1933
Giveaway

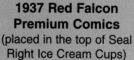

1937 Red Falcon Premium Comics
(placed in the top of Seal Right Ice Cream Cups)

Comic Book Giveaways

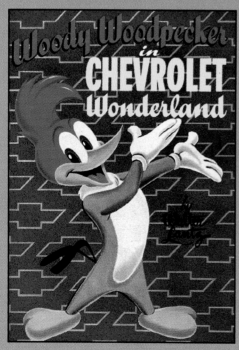

1954 Woody Woodpecker Comic
(from Chevrolet car company)

1949 Lassie Comic
(from Red Heart dog food)

Comic Character Paper Premiums

1939 Chicago Tribune/N.Y. News Giveaway
featuring 15 major comic stars (front cover)

**War Item from
Green Lama 1943
Club Kit**
(second version)

1939 Chicago Tribune/N.Y. News Giveaway
featuring 15 major comic stars (book open)

Comic Character Pocket Knives

Dick Tracy

Frank Buck

Hopalong Cassidy

Mickey Mouse

Lone Ranger
(front & back)

Rin-Tin-Tin & Rusty

Tom Mix

Buster Brown

Tom Mix Ralston

Roy Rogers & Trigger
2 styles

Character Beanies

Captain Marvel (boy's style)
1940s

Dumbo (Disney movie)

1950s Li'l Abner

1948 Donald Duck Ice Cream

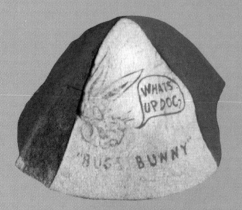

1950s Bugs Bunny

1932 Skippy Club

1950s Turtles (television)

Mickey Mouse

Radio & Television Characters Hats

1938 Lone Ranger
Military hat with
button

Rin-Tin-Tin & Rusty

Robin Hood

Tom Corbett
Space Cadet
with sunglasses

Annie Oakley

Zorro
with
mask

Howdy Doody

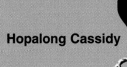

Hopalong Cassidy

Archie

Flash Gordon

Prince Valiant

Annie Rooney

Dagwood

Blondie

Little King

Barney Google

Tim Tyler

Phantom (purple costume)

Jiggs

Olive Oyl

Popeye

Wimpy

Set of Pinocchio Multi-Products Figures 1945

Figaro

Giddy

Geppetto

Jiminy Cricket

Jiminy Cricket
United Fund Award

Pinocchio

Geppetto

Lampwick

Comic Character Dolls

Aunt Jemima

Rin-Tin-Tin

Smitty

Moon Mullins

Mighty Mouse

Nancy

Sluggo

Comic Character Figures

1995 Donald Duck with Gong from the Disneyana Convention

1944 Rosie Syroco Figure

1930s Mickey & Minnie with Donald Toothbrush Holder

1945 Alley Oop Test Product Statuette

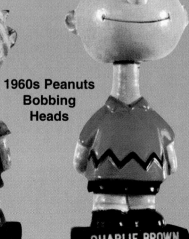

1960s Peanuts Bobbing Heads

Donald Duck Display Posters and Sign

Donald Duck Icy-Frost Twin
Pops die cut sign

Donald Duck Sylvania Cardboard Display
by Einson-Freeman 1940s
20.5"x 36"

1944 Donald Duck Bond
Poster 17"x 20"

Premium Glasses & Mugs

1940s Lightning Jim

1930s Ovaltine Mixer

1938 Lone Ranger

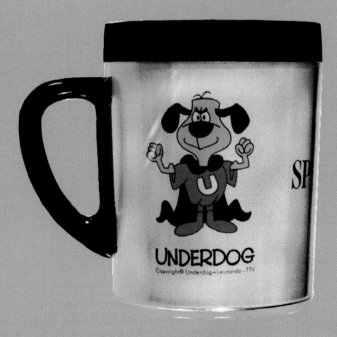

Underdog Mug

1960s Hi-C Missile
Game Set

14"x16" Vernon Grant
Poster Display
(Rice Krispies)

13"x19" 1938 Snow White Post
Toasties Banner

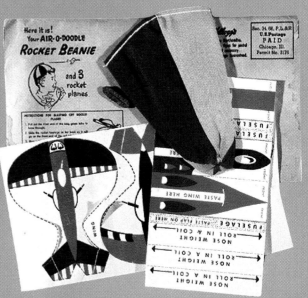

Kellogg's 1950s Air-O-Doodle Rocket Beanie

Whirl-erang with Box Back 1950s
(Canceled because children were hurt by the toy)

Promotional Items

**Red Goose Shoes 1950s Display
with Sign 8"x 28" tall**
(Golden Egg with prize inside)

Omar the Mystic 1936 Decoder

**Ken Maynard 1933
Einson-Freeman
Mask**

1951 Pop-up

Enlargement of front row of characters

Scarce 1951 Pop-up Cardboard Ad display featuring 29 comic characters from Metro Sunday Newspapers.

4 Piece Character Standee

1950s Fearless Fosdick Standee Promoting Wildroot Hair Tonic

Famous Heroes of Television & Radio

Mailer & 18 Picture Cards-1950s Quaker Cereal
(detailed information on each Indian chief on back of card)

**Rocky Lane Posse Club
Decal 1950s**

1940s Sky Blazers Radio Promo

**Sergeant Preston of the Yukon
Small Picture Premium 1950s**

Character Cereal Boxes

1966 Kellogg's OKs cereal uses Yogi Bear and Batman to promote their product

1940 Post Toasties features highlights from Disney's film *Pinocchio* on the back of some boxes

1957 Wheaties Lone Ranger & Tonto poster offer

1933 Wheaties Jack Armstrong grip developer offer

Jack Armstrong front

Character Cereal Boxes

1957 U.S.Soldiers offer on back of Sugar Smacks box

1961 Sugar Pops Dennis the Menace Spoon offer

1966 Kellogg's Frosted Flakes with Batman offer on back
(note the Tony mug & bowl offer on side)

1934 Mickey Mouse used to promote Post Toasties
(back has Mickey at the Circus)

TV Heroes Poster

Unique 1957 single poster of the Lone Ranger and Tonto that was displayed in the General Mills lobby. Wheaties offered separate posters of each character in a "big as life" promotion. Both individual posters could be acquired for fifty cents and three Wheaties box tops. The single poster of both characters, as pictured above, was not offered to the general public.

1957 Lone Ranger Cardboard 6' Standee Promoting several General Mills Cereals

588

Grape-Nuts Flakes Small Kites Offer

1950s Grape-Nuts Flakes
Fireball Twigg Kite
Premium Sign

1950s Grape-Nuts Flakes
Fireball Twigg Midget Kite
Kit

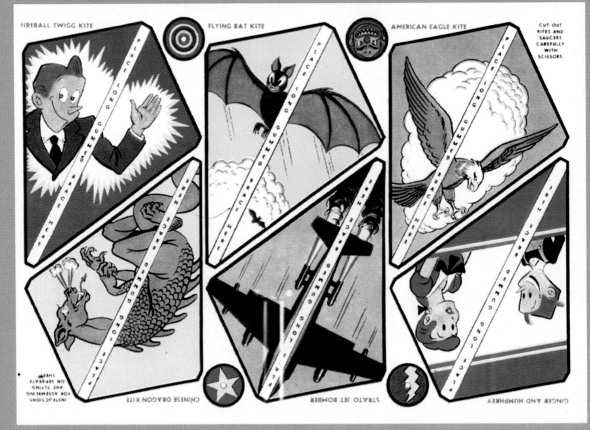

Famous Faces of the Comics

Roy Rogers 1955-1956 Product Manual
full color inside

Little Lulu Mask 1950s

Tubby Mask 1950s

Dumbo DX Gasoline Mask 1942

Roy Rogers 1954-1955 Product Manual
full color inside

Indian Theme Premiums

1950 Straight Arrow Radio/Comic Strip Pressbook
(contains rare comic strips)

1950 Straight Arrow Coloring Book

**1950s Lone Ranger
Deputy Chief Badge**

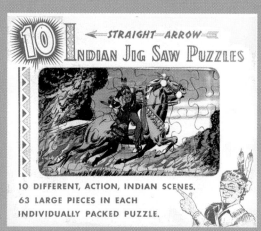

1949 Straight Arrow Jigsaw Puzzle
(boxed set of 10)

Young Forty-Niners Indian Village
Sheet opens to 19"x37" unpunched

Movie Standee

Rare 1951 "The Day the Earth Stood Still" 5 foot Movie Standee

1954 Snap,
Crackle & Pop
Cloth Pattern Dolls

1950s Model Airplanes with Mailer

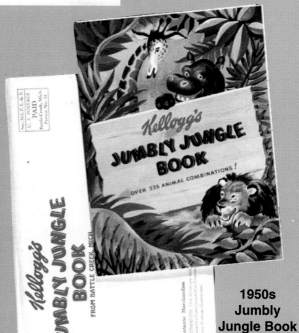

1950s
Jumbly
Jungle Book
with Mailer

1950 Billy West Promo Card

1930s Black Flame Paper Mask
(Hi-Speed Gasoline)

1950s Breakfast Club "Kiddie Party Ideas" Booklet
(Fritos)

1950s Flap Happy Bird with Mailer
(Post Toasties Premium)

1965 Man from U.N.C.L.E. Membership Kit

1955 Captain 11 Super Zoom Decoder

Character Paper Items

1954 Howdy Doody
"Comic Circus" Picture
Toy
(Poll Parrot Shoes)

1934 Tarzan of the Air Promo with
Mailer

1940s Kayo Bottle
Top Chocolate Drink
Display Sign

1950s Howdy Doody Large Postcard

1920s Little Jimmy Writing Tablet

Character Spoons

Star Trek

Dennis the Menace

Mary Poppins

Kukla
(Television show)

Woody Woodpecker

Ollie
(Television show)

Green Hornet

Pinocchio

SpaghettiOs

Famous Faces in Comics

11"x 20" Burns & Allen
Banner (double sided)

13"x 18" Hop Harrigan Sign

3"x 6" Danny
Thomas Flicker
promo for Post
Toasties

1950s Television
Cisco Kid Lariat
Toy

First standee ever made to promote Superboy. The Super Powers collection
of figures and various accessories including VHS and Beta video tapes was
offered in 1984 and 1985.

On the convention trail?
Let **Geppi's International Travel**
be your guide!

BIBLIOGRAPHY

Bordman, Gerald. *American Musical Theatre*. New York: Oxford University Press, 1978.

Brooks, Tim & Marsh, Earle. *The Complete Directory to Prime Time Network TV Shows*. 3rd ed. New York: Ballantine Books, 1985

Brown, Hy. *Comic Character Timepieces: Seven Decades of Memories*. West Chester, PA.: Schiffer Publishing, Ltd. 1992.

Bruce, Scott. *Cereal Box Bonanza: The 1950s*. Paducah, KY.: Collector Books, 1995.

Bruce, Scott & Crawford, Bill. *Cerealizing America*. Boston: Faber & Faber, 1995.

Bruce, Scott. *Flake: The Breakfast Nostalgia Magazine*. Cambridge, MA. 1990-1995.

Claggett, Tom, ed. *The Premium Exchange*. St. Clair Shores, MI.: December 1976-January 1978.

Davis, Stephen. *Say Kids! What Time Is It? Notes From The Peanut Gallery*. Boston: Little, Brown and Company, 1987.

Dinan, John A. *The Pulp Western*. San Bernardino, CA.: Borgo Press, 1983.

Douglas, George H. *The Early Days of Radio Broadcasting*. Jefferson, NC.: McFarland & Co., 1987.

Dunning, John. *Tune in Yesterday*. Englewood Cliffs, NJ.: Prentice-Hall, 1976.

Fenin, George N. & Everson, William K. *The Western*. New York: Orion Press, 1962.

Fischer, Stuart. *Kids' TV: The First 25 Years*. New York: Facts on File, 1983.

Geissman, Grant. *Collectibly Mad: The Mad And EC Collectibles Guide*. Northhampton, MA.: Kitchen Sink Press, 1995.

Goulart, Ron. *Cheap Thrills*. New Rochelle, NY.: Arlington House, 1972.

Goulart, Ron, ed. *Encyclopedia of American Comics*. New York: Facts on File, 1990.

Goulart, Ron. *Great History of Comic Books*. Chicago: Contemporary Books, 1986.

Grossman, Gary H. *Saturday Morning TV*. New York: Dell, 1981.

Hake, Ted. *Hake's Americana & Collectibles Auction Catalogues Nos. 17-133*. York, PA., 1971-1995.

Hake, Ted. *Hake's Guide to Advertising Collectibles*. Radnor, PA.: Wallace-Homestead, 1992.

Hake, Ted. *Hake's Guide to Comic Character Collectibles*. Radnor, PA.: Wallace-Homestead, 1993.

Hake, Ted. *Hake's Guide to Cowboy Character Collectibles*. Radnor, PA.: Wallace-Homestead, 1994.

Hake, Ted. *Hake's Guide to TV Collectibles*. Radnor, PA.: Wallace-Homestead, 1990.

Hake, Ted & King, Russell. *Collectible Pin-Back Buttons 1896-1986*. Radnor PA.: Wallace-Homestead, 1991.

Halliwell, Leslie. *Halliwell's Film Guide. 7th ed*. New York: Harper & Row, 1990.

Heide, Robert & Gilman, John. *Cartoon Collectibles*, Garden City, NY.: Doubleday, 1983.

Hickerson, Jay *The Ultimate History of Network Radio Programming and Guide to All Circulating Shows*. 2nd ed. Hamden, CT.: Presto Print II, 1992.

Hirschhorn, Clive. *The Warner Bros. Story*. New York: Crown, 1979.

Horn, Maurice, ed. *The World Encyclopedia of Comics*. New York: Avon Books, 1977.

Inman, David. *The TV Encyclopedia*. New York: Putnam, 1991.

Lenburg, Jeff. *The Encyclopedia of Animated Cartoon Series*. Westport, CT.: Arlington House, 1981.

Levin, Marshall N. and Hake, Theodore L. *Buttons In Sets 1896-1972*. York PA.: Hake's Americana & Collectibles Press, 1984

Maltin, Leonard. *Of Mice and Magic*. New York: McGraw-Hill, 1980.

Maltin, Leonard. *TV Movies and Video Guide*. 1991 ed. New York: Penguin, 1990.

Mandelowitz, Hy. *The Premium Guide*. New York: November 1977-August 1979.

Matetsky, Amanda Murrah. *The Adventures Of Superman Collecting*. West Plains, MO.: Russ Cochran, Ltd., 1988.

Melcher, Jack, ed. *Radio Premium Collectors Newsletter*. Waukegan, IL.: January 1973-September 1975.

Mix, Paul E. *The Life and Legend of Tom Mix*. South Brunswick & NY: A.S. Barnes, 1972.

Morgan, Hal. *Symbols of America*. New York: Viking Penguin, 1986.

Moskowitz, Milton, Levering, Robert & Katz, Michael. *Everybody's Business*. New York: Doubleday, 1990.

Norris, M.G. "Bud." *The Tom Mix Book*. Waynesville, NC.: The World Of Yesterday, 1989.

Olson, Richard D., ed. *Little Orphan Annie Reader*. New Orleans, LA.: 1979-1980.

Olson, Richard D., ed. *The R.F. Outcault Reader: The Official Newsletter Of The R.F. Outcault Society*. Slidell, LA.:1993.

Overstreet, Robert M. *The Overstreet Comic Book Price Guide. 25th ed*. New York: Avon, 1995.

Overstreet, Robert M. *Overstreet Premium Ring Price Guide*. Timonium, MD.: Gemstone Publishing, Inc. 1994.

Paquin, Mike. *"Put on a 'Funny Face,'" Collecting Figures*, pp. 74-75, June, 1995.

Penzler, Otto, Steinbrunner, Chris & Lachman, Marvin, eds. *Detectionary*. Woodstock, NY.: Overlook Press, 1977.

Rinker, Harry L. *Hopalong Cassidy King Of The Cowboy Merchandisers*. Atglen, PA.: Schiffer Publishing, Ltd., 1995.

Santelmo, Vincent. *The Official 30th Anniversary Salute To GI Joe 1964-1994*. Iola, WI.: Krause Publications, 1994.

Sarno, Joe, ed. *Space Academy Newsletter*. Chicago: July 1978-October, 1981.

Scarfone, Jay and Stillman, William. *The Wizard of Oz Collector's Treasury*. West Chester, PA.: Schiffer Publishing, Ltd. 1992.

Selitzer, Ralph. *The Dairy Industry in America*. New York: Magazines for Industry, 1976.

Smilgis, Joel, ed. *Box Top Bonanza*. Moline, IL.: December 1983-No. 49, 1991.

Stedman, Raymond William. *The Serials. 2nd ed*. Norman, OK.: University of Oklahoma Press, 1977.

Swartz, Jon D. & Reinehr, Robert C. *Handbook of Old-Time Radio*. Metuchen, NJ.: Scarecrow Press, 1993.

Terrace, Vincent. *Radio's Golden Years*. San Diego, CA.: A.S. Barnes, 1981.

Thompson, Steve. *The Walt Kelly Collector's Guide: A Bibliography and Price Guide*. Richfield, MN.: Spring Hollow Books.

Tumbusch, Tom. *Tomart's Price Guide to Radio Premium and Cereal Box Collectibles*. Dayton, OH.: Tomart Publications, 1991.

Weiss, Ken & Goodgold, ed. *To Be Continued....* New York: Bonanza Books, 1972.

Woolery, George W. *Animated TV Specials*. Metuchen, NJ.: Scarecrow Press, 1989.

Woolery, George W. Children's *Television: The First Thirty-Five Years, 1946-1981*. Part I. Metuchen, NJ.: Scarecrow Press, 1983.

Woolery, George W. Children's *Television: The First Thirty-Five Years, 1946-1981*. Part II. Metuchen, NJ.: Scarecrow Press, 1985.

INDEX

This index covers the subject histories and listed items in all 302 category sections. Actual people are entered alphabetically by last name. All other entries are alphabetical by the first word, disregarding articles A, An, and The.